SECOND EDITION

TOP NOTCH
3

Teacher's Edition and Lesson Planner

with ActiveTeach

Joan Saslow • Allen Ascher

With Silvia Carolina Tiberio

PEARSON

Longman

PEARSON

Test preparation that develops real English skills

As educators we spend a lot of time and energy preparing students for the rigors of study or work in an English-speaking setting. We design our courses and choose our materials carefully in order to teach the strategies that students will need to communicate effectively in English. However, when it comes to assessing their English skills, we realize that many high-stakes tests are simply a means to an end in which students dedicate valuable time to passing the test without developing real English skills.

There is a new academic test of English that matches our efforts in the classroom, Pearson Test of English Academic (PTE Academic), already recognized by institutions around the world and the UK Border Agency, it is endorsed by, and is the preferred English language test of GMAC®.

Why are educators so excited about the new test? This state-of-the-art test breaks many of the barriers in testing, but the key concern to teachers is that it truly helps students to become effective communicators in English.

"PTE Academic score data on the enabling language skills such as fluency, grammar, vocabulary and pronunciation, gives us a great tool to assess the language abilities of incoming MBA applicants to ensure they can interact at the levels expected in a small, experienced group of professionals on the Ashridge MBA program."

Amy Armstrong, Director of Marketing
Ashridge Business School

Relevant tasks
Comprising 20 different and often innovative items types, PTE Academic assesses the communicative skills of Listening, Reading, Speaking and Writing in a great number of ways. It assesses a range of enabling skills; grammar, oral fluency, pronunciation, spelling, vocabulary and written discourse to create a detailed profile of test takers' strengths and weaknesses.

Many of the 20 item types integrate these communicative and enabling skills to provide a real-life measure of a test taker's ability to deal with academic English language in communication.

International English
PTE Academic reflects the international world in which we live. Measures are taken to ensure that the material in the test is representative of international academic English. Not only are test development professionals based in several regions, including the United Kingdom, Australia, and the United States, but test items are internationally cross-validated to ensure that there is no regional bias.

Targeted preparation for test takers
A variety of dedicated test preparation materials are available for test takers. These include:

- Two fully-scored online practice tests with same-day score reporting, providing an authentic predictor of official PTE Academic test performance
- An unscored online practice test with sample answers
- a free PTE Academic Tutorial providing an overview of the test, instruction on each item type that the test taker will encounter and tips on how to navigate through the test
- The *Official Guide to PTE Academic* providing detailed information on administration, descriptions of all item types, analysis of sample answers, test-taking strategies and a wealth of practice items on the accompanying CD-ROM

The skills that students acquire in preparing for PTE Academic will serve them greatly once they arrive at their higher education institutions, or professional and government organizations.

"As we evaluate candidates, PTE Academic will give us an important tool for measuring their ability to study in an academic environment where English is the primary language of instruction."

Randall Sawyer, Director of Admissions
Cornell University, The Johnson School

For free PTE Academic teaching resources visit www.pearsonpte.com/success

Contents

NOTE: Workbook Answer Key is available on ActiveTeach

METHODS HANDBOOK

What Is *Top Notch*?

Instructional levels

Top Notch (together with *Summit*) is a six-level communicative English course for adults and young adults.

- *Top Notch* Fundamentals: for true beginners or very weak false beginners
- *Top Notch* 1: for false beginners or for students who have completed *Top Notch* Fundamentals
- *Top Notch* 2: for pre-intermediate students
- *Top Notch* 3: for intermediate students
- *Summit* 1: for high-intermediate students
- *Summit* 2: for advanced students

The following chart shows the correlation of *Top Notch* and *Summit* to International Standards and Tests. For detailed correlations to the "Can do" statements of the Common European Framework (CEFR) and to U.S. federal and state standards, please consult the *Top Notch* website at: pearsonlongman.com/topnotch.

Correlations to International Standards and Tests

Course Level	TOEFL (Paper)	TOEFL (iBT)	TOEIC
Top Notch Fundamentals (true beginner)			110 – 250
Top Notch 1 (false beginner)	380 – 425	26 – 38	250 – 380
Top Notch 2 (pre-intermediate)	425 – 475	38 – 52	380 – 520
Top Notch 3 (intermediate)	475 – 525	52 – 70	520 – 700
Summit 1 (high-intermediate)	525 – 575	70 – 90	700 – 800
Summit 2 (advanced)	575 – 600	90 – 100	800 +

Course Level	Common European Framework (CEF)
Top Notch Fundamentals (true beginner)	A1/Breakthrough
Top Notch 1 (false beginner)	A2/Level 1
Top Notch 2 (pre-intermediate)	A2/Level 1
Top Notch 3 (intermediate)	B1/Level 2
Summit 1 (high-intermediate)	B2/Level 3
Summit 2 (advanced)	C1/Level 4

Course Level	Cambridge Exams IELTS	Exam Level
Top Notch Fundamentals (true beginner)		
Top Notch 1 (false beginner)	3.0	KET
Top Notch 2 (pre-intermediate)	4.0	PET
Top Notch 3 (intermediate)	4.0	PET
Summit 1 (high-intermediate)	5.0	FCE
Summit 2 (advanced)	6.0	CAE

Scope

Each level of the *Top Notch* course contains enough material for 60 to 90 hours of classroom instruction. Split editions are also available. A wide choice of supplementary components makes it easy to tailor *Top Notch* to the needs of diverse classes and programs or to expand the total number of hours.

Goal

The goal of the course is to make English unforgettable, enabling learners to understand, speak, read, and write English accurately, confidently, and fluently. Three key features are emblematic of the *Top Notch* course:

- Multiple exposures to new language
- Numerous opportunities to practice it
- Deliberate and intensive recycling

Content

Top Notch has a classic sequential grammatical syllabus. Grammar, vocabulary, and social language are integrated within topical, communicative units. Offering a balance of practical and informational topics, the content is designed to be consciously appealing to the student learning English.

Language and culture

Since English is the primary language of international communication, the *Top Notch* course goes beyond the traditional cultural and linguistic features of English. It prepares students to communicate with the diverse array of English language speakers around the world—more than two-thirds of whom are not native speakers of English.

Although the spellings, pronunciation, and usage in *Top Notch* language models for students are in standard American English, *Top Notch* integrates a variety of regional, national, and non-native accents throughout the listening texts and in the video program, *Top Notch TV*, beginning at the *Top Notch* 1 level. The first language of speakers with non-native accents is identified for you and your students. In addition, the Teacher's Edition contains a wealth of information, clarifying relevant differences between American and British usage.

In contrast to a focus on native language culture, *Top Notch* emphasizes "cultural fluency." This emphasis helps students build the communication skills and self-confidence needed to navigate social, travel, and business situations in unfamiliar cultural settings.

All spoken language models in *Top Notch* are informed by and confirmed with the Longman Corpus Network, which collects both spoken and written samples of authentic language. *Top Notch* students can be assured that the language they are learning is authentic and appropriate.

Instructional design

The following is a synopsis of the *Top Notch* instructional design.

A communication goal for each class session. Each of the four numbered two-page lessons in a *Top Notch* unit is designed for one class session of 45–60 minutes, and has a clearly stated communication goal.

Three reasons for having a communication goal are to make each class purposeful, to demonstrate progress in each class session, and to enable a more focused evaluation. When teachers and students are unaware of the purpose of each lesson, they often just "go through the motions." Conversely, when teachers and students know the purpose of the lesson, they see value in it and are motivated to achieve a successful outcome.

Integration of skills and content. Research has confirmed that when students encounter new language only once or twice, they find it difficult to master or even remember. For that reason, new vocabulary and grammar are embedded in exercises, conversation models, pair work activities, listening comprehension texts, readings, and other activities to make them unforgettable. In each lesson, new language is examined, explained, integrated, expanded on, and applied so that students receive multiple exposures to the language as well as numerous opportunities to practice it in all skill areas.

Confirmation of progress. The culmination of each of the four lessons is a carefully constructed, guided communication activity called Now You Can. Each of these activities is a semi-controlled or free conversation, discussion, or role play in which students demonstrate their achievement of the goal of the lesson. Students are motivated by their success, and in keeping with the aims of the "Can do" statements of the Common European Framework, continually see the practical value of their instruction.

Explicit presentations of vocabulary, grammar, and social language. In order to allow the *Top Notch* Student's Books to double as both a teaching and a reviewing tool, language is presented explicitly. Explicit presentations take the guesswork out of understanding meaning, form, and use and provide a concrete reference for students to review. For those who prefer an inductive presentation of grammar, there are printable "Inductive Grammar Charts" on the ActiveTeach multimedia disc at the back of this Teacher's Edition. These charts provide an alternative (inductive) approach to each grammar presentation in the Student's Book. In addition, Vocabulary Flash Cards on the ActiveTeach multimedia disc can also be used for an alternative approach to presenting vocabulary.

A model-based social language syllabus. Each unit in the *Top Notch* course contains at least two models of essential social language in short conversations. Each of these Conversation Models serves a clear communicative purpose by embedding key conversation strategies. A full list of conversation strategies can be found in the Learning Objectives charts on pages iv–vii of the Student's Book. The Conversation Models in *Top Notch* are designed to be changed and personalized by pairs or groups of students, using the target grammar and vocabulary. This practice activates and engraves the language in students' memories, providing them with "language in their pockets;" in other words, language that is accessible and ready to use in real life.

A systematic approach to developing free expression. *Top Notch* features a four-pronged approach to discussion: *idea framing, notepadding, text-mining,* and *wordposting* (described in *Methodology for a Communicative Classroom,* pages Tx–Txi). These four techniques enable students to actively access, use, remember, and recycle previously learned language as they express their ideas. This approach results in confident and highly productive free expression and rehearses students for the real world.

A strategy-based focus on reading and listening comprehension. In addition to the rigorous practice of reading and listening, there is an emphasis on learning strategies. The strategies include such things as understanding meaning from context, distinguishing main ideas from details, comparing and contrasting, determining points of view, drawing conclusions, paraphrasing, and summarizing—all of which enrich students as learners and as communicators.

A systematic writing syllabus. The *Top Notch* course also contains guided writing practice. Beginning with *Top Notch* 1, writing activities guide students in the conventions of written English. The activities evolve with each level, taking student writings from mere written production of what students can say to carefully constructed and correctly written sentences, paragraphs, and essays.

A complete course. *Top Notch* is a complete course with a wealth of supplementary components and a simple integrated technology, allowing the maximum flexibility for all teaching styles, learning settings, and course needs.

For a pictorial presentation of all components of the *Top Notch* course, please see Student's Book pages ix–xi.

Methodology for a Communicative Classroom

The goal of any communicative language course should be to enable students to express themselves confidently, accurately, and fluently in speaking and writing; to understand spoken and written English as it is used in the world today; and to function socially in English in a variety of settings, both familiar and unfamiliar. Much practice is needed to reach those goals.

Because the typical student has limited opportunities to observe and practice English outside of class, the goal of the classroom must be to provide rich sources of input for observation as well as intensive opportunities for controlled and free practice. In other words, the classroom must become both a microcosm of, as well as a rehearsal for the "real world." It is the goal of this section and the goal of the *Top Notch* course to suggest a methodology which makes that possible.

Permitting active observation of language

Although the world is saturated with English (through the Internet, films, music, and television), much of it is incomprehensible to beginning and intermediate students and difficult and frustrating to learn from. Nevertheless, students should be encouraged to seek out and observe English outside of class whenever possible.

On the other hand, students benefit greatly and learn easily from exposure to models of spoken and written English at their own productive level or language just above that level. The level of challenge that benefits students most is often called "i+1" (Krashen and Terrell, 1983*) or "comprehensible input." Comprehensible input is language that

---

* Krashen, Stephen and Terrell, Tracy D. 1983. *The Natural Approach: Language Acquisition in the Classroom.* Oxford: Pergamon Press.

contains some unknown words or structures, but is still at a level that students can understand. Such language, especially when it is authentic, is extremely valuable for student progress and is abundant in the *Top Notch* course.

Although current methodologies often expect immediate production of target language, we believe that each class session should provide students with an opportunity to observe language by reading it and hearing it as well.

In order to benefit from the observation process, students should be encouraged to look at and/or listen to reading and listening material for several minutes in order for them to process it and to make connections between what they know and what is new. Only after students have had ample opportunity to immerse themselves in the observation process should they begin discussing the text or answering questions about it. And to maximize the value of observation, we strongly suggest that students support their opinions or answers by indicating where in an observed text or listening they got the information they needed to answer or to form an opinion. In this way, observation becomes an active process rather than simply a receptive activity.

Encouraging repetition of new language

Some people believe that repetition of language is indicative of an outdated behaviorist audio-lingual approach. Consequently, recent trends in language teaching tend to de-emphasize or discourage repetition of language being learned. However, we have observed that repeating new language is valuable as long as it is not overused and does not interfere with awareness of meaning. Repetition helps students remember correct pronunciation, stress, and intonation. It is recommended that students listen and repeat new language being learned for production.

For this reason, when students are learning new vocabulary or new social language, they should be encouraged to listen, or to read and listen, and then to listen again and repeat. When using audio materials as models, students appreciate the opportunity to compare their pronunciation, stress, and intonation with those of the speakers on the audio. We recommend that repetition be a regular feature of the presentation of vocabulary and model conversations.

For activities requiring students to listen and repeat, we suggest having students listen the first time while looking at the written form in their textbooks. This allows students to link the written form in the textbook to the sounds they hear. Next, as students are asked to listen and repeat, have

them do it with their textbooks closed. This serves to reduce distractions and allows students to focus exclusively on listening and repeating, rather than reading. It also reduces the confusing effect of English spelling on pronunciation. However, if students find this difficult, allow them to keep their books open for visual support.

It is always beneficial to vary the method and sequence of repetition. Using alternative approaches does not diminish the value of repetition; the approaches add variety and help maintain interest. For example, it is not necessary to limit repetition to simply mimicking the words in the textbook. Occasionally, and within reason, students can practice by making small changes in conversation models as they are repeated. For instance, if the Conversation Model is "How have you been?" "Well, actually, I have a headache," students can be encouraged to change the model, substituting another ailment such as "backache." In this way, the original model is heard and used, yet not parroted mechanically, and still reinforces correct rhythm, intonation, and pronunciation.

It is best to keep the pace of repetition and personalization lively so that the greatest number of students have a chance to participate, maximizing their exposure to new language.

It is also beneficial to vary the number of people being asked to repeat. Sometimes it is helpful to have students repeat individually; at other times the whole class, half the class, all the males, all the females, etc. can be asked to repeat as a group. The goal is always served, no matter how the repetition is structured.

It is important, however, not to exaggerate the amount of class time devoted to repetition. A lively pace and a short time period will achieve the desired results; then it is time to move on to more substantive activities.

Ensuring that students use learning strategies

It is important to provide opportunities for students to work toward goals, to access prior knowledge, and to practice strategies such as planning, self-assessing, predicting, etc. These strategies have been proven to have positive results on students' learning. Knowing learning strategies is not enough, however. Research has shown that unless students are aware of the value of strategies, they are unlikely to incorporate them into their own learning initiatives.*

---

* The foundational learning strategies that folllow are an intrinsic part of the *Top Notch* Student's Book. For teachers who would like to teach additional reading, listening, and vocabulary-building strategies, there are numerous printable extension activities on the ActiveTeach multimedia disc in the back of this Teacher's Edition.

Working toward goals. At the beginning of each term, before beginning instruction, probe students' individual personal goals in learning English. This discussion can be conducted in English or in the students' native language, depending on their level. Common goals could be for their profession, travel, academic study, etc. Help students become aware of how their course and/or their textbook will help them reach those goals; for example, by helping them learn to understand and communicate in spoken and written English. It is also worthwhile to encourage students to brainstorm a specific list of what they want to be able to do in English in practical or specific terms. For example:

I want to learn English because I want to:

- o *order meals in a restaurant.*
- o *get directions when I travel.*
- o *give directions to foreign visitors to my city.*
- o *check in and out of hotels.*
- o *read academic journals or articles.*
- o *write e-mails or letters.*
- o *discuss news and current events.*
- o *have social conversations.*
- o *use the Internet.*

Have students look through their textbook to see if it will fulfill any of their goals. Ask them to point out lessons or units that they look forward to learning from.

Make goal-setting or goal awareness an important part of each unit and lesson. Before beginning a unit or lesson, have students look it over and brainstorm what they will be able to do at the end of it. Such awareness builds expectation of results, focuses students' attention on the purpose of instruction, and results in greater satisfaction with each class. Specific techniques for using the goals in class are covered in *Applied methods: How to teach a* Top Notch *unit* on pages Txviii and Txx.

Observing progress and self-assessing. When a brief discussion of goals takes place at the beginning of a class session, it then becomes easy for students to observe and confirm their progress that day. One simple way to ensure this is to ask "Did you learn how to give someone directions?" "What did you learn today?" and so on. When students confirm that the lesson's goal has been achieved, they value their instruction. Similarly, regularly review progress at the end of each full unit. In general, cumulative positive reinforcement of their study motivates learners to persevere. See a detailed explanation in *Applied methods: How to teach a* Top Notch *unit* on page Txxiii.

Being aware of the instructional process. Make students aware that presentations and activities in class, as well as those assigned for work outside of class (homework, projects, laboratory activities), have a definite purpose and are not random or accidental.

Effective lessons offer students presentations and activities that integrate target content. However, merely *offering* students such lessons is often not enough. The lesson will be more effective if students are *cognitively aware* of the value of each section of the lesson in achieving the lesson goals.

When finishing tasks, projects, and homework, take a moment to review the language students used in the task; for example, ask "Where did you use the present perfect today?" When students become aware that they actually used the present perfect in their conversations, practicing it becomes valuable to them. It is surprising how often students are not aware of the way in which activities help reinforce what they are learning. They often see a conversation practice session as isolated from grammar or vocabulary content, viewing it as just for fun or something to do to fill time.

Reflecting on one's learning. A number of hurdles must be overcome in learning a foreign or second language. One such hurdle is confusing the difference between *understanding* a word and *being able to translate* it into one's own (native) language.

Learners instinctively attempt to translate everything they read or hear, word for word. This is futile for two reasons. First, no one can possibly translate word-for-word quickly enough to follow a speaker speaking at a natural pace. Second, word-for-word translations are impossible for idioms, expressions, metaphors, or other figurative language.

In order to build students' awareness of this fact, we must help them reflect on the meaning of "understanding." Help them to see that they can in fact derive both general and specific meaning from spoken and written texts that contain words they have not heard or seen before. If students say they do not understand the meaning of a new word being learned, help them to describe its meaning, rather than to try to translate it. For example: assume you have presented the word *tight* (for clothing size) through an illustration depicting a person in a shirt that is too small. The caption states, "The shirt is tight." Because students already know the word *small,* they may be puzzled at seeing *tight* used here, instead of *small.* The natural impulse of learners is to search for a word in their own language that means *tight.* They will probably ask "What's *tight*?" To help students grasp the difference between understanding and translating, ask them to explain the meaning of "The shirt is tight." They will say "The shirt is too small." Point out to students that they in fact do understand the meaning of *tight* and that not being able to translate a word is different from not understanding it.

This is a profound awareness on which every learner of a new language needs to reflect. This awareness creates the desire and need to depend on context to infer meaning, promoting the development of one of the most important strategies for language learners—understanding meaning from context.

Managing pair, group, and collaborative activities

Collaborative activities, as well as pair and group work, facilitate interaction in English and are a hallmark of communicative language teaching. These activities encourage students to use their own language resources, which in turn makes the lesson more personal and meaningful. They also ensure that students initiate as well as respond in English. Also, by working together, students get to know each other faster and become more independent; they rely on the teacher less for guidance and ultimately take more responsibility for their own learning. We recommend the following approaches for activities featuring pair and group work.

Creating a student-centered environment. Some students, particularly those accustomed to teacher-centered lessons in which teachers spend a lot of time explaining, may not immediately see the benefits of working in pairs or groups. Remind students that working together allows them more time to practice their English and allows you to listen to more students individually. Reassure students that you will circulate to give them individual attention and that this will make you aware of any points that need explanation.

Encouraging cooperative learning and collaboration. Encourage students to help and learn from each other; in other words, to create a community of learners in the classroom. Whenever possible, try to elicit answers from other students before answering a question yourself. If a student asks a question that was previously asked by another student, direct him or her to the person who first asked that question. Also, before asking students to speak in front of the class, build their confidence by having them rehearse language in pairs, small groups, or chorally as a class. Students can also collaborate on written exercises with a partner or group, either by completing the activity together or by comparing their answers.

Facilitating a flexible seating arrangement. To ensure that students interact with a variety of partners, have them sit in a different location for each class. When dividing the class into pairs or groups, try to match students of different abilities. One method of forming groups is to have students count off according to the number of groups needed. The "1"s work together, the "2"s work together, and so on.

Monitoring activities. During pair and group work activities, monitor students by moving around the room to keep them on task and to provide help as needed. When possible, avoid participating in pair work yourself, as this will limit your ability to monitor and offer assistance to the rest of the class. If you are faced with an odd number of students, create a group of three students. The third student can work as a helper to encourage eye contact and other socially appropriate behavior and to correct mistakes.

Managing time. To keep students on task, it is best to set time limits for each activity. End activities when most of the class has finished to avoid "dead time" during which students are waiting for others to finish. For students who finish a conversation activity early, have them write out the conversation they created. If you use supplementary activities, it is a good idea to have some of those photocopied and on hand.

Correcting errors purposefully

In general, language learners—particularly adults—like feedback and expect to be corrected when they make a mistake. However, recent research (Brown, 2007*) suggests that correcting errors in students' speech and writing may not be as effective in promoting correct language use as is commonly believed. In fact, research indicates that excessive correction in a communicative course can embarrass or dishearten students and discourage them from attempting the experimentation and practice that is essential for language acquisition.

In view of these findings, we recommend striking a balance between the need for correction and maintaining feelings of success. The following are approaches to provide effective and positive feedback.

Promoting accuracy. For activities where accuracy is the focus, such as controlled conversation pair work, address mistakes shortly after they occur. Students need guidance as they attempt to use new words, phrases, and grammar; immediate correction is important. Ask students to incorporate the corrections as they continue their pair work.

---

* Brown, H. Douglas. 2007. *Teaching By Principles: An Interactive Approach to Language Pedagogy* (3rd ed.). White Plains: Pearson Education.

Promoting fluency. For freer and more challenging activities where fluency and free expression are the focus (discussions and role plays), refrain from stopping the flow of student discussion with corrections. In these activities, accuracy is less important than communicating ideas, improvising, and remembering and using the full range of language students have learned. Developing the ability to retrieve and use previously learned language is critical if students are to convert the English they have learned in the classroom into the English they need in their own lives. Interrupting students with corrections discourages this experimentation. Instead, take notes on common student mistakes and then review those errors with the entire class at the end of the activity.

Encouraging self-correction. If allowed, students are often able to correct their own mistakes. First let the student finish the thought, then indicate by sound or gesture that there has been a mistake. Try to point out where the mistake was to give the student an opportunity to self-correct.

Some techniques for eliciting self-correction include counting each word of the phrase on your fingers and pausing at the mistake, or repeating the student's sentence and pausing at the mistake; for example, S: "He has two child." T: "He has two ….?" S: "He has two *children*."

A less intrusive method is to correct the student's mistake by reformulating what the student said without stopping the flow of conversation; for example, S: "He have a car." T: "Oh, he *has* a car?" S: "Yes, he has a car." Note that these techniques often prompt the student to self-correct.

Being selective. Do not try to correct every mistake. Doing so could discourage or overwhelm students. Instead, focus corrections on the skills that are being taught in that particular lesson or on mistakes that interfere with comprehensibility.

Providing emotional support. Above all, be careful not to embarrass students. Be aware that students may be sensitive to criticism in front of their peers and may prefer more private feedback. Give students enough time to think before they answer to avoid making them feel pressured. There is nothing more effective in promoting student participation than reinforcing their belief that you are "on their side." To that end, we suggest that you show approval for student experimentation, even when language is inaccurate. Correction can come later. Experimentation is an essential step on the road to mastery.

Checking and managing homework. Maximizing the amount of time students have to interact and practice English is essential in a classroom environment. It is best to limit the amount of class time devoted to checking answers and correcting homework. For exercises done in class, have students check their answers with a partner. This increases interaction time, ensures that errors get corrected, and encourages students to correct their own mistakes. It also helps students avoid the possible embarrassment of giving incorrect answers in front of the entire class.

When the class has finished comparing answers, review the correct answers as a class, either by eliciting the answers from individual students or by having volunteers write their answers on the board. In classes with time constraints, we recommend that you write the answers on the board, as this method is faster.

We suggest that you follow a similar approach with homework by quickly reviewing correct answers. In large classes, you may prefer to systematically select which papers to review out of class in order to give individual feedback and check progress. If five to ten papers are collected every session, each student will receive individual feedback several times per term.

Actively developing free expression

One of the greatest challenges in the English language classroom is successfully engaging learners in free discussions and role plays. Teachers often find that students sit silently, produce single short "fossilized" utterances, or resort to using their first language. Some impediments to students' success are lack of vocabulary, grammar, subject knowledge, or interest—or forgetting previously learned language. There are psychological and psychosocial hurdles as well. Adult and young-adult students have many ideas to express but worry that they will be judged by both their teachers as well as their peers.

The following four techniques form part of a process approach to discussion and are recommended to mitigate the challenge of free discussions and role plays. They support learner confidence and increase quantity, quality, and complexity of expression.

Idea framing. When students are presented— unprepared—with a discussion topic, they typically approach it narrowly; for example, if you propose a discussion of vacation preferences, students may only think about one particular aspect of vacations. Worse, students often worry about what you consider appropriate to include in the discussion.

Providing students with a stimulus such as an online or magazine survey or questionnaire can help them frame their ideas by indirectly suggesting topics to be included in the discussion to follow. Surveys and questionnaires you provide also reduce student anxiety by clarifying your expectations of what is appropriate to include in the discussion.

Notepadding. Giving students an opportunity to write notes helps them consider how they will express their ideas. Here again, students may start with a narrow view of what to include in the discussion, but when they are given preparation time beforehand, they will broaden their ideas and plan how they want to express them. Notepadding builds confidence and yields more complex statements than discussion without preparation does.

Text-mining. Although language textbooks usually contain readings that provide students with an opportunity to confront "i+1" comprehensible language, using these readings solely for reading comprehension can be a missed opportunity. One way to make the most of a textbook reading is to ask students to notice and select language from it ("mining its text") that they can use in a discussion or role play. Permit students to circle, underline, or copy "mined" language prior to classroom discussions. Text-mining greatly enhances students' ability to acquire and use language slightly above the level they have learned.

Wordposting. Another huge challenge to students is remembering known language—even recently learned language—and using it in discussions and role plays. But when students do not use and reuse learned language, they inevitably forget it.

To ensure that students recycle previously taught language, we suggest that you (or the students themselves) make and keep "wordposts"—lists of relevant recyclable language.* Wordposts can be written on the board or photocopied and distributed. To encourage the use of the wordposts during the discussion, you or your students can write a checkmark, cross out, or circle each word or phrase as it is used. Wordposting is one effective recycling technique that makes English unforgettable.

Teaching the receptive skills: reading and listening

Reading and listening are sometimes thought of as receptive skills. In a communicative classroom, however, reading and listening activities can greatly enhance speaking and writing, provide growth of comprehension, and help students cope with authentic language containing unknown words and complex ideas. The following are suggestions for approaching reading and listening in order to gain maximum benefit.

Authentic reading and listening passages will always contain a quantity of unknown language. We know that students can understand more language than they can produce, but they are often frightened to tackle readings or listening activities that include unknown language. (See the earlier discussion of the value of "i+1" comprehensible input on pages Tvi–Tvii.)

Readings and listening activities should represent real language. However, it is important to avoid language that falls significantly above the comprehensible level. Identifying a zone of comprehensibility enables readings and listening activities to maximize the building of comprehension skills and vocabulary.

As stated earlier, it is important to recognize that most language learners instinctively try to translate every word as they read and are frustrated by their inability to create a one-to-one correspondence of the English words to their native language. Adopting an approach that respects the amount of challenge a reading or listening activity presents, discouraging translation, and teaching reading and listening skills and strategies can help students read and listen successfully.

Reading strategies and applied comprehension skills. Reading skills and strategies that help students cope with the challenge of foreign- or second-language reading help prepare them to confront such readings with confidence. Some are practiced before, others during, and still others, after the actual reading.

Before a reading activity, encourage students to explore their ideas about the topic of the reading. To pique their interest in the reading, get them to access any knowledge they already have about the topic. Another strategy that helps students cope with a reading is identifying its source; for example, is it a magazine article, a website, a series of letters, an advertisement, etc.? These pre-reading strategies will help students approach a reading with the confidence that they know what is coming and will discourage them from focusing on every unknown word.

Some strategies and skills that help students while they read are *skimming, scanning,* and *focusing on the context* in which unknown words occur, to help students understand meaning (instead of trying to translate those words). Encourage students to quickly read the passage from beginning to end

* In *Top Notch* units, wordposts are listed within a box called *Be sure to recycle this language.*

without stopping for details. One way to teach skimming is to have students read the first sentence of each paragraph and the first few sentences at the beginning and the end of the passage.

Scanning for specific information is another helpful skill. Before students read line for line, they can be asked to find information about dates, names, ages, times, etc. Such information usually identifies itself by format—numbers, isolated words, charts, and the like. Keep in mind, though, that not all readings lend themselves naturally to skimming or scanning. Only choose skimming or scanning with readings that naturally lend themselves to that sort of examination.

As students read and encounter unknown words, help them to find the context clues that "explain" the meaning of those words. In the following sentence, the general meaning of the word *dousing* can be understood from the context: "Songkran is a wild and wonderful festival in which people of all ages have fun *dousing* each other with water for three solid days." Many students would instinctively reach for the bilingual dictionary to look up *dousing* or simply decide the reading was too hard. But asking them to look for the meaning in the surrounding text (the "context," where they will find "with water") helps build the habit of searching for context clues and taking educated guesses.

A good way to help students see the value of searching for context clues is to ask them to explain their reasons for guessing the meaning of a word. Ask them to go into the text to provide support for their opinions. In the case above, students would cite "with water" to support their opinions. Note that a precise definition or translation is not necessarily the goal. Students should also be encouraged to guess the "sense" of a word; for example, whether it is positive or negative, male or female, something you eat or wear, etc. If this is done regularly, students will develop the habit of looking for meaning in the context.

After reading, *summarizing* a text is a valuable applied reading comprehension skill. When students are able to summarize a reading, it indicates that they have identified the main idea and can distinguish it from random facts or details that are included in the article.

One way to provide practice in distinguishing main ideas from details is to ask students to *take notes* as they read and to organize or separate their notes into categories; for example, in a reading about the experiences of a woman with physical challenges, students can be asked to take notes about her habitual activities in the morning, in the afternoon, and in the evening. In a reading about healthy eating habits, students can be asked to jot down information about foods that are good for you and those that are not good for you. Putting notes into categories helps students perceive the details that support the main ideas of a reading and can provide a framework for a logical and articulately expressed summary. A further way to help students understand the main idea of or the point of view expressed in a reading is to ask them to try to *paraphrase* what the author's idea is. As they read, ask students to put the author's words into their own words.

The input/task ratio. When asking comprehension questions about a reading (or a listening activity; see below) it is helpful to keep in mind the relative difficulty of the text. If a text is very challenging and has a lot of difficult or unfamiliar language and complex ideas, questions and tasks should be relatively easy and receptive, such as determining general or main ideas. If a text is relatively easy, the tasks and questions should be commensurately more difficult, productive, and inferential, and should require more critical thinking. In other words, the difficulty of the task should be inversely proportional to the difficulty of the text. If this ratio is respected, even very difficult texts can be used by students at lower levels.

Listening skills and strategies. Listening is often frustrating to students because of factors such as speed, accent, background interference, and the fact that in the real world, a listener usually has only one opportunity to understand. In contrast, a reading text—even if difficult—can be explored, studied, and re-read at the learner's pace.

For most learners, understanding spoken language can be very difficult, especially when the speaker is not seen, as during a phone conversation or when listening to the radio, a podcast, or a classroom audio program. Listening skills and strategies can help reduce the natural panic that occurs when students listen to challenging speech.

If we want students to be able to cope with real spoken language, it is crucial to expose them to listening passages recorded at a normal rate of speed and in a variety of accents. When students are presented with unnaturally slow and over-enunciated listening passages, they may understand them easily and perform well on comprehension exercises. Unfortunately, however, this apparent success is misleading because it does not indicate that students will be able to understand authentic speech, which is inevitably faster and less enunciated. As language educators, it is important for us to ask ourselves what the purpose of listening comprehension exercises is in a communicative classroom. Is it to get students to understand every word they hear in a comprehension exercise or is it to help them learn how to successfully understand real spoken English in the world outside the classroom? Although we know the answer is the latter, we struggle with our own feelings of "failure" when students are unable to easily understand the listening texts we bring to class.

To offset our own fears as educators, it is important to explain to students the value of challenging listening experiences and to reassure them that the exercise is not a test of whether or not they understood everything the first time. Be sure students understand that the purpose of this practice is to help them obtain meaning, even from something that is not completely understood, and not simply to answer questions.

In presenting listening comprehension practice in class, be sure students have several opportunities to listen to each passage. Focus students' attention by having them listen for a different purpose each time they listen. Build up the progression of tasks from easier to more challenging ones. Add an extra listening opportunity again after other tasks in order to let students check their work.

The input/task ratio especially applies to constructing listening activities in the classroom. (See page Txii.) If the listening passage is fast, accented, or otherwise difficult, present a less challenging or receptive task, such as understanding main ideas or identifying the global purpose. On the other hand, if the listening passage is slow or otherwise easy, present more productive or difficult exercises. A convenient way to apply the input/task ratio to listening comprehension exercises is to compare them to the reading skills of skimming and scanning: for more difficult listening passages, expect students to "skim" by listening and getting the main idea, but few details, inferences, or complexities. For easier listening passages, expect them to "scan" for details, make inferences, and draw conclusions based on those.

In all cases, however, make sure students realize that these exercises are meant to increase their ability to cope with natural spoken speech, not a means to judge what they can understand on one listening.

Improving written expression

Writing tasks perform a number of useful functions in a communicative classroom:

- First, they offer yet another vehicle for students to remember, practice, and consolidate language they are learning, reinforcing vocabulary and grammatical conventions.
- Second, they promote the development of accuracy because students and instructors read and edit the writing; errors are visible and can be meticulously corrected.
- Third, they can prepare students for the real writing they will do in their work and

social lives: letters, e-mails, reports, articles, messages, and the like.
- Fourth, tasks based on a writing syllabus can teach students the conventions of standard written expression, such as sentence and paragraph development, use of topic sentences, and written rhetorical devices. These cannot be learned through speaking activities.

Students should have frequent opportunities to write. In every class session, they should be offered grammar, vocabulary, reading, and listening comprehension exercises that require a written response. Exercises should include word and phrase-level cloze or fill-in-the-blanks exercises; sentence-level exercises that require one or several sentences; and other controlled writing tasks. Such exercises should be corrected for grammar, usage, punctuation, and capitalization errors, either through peer-correction or through self-correction by seeing the correct responses on the board. Alternatively, exercises that have written responses can be collected and corrected periodically. (See section on checking and managing homework on page Tx.)

Students should also be given topics to write about. Even beginning-level learners can write short paragraphs based on the topic or theme of the textbook unit as long as the goal is specific; for example, if beginning-level students have learned the vocabulary of daily activities, the simple present tense, and frequency adverbs, a good writing assignment would be for them to write about their "typical day."

Expect an increase in both quality and quantity as students develop their writing skills. Students should be reminded and encouraged to actively use the language they have learned, and they should try to vary the vocabulary they use and the way they express themselves. In addition, they should always be encouraged to try and write a little more. If students share their writing in pairs or groups, have other students ask questions about information they want to know more about. Do the same when you read students' work.

Writing is a process that begins with ideas. Encourage students to brainstorm ideas, write lists, take notes, organize their thoughts, use graphic organizers, etc. before they begin writing a first draft. Encourage revision as a regular habit in writing. Students should get feedback from others and look at their own writing critically for clarity of ideas. Then they should rewrite to try and improve what they wrote in the first draft.

When you first read your students' writing, respond to the ideas they are trying to express, rather than focusing on errors. Ask questions that encourage students to say more and clarify what they are saying. Focus on accuracy only after students have had an opportunity to revise and improve the content of their own work.

Intermediate-level and advanced-level learners can cope with more challenging assignments; for example, if students have completed a unit in their textbook on the unreal conditional, government, politics, and global issues, they can write an essay about what they would do about corruption if they were in government.

At all levels of instruction, however, it is important to construct a writing assignment that students are prepared to write about. Many failures in writing occur when students begin translating their ideas from their own language into English, instead of using the words, expressions, and grammar they are familiar with. When assigning a writing task, ask yourself if it will require students to use known language or whether the subject is unrelated to what they know.

To help develop students' abilities in the conventions of writing, it is helpful to link each writing assignment to a particular skill to be applied, such as correct capitalization or punctuation, the use of connecting or sequencing words, the inclusion of topic sentences, and introductory and concluding statements, and other features of effective writing. In this way, students practice the language they are learning as well as the conventions expected in English writing. Finally, so that students become familiar with the conventions of formal and informal written expression, vary the text types in assignments, from e-mails to formal letters and essays.

Commonsense Testing and Evaluation

One of a teacher's most difficult challenges is to construct tests that fairly evaluate global student progress. Without pretending to present an exhaustive approach to testing and evaluation, we offer a few principles. First of all, although all teachers accept the principle that "we should test only what we teach," this is easier said than done in a communicative classroom, where more than 50% of class time is spent practicing the oral/aural skills. If we were to "test what we taught" this would require more than 50% of our test items to evaluate listening and speaking. However, oral tests take a lot of time because each student must be tested individually; few programs provide enough time for such testing. For this reason, most programs rely on tests that are largely written.

We would like to suggest procedures that answer the following two questions:

- How can students receive credit for their progress in speaking— the aspects of language learning that have received the most emphasis in class? In other words, how can we evaluate speaking?

- How can we construct a written test that permits students of all ability levels to demonstrate their knowledge of the language they've studied and which measures their abilities in listening and reading comprehension as well as written expression?

Oral tests

As mentioned above, formal oral tests are very time-consuming. In a class of thirty students, administering a five-minute unit oral test to each student would take 150 minutes (two and a half hours). Almost no program could dedicate that much time to oral testing at the end of each textbook unit, so it's only possible to administer a few oral tests per term. However, teachers report that when there are very few oral tests, students tend to panic and perform poorly because the stakes are too high. And a test on which students underperform doesn't accurately assess their progress. A more practical and effective way to measure students' progress is to provide an ongoing, less formal, in-class assessment of speaking skills.

One approach is to keep a record of students' progress in each class session. If a class has thirty students, we suggest focusing on ten students in each session, making a mental note of their spoken responses in whole class, small group, and pair work activities. At the end of the session, make a notation in your record book in a form that makes most sense to you. One simple notation system is to give each student you evaluated a "plus," a "check," or a "minus" for that day's oral work. In the following class session, focus on the next ten students, and in the following session, focus on the final third of the students. In that way, students receive credit for their progress as they begin to retrieve and use target language to communicate in class. You can determine the criteria you wish to use to evaluate your students (e.g. fluency, accuracy, clarity, etc.). The important thing is that you have a record of each student's ongoing progress. This set of records can then be factored into the grade each student receives for the marking period, unit, term, etc. The percentage of weight you wish to give to this ongoing oral evaluation in relation to the written test is up to you and your program.

Written tests

How can we construct a written test that enables us to fairly evaluate the progress of all students—those who are gifted as well as those who struggle? All students learn, though not at the same rate, and some learn more from a textbook unit or from a lecture, etc. than others. We suggest that test items in written tests be weighted as follows so that all students who have progressed acceptably can demonstrate that growth on the test. (Note that the item types described below can be mixed throughout the test.)

We propose that 80% of the test items be receptive and literal ones. Examples of these item types would include such things as true and false, multiple choice, and cloze sentences with word banks from which to choose items. These items should "test" students' knowledge of the target vocabulary and grammar they studied in the unit. In terms of difficulty, these items should be at a level that all students who have studied and learned the material can answer successfully.

In turn, 10% of test items should be items that require more thought and more productive responses than those mentioned above. Examples of these items would be an answer to a question, a completion of a conversation response, or cloze sentences in which students have to complete items without benefit of a word bank or a set of choices. These items should "test" students' knowledge and use of vocabulary and grammar learned in the unit. Regarding difficulty level, these items should target average and above-level students. While it is possible that weaker students will correctly complete these items, it is not probable. It is worth noting that all students sometimes perform above expectation, and that performance should be encouraged.

The final 10% of test items should require responses of multiple sentences or paragraphs, etc. that indicate mastery of vocabulary and grammar and that may require critical thinking, such as inferential understanding of language and ideas in context from reading passages. These items would typically target the strongest students in the class. Again, it is possible, however unlikely, that some weaker and average-ability students might perform well on these items. Any success should be supported.

If a written test is constructed using items apportioned as above, all students can demonstrate progress, with the weakest students (who have worked to their capacity) probably achieving a potential 80% score, average-ability students achieving a potential 90% score, and the best students achieving a potential 100%. Of course, these percentages are not guaranteed, but they do permit even the weakest students to see their progress and the best ones to demonstrate their mastery.

A compelling reason for this approach to constructing written tests is to address teachers' frequent concern that their students don't "do well on the test." Research has shown that teachers often write tests that provide items weighted on the side of the most difficult content taught, under the rationale that "if students can answer these questions, I can assume they could have answered easier items." The consequence of this assumption is that many students don't receive recognition for the language they <u>have</u> learned because they are unable to answer the most difficult and productive items perfectly. However, it is our contention that the easier content, such as the knowledge of the target vocabulary, is at least as important as the ability to use the most difficult grammar. We believe that all of the content should be evaluated.

Once a score on a written test has been determined, you (or your program) can decide how much weight to give oral tests or the ongoing oral assessment in the student's global evaluation. If we are to truly test what we taught, and the amount of time spent on the oral/aural skills was 75%, then a case could be made for "counting" the written test for 25% of the grade, although few programs would adopt such a scale, for reasons of expediency. Our purpose here is to provide a starting point for discussion to enable programs to consider what weight to assign the oral and written tests so that each student's evaluation meets the goals of the program.

ActiveTeach Multimedia Disc For more information on the topics in this section, please consult the ActiveTeach multimedia disc in the back of this Teacher's Edition and Lesson Planner. You will also find four academic articles written by Joan Saslow and Allen Ascher:

- "Making English Unforgettable: Enhancing Acquisition in the EFL Setting"
- "The Purposeful Use of Songs in Language Instruction"
- "A Process Approach to Discussion: Four Techniques that Ensure Results"
- "From Awareness to Application: Five Essential Aids to Learner Training"

Top Notch Unit Format

Top Notch units contain six two-page lessons, described in detail on pages Txviii–Txxviii.

UNIT 3

Getting Things Done

Preview

Are you a PROCRASTINATOR?

Take the survey.

1 At the beginning of every week, you ___.
- a. always make to-do lists for your calendar
- b. sometimes make to-do lists, but you often forget
- c. don't bother with planning and just let things happen

2 When you need to buy someone a gift, you ___.

4 When you have a lot of things you need to do, you do ___.
- a. the hardest things first
- b. the easiest things first
- c. anything but what you need to do

5 When you need to get something done in a short amount of time, you ___.
- a. feel motivated to work even harder
- b. feel a little nervous, but you get to work
- c. have a hard time doing it

6 You ___ feel bad when there are things you haven't gotten done yet.
- a. always
- b. sometimes
- c. rarely

If you answered "c" four or more times:
You are a classic procrastinator! You tend to put things off.
If you answered "b" four or more times:
You are a bit of a procrastinator, but you try to get things done on time.
If you answered "a" four or more times:
You are organized and self-motivated. You never put off what you can get done now.

Source: adapted from www.blogthings.com.

A Pair work Compare responses on the survey with a partner. Does your score accurately describe the kind of person you are? Explain, using examples.

B Discussion Based on the survey questions, what is a procrastinator? What do you think it means to be an "organized and self-motivated" person? What do you think are the advantages of being that type of person?

26 UNIT 3

C Photo story Read and listen to some customers placing orders at a copy shop.

English For Today's World connecting people from different cultures and language backgrounds

Manager: What can I do for you today, Ms. Krauss?
Customer 1: I need to get these documents copied a.s.a.p.* Think I could get 300 copies done by 11:00?
Manager: I'm afraid that might be difficult. I've got a lot of orders to complete this morning.
Customer 1: Sorry. I know this is last minute. But it's really urgent.
Manager: Well, you're a good customer. Let me see what I can do.
Customer 1: Thanks a million. You're a lifesaver!

Manager: Excuse me . . . Hello. Happy Copy.
Customer 2: Hi, Sam. Ken Li here.
Manager: Hi, Mr. Li. How can I help you today?
Customer 2: Well, I'm going through my to-do list, and I just realized I need to get fifty 30-page sales binders made up for our meeting next week. Any chance I could get them done by first thing tomorrow morning?
Manager: Tomorrow morning? No sweat. Can you get the documents to me before noon?
Customer 2: Absolutely. I owe you one, Sam!

Manager: Sorry to keep you waiting Ms. Krauss.
Customer 1: Well, I see that you've got a lot on your plate today. I won't keep you any longer.
Manager: Don't worry, Ms. Krauss. We'll get your order done on time.
Customer 1: Should I give you a call later?
Manager: No need for that. Come at 11:00 and I'll have your documents ready.
Customer 1: Thanks, Sam.

*a.s.a.p. = as soon as possible   Customer 2: Chinese speaker

D Paraphrase Say each of the following statements from the Photo Story in your own way.

1 "… this is last minute."
2 "… it's really urgent."
3 "You're a lifesaver!"
4 "No sweat."
5 "I owe you one!"
6 "… you've got a lot on your plate …"
7 "I won't keep you any longer."

E Discussion Based on the survey on page 26, how would you describe each character in the Photo Story? Complete the chart. Then compare charts with your classmates.

	Procrastinator?	Organized?	Explain
Ms. Krauss	☐	☐	
Sam	☐	☐	
Mr. Li	☐	☐	

Preview Lesson
- Previews content of the unit
- Activates prior knowledge
- Gets students thinking and talking

LESSON 1

GOAL Get

GRAMMAR Causatives get, have

Use a causative to express the idea that

Get: Use an object and an infinitive.
object   infinitive
I got the company   to ag
They got the students   to cle

Have: Use an object and the base for
object   base
I had my assistant   plan
They had the bellman   brin

Make: Use an object and the base f
object   bas
I made my brother   he
They made him   si

Grammar practice Complete each s

1 (have / call) Why don't you …
2 (get / do) I'll never be able to …
3 (have / clean) Why didn't you …
4 (get / give) You should …
5 (make / wash) Why don't you …
6 (get / sign) I'm sure we can …

VOCABULARY Some wa

A Read and listen. Then listen

My car's at the repair shop. Could you possibly **give** me a **ride** to work?

give [someone]

I need to u men's roo you **keep** on my thi get back?

keep [somethi

Txvi

28 UNIT 3

LESSON 2

GOAL Request express service

VOCABULARY Services

A Read and listen. Then listen again and repeat.

 1 dry-clean a suit

2 repair shoes

3 frame a picture

 4 deliver a package

5 lengthen / shorten a skirt

6 print a sign

7 copy a report

B Pair work Name other things you can get these services for.

You can also dry-clean sweaters or pants.

GRAMMAR The passive causative

Use a form of have or get with an object and a past participle to talk about arranging services. There is no difference in meaning between have and get.

	object	past participle
I had	my suits	dry-cleaned.
They're having	the office	painted tomorrow.
She can get	her sandals	repaired in an hour.

Remember: In the passive voice, a by phrase is used when the information is important.
We had the office painted last week. It looks great. (no by phrase)
We're having the office painted by Royal Painting Services. They're the best!

GRAMMAR BOOSTER • p. 126
• The passive causative: the by phrase

A Grammar practice Write questions using the passive causative. Write three questions with have and three with get.

1 Would it be possible to / these pictures / frame?
2 Could I / these sandals / repair / here?
3 Where can I / this bowl / gift wrap?
4 Can I / these shirts / dry-clean / by tomorrow?
5 Is it possible to / my hair / cut / at 3:00 / by George?
6 Would you / these photos / print / before 6:00?

B Complete each sentence with one of the v... phrases from the Vocabulary.
... until 5:00. Do...

30 UNIT 3

Lessons 1 and 2
- Goal and achievement based
- Integrate grammar, vocabulary, pronunciation, and social language
- End with a guided conversation

CONVERSATION MODEL

A Read and listen to someone requesting express service.

A: Do you think I could get this jacket dry-cleaned by tomorrow?
B: Tomorrow? That might be difficult.
A: I'm sorry, but it's pretty urgent. My friend is getting married this weekend.
B: Well, I'll see what I can do. But it won't be ready until after 4:00.
A: I really appreciate it. Thanks!

B Rhythm and intonation Listen again and repeat. Then practice the Conversation Model with a partner.

NOW YOU CAN Request express service

A Pair work Change the Conversation Model. Use the ideas to request an express service and give a reason for why it's urgent. Then change roles.

A: Do you think I could …… by ……?
B: ……? That might be difficult.
A: I'm sorry, but it's pretty urgent. ……
B: Well, I'll see what I can do. But it won't be ready until ……
A: ……

Ideas for express services
• frame a [photo / painting / drawi
• dry-clean a [suit / dress / sweater
• lengthen or shorten a [dress / ski

Ideas for why it's urgent
• Someone is coming to visit.
• You're going on [a vacation / a bu
• There's going to be [a party / a me
• Your own idea: ___

Don't stop!
• Say you need to have the service completed earlier.
• Ask how much it will cost.

Be sure to recycle this language.
I owe you one!   I know this is last minute.
Thanks a million.   I won't keep you any longer.
You're a lifesaver!

B Change partners Request other express services.

BEFORE YOU READ

Warm-up Have you or someone you know ever h...
something to wear or something for your home? If...

READING 🔊 2:11

The Tailors of Hong Kong

The famous Hong Kong 24-hour suit is a thing of th...
but tailors there are still reliable: You can trust them...
if they say they'll have your clothes custom-made...
in just a few days.

Today, prices are quite
reasonable—not as low as
they used to be, but they're
often about what you'd pay
for a ready-made garment
back home. The difference,
of course, is that a tailor-
made garment should fit
you perfectly. Most tailors
are extremely professional.
The workmanship and
quality of the better
established shops rival even
those of London's Savile
Row—but at less than half
the price!

Tailors in Hong Kong are
very helpful and are willing
to make almost any garment
you want. Most offer a wide
range of fabrics from which to choose, from...
and linen to very fine wools, cashmere, an...

At your first f...
tailor will take...
measurement...

Source: Information from *Frommer's Hong K...

A Identify supporting details C...
the article. Find information in th...

1 ☐ You used to be able to get...
day in Hong Kong.

2 ☐ Having a suit custom-mad...
always less expensive than...

3 ☐ If you buy a garment on...
you will pay about twice...
pay for one custom-mad...

BEFORE YOU LISTEN

A 🔊 2:13 **Vocabulary • Planning an event** Read and listen. Then listen again and repeat.

make a list of attendees   pick a date, time, and place   make a budget   assign responsibilities

plan an agenda   send out an announcement   arrange catering   set up the room

B Pair work Have you ever taken any of these steps to plan an event, such
as a meeting or party? Which of the activities do you think you would be
the best at doing? Use the Vocabulary.

LISTENING COMPREHENSION

A 🔊 Listen for main ideas Listen to the
conversation and answer the questions.

1 What kind of event are they planning?
....

2 How many people will come to the event?
....

3 Is it a formal or informal event?
....

4 Which of the following are mentioned
as part of the event? (music / food /
a lecture / dancing / meetings)

B 🔊 2:15 Listen for order of details Listen again and
number the activities in the order they will occur.
Circle the activities she'll do herself.

	make a list of attendees
1	pick a date and time
	pick a location
	make a budget
	assign responsibilities
	send out announcements
	arrange catering
	arrange music
	set up the room

B Activate language from a text Find these adjectives in
the Reading on page 32. Complete the descriptions, using
the adjectives.

reliable   reasonable   helpful   professional

1 I find Portello's to...really...
compared to oth...
and I can't find a...
prices.

2 What I like abou...
they're so...
is a bit unusual,

3 Jamco Design is extremely......................
You never have to worry about their doing

Lessons 3 and 4
- Goal and achievement based
- Build reading or listening skills and strategies
- End with a role play or free discussion

NOW YOU CAN Plan a meeting or a social event

A Frame your ideas Take the survey. Compare answers with a partner.

Check which event
activities you would
rather do. Choose
from Column A or B.

**What type of
person are
YOU?**

Column A
○ make a budget
○ assign responsibilities
○ plan an agenda
○ arrange catering
○ get people to set up the room
○ leave before cleanup

○ spend
○ take res
○ be a pre
○ cook foo
○ set up th
○ stick aro

If you chose four or more from Column A, you're a...
If you chose four or more from Column B, you're a...

B Notepadding In a group, plan a meeting or social event for your class.
Choose the type of event and discuss what needs to be done. Write the
activities and assign responsibilities. Discuss dates, times, and locations.

Type of event:	Location:
Date and time:	
Activity	**Name**

• A s
• An

Be sure to recycle this language.

Why don't we ___ ?	What needs to be done [first]?
Why don't you ___ ?	That's a [good idea. / great idea. / good point.]
How about ___ ?	That would be great.
What about ___ ?	That sounds ___ .
I think ___ .	

An en...
New...

*Thank...

C Discussion Present your plans to your class. Then choose the best plan.

A Top Notch Pop

Review

A 🔊 2:16 **Listening comprehension** Listen to each conversation.
Write a sentence to describe what the customer needs and when.
Listen again if necessary.

Example: He'd like to get his shoes shined by tomorrow morning.

1 ....
2 ....
3 ....
4 ....

B Complete each question or request with any noun that makes sense with
the passive causative verb.

1 Can I get my .... dry-cleaned by tomorrow?

Review Lesson
- Reviews content of the unit
- Evaluates readiness for assessment
- Enables students to confirm their
  achievement of the unit's goals

More Practice
ActiveBook Self-Study Disc
grammar · vocabulary · listening
reading · speaking · pronunciation

*Notch Pop
*et Back to You"
*s p. 149

2 We got the travel agent ....
3 When I was young, my mother always made me ....
4 When you arrive, you should get the hotel ....
5 Don't forget to have the gas station attendant ....
6 I can never get my friends ....

D Writing Do you think being a procrastinator is a serious problem?
On a separate sheet of paper, explain your views by giving examples
from personal experience.

Some possible examples
- getting things repaired
- having things cleaned
- paying bills
- making plans for a vacation
- keeping in touch with people

WRITING BOOSTER • p. 142
- Supporting an opinion with
  personal examples
- Guidance for Exercise D

ORAL REVIEW

Game Study the pictures for one minute, paying
attention to the time in each picture. Then close your
books. Ask and answer questions about the photos,
using the causative. Start like this:
What does Paul need to get done at 2:00?

Pair work Create a conversation for each situation.
Start like this:
Do you think I could get this ___ by ___?

Story Close your books. In a small group, tell the
story of Paul's day. Start like this:
At 9:00, Paul needed to get ___ ...

Paul's Difficult Day

NOW I CAN...
☐ Get someone else to do something.
☐ Request express service.
☐ Evaluate the quality of service.
☐ Plan a meeting or social event.

Applied Methods: How to Teach a *Top Notch* Unit

See pages Txvi–Txvii for pictorial examples of the following lessons.

Preview Lesson

The purpose of the Preview Lesson is to provide an introduction to the topic and social language of the unit. A Goals list at the top right of the first page announces the communication goals that are presented in the unit, building students' anticipation of what they will learn in the unit. We suggest that the four goals be pointed out at the beginning of the unit and then individually as each of the four numbered lessons begins.

The Preview Lesson includes highly authentic "i+1" language which should be comprehensible yet challenging for a student at that level of the *Top Notch* series. It is well-known that students make good progress when they are exposed to such language as long as they are not expected to produce it right away. When students see that they can cope with somewhat challenging language, their confidence grows and they enter the unit motivated with the expectation of success. The Preview Lesson contains embedded illustrations, contextual photographs, and other visual cues to meaning.

The material included in each Preview Lesson helps students activate prior knowledge of themes, topics, and language. It also actively helps them build the strategy of determining meaning from context. Encouraging students to use visual cues as well as the surrounding context will help them understand any unknown language in what they are reading or listening to in this first part of the unit.

Preview text. The first page of the Preview Lesson contains a text for students to observe, read, and think about. It may be a website, a menu, a self-test, an advertisement, or something similar. When important topical vocabulary is included, there is an audio icon ◀)) indicating that the vocabulary is recorded on the Classroom Audio Program and provides whole-class pronunciation practice of these words. Alternatively, you might ask students to access the audio directly from their ActiveBook for individual practice. In addition to the preview text and vocabulary, you will find one or more exercises that provide practice with the content and language of the preview text.

FYI: There are several options for accessing the audio. If you are using the Classroom Audio Program audio CDs, CD and track numbers are listed directly above the audio icon on the Student's Book pages; for example, 4:15 indicates

that the recording is on CD 4, track 15. If you are using the Digital Student's Book on your ActiveTeach multimedia disc, you can click on the audio icons for instant play. Your students can do the same when using their own Digital Student's Book on the ActiveBook. Alternatively, your students can download individual MP3 files of each track directly from a folder on their ActiveBook. These files have the same CD and track numbers used in the Student's Book.

▶ **Teaching tips**   Before discussing the preview text or doing the exercises, allow a few minutes for students to silently familiarize themselves with its content and form and explore its details. Always remind students to use the illustrations and context to help determine the meaning of unfamiliar words and phrases. This is an important learning strategy for understanding material above one's productive level. When students have had a few minutes to take in the preview text, ask a few questions about the content of the text. (Specific questions for each preview text are provided in the interleaved section of this Teacher's Edition—the "Lesson Planner.")

The exercises that follow the preview text are designed to get students to start talking about the unit topic. These discussion activities help students use both familiar and unfamiliar (new) language from the preview text. Students can discuss in pairs or small groups. After students have concluded their discussions, review by asking a few students to share their ideas with the whole class.

Photo Story. On the second page of the Preview Lesson, a short Photo Story permits students to see an illustrated conversation that contains natural, authentic, corpus-informed social language in a story context. The Photo Story is not intended to be a conversation model for students to repeat and "learn." Rather, it is an opportunity to observe, read, and listen in order to notice language and how it is used. These examples of natural language will promote comprehension of real spoken English and will ready students for productive social language they will learn in the numbered integrated-skills lessons that follow the Preview Lesson. *Top Notch* Photo Stories contain highly appealing idiomatic language that many students will pick up and make their own.

A note about accented speakers in *Top Notch:* As mentioned on page Tv, in order to accustom students to listening to English in today's world, where native speakers of English have a variety of accents and more than two-thirds of English speakers are non-native speakers of the language, *Top Notch* listening selections include regionally accented native speakers (British, Australian, Canadian, U.S. regional, etc.) as well as accented speakers from a variety of other languages. The first language of any non-native speakers in the Photo Stories is indicated on the Student's Book page. The Teacher's Edition identifies the regional or language background of all other speakers included in listening comprehension on the audio. We encourage you to share this information with your class and to remind students that English is an international language that is used to connect speakers from a variety of cultures and language backgrounds. Important: anything students are supposed to repeat (productive language models), such as vocabulary and Conversation Models are <u>always</u> in standard American English.

▶ **Teaching tips**   Before students read and listen to the Photo Story conversation, ask questions about the photos, if possible. For variety, and to provide listening practice, you may sometimes want to have students listen with books closed. Another option is to have students read the Photo Story silently first, then read and listen, or listen without reading. (Specific suggestions for each Photo Story are given in the Lesson Planner, but we encourage you to use the approach you feel is best for your group.) No matter which approach you elect to use, however, it is always worthwhile to have students listen to the Photo Story, whether before or after reading it. (See FYI on page Txviii for alternative ways to access *Top Notch* audio.)

After students have become familiar with the Photo Story, ask questions to check comprehension. Use the questions that are provided in the Lesson Planner or your own questions. Questions can be presented to the full class, written on the board for students to answer with a partner, or read aloud for students to write answers to. If appropriate, ask additional questions that relate the content of the Photo Story conversation to students' own lives. Then proceed to the exercises that follow the Photo Story.

Photo Story exercises. A series of intensive exercises following each Photo Story provides practice in determining meaning of new language from context as well as activating previously learned language. One important feature of the second edition of *Top Notch* is an emphasis on asking students to **explain** their answers. In exercises called Think and Explain, students are asked to notice and cite key language from the Photo Story to explain the basis of their answers. In addition to building critical thinking skills, explaining provides an opportunity to make receptive exercises productive; it stimulates discussion in class and trains students to use

context to support an answer. An added benefit of asking students to find support for answers within a passage is improved performance on standardized tests that expect students to delve into texts to extract meaning.

Other exercises ask students to classify or paraphrase language encountered in the Photo Story in order to demonstrate understanding. Many of these are called Focus on Language. These productive exercises build the essential skills of determining meaning from context and of using known language to "talk around" words not yet known.

The final exercise in the Preview Lesson usually asks students to consolidate the information, personalize it, or discuss it before moving on to Lesson 1.

▶ **Teaching tips**   The exercise questions can be asked in open class, written on the board for students to answer with a partner, or read aloud for students to write answers to. Specific suggestions are made in the Lesson Planner. When time is short, these exercises can be done as homework and reviewed quickly in class. They remain in the book, however, as a convenient reminder of meaning when students study and prepare for tests.

Lessons 1 and 2

FYI: All parts of these lessons are described below. The order of the parts may vary from lesson to lesson.

Lessons 1 and 2 contain a combination of rich input of social language as well as presentations and exercises in several of the following skill areas: grammar, vocabulary, pronunciation, and listening comprehension. These lessons always feature a Conversation Model and Pair Work in which students personalize and change the Conversation Model by using target grammar and vocabulary. Each lesson begins with the statement of its communication goal and concludes with Now You Can, which provides an opportunity for students to demonstrate their achievement of the goal. Each goal corresponds to the goals that are listed in the Preview Lesson. All content within any lesson is designed to lead students to, and is important for, the achievement of the goal.

Lessons have been organized to make full use of the interplay between vocabulary, grammar, and social language, and to provide variety from lesson to lesson. The sequencing of the internal elements of each lesson is approached logically, sometimes starting with the Conversation Model and other times with the Vocabulary or the Grammar. However, you may wish to use a different sequence from time to time. This is possible because all parts of the lesson lead to its conclusion, Now You Can.

▶ **Teaching tips** Before beginning each lesson, be sure students focus on the goal of the lesson so that they will appreciate achieving it by the end of the lesson. Students should always be aware of their goals and their achievement.

Below are general suggestions for teaching all parts of Lessons 1 and 2. (Specific suggestions are given in the Lesson Planner.)

Conversation Model. A key element of the *Top Notch* pedagogy is the Conversation Model, which includes natural social language and conversation strategies. The models are appealing to students because their practical value is obvious. All Conversation Models provide at least one example of the target grammar and/or vocabulary from the lesson. The aim of each Conversation Model is to provide language students can "carry in their pockets" and can make their own. All Conversation Models are recorded so students can listen to the natural stress and intonation of spoken English.

▶ **Teaching tips** To build awareness and facilitate comprehension, begin by asking questions about the photo, if possible. Many questions are provided in the Lesson Planner, but it is not necessary to stop there. When you ask questions, however, be mindful of what students are capable of answering. Avoid eliciting language or information that students would not know prior to reading the Conversation Model.

One presentation technique is to play the audio of the Conversation Model or read it aloud yourself with a more confident student while the other students read and listen with books open (or closed). Then check students' understanding of the conversation by asking comprehension questions. The questions provided in the Lesson Planner help students focus on the essential information in the conversation and determine the meaning of any new language from context. Because at least one example of the lesson's grammar and/or vocabulary is embedded in the Conversation Model, the questions will also build familiarity, understanding, and correct usage of the lesson's target language.

An alternative presentation technique, especially in stronger groups, is to have students listen to the Conversation Model the first time with books closed in order to build comprehension and avoid being distracted by the written word. When choosing this option, have students begin by looking at the picture to raise awareness of the social situation of the conversation.

Rhythm and intonation. This activity directly follows the Conversation Model. It contains the same recording of the Conversation Model, but with pauses between the utterances so students can focus on and practice imitating the pronunciation, rhythm, stress, and intonation of the speakers on the audio. The Conversation Models have been recorded by native speakers who have standard American accents and speak naturally, but slowly enough so students can repeat at the same pace. It is important to make sure that students practice using socially appropriate pitch and intonation when they imitate the model. The teaching suggestions in the Lesson Planner provide specific rhythm, stress, and intonation points to pay attention to.

▶ **Teaching tips** Some instructors like to have students look at the text for support as they repeat. Some prefer to have students do the rhythm and intonation practice with books closed to avoid any interference caused by English spelling. We encourage experimentation to see which is more effective in your classroom. This exercise can be done chorally, with the whole class participating. Alternatively, or additionally, it can be done by students using their own MP3 audio from the ActiveBook self-study disc in the back of their Student's Book.

With books open or closed, students listen and repeat after each utterance. Encourage students to imitate the rhythm, stress, and intonation of the conversation as closely as possible. Once students are more familiar with the model, you might want to have them continue practicing by playing a particular role in groups or individually; for example, one half of the class can be the first speaker and the other half the second speaker. Finally, have students practice the Conversation Model in pairs on their own, using the words of the original speakers. Correct their pronunciation, stress, or intonation when necessary. In this way students will be thoroughly familiar with the model and will be better prepared to change it and make it their own.

Another, more dynamic, approach to rhythm and intonation practice can be found in "Speaking Practice" in the *More Practice* section of the student's ActiveBook. Instruct students to go to the Conversation Model for this lesson in "Speaking Practice" and have them select "Record and Compare." There they will be able to repeat each utterance of the

Conversation Model, record their voice, and compare it with the speaker on the audio. (See a description of the ActiveBook on page ix of the Student's Book.)

Grammar. In the Grammar boxes, rules for new structures are presented through explanations of form, meaning, and use. Following each explanation are one or more examples so students can visualize the grammar in actual sentences or in patterns. Certain words and phrases are in bold color type in order to focus students' attention on those words within examples that show the form.

The Grammar boxes in the Student's Book present grammar deductively so that each presentation can serve as a reference for future review or study. However, if you prefer an inductive approach to grammar, an alternative inductive presentation of the grammar is also available as a printable extension activity on the ActiveTeach multimedia disc (click on "Inductive Grammar Charts"). (See a full explanation of your ActiveTeach multimedia disc and its contents on pages Txxix–Txxx.)

▶ **Teaching tips**   The Lesson Planner provides teaching suggestions and guidance for teaching the grammar in each Grammar box. However, it is important to remember that although focused presentations of grammar are essential, actual use of grammar greatly enhances its learning and activation.

Each new grammar structure is included at least one time within the Conversation Model so students always read, hear, and understand the structure in a conversational context. If you have presented the Conversation Model prior to presenting the Grammar, revisit the model and ask students to find the grammar they have just learned. Seeing the grammar in conversational use will help students remember it. If you haven't yet presented the Conversation Model, take a moment to ask students to find the grammar within the model after they have read and listened to it. At the end of the lesson, after students have completed the conversation practice in Now You Can, be sure to ask them to find the grammar again in their personalized conversations. (See "Now You Can" on page Txxiii.)

Grammar Booster. Everything students need to be successful in the lesson is covered in the Grammar box. However, following most Grammar boxes is an icon referring students to the optional Grammar Booster. Teachers and programs differ, so the Grammar Booster is an option for teachers who want to go beyond what is normally included in a textbook for this level.

Each Grammar Booster icon indicates the content of the Grammar Booster for that lesson. In some cases, the Grammar Booster expands on the specific grammar point taught in the lesson. In others, it includes related grammar concepts, some of which will be presented in more detail at a later stage in the series. In still other cases, the Grammar Booster provides targeted review of related concepts students have learned earlier. The Grammar Booster contains confirming exercises for each grammar point presented. Answers are printed in green on the Grammar Booster pages in this Teacher's Edition, or included in the lesson plan on the page facing the exercise, just as they are within the unit lesson. Please note that the Workbook has a separate section for optional extra Grammar Booster practice.

▶ **Teaching tips**   The Lesson Planner provides teaching suggestions for all grammar presentations and exercises in the Grammar Booster. We suggest that even if you decide not to use the Grammar Booster or if you elect to use only some, but not all of it, that students be made aware that there is extra material in the back of the book. Stronger students may be encouraged to work through this material on their own.

Grammar practice.   One or more individual pair work or group work exercises always follow the Grammar presentations. There are several types in *Top Notch*. Grammar Practice exercises provide written or oral practice of the structures being taught. Find the Grammar exercises direct students to look for examples of the structures in the Conversation Models or the Photo Stories. Understand the Grammar exercises have students demonstrate that they grasp the meaning of the grammar or how it works. Some exercises require listening comprehension of the grammar in context. (For general suggestions for teaching listening skills and strategies, see "Listening skills and strategies" within *Methodology for a communicative classroom* on page Txii. For information on managing listening comprehension exercises, see "Listening Comprehension" on page Txxiv.)

▶ **Teaching tips**   You may wish to complete the exercises with the class as a whole or you may prefer that students complete the exercises independently. If necessary, model how to complete the first item in each task. In large groups, you might divide the class so half of the class is working on those exercises that require an individual written response and the other half is working on those that entail pair or group oral work. With fewer students doing pair or group work at once, you will have more time to circulate so you can monitor, assist, and correct the pairs and groups. Then have the groups change tasks, allowing you to monitor and assist the oral work of the other students.

Specific suggestions are offered in the Lesson Planner for each exercise. When all the practice exercises are complete, you may wish to review answers with the whole class or have students check their answers with a partner.

If you would like your students to have even more practice of each grammar concept, encourage them to use their ActiveBook, where they will find numerous additional interactive grammar exercises with instant feedback. Students will find those by clicking on "Grammar and Vocabulary Practice." The *Top Notch* Workbook and the activities in the accompanying Copy & Go also include more grammar practice.

Vocabulary. Throughout *Top Notch*, new vocabulary is explicitly presented through captioned pictures, definitions, or in the context of example sentences. The vocabulary presentations in the Student's Book serve to convey clear meaning of each new vocabulary item and to provide a reference for self-study, especially valuable as students prepare for tests. Vocabulary in *Top Notch* is presented at word, phrase, and sentence level—including expressions, idioms, and collocations.

▶ **Teaching tips** Begin by focusing students' attention on the illustrations, definitions, or example sentences. An option is to have students cover the words with a sheet of paper and look only at the pictures. Pairs can test themselves to check which words and phrases they already know. Play the audio program from one of the available sources. (See FYI on page Txviii for alternative ways to access *Top Notch* audio.) If you don't have access to the audio, read the words aloud as a model. Alternatively, or in addition, students can study the words and phrases individually, using the MP3 audio files from their ActiveBook. Students should listen and repeat. Note that in the vocabulary presentations, singular count nouns are generally shown with the indefinite article *a/an*. Students should use the article when they repeat. Depending on your students' language background, the concept of count and non-count nouns may present a challenge. Using the indefinite article to contrast singular count nouns with non-count nouns will help reinforce this concept. For vocabulary that is presented as collocations or in the context of sentences, students should repeat the whole collocation or sentence as well.

If necessary, clarify the meaning of any words or phrases students have difficulty understanding. For lower-level students, convey the meaning physically—through gestures, mime, or reference to people or objects in the room—or give examples or a simple definition. Specific ideas for each vocabulary presentation are in the Lesson Planner.

When possible, personalize the vocabulary or use the vocabulary to talk about or ask questions about content familiar to your students. Many of the activities that immediately follow vocabulary presentations provide these opportunities.

Vocabulary presentations are followed by one or more exercises that may include written or oral responses. Many vocabulary presentations are followed by a listening comprehension exercise to reinforce and practice the new vocabulary. (For general suggestions for teaching listening skills and strategies, see *Methodology for a communicative classroom* on page Txii. For information on managing listening comprehension exercises, see "Listening comprehension" on page Txxiv.)

For review and reinforcement of vocabulary or as an alternative way to present it, use the "Vocabulary Flash Cards" from the printable *Extension Activities* section of the ActiveTeach multimedia disc. The Teaching Ideas found in the "Vocabulary Flash Cards" folder also contain a wealth of ideas for using the cards. In addition, the *Extension Activities* section of the ActiveTeach multimedia disc provides printable vocabulary-building strategies activity worksheets for many of the units. (See the "Learning Strategies" folder on ActiveTeach.) Another option is to ask students to use the *More Practice* section of their ActiveBook. Many of the activities in the Workbook and the interactive activities in Copy & Go provide more practice of the vocabulary as well.

Pronunciation. In addition to the rhythm and intonation practice that follows each Conversation Model, each unit presents and provides practice of a specific pronunciation point. Pronunciation points and activities are usually related to the lesson's content. Suggestions for extending this pronunciation practice are frequently given in the Lesson Planner as well.

▶ **Teaching tips** Play the audio from one of the sources, or model the pronunciation yourself. Have students first read and listen, then listen again and repeat. After students repeat, have them read the sentences to their partners. One technique is to have students exaggerate when they practice correct intonation, pronunciation, or stress to be sure they are focused on the pronunciation point. Remind them however, not to exaggerate the pronunciation point when they are really speaking. Remind students to practice the pronunciation point as well when they do the pair work activity in Now You Can.

To extend practice of the pronunciation point in a pair work activity, print out the corresponding "Pronunciation Activity" from the *Extension Activities* section of your ActiveTeach multimedia disc. If you would like do even more pronunciation work, print out the "Supplementary Pronunciation Lesson"* from the same source.

Now You Can. Each of the four integrated-skills lessons within *Top Notch* units ends with a feature called Now You Can. It is here, at the end of the lesson, that students demonstrate the achievement of the communication goal of the lesson. As students work through the exercises in this section, meaningfully activating the language of the lesson, they will feel motivated by their success and see confirmation of their efforts in achieving the goal. Because each goal has obvious practical and communicative value, students will see their English lessons as worthwhile. Cognitive awareness of progress is exhilarating for language learners and keeps them interested and learning.

Pair work activities. Now You Can sections in Lessons 1 and 2 always provide a guided conversation pair work, which is fashioned after the Conversation Model from the lesson. In the guided pair work, pairs of students personalize or role-play the Conversation Model, inserting their own choice of information in the blank spaces (gaps) so they can make the conversation their own. The gaps have been carefully placed within the conversation to offer a number of possibilities based on what the students have learned, so they are largely foolproof. The importance of this activity cannot be overstated, for it is in producing their own language in this controlled activity that students transfer language to reflect their own ideas, taking their first steps toward truly free language use.

Throughout Lessons 1 and 2 in *Top Notch*, the gaps in the Now You Can pair work activities perform a variety of roles. Some are included specifically because they enable students to substitute target vocabulary or grammar. Others are there so students can address each other with their own names. Still others are there so students can insert their own preferences; for example, foods or activities. Finally, others are there simply because students have already learned a number of ways to

express a particular thought. For instance, following "Thank you," a gap for a response is provided because students can respond in a number of previously learned ways, such as "You're welcome," "No problem," or "Sure!" Each gap has been tested to be sure students have enough language "in their pockets" to provide one or more responses.

This controlled communication practice makes the Conversation Model even more memorable. Additionally, it is of great value for pronunciation and intonation practice. Illustrations and other concrete cues are often provided to keep the ideas flowing.

So that students have more than one opportunity to personalize the conversation and practice several times, each time differently, Now You Can almost always directs students to first change roles and then change partners. With another partner or role, students access and activate even more language, making it unforgettable.

Don't Stop! So that students extend the conversation, a Don't stop! activity box suggests ways students could move beyond the actual Conversation Model, making it longer or taking it in another direction. Instructions have been carefully written to ensure that students have already learned any language they need in order to continue. In some cases, students are asked to continue the conversation by moving on to another subject that might naturally follow. Other Don't Stop! activities encourage students to ask and answer additional questions.

▶ **Teaching tips** Begin by focusing students on the title of the Now You Can activity. Remind them of, or solicit from them, the goal of the lesson so they are aware that they are about to achieve the goal. Then read the instructions aloud so students understand the purpose of the task and are reminded of the original Conversation Model and the vocabulary and grammar to use in performing the pair work activity. Show them the gaps in the pair work activity in which they need to use the grammar or the vocabulary from the lesson. Emphasis has been placed on building students' cognitive awareness of what they are doing. Research has shown that awareness greatly contributes to learning. To this end, ask students to look back at the vocabulary and grammar they learned in this lesson and encourage them to use it here.

Model the conversation with a more confident student to demonstrate that students should change the Conversation Model by filling in new language from the lesson or from other sources. *Be sure students do not think the point of the practice is to test their "memory" of the original Conversation Model.* The purpose is exactly the opposite. The point is

---

* Supplementary Pronunciation Lessons by Bertha Chela-Flores.

personalization and experimentation. The most effective way to encourage experimentation is to show approval when students use imagination and variety in their "gap fillers."

Students practice the conversation with a partner and then change roles. Encourage students to vary their partners from lesson to lesson. As students practice, circulate and offer help and encouragement as needed. Make sure students are aware of the social situation of the conversation so that they use socially appropriate pronunciation and tone. To encourage active listening and socially appropriate body language, remind students to make eye contact during conversations. An option is to have pairs role-play their conversations for the class or for each other. Having different pairs of students perform their conversations in front of the class reminds all students of how much social language they have learned. Specific suggestions for each Now You Can section are provided in the Lesson Planner.

For additional reinforcement in class, direct students either before or after the pair work activity in Now You Can to the "Speaking Practice" section of their ActiveBooks. There they will find every Conversation Model in a format that permits them to role-play the conversation, recording their own voices as either Speaker A or Speaker B and responding in their own way, which they can play back as a complete conversation with the other recorded voice. This activity has limitless possibilities and is a lot of fun.

Another option or alternative is to print out and photocopy the "Conversation Pair Work Cards" from the *Extension Activities* section of your ActiveTeach multimedia disc (see page Txxix), assigning Speaker A's role to one student and Speaker B's role to his or her partner. This allows you to get students "out of the book" and actively listening to each other. Teaching Ideas are provided on your ActiveTeach multimedia disc to maximize the impact of this practice. (See the "Conversation Pair Work Cards" folder.) In addition, the *Extension Activities* section offers some printable activity worksheets for building conversation strategies (in the "Learning Strategies" folder).

Lessons 3 and 4

Lessons 3 and 4 provide integrated skills with a listening or reading focus. They begin with a communication goal and a pre-listening or pre-reading activity. Then each lesson culminates in a Now You Can activity, which is an opportunity for students to demonstrate their achievement of the goal.

Before You Listen and Before You Read. A Before You Listen (or Before You Read) feature prepares students for the reading or listening passage that follows. In some places vocabulary is presented prior to the passage. This vocabulary is taken from the passage and should be learned and used productively by the student both before and after reading or listening. Elsewhere, there are discussion activities that tap into prior knowledge or explore students' ideas on the topic of the reading or listening passage.

▶ **Teaching tips** The Lesson Planner suggests a procedure for each Before You Listen (or Before you Read) activity. In addition to the suggested procedure in the Lesson Planner, options and alternatives are also presented to help you approach these activities in a varied way. As always, we encourage you to use your own procedures with all activities and presentations if preferable.

Another pre-listening or pre-reading technique you can use in addition to what is already on the Student's Book page is to give students a few minutes to examine any photos, captions, headings, or charts in the reading passage or accompanying the listening exercise that follows.

Listening Comprehension. Listening passages and the exercises that follow them in Lessons 3 and 4 provide the core listening practice of the unit and focus on the building of listening comprehension skills and strategies such as listening for main ideas, details, point of view, prediction, and the like. (The Learning Objectives charts on pages iv–vii show the full range of skills and strategies covered in this level of *Top Notch*.)

Listening passages contain language at students' productive level as well as at the more challenging "i+1" level. Context, intonation, and similarity to language students already know all aid them in comprehending the listening passages.

▶ **Teaching tips** Point out to students that a major cause of lack of comprehension is the natural panic that occurs when learners hear unknown words. Be sure that they understand that the instructional purpose of a listening comprehension activity is to build their ability to derive meaning from listening *even when they don't understand every word.* Make sure students understand that the listening comprehension activities are not meant to be tests, but rather skill-building activities.

To maximize the effectiveness of these activities, avoid providing students with explanations of new language beyond any vocabulary that was taught prior to the actual listening. If a student specifically asks about a new word, give the meaning, but do not spend a lot of time on it. Exposure to "i+1" language promotes students' language development and prepares them to fend for themselves outside a classroom, where there will be no one to explain language to them prior to hearing it.

If information about the speakers, setting, or situation is provided in the directions to the exercise, read it aloud before listening. In general, we recommend that students listen to the passage the first time with books closed. (In some cases, the Lesson Planner provides an alternative approach.) In this way, students can focus on the "big picture" without the distraction of completing the exercise. Alternatively, you might prefer to ask general questions (after the first listening), such as "Who's talking?" "Where are the people?" "What are the people doing?" If students are not forthcoming with answers to these questions, you can restate a question, providing two answers from which to choose. The value of this approach is to convince students that they have, in fact, understood a good deal, even if they have not understood everything. Demonstrating to students that they have understood something challenging builds their confidence and helps reduce their fear of listening.

Before students listen again and complete an exercise, have them look at the exercise to focus their attention on the specific listening task, such as listening for locations, for opinions, in order to predict, and the like. Play the audio as many times as necessary for students to complete the activity. Try not to approach these exercises as "tests." Repeated exposure to each listening passage has substantial instructional value. Increasing students' exposure to challenging language enhances their comprehension and confidence.

Review answers with the whole class, or have students check their answers with a partner. Be sure to ask students to explain their answers.

Please note that all listening passages are accessible on the student's ActiveBook. If, to save time, you wish students to listen individually and complete the exercises on their own, they can do that out of class. If an exercise is in the form of pair work or discussion, however, we recommend that it be completed during class time.

If you would like more exercises for the listening passage, there may be a corresponding listening comprehension strategy worksheet in the *Extension Activities* section of your ActiveTeach multimedia disc. (See the "Learning Strategies" folder.) If you want even more listening practice, there are additional listening passages and exercises for every unit, including dictation practice, in the *More Practice* section of the Student's ActiveBook.

Readings. Readings and the exercises that follow them provide the core reading experience in the *Top Notch* units. All readings are based on authentic sources. To avoid frustrating students at this level, we have adapted and simplified some of the language from the original sources, but have taken care to maintain the authentic character of the material. The readings in each unit are related to the content of the other lessons within the unit to facilitate discussion using previously learned language.

Exercises have been developed to go beyond simple factual comprehension questions and engage students in skills and strategies such as recognizing point of view, critical thinking, inference, and the like. Exercises are challenging and provide both receptive and productive responses. The exercises will not only build and check comprehension, they will stimulate discussion and help students build the skills they need to perform well on standardized tests.

▶ **Teaching tips** As with the listening passages, students should be reminded that it is not necessary to know every word in a reading in order to understand it. They should be encouraged to read without looking up every new word in the dictionary. Remind students that reading in a foreign or second language always presents the challenge of some unknown language. Students need to learn that they can comprehend main ideas, get specific information, and infer information even without knowing every word. If students are apprehensive about not being able to "translate" every word into their own language (which students sometimes confuse with comprehension—see "Teaching the receptive skills: reading and listening" in *Methodology for a Communicative Classroom* on page Txi for a discussion of this problem), encourage them to guess the meaning of new words as much as possible, or to comprehend as much as they can without understanding every word. After students read, ask questions or use activities that lead them to figure out the meaning of new language and that help them identify the essential information from the reading. The Lesson Planner makes specific suggestions to help students build the skill of understanding vocabulary from context.

Please note that all readings are recorded on the Classroom Audio Program for optional listening practice. Listening to the readings gives excellent ear training for the rhythm, stress, and intonation of narrative (as opposed to conversational) speech. It also builds students' awareness of collocations (words that "go together" as phrases.) Several optional alternatives for using the audio of the readings follow: If you choose to use the audio of the reading, you may play it as students read along for the first time, or not until after students have done all other strictly-reading applications. Or you may choose to have them listen with books closed for listening comprehension practice. Another approach is to use the audio as a model for reading aloud, which provides another level of pronunciation practice. The possibilities are numerous. We encourage you to use the reading audio in a way that matches your needs and your teaching philosophy. We also encourage you to experiment and try a variety of approaches. The Lesson Planner provides suggestions for using the audio as an alternative or additional activity.

For exercises following the reading, read the directions aloud, or ask volunteers to read them. Have students read the exercise items and then reread the reading passage independently. As students read, they can underline words or information that will help them complete the exercise. Allow students a set period of time to refer to the reading to complete the exercise individually, in pairs, or in small groups. Have students check their work with another pair or group, or review answers as a class. For a challenge, have students practice reading the passage or parts of it aloud in small groups.

In addition to the exercises on the page, optional basic comprehension and critical-thinking exercises on the same reading passage ("Extra Reading Comprehension Questions") can be printed out from the student's ActiveBook. There are also extra reading exercises for the same passage in the Workbook. To teach strategies and prepare students for tests, there are printable activity worksheets for reading strategies in the *Extension Activities* section of your ActiveTeach multimedia disc. (See the "Learning Strategies" folder.) Printable "Extra Reading Comprehension Questions" are also in the *Extension Activities* section of your ActiveTeach multimedia disc.

If you are looking for even more reading practice, there are additional reading passages and exercises in the *More Practice* section of the student's ActiveBook.

Now You Can. As in Lessons 1 and 2, Now You Can is an activity in which students demonstrate the achievement of the communication goal of the lesson. In Lessons 3 and 4, Now You Can is an integrated free-speaking activity based on the content and theme of the reading or listening passage. Surveys, questionnaires, and notepadding activities are included to help students frame their thoughts and prepare what they will say.

▶ **Teaching tips** Success in the discussion or role play will be greatly enhanced by allowing students adequate time to complete any surveys and notepadding activities. (For an expanded discussion of this, see "Actively developing free expression" in the section entitled *Methodology for a communicative classroom* on pages Tx–Txi.) In every case, the Lesson Planner provides detailed suggestions and alternatives.

Be Sure to Recycle This Language. When language is out of sight it is often out of mind. The Be Sure to Recycle This Language feature, which represents a major instructional strategy of the *Top Notch* course, ensures that students get multiple opportunities to use previously learned language, making it unforgettable. The language listed in the form of "wordposts" has been included because it will support students in their discussions within Now You Can. (See a discussion of wordposting in "Actively developing free expression" on page Txi.) Be Sure to Recycle This Language boxes cumulatively gather language from the unit as well as from previous units, listing it to be used as wordposts. *No unknown language is included.*

▶ **Teaching tips** Focus students' attention on the wordposts and encourage them to look at the words and phrases as they conduct their discussions, role plays, and the like. One option is to have students check each one off as it is used. Alternatively, have students report which language they used after the activity is completed. Give students positive feedback when they use the wordposts, and encourage them to remember and use all the language that is, or should be, in their repertoire. To further elevate the importance of the wordposts, ask students to use the *Unit Study Guides* (which can be printed from the student's ActiveBook or from your ActiveTeach multimedia disc) for each Now You Can activity, adding other language they have used and want to remember. If your class always meets in the same classroom, you may wish to have a permanent "word wall"—wordposts on large paper displayed on the classroom walls—that students can consult for support. (See "Wordposting" on page Txi.)

Review

The left-hand page reviews essential content and skills from the unit and provides exercises that require a written response. The first activity is always a listening comprehension exercise, and the page always ends with a writing assignment in which students use the language content of the unit in a formal piece of writing that contains one or more paragraphs.

Writing Booster. An optional Writing Booster teaches and practices the conventions of written English and provides guidance for the writing activity on the page. (To see a list of the scope and sequence of writing skills in this level of *Top Notch*, see the Learning Objectives charts on pages iv-vii.) We suggest that even if you decide not to use the Writing Booster, or if you elect to use only some, but not all of it, students be made aware of it. Stronger students may be encouraged to work through this material on their own.

Oral Review. The right-hand page contains the Oral Review, a signature feature of the *Top Notch* course—a full-page illustration or a set of photos with instructions to use it as a stimulus for an oral review of the entire unit. The picture provides a clear visual context for practice and helps bridge the gap between practice and authentic language use. Activities on the page prompt students to find and name items in the picture, ask and answer questions about the picture, create conversations between people in the picture, tell stories about the people or situations in the picture, and more.

▶ **Teaching tips** Have students work individually to complete the exercises. Move around the room to offer help as needed. Review the correct answers as a class. Alternatively, or to save time, you may wish to have students complete these exercises as homework, reviewing the answers quickly the next day. Note any areas of difficulty and provide additional instruction and practice as necessary.

For the writing activity, there are optional "Writing Process Worksheets" you can print out from the *Extension Activities* section of your ActiveTeach multimedia disc.

▶ **Teaching tips** Specific suggestions for getting full value out of each illustration are provided in the Lesson Planner for each Oral Review. Depending on the focus of the picture(s), the Lesson Planner indicates responses your students should be able to produce as they follow the directions at the top of the page. This information is enclosed in a text box on the Lesson Planner page and is called "Possible responses."

Begin by having students read the directions for each activity. Be sure they review the example provided to feel confident they know what is expected. You may wish to have all students do each activity at the same time, or alternatively, you may wish to divide the class so that groups of students are working on different activities. Divide students into pairs or small groups. Move around the room and offer help as needed. To encourage risk-taking and improvisation, avoid interrupting students with corrections. Instead, take notes on common student mistakes and review them as a class at the end of the activity. Encourage students to say as much as they can and to extend the suggested tasks as much as possible. The following are some techniques that teachers have found successful with the Oral Review:

- **Word Memory Game.** Allow students to look at the picture for one minute. Then have them close their books and write down all the vocabulary items they can remember from the picture. See who remembers the most items.

- **Groups of Four.** In pairs, students write three true statements and three false statements about the picture. Regroup students into groups of four. One pair reads their statements, in random order, to the other pair, who replies *true* or *false*.

- **Chain Story.** One group (or pair) begins by saying a sentence about the picture, and the next group follows by saying another sentence. Groups that can no longer say anything are eliminated until only one group (or pair) remains.

- **Content Memory Game.** Give students one minute to study the picture and remember all they can about it. Then have students close their books and form small groups. Ask questions about the picture and keep a record of the correct answers. After each question, allow the groups time to discuss and write down an answer. Review as a class and see which group has the most correct answers.

- **"Who Said It?" Game.** Give each character in the picture a name. Working in pairs, students write one line of conversation for each person in the picture. Then each pair of students joins another pair. Pairs take turns reading their lines and guessing who in the picture is speaking. Students may answer with the name of the character, by pointing, or by describing the character; for example, "the short woman."

- **Mystery Characters.** Have volunteers act out one of their conversations in front of the class. Students listen and guess which people in the picture are being portrayed.

- **"What Did They Say?" Game.** Have two volunteers act out their conversation in front of the class. The class listens and tries to remember exactly what was said. Working in pairs, students try to re-create the exact conversation they heard.

- **Script-Scramble.** In pairs, students write their conversation in dialogue form. Each pair then writes each line of its conversation on a separate slip of paper, mixes up the order of the slips, and gives them to another pair. The other pair must then put the conversation back in the correct order.

- **This is Your Life.** Have students choose one person in the picture and write his or her biography. The details of the person's life should be based on what is in the picture, but students will have to make up much of the information. Have volunteers read their biographies to a group or to the class and have students guess who in the picture is being described.

Oral Progress Assessment. An optional Oral Progress Assessment based on the full-page picture is provided in the Lesson Planner.

▶ **Teaching tips** The Oral Progress Assessment is designed to take no more than five minutes per student. These short tests make it possible to check class progress quickly. The *Oral Progress Assessment Charts* can be printed from your ActiveTeach multimedia disc and used to guide your assessment. Please note that the Complete Assessment Package provides Speaking Tests after Unit 5 and Unit 10.

Now I Can. This check box is provided for students to self-assess and demonstrate that they have achieved the communication goals of the unit. These goals appear in the Preview Lesson and then again at the beginning of the four integrated-skills lessons (Lessons 1–4). The check-box format is used in the spirit of the Common European Framework's "Can do" statements. Allowing students to check off each achieved goal is a motivating and success-confirming experience.

▶ **Teaching tips** Students can check the goals off at the end of the unit, demonstrating to themselves how much they've learned. Alternatively, they can check each one off at the end of each of the four lessons. We recommend that time be taken for informal congratulations to the students for their progress. One extension is to ask students where and when they imagine they can use their new communication abilities.

How to Use *ActiveTeach*

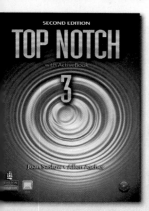

SECOND EDITION

TOP NOTCH
with ActiveBook

3

Joan Saslow • Allen Ascher

Digital Student's Book with

- Interactive Whiteboard Software
- More Practice (from *ActiveBook*)
- Complete Classroom Audio Program
- *Top Notch TV*

Other Resources (printable)

- How to use the Digital Student's Book
- Extension Activities
- *Top Notch TV* Activity Worksheets
- • Unit Study Guides
  • Pronunciation Table
  • Reference Charts
  • Oral Progress Assessment Charts
- • Audioscripts
  • Workbook Answer Key
- Authors' Academic Articles

ActiveTeach menu screen

Insert the disc into a computer and choose the Digital Student's Book or one of the printable resources.

The Digital Student's Book

Choose a unit and open any two-page lesson.

Choose any of the interactive activities in the student's *ActiveBook*.

Open any segment of the *Top Notch TV* video program.

Enlarge any section of the page.

Play the audio.

Click on ◀ to instantly go to that lesson's Grammar Booster.

Write, highlight, erase, create notes, etc.

Note: If you'd prefer to view *Top Notch TV* as a DVD, insert the disc into a DVD player instead.

Save any work you've created in class.

Other Resources (printable)

How to use the Digital Student's Book

Extension Activities

Top Notch TV Activity Worksheets

- Unit Study Guides
- Pronunciation Table
- Reference Charts
- Oral Progress Assessment Charts

- Audioscripts
- Workbook Answer Key

Authors' Academic Articles

ware
Book)
o Program

Extension Activities
Choose activities that suit your own teaching situation and style.

- Vocabulary Flash Cards
- Conversation Pair Work Cards
- Learning Strategies
- Pronunciation Activities
- Supplementary Pronunciation Lessons
- Inductive Grammar Charts
- Extra Reading Comprehension Questions
- Graphic Organizers
- Just for Fun
- Writing Process Worksheets
- *Top Notch Pop* Song Activities

Services
— a suit

Services
— shoes

DATE: _____

Writing Process Worksheet
(Accompanies Unit 3, page 36)

ASSIGNMENT: Write an explanation, giving examples from personal experience, of whether or not you are a procrastinator.

1. PREWRITING

Check the box that is true for you.

❑ I get things repaired as soon as they get damaged.	❑ I usually wait a few months to get something repaired.	❑ After a year or so, I just buy a new item.
❑ I get things cleaned right away.	❑ I wait until I need to wear something, then get it cleaned.	❑ Stuff just sits in my closet! I never get it cleaned.
❑ I always pay my bills on time.	❑ Every now and then, I'm a little late paying my bills.	❑ I can never seem to pay my bills on time.
❑ I plan my vacation months in advance.	❑ I like to plan vacations at the last minute, right before I leave.	❑ I never plan vacations! I just get up and go!
❑ I'm really good about keeping in touch with people	❑ Sometimes I let a lot of time go by, but then send an e-mail or call my friends.	❑ I just can't seem to keep up with my friends.

2. WRITING

On a separate sheet of paper, write a first draft of the paragraph. Use the information in the chart from Prewriting to support your opinions.

3. PEER FEEDBACK

Meet with a partner. Read each other's paragraph. After reading the paragraph, complete the Peer Feedback Checklist. Then give your partner your feedback.

Top Notch 3, Second Edition
Copyright ©2011 by Pearson Education. Permission granted to reproduce for classroom use.

Unit 3

NAME: _____ DATE: _____

Learning Strategy
(Unit 10, page 118, Reading)

READING STRATEGY: identifying causes and effects

Understand the relationship between causes (why something happens or is true) and effects (results of the causes) to improve comprehension of a text.

PRACTICE

Fill in the chart with causes and effects from the Reading on page 118 in the Student's Book.

Causes	Effects
An increase in the amount of CO_2 in the air…	contributes to global warming.
Choosing clean energy…	will use less gasoline and save money.
Replacing an old refrigerator or air-conditioner with an energy efficient model…	will use 25% less electricity.
Using products that are recycled from old paper, glass, and metal…	
Shipping foods over long distances…	causes flooding in coastal areas.
	endangers sea life.
The shrinking of glaciers…	leads to famine.

Unit 10

Top Notch 3, Second Edition
Copyright ©2011 by Pearson Education. Permission granted to reproduce for classroom use.

DATE: _____

Graphic Organizer
(Unit 9, page T107, Debate)

Pros   Co

Unit Study Guides help students review and prepare for tests.

DATE: _____

NAME: _____

Unit Study Guide
(Unit 3)

Self-Check Write a checkmark ✔ next to the language you know. Return to the unit in your Student's Book to find and study the language you are not yet sure of.

GRAMMAR
❑ Causatives *get*, *have*, and *make* (page 28)
❑ The passive causative (page 30)

VOCABULARY
Some ways to help out another person
❑ give [someone] a ride
❑ keep an eye on [something or someone]
❑ lend [someone] [something]
❑ fill in for [someone]
❑ pick up [someone or something]

...vices
...ry clean [a suit]
❑ repair [shoes]
❑ frame [a picture]
❑ deliver [a package]
❑ lengthen / shorten [a skirt]

Adjectives to describe good service
❑ reliable
❑ reasonable
❑ helpful
❑ professional

Planning an event
❑ make a list of attendees
❑ pick a date, time, and place
❑ make a budget
❑ assign responsibilities
❑ plan an agenda
❑ send out an announcement
❑ arrange catering
❑ set up the room

Other language
❑ repair shop
❑ doctor's appointment

SOCIAL LANGUAGE
❑ I know this is really last minute.
❑ It's really urgent.
❑ You're a lifesaver.
❑ No sweat.
❑ Thanks a million.
❑ I owe you one.
❑ I see you've got a lot on your plate today.
❑ I won't keep you any longer.
❑ I wonder if you could do me a favor.
❑ Sure. What do you need?
❑ Do you think [you could give me a ride]?
❑ I would, but [I have a doctor's appointment 2:00].
❑ Oh, that's OK. I understand.
❑ Maybe you could [get Jack to take you].
❑ Good idea.
❑ I'll see what I can...
❑ I really appreciate... Thanks!

Txxx

Top Notch TV Activity Worksheets build comprehension skills.

Name _____

UNIT 2

Interview: *Are you traditional in your medical ideas?*

A. Read the interviewer's question. Then match each ... person who said it.

Are you traditional in your medical ideas … or do you like to explore nontraditional treatments, such as acupuncture or homeopathic medicine?

a.   b.

_____ 1. "I'm more for the naturalistic approach ...
_____ 2. "I don't explore nontraditional treatm...
_____ 3. "I'm more traditional than anything el...

B. Check the things Vanessa does when she fee...
❑ gets a lot of rest
❑ takes an herbal medicine
❑ takes vitamins
❑ drinks a lot of orange juice
❑ drinks a lot of tea

Academic articles from the Top Notch Professional Development Series by Saslow and Ascher

TOP NOTCH PROFESSIONAL DEVELOPMENT SERIES

Issue 1

MAKING ENGLISH UNFORGETTABLE

Enhancing Acquisition in the EFL Setting

Joan Saslow and Allen Ascher

These "three R's" ensure memorability in the EFL setting:

RELEVANCE

"English? I studied it for ten years and I can't speak a word!" Such is the self-critical lament heard outside of...

SECOND EDITION

TOP NOTCH

English for Today's World

3

Joan Saslow • Allen Ascher

With *Top Notch Pop Songs and Karaoke*
by Rob Morsberger

PEARSON
Longman

About the Authors

Joan Saslow

Joan Saslow has taught in a variety of programs in South America and the United States. She is author of a number of multi-level integrated-skills courses for adults and young adults: *Ready to Go: Language, Lifeskills, and Civics; Workplace Plus: Living and Working in English;* and of *Literacy Plus*. She is also author of *English in Context: Reading Comprehension for Science and Technology*. Ms. Saslow was the series director of *True Colors* and *True Voices*. She participates in the English Language Specialist Program in the U.S. Department of State's Bureau of Educational and Cultural Affairs.

Allen Ascher

Allen Ascher has been a teacher and a teacher trainer in China and the United States and taught in the TESOL Certificate Program at the New School in New York. He was also academic director of the International English Language Institute at Hunter College. Mr. Ascher is author of the "Teaching Speaking" module of *Teacher Development Interactive*, an online multimedia teacher-training program, and of *Think about Editing: A Grammar Editing Guide for ESL*.

Both Ms. Saslow and Mr. Ascher are frequent and popular speakers at professional conferences and international gatherings of EFL and ESL teachers.

Authors' Acknowledgments

The authors are indebted to these reviewers who provided extensive and detailed feedback and suggestions for the second edition of *Top Notch* as well as the hundreds of teachers who participated in surveys and focus groups.

Manuel Aguilar Díaz, El Cultural Trujillo, Peru • **Manal Al Jordi,** Expression Training Company, Kuwait • **José Luis Ames Portocarrero,** El Cultural Arequipa, Peru • **Vanessa de Andrade,** CCBEU Inter Americano, Curitiba, Brazil • **Rossana Aragón Castro,** ICPNA Cusco, Peru • **Jennifer Ballesteros,** Universidad del Valle de México, Campus Tlalpan, Mexico City, Mexico • **Brad Bawtinheimer,** PROULEX, Guadalajara, Mexico • **Carolina Bermeo,** Universidad Central, Bogotá, Colombia • **Zulma Buitrago,** Universidad Pedagógica Nacional, Bogotá, Colombia • **Fabiola R. Cabello,** Idiomas Católica, Lima, Peru • **Emma Campo Collante,** Universidad Central Bogotá, Colombia • **Viviane de Cássia Santos Carlini,** Spectrum Line, Pouso Alegre, Brazil • **Fanny Castelo,** ICPNA Cusco, Peru • **José Luis Castro Moreno,** Universidad de León, Mexico • **Mei Chia-Hong,** Southern Taiwan University (STUT), Taiwan • **Guven Ciftci,** Faith University, Turkey • **Freddy Correa Montenegro,** Centro Colombo Americano, Cali, Colombia • **Alicia Craman de Carmand,** Idiomas Católica, Lima, Peru • **Jesús G. Díaz Osío,** Florida National College, Miami, USA • **Ruth Domínguez,** Universidad Central Bogotá, Colombia • **Roxana Echave,** El Cultural Arequipa, Peru • **Angélica Escobar Chávez,** Universidad de León, Mexico • **John Fieldeldy,** College of Engineering, Nihon University, Aizuwakamatsu-shi, Japan • **Herlinda Flores,** Centro de Idiomas Universidad Veracruzana, Mexico • **Claudia Franco,** Universidad Pedagógica Nacional, Colombia • **Andrea Fredricks,** Embassy CES, San Francisco, USA • **Chen-Chen Fu,** National Kaoshiung First Science Technology University, Taiwan • **María Irma Gallegos Peláez,** Universidad del Valle de México, Mexico City, Mexico • **Carolina García Carbajal,** El Cultural Arequipa, Peru • **Claudia Gavancho Terrazas,** ICPNA Cusco, Peru • **Adriana Gómez,** Centro Colombo Americano, Bogotá, Colombia • **Raphaël Goossens,** ICPNA Cusco, Peru • **Carlo Granados,** Universidad Central, Bogotá, Colombia • **Ralph Grayson,** Idiomas Católica, Lima, Peru • **Murat Gultekin,** Fatih University, Turkey • **Monika Hennessey,** ICPNA Chiclayo, Peru • **Lidia Hernández Medina,** Universidad del Valle de México, Mexico City, Mexico • **Jesse Huang,** National Central University, Taiwan • **Eric Charles Jones,** Seoul University of Technology, South Korea • **Jun-Chen Kuo,** Tajen University, Taiwan • **Susan Krieger,** Embassy CES, San Francisco, USA • **Robert Labelle,** Centre for Training and Development, Dawson College, Canada • **Erin Lemaistre,** Chung-Ang University, South Korea • **Eleanor S. Leu,** Soochow University, Taiwan • **Yihui Li (Stella Li),** Fooyin University, Taiwan • **Chin-Fan Lin,** Shih Hsin University, Taiwan • **Linda Lin,** Tatung Institute of Technology, Taiwan • **Kristen Lindblom,** Embassy CES, San Francisco, USA • **Ricardo López,** PROULEX, Guadalajara, Mexico • **Neil Macleod,** Kansai Gaidai University, Osaka, Japan • **Robyn McMurray,** Pusan National University, South Korea • **Paula Medina,** London Language Institute, Canada • **María Teresa Meléndez de Elorreaga,** ICPNA Chiclayo, Peru • **Sandra Cecilia Mora Espejo,** Universidad del Valle de México, Campus Tlalpan, Mexico City, Mexico • **Ricardo Nausa,** Centro Colombo Americano, Bogotá, Colombia • **Tim Newfields,** Tokyo University Faculty of Economics, Tokyo, Japan • **Mónica Nomberto,** ICPNA Chiclayo, Peru • **Scarlett Ostojic,** Idiomas Católica, Lima, Peru • **Ana Cristina Ochoa,** CCBEU Inter Americano, Curitiba, Brazil • **Doralba Pérez,** Universidad Pedagógica Nacional, Bogotá, Colombia • **David Perez Montalvo,** ICPNA Cusco, Peru • **Wahrena Elizabeth Pfeister,** University of Suwon, South Korea • **Wayne Allen Pfeister,** University of Suwon, South Korea • **Cecilia Ponce de León,** ICPNA Cusco, Peru • **Andrea Rebonato,** CCBEU Inter Americano, Curitiba, Brazil • **Elizabeth Rodríguez López,** El Cultural Trujillo, Peru • **Olga Rodríguez Romero,** El Cultural Trujillo, Peru • **Timothy Samuelson,** BridgeEnglish, Denver, USA • **Enrique Sánchez Guzmán,** PROULEX, Guadalajara, Mexico • **Letícia Santos,** ICBEU Ibiá, Brazil • **Lyndsay Shaeffer,** Embassy CES, San Francisco, USA • **John Eric Sherman,** Hong Ik University, South Korea • **João Vitor Soares,** NACC, São Paulo, Brazil • **Elena Sudakova,** English Language Center, Kiev, Ukraine • **Richard Swingle,** Kansai Gaidai College, Osaka, Japan • **Sandrine Ting,** St. John's University, Taiwan • **Shu-Ping Tsai,** Fooyin University, Taiwan • **José Luis Urbina Hurtado,** Universidad de León, Mexico • **Monica Urteaga,** Idiomas Católica, Lima, Peru • **Juan Carlos Villafuerte,** ICPNA Cusco, Peru • **Dr. Wen-hsien Yang,** National Kaohsiung Hospitality College, Kaohsiung, Taiwan • **Holger Zamora,** ICPNA Cusco, Peru.

Learning Objectives

Unit	Communication Goals	Vocabulary	Grammar
1 **Make Small Talk** page 2	• Make small talk • Describe a busy schedule • Develop your cultural awareness • Discuss how culture changes over time	• Ways to ask about proper address • Intensifiers • Manners and etiquette	• Tag questions: usage, form, and common errors • The past perfect: meaning, form, and usage **GRAMMAR BOOSTER** • Tag questions: short answers • Verb usage: present and past (review)
2 **Health Matters** page 14	• Call in sick • Make a medical or dental appointment • Discuss types of treatments • Talk about medications	• Dental emergencies • Symptoms • Medical procedures • Types of medical treatments • Medications	• Modal <u>must</u>: drawing conclusions • <u>Will be able to</u> • Modals <u>may</u> and <u>might</u> **GRAMMAR BOOSTER** • Other ways to draw conclusions: <u>probably</u>, <u>most likely</u>; common errors • Expressing possibility with <u>maybe</u>; common errors
3 **Getting Things Done** page 26	• Get someone else to do something • Request express service • Evaluate the quality of service • Plan a meeting or social event	• Ways to help out another person • Ways to indicate acceptance • Services • Planning an event	• Causatives <u>get</u>, <u>have</u>, and <u>make</u> • The passive causative **GRAMMAR BOOSTER** • <u>Let</u> to indicate permission • Causative <u>have</u>: common errors • The passive causative: the <u>by</u> phrase
4 **Reading for Pleasure** page 38	• Recommend a book • Offer to lend something • Describe your reading habits • Discuss the quality of reading materials	• Types of books • Ways to describe a book • Ways to enjoy reading	• Noun clauses: usage, form, and common error • Noun clauses: embedded questions ◦ Form and common errors **GRAMMAR BOOSTER** • Verbs and adjectives that can be followed by clauses with <u>that</u> • Embedded questions: usage and common errors, punctuation, with infinitives • Noun clauses as subjects and objects
5 **Natural Disasters** page 50	• Convey a message • Report news • Describe natural disasters • Prepare for an emergency	• Severe weather and other natural disasters • Adjectives of severity • Emergency preparations and supplies	• Indirect speech: ◦ Imperatives ◦ <u>Say</u> and <u>tell</u> ◦ Tense changes **GRAMMAR BOOSTER** • Direct speech: punctuation rules • Indirect speech: optional tense changes ◦ Form and common errors

Conversation Strategies	Listening / Pronunciation	Reading	Writing
• Talk about the weather to begin a conversation with someone you don't know • Use question tags to encourage someone to make small talk • Ask about how someone wants to be addressed • Answer a <u>Do you mind</u> question with <u>Absolutely not</u> to indicate agreement • Say <u>That was nothing</u> to indicate that something even more surprising happened • Use <u>Wow!</u> to indicate that you are impressed	**Listening Skills:** • Listen for main ideas • Listen to summarize • Confirm the correct paraphrases **Pronunciation:** • Rising and falling intonation of tag questions	**Texts:** • A business meeting memo and agenda • A magazine article about formal dinner etiquette of the past • A survey about culture change • A photo story **Skills/Strategies:** • Predict • Confirm facts • Summarize	**Task:** • Write a formal and an informal e-mail message **WRITING BOOSTER** • Formal e-mail etiquette
• Introduce disappointing information with <u>I'm afraid …</u> • Express disappointment with <u>I'm sorry to hear that</u> • Show concern with <u>Is something wrong?</u> and <u>That must be awful</u> • Begin a request for assistance with <u>I wonder if …</u> • Use <u>Let's see …</u> to indicate you are checking for something • Confirm an appointment with <u>I'll / We'll see you then</u> • Express emphatic thanks with <u>I really appreciate it</u>	**Listening Skills:** • Auditory discrimination • Listen for details **Pronunciation:** • Intonation of lists	**Texts:** • A travel tips website about dental emergencies • A brochure about choices in medical treatments • A patient information form • A medicine label • A photo story **Skills/Strategies:** • Understand from context • Relate to personal experience • Draw conclusions	**Task:** • Write an essay comparing two types of medical treatments **WRITING BOOSTER** • Comparisons and contrasts
• Use <u>I would, but …</u> and an excuse to politely turn down a request • Indicate acceptance of someone's excuse with <u>That's OK. I understand</u> • Suggest an alternative with <u>Maybe you could …</u> • Soften a request by beginning it with <u>Do you think you could …</u> • Soften an almost certain <u>no</u> with <u>That might be difficult</u> • Use <u>Well, …</u> to indicate willingness to reconsider	**Listening Skills:** • Listen for specific information • Listen for main ideas • Listen for order of details • Listen to summarize **Pronunciation:** • Emphatic stress to express enthusiasm	**Texts:** • A survey about procrastination • A travel article about tailoring services • A photo story **Skills/Strategies:** • Identify supporting details • Activate language from a text	**Task:** • Write an essay expressing a point of view about procrastination **WRITING BOOSTER** • Supporting an opinion with personal examples
• Use <u>Actually</u> to show appreciation for someone's interest in a topic • Soften a question with <u>Could you tell me …?</u> • Indicate disappointment with <u>Too bad</u> • Use <u>I'm dying to …</u> to indicate extreme interest • Say <u>That would be great</u> to express gratitude for someone's willingness to do something	**Listening Skills:** • Listen to take notes • Listen to infer a speaker's point of view and support your opinion **Pronunciation:** • Sentence stress in short answers with <u>so</u>	**Texts:** • An online bookstore website • Capsule descriptions of four best-sellers • A magazine article about comics • A photo story **Skills/Strategies:** • Recognize points of view • Critical thinking	**Task:** • Write a summary and review of something you've read **WRITING BOOSTER** • Summarizing
• Use <u>I would, but …</u> to politely turn down an offer • Say <u>Will do</u> to agree to a request for action • Use <u>Well</u> to begin providing requested information • Say <u>What a shame</u> to show empathy for a misfortune • Introduce reassuring contrasting information with <u>But, …</u> • Say <u>Thank goodness for that</u> to indicate relief	**Listening Skills:** • Listen for main ideas • Listen for details • Listen to paraphrase • Listen to infer meaning **Pronunciation:** • Direct and indirect speech: rhythm	**Texts:** • News headlines • A textbook article about earthquakes • Statistical charts • A photo story **Skills/Strategies:** • Paraphrase • Confirm facts • Identify cause and effect • Interpret data from a chart	**Task:** • Write a procedure for how to prepare for an emergency **WRITING BOOSTER** • Organizing detail statements by order of importance

Unit	Communication Goals	Vocabulary	Grammar
6 **Life Plans** page 62	• Explain a change in life and work plans • Express regrets about past actions • Discuss skills, abilities, and qualifications • Discuss factors that promote success	• Reasons for changing plans • Skills and abilities	• Future in the past: <u>was / were going to</u> and <u>would</u> ◦ Usage, form, and common errors • Perfect modals **GRAMMAR BOOSTER** • Expressing the future (review) • The future with <u>will</u> and <u>be going to</u> (review) • Common errors • Regrets about the past: ◦ <u>Wish</u> + the past perfect ◦ <u>Should have</u> and <u>ought to have</u>
7 **Holidays and Traditions** page 74	• Wish someone a good holiday • Ask about local customs • Exchange information about holidays • Explain wedding traditions	• Types of holidays • Ways to commemorate a holiday • Ways to give good wishes on holidays • Getting married: events and people	• Adjective clauses with subject relative pronouns <u>who</u> and <u>that</u> ◦ Usage, form, and common errors • Adjective clauses with object relative pronouns <u>who</u>, <u>whom</u>, and <u>that</u> ◦ Form and common errors **GRAMMAR BOOSTER** • Adjective clauses: common errors • Reflexive pronouns • Reciprocal pronouns • Adjective clauses: <u>who</u> and <u>whom</u> in formal English
8 **Inventions and Discoveries** page 86	• Describe technology • Take responsibility for a mistake • Describe how inventions solve problems • Discuss the impact of inventions / discoveries	• Describing manufactured products • Descriptive adjectives	• Conditional sentences (review and common errors) • The past unreal conditional ◦ Usage, form, and common errors **GRAMMAR BOOSTER** • Real and unreal conditionals (review) • Clauses after <u>wish</u> • <u>Unless</u> in conditional sentences • The unreal conditional: variety of forms
9 **Controversial Issues** page 98	• Bring up a controversial subject • Discuss controversial issues politely • Propose solutions to global problems • Debate the pros and cons of issues	• Political terminology • A continuum of political and social beliefs • Introducing sticky questions • Controversial issues • Ways to agree or disagree • How to debate an issue politely	• Non-count nouns that represent abstract idea • Verbs followed by objects and infinitives **GRAMMAR BOOSTER** • Count and non-count nouns: review and extension • Gerunds and infinitives: ◦ Review of form and usage ◦ Review of usage after certain verbs
10 **Beautiful World** page 110	• Describe a geographical location • Warn about a possible risk • Describe a natural setting • Discuss solutions to global warming	• Geographical features • Geographical directions • Ways to recommend or criticize a place • Ways to describe possible risks • Dangerous animals and insects • Geographic nouns and adjectives • Ways to talk about the environment	• Prepositions of geographical place • <u>Too</u> + adjective and infinitive ◦ Usage, form, and common errors **GRAMMAR BOOSTER** • Prepositions of place: more usage • Proper nouns ◦ Capitalization ◦ Use of <u>the</u> • Infinitives with <u>enough</u> ◦ Usage and common errors

Conversation Strategies	Listening / Pronunciation	Reading	Writing
• Say <u>No kidding!</u> to indicate delight or surprise • Say <u>How come?</u> to ask for a reason • Express a regret with <u>I should have ...</u> • Use <u>You never know...</u> to reassure someone • Accept another's reassurance with <u>True</u>	**Listening Skills:** • Listen to infer a speaker's motives • Listen for details • Listen to classify information **Pronunciation:** • Reduction of <u>have</u> in perfect modals	**Texts:** • Career and skills inventories • A magazine article with tips for effective work habits • A photo story **Skills/Strategies:** • Understand from context • Confirm content	**Task:** • Write a short autobiography **WRITING BOOSTER** • Dividing an essay into topics
• Show friendliness by wishing someone a good holiday • Reciprocate good wishes with <u>Thanks! Same to you!</u> • Preface a potentially sensitive question with <u>Do you mind if I ask you ...</u> • Ask about socially appropriate behavior in order to avoid embarrassment • Express appreciation with <u>Thanks. That's really helpful</u>	**Listening Skills:** • Listen for the main idea • Listen for details • Infer information **Pronunciation:** • "Thought groups"	**Texts:** • A magazine article about holidays around the world • Proverbs about weddings • Factoids on holidays • A photo story **Skills/Strategies:** • Preview • Scan for facts • Compare and contrast • Relate to personal experience	**Task:** • Write a detailed description of two holidays **WRITING BOOSTER** • Descriptive details
• Congratulate someone for a major new purchase • Apologize for lateness and provide an explanation • Indicate regret for a mistake by beginning an explanation with <u>I'm ashamed to say ...</u> • Reduce another's self-blame with <u>That can happen to anyone</u> and <u>No harm done</u>	**Listening Skills:** • Infer the correct adjective • Listen for main ideas • Listen to associate • Listen to infer meaning **Pronunciation:** • Contractions with <u>'d</u> in spoken English	**Texts:** • Case studies of poor purchasing decisions • A book excerpt about the printing press • Factoids on famous inventions • A photo story **Skills/Strategies:** • Infer information • Identify cause and effect	**Task:** • Write an essay about the historical impact of an important invention **WRITING BOOSTER** • Summary statements
• Ask for permission when bringing up a sticky subject • Politely indicate unwillingness with <u>No offense, but ...</u> • Apologize for refusing with <u>I hope you don't mind</u> • Use <u>How do you feel about...</u> to invite someone's opinion • Use <u>Well, ...</u> to introduce a different point of view • Use <u>So ...</u> to begin a question clarifying someone's statement	**Listening Skills:** • Infer a speaker's political and social beliefs • Infer a speaker's point of view • Listen to summarize • Auditory discrimination **Pronunciation:** • Stress to emphasize meaning	**Texts:** • A self-test of political literacy • A textbook introduction to global problems • A photo story **Skills/Strategies:** • Activate language from a text • Understand from context • Critical thinking	**Task:** • Write an essay presenting the two sides of a controversial issue **WRITING BOOSTER** • Contrasting ideas
• Show interest in someone's plans by asking follow-up questions • Indicate possible intention with <u>I've been thinking about it</u> • Qualify a positive response with <u>Sure, but ...</u> • Elaborate further information using <u>Well, ...</u> • Express gratitude for a warning	**Listening Skills:** • Infer a speaker's point of view • Listen for main ideas • Listen for details • Listen to summarize **Pronunciation:** • Voiced and voiceless <u>th</u>	**Texts:** • Maps • A magazine article about ways to curb global warming • A photo story **Skills/Strategies:** • Interpret maps • Understand from context • Critical thinking • Summarize	**Task:** • Write a geographic description of your country, state, or province **WRITING BOOSTER** • Organizing by spatial relations

What is *Top Notch*?

Top Notch is a six-level* communicative course that prepares adults and young adults to interact successfully and confidently with both native and non-native speakers of English.

The goal of the *Top Notch* course is to make English unforgettable through:

► Multiple exposures to new language
► Numerous opportunities to practice it
► Deliberate and intensive recycling

The *Top Notch* course has two beginning levels: *Top Notch* Fundamentals for true beginners and *Top Notch* 1 for false beginners.

Each full level of *Top Notch* contains enough material for 60 to 90 hours of classroom instruction. A wide choice of supplementary components makes it easy to tailor *Top Notch* to the needs of your classes.

Summit 1 and *Summit* 2 are the titles of the fifth and sixth levels of the *Top Notch* course.
All Student's Books are available in split editions with bound-in workbooks.

The *Top Notch* instructional design

Daily confirmation of progress

Each easy-to-follow two-page lesson begins with a clearly stated communication goal. All lesson activities are integrated with the goal and systematically build toward a final speaking activity in which students demonstrate achievement of the goal. "Can-do" statements in each unit ensure students' awareness of the continuum of their progress.

A purposeful conversation syllabus

Memorable conversation models provide essential and practical social language that students can carry "in their pockets" for use in real life. Guided conversation pair work enables students to modify, personalize, and extend each model so they can use it to communicate their <u>own</u> thoughts and needs. Free discussion activities are carefully crafted so students can continually retrieve and use the language from the models. All conversation models are informed by the Longman Corpus of Spoken American English.

An emphasis on cultural fluency

Recognizing that English is a global language, *Top Notch* actively equips students to interact socially with people from a variety of cultures and deliberately prepares them to understand accented speakers from diverse language backgrounds.

Intensive vocabulary development

Students actively work with a rich vocabulary of high-frequency words, collocations, and expressions in all units of the Student's Book. Clear illustrations and definitions clarify meaning and provide support for independent study, review, and test preparation. Systematic recycling promotes smooth and continued acquisition of vocabulary from the beginning to the advanced levels of the course.

A dynamic approach to grammar

An explicit grammar syllabus is supported by charts containing clear grammar rules, relevant examples, and explanations of meaning and use. Numerous grammar exercises provide focused practice, and grammar usage is continually activated in communication exercises that illustrate the grammar being learned.

A dedicated pronunciation syllabus

Focused pronunciation, rhythm, and intonation practice is included in each unit, providing application of each pronunciation point to the target language of the unit and facilitating comprehensible pronunciation.

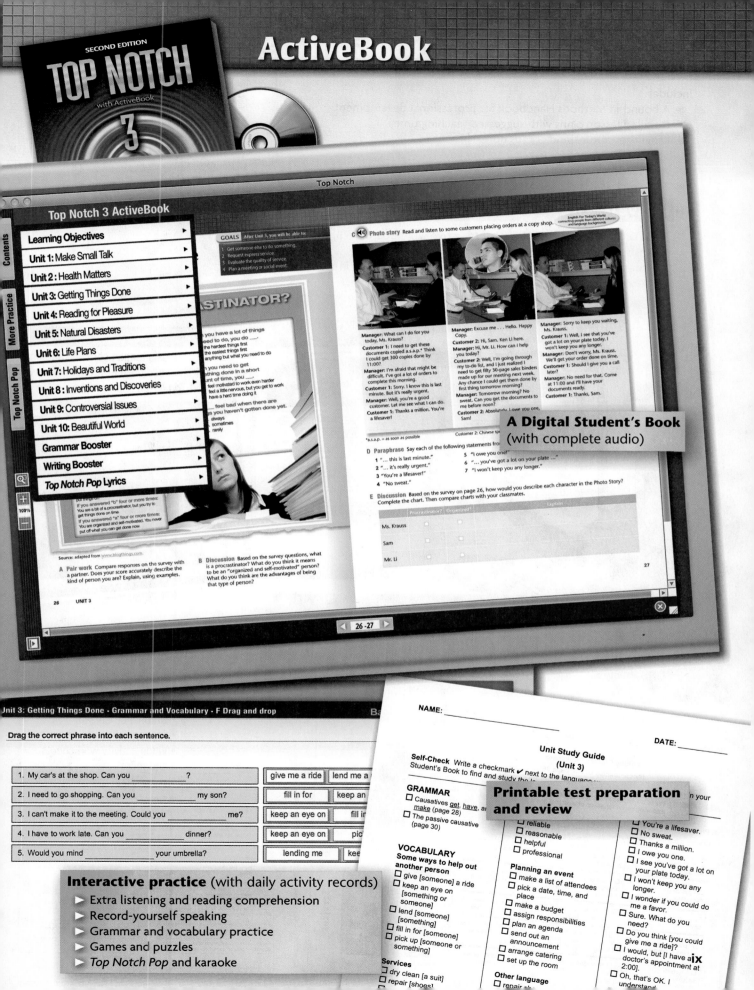

SECOND EDITION

TOP NOTCH
with ActiveBook
3

ActiveBook

A Digital Student's Book
(with complete audio)

Printable test preparation and review

Interactive practice (with daily activity records)
- ► Extra listening and reading comprehension
- ► Record-yourself speaking
- ► Grammar and vocabulary practice
- ► Games and puzzles
- ► Top Notch Pop and karaoke

The Teacher's Edition and Lesson Planner

Includes:
- ► A bound-in Methods Handbook for professional development
- ► Detailed lesson plans with suggested teaching times
- ► Language, culture, and corpus notes
- ► Student's Book and Workbook answer keys
- ► Audioscripts
- ► *Top Notch TV* teaching notes

ActiveTeach
- ► A Digital Student's Book with interactive whiteboard (IWB) software
- ► Instantly accessible audio and *Top Notch TV* video
- ► Interactive exercises from the Student's *ActiveBook* for in-class use
- ► A complete menu of printable extension activities

Teacher's Edition and Lesson Planner with ActiveTeach
SECOND EDITION
TOP NOTCH 3
Joan Saslow • Allen Ascher

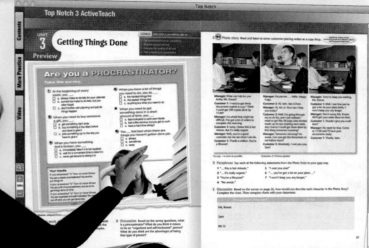

The Digital Student's Book
With zoom, write, highlight, save and other IWB tools.

Top Notch TV
A hilarious situation comedy, authentic unrehearsed on-the-street interviews, and *Top Notch Pop* karaoke.

Printable Extension Activities
Including:
- • Writing process worksheets
- • Vocabulary flashcards
- • Learning strategies
- • Graphic organizers
- • Pronunciation activities
- • Video activity worksheets and more . . .

Page 1 of 2

NAME: _____ DATE: _____

Writing Process Worksheet
(Accompanies Unit 3, page 36)

ASSIGNMENT: Write an explanation, giving examples from personal experience, of whether or not you are a procrastinator.

1. PREWRITING
Check the box that is true for you.

❑ I get things repaired as soon as they get damaged.	❑ I usually wait a few months to get something repaired.	After a year or so, I ju__ buy a new item.
❑ I get things cleaned right away.	❑ I wait until I need to wear something, then get it cleaned.	❑ Stuff just sits in my closet! I never get it cleaned.
❑ I always pay my bills on time.	❑ Every now and then, I'm a little late paying my bills.	❑ I can never seem to pay my bills on time.
❑ I plan my vacation months in advance.	❑ I like to plan vacations at the last minute, right before I leave.	❑ I never plan vacatio__ I just get up and go!
❑ I'm really good about keeping in touch with	❑ Sometimes I let a lot of time go by, but then send an e-mail or call my friends.	❑ I just can't seem to keep up with my frien__

— a suit

Services

— shoes

Services

NAME: _____

Learning Strategy
(Unit 10, page 118, Reading)

READING STRATEGY: identifying causes and effects

Understand the relationship between causes (why something happens or is true) and effects (results of the causes) to improve comprehension of a text.

PRACTICE
Fill in the chart with causes and effects from the Reading on page 118 in the Student's Book.

Causes	Effects
An increase in the amount of CO_2 in the air...	contributes to global warming.
Choosing clean energy...	
	will use less gasoline and save money.
Replacing an old refrigerator or air-conditioner with an energy efficient model...	will use 25% less electricity.
Using products that are recycled from old paper, glass, and metal...	
Shipping foods over long distances...	

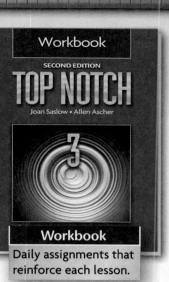

Workbook

Daily assignments that reinforce each lesson.

Classroom Audio Program

Includes a variety of authentic regional and non-native accents.

Complete Assessment Package

Ready-made achievement tests. Software provides option to edit, delete, or add items.

Full-Course Placement Tests

Choose printable or online version.

Copy & Go

Board games, role plays, information gaps, and "find someone who. . ." for every lesson.

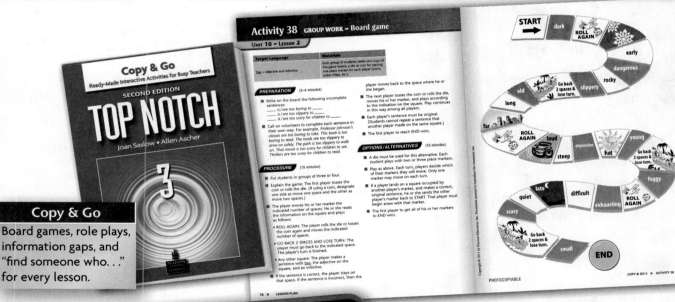

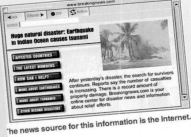

MyTopNotchLab

An optional online learning tool with:

► An interactive *Top Notch* Workbook
► Speaking and writing activities
► Pop-up grammar help
► Student's Book *Grammar Booster* exercises
► *Top Notch TV* with extensive viewing activities
► Automatically-graded achievement tests
► Easy course management and record-keeping

Make Small Talk

GOALS After Unit 1, you will be able to:

1 Make small talk.
2 Describe a busy schedule.
3 Develop your cultural awareness.
4 Discuss how culture changes over time.

ROWAN PAPER
International

Annual Meeting for Affiliates
Bangkok, Thailand
March 24 – 27

Meeting Etiquette

WELCOME TO OUR AFFILIATES FROM
ALL PARTS OF THE WORLD!

Since we all come together from different traditions and cultures,
here are some guidelines to make this meeting run smoothly:

• Please arrive promptly for meetings.

• Dress is business casual: no ties or jackets required.
However, no denim or shorts, please. Ladies should feel free
to wear slacks.

• Please refrain from making or taking calls during meetings.
Put all cell phones and pagers on vibrate mode. If you have
an urgent call, please step outside into the corridor.

• Note: Everyone is on a first-name basis.

FYI: Food is international style. All meals will provide
non-meat options. If you have a special dietary requirement,
please speak with Ms. Parnthep at the front desk.

ROWAN PAPER
International

Agenda–March 24

8:30:	Breakfast buffet in Salon Bangkok	Ballroom
9:15:	Welcome and opening remarks Philippe Martin President and CEO	Ballroom
9:45:	First quarter results and discussion Angela de Groot CFO	
10:30:	Coffee break	Ballroom
11:00:	International outlook and integrated marketing plans Sergio Montenegro	
11:00:	Regional marketing plans • U.S. and Canada Group • Mexico and Central America Group • Caribbean Group • South America (Southern Cone and Andes) Group • Brazil	Salon A Salon B Salon C Salon D Salon E

A Read and summarize the etiquette guidelines
for an international business meeting. Write
four statements beginning with <u>Don't</u>.

B **Discussion** Why do you think Rowan Paper
International feels it's necessary to tell
participants about meeting etiquette? What
could happen if they didn't clarify expectations?

UNIT 1

Make Small Talk

Preview

How to plan a *Top Notch* lesson

The teaching suggestions for each two-page lesson add up to a total teaching time of 45–60 minutes. Your actual teaching time will vary from the times suggested, according to your needs, your schedule, and the needs of your class.

Activities labeled "Option" are additional to the 45–60 minutes, and the estimated teaching time for each is noted with the activity.

In addition, you will see other optional extensions to the material on the Student's Book page. These of course will also increase the time allotted to the lesson:

ActiveTeach Multimedia Disc An extension activity from the *ActiveTeach Multimedia Disc* in the back of this Teacher's Edition

GRAMMAR BOOSTER An optional feature at the end of the Student's Book

WRITING BOOSTER An optional feature at the end of the Student's Book

EXTRAS (optional) Available supplementary components to support the lesson

These optional activities can be assigned as homework or class work. They come from the Workbook, Copy & Go, Top Notch TV, and the Complete Assessment Package.

Oral Progress Assessment and *Top Notch* Project

At the end of each unit there is also an optional oral progress assessment and Top Notch project. Time for these activities depends on the size of your class.

The Top Notch authors strongly encourage you to view these lesson plans and accompanying options and extensions as a menu of possibilities in creating the best lesson plan for you. You may wish to construct your lesson entirely without the options and extensions, or to extend the lesson to do all possible activities. The suggested teaching times are provided to help you do that.

Before Exercise A, give students a few minutes of silent time to observe the meeting guidelines and agenda.

A Read and summarize . . .

Suggested teaching time:	10 minutes	Your actual teaching time:	

• After students observe the text, check comprehension of key information by asking *What is this text about?* (Meeting etiquette.) Then ask:
Who is it addressed to? (Participants of an international business meeting.)

Where and when will the meeting take place? (In Thailand in March.)
Who has organized the meeting? (Rowan Paper International.)

• To personalize, ask students if they know anyone who has ever been to an international meeting. Encourage students to briefly talk about it by saying where and when the meeting took place.

• To model the activity, write the first guideline on the board: *Please arrive promptly for meetings.* Have students restate the guideline starting with the word *Don't.* (Don't arrive late for meetings.)

• Tell students to choose any four guidelines and rewrite them individually. Encourage students to use information in the text to help them figure out the meaning of words they don't know. Students may need help with the following words: *affiliate* (A small company that is related or controlled by a larger one.); *run smoothly* (If an event runs smoothly, there are no problems to spoil it.); *promptly* (On time.); *refrain from [doing something].* (To not do something that you want to do.)

• To review, have students compare statements with a partner. Then ask volunteers to say one of their statements aloud.

B Discussion

Suggested teaching time:	8–13 minutes	Your actual teaching time:	

• Form groups of three. Encourage students to write two or three reasons why it is necessary to provide etiquette guidelines. (Possible answers: Because customs vary from country to country. Because levels of formality differ from country to country. Because what is appropriate in one culture might not be appropriate in another culture.)

• Ask several groups to say their reasons. Then write them on the board.

• To wrap up, have volunteers from different groups describe what could happen if a person didn't know a country's etiquette guidelines.

Option: [+10 minutes] To extend the activity, have students think of useful etiquette guidelines for an international meeting in their country. Form small groups. Ask different groups to report their ideas to the class. You may want to list a few on the board.

FYI: All recorded material is indicated with the following icon ◀))). CD track numbers for all recorded material can be found on the Student's Book pages, above this icon. For example, 1:02 indicates that the recording is located on CD1, track 02.

C ◀)) Photo story

Suggested teaching time:	5–7 minutes	Your actual teaching time:

* As a warm-up, ask students to cover the conversations and look at the pictures. Have students predict answers to this question and write their answer on the board. *What are the people in the photos doing?* (Possible answers: Clapping, greeting each other, praying.)

* Ask students to answer the same question after they have read and listened. Then compare the answer with their prediction. (They are greeting each other.)

* Have students read and listen again. To check comprehension, ask:
  Does Surat introduce himself first? (No, Teresa introduces herself first.)
  What does Teresa want to know? (If Thais use their first names to address each other.)
  When does Surat say it's OK to use first names? (At company meetings held in English.)

* Tell students that the *wai* is the name of the gesture Thais use to greet each other. Point out that men and women say the greeting a bit differently. (See the *Language and culture* box.)

* Ask students to describe common formal and informal greetings in their country and greetings they are familiar with from other countries; for example, *In English-speaking countries people often shake hands in formal and informal situations. In Japan, people usually bow to each other in formal situations.*

ENGLISH FOR TODAY'S WORLD The oval at the top of this page, titled "English for Today's World," indicates that one or both of the speakers in the Photo Story is not a "native speaker" of English. Remind students that in today's world, they must learn to understand both a variety of standard and regional spoken "native" accents as well as "non-native" accents, because most English speakers in the world are not native-speakers of the language. Language backgrounds are shown in a footnote so you can point them out to students.

FYI: The subtitle of the *Top Notch* series is *English for Today's World*. This is in recognition of the fact that English is a language for communication between people from a variety of language backgrounds.

Language and culture
FYI: Language and culture notes are provided to offer students enrichment or more information about language and / or culture. Their use is optional.
* *M-hmm* is an informal way of saying *yes*.
* In Thailand, people greet each other with the *wai* (putting their hands together as in the photo), nodding slightly. A woman says *Sawatdee-Kaa* and a man says *Sawatdee-Khrab*. The *wai* hand position is also used when making an apology and when expressing thanks.

* *You know what they say* is almost always used to introduce a common expression, proverb, or piece of information that the listener probably already knows.
* The quote, *When in Rome do as the Romans do* is so universally known that just the first half of it is said.
LCN **From the Longman Corpus:** Two people can *be on a first-name basis* or a person can be *on a first-name basis with [someone]*. Each has about the same level of frequency in American English.

D Think and explain

Suggested teaching time:	5–10 minutes	Your actual teaching time:

* Have students discuss the questions in pairs.
* If students need help with item 5, ask *What should you do in a foreign country—follow the local customs or do things the way you do them in your country?*

Answers for Exercise D
Answers will vary, but may include the following:
1. He was surprised because she is Chilean, but greeted him with the *wai.* He asked her where she learned it.
2. Because she knew he was from Thailand.
3. She meant that he didn't need to call her "Ms. Segovia."
4. "People <u>tend</u> to be . . ." means people are <u>usually</u> (but not always) a little more formal. "People <u>are</u> . . ." means people are <u>always</u> a little more formal.
5. It means when you are in a new place you should follow the local customs.

E Personalization

Suggested teaching time:	7–10 minutes	Your actual teaching time:

* Explain to students who checked the column *In some situations* that they need to identify the situations where they may want to be addressed differently; for example, on business trips or on school trips.

Language and culture
* A nickname is a shorter version of your name. It can also be a silly name or an endearing name usually used by your friends or family.
* In English-speaking countries, the order for names is first name (also known as your *given name*), middle name, and then last name (also known as your *surname* or *family name*). In the U.S., people usually call each other by their first names. In business situations, someone will often introduce a colleague with his or her full name and title, but then use the person's first name.

F Discussion

Suggested teaching time:	10 minutes	Your actual teaching time:

* Form groups of three. Ask students to share their opinions about each question. Point out that there are no correct or incorrect answers.

EXTRAS (optional)
* Workbook: Exercises 1–3

C 🔊 **Photo story** Read and listen to a conversation between two participants at the meeting in Bangkok.

ENGLISH FOR TODAY'S WORLD
connecting people from different cultures
and language backgrounds

Teresa: Allow me to introduce myself. I am Teresa Segovia from the Santiago office. *Sawatdee-Kaa.*

Surat: Where did you learn the *wai**? You're Chilean, aren't you?

Teresa: Yes, I am. But I have a friend in Chile from Thailand.

Surat: Well, *Sawatdee-Khrab.* Nice to meet you, Ms. Segovia. I'm Surat Leekpai.

Teresa: No need to be so formal. Please call me Terri.

Surat: And please call me Surat.

Teresa: OK. Surat, do you mind my asking you a question about that, though?

Surat: Not at all.

Teresa: Is it customary in Thailand for people to be on a first-name basis?

Surat: Well, at company meetings in English, always. In other situations, though, people tend to be a little more formal. It's probably best to watch what others do. You know what they say: "When in Rome, . . . "

Teresa: Mm-hmm . . ., "do as the Romans do!"

Teresa: Spanish speaker / Surat: Thai speaker
*Thais greet each other with a gesture called the <u>wai</u> and by saying "Sawatdee-Kaa" (women) / "Sawatdee-Khrab" (men).

D Think and explain Answer the following questions. See page T3 for answers.

1 Why was Surat surprised about the way Teresa greeted him? How do you know he was surprised?

2 Why do you think Teresa decided to say "Sawatdee-Kaa"?

3 What did Teresa mean when she said, "No need to be so formal"?

4 What do you think the difference is between "People *tend to be* a little more formal" and "People *are* a little more formal"?

5 What do you think the saying "When in Rome, do as the Romans do" means?

E Personalization Look at the chart. If you took a trip to another country, how would you like to be addressed? Explain your reasons.

I'd like to be called . . .	Always	In some situations	Never
by my title and my family name.	☐	☐	☐
by my first name.	☐	☐	☐
by my nickname.	☐	☐	☐
I'd prefer to follow the local customs.	☐	☐	☐
Other	☐	☐	☐

F Discussion Talk about the following questions.

1 In your opinion, is it inappropriate for two people of very different status (such as a CEO and an assistant) to be on a first-name basis? Explain.

2 In general, when do you think people should use first names with each other? When should they use titles and last names? Explain your reasons.

GOAL   Make small talk

CONVERSATION MODEL

A ◀)) 1:03 Read and listen to two people meeting and making small talk.

A: Good morning. Beautiful day, isn't it?

B: It really is. By the way, I'm Kazuko Toshinaga.

A: I'm Jane Quitt. Nice to meet you.

B: Nice to meet you, too.

A: Do you mind if I call you Kazuko?

B: Absolutely not. Please do.

A: And please call me Jane.

◀)) 1:05 **Ways to ask about proper address**
Do you mind if I call you [Kazuko]?
Would it be rude to call you [Kazuko]?
What would you like to be called?
How do you prefer to be addressed?
Do you use <u>Ms</u>. or <u>Mrs</u>.?

B ◀)) 1:04 **Rhythm and intonation** Listen again and repeat.
Then practice the Conversation Model with a partner.

GRAMMAR   *Tag questions: use and form*

Be careful!
Use <u>aren't I</u>? for negative tag questions after <u>I am</u>.
   I'm on time, **aren't I**? BUT I'm not late, **am I**?
Use pronouns, not names or other nouns, in tag questions.
   Bangkok is in Thailand, isn't **it**?
   NOT isn't Bangkok?

Use tag questions to confirm information you already think is true or to encourage someone to make small talk with you.
   (It's a) beautiful day, **isn't it**?

When the statement is affirmative, the tag is negative. When the statement is negative, the tag is affirmative.

affirmative		negative	
You're Lee,	**aren't you?**	You're not Amy,	**are you?**
She speaks Thai,	**doesn't she?**	I don't know you,	**do I?**
He's going to drive,	**isn't he?**	We're not going to eat here,	**are we?**
They'll be here later,	**won't they?**	It won't be long,	**will it?**
You were there,	**weren't you?**	He wasn't driving,	**was he?**
They left,	**didn't they?**	We didn't know,	**did we?**
It's been a great day,	**hasn't it?**	She hasn't been here long,	**has she?**
Ann would like Quito,	**wouldn't she?**	You wouldn't do that,	**would you?**
They can hear me,	**can't they?**	He can't speak Japanese,	**can he?**

GRAMMAR BOOSTER ▶ p. 122

• *Tag questions: short answers*

A Find the grammar Find a tag question in the Photo Story on page 3.
   You're Chilean, aren't you?

B Grammar practice Complete each statement with a tag question.

1 Rob is your manager, ...isn't he......?

2 I turned off the projector, ...didn't I.......?

3 Tim is going to present next, ...isn't he......?

4 She won't be at the meeting before 2:00, ...will she......?

5 We haven't forgotten anything, ...have we......?

6 There was no one here from China, ...was there......?

7 The agenda can't be printed in the business center before 8:00 A.M., ...can it......?

8 They were explaining the etiquette rules, ...weren't they......?

9 She wants to be addressed by her first name, ...doesn't she......?

10 It was a great day, ...wasn't it......?

CONVERSATION MODEL

A ◄))) Read and listen . . .

Suggested teaching time:	3–5 minutes	Your actual teaching time:

These conversation strategies are implicit in the model:
• Talk about the weather to begin a conversation with someone you don't know.
• Use question tags to encourage someone to make small talk.
• Ask about how someone wants to be addressed.
• Answer a "Do you mind" question with "Absolutely not" to indicate agreement.

• Before students read and listen, have them look at the picture and ask *What gesture are the women using to greet each other?* (Shaking hands.)

• After students read and listen, check comprehension by asking *What are the women's first names?* (Kazuko and Jane.) *How do they prefer to be addressed—by their family names or first names?* (By their first names.)

• Have students listen, and then repeat the questions in the box about addressing someone. Tell students that the questions are transferable to other situations. Point out that using these questions in real exchanges will help students engage in polite and friendly conversations with the people they meet.

• To introduce the topic of small talk, ask *How does Jane start the conversation?* (She says *Good morning* and talks about the weather.) Tell students that talking about the weather helps Jane engage in an informal conversation with a stranger. This is small talk.

Language and culture
• Appropriate topics for small talk vary from country to country. In many English-speaking countries, appropriate topics are the weather, the food you are eating, the place you are visiting, sports, popular movies, and music.

B ◄))) Rhythm and intonation

Suggested teaching time:	3 minutes	Your actual teaching time:

• Have students repeat each line chorally. Make sure students:
  ○ use rising intonation for *isn't it?* and *Do you mind if I call you Kazuko?*
  ○ link the *t* and *y* in *meet you* to form *ch*.

GRAMMAR

Suggested teaching time:	10–15 minutes	Your actual teaching time:

• To focus students' attention, have them read the first explanation and study the example. Ask students to identify the tag question. (Isn't it?) Point out that a tag question comes after a statement.

• Direct attention to the second explanation and have students study the examples. Point out the tag questions in blue. Explain that the auxiliary or verb in the tag question is the same as the verb in the statement.

• Have students look at example 1 in both the affirmative column and the negative column. The verb *be* is used in the statement, so *be* is needed in the tag question. Have students look at example 2 in both columns. The verb in the statement is in the present tense, but it is not *be*, so the tag question needs the auxiliary *does*.

• Have students read the explanations in the *Be careful!* box. To check comprehension, write the following questions and have students complete the sentences:
  I'm not going to pass this class. ___? aren't I? / am I?
  Jane went shopping yesterday. ___? didn't Jane? / didn't she?

Language and culture
• In British English, it is possible to use an affirmative tag question after an affirmative statement to confirm information; for example, *You're here on business, are you?*

LCN From the Longman Corpus: It is common for many learners to get confused when forming tag questions with sentences using the possessive *your*; for example, *Your favorite sport is baseball, aren't you?* rather than *Your favorite sport is baseball, isn't it?*

Option:  **GRAMMAR BOOSTER** (Teaching notes p. T122)

ActiveTeach Multimedia Disc • Inductive Grammar Charts

A Find the grammar

Suggested teaching time:	2 minutes	Your actual teaching time:

• To clarify how to reply to tag questions, point out that when responding to a tag question, the listener should agree or disagree with the information in the statement, not in the tag question. To exemplify, address a student and say *You're [student's correct name], aren't you?* The student should say *Yes, I am.* Address another student and say *You're [student's incorrect name], aren't you?* The student should say *No, I'm not.* Address a third student and say *This class starts at [incorrect time], doesn't it?* The student should say *No, it doesn't.*

Language and culture
• If a speaker asks a tag question someone agrees with, for example, *It's a great concert, isn't it?* the response can be *Yes, it (really) is. / Yes. / It sure is (ly). / I agree.* If someone doesn't agree, it is polite to give an opinion or a reason why; for example, *Well, I think the music is too loud. / No, it really isn't. / I don't like this kind of music.*

B Grammar practice

Suggested teaching time:	3–4 minutes	Your actual teaching time:

• To model the activity, complete the first item with the class. Clarify that the correct answer is *isn't he* by pointing out that the statement uses *is* in the affirmative form, so the tag question requires *is* in the negative form. Also, the pronoun *he* is needed, not the person's name (Robert) which should not be repeated.

• Encourage students to underline the verb in each statement before writing the tag questions.

PRONUNCIATION

A 🔊 Rising intonation . . .

Suggested teaching time:	2–3 minutes	Your actual teaching time:

- First listening: Have students listen. To check understanding, ask *Does intonation rise or fall at the end of each question?* (It rises.) *Are the speakers sure about the answers to their questions?* (No.)

- Second listening: Stop at the end of each tag question and have students repeat. Make sure students use rising intonation.

B 🔊 Falling intonation . . .

Suggested teaching time:	2–3 minutes	Your actual teaching time:

- First listening: Have students listen and ask if they notice a difference in intonation. To check understanding, ask *Does intonation rise or fall at the end of each question?* (It falls.) *Does the speaker expect the listener to agree or disagree?* (To agree.)

- Second listening: Stop at the end of each question and have students repeat. Make sure students use falling intonation.

Option: [+3 minutes] To extend the activity, have students practice saying a statement twice—first using rising intonation and then using falling intonation.

C Pair work

Suggested teaching time:	5 minutes	Your actual teaching time:

- To prepare students for the activity, you may want to read aloud a few examples from the grammar chart on page 4 using either rising or falling intonation and then have students identify which kind of intonation you are using.

FYI: Reassure students that the difference is very subtle and if incorrectly intoned will not lead to a breakdown in communication. This pattern can be different from the pattern used by some speakers of British English.

 • Pronunciation Activities

NOW YOU CAN | Make small talk

A Pair work

Suggested teaching time:	5–10 minutes	Your actual teaching time:

- To prepare students for the activity, have them read the Conversation Model on page 4 again. You may also want to have students listen to the model.

- Review the *Ideas for tag questions* in the box. Ask several students to provide new options for the words in brackets and to complete the tag questions. For example:
  Great weather, isn't it?
  Nice day, isn't it?
  Great book, isn't it?

Delicious food, isn't it?
The movie was really interesting, wasn't it?

- Be sure to reinforce the use of the conversation strategies. Encourage students to use question tags to make small talk. Remind students that the intonation they use "sends a message."

Don't stop! Extend the conversation. Review the ideas in the box. Explain that these are tips for keeping the conversation going. Have students give examples of questions they could ask. You may want to write some of the questions on the board:
  Are you from [Japan]?
  You are [Japanese], aren't you?
  Are you here on vacation / on business?
  How do you like it here?
  Do you work near here?
  When did you start studying English?
  You've taken English before, haven't you?

- To model the activity, role-play and extend the conversation with a more confident student.

- Encourage students to use the correct rhythm and intonation and to continue their conversations by asking follow-up questions. Then tell students to change partners.

 • Conversation Pair Work Cards
• Learning Strategies

B Extension

Suggested teaching time:	10 minutes	Your actual teaching time:

- Review the written model with the class. Then read aloud the question in the speech balloon.

- Ask students to provide other possible tag questions; for example, *You grew up here, didn't you? You started studying English long ago, didn't you?*

- Tell students to write at least five or six facts about themselves and their families. Point out that they should include present and past information. Remind students that they will ask tag questions to confirm their partner's information.

- Encourage students to use falling intonation in their tag questions because they are confirming information.

Option: [+10 minutes] To extend the activity, tell students to write two true statements and two false statements about themselves or their family on a sheet of paper. (The information should be different from the one used in the previous activity.) Ask students to exchange sheets of paper with a partner and take turns asking and answering tag questions; for example, Student A wrote *I speak French.* If Student B thinks the information is true, he or she asks *You speak French, don't you?* If Student B thinks the information is false, he or she asks *You don't speak French, do you?*

EXTRAS (optional)

- Workbook: Exercises 4–8
- Copy & Go: Activity 1

A 🔊 1:06 Rising intonation usually indicates that the speaker is confirming the correctness of information. Read and listen. Then listen again and repeat.

1 People use first names here, don't they?
2 That meeting was great, wasn't it?
3 It's a beautiful day for a walk, isn't it?

B 🔊 1:07 Falling intonation usually indicates that the speaker expects the listener to agree. Read and listen. Then listen again and repeat.

1 People use first names here, don't they?
2 That meeting was great, wasn't it?
3 It's a beautiful day for a walk, isn't it?

C Pair work Take turns reading the examples of tag questions in the grammar chart on page 4. Read each with both rising and falling intonation.

NOW YOU CAN Make small talk

A Pair work Change the Conversation Model to greet a classmate. Make small talk. Ask each other about how you would like to be addressed. Then change partners.

A: Good ...., isn't it?
B: It really is. By the way, I'm ....
A: I'm ....

Ideas for tag questions
• [Awful] weather, …
• Nice [afternoon], …
• Great [English class], …
• [Good] food, …
• The food is [terrible], …

Don't stop!
• Continue making small talk.
• Get to know your new classmates.
• Ask about families, jobs, travel, etc.

B Extension Write your name and a few facts about yourself on a sheet of paper and put it on a table. Choose another classmate's paper, read it quickly, and put it back on the table. Then meet that person and confirm the information you read, using tag questions.

> Maria Carbone
>
> I grew up here, but my parents are from Italy. I started studying English when I was in primary school.

❝ Maria, hi! I'm Deborah. Your parents are from Italy, aren't they? ❞

5

GOAL **Describe a busy schedule**

GRAMMAR *The past perfect: meaning, form, and use*

Use the past perfect to describe an action that happened (or didn't happen) before another action or before a specific time in the past.

Our flight **had arrived** by noon.
The meeting **hadn't** yet **begun** when we arrived.

Past perfect form: had + past participle

Use the past perfect with the simple past tense to clarify which of two past events occurred first.

The meeting **had ended** late, so we had a short lunch.
(First action: The meeting ended; later action: we had lunch.)
When the tour **started**, Ann **had** already **met** Kazuko.
(First action: Ann and Kazuko met; later action: the tour started.)

Note: In informal speech, it's common to use the simple past tense instead of the past perfect. The words <u>by</u>, <u>before</u>, and <u>after</u> often clarify the order of the events.

By April, he **started** his new job.
Before I got married, I **got** a degree in marketing.
After I learned to make presentations, they **promoted** me.

GRAMMAR BOOSTER ▶ p. 123

• Verb usage: present and past (review)

A Grammar practice Choose the correct meaning for each statement.

1 "Before they decided to have the meeting in Bangkok, I had already decided to take my vacation there."
☐ First they decided to have the meeting in Bangkok. Then I decided to take my vacation there.
☑ First I decided to take my vacation in Bangkok. Then they decided to have the meeting there.

2 "By the time she got to the meeting, she had already reviewed the agenda."
☑ First she reviewed the agenda. Then she got to the meeting.
☐ First she got to the meeting. Then she reviewed the agenda.

3 "They had already asked us to turn off our cell phones when the CEO began her presentation."
☑ First they asked us to turn off our cell phones. Then the CEO began her presentation.
☐ First the CEO began her presentation. Then they asked us to turn off our cell phones.

4 "I had changed into business casual dress before the meeting started."
☐ First the meeting started. Then I changed into business casual dress.
☑ First I changed into business casual dress. Then the meeting started.

B Accept answers with or without contractions (unless specified in the directions.)

Meg Ash has to travel to a sales meeting in Seoul tomorrow. It's now 7:00 P.M. Read her to-do list and complete the statements, using <u>already</u> or <u>yet</u>.

Monday, January 4	
8:00	Drop off the laundry at Minute Wash.
9:00	
10:00	Take the cat to Mom's house.
11:00	Pack for the meeting.
12:00	Pick up the sales binders at Office Plus.
1:00	Lunch with Adam
2:00	Return the DVDs to FilmPix.
3:00	
4:00	See dentist. ☹
5:00	5:30 Pick up the laundry from Minute Wash.
6:00	Get a manicure if there's time!
7:00	
8:00	

1 At 8:30 Meg ___had already dropped off___ her laundry, but she ___hadn't yet taken___ the cat to her mom's house.

2 By 10:45 she ___had already taken___ the cat to her mom's house, but she ___hadn't yet packed___ for the meeting.

3 By 12:15 she ___had already picked up___ the sales binders at Office Plus, but she ___hadn't yet had/eaten___ lunch with Adam.

4 At 1:30 she ___had already had/eaten___ lunch with Adam, but she ___hadn't yet returned___ the DVDs to FilmPix.

5 By 2:15 she ___had already returned___ the DVDs to FilmPix, but she ___hadn't yet seen___ the dentist.

6 At 5:55 she ___had already seen___ the dentist, but she ___hadn't yet gotten___ a manicure.

GRAMMAR

Suggested teaching time:	10–15 minutes	Your actual teaching time:

- Direct attention to the small box in the chart about how the past perfect is formed. Write two examples of the past perfect on the board: *had met / had opened*. Review how past participles are formed: *What verb is met the past participle of?* (Meet.) *Is meet a regular or an irregular verb?* (Irregular.) *What verb is opened the past participle of?* (Open.) *Is open a regular or an irregular verb?* (Regular.)

- Have students read and study the first explanation. To make sure students understand the order of when each event happened, ask *What specific past time is mentioned in the first example?* (By noon.) *What happened before noon?* (Their flight arrived.)

- Direct attention to the second example. Point out that *yet* in negative statements adds emphasis about something not completed. Point out its placement—between *hadn't* and the past participle.

FYI: It is more common in spoken English to insert *yet* at the end of the sentence; for example, *She hadn't taken the cat to her mom's house yet.*

- Point out that the specific time in the past is often a phrase starting with *By* [point in time]; for example, *By Saturday, By yesterday afternoon, By lunch time.* To check comprehension, ask students the following question *What had you already done by [eight] o'clock this morning?* (Possible answers: I had eaten breakfast. I had taken the dog for a walk. I had taken a shower.) Say a different time each time you ask a new student.

- Have students read the second explanation (the use of the past perfect with the simple past) and study the example. To convey the time relationship between the two past events, draw a time line on the board and write the following information:

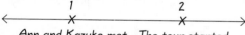

Ann and Kazuko met.   The tour started.

- Review the timing of the two events by saying *First Ann met Kazuko. Then the tour started. When the tour started Ann had already met Kazuko,* or *Ann had already met Kazuko when the tour started.*

- To make sure students understand how to use the past perfect with the simple past, ask students to make a time line and write three sentences about their own lives using the simple past and the past perfect with *when, by,* or *yet.* Form pairs and have students share their sentences.

- Ask students to read the note and study the examples. To check comprehension, ask *When can the simple past be used instead of the past perfect?* (In informal speech.) Then ask students to rewrite the first example with the past perfect instead of the simple past tense. (By April, he had started his new job.)

Option: [+5 minutes] To extend the activity, ask students to say the past participle of several verbs and write them on

the board: *choose (chosen), live (lived), introduce (introduced), call (called).* Then have students write sentences using the past perfect with the verbs on the board. Encourage them to make up the information; for example, *By June, I had already chosen my next vacation destination. By the time I was twelve, I had lived in three different countries.*

Option: **GRAMMAR BOOSTER** (Teaching notes p. T123)

 • Inductive Grammar Charts

A Grammar practice

Suggested teaching time:	3–5 minutes	Your actual teaching time:

- Ask students to complete the first item and review the correct answer with the class. Ask *What happened first—they decided to have the meeting in Bangkok, or the person decided to take his or her vacation there?* (The person decided to take his or her vacation there.)

- Have students compare answers with a partner. Then review with the class.

> **Language and culture**
> - In British English a cell phone, or a cellular phone, is called a mobile, or a mobile phone.

B Meg Ash has to travel . . .

Suggested teaching time:	7–10 minutes	Your actual teaching time:

- To clarify the use of *already*, point out that *already* is placed between *had* and the past participle. Tell students that *already* is not necessary, but adds emphasis to show that something has finished.

- Remind students that *yet* can be placed between *had not / hadn't* and the past participle.

- You may want to tell students that they will need to use the past perfect tense because it is almost the end of the day and they are describing what happened before specific times in the past.

- Encourage students to pay attention to the verbs used in the to-do list, as they will need them to write the answers. Ask students which verbs are needed for *Lunch with Adam* and *dentist.* (Have or eat lunch with someone, see the dentist.)

- To review, have students check answers with a partner.

Option: [+10 minutes] For a challenge, write on the board:
1. *You had invited friends to dinner at your house at 6:00 P.M. They arrived at 5:00.*
2. *You had called for a car service to pick you up at 9:00 A.M. to take you to the airport. The car arrived at 8:00 A.M.*

Form pairs and have students take turns telling a short story about what happened in each situation. Encourage students to talk about what they had or hadn't done up to the earlier point in time in each situation. Remind students they will use the past perfect and the simple past; for example, *When the doorbell rang, I had already set the table but I hadn't finished cooking yet. I had taken a shower already, so I was lucky!*

CONVERSATION MODEL

A 🔊 Read and listen . . .

Suggested teaching time:	4–5 minutes	Your actual teaching time:	

> These conversation strategies are implicit in the model:
> • Say "That was nothing" to indicate that something even more surprising happened.
> • Use "Wow!" to indicate that you are impressed.

• After students read and listen to check comprehension and reinforce the past perfect, ask *What had the man already done before 9:00?* (He had already taken the placement test, registered for class, and bought his books.) *What else had he done before 1:00?* (He had been across town for a meeting.) *Had he eaten lunch when he got to class?* (No, he hadn't.)

• Have students listen, study, and then repeat the *Intensifiers* in the box.

• To practice, ask several students *So how was your day?* Encourage them to answer with an intensifier and the word *busy* or an adjective of their choice. (Possible answers: Incredibly long. Really interesting. So tiring. Pretty boring.)

• Point out that Speaker A shows interest in Speaker B by asking questions and making relevant comments. Ask students to find examples in the conversation. (Possible answers: So how was your day? That's a lot to do before 9:00! What did you do about lunch? You must be pretty hungry by now!)

• Tell students they can do the same when they engage in real conversations to show interest and friendliness.

> #### Language and culture
> • *Yet* can come between *had not* and the past participle or at the end of the statement, as it appears in the Conversation Model *I hadn't eaten yet.*

B 🔊 Rhythm and intonation

Suggested teaching time:	3 minutes	Your actual teaching time:	

• Have students repeat each line chorally. Make sure students:
  ○ use falling intonation for *So how was your day?*
  ○ put extra stress on *Unbelievably* and *busy.*
  ○ use falling intonation for *What did you do about lunch?*

NOW YOU CAN   Describe a busy schedule

A Pair work

Suggested teaching time:	8–10 minutes	Your actual teaching time:	

• Remind students they should use the past perfect to express what they had already done by a particular time.

• Be sure to reinforce the use of the conversation strategies. Remind students to show enthusiasm when saying "Wow!" to indicate that they are impressed.

> **Don't stop!** Extend the conversation. Review the ideas in the box. Explain that these are tips for keeping the conversation going. Have students write three more questions to ask. For example:
> *Did you get there by bus?*
> *How did the meeting go?*
> *Were you able to find a parking space?*

• To model the activity, role-play and extend the conversation with a more confident student.

 • Conversation Pair Work Cards

B Change partners

Suggested teaching time:	10–12 minutes	Your actual teaching time:	

• Encourage students to play a different role.

• Remind students to use other times and activities. To add variety to the exercise, ask students to be creative and talk about an imaginary day.

EXTRAS (optional)

• Workbook: Exercises 9–12
• Copy & Go: Activity 2

A 🔊 **1:08** Read and listen to someone describing a busy schedule.

A: So how was your day?

B: Unbelievably busy. By 9:00 I had already taken the placement test, registered for class, and bought my books.

A: That's a lot to do before 9:00!

B: That was nothing. At 10:00 I had to be across town for a meeting.

A: Wow!

B: And then I had to get back for the class at 1:00.

A: What did you do about lunch?

B: Well, when I got to class, I hadn't eaten yet, so I just got a snack.

A: You must be pretty hungry by now!

1:10 🔊 **Intensifiers**

+++ unbelievably
+++ incredibly
++ really
++ so
+ pretty

B 🔊 **1:09** **Rhythm and intonation** Listen again and repeat. Then practice the Conversation Model with a partner.

NOW YOU CAN | Describe a busy schedule

A Pair work Change the Conversation Model to describe a busy day, morning, afternoon, evening, week, or any other period of time in the past. Then change roles.

A: So how was your ....?

B: .... busy. By .... I .... already ....

A: That's a lot to do before ....!

B: That was nothing. ....

A: Wow!

B: And then I ....

A: What did you do about ....?

B: ....

A: You must be ....!

Don't stop!
• Ask more questions about your partner's activities.
• Provide more details about the activities.

B Change partners Practice the conversation again. Ask other classmates to describe their busy schedules.

GOAL | Develop your cultural awareness

1:11
A 🔊 **Vocabulary • Manners and etiquette** Read and listen. Then listen again and repeat.

etiquette the "rules" for polite behavior in society or in a particular group

cultural literacy knowing about and respecting the culture of others

table manners rules for polite behavior when eating with other people

punctuality the habit of being on time

impolite not polite, rude

offensive extremely rude or impolite

customary usual or traditional in a particular culture

taboo not allowed because of very strong cultural or religious rules

B Complete each sentence with the correct word or phrase from the Vocabulary.

1 It's (taboo / impolite) to eat pork in some religions. No one would ever do it.

2 Many people believe that (cultural literacy / punctuality) is important and that being late is impolite.

3 In some cultures, it's (offensive / customary) to take pictures of people without permission, so few people do that.

4 Some people think that talking with a mouth full of food is an example of bad (cultural literacy / table manners).

5 In some cultures, it's (customary / offensive) to name children after a living relative, and most people observe that tradition.

6 Each culture has rules of (cultural literacy / etiquette) that are important for visitors to that country to know.

7 In more conservative cultures, it's slightly (impolite / taboo) to call someone by his or her first name without being invited, but it isn't truly offensive.

8 The most successful global travelers today have developed their (punctuality / cultural literacy) so they are aware of differences in etiquette from culture to culture.

Some people eat with a fork, some with chopsticks, and some with their hands.

C **Discussion** Discuss your opinions, using the Vocabulary.

1 What are some good ways to teach children etiquette? Give examples.

2 Do you know of any differences in etiquette between your culture and others? Give examples.

3 Why are table manners important in almost all cultures? How would people behave if there were no rules?

1:12
A 🔊 **Listen for main ideas** Look at the subjects on the chart. Listen to three calls from a radio show. Check the subjects that are discussed during each call.

1:13
B 🔊 **Summarize** Listen again. On a separate sheet of paper, take notes about the calls. Then, with a partner, write a summary of each call. Use the Vocabulary.

Subjects	1 Arturo / Jettrin	2 Hiroko / Nadia	3 Javier / Sujeet
table manners	☐	☐	☑
greetings	☑	☐	☐
dress and clothing	☐	☑	☐
male / female behavior	☐	☑	☐
taboos	☑	☐	☑
offensive behavior	☑	☑	☑
punctuality	☐	☐	☐
language	☐	☑	☐

BEFORE YOU LISTEN

A 🔊 Vocabulary

Suggested teaching time:	2–3 minutes	Your actual teaching time:

- Point out the photograph of the fork and chopsticks. Ask students *In what countries do people eat with a fork, a hand, or chopsticks?* (Possible answers: fork—Canada, Italy, Argentina; hand—India, Nepal, Ethiopia; chopsticks—China, Japan, Korea, Thailand.)

- To check comprehension, ask the following questions and encourage students to give examples.
  What are some basic rules of etiquette in this country?
  Is punctuality considered important here?
  What is considered offensive in this country?
  Are handshakes customary here?

> **Language and culture**
>
>  **From the Longman Corpus:** *Impolite* is more commonly used in the phrase *impolite to [do something]* than *impolite to [someone]*. However, it is more common to say *offensive to [someone]* than *offensive to [do something]*.

ActiveTeach Multimedia Disc
- **Vocabulary Flash Cards**
- **Learning Strategies**

B Complete each sentence . . .

Suggested teaching time:	3 minutes	Your actual teaching time:

- Complete the first item with the class. Then have students compare answers with a partner.

C Discussion

Suggested teaching time:	3–5 minutes	Your actual teaching time:

- Form small groups. Encourage students to take notes as they discuss each question and to use as many of the vocabulary words as they can.

- Ask a few groups to answer one of the questions.

LISTENING COMPREHENSION

A 🔊 Listen for main ideas

Suggested teaching time:	10 minutes	Your actual teaching time:

- To familiarize students with the format and purpose of the radio show, first have them listen to the radio announcer introducing the show and the guests. Ask students to listen for the answers to these questions: *How many guests are there in the studio?* (Three.) *Where are they from?* (Thailand, Dubai, and Nepal.) If there is a map in the room, point out the countries.

- Then have students listen to Call 1 and check the boxes in the first column of the chart. Ask them to compare answers with a partner.

- Review the answers with the class. Then have students listen to Calls 2 and 3.

FYI: You may want to tell students there is one distracter—one item on the list of subjects that is not talked about in any conversation. (Punctuality.)

AUDIOSCRIPT

CALL 1 ARTURO AND JETTRIN [F1 = British English, M1 = Thai, F2 = Arabic, M2 = Indian, M3 = Spanish]

F1: Good morning, world. This is Millicent McKay in Brussels with today's worldwide Cultural Literacy Update. If you're new to the program, here's the format: In the studio three people take your phone calls and answer your questions about etiquette in their countries. Today's guests are Jettrin from Thailand, Nadia from Dubai in the United Arab Emirates, and Sujeet from Nepal. We're all first-name here, so let me welcome Jettrin, Nadia, and Sujeet.

M1: Sawatdee Khrab, Millicent. Good morning! I'm Jettrin from Thailand.

F2: Hello. It's nice to be with you. I'm Nadia from Dubai.

M2: And good morning, Millicent, Jettrin, and Nadia. Sujeet here from Nepal.

F1: OK. Let's get started. I see our first caller is on the line. Hello, Arturo from Montevideo. You're on the air.

M3: Good morning—actually, good evening. It's 10:30 at night here in Montevideo. Here's my question: I'm traveling on business to Thailand next month, and I'll be working with Thai business managers from my company. What should I know?

M1: Hello, Arturo. Jettrin here. Just a couple of things: First, a taboo: —Don't touch anyone's head, not even a child's.

M3: Hmm? Well, I don't ordinarily touch people's heads, but if you don't mind my asking, what's wrong with touching someone's head?

M1: Well, we believe the head is where the person's soul lives. So it's very disrespectful and offensive to touch a person's head.

AUDIOSCRIPT continues on page T9.

B 🔊 Summarize

Suggested teaching time:	12–14 minutes	Your actual teaching time:

- To help students focus on key information as they listen, write the following questions on the board:
  1. *Where is Jettrin from? What two taboos does he talk about? What does he say about the wai?*
  2. *Where is Nadia from? What does she say about clothing and taking pictures?*
  3. *Where is Sujeet from? What are some taboos and behaviors to know about when in Nepal?*

- Have students listen for the answers to the questions and take notes about them. (1. Thailand. Visitors should not touch people's heads or show the bottom of their feet. Thais appreciate it when foreigners do the *wai*, even if they don't do it right. 2. The United Arab Emirates. Visitors should dress modestly. They should not take pictures of Muslim women, and they need to ask a man for permission to take his picture. 3. Nepal. People eat with their right hands; visitors can use a fork. People from Nepal don't eat beef. When visiting a temple, visitors should ask if they are allowed to enter, take off their shoes or wear open sandals, and ask before using a camera. They should not take leather things near a temple.)

ActiveTeach Multimedia Disc
- **Learning Strategies**

NOW YOU CAN   Develop your cultural awareness

A Frame your ideas

Suggested teaching time:	5–10 minutes	Your actual teaching time:

• Encourage students to write brief notes for each item on the notepad.

B Discussion

Suggested teaching time:	5 minutes	Your actual teaching time:

• As students share their answers, encourage them to use the vocabulary whenever possible; for example, *In our culture it's customary to shake hands.*

• Identify the items students did not agree on with a check mark or other symbol. Encourage a friendly discussion.

C Group work

Suggested teaching time:	5–10 minutes	Your actual teaching time:

• To prepare students for the activity, review the speech balloons with the class.

• Remind students to use language that they learned in Lesson 1; for example, making small talk, using tag questions, and ways to meet and greet people.

• To model the activity, role-play a conversation with a more confident student.

• Encourage students to keep the conversation going by asking questions or making relevant comments about what is customary in their cultures; for example, *In this country, the woman should extend her hand first.*

• To review, ask a few groups to role-play one of their conversations to the class.

EXTRAS (optional)

• **Workbook:** Exercises 13–15
• **Copy & Go:** Activity 3

AUDIOSCRIPT Continued, for page T8 (**A** Listen for main ideas)

M3: Any other tips?

M1: Well, when you are seated, be sure not to cross your legs in such a way that others can see the bottom of your foot.

M3: Actually, I knew that. But don't worry. It's good to be reminded. I do have one more specific question before I hang up.

M1: Sure. What's that?

M3: In Uruguay it's customary to shake hands, and I know Thai people greet each other with the wai. Will it seem impolite for a foreigner to do the wai?—and what happens if I don't do it right? Will that be offensive?

M1: Absolutely not! Just put the palms of your hands together on your chest and bow slightly. Say "Sawatdee– khrab." For the women listening, you say "Sawatdee kaa." You will warm our hearts with that. Don't worry if you don't do it exactly the way Thais do it. And don't worry about the pronunciation. Have a wonderful trip to Thailand. Try to do some sightseeing. And taste our wonderful food!

M3: Thanks so much.

F1: Thank YOU, Jettrin and Arturo, for a good lesson in cultural literacy. Let's take a break and then another call.

CALL 2 HIROKO AND NADIA [F3 = Japanese]

F1: Welcome back, listeners. This is Millicent McKay with a worldwide town meeting, answering all your questions about do's and taboos around the world. Let's say hello to Hiroko from Osaka, Japan. Hiroko, you're on the air.

F3: Thank you, Millicent. My husband and I are going to Dubai. He's a banker and has business there, but I'm going with him as a tourist. I'm very interested in all kinds of culture, and I understand Dubai is very different from Japan. I have three questions.

F2: Hello, Hiroko. Nadia on the line.

F3: Thanks, Nadia. If I'm alone, can I walk on the street or drive a car? When we went to Saudi Arabia, women were not permitted to go out alone or drive.

F2: Absolutely. As a woman traveler, you will have no difficulty getting around, even if you are alone. You can drive, and as long as you dress modestly, you can wear whatever you like.

F3: Second question: I don't speak any Arabic.

F2: Again, no problem. As you know, Arabic is the official language of Dubai, but English is commonly used in tourism and commerce.

F3: You speak very good English, Nadia. Where did you learn it?

F2: I actually am an English teacher. I learned my English in the United States, at the University of Wisconsin.

F3: And my last question: I'm an amateur photographer. Will I be able to take pictures in Dubai?

F2: Well, yes, but you should know that it is considered offensive to take pictures of Muslim women here.

F3: Oh. I'm glad I asked. What about pictures of men?

F2: Well, yes, just be sure to ask permission.

F3: I don't know how to thank you. I'm really looking forward to the trip!

F1: We'll be right back with our final call.

CALL 3 JAVIER AND SUJEET [M4 = Spanish]

F1: I think we have time for one more caller. Javier from Mexico City! Welcome to the show. How can we help you?

M4: I'm going to Nepal next month on an international trek. I will be staying with a Nepalese family for a weekend, and I want to be sure I don't offend anyone. Mexico is very different from Nepal.

F1: Well . . . let's ask Sujeet to comment.

M2: Hi, Javier. Let's talk about table manners. First of all, Nepalese don't usually use spoons, forks, or knives.

M4: No? So how do the people eat? How will I eat?

M2: Well, your hosts will eat with their right hand, never the left hand. But I'm sure they'll provide you with spoons and forks. If they are welcoming foreigners into their home, they'll want you to be comfortable. But remember one

A Frame your ideas With a partner, look at the questions about your culture on the notepad. Discuss each question and write your answers to the questions.

How do people greet each other when they meet for the first time?

How do they greet each other when they already know each other?

Are greeting customs different for men and women? How?

When and how do you address people formally?

When and how do you address people informally?

What are some do's and don'ts for table manners?

Are certain foods or beverages taboo?

What are some taboo conversation topics?

What are the customs about punctuality?

What is a customary gift if you are visiting someone's home?

Are there any gift taboos (kinds of flowers, etc.)?

Are there places where certain clothes would be inappropriate?

Is there an important aspect of your culture that's not on this list?

C Group work Role-play a conversation with a visitor to your country. Tell the visitor about your culture. Use the answers to the questions on the notepad.

> ❝ It's bad table manners to pick up a soup bowl and drink soup from it. You have to use a spoon. ❞

> ❝ It's not customary for a man to extend his hand to shake hands with a woman. He should wait for the woman to do that. ❞

B Discussion Combine classmates' notes on the board for the class to share. Does everyone agree? Discuss your differences of opinion.

GOAL Discuss how culture changes over time

A Use prior knowledge In what ways do you think table manners have changed since the days when your grandparents were children?

B Predict the topic Look at the title of the article, the original date of publication, and the internal headings. Use those cues to predict what the article will be about.

READING 1:14

Formal Dinner Etiquette

*I*t is very discourteous for a guest to be late. Arrive at least five minutes before the hour set for the dinner. If for some unavoidable reason you cannot arrive on time, telephone the hostess and explain the reason to her. Etiquette only requires that she wait for fifteen minutes before beginning the meal. If it has been impossible for you to notify her and she has started the meal, go to her, offer apologies, and take your place at the table as quickly as possible.

SEATING

The hostess leads the female guests into the dining room. The host and the male guests follow. The hostess then tells her guests where to sit. She must always have the seating arrangement planned in advance in order to avoid confusion and delay.

Each person stands casually behind his chair until the hostess starts to take her seat. The man helps his dinner partner to be seated and also helps move her chair as she rises. Each person moves to the left of the chair to be seated and also rises from the left.

Originally published in 1940 in the United States

THE MEAL

At a small dinner party, do not start to eat until all guests are served. At a large dinner party, you may start to eat as soon as those near you have been served. Do not eat too fast. Do not talk while you have food in your mouth, and keep the mouth closed while you chew your food. Elbows should not be put on the table when you are eating (however, between courses at a restaurant, if you cannot hear your companion, it is permissible to lean forward on your elbows).

If silver is dropped on the floor, leave it there. If an accident happens at the table, apologize briefly to your hostess.

The hostess continues to eat as long as her guests do. When all have finished, she rises from the table and the others follow.

DEPARTING

If you have no dinner partner, push your chair from the table by taking hold of each side of the seat of the chair. Don't rest your hands or arms on the table to push yourself up.

It is not necessary to remain longer than thirty minutes after a dinner if the invitation does not include the entire evening. However, one should avoid appearing in a hurry to leave.

Source: www.Oldandsold.com

A Confirm facts On a separate sheet of paper, answer the questions about dinner party etiquette in the 1940s.
See page T10 for answers.

1 If the dinner party invitation is for 8:00, what time should guests arrive?

> *Guests should arrive by 7:55 at the latest.*

2 If a guest is going to be late, what should he or she do?

3 Who decides where guests should sit at the table?

4 What are the different roles or expectations of men and women at a dinner party?

5 When should a guest begin eating?

6 What should a guest do if a fork or a knife falls to the floor?

7 What should a guest do if he or she spills a drink on the table?

8 How long should the host or hostess continue eating?

9 What should a guest do when the host or hostess leaves the table?

10 How long should guests stay after dinner is over?

LESSON 4

BEFORE YOU READ

A Use prior knowledge

Suggested teaching time:	2–3 minutes	Your actual teaching time:

- To prompt students, ask the following questions and have selected students answer them:

  Could children always speak when sitting at a table with adults?

  Could they complain about the food?

  Could people leave the table before everyone was done eating?

  Did members of the same family have dinner at different times?

  Did people use paper napkins?

  Did they use tablecloths or placemats?

  What kind of dishes were used?

B Predict the topic

Suggested teaching time:	3–5 minutes	Your actual teaching time:

- Write students' ideas on the board. (Possible answers: Table manners in 1940. Etiquette guidelines for a dinner party. Polite and impolite behavior at a formal dinner.)

- You may follow up by asking students to give examples of specific impolite behavior they predict will be in the article. (Possible answers: Arriving late. Taking a seat before being told where to sit. Leaving the table without asking permission. Telling jokes at the table. Leaving earlier than the other guests.)

READING

Suggested teaching time:	10–12 minutes	Your actual teaching time:

- To help students focus on the Reading, ask them to look for interesting information. It can be something they consider funny, strange, unusual, impractical, etc.

- After students read, have volunteers share information that interested them. Encourage them to explain why.

- To wrap up, have students compare the predictions on the board with the information in the article. Were they correct?

ActiveTeach Multimedia Disc
- Extra Reading Comprehension Questions
- Learning Strategies

A Confirm facts

Suggested teaching time:	10 minutes	Your actual teaching time:

- Tell students to scan the article to find the answers to the questions. You may want to ask students to underline relevant information.

- To model the activity, review the example with the class.

- Have students compare answers with a partner. Then review with the class.

Option: [+10 minutes] For a different approach, draw the following chart on the board (without the answers) or print out this Graphic Organizer for each student from the ActiveTeach Multimedia Disc. Ask students to read the statements and then have them quickly read the article to decide if they are true or false. Correct the false statements. (The blue text in the chart represents examples of possible answers.)

Statements	True	False	Corrections
If a guest is late, the hostess will wait 5 minutes before beginning the meal.		X	She will wait for fifteen minutes.
The host is the first to go into the dining room.		X	The hostess is the first to go in.
Guests take their seats before the hostess.		X	They take their seats as soon as the hostess starts to take hers.
People should take a seat and rise from the left.	X		
Guests should never start eating until all the guests are served.		X	At a large dinner party, guests can start eating as soon as those near them are served.
The hostess is the first to finish eating.		X	The hostess continues to eat as long as her guests do.
Guests shouldn't rest their hands on the table to push themselves up.	X		

Answers for Exercise A

Answers will vary slightly, but may include the following:

2. He or she should telephone the hostess and explain the reason to her.
3. The hostess.
4. The man helps his dinner partner to be seated and also helps move her chair when she rises.
5. At a small dinner party, when all the guests are served. At a large dinner party, when those near him or her have been served.
6. Leave it there.
7. Apologize briefly to the host.
8. As long as his or her guests do.
9. Leave the table too.
10. Thirty minutes.

ActiveTeach Multimedia Disc
- Graphic Organizers

B Summarize

Suggested teaching time:	5–10 minutes	Your actual teaching time:

- To help students prepare for the discussion, draw the following chart on the board or print out a copy for each student from the ActiveTeach Multimedia Disc.

	Now	1940
1. Punctuality		
2. Seating		
3. Starting to eat		
4. Dropping silverware		
5. Leaving the table		
6. Leaving the dinner party		
7. Other		

- Have students complete the chart with notes from the Reading. Tell them to use their own ideas for row 7.
- Form groups of four. Encourage students to discuss the topics in the chart one at a time.
- To wrap up, ask a few groups to say what has changed. You may want to add students' ideas to the chart on the board.

 • Graphic Organizers

---

NOW YOU CAN **Discuss how culture changes over time**

A Frame your ideas

Suggested teaching time:	5–10 minutes	Your actual teaching time:

- Direct attention to *Are you a dinosaur...* on the right and have students read it.
- To check comprehension, ask *Why do you think the dinosaur is used to describe someone who doesn't like change?* (Because it's an animal that no longer exists because it couldn't adapt to change.) *Why is the chameleon used to describe someone who adapts to change?* (Because this animal can change its color to match the colors around it to survive.)
- Tell students to fill in the survey, count the number of *yes* answers, and then find the information that describes how they feel about change.

Option: [+5 minutes] Form small groups. To challenge students, write on the board: *Do you feel the description is true? Not true? Why?* Elicit students' opinions of the results of their survey. Have them compare which description—dinosaur or chameleon—their scores earned and discuss the questions on the board.

Language and culture

- The expression *If it isn't broken, don't fix it!* means if something is working OK, then don't change anything. Often the slang version is used: *If it ain't broke, don't fix it!*
- The expression *Easy does it!* is usually used to tell someone to slow down and / or be careful.
- The expression *Out with the old, in with the new!* means someone looks forward to and makes changes easily.

B Pair work

Suggested teaching time:	5 minutes	Your actual teaching time:

- To help students prepare for the activity, review the speech balloon with the class.
- Remind students that they should give examples to support why they think each of the cultural items has changed a little or a lot; for example, *I think table manners have changed a lot. Young people don't seem to have any.*
- Remind students to use the past perfect if they can; for example, *When my grandmother was young, women didn't work outside the home. By the time my mother was my age, women had already started working at certain types of jobs. Now women do a lot of different jobs.*

C Discussion

Suggested teaching time:	5 minutes	Your actual teaching time:

- Have pairs of students combine to form groups of four.
- Point out the *Be sure to recycle...* box and review the expressions. You may want to have students repeat them before starting the discussion.
- Encourage students to give examples and to ask each other follow-up questions.
- To wrap up, ask a few groups to say if they agreed with each other or not and to explain why.

EXTRAS (optional)

- Workbook: Exercises 16–19
- Copy & Go: Activity 4

B Summarize Summarize how dinner party etiquette has changed since the 1940s. Use the questions in Exercise A on page 10 as a guide.

On your *ActiveBook* Self-Study Disc:
Extra Reading Comprehension Questions

NOW YOU CAN Discuss how culture changes over time

A Frame your ideas Think about how culture has changed since your grandparents were your age. Complete the survey.

Culture Survey	have changed a little	have changed a lot	Is the change for the better? (YES or NO)	
1. Table manners	☐	☐	☐	☐
2. Musical tastes	☐	☐	☐	☐
3. Dating customs	☐	☐	☐	☐
4. Clothing customs	☐	☐	☐	☐
5. Rules about formal behavior	☐	☐	☐	☐
6. Rules about punctuality	☐	☐	☐	☐
7. Forms of address	☐	☐	☐	☐
8. Male / female roles in the workplace	☐	☐	☐	☐
9. Male / female roles in the home	☐	☐	☐	☐
		Total YES answers: _____		

Are you a dinosaur or a chameleon?

How many times did you check YES in the third column?

0–3 = Definitely a dinosaur. You prefer to stick with tradition. Your motto: "If it isn't broken, don't fix it!"

4–6 = A little of both. You're willing to adapt to change, but not too fast. Your motto: "Easy does it!"

7–9 = Definitely a chameleon. You adapt to change easily. Your motto: "Out with the old, in with the new!"

B Pair work Compare and discuss your answers. Provide specific examples of changes for each answer. Use the past perfect if you can.

> ❝I think clothing customs have become less modest. My mother had to wear a uniform to school. But by the time I started school, girls had stopped wearing them. Now girls can go to school in jeans and even shorts!❞

C Discussion Talk about how culture has changed. Include these topics in your discussion:

- Which changes do you think are good? Which changes are not good? Explain your reasons.

- How do you think older people feel about these changes?

- Do you think men and women differ in their feelings about cultural change? If so, how?

♻ **Be sure to recycle this language.**

Formality	**Tag questions**	**Agreement / Disagreement**
be on a first-name basis	[People don't ___ as much], do they?	I agree.
prefer to be addressed by ___	[Customs used to be ___], didn't they?	I think you're right.
It's impolite to ___ .		I disagree.
It's offensive to ___ .		Actually, I don't agree because ___ .
It's customary to ___ .		Really? I think ___ .
It isn't customary to ___ .		

Review

More Practice

ActiveBook *Self-Study Disc*

grammar · vocabulary · listening
reading · speaking · pronunciation

A 🔊 **Listening comprehension** Listen to the conversations between
people introducing themselves. Check the statement that correctly
paraphrases the main idea.

1 ☐ She'd like to be addressed by her title and family name.
☑ She'd like to be addressed by her first name.

2 ☐ She'd prefer to be called by her first name.
☑ She'd prefer to be called by her title and last name.

3 ☑ It's customary to call people by their first name there.
☐ It's not customary to call people by their first name there.

4 ☑ He's comfortable with the policy about names.
☐ He's not comfortable with the policy about names.

5 ☐ She prefers to use the title "Mrs."
☑ She prefers to use the title "Dr."

1:16 / 1:17

🎵 ***Top Notch Pop***
"It's a Great Day for Love"
Lyrics p. 149

B Complete each sentence with a tag question.

1 You're not from around here, ...*are you*........ ?

2 You were in this class last year, ...*weren't you*........ ?

3 They haven't been here since yesterday, ...*have they*........ ?

4 Before the class, she hadn't yet told them how she wanted to be addressed, ...*had she*........ ?

5 I can bring flowers as a gift for the hosts, ...*can't I*........ ?

6 You won't be back in time for dinner, ...*will you*........ ?

7 I met you on the tour in Nepal, ...*didn't I*........ ?

8 We'll have a chance to discuss this tomorrow, ...*won't we*........ ?

9 They were going to dinner, ...*weren't they*........ ?

10 My friends are going to be surprised to see you, ...*aren't they*........ ?

C Complete each statement with the correct word or phrase.

1 Offending other people when eating a meal is an example of bad ....*table manners*........ .

2 Each country has customs and traditions about how to behave in social situations.
The rules are sometimes called ....*etiquette*........ .

3 Each culture has its own sense of ....*punctuality*........ . It's important to
understand people's ideas about lateness.

D Writing On a separate sheet of paper, write two e-mail messages—one
formal and one informal—telling someone about the cultural traditions in
your country. Review the questionnaire about cultural traditions on
page 9 for information to select from.

- For the formal e-mail, imagine you are writing to a businessperson who
is coming to your country on a business trip.

- For the informal e-mail, imagine you are writing to a friend who is
visiting your country as a tourist.

WRITING BOOSTER ▸ p. 141

- *Formal e-mail etiquette*
- *Guidance for Exercise D*

Review

A 🔊 Listening comprehension

Suggested teaching time:	5–10 minutes	Your actual teaching time:

- To prepare students for listening, have them read the statements.
- To help students focus their attention, ask *What do you think the conversations are about?* (People's names and ways to be addressed.)
- Have students compare answers with a partner. Then review with the class.

Option: [+5 minutes] To extend the activity, have students listen to the recording and write the information that supports each answer. (1. Please call me *Ana*. 2. *Mrs. Denman* would be fine. 3. The policy is generally first name. 4. Not at all. *Robert's* fine with me. 5. I use *doctor*.)

AUDIOSCRIPT

CONVERSATION 1 [F = Spanish]
F: Good morning. I'm Dr. Ana Montoya.
M: Good morning, Dr. Montoya.
F: Please call me Ana.

CONVERSATION 2 [F = British English]
M: Hi. I'm Larry Lockhart.
F: Hi. I'm Winnie Denman. Nice to meet you.
M: Nice to meet you, too. By the way, how would you prefer to be addressed?
F: "Mrs. Denman" would be fine.

CONVERSATION 3 [F1 = Portuguese]
F1: Excuse me. I'm Sofia Peres. I'm looking for Martin Page.
F2: Certainly, Ms. Peres. I'm Ramona Wright. Martin's right over there. Come. I'll introduce you.
F1: Thanks. And would it be rude if I called him Martin?
F2: No, that's fine. And while you're at it, feel free to call me Ramona.
F1: And please call me Sofia.

CONVERSATION 4
M: Hi. I'm Robert Morse, the new English instructor.
F: Oh, hello, Dr. Morse. I'm Laura Lane, the department secretary. I'll take you to your class. By the way, how would you like to be introduced to the class?
M: Well, what's the custom here?
F: We're pretty informal. The policy is generally first name. We think it makes for a more conversational English class. Do you mind?
M: Not at all. "Robert's" fine with me!

CONVERSATION 5 [F1 = Japanese]
F1: Hello. I'm Mayumi Sato. I'm pre-registered for the conference.
F2: Certainly. Let me make up your name badge. Do you prefer Ms. or Mrs.?
F1: Actually, neither. I use "doctor."
F2: Of course, Dr. Sato. Here you go.
F1: Thanks!

B Complete each sentence . . .

Suggested teaching time:	3–5 minutes	Your actual teaching time:

- Before students complete the sentences, review tag questions on page 4.
- Ask volunteers to read their sentences aloud.

Option: [+5 minutes] To extend the activity, write true and false information about yourself on the board; for example, *I live in a house / an apartment. I'm going to [the mall] / [the beach] this weekend.* Ask students to make tag questions to check which information is true. Remind students that falling intonation means the speaker is confirming information he or she knows, and rising intonation means the speaker doesn't know and wants the correct information. For example:
Student A: *You live in a house, don't you?* [falling intonation]
Teacher: *Actually, I don't. I live in an apartment.*
Student B: *You're going to the beach this weekend, aren't you?* [rising intonation]
Teacher: *Why yes, I am.*

C Complete each statement . . .

Suggested teaching time:	2 minutes	Your actual teaching time:

- Before students complete the sentences, review the Vocabulary on page 8.

Option: [+5 minutes] To challenge students, call out key phrases and ask students to say the matching words from the vocabulary on page 8. Say *Arriving on time* (Punctuality.); *Insulting someone* (Offensive.); *Chewing with your mouth open* (Bad table manners.); *Rules of polite behavior* (Etiquette.); *Not saying Thank you* (Impolite.); *Eating beef in India* (Taboo.); *Saying Good morning.* (Customary.)

D Writing

Suggested teaching time:	10–15 minutes	Your actual teaching time:

- Before students write, list the following topics on the board:
  Greetings
  Addressing people
  Food and table manners
  Conversation topics
  Punctuality
  Gifts
  Clothing
- Ask students to choose three or four topics that they would like to write about and then look at the questionnaire on page 9 and review their notes. Encourage students to think about which topics would be useful for a businessperson and which ones would be useful for a friend.

Option: **WRITING BOOSTER** (Teaching notes p. T141)

 • Writing Process Worksheets

ORAL REVIEW

Before the first activity, give students a few minutes of silent time to explore the pictures and become familiar with them.

Tell a story

Suggested teaching time:	10–13 minutes	Your actual teaching time:

- Have students identify the Itos and the Garzas in the pictures and then read the itineraries.

- Before students tell the story in pairs, encourage them to use the information in the itineraries as well as their imaginations. Encourage students to add information about tours, dining experiences, etc.

- To wrap up, have selected students share their stories with the class.

> **Language and culture**
> - Machu Picchu, the remains of an ancient city of the Inca Empire, is situated in the Andes Mountains in Peru. The site is believed to have been built in the mid-1400s. The ruins are located about 2,400 meters (8,000 feet) above sea level and cover about 13 square kilometers (5 square miles). It was rediscovered by archeologists in 1911 and has become a popular tourist destination.

Pair work 1

Suggested teaching time:	5 minutes	Your actual teaching time:

- To help students prepare for the activity, have them describe what the people are doing in the pictures. (Possible answers: In the first picture they are greeting each other. In the second picture they are making small talk. In the third picture they are sharing photos.)

- Before students create the conversations, you may want to choose three students and model the conversation.

> **Possible responses ...** *
> **A:** Beautiful place, isn't it? **B:** Yes. It's great. By the way, I'm Haru Ito. **A:** I'm Antonio Garza. Nice to meet you. **B:** Nice to meet you, too.

*Here and throughout this Teacher's Edition, possible responses provide a sample of the quantity and quality of response students have been prepared for. *Actual* responses will vary.

Pair work 2

Suggested teaching time:	5 minutes	Your actual teaching time:

- Model this activity. Remind students that the women are making small talk.

> **Possible responses ...**
> **A:** This place is fantastic, isn't it? **B:** It really is. You know, you look familiar. You're staying at the Hanaq Pacha Hotel, aren't you? **A:** Oh, yes, I am. Are you staying there, too? **B:** Yes. Great hotel, isn't it? **A:** It really is.

Pair work 3

Suggested teaching time:	5 minutes	Your actual teaching time:

- Model this activity. Suggest that students refer to the itineraries on this page. Remind them to use the past perfect when possible.

> **Possible responses ...**
> **A:** How long have you been in Peru? **B:** For about two weeks. **A:** Have you visited many places? **B:** Oh, yes. By the end of our first week here, we had already been to Lima, Puno, and Cusco. **A:** Wow! That's a lot!

Option: [+5 minutes] To challenge students, have pairs talk about the places they had already visited at different times in their lives. Ask students to use the past perfect.

Option: Oral Progress Assessment

Use the photographs on page 13. Encourage students to use the language practiced in this unit and previous units.

- Tell the student to ask you four questions about the photograph using tag questions. Encourage him or her to practice using rising and falling intonation; for example, **S:** *This is Machu Picchu, isn't it?* **T:** *Yes, it is.*

- Point to one of the pictures of people talking and tell the student that together you are going to role-play a conversation. Tell him or her you will start with small talk and he or she should continue; for example, **T:** *Hi. Nice place, isn't it?* **S:** *Yes, it is. I'm [Thomas] [Martin].*

- Tell the student you will ask questions using the present perfect about the Itos. Tell him or her to answer in complete sentences. Ask *What cities had the Itos visited by May 31?*

- Evaluate the student on intelligibility, fluency, correct use of target grammar, and appropriate use of vocabulary.

 • Oral Progress Assessment Charts

Option: *Top Notch* **Project**

Have students work in small groups and create a cultural literacy guidebook.

Idea: With the class, brainstorm topics that could be included in a cultural literacy guidebook. Encourage students to assign tasks; for example, researching, writing and editing, finding photographs and illustrations, and putting together the guidebook. Have groups present their guidebooks to the class.

EXTRAS (optional)

- Complete Assessment Package
- Weblinks for Teachers: pearsonlongman.com/topnotch/

And on your ActiveTeach Multimedia Disc:
    Just for Fun
    Top Notch Pop Song Activities
    Top Notch TV Video Program and Activity Worksheets
    Supplementary Pronunciation Lessons
    Audioscripts
    Unit Study Guides

Tell a story First, look at the pictures and tell the story of the Garzas and the Itos on June 10. Then, look at the itineraries below and use the past perfect to talk about what they had done by June 5. Start like this:

By June 5, the Itos had been to . . .

Pair work Create conversations.

1 Create a conversation for the two men in the first picture. Each man tells the other how he'd like to be addressed.

2 Create a conversation for the two women in the second picture. The women are making small talk.

3 Create a conversation for the people in the third picture. Ask and answer questions about the their trips to Peru. Use the past perfect when possible.

JUNE 10, 10:00 A.M.

María and Antonio Garza

Haru and Kimi Ito

LATER THAT DAY

GLOBAL ADVENTURES, INC.

Haru and Kimi Ito—Peru Itinerary

May 29
Lima: María Angola Hotel
La Paz 610, Miraflores

May 31
Puno: Casa Andina Classic
Jr. Independencia 185, Plaza de Armas

June 4
Cusco: Novotel
San Agustín 239

June 9
Machu Picchu: Hanaq Pacha Hotel
(Aguas Calientes)

GetAway Travel, Inc.

**María and Antonio Garza—
Peru itinerary**

May 30
Lima: María Angola Hotel
La Paz 610, Miraflores

June 3
Arequipa: Tierra Sur Hotel
Consuelo 210

June 6
Nasca: Brabant Hostel
Calle Juan Matta 978

June 9
Machu Picchu: Hanaq Pacha Hotel
(Aguas Calientes)

NOW I CAN...

☐ Make small talk.
☐ Describe a busy schedule.
☐ Develop cultural awareness.
☐ Discuss how culture changes over time.

Health Matters

GOALS After Unit 2, you will be able to:

1 Call in sick.
2 Make a medical or dental appointment.
3 Discuss types of treatments.
4 Talk about medications.

TravelTips

http://www.traveltips.com

| Travel Documents | Travel Insurance | Medical | **Dental** | Optical | FAQS |

Travel Tips.com
Know Before you Go!

WHAT IF YOU HAVE A DENTAL EMERGENCY WHEN YOU'RE OVERSEAS?

Nothing can spoil a trip faster than a dental emergency. So <u>before</u> you go on a trip, visit your dentist and make sure your teeth are in good shape. But if you have a dental problem during your trip, here are some temporary solutions.

Note: If you think it's an emergency, see a dentist as soon as possible. Otherwise, be sure to call your own dentist as soon as you get back home.

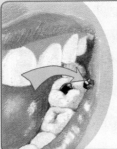

What if I lose a filling?

Put some sugarless chewing gum in its place. (Don't use regular gum. The sugar will hurt!)

more

What if my gums are swollen?

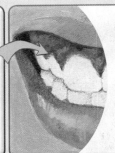

Rinse your mouth with mild salt water or apply a warm moist tea bag to the gums.

more

What if my tooth comes loose?

Apply a cold compress to the outside of your mouth and take aspirin or painkillers as needed. Do not eat any crunchy or chewy foods.

more

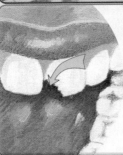

What if I break a tooth?

Depending on how much of your tooth has broken off, you may be able to wait till you return home to see your dentist. If you feel any pain, apply a washcloth dipped in very cold water to the outside of the mouth and take aspirin or another painkiller.

more

What if I have a lot of tooth pain?

If you have a toothache, rinse your mouth with warm water and put a cold compress against your cheek. In some cases, flying in a plane can make a toothache worse, so make sure you have aspirin or another painkiller with you.

more

Information source: www.webmd.com

A Discussion Do you think the information in the website is useful? Why do you think some people would wait until they got back home to see a dentist?

B Pair work Discuss each of the situations described in the website and what you would do. Circle <u>yes</u> or <u>no</u>.

I would . . .		
• ignore the problem.	yes	no
• make an appointment to see a dentist right away.	yes	no
• call or e-mail my own dentist and ask for advice.	yes	no
• use the remedy suggested in the website.	yes	no
• use my own remedy (explain).	yes	no

UNIT 2

Preview

Health Matters

Suggested teaching time:	10–15 minutes	Your actual teaching time:

Before Exercise A, give students a few minutes of silent time to observe the website.

- After students observe the website, check comprehension of key information by asking *What's the name of the website?* (Traveltips.com.) *What kind of tips does it give?* (What you should do if you have dental problems.) *Who are the tips for?* (International travelers.)

- Ask students to quickly read the text to find the five dental problems for which tips are given. (You lose a filling, your gums are swollen, your tooth comes loose, you break a tooth, you have a toothache.) As students say the problems, write them on the board. Clarify any confusion students may have about the vocabulary.

- Have students scan the website for a tip to solve each problem. Encourage students to use the text to help them figure out the meaning of words they don't know. Students may need help with the following words: *rinse* (To clean quickly with water.); *moist* (Slightly wet.); *compress* (A small thick piece of wet cloth that you put on an injured part of your body to make it less painful.); *painkiller* (A medicine that reduces pain.); and *washcloth* (A small square towel used for washing your hands and face.).

- Ask several students to read a tip aloud.

A Discussion

Suggested teaching time:	2–3 minutes	Your actual teaching time:

- Form groups of three or four. To help students generate ideas for the discussion, have them think of the answers to the following questions:
    Did you already know what to do in the situations described in the website?
    Did you learn anything new?
    Do you think the tips are practical?
    Why would some people decide to wait and see a dentist when they got back home?

- Ask several groups to answer one of the questions aloud.

Option: [+3 minutes] To personalize the activity, ask students if they have ever had the problems described on the website during a trip (or if they know someone who has). Have them briefly talk about their experiences by saying what the problem was and where they were.

Option: [+5 minutes] To extend the activity, point out the beginning of the first paragraph *Nothing can spoil a trip faster than a dental emergency.* Ask students to tell about other emergencies or events that could spoil a trip; for example, *breaking a [leg], needing an operation, losing a passport, having your rented car break down on a back road,* etc.

B Pair work

Suggested teaching time:	5–7 minutes	Your actual teaching time:

- Have students spend a few minutes thinking about what they would do in each situation and then ask them to complete the chart.

- To help students with the language they will need during the discussion (and to review unreal conditional sentences), write on the board:

If	I lost a filling,	I would . . .
	my gums were swollen,	
	my tooth came loose,	
	I broke a tooth,	
	I had a toothache,	

- Have students work in pairs. Walk around the room and provide help as needed. Ask several students to say what they would do in one of the situations.

Option: [+10 minutes] To challenge students, brainstorm with the class and write on the board a list of things to do to prepare for an international trip; for example, *booking a hotel, making airline reservations, collecting / preparing necessary travel documents, packing your suitcase(s), finding out about local customs and etiquette, finding out about the local currency.* Ask students to work in pairs and write a few tips about a task. Have pairs combine with other pairs to share their tips. For example:
    Booking a hotel: Check where the hotel is located before you make your reservations.
    Book in advance. Reconfirm your reservation a week before you leave.
    Print a copy of your reservation and take it with you.
    Travel documents: Make sure you have a valid passport.
    Find out if you need a visa.
    Get an international driver's license.

C 🔊 Photo story

Suggested teaching time:	3–5 minutes	Your actual teaching time:	

- As a warm-up, have students cover the conversations and look at the pictures. Ask them to make predictions for the following questions: *Where are the people in the first picture? Who do you think they are? What do you think they are talking about?* (Possible answers: At the front desk in a hotel. A hotel guest and a hotel clerk. The guest is asking for something / maybe he has a problem.) *Who is the woman in the other two pictures and where is she?* (Possible answers: A dentist. In a dentist's office. In a hospital.) *What kind of problem do you think the man has?* (Possible answers: He lost a filling. He has a toothache.)

- After reading and listening to the conversation, ask students the same questions and have them compare their answers with their predictions.

- Write on the board:
  What does the guest ask the clerk to recommend?
  Who calls the dentist?
  Why is the guest able to make an appointment?

- To check comprehension, ask students to read and listen again and then answer the questions. (1. A dentist who speaks English; 2. the hotel clerk; 3. another patient canceled / didn't come.)

Language and culture

LEN From the Longman Corpus

- *Could you recommend. . .* is much more common than *I was wondering if you might be able to recommend. . .* However, the latter is considered much more polite.
- In the expression *I hear [noun clause]. . .,* the word *that* is frequently deleted. For example, *I hear ~~that~~ you are from overseas.*

D Focus on language

Suggested teaching time:	5–10 minutes	Your actual teaching time:	

- Encourage students to identify who says the phrases and to use the context of the conversation to help figure out the meaning.

E Personalize

Suggested teaching time:	10 minutes	Your actual teaching time:	

- Ask students to use the chart to help them organize their ideas about an emergency they had. Alternatively, students can write about events that happened to someone they know.

- Encourage students to use a dictionary if necessary. Walk around the room to provide help as needed.

F Group work

Suggested teaching time:	10 minutes	Your actual teaching time:	

- Model the activity by role-playing with a student. Ask the student to read aloud the model in the speech bubble and then ask him or her a follow-up question; for example, *Did you stay in the hospital?* or *What did the doctor do?*

- Have students work in small groups. Ask them to use their notes as a guide to talk about their experiences. Encourage students who are listening to ask follow-up questions.

- Walk around the room and provide help as needed. Ask several students to give a brief summary of their emergency experiences to the class.

EXTRAS (optional)

- **Workbook:** Exercises 1–3

C 🔊 **Photo story** Read and listen to someone with a dental emergency during a trip.

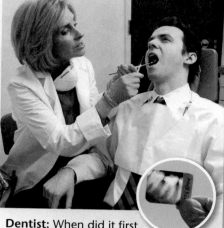

Guest: I need to see a dentist as soon as possible. I think it's an emergency. I was wondering if you might be able to recommend someone who speaks English.

Clerk: Let me check. Actually, there is one not far from here. Would you like me to make an appointment for you?

Guest: If you could. Thanks. I'm in a lot of pain.

Dentist: So I hear you're from overseas.

Patient: From Ecuador. Thanks for fitting me in.

Dentist: Luckily, I had a cancellation. So what brings you in today?

Patient: Well, this tooth is killing me.

Dentist: When did it first begin to hurt?

Patient: It's been bothering me since last night.

Dentist: Let's have a look. Open wide.

Patient: Ah . . .

Dentist: Well, let's take an X-ray and see what's going on.

Guest (Patient): Spanish speaker / Clerk and dentist: Russian speakers

D **Focus on language** Find the underlined statements in the Photo Story. Then use the context to help you restate each one in your own words.

1 I was wondering if you might be able to recommend someone who speaks English.
   Could you please

2 If you could. Thanks.   Yes, please.

3 Thanks for fitting me in.
   seeing me / giving me an appointment so quickly

4 This tooth is killing me.   so painful / hurting very badly

5 It's been bothering me since last night.   hurting

6 Let's have a look.   I'll examine you now. / Let me check.

7 Let's take an X-ray and see what's going on.
   see what the problem is

E **Personalize** Have you—or has someone you know—ever had an emergency that required dental or medical attention? Complete the chart.

Where did it happen?	When did it happen?	What happened?

F **Group work** Tell your classmates about your emergency.

❝Last year, I went skiing and I broke my arm. I had to go to the emergency room at the hospital.❞

GOAL   Call in sick

VOCABULARY   *Symptoms*

A 🔊 ^1:19 Read and listen. Then listen again and repeat.

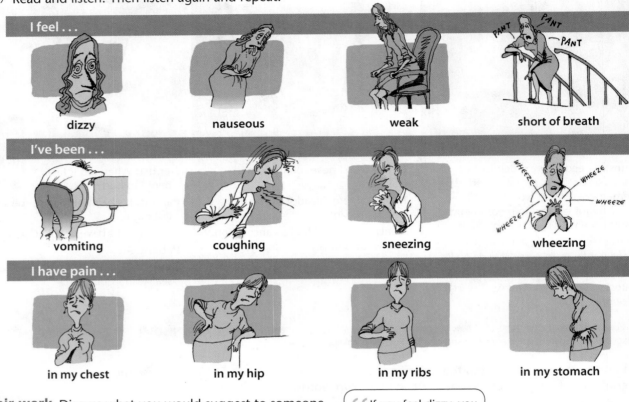

| I feel . . . | | | |
| dizzy | nauseous | weak | short of breath |

| I've been . . . | | | |
| vomiting | coughing | sneezing | wheezing |

| I have pain . . . | | | |
| in my chest | in my hip | in my ribs | in my stomach |

B **Pair work** Discuss what you would suggest to someone with some of the symptoms in the Vocabulary.

> ❝If you feel dizzy, you should lie down.❞

C 🔊 ^1:20 **Listening comprehension** Listen and check the symptoms each patient describes. Then listen again. If the patient has pain, write where it is.

	dizziness	nausea	weakness	vomiting	coughing	sneezing	wheezing	pain	If pain, where?
1	✓	☐	✓	☐	☐	☐	☐	✓	shoulder
2	☐	☐	☐	☐	✓	☐	☐	✓	back of neck
3	☐	☐	☐	☐	☐	✓	☐	✓	back
4	☐	✓	☐	✓	☐	☐	☐	☐	
5	☐	☐	☐	☐	☐	☐	✓	☐	
6	☐	☐	☐	☐	☐	☐	☐	✓	hip

PRONUNCIATION   *Intonation of lists*

A 🔊 ^1:21 Use rising intonation on each item before the last item in a list. Use falling intonation on the last item. Read and listen. Then listen again and repeat.

1 I feel weak and dizzy.

2 I've been sneezing, coughing, and wheezing.

3 I have pain in my neck, my shoulders, my back, and my hip.

VOCABULARY

A ◀)) Read and listen . . .

Suggested teaching time:	3–5 minutes	Your actual teaching time:

- To prepare students for the activity, ask them to listen and study the words and pictures. Then have students listen and repeat chorally.

- Point out that the second group of symptoms uses *I've been + ___ ing*. You may also want to tell students that *I've been [cough]ing* usually includes *a lot, for [two] hours, for the last few days,* etc. to give information about how long they've had the symptom.

 ActiveTeach Multimedia Disc
- **Vocabulary Flash Cards**
- **Learning Strategies**

B Pair work

Suggested teaching time:	5 minutes	Your actual teaching time:

- To help students generate ideas, as a class brainstorm things people usually do / don't do when they have some kind of health problem. Write students' ideas in two columns on the board. For example:

Do's	Don'ts
eat a light meal	go out
drink some tea	eat too much
go to bed	do exercise
stay at home	go to work
see a doctor	lift heavy objects
take some medication	drink coffee

- Read the speech balloon aloud. Encourage students to discuss suggestions for all of the symptoms. Remind them that they can use ideas from the board.

Language and culture
- In the sentence *If you feel dizzy, you should lie down,* <u>you</u> is used impersonally to give general advice.

C ◀)) Listening comprehension

Suggested teaching time:	8–10 minutes	Your actual teaching time:

- To prepare students for listening, have them study the chart. Point out that the first three column heads in the chart use the noun forms of the symptoms. Ask students to provide the adjective forms. (Dizzy, nauseous, weak.)

FYI: *Nausea* and *nauseousness* are both noun forms.

- Pause after each conversation to allow students time to check the columns and write about the pain.

AUDIOSCRIPT

CONVERSATION 1
- **M:** What seems to be the problem today, Mrs. Gilles?
- **F:** Well, I've been feeling pretty dizzy for the last few days. I have to lie down all the time. I feel really weak and I have so little energy—I can't even make myself lunch or dinner.
- **M:** I'm sorry to hear that.

- **F:** And I can hardly walk up stairs. I'm so short of breath whenever I try.
- **M:** Any pain?
- **F:** Funny you should ask. I have pain in my shoulder, too.

CONVERSATION 2 [F = Chinese]
- **F:** Is there anything bothering you today, Mr. Baker?
- **M:** Well, when I woke up this morning I felt terrible. I had this pain in the back of my neck, and I thought I'd better get in to see the doctor right away.
- **F:** Have you been coughing?
- **M:** A lot, actually. I've had a bad cold for over a week now.
- **F:** That might explain the pain you've been feeling in your neck. I'm going to give you something for that cold.

CONVERSATION 3 [M = Australian English]
- **M:** The doctor will be right with you, Ms. Rice. Have you not been feeling well?
- **F:** Not great, actually. And I've been sneezing like crazy.
- **M:** Oh, that's too bad.
- **F:** Anyway, today my back is killing me. So I thought, that's it, I'd better come in.
- **M:** Come. I'll take you in to see the doctor.

CONVERSATION 4
- **F:** You're here to see Dr. Fox?
- **M:** Yes, I am. I've been really sick.
- **F:** Oh, I'm sorry to hear that. Have you been nauseous?
- **M:** Oh, yeah.
- **F:** Any vomiting?
- **M:** Yes. I'm afraid I've been throwing up everything I eat.
- **F:** Any dizziness?
- **M:** Not really. Just nauseousness.
- **F:** Well, Dr. Fox will be with you in a moment.

CONVERSATION 5
- **M:** You're Ms. Pearlman?
- **F:** Yes, I am.
- **M:** The doctor will be with you soon. Can I ask you a few questions?
- **F:** OK.
- **M:** What brings you in today?
- **F:** Well, I've been wheezing a lot since yesterday. I don't know what's wrong. It's really annoying.
- **M:** Are you allergic to anything?
- **F:** Not that I can think of.
- **M:** Any other symptoms?
- **F:** Not really.

CONVERSATION 6 [M = Arabic]
- **F:** Mr. Rashid?
- **M:** That's me.
- **F:** Hello, Mr. Rashid. The doctor will see you in just a moment. Are you in a lot of pain?
- **M:** Well, my hip has been bothering me a lot for the past two days. It hurts all the time.
- **F:** Hmm. Did you fall or have an accident?
- **M:** Not that I can remember.
- **F:** Any pain anywhere else? In your knees? Your elbows?
- **M:** No.

PRONUNCIATION

A ◀)) Use rising intonation . . .

Suggested teaching time:	2 minutes	Your actual teaching time:

- Make sure students identify the difference in intonation between the first item(s) and the last item. To check understanding, ask *Does rising intonation show that the list is complete or incomplete?* (Incomplete.) *What does falling intonation at the end of a list show?* (That the list is complete.)

B Pair work

Suggested teaching time:	5 minutes	Your actual teaching time:	

- Tell students they can be dramatic and encourage them to combine the Vocabulary; for example, *I feel weak and nauseous, and I've been coughing, sneezing, and vomiting.*
- If necessary, have students write their sentences first before reading them aloud.

 • Pronunciation Activities

GRAMMAR

Suggested teaching time:	5–10 minutes	Your actual teaching time:	

- Direct attention to the chart and have students read the explanation and study the examples. To help students understand, write two column heads on the board: *Situation / Conclusion.* Then have students look at the examples and identify the situation and the conclusion in each case. (Possible answers: Example 1: Situation: I broke a tooth. Conclusion: That must hurt. Example 2: Situation: The doctor said I can wait until next week. Conclusion: It must not be an emergency.) List students' answers under each column head on the board.
- To help clarify, say *Use must when you are not 100% certain, but you are almost sure that something is true.* Point out that the negative is *must not.*

Language and culture

- The contraction of *must not* (*mustn't*) is only used for prohibiting, not for drawing a conclusion.

Option: **GRAMMAR BOOSTER** (Teaching notes p. T124)

 • Inductive Grammar Charts

Grammar practice

Suggested teaching time:	2–3 minutes	Your actual teaching time:	

- To model the activity, complete the first item with the class.
- Have students compare answers with a partner. Then review with the class.

CONVERSATION MODEL

A ◄)) Read and listen . . .

Suggested teaching time:	2–3 minutes	Your actual teaching time:	

These conversation strategies are implicit in the model:
- Introduce disappointing information with "I'm afraid...."
- Express disappointment with "I'm sorry to hear that."
- Show concern with "Is something wrong?" and "That must be awful."

- Have students look at the photographs and describe what is happening. Ask *What is the man doing?* (Looking at a thermometer.) *What is the woman doing?* (Talking on the phone to the man.)
- After students read and listen, check comprehension by asking *What problem does the man have?* (He's not feeling well. He's been coughing and sneezing for a couple of days.) *What does the woman suggest?* (She says he should see a doctor.)

B ◄)) Rhythm and intonation

Suggested teaching time:	3–5 minutes	Your actual teaching time:	

- Have students repeat each line chorally. Make sure students:
  - use rising intonation for *Is something wrong?*
  - put extra stress on *awful* in *That must be awful.*
  - use rising intonation for *OK?*

NOW YOU CAN Call in sick

A Pair work

Suggested teaching time:	5–7 minutes	Your actual teaching time:	

- If necessary, review the Vocabulary for symptoms by having students take turns acting out problems and guessing symptoms.
- Be sure to reinforce the use of the conversation strategies. Have students brainstorm ways they can use *I'm afraid . . .* to introduce disappointing information. Write on board *I'm afraid I'm not going to be able to ___ today.* (Possible answers: Come to your party, help you with your homework, drive you to work.)

Don't stop! Extend the conversation. Review the language in the *Be sure to recycle . . .* box. Give students a few minutes to skim the *wordposts* (language in the Recycle box). For more information on wordposting, see the Actively Developing Free Expression section of the Introduction.

- To model the activity, role-play and extend the conversation with a more confident student.

 • **Conversation Pair Work Cards**
• **Learning Strategies**

B Change partners

Suggested teaching time:	5 minutes	Your actual teaching time:	

- Assign students new partners. Remind them to substitute other situations.

EXTRAS (optional)

- **Workbook:** Exercises 4–7
- **Copy & Go:** Activity 5

B Pair work Take turns using the Vocabulary to make lists of symptoms. Practice correct intonation for lists.

> ❝ I feel dizzy, weak, and short of breath. ❞

GRAMMAR   *Modal <u>must</u>: drawing conclusions*

Use <u>must</u> and the base form of a verb to indicate that you think something is probably true.
A: I think I just broke my tooth!   A: The doctor said I should come in next week.
B: Oh, no. That **must hurt**.   B: Oh, good. It **must not be** an emergency.

> **GRAMMAR BOOSTER** ▸ p. 124
> • Other ways to draw conclusions:
>   <u>probably</u>; <u>most likely</u>

Grammar practice Complete the conversations by drawing conclusions, using <u>must</u> or <u>must not</u>.

1 A: You look awful! You ....**must be**........
       in a lot of pain.
                                    be

   B: I am.

2 A: Gary just called. He has a bad headache.

   B: Too bad. He ......**must not want**...... to go running.
                              want

3 A: My doctor says I'm in perfect health.

   B: That's great. You ......**must feel**...... really good.
                                    feel

4 A: Did you call the dentist?

   B: Yes, I did. But no one's answering. She
       ......**must not be**...... in today.
                    be

CONVERSATION MODEL

A 🔊 *1:22* Read and listen to someone calling in sick.

A: I'm afraid I'm not going to be able to come in today.

B: I'm sorry to hear that. Is something wrong?

A: Actually, I'm not feeling too well. I've been coughing and wheezing for a couple of days.

B: That must be awful. Maybe you should see a doctor.

A: I think I will.

B: Good. Call me tomorrow and let me know how you feel. OK?

B 🔊 *1:23* **Rhythm and intonation** Listen again and repeat. Then practice the Conversation Model with a partner.

NOW YOU CAN   Call in sick

A Pair work Change the Conversation Model to describe other symptoms. Use <u>must</u> or <u>must not</u> to draw conclusions. Then change roles.

   A: I'm afraid I'm not going to be able
          to .... today.

   B: .... Is something wrong?

   A: Actually, I'm not feeling too well. I ....

   B: That must be .... Maybe you should ....

   A: ....

   B: .... Call me tomorrow and let me
          know how you feel. OK?

B Change partners Call in sick for other situations such as school or social events.

Don't stop!
• Ask more questions about your partner's symptoms.
• Give your partner more suggestions about what to do.

 Be sure to recycle this language.

Ask questions
Are you [coughing]?
Did you try ___?
Make suggestions
You should / You'd better ___.
Why don't you try ___?
How about ___?
Draw conclusions
You must feel awful / terrible.
That must hurt.

GOAL | **Make a medical or dental appointment**

GRAMMAR | **Will be able to; Modals may and might**

Will be able to + base form: future ability
The doctor **will be able to see** you tomorrow. (= The doctor can see you tomorrow.)
She**'ll be able to play** tennis again in a week or so. (= She can play tennis again in a week or so.)

May or might + base form: possibility
The dentist **might have** some time to see you this afternoon.
You **may need** to come in right away.

Note: You can use be able to with may and might for possibility or with must for drawing conclusions.

The doctor	may be able to	see you today.
I	might not be able to	get there till 6:00.
We	must be able to	park here—see the sign?
They	must not be able to	cancel the appointment.

GRAMMAR BOOSTER ▸ p. 125
• Expressing possibility with *maybe*

Grammar practice   Complete each conversation. Use <u>might</u>, <u>be able to</u>, <u>might be able to</u>, or <u>must not be able to</u> and the base form.

1 A: I'd like to see a dentist right away. I think it's an emergency.

   B: Well, I .... might be able to get .... you an appointment at 2:00. Would that be OK?
   get

2 A: Is Dr. Lindt in this morning? I'm not feeling very well.

   B: She is, but she doesn't have any openings. However, she .... might have .... time to see you this afternoon.
   have

3 A: I think I .... might be .... allergic to strawberries. I had some for breakfast, and I have a rash all over my body.
   be

   B: Then you'd better come in this morning. I .... might be able to fit .... you in right before noon.
   fit

4 A: I've been calling Mr. Reis for an hour. I know he's home, but no one's answering.

   B: That's strange. He .... must not be able to hear .... the phone.
   hear

VOCABULARY | **Medical procedures**

A 🔊 **1:24**   Read and listen. Then listen again and repeat.

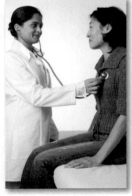
a checkup /
an examination

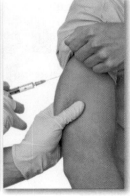
a shot /
an injection

an EKG /
an electrocardiogram

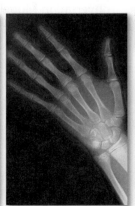
an X-ray

a blood test

GRAMMAR

Suggested teaching time:	10–15 minutes	Your actual teaching time:

- Direct attention to the chart and have students read the first explanation and study the examples. To help clarify, tell students that *be able to* and *can* have the same meaning. Point out that *can* is not used with *will*.

- To check comprehension, ask several students to say what they will be able to do later today, tomorrow, etc.; for example, *I'll be able to leave work early today. We'll be able to get tickets tonight for the concert tomorrow.*

- Have students read the second explanation and study the examples. To help clarify, write on the board:
    Kevin may / might come tomorrow.
    Maybe Kevin will come tomorrow.

- Tell students that both sentences mean we're not sure if Kevin will come tomorrow.

- To check comprehension, write on the board: *Saturday morning, go shopping / Sunday afternoon, go to the movies.* Form pairs and ask students to write sentences using *may* and *might* with the information on the board. Encourage students to add information about who else is going, why they are going, etc. To review, ask several students to say one sentence about each day. Make necessary corrections.

- Have students read the Note and study the examples. Point out that *may, might,* and *must* come before *be able to.* Also point out that *be able to* is followed by a base form.

- To check understanding, say *Maybe I will see her today* and ask students to restate the sentence using *may* or *might* and *be able to.* (I may / might be able to see her today.) Then say *Probably we can get some time off* and have students restate the sentence using *must* and *be able to.* (We must be able to get some time off.)

- Tell students that the negatives of *may* and *might* are *may not* and *might not.* Write on the board: *The dentist may / might not have a cancellation.* The negative of *will be able to* is *will not be able to.* Add to the board: *He will not be able to see you tomorrow.* The contraction for *will not be able to* is *won't be able to. May not* and *might not* cannot be contracted.

Option: [+5 minutes] To challenge students, ask them to write a list of four things they would ideally like to do this weekend; for example, *Go away for the weekend. Go out for dinner.* Then ask volunteers to say what they think they may / might be able to do. (Possible answers: I won't be able to go away for the weekend, but I might be able to go out for dinner.) Make necessary corrections.

Option:  (Teaching notes p. T125)

ActiveTeach Multimedia Disc • **Inductive Grammar Charts**

Grammar practice

Suggested teaching time:	3–5 minutes	Your actual teaching time:

- To model the activity, complete the first item with the class.

- Have students compare answers with a partner. Then review with the class.

A 🔊 Read and listen . . .

Suggested teaching time:	2 minutes	Your actual teaching time:

- Have students listen and study the words and pictures. Then have students repeat chorally.

- If you feel it is appropriate, ask several students questions about their own lives; for example, *Have you ever had an X-ray? When did you last get an injection?*

Option: [+3 minutes] To extend the presentation, review *verb + noun* combinations, and tell students that the medical procedures in this section are normally used with *have.* Write on the board: *have + medical procedure.* Have students work in pairs and ask questions about medical procedures. For example:

Student A: *When did you last have a checkup?*
Student B: *I had a checkup last year.*
Student B: *When did you have a shot?*
Student A: *I had an injection when I went to South Africa in April.*

ActiveTeach Multimedia Disc • **Vocabulary Flash Cards**

B Pair work

Suggested teaching time:	5–8 minutes	Your actual teaching time:

- Read the speech balloon aloud. Encourage students to think of two situations that might need each medical procedure.

- Then ask several students to say a situation. For example:
  You may need a checkup / an examination if you have a fever.
  You might need a shot if you travel to [India].
  You may need an EKG / electrocardiogram if you have pain in your chest.
  You might need an X-ray if you have a car accident.
  You may need a blood test if you feel weak.

CONVERSATION MODEL

A ◀») Read and listen . . .

Suggested teaching time:	2 minutes	Your actual teaching time:

These conversations strategies are implicit in the model:
- Begin a question of possibility with "I wonder if. . . ."
- Use "Let's see if . . ." to indicate you are checking for something.
- Confirm an appointment with "I'll / We'll see you then."
- Express emphatic thanks with "I really appreciate it."

- Before students read and listen to the conversation, have them look at the photographs. Ask *Where is the man?* (At a hospital. In a doctor's office.) *Where is the woman?* (At home.)

- After students read and listen, check comprehension by asking:
  What does the woman need to make an appointment for? (A blood test.)
  When does she want the appointment? (Early next week.)
  When is the appointment? (Tuesday at 10:00.)

- It is important for students to understand that the use of these conversation strategies will help them engage in socially appropriate conversations and communicate effectively.

B ◀») Rhythm and intonation

Suggested teaching time:	3 minutes	Your actual teaching time:

- Have students repeat each line chorally. Make sure students:
  ○ use falling intonation for *How about Tuesday?*
  ○ use rising intonation for *Could I come in the morning?* and *Would you be able to be here at 10:00?*
  ○ put extra stress on *really* in *I really appreciate it.*

NOW YOU CAN Make a medical or dental appointment

A Pair work

Suggested teaching time:	10–15 minutes	Your actual teaching time:

- Read aloud the words and phrases in the *Ideas* box. Then review the Vocabulary on page 18 and have students look at the medical procedures listed on the schedule.

- Be sure to reinforce the use of the conversation strategies. For example, make sure students express thanks using *I really appreciate it* emphatically.

Don't stop! Extend the conversation. Have students give examples of what they can say to discuss other days and times. For example:
  I'm sorry, but I can't make it at 5:00.
  Can I get an appointment later today?
  I'm sorry, but I have a meeting at 3:00.
  Can I have an appointment earlier than that?

- You may also want to review other questions an assistant might ask. For example:
  Have you been here before?
  Could I have your name, please?
  Are you from out of town?
  Where are you from?

- Choose a student and role-play the conversation. Then walk around the room and provide help as needed. Encourage students to use the correct rhythm and intonation and to continue their conversations by asking follow-up questions.

 ActiveTeach Multimedia Disc • Conversation Pair Work Cards

B Change partners

Suggested teaching time:	10 minutes	Your actual teaching time:

- To form new pairs, have students count off, alternating A and B. Then have them find a new partner with the same letter.

- Walk around and provide help as needed. Remind students to make new appointments for different medical procedures and at different times.

EXTRAS (optional)

- Workbook: Exercises 8–12
- Copy & Go: Activity 6

B Pair work Discuss when a person might need each medical procedure from the Vocabulary.

> " If you have pain in your arm, you might need an X-ray. "

A 🔊 **1:25** Read and listen to someone making an appointment.

A: Hello. Doctor Star's office. Can I help you?

B: Hello. I need to make an appointment for a blood test. I wonder if I might be able to come in early next week.

A: Let's see if I can fit you in. How about Tuesday?

B: Could I come in the morning?

A: Let me check . . . Would you be able to be here at 10:00?

B: That would be perfect.

A: We'll see you then.

B: Thanks! I really appreciate it.

B 🔊 **1:26** **Rhythm and intonation** Listen again and repeat. Then practice the Conversation Model with a partner.

NOW YOU CAN   Make a medical or dental appointment

A Pair work Make an appointment to see a doctor or dentist. Suggest a day. Write the appointment on the schedule. Then change roles.

A: Hello. Doctor .... 's office. Can I help you?

B: Hello. I need to make an appointment for .... I wonder if I might be able to come in ....

A: Let's see if I can fit you in. Would you be able to be here at .... ?

B: ....

Don't stop!
• Say you can't be there today.
• Discuss other days and times.

Ideas
• tomorrow
• next week
• early next week
• at the end of next week
• the week of [the 3rd]

B Change partners Make another appointment.

	Patient's name	Medical procedure
8:00	Bill Reed	blood test
9:00	Marie Petton	chest X-ray
10:00		
11:00		
12:00		
1:00	Angela Baker	checkup
2:00	Victor Gaines	flu shot
3:00		
4:00	Teresa Keyes	EKG
5:00		
6:00	Anna Holmes	chest X-ray
7:00		
8:00		
9:00		

19

GOAL   Discuss types of treatments

BEFORE YOU READ

Warm-up What do you do when you get sick or you're in pain? Do you treat the problem yourself or see a doctor right away?

READING 1:27

Consider the choices . . .

CONVENTIONAL MEDICINE

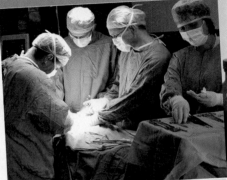

The beginnings of conventional medicine can be traced back to the fifth century B.C.E. in ancient Greece. It is based on the scientific study of the human body and illness.

In the last century, there has been great progress in what doctors have been able to do with modern surgery and new medications. These scientific advances have made conventional medicine the method many people choose first when they need medical treatment.

HOMEOPATHY

Homeopathy was founded in the late eighteenth century in Germany. It is a low-cost system of natural medicine used by hundreds of millions of people worldwide.

In homeopathy, a patient's symptoms are treated with remedies that cause similar symptoms. The remedy is taken in very diluted form: 1 part remedy to one trillion (1,000,000,000,000) parts water.

HERBAL THERAPY

Herbal medicine, often taken as teas or pills, has been practiced for thousands of years in almost all cultures around the world. In fact, many conventional medicines were discovered by scientists studying traditional uses of herbs for medical purposes.

The World Health Organization claims that 80% of the world's population uses some form of herbal therapy for their regular health care.

ACUPUNCTURE

An acupuncturist inserts needles at certain points on the body.

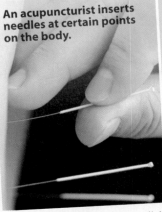

Acupuncture originated in China over 5,000 years ago. Today, it is used worldwide for a variety of problems.

Acupuncture needles are inserted at certain points on the body to relieve pain and/or restore health. Many believe acupuncture may be effective in helping people stop smoking as well.

SPIRITUAL HEALING

Many believe meditation or prayer may help heal disease.

Also known as faith healing, or "mind and body connection," various forms of spiritual healing exist around the world. This is a form of healing that uses the mind or religious faith to treat illness.

A number of conventional doctors say that when they have not been able to help a patient, spiritual healing just may work.

Sources: www.alternativemedicine.com and www.holisticmed.com

BEFORE YOU READ

Warm-up

Suggested teaching time:	2–3 minutes	Your actual teaching time:

- In small groups, have students take turns saying what they do when they get sick or when they are in pain. For example:

  Student A: *When I get sick, I go to bed.*
  Student B: *When I'm in pain, I usually take some medicine.*
  Student C: *When I feel nauseous, I drink some cold water.*
  Student D: *When I don't feel well, I see a doctor right away.*

- Encourage students to offer information about more than one situation. Ask several students to share one of their situations with the class.

READING

Suggested teaching time:	10–15 minutes	Your actual teaching time:

- To activate students' prior knowledge, have them look at the pictures and subheadings and make simple statements about what they already know about each medical treatment. For example:

  I drink herbal tea when my stomach hurts.
  Acupuncture uses needles.
  My sister believes in meditation.

- Then draw the following chart on the board (without the answers) or print it out from the ActiveTeach Multimedia Disc and distribute it to students. Ask students to fill it in as they read and listen to the article. Point out that no information is given about where two of the treatments originated. (The blue text represents example answers.)

Treatment	What does it use? / What is done?	Where did it start?
Conventional medicine	medications, surgery	Greece
Homeopathy	natural medicine	Germany
Herbal therapy	teas, pills	no information
Acupuncture	needles	China
Spiritual healing	the mind, religious faith	no information

FYI: The acronym *B.C.E.* means *Before the Common Era*

- To check comprehension, have students answer the following questions about the treatments. Tell them they can look back at the article for the answers.

  1. *When did conventional medicine begin?* (Fifth century B.C.E.)

  2. *Which treatment uses teas and pills?* (Herbal therapy.)

  3. *What is conventional medicine based on?* (Scientific study of the human body.)

  4. *What is spiritual healing also known as?* (Faith healing or "mind and body connection".)

  5. *When was homeopathy founded?* (Late eighteenth century.)

  6. *Which treatment is said to help people stop smoking?* (Acupuncture.)

Option: [+5 minutes] For a different approach, have students work in small groups. Ask the groups to look at the photograph of each treatment and describe it. (Spiritual healing: two women meditating, sitting on the floor, looking very peaceful with their eyes closed.) Then ask each group to discuss whether they think the photograph illustrates the treatment accurately. Elicit suggestions of other photographs or illustrations that would describe the treatments.

ActiveTeach Multimedia Disc
- **Extra Reading Comprehension Questions**
- **Learning Strategies**
- **Graphic Organizers**

A Understand from context

Suggested teaching time:	3–5 minutes	Your actual teaching time:	

- If students need help, tell them to find five words that are related to restoring health or treating illness.
- Have students compare answers with a partner. Then review with the class.

B Relate to personal experience

Suggested teaching time:	10 minutes	Your actual teaching time:	

- Ask students to form groups of three or four. Have them use the Vocabulary from previous lessons, such as the symptoms on page 16, medical procedures on page 18, and the information in the reading.
- For question 1, encourage students to make a list of the treatments they or their family have tried.
- For question 2, encourage students to use their own experiences to talk about the effectiveness of treatments. To help students with the language they need, brainstorm ways to describe how treatments helped / didn't help. Write students ideas' on the board. For example:

  It helped me with my [back] pain.
  It stopped my [cough] right away.
  It didn't relieve my pain.
  It just didn't work.
  It didn't help at all.
  It helped me feel better.

- Then ask volunteers to share their experiences with a type of treatment and say why they think it is or it is not effective. Encourage the class to ask follow-up questions and share their own experiences with the same treatment.

C Draw conclusions

Suggested teaching time:	5–7 minutes	Your actual teaching time:	

- Remind students to choose at least two types of treatment for each patient—one that the patient might not want to use and one that the patient might prefer to use. Encourage them to give reasons why they chose their particular answers.
- Have students compare answers with a partner. Then ask several students to tell the class the treatments they chose for each person.

Option: [+3 minutes] To extend the activity, have students work in pairs. Ask them to take turns saying if they agree or disagree with the opinions of the people in the pictures and explain why.

NOW YOU CAN Discuss types of treatments

A Notepadding

Suggested teaching time:	10 minutes	Your actual teaching time:	

- Review the list of *Practitioners* in the box.
- Clarify the task: First ask students to fill in the first column with their own information. Then discuss their answers and take notes about their partner. Encourage students to explain their choices.

B Discussion

Suggested teaching time:	5–10 minutes	Your actual teaching time:	

- Select several students to read the speech balloons aloud for the class.
- Form groups of four. Before students begin their discussions, review the different ways to say whether a treatment works or not. For example:

  It works for me.
  It helped me with [headaches].
  It helped my body to heal itself.
  It relieved my pain.
  I felt a lot better.

- Walk around the room and provide help as needed. Then take a poll to find out which type of treatment is the most popular in the class.

EXTRAS (optional)

- **Workbook:** Exercises 13–16
- **Copy & Go:** Activity 7

A Understand from context Five of these words have similar meanings. Cross out the three words that don't belong. Look at the article again for help.

| remedy | treatment | therapy | ~~advances~~ |
| ~~resources~~ | healing | care | ~~purposes~~ |

B Relate to personal experience Talk about the following questions.

1 Which of the treatments in the Reading have you or your family tried?

2 Which treatments do you think are the most effective? Why?

C Draw conclusions Decide which treatment or treatments each patient would probably NOT want to try and which he or she might prefer. Explain your answers, using <u>might</u> or <u>might not</u>. (More than one therapy might be appropriate.)

1 **"**I definitely want to see a doctor when I have a problem. But I want to avoid taking any strong medications or having surgery. **"** herbal therapy, acupuncture

2 **"**I believe you have to heal yourself. You can't just expect a doctor to do everything for you. **"** homeopathy, spiritual healing

3 **"**I think it would be crazy to try a health care method that isn't strongly supported by scientific research. **"** conventional medicine

On your *ActiveBook* Self-Study Disc:
Extra Reading Comprehension Questions

NOW YOU CAN Discuss types of treatments

A Notepadding With a partner, discuss treatments you would choose for each ailment. What kind of practitioner would you visit? Complete your notepad.

Practitioners
- a conventional doctor
- a homeopathic doctor
- an acupuncturist
- an herbal therapist
- a spiritual healer

Ailment	You	Your partner
a cold		
a headache		
nausea		
back pain		
a high fever		
a broken finger		

B Discussion Compare the kinds of treatments you and your classmates would use. Say what you learned about your partner.

"I would never try herbal therapy. I just don't think it works. My partner agrees. **"**

"My partner has been to an acupuncturist a number of times. It really helped with her back pain. **"**

"I see a homeopathic doctor regularly, but my partner doesn't believe in that. He prefers a conventional doctor. **"**

21

1:29
🔊 **Medicine label information**
Dosage: Take 1 tablet by mouth every day.
Warnings: Do not take while driving or operating machinery.
Side effects: May cause dizziness or nausea.

a prescription

BEFORE YOU LISTEN

A 🔊 **Vocabulary • *Medications*** Read and listen.
1:28
Then listen again and repeat.

a painkiller

cold tablets

**a nasal spray /
a decongestant**

eye drops

an antihistamine

cough medicine

an antibiotic

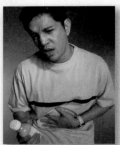

an antacid

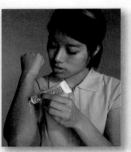

an ointment

vitamins

B   Pair work Discuss what you might use
each medication for.

> ❝I might take an antacid
> for a stomachache.❞

LISTENING COMPREHENSION

A 🔊 **Listen for key details** Listen to each conversation with a doctor.
1:30
Use the medications Vocabulary above and the symptoms Vocabulary from
page 16 to complete the chart for each patient.

Name: *Didem Yilmaz*

What are the patient's symptoms?
back pain

Is the patient currently taking any
medications? ☑Yes ☐No

If so, which ones?
painkillers

Did the patient get a prescription?
☑Yes ☐No

Name: *Lucy Fernández*

What are the patient's symptoms?
headache, nauseous

Is the patient currently taking any
medications? ☑Yes ☐No

If so, which ones?
antacid, painkillers

Did the patient get a prescription?
☑Yes ☐No

Name: *Mark Goh*

What are the patient's symptoms?
red eyes

Is the patient currently taking any
medications? ☑Yes ☐No

If so, which ones?
eye drops

Did the patient get a prescription?
☑Yes ☐No

BEFORE YOU LISTEN

A 🔊 Vocabulary

Suggested teaching time:	3–5 minutes	Your actual teaching time:

- Ask students which medicine they use or someone they know uses.

- Draw students' attention to the medicine label information. Tell them that a prescription is a medicine ordered by a doctor for an illness.

- Have students read the label of the prescription container. Then write on the board:

    1. dosage   a. things you shouldn't do
    2. warnings   b. symptoms a medication can cause
    3. side effects   c. how much medicine to take and when to take it

- To check comprehension, ask students to match the words with the definitions. (1. c; 2. a; 3. b.)

- Have students listen and study the medications. Then have them listen and repeat chorally.

- **Vocabulary Flash Cards**
- **Learning Strategies**

B Pair work

Suggested teaching time:	5 minutes	Your actual teaching time:

- To prepare students for the activity, read the speech balloon and review the Vocabulary for symptoms on page 16. Brainstorm other symptoms or illnesses and write them on the board: *flu, a cold, a fever, a sore throat, a headache, red eyes, a rash, a burn.*

- To help students with the language they will need, point out the following *verb + noun* combinations and write them on the board:

    get a prescription for ___
    use [a nasal spray / eye drops / an ointment]
    take [a painkiller / cold tablets / an antihistamine / cough medicine / an antibiotic / an antacid / vitamins]

- To review, have volunteers say when they would take one or more medications.

Language and culture

- In American English, the store where you buy medicine is called a *drugstore* or *pharmacy*. In British and Australian English, a pharmacy is called a *chemist's*.
- In North America, a doctor's prescription is required for many medications. Medicines that don't need a prescription are called *over-the-counter* medicines or *OTCs*. Antibiotics, for example, require a prescription and are never sold over-the-counter at a pharmacy.

LISTENING COMPREHENSION

A 🔊 Listen for key details

Suggested teaching time:	7–10 minutes	Your actual teaching time:

- To prepare students for listening, have them look at the charts to check which information they should listen for. Pause after each conversation so that students can complete each chart.

- To help focus attention, you may choose to have students listen each time for different information in the charts.

- To review, have students compare answers with a partner and then with the class.

AUDIOSCRIPT See page T23.

B 🔊)) Listen for more details

Suggested teaching time:	7–10 minutes	Your actual teaching time:

• Follow the same procedure as for Exercise A.

NOW YOU CAN Talk about medications

A Preparation

Suggested teaching time:	5–10 minutes	Your actual teaching time:

• Point out that students should complete the form with imaginary information.

B Group work

Suggested teaching time:	10 minutes	Your actual teaching time:

• Form groups of four. Have students read the list of *Roles* in the box and the descriptions of the three scenes.

• Point out the *Be sure to recycle . . .* box and review the wordposts. As you review each expression, you may want to have students say who is likely to say it (the patient, the friend, the doctor, or the receptionist); for example, you or a student reads *I've been wheezing / coughing / dizzy.* The class says: *The patient.*

• Encourage students to use as many of the expressions in the box as they can. Ask them to check off the ones they use.

C Presentation

Suggested teaching time:	8–10 minutes	Your actual teaching time:

• Ask students to practice their scenes before performing them for the class.

EXTRAS (optional)

• Workbook: Exercises 17–19
• Copy & Go: Activity 8

AUDIOSCRIPT for page T22 (**A** Listen for key details)

CONVERSATION 1 [M = Korean, F = Turkish]
M: Ms. Yilmaz? I'm Dr. Lee. I understand you're here on business.
F: That's right. I'm from Turkey, actually.
M: And you're not feeling well?
F: No, I'm afraid not. My back has been killing me for several days now.
M: Are you taking anything?
F: Just some painkillers. But they're not really helping.
M: Let me give you a prescription for a stronger painkiller. I think you might find it very helpful.
F: Does it have any side effects?
M: Well, for very few patients it causes nausea or vomiting. But that's very rare. I really don't think you'll have to worry. Call me if you feel at all nauseous, OK?
F: OK. Thanks.
M: The dosage is one tablet in the morning, one in the evening, with food. The pharmacist will give you a full set of instructions when you pick up your prescription.
F: Thank you, Dr. Lee.

CONVERSATION 2 [M = Japanese, F = Spanish]
M: Lucy Fernández? I'm Dr. Hirano.
F: Thanks so much for fitting me in.
M: My pleasure. Where are you from?
F: Mexico. I'm here on business.
M: You're a long way from home! What can I do for you today?
F: Well, I've got a splitting headache, and I've been kind of nauseous since Monday.
M: You must feel terrible. Are you currently taking any medication?
F: I've been taking an antacid and a painkiller.
M: Are you allergic to any medications?
F: I think I might be allergic to penicillin. But I'm not sure.
M: Well, that's OK. Keep taking the painkiller for that headache. But you can stop taking the antacid. I'm going to give you a prescription for your nausea. Take it twice a day.
F: Will there be any side effects?
M: It might make you a little tired during the day. But chances are you'll be fine. Call me if you don't feel better.

CONVERSATION 3 [M = Chinese]
M: Dr. Benson? Hi, I'm Mark Goh.
F: Hello, Mr. Goh. I hear you're not from around here.
M: Right. I'm visiting from Hong Kong for a few weeks.
F: You've come a long way to see a doctor! Well, what can I do for you today?
M: My eyes have been really red for about a week now.
F: Have you been using any medication?
M: Well I got some eye drops at the drugstore, but they aren't helping.
F: For your condition, I think you might want something stronger. I'm going to give you a prescription for an eye ointment. Use it twice a day, and wash your eyes several times a day.
M: OK.
F: It's a strong medication, but there aren't any side effects you need to worry about. If you keep your eyes clean, the ointment should do the trick.
M: Thanks.
F: Will you still be here next week? I'd like you to come back to see me.
M: Yes, I'll still be here.
F: Good. You can make an appointment at the front desk on your way out.
M: Thanks, Doctor.

B 🔊 **Listen for more details** Listen again. Complete the information about each patient.

Didem Yilmaz
Dosage: One tablet _____twice_____ a day
Side effects: ☑Yes ☐No
If so, what are they? ___nausea, vomiting___
_____

Lucy Fernández
Dosage: _____twice_____ a day
Side effects: ☑Yes ☐No
If so, what are they? _tiredness_____
OR may make you tired
_____

Mark Goh
Dosage: Apply ointment _____twice_____ a day
Side effects: ☐Yes ☑No
If so, what are they? _____
_____
_____

NOW YOU CAN Talk about medications

A Preparation Imagine you are visiting the doctor. Complete the patient information form.

B Group work With three other classmates, role-play a visit to a doctor. First, choose roles. Then role-play the three scenes below. Use the patient information form.

Roles
• a patient
• a friend, colleague, classmate, or relative
• a receptionist
• a doctor

Scene 1: The colleague, classmate, friend, or relative recommends a doctor.
Scene 2: The patient calls the receptionist to make an appointment.
Scene 3: The doctor asks about the symptoms and recommends medication, etc.

Patient Information Form

Last name	First name

1. What are your symptoms?

☐ dizziness	☐ coughing	☐ nausea	☐ weakness
☐ sneezing	☐ vomiting	☐ shortness of breath	
☐ wheezing	☐ pain (where?)		
☐ other:			

2. How long have you had these symptoms?

3. Are you currently taking any medications? ☐ Yes ☐ No
If so, which ones?

4. Are you allergic to any medications? ☐ Yes ☐ No
If so, which ones?

♻ **Be sure to recycle this language.**

Scene 1
I've been [wheezing / coughing / dizzy].
I'm in a lot of pain.
Could you recommend ___ ?
I think you should try ___ .
Why don't you ___ ?
You may have to ___ .
I hope you feel better soon.

Scene 2
I need to make an appointment for ___ .
I wonder if I might be able to ___ .
Let me check.
Let's see if I can fit you in.
Would you be able to be here ___ ?
I really appreciate it.

Scene 3
Thanks for fitting me in.
Luckily, I had a cancellation.
Let's have a look.
Are you taking any medications?
Are you allergic to any medications?
Are there any side effects?
Call me tomorrow.

C Presentation Perform your role play for the class.

Review

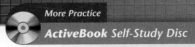
A ◀)) **Listening comprehension** Listen to each conversation and complete the statements. Then listen again to check your answers.

The patient lost .... a filling .... when she was eating .... candy ....

The patient has ...... been sneezing all day .... She needs to take ...... an antihistamine ....

The patient needs ...... an x-ray ...... of his .... leg ....

The patient would like to try .... acupuncture .... for pain in her .... back ....

B Suggest a medication for each person. (Answers will vary.)

1 .... a painkiller ....

2 ...... an antihistamine ......

3 ...... an antacid ......

4 ...... eye drops ......

5 ...... cold tablets ......

C Complete each conversation by drawing your own conclusion with <u>must</u>. Answers will vary slightly, but may include the following:

1 A: I feel really nauseous. I've been vomiting all morning.
   B: You *must feel terrible* ....

2 A: My dentist can't fit me in till next month.
   B: Your dentist ...... must be busy ....

3 A: My daughter was sick, but it wasn't anything serious, thank goodness.
   B: You ...... must be happy ....

4 A: My husband fell down and broke his ankle.
   B: He ...... must be in pain ...... !

D On a separate sheet of paper, rewrite each statement, using <u>may</u> (or <u>might</u>) and <u>be able to</u>. Answers will vary slightly, but may include the following: (Accept answers with <u>may</u> or <u>might</u>.)

1 Maybe the doctor can see you tomorrow.

   The doctor might be able to see you tomorrow.

2 Maybe an acupuncturist can help you.
   An acupuncturist may be able to help you.
3 Maybe the hotel can recommend a good dentist.
   The hotel might be able to recommend a good dentist.
4 Maybe she can't come to the office before 6:00.
   She may not be able to come to the office before 6:00.
5 Maybe you can buy an antihistamine in the hotel gift shop.
   You might be able to buy an antihistamine in the gift shop.

E **Writing** On a separate sheet of paper, compare two types of medical treatments. Use the Reading on page 20 and your own experiences and ideas. Consider the following questions:

- How are the two medical treatments similar or different?

- Which treatment do you think is more effective?

- Why might people choose each treatment?

- Which treatments do you—or people you know—use? Why?

1:33/1:34
♪ **Top Notch Pop**
"X-ray of My Heart"
Lyrics p. 149

WRITING BOOSTER ▶ p. 141

- *Comparisons and contrasts*
- *Guidance for Exercise E*

Review

A 🔊 Listening comprehension

Suggested teaching time:	5–10 minutes	Your actual teaching time:

- **First listening:** To prepare students for the activity, have them identify which problem each patient has. (First patient: She has some pain in her tooth. Second patient: She's been sneezing all day. Third patient: His leg hurts. Fourth patient: Her back has been killing her.)
- **Second listening:** Have students read the incomplete statements and then listen again to complete them.
- Ask students to compare answers with a partner. Then review with the class.

Option: [+5 minutes] To extend the activity, tell students that the cause or reason for the problem is given for three of the patients. Have them listen to the conversations again and write the cause or reason. (1. Eating candy / something hard; 2. allergies; 3. skiing fast and falling down; 4. not known.)

AUDIOSCRIPT

CONVERSATION 1
M: So, what's bothering you today?
F: Well, I've had some pain in my tooth. Here, on the right side.
M: Let's have a look. Hmm . . . Looks like you lost a filling.
F: Really? My regular dentist just put that in a month ago!
M: Have you eaten anything hard or chewy or crunchy lately?
F: Uh-oh. I think that's it. It was probably that candy I ate two days ago.
M: Well, how about we take care of that right now, OK?
F: Thanks.

CONVERSATION 2
F: Thanks for fitting me in. I've been sneezing like crazy all day. I thought I'd better come in and get something.
M: Allergies?
F: Mm-hmm. I get them every spring at this time. I don't know if it's the trees or the flowers or what. But my eyes get red. I sneeze.
M: Well, I can give you a prescription to take care of that. ClearAid is a very good antihistamine.
F: Thanks. I'd really appreciate that.

CONVERSATION 3
F: You must be in a lot of pain.
M: I am. My leg really hurts a lot.
F: You said you were skiing?
M: Yes. I guess I went a little too fast.
F: Well, don't worry about that now. Let's get you into radiology and then we'll know if you've broken anything or not. Have you ever been X-rayed before?
M: Just for my teeth.

CONVERSATION 4
M: You look like you're in a lot of pain.
F: Yes. My back's been killing me for several days now. I've been taking painkillers several times a day.
M: And that hasn't helped?
F: Not really. I still can't sit. I can't stand. All I can do is lie down.
M: Well, I could write you a prescription for a stronger medication if you like. That might help.
F: I don't know. Everyone says acupuncture is good for pain. Do you think I should try that?
M: Sometimes it helps. I could give you a referral if you like.
F: I'd like that. I need to try something else.

B Suggest a medication for . . .

Suggested teaching time:	3 minutes	Your actual teaching time:

- Encourage students to look at the part of the body that has the problem.
- To review, ask students to use complete sentences to say what the problem is and which medication the person should take; for example, *She has a headache. She needs a painkiller. He has allergies. He needs an antihistamine.*

Option: [+5 minutes] To extend the activity, write the following ailments and medications in two columns on the board. Ask students to match them. Have students compare answers with a partner and review with the class. (1. b; 2. d or a; 3. a or d; 4. f; 5. e; 6. c.)

1. a burn
2. a stuffy nose
3. an allergy
4. a burning feeling in your stomach
5. a headache
6. a cold

a. antihistamine
b. ointment
c. cold tablets
d. nasal spray / decongestant
e. painkiller
f. antacid

C Complete each conversation . . .

Suggested teaching time:	2 minutes	Your actual teaching time:

- First review the example.
- Then have pairs of students read the sentences aloud to each other in order to complete them.

Option: [+2 minutes] To extend the activity, ask students to take turns role-playing the corrected conversations.

D On a separate sheet . . .

Suggested teaching time:	5 minutes	Your actual teaching time:

- First review the example. Then restate the example using *may: The doctor may be able to see you tomorrow.* Remind students that *may* and *might* usually have the same meaning.
- Ask students to compare answers with a partner. Call on several students to read their answers aloud.

E Writing

Suggested teaching time:	10 minutes	Your actual teaching time:

- Before students begin, ask them to name the different medical treatments they have discussed in this unit. (Conventional medicine, homeopathy, herbal therapy, acupuncture, spiritual healing.)
- Have students choose two treatments to compare and answer the questions. Walk around the room as students write and provide help as needed.

Option: **WRITING BOOSTER** (Teaching notes p. T141)

 ActiveTeach Multimedia Disc • Writing Process Worksheets

ORAL REVIEW

Before the first activity, give students a few minutes of silent time to explore the pictures and become familiar with them.

Pair work 1

Suggested teaching time:	5–10 minutes	Your actual teaching time:

- To help students prepare for the activity, ask *Where are the people?* (The man is at home, and the woman is at work.) *What seems to be the problem?* (The man has a cold and won't be able to come in today.)
- Have pairs of students choose roles. Remind them that the person who calls in sick should explain what is wrong. His or her boss should show sympathy and make a suggestion.
- Before students create the conversations, you may want to model one with a student.

Possible responses . . .

A: I'm afraid I'm not going to be able to come in today. I have a cold / a high fever. **B:** I'm sorry to hear that. **A:** I've been coughing and wheezing all night. **B:** That must be awful / terrible. Maybe you should see / You'd better see a doctor. **A:** I think I will. **B:** Call me tomorrow and let me know how you feel. OK?

Pair work 2

Suggested teaching time:	5–10 minutes	Your actual teaching time:

- Choose a student and role-play the conversation.
- Walk around the room monitoring students' work. Make sure each student plays both roles. Then ask one or two pairs to role-play their conversations for the class.

Possible responses . . .

A: Hello. Can I help you? **B:** I wonder if I might be able to get an appointment for a checkup today. **A:** Are you in pain? **B:** Yes, actually, I am. [My stomach really hurts. I've been vomiting a lot.] **A:** Well, don't worry. I'm sure Dr. [Jones] can help you. Could you be here at [3:00]? **B:** Yes. That would be fine. Thanks for fitting me in.

A: Hello. Can I help you? **B:** I wonder if I might be able to get an appointment for [a blood test / a chest X-ray / a flu shot / an EKG]. **A:** Well, let me check. Would you be able to be here at 5:00? **B:** That would be perfect. **A:** We'll see you then. **B:** Thanks.

Game

Suggested teaching time:	10 minutes	Your actual teaching time:

- Before students create the conversation, ask *Where are these people?* (At a medical office / at a clinic.)
- Have students work in groups and take turns describing a patient and drawing a conclusion.

Possible responses . . .

The man is going to have an X-ray. He may have pain in his chest. The woman is having a blood test. She might feel weak. The man is getting a shot. He might be going on a trip. The man is coughing. He must have a cold. The woman is touching her hip. She must be in pain.

Option: [+5 minutes] To extend the activity, tell students to create a new conversation to make a dental appointment. Explain that the assistant should ask what is wrong and the patient should describe the problem. Remind students of the vocabulary they practiced on page 14.

Option: [+5 minutes] To challenge students, ask them to create conversations for the people in the different medical examination rooms. For example (first room):

Student A: *Hello, [Mr. Black]. Tell me what happened.*
Student B: *Well, I was [washing the car]. I slipped and fell down and now I have pain in my [back].*
Student A: *I understand. Are you in a lot of pain now?*
Student B: *It isn't too bad.*
Student A: *Well, we'd better take an X-ray.*

Option: Oral Progress Assessment

Use the illustration on page 25. Encourage students to use the language practiced in this unit and previous units.

- Tell the student you are going to role-play a conversation between the man and the woman in the first picture. The student should play the man. Tell him or her to start by saying *I'm afraid I'm not going to be able to come in today.*
- Tell the student you are going to ask questions about several people in the waiting area and have him or her make a statement of deduction using *may, might,* or *must*; for example, **T:** *Why does the man on the telephone need an appointment?* **S:** *He might be on a business trip and he feels weak and nauseous.*
- Evaluate the student on intelligibility, fluency, correct use of target grammar, and appropriate use of vocabulary.

 • Oral Progress Assessment Charts

Option: *Top Notch* Project

Have students prepare a presentation on a world health problem such as AIDs, malaria, or tuberculosis.

Idea: Encourage students to include visual aids such as photographs and drawings to help illustrate the ideas. Have students keep a list of new medical vocabulary and look up their definitions. Ask them to copy and hand out the list before giving the presentation.

EXTRAS (optional)

- Complete Assessment Package
- Weblinks for Teachers: pearsonlongman.com/topnotch/

And on your ActiveTeach Multimedia Disc:
  Just for Fun
  Top Notch Pop Song Activities
  Top Notch TV Video Program and Activity Worksheets
  Supplementary Pronunciation Lessons
  Audioscripts
  Unit Study Guides

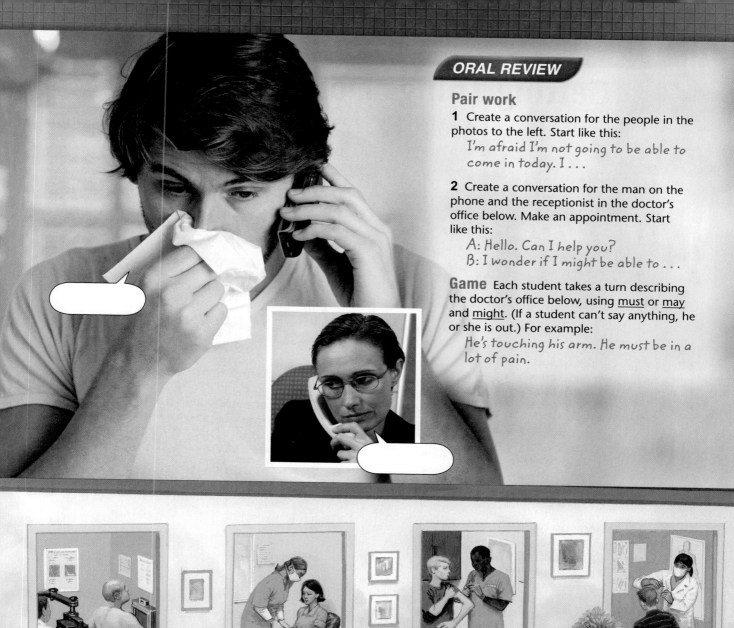

Pair work

1 Create a conversation for the people in the photos to the left. Start like this:

I'm afraid I'm not going to be able to come in today. I . . .

2 Create a conversation for the man on the phone and the receptionist in the doctor's office below. Make an appointment. Start like this:

A: Hello. Can I help you?
B: I wonder if I might be able to . . .

Game Each student takes a turn describing the doctor's office below, using <u>must</u> or <u>may</u> and <u>might</u>. (If a student can't say anything, he or she is out.) For example:

He's touching his arm. He must be in a lot of pain.

NOW I CAN...

- ☐ Call in sick.
- ☐ Make a medical or dental appointment.
- ☐ Discuss types of treatments.
- ☐ Talk about medications.

Getting Things Done

GOALS | After Unit 3, you will be able to:
1 Get someone else to do something.
2 Request express service.
3 Evaluate the quality of service.
4 Plan a meeting or social event.

Are you a PROCRASTINATOR?

Take the survey.

1 At the beginning of every week, you ___.
- ☐ a. always make to-do lists for your calendar
- ☐ b. sometimes make to-do lists, but you often forget
- ☐ c. don't bother with planning and just let things happen

2 When you need to buy someone a gift, you ___.
- ☐ a. get something right away
- ☐ b. buy something a few days before you have to give it
- ☐ c. pick something up on the day you have to give it

3 When you have something that's broken, you ___.
- ☐ a. immediately take it in to be repaired
- ☐ b. wait for a convenient time to take it in
- ☐ c. never get around to taking it in

4 When you have a lot of things you need to do, you do ___.
- ☐ a. the hardest things first
- ☐ b. the easiest things first
- ☐ c. anything but what you need to do

5 When you need to get something done in a short amount of time, you ___.
- ☐ a. feel motivated to work even harder
- ☐ b. feel a little nervous, but you get to work
- ☐ c. have a hard time doing it

6 You ___ feel bad when there are things you haven't gotten done yet.
- ☐ a. always
- ☐ b. sometimes
- ☐ c. rarely

Your results

If you answered "c" four or more times:
You are a classic procrastinator! You tend to put things off.

If you answered "b" four or more times:
You are a bit of a procrastinator, but you try to get things done on time.

If you answered "a" four or more times:
You are organized and self-motivated. You never put off what you can get done now.

Source: adapted from www.blogthings.com.

A Pair work Compare responses on the survey with a partner. Does your score accurately describe the kind of person you are? Explain, using examples.

B Discussion Based on the survey questions, what is a procrastinator? What do you think it means to be an "organized and self-motivated" person? What do you think are the advantages of being that type of person?

UNIT 3

Getting Things Done

Preview

Suggested teaching time:	10–15 minutes	Your actual teaching time:

Before Exercise A, give students a few minutes of silent time to observe the survey.

• Direct students' attention to the title and ask *What will you find out by completing this survey?* (Something about yourself.)

FYI: Do not clarify the meaning of *procrastinator*. Instead tell students that the survey will help them figure out its meaning. Students will be discussing what a procrastinator is in Exercise B.

• Write two column heads on the board:
  Things I try to do right away
  Things I tend to put off

• Ask students to read both heads and guess what "put off" means. Ask *What's the opposite of doing things right away?*

• To help students prepare for the survey, ask them to list examples of things they tend to put off and things they do right away. Then ask students to fill in the survey, count the number of "a," "b," and "c" answers, and then look at the results. Have students use examples from their lists to explain if their scores accurately describe the kind of people they are.

A Pair work

Suggested teaching time:	8–10 minutes	Your actual teaching time:

• After pairs compare their responses on the survey, have volunteers tell the class why they agree or don't agree with the results.

Option: [+5 minutes] To extend the activity, have students form small groups and choose a question from the survey. Then ask each group to give an example to back up the answer they chose; for example, *I usually buy gifts on the day I have to give them. It was my brother's birthday last week. I remember I was late for his dinner party because I had to go to the mall to pick up a gift.*

B Discussion

Suggested teaching time:	8–10 minutes	Your actual teaching time:

• To reinforce the concept of what a procrastinator is, write the following statements on the board and have students choose the correct words to complete them.
  A procrastinator . . .
    a. puts / doesn't put things off.
    b. does / doesn't do things right away.
    c. is / is not organized.
    d. is / is not self-motivated.
    (a. Puts; b. doesn't do; c. is not; d. is not.)

• To help students explain what an organized and self-motivated person is, have them choose examples from the survey; for example, *An organized person always makes to-do lists. A self-motivated person does the hardest things first.*

• To check students' understanding, ask volunteers to answer one of the discussion questions.

C 🔊 Photo story

Suggested teaching time:	5 minutes	Your actual teaching time:

- To help students prepare, have them cover the conversations and look at the pictures. Ask *Where are the people?* (Two of the people are in a copy shop. A third man is somewhere else.) *Is it a quiet day or a busy day in the shop?* (A busy day.) *Why?* (Possible answer: There is a customer in the shop and another customer is calling the shop.)

- After reading and listening, check comprehension by having students summarize the conversations using the questions as a guide. For example:
  ○ Conversation 1: Ms. Krauss needs 300 copies of a document by 11:00. The manager is very busy, but agrees to do the work because she is a good customer.
  ○ Conversation 2: Mr. Li needs fifty sales binders for tomorrow morning. The manager says he can do the work.

- Point out that *a.s.a.p.* is said with the four letters A-S-A-P.

Option: [+5 minutes] For an initial presentation based on listening, follow the discussion of the pictures by writing the following questions on the board:

What does each customer need?
When does he or she need it by?
How is each situation resolved?

Ask students to listen for the answers to these questions.

Language and culture

- The omission of words that are not necessary for understanding the message is common in rapid, spoken English. The full forms of *Any chance I could* and *No need for that* are *Is there any chance I could get them done by first thing tomorrow morning?* and *There is no need for that.*

LEN **From the Longman Corpus:** The acronym *a.s.a.p.* is used frequently in spoken English and informal writing, such as in e-mails. The use of *first thing* as an adverb is especially common in spoken and informal English.

D Paraphrase

Suggested teaching time:	5–7 minutes	Your actual teaching time:

- To check understanding, ask students to identify who says the phrases and to use the context of the conversation to help figure out the meaning.

- Have students compare answers with a partner. Then review with the class.

Answers for Exercise D
1. I should have come earlier / before.
2. It must be done immediately.
3. You really helped me out.
4. No problem.
5. Thank you. I appreciate it.
6. You have a lot to do. / You are very busy.
7. I won't delay you.

E Discussion

Suggested teaching time:	9–13 minutes	Your actual teaching time:

- To help students generate ideas to complete the chart ask:

Who makes to-do lists? (Mr. Li.)
Who needs to get a job done right away? (Ms. Krauss.)
Who needs to get a job done for the next day? (Mr. Li.)
Who is busy, but feels motivated to work hard? (Sam, the manager.)

- To describe the characters, ask students to use the chart to help them organize their ideas. Walk around the room to provide help as needed. Then ask three volunteers to describe a character.

Option: [+5 minutes] For a different approach, have students form small groups and share their own experiences. Ask them to think of a day when they needed to do something right away. Then have them explain what they needed and if they managed to do it on time. Encourage students to ask follow-up questions.

EXTRAS (optional)

- **Workbook:** Exercises 1 and 2

C 🔊 **Photo story** Read and listen to some customers placing orders at a copy shop.

English For Today's World
connecting people from different cultures
and language backgrounds

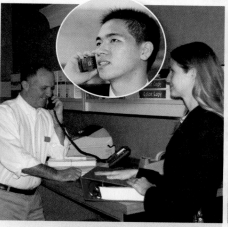

Manager: What can I do for you today, Ms. Krauss?

Customer 1: I need to get these documents copied a.s.a.p.* Think I could get 300 copies done by 11:00?

Manager: I'm afraid that might be difficult. I've got a lot of orders to complete this morning.

Customer 1: Sorry. I know this is last minute. But it's really urgent.

Manager: Well, you're a good customer. Let me see what I can do.

Customer 1: Thanks a million. You're a lifesaver!

Manager: Excuse me . . . Hello. Happy Copy.

Customer 2: Hi, Sam. Ken Li here.

Manager: Hi, Mr. Li. How can I help you today?

Customer 2: Well, I'm going through my to-do list, and I just realized I need to get fifty 30-page sales binders made up for our meeting next week. Any chance I could get them done by first thing tomorrow morning?

Manager: Tomorrow morning? No sweat. Can you get the documents to me before noon?

Customer 2: Absolutely. I owe you one, Sam!

Manager: Sorry to keep you waiting, Ms. Krauss.

Customer 1: Well, I see that you've got a lot on your plate today. I won't keep you any longer.

Manager: Don't worry, Ms. Krauss. We'll get your order done on time.

Customer 1: Should I give you a call later?

Manager: No need for that. Come at 11:00 and I'll have your documents ready.

Customer 1: Thanks, Sam.

*a.s.a.p. = as soon as possible   Customer 2: Chinese speaker

D Paraphrase Say each of the following statements from the Photo Story in your <u>own</u> way.

See page T27 for answers.

1 "… this is last minute."

2 "… it's really urgent."

3 "You're a lifesaver!"

4 "No sweat."

5 "I owe you one!"

6 "… you've got a lot on your plate …"

7 "I won't keep you any longer."

E Discussion Based on the survey on page 26, how would you describe each character in the Photo Story? Complete the chart. Then compare charts with your classmates. Answers will vary slightly, but may include the following:

	Procrastinator?	Organized?	Explain
Ms. Krauss	✓	☐	She waited until the last minute to order the copies.
Sam	☐	✓	He will work hard to complete all of his orders. / He needs to get a lot of things done in a short amount of time and he feels motivated to work hard.
Mr. Li	☐	✓	He wrote a to-do list.

GOAL | Get someone else to do something

GRAMMAR | *Causatives get, have, and make*

Use a causative to express the idea that one person causes another to do something.

Get: Use an object and an infinitive.

	object	infinitive
I got	**the company**	**to agree** to a new date for the meeting.
They got	**the students**	**to clean up** after the party.

Have: Use an object and the base form of a verb.

	object	base form
I had	**my assistant**	**plan** the meeting.
They had	**the bellman**	**bring** the guests' bags to their rooms.

Make: Use an object and the base form of a verb.

	object	base form
I made	**my brother**	**help** me finish the job.
They made	**him**	**sign** the form.

> **Causatives: meaning**
> • The causative <u>get</u> implies that someone convinced another person to do something.
> • The causative <u>have</u> implies that instructions were given.
> • The causative <u>make</u> implies an obligation.

> **GRAMMAR BOOSTER** ▸ p. 125
> • *Let to indicate permission*
> • *Causative have: common errors*

Grammar practice Complete each sentence with a causative.

1 (have / call) Why don't you ...*have*... your assistant ....*call*......... them?
2 (get / do) I'll never be able to ...*get*... my brother ....*to do*......... the laundry.
3 (have / clean) Why didn't you ...*have*... your friends ....*clean*......... up after the party?
4 (get / give) You should ...*get*... the hotel ....*to give*......... you your money back.
5 (make / wash) Why don't you ...*make*... your brother ....*wash*......... the dishes?
6 (get / sign) I'm sure we can ...*get*... the teacher ....*to sign*......... these forms.

VOCABULARY | *Some ways to help out another person*

2:03
A ◀))) Read and listen. Then listen again and repeat.

My car's at the repair shop. Could you possibly *give me **a ride*** to work?

I need to use the men's room. Could you ***keep an eye on** my things* till I get back?

Excuse me. Would you mind ***lending** me your pen?*

I can't play soccer this afternoon. You're a good player. Do you think you could ***fill in for** me?*

I'm too busy to go out for lunch. Do you think you could ***pick up** a sandwich* for me?

give [someone] **a ride**

keep an eye on [something or someone]

lend [someone] [something]

fill in for [someone]

pick up [something or someone]

GRAMMAR

Suggested teaching time:	10–15 minutes	Your actual teaching time:

- Direct attention to the chart and have students read the explanation and study the examples. Write on the board: *get + [person] + infinitive*. To help clarify how to form the causative with *get*, point to the items on the board as you say *I got my sister to make the cake*.

- Write on the board: *I finally convinced my brother to help, and he mailed the invitations*. To check comprehension, ask students to rewrite the sentence starting with *I got*. (I got my brother to mail the invitations.)

- Have students read the second explanation and study the examples. Write on the board: *have + [person] + base form*. To help clarify how to form the causative with *have*, point to the items on the board as you say *I had my sister organize my closet*.

- Write on the board: *I asked my assistant to send the announcement*. To check comprehension, ask students to rewrite the sentence starting with *I had*. (I had my assistant send the announcement.)

- Have students read the third explanation and study the examples. Write on the board: *make + [person] + base form*. To help clarify how to form the causative with *make*, point to the items on the board as you say *His mother made him water the plants*.

- Write on the board: *His father told him to wash the car*. To check comprehension, ask students to rewrite the sentence starting with *His father made*. (His father made him wash the car.)

- Review the implied meanings of the causatives *get*, *have*, and *make* in the box. To help clarify ask a volunteer to explain the differences using the examples in the chart.

Language and culture

LEN **From the Longman Corpus:** Among learners of English, using an infinitive after *make* and an object instead of a base form, is a common error; for example, *He made them to finish the job early*.

Option: GRAMMAR BOOSTER (Teaching notes p. T125)

 **ActiveTeach Multimedia Disc** • Inductive Grammar Charts

Grammar practice

Suggested teaching time:	3 minutes	Your actual teaching time:

- Remind students that the causative *get* needs the infinitive, and the causatives *have* and *made* need the base form.

- Have students compare answers with a partner and then review with the class.

Option: [+3 minutes] To extend the activity and reinforce the use of causatives, have students work in pairs. Ask students to take turns restating the sentences using a different causative.

VOCABULARY

A 🔊 Read and listen . . .

Suggested teaching time:	2–3 minutes	Your actual teaching time:

- To focus students' attention, ask them to study the words and examples first. Then have students listen and repeat chorally.

- Direct attention to the phrases below each photo. To build confidence, read the first phrase aloud and encourage several students to provide substitutes for the words in brackets; for example, **A:** *Give me a ride*. **B:** *Give my daughter a ride*. **C:** *Give my friend a ride*. Do the same with the other phrases.

Option: [+5 minutes] For a different approach, ask questions that need the correct verbal phrases as a response. For example:

[Kim] is not going to be able to play soccer today, so what does she ask a friend? (Fill in for her.)

[Tanya] can't go out for lunch, so what does she ask a colleague? (Pick up a sandwich for her.)

[Max] needs to use the men's room, so what does he ask a person sitting nearby? (Keep an eye on his things.)

[Denise] needs something to write with, so what does she ask a colleague? (Lend her a pen.)

[Ray's] car is in the repair shop, so what does he ask a neighbor? (Give him a ride to work.)

Language and culture

- *Pick up* is a separable phrasal verb. When a pronoun is used, the phrasal verb is separated. Compare: *Could you pick up a magazine at the newsstand? Can you pick me up around four?*

B Complete each sentence . . .

Suggested teaching time:	3–4 minutes	Your actual teaching time:

- Complete the first item with the class.
- Call on several volunteers to read their answers aloud.

Option: [+5 minutes] To extend the activity and reinforce the Vocabulary, write on the board:

give me a ride
keep an eye on
lend me
fill in for me
pick up
	my bag
	your cell phone
	to the station
	while I go out
	  for lunch
	a snack
	my son
	to school
	while I'm at
	  the meeting

Ask students to work in pairs and combine phrases from the boxes to write requests; for example, *Can you give me a ride to school?*

CONVERSATION MODEL

A ◀») Read and listen . . .

Suggested teaching time:	3–5 minutes	Your actual teaching time:

These conversation strategies are implicit in the model:
- Use "I would, but . . ." and an excuse to politely turn down a request.
- Indicate acceptance of someone's excuse with "That's OK. I understand."
- Suggest an alternative with "Maybe you could . . .".

- To introduce the activity tell students to look at the photograph. Ask *Where are the people?* (At work. In an office.)
- After students read and listen, check comprehension by asking:
  Where does the woman need to go? (To the repair shop.)
  Can the man give her a ride? (No.)
  Why not? (Because he has a doctor's appointment.)
  What does he suggest? (Ask Jack.)
- Have students listen, study, and then repeat the *Ways to indicate acceptance* in the box. Remind students that the expressions in the box are transferable to other situations. Point out that using them in real exchanges will help students engage in polite conversations.

B ◀») Rhythm and intonation

Suggested teaching time:	2–3 minutes	Your actual teaching time:

- Have students repeat each line chorally. Make sure students:
  ○ use rising intonation for *What do you need?*
  ○ use falling intonation for *Do you think you could give me a ride?*

○ pause slightly after *I would* in *I would, but I have a doctor's appointment at 2:00.*
○ put extra stress on *Jack* in *Maybe you could get Jack to take you.*

NOW YOU CAN   Get someone else to do something

A Review the Vocabulary . . .

Suggested teaching time:	7–10 minutes	Your actual teaching time:

- To review the Vocabulary, have students look at Exercise A on page 28.
- Before students write their lists, ask them to think of actual favors they have had to ask recently. Remind them to start their requests with *Do you think you could . . .?*

B Pair work

Suggested teaching time:	5–7 minutes	Your actual teaching time:

- Review the *Reasons to turn down a request* in the box. Have students add more reasons; for example, *I'm leaving right away. I have to work right now. I have to meet my sister.*
- Remind students to use causatives whenever possible.
- Be sure to reinforce the use of the conversation strategies. Remind students that they have learned different ways to indicate acceptance of another person's excuse. (I understand. No problem. Don't worry about it.)

Don't stop! Extend the conversation. Review the ideas in the box. Explain that these are tips for keeping the conversation going. Ask students to write two more questions they could ask; for example, *Maybe you could have George help you? Why don't you ask Sarah?*

- To model the activity, role-play and extend the conversation with a more confident student.
- Walk around the room and provide help as needed. Encourage students to use the correct rhythm and intonation and to continue their conversations by asking follow-up questions.

 • Conversation Pair Work Cards

C Change partners

Suggested teaching time:	10 minutes	Your actual teaching time:

- Make sure students change roles and partners.
- Remind students to use different reasons for turning down requests.

EXTRAS (optional)

- Workbook: Exercises 3–6
- Copy & Go: Activity 9

B Complete each sentence with one of the verb phrases from the Vocabulary.

1 The meeting doesn't end until 5:00. Do you think you could ....*pick up*.... my kids from school at 4:00?

2 Janus usually answers the phones but he's out sick today. Could you possibly ....*fill in for*.... him?

3 Oops. I'm completely out of cash! Do you think you could ....*lend*.... me some money for lunch?

4 I have to make an important phone call. Could you ....*keep an eye on*.... my daughter for about ten minutes?

5 Doris is catching a flight at 9:00. Do you think you might be able to ....*give*.... her ....*a ride*.... to the airport?

CONVERSATION MODEL

A 2:04 Read and listen to someone asking for a favor.

A: Martin, I wonder if you could do me a favor.

B: Sure. What do you need?

A: My car's at the repair shop and I need to pick it up at 3:00. Do you think you could give me a ride?

B: I would, but I have a doctor's appointment at 2:00.

A: Oh, that's OK. I understand.

B: Maybe you could get Jack to take you.

A: Good idea.

> **2:06**
> **Ways to indicate acceptance**
> I understand.
> No problem.
> Don't worry about it.

B 2:05 **Rhythm and intonation** Listen again and repeat. Then practice the Conversation Model with a partner.

NOW YOU CAN Get someone else to do something

> I wonder if you could do me a favor . . .

A Review the Vocabulary. On a separate sheet of paper, write a list of three requests for a favor.

B Pair work Change the Conversation Model to create a new conversation. Use one of the favors from your list. Your partner gives a reason for turning down your request and suggests getting someone else to do it. Then change roles.

A: ...., I wonder if you could do me a favor.

B: .... What do you need?

A: .... Do you think you could ....?

B: I would, but ....

A: Oh, that's OK. ....

B: Maybe you could get ....

A: ....

> **Reasons to turn down a request**
> • I'm running late for an appointment.
> • I have a meeting in an hour.
> • I'm expecting an important phone call.
> • Your own reason: ___

> **Don't stop!** Make other suggestions.
> What about ___ ?
> Why don't you ask ___ ?

C Change partners Try to get someone else to do you a favor.

GOAL Request express service

A 🔊 2:07 Read and listen. Then listen again and repeat.

1 dry-clean a suit

2 repair shoes

3 frame a picture

4 deliver a package

5 lengthen / shorten a skirt

6 print a sign

7 copy a report

B **Pair work** Name other things you can get these services for.

> ❝ You can also dry-clean sweaters or pants. ❞

GRAMMAR   *The passive causative*

Use a form of <u>have</u> or <u>get</u> with an object and a past participle to talk about arranging services. There is no difference in meaning between <u>have</u> and <u>get</u>.

	object	past participle
I **had**	my suits	**dry-cleaned**.
They're **having**	the office	**painted** tomorrow.
She **can get**	her sandals	**repaired** in an hour.

Remember: In the passive voice, a <u>by</u> phrase is used when the information is important.

We had the office painted last week. It looks great. (no <u>by</u> phrase)
We're having the office painted **by Royal Painting Services**. They're the best!

GRAMMAR BOOSTER ▸ p. 126

• *The passive causative: the <u>by</u> phrase*

A **Grammar practice** Write questions using the passive causative. Write three questions with <u>have</u> and three with <u>get</u>.

1 Would it be possible to / these pictures / frame?
Would it be possible to get/have these pictures framed?

2 Could I / these sandals / repair / here?
Could I have/get these sandals repaired here?

3 Where can I / this bowl / gift wrap?
Where can I have/get this bowl gift-wrapped?

4 Can I / these shirts / dry-clean / by tomorrow?
Can I get/have these shirts dry-cleaned by tomorrow?

5 Is it possible to / my hair / cut / at 3:00 / by George?
Is it possible to have/get my hair cut at 3:00 by George?

6 Would you / these photos / print / before 6:00?
Would you be able to get/have these photos printed before 6:00?

VOCABULARY

A  Read and listen . . .

| Suggested teaching time: | 2 minutes | Your actual teaching time: |

- Ask students to listen and study the phrases. Then have students listen and repeat chorally.

Option: [+10 minutes] To provide practice, ask students to describe the pictures without using the Vocabulary or saying which service it is to a partner. Have partners guess which service is being described. Then change roles. Point out that the student describing can talk about people or objects, and use any tense, but the person guessing only needs to say *the service*. For example:

Student A: *This person works with clothes. She cleans them, but she doesn't wash them in water.*
Student B: *Dry-clean.*
Student B: *This person makes a lot of the same thing. If I have one, but I want fifty, this person does this.*
Student A: *Copy. (OR Make copies.)*

ActiveTeach Multimedia Disc
- Vocabulary Flash Cards
- Learning Strategies

B Pair work

| Suggested teaching time: | 3 minutes | Your actual teaching time: |

- To prepare students for the activity, ask them to brainstorm other nouns that can be used with the verbs. Write the nouns (without the verbs) in random order on the board; for example, *dry-clean—a jacket, a raincoat, a blouse; repair—a car, a copier; frame—a painting, a photo; deliver—a letter, a box; lengthen / shorten—pants, a dress; print—a document, a card; copy—a document, a letter.*

- Review the speech balloon. Then ask students to create sentences using the nouns on the board or their own ideas.

Language and culture
- Other ways to say *get a document copied* are *get it duplicated* or *get it Xeroxed* (/'zir·akst/). To *xerox something* comes from the trademark Xerox, which is the name of a company that makes copy machines.

GRAMMAR

| Suggested teaching time: | 10–15 minutes | Your actual teaching time: |

- Direct students' attention to the chart and ask them to read the first explanation and study the examples. Write on the board:
  I *got* my shoes *repaired.*
  I *had* my shoes *repaired.*

- Point out that the passive causative is formed with *had* or *got* + object (*shoes*) + past participle (*repaired*). Write on the board:
  Kim cleaned the carpet.
  Kim had the carpet cleaned.

- To check comprehension of the usage of the passive causative, ask students to identify the difference

between the two sentences. (Kim cleaned the carpet herself. / Someone else cleaned Kim's carpet.)

- Direct attention to the different forms of *get* and *have* in the chart. Point out that the passive causative can be used in all tenses. Write on the board:

| I | had am getting will have | my car repaired. |

- Clarify that the past participle (*repaired*) remains the same with the different tenses and modals.

- Have students read the last explanation and study the examples. Write on the board:
  Sue needs to get this report copied.
  Sue needs to get this report copied by Frank.

- Point out that in the first example, what is important to know is that Sue needs copies. In the second example, *by Frank* is included because *who's* doing the copying is important for the reader / listener.

Language and culture

LEN From the Longman Corpus: The passive causative with *get* is much more frequently used in speech than in writing. *Have* is used more frequently in written English.

Option: [+15 minutes] For a different approach, draw the following chart on the board or print out one for each student from the ActiveTeach Multimedia Disc.

Activity	Me	My partner
Clean the house / apartment		
Paint the house / apartment		
Get a haircut		
Wash the car		
Wash clothes		
Other		
Other		

Have students work in pairs. First ask students to add two more activities to the bottom of the chart. Then have them identify which activities they do themselves and which they use services for. Combine the pairs and have students take turns sharing information about themselves and their partners; for example, *I always clean my house on Fridays. Gina doesn't have time to clean, so she has it cleaned once a week—usually on Mondays.*

Option:  **GRAMMAR BOOSTER** (Teaching notes p. T126)

ActiveTeach Multimedia Disc
- Inductive Grammar Charts
- Graphic Organizers

A Grammar practice

| Suggested teaching time: | 5–7 minutes | Your actual teaching time: |

- Complete the first item with the class. Remind students that they should write three questions with *have* and three with *get*.

B 🔊 Listening comprehension

Suggested teaching time:	3–5 minutes	Your actual teaching time:

- Pause after each conversation to allow students time to complete the statements.
- To review the answers with the class, have students say the complete sentences. Make sure they use passive causative correctly.

AUDIOSCRIPT

CONVERSATION 1 [F1 = U.S. regional, F2 = Spanish]
F1: Look at these pants. They're way too short.
F2: You should get them lengthened.
F1: Do you know a good tailor?
F2: You should take them to mine. They do good work there.

CONVERSATION 2
M1: Can you recommend a good dry-cleaner? I need to get my shirts done and I'm not too happy with the place I'm using now.
M2: Well, you could try Downtown Cleaners. That's who I use, and I think they're pretty good.

CONVERSATION 3 [F = Russian]
M: Where'd you take that photo?
F: This one? Oh, I took that last year when we were in the south of France.
M: You really should have it framed. It's really nice.
F: I'm thinking about it. I like it, too.

CONVERSATION 4 [M = Australian English]
M: OK. Smile! Say cheese!
F: Cheese!
M: Uh-oh.
F: What's the matter?
M: My camera hasn't been working right the last few days. I think I need to have it repaired.
F: That's too bad. Well, you can try bringing it to Hoyt Camera. I've heard they're very good.

CONVERSATION MODEL

A 🔊 Read and listen . . .

Suggested teaching time:	2 minutes	Your actual teaching time:

These conversation strategies are implicit in the model:
- Soften a request by beginning it with "Do you think you could . . .".
- Soften an "almost certain" no with "That might be difficult."
- Use "Well, . . ." to indicate a willingness to reconsider.

- Before students read and listen, use the photograph to predict what will happen in the Conversation Model. Ask *Where does the conversation occur?* (At the dry-cleaners.) *What do you think is happening?* (The woman needs her jacket cleaned.)
- After students read and listen, ask *Why does the woman need her jacket cleaned so quickly?* (She needs it for a friend's wedding on the weekend.) *When will the jacket be ready?* (By Thursday, but after four o'clock.)

Language and culture

LEN **From the Longman Corpus:** *I'll see what I can do* has the same meaning as *I'll try*, but *I'll see what I can do* is typically used in conversation.

B 🔊 Rhythm and intonation

Suggested teaching time:	3 minutes	Your actual teaching time:

- Have students repeat each line chorally. Make sure students:
  - use rising intonation for *Do you think I could get this jacket dry-cleaned by tomorrow?* and *Tomorrow?*
  - put extra stress on *really* in *I really appreciate it.*

NOW YOU CAN Request express service

A Pair work

Suggested teaching time:	9–13 minutes	Your actual teaching time:

- Review the *Ideas for express services* and *Ideas for why it's urgent* in the boxes. Have students brainstorm other ideas; for example, *Ideas for express service: repair a suitcase / a bag; copy a report / documents; clean a room / an office. Ideas for why it's urgent: You promised to get it done and forgot about it. You need it for a job interview. You need it for your graduation. It's a gift for someone.*
- Be sure to reinforce the use of the conversation strategies. Make sure students say *That might be difficult* politely and then use *Well, I'll see what I can do* to provide an option.
- Review the expressions in the *Be sure to recycle . . .* box. Remind students to use the passive causative whenever possible.

Don't stop! Extend the conversation. Review the ideas in the box. Explain that these are tips for keeping the conversation going. Ask students to write two more questions; for example, *Could I [get them done] earlier than that? Should I give you a call later? How much will it cost?*

- To model the activity, role-play and extend the conversation with a more confident student. Encourage students to use the correct rhythm and intonation and to continue their conversations by asking follow-up questions.

 • **Conversation Pair Work Cards**

B Change partners

Suggested teaching time:	8–10 minutes	Your actual teaching time:

- Challenge students to keep the conversation going. Tell them that once they get the service they need, they should ask for a new one; for example, *And just one more thing. Do you think you could also . . .?*

EXTRAS (optional)
- Workbook: Exercises 7–11
- Copy & Go: Activity 10

B 🔊 **Listening comprehension** Listen to the conversations. Complete each statement with the item and the service. Use passive causatives.

1 She needs to get her .... pants .... lengthened ....

2 He wants to get his .... shirts .... done ....

3 She's thinking about having a .... photo .... framed ....

4 He needs to have his .... camera .... repaired ....

CONVERSATION MODEL

2:09

A 🔊 Read and listen to someone requesting express service.

A: Do you think I could get this jacket dry-cleaned by tomorrow?

B: Tomorrow? That might be difficult.

A: I'm sorry, but it's pretty urgent. My friend is getting married this weekend.

B: Well, I'll see what I can do. But it won't be ready until after 4:00.

A: I really appreciate it. Thanks!

2:10

B 🔊 **Rhythm and intonation** Listen again and repeat. Then practice the Conversation Model with a partner.

NOW YOU CAN   Request express service

A Pair work Change the Conversation Model. Use the ideas to request an express service and give a reason for why it's urgent. Then change roles.

A: Do you think I could .... by ....?

B: ....? That might be difficult.

A: I'm sorry, but it's pretty urgent. ....

B: Well, I'll see what I can do. But it won't be ready until ....

A: ....!

Ideas for express services
- frame a [photo / painting / drawing / diploma]
- dry-clean a [suit / dress / sweater]
- lengthen or shorten a [dress / skirt / pants]

Ideas for why it's urgent
- Someone is coming to visit.
- You're going on [a vacation / a business trip].
- There's going to be [a party / a meeting].
- Your own idea: ___

Don't stop!
- Say you need to have the service completed earlier.
- Ask how much it will cost.

 Be sure to recycle this language.

I owe you one!	I know this is last minute.
Thanks a million.	I won't keep you any longer.
You're a lifesaver!	

B Change partners Request other express services.

GOAL   Evaluate the quality of service

Warm-up Have you or someone you know ever had something custom-made—for example, something to wear or something for your home? If so, how was the quality of workmanship?

READING 2:11

The Tailors of Hong Kong

The famous Hong Kong 24-hour suit is a thing of the past, but tailors there are still reliable: You can trust them if they say they'll have your clothes custom-made in just a few days.

Today, prices are quite reasonable—not as low as they used to be, but they're often about what you'd pay for a ready-made garment back home. The difference, of course, is that a tailor-made garment should fit you perfectly. Most tailors are extremely professional. The workmanship and quality of the better established shops rival even those of London's Savile Row—but at less than half the price!

Tailors in Hong Kong are very helpful and are willing to make almost any garment you want. Most offer a wide range of fabrics from which to choose, from cotton and linen to very fine wools, cashmere, and silk.

At your first fitting, the tailor will take your measurements.

You should allow three to five days to have a garment custom-made, with at least two or three fittings. You will pay a deposit of about 50% up front. But if you are not satisfied with the finished product, you don't have to accept it. Your only expense will be the deposit.

You can choose from a variety of fabrics.

With more than 2,500 tailoring establishments in Hong Kong, it shouldn't be any problem finding one. Some of the most famous are located in hotel arcades and shopping complexes, but the more upscale the location, the higher the prices.

Once you've had something custom-made and your tailor has your measurements, you will more than likely be able to order additional clothing online, even after you've returned home!

Tailors will make almost any garment you want—suits, evening gowns, wedding dresses, leather jackets, and shirts.

Source: Information from *Frommer's Hong Kong*

A Identify supporting details Check the statements that are true, according to the article. Find information in the Reading to support your answers.
See page T32 for answers.

1 ☑ You used to be able to get a suit made in one day in Hong Kong.

2 ☐ Having a suit custom-made in Hong Kong is always less expensive than buying one at home.

3 ☑ If you buy a garment on Savile Row in London, you will pay about twice as much as you would pay for one custom-made in Hong Kong.

4 ☑ If you are not satisfied with the finished garment, you can refuse to accept it and pay only 50% of the total cost.

5 ☐ If you want to pay a lower price for a custom-made garment, go to an upscale hotel shopping arcade.

BEFORE YOU READ

Warm-up

Suggested teaching time:	3–5 minutes	Your actual teaching time:

- To help students generate ideas, brainstorm things that can be custom-made. If necessary, explain that when something is custom-made, it has been made especially for you. Draw the following chart on the board (without the answers). Write the students' ideas in the correct column.

Clothing	Things for the home
suits	curtains
wedding dresses	drapes
evening dresses	built-in cabinets
shirts	chests
skirts	bookcases
suits	
coats	

- Elicit reasons to have something custom-made; for example, *The quality / fit is better. You can get exactly what you want / need. The items are unique. You can choose the design / materials.*

- Ask several students to name custom-made items that they or someone they know had made. Elicit descriptions of the item and its quality. Ask students to explain why it was custom-made.

READING))

Suggested teaching time:	10–15 minutes	Your actual teaching time:

- To practice the reading strategy of scanning, have students look at the headline, the photos, and the captions to answer these questions: *What is the article about?* (Hong Kong tailors, clothes you can have made in Hong Kong.) *What can the tailors make?* (Suits, gowns, wedding dresses, jackets, shirts.) *Do they offer a wide range of fabrics?* (Yes.) *Do customers have to attend fittings? Why?* (Yes, so the tailor can take your measurements.)

- Point to clothes made of different fabrics in the classroom. If you need to clarify the different fabrics, give examples of clothes that are typically made from them. For example:
  Many T-shirts are made of cotton.
  Jackets and dresses are often made of linen.
  Warm sweaters are made of wool or cashmere.
  Some ties and scarves are made of silk.

- Before students read and listen, ask *Do you think the author recommends Hong Kong tailors?* Have students read and listen to find out.

- After students read and listen, ask them if the author recommends Hong Kong tailors and have students give one or two reasons why. (Possible answers: Yes. They are good. They are professional.) Note: Do not go into details at this point.

Option: [+3 minutes] To extend the activity, ask students to imagine they won a prize—a garment of their choice, custom-made by a Hong Kong tailor. Have students work in pairs and take turns saying what garment they would like to have custom-made and when they would wear the garment; for example, *I'd like a silk shirt, and I'd wear it at important business meetings. I'd like an evening gown for my sister's wedding.* Ask several students to report to the class about the garments their partners would like to have custom-made.

Language and culture

- In British English *pants* are called *trousers*, an *undershirt* is called a *vest*, a *vest* is called a *waistcoat*, and the term *custom-made* can also be referred to as *made-to-measure*.

 **ActiveTeach** Multimedia Disc
- **Extra Reading Comprehension Questions**
- **Learning Strategies**

A Identify supporting details

Suggested teaching time:	5–10 minutes	Your actual teaching time:

- Ask students to underline any information in the text that supports their answers.

- Have students compare answers with a partner and then review with the class.

Answers for Exercise A
Answers will vary slightly, but may include the following:
1. The famous Hong Kong 24-hour suit is a thing of the past, . . .
2. Prices are . . . often about what you'd pay for a ready-made garment back home.
3. The workmanship and quality . . . rival even those of London's Savile Row—but at less than half the price.
4. You will pay a deposit of about 50% up front. But if you are not satisfied . . . you don't have to accept it. Your only expense will be the deposit.
5. . . . the more upscale the location, the higher the prices.

B Activate language from a text

Suggested teaching time:	5–10 minutes	Your actual teaching time:

- Have students find the adjectives in the text and circle them. Ask *Who or what does each adjective refer to?* (Reliable, helpful, professional: Hong Kong tailors; reasonable: prices for custom-made clothes.)

- To help students figure out the meaning of each adjective, have them find the answers to these questions in the text: *Why are Hong Kong tailors reliable?* (Because you can trust them if they say they'll have your clothes made in just a few days.) *Why are their prices reasonable?* (Because they are about the same price as a ready-made garment.) *Why are Hong Kong tailors professional?* (Because of the good quality of their workmanship.) *Why are they helpful?* (Because they are willing to make almost any garment you want.)

Option: **[+10 minutes]** For a different approach, ask students to close their books. Then write the following sentences on the board:

- a. *Now you can order more clothes without having to travel to Hong Kong.*
- b. *Tell the tailor the type of garment you want.*
- c. *Pick up the garment and pay the remaining 50% of the price.*
- d. *Pay a deposit of about 50% of the total cost.*
- e. *Attend two or three fittings to try on the garment.*

Read the sentences aloud and have students put them in the order in which they occurred. Ask several students to read the sentences aloud to confirm the correct order. (1. b; 2. d; 3. e; 4. c; 5. a.)

Option: **[+10 minutes]** To challenge students, ask them to scan the text for at least four advantages in having a garment custom-made in Hong Kong. Have pairs compare answers with other pairs. (1. You can have the garment custom-made in only three to five days. 2. The garment will cost about as much as a ready-made garment at home. 3. The garment will cost less than half the price it costs in London. 4. The garment will fit you perfectly. 5. You can easily find a tailoring establishment, because there are over 2,500 of them. 6. You can find a tailor that suits your price needs. 7. Hong Kong tailors will make almost any kind of garment you want. 8. Hong Kong tailors offer a variety of fabrics to choose from. 9. You don't have to accept the garment if you're not fully satisfied. 10. You can order another garment online when you're back home.) Finally, ask several students to say whether they would have a garment custom-made if they ever visited Hong Kong.

PRONUNCIATION

🔊 Read and listen . . .

Suggested teaching time:	2 minutes	Your actual teaching time:

- Have students listen and study the examples.

- Write on the board: *They're REALly reliable.*

- Point out that the underlined word is spoken louder to make it stand out. Explain that when you say *REALLY reliable* and stress *really*, you want to give the message

that the person is very, very reliable (not just reliable). Point out that stress affects the meaning of a message.

Option: **[+5 minutes]** To extend the activity and provide more practice, have pairs take turns asking and answering questions about services, using emphatic stress in their answers; for example, **A:** *Why do you have your clothes dry-cleaned at Brenda's?* **B:** *Because they're incredibly fast.*

 • **Pronunciation Activities**

NOW YOU CAN Evaluate the quality of service

A Frame your ideas

Suggested teaching time:	5–8 minutes	Your actual teaching time:

- To prepare students for the activity, review the *Reasons for choosing a business* in the box. Point out that *speed* refers to how fast something is done, *reliability* means you can depend on something, *workmanship* refers to the skill in making things, and *professionalism* refers to the qualities and skills that someone is expected to have.

- To help students with the vocabulary they will need, brainstorm adjectives that can be used to describe the reasons for choosing a business; for example, *fast, efficient, reliable, honest, reasonable, low cost, professional, helpful, near, accessible.* Remind students to use some of these adjectives when they complete the chart.

- Encourage students who don't remember the name of a business to think of another way to identify it; for example, *the one on the corner, the one at the mall, the one opposite my office.*

B Discussion

Suggested teaching time:	10 minutes	Your actual teaching time:

- To prepare students for the discussion, read aloud the speech balloons. Point out the causatives and remind students to use them.

- Form small groups. Ask students to use their charts as a guide to recommend a local business. Encourage them to include as many adjectives as they can.

- Walk around the room and provide help as needed. Make sure students use the causatives *have, get,* and *make* correctly. Encourage them to keep the conversation going by asking questions or making relevant comments based on personal experiences. For example:
  What kinds of clothes do you get dry-cleaned there?
  Have you ever brought in a leather jacket to be cleaned?
  Are their prices reasonable?
  I also have my shoes repaired there.
  I have my shoes repaired at High Heels.
  They are fast and reliable too, but they are not as cheap.

EXTRAS (optional)

- Workbook: Exercises 12–16
- Copy & Go: Activity 11

B **Activate language from a text** Find these adjectives in the Reading on page 32. Complete the descriptions, using the adjectives.

| reliable | reasonable | helpful | professional |

1 I find Portello's to be really ....reasonable........... compared to other places. I've shopped around and I can't find another service with such low prices.

2 What I like about Link Copy Services is that they're so ....helpful........... . Even if the job is a bit unusual, they're willing to try.

3 Jamco Design is extremely ....professional........... . You never have to worry about their doing anything less than an excellent job.

4 Dom's Auto Repair is incredibly ....reliable........... . If they promise to have a job ready in an hour, you can be sure that they will.

> On your *ActiveBook* Self-Study Disc:
> **Extra Reading Comprehension Questions**

PRONUNCIATION   *Emphatic stress to express enthusiasm*

2:12

🔊 Read and listen. Then listen again and repeat. Finally, read each statement on your own, using emphatic stress.

1 They're REALly reliable.

2 They're inCREDibly helpful.

3 They're exTREMEly professional.

4 They're SO reasonable.

NOW YOU CAN   Evaluate the quality of service

> **Reasons for choosing a business**
> • speed
> • reliability
> • price
> • workmanship
> • location
> • efficiency
> • professionalism
> • other: ___

A **Frame your ideas** Complete the chart with services you or someone you know uses. Write the name of the business and list the reasons why you use that business. Then compare charts with a partner.

Service	Name of business	Reason
laundry / dry cleaning		
repairs		
tailoring		
delivery		
haircuts		
copying		
other: _____		

B **Discussion** Recommend local businesses from your chart. Explain why you or other people use them. Use the active and passive causatives.

> ❝I always get my clothes dry-cleaned at Quick Clean. They're near my home and their prices are reasonable.❞

> ❝I rarely have my shoes repaired. But I hear that Al's Shoes is fast and reliable.❞

33

GOAL **Plan a meeting or social event**

A ◀») Vocabulary • *Planning an event* Read and listen. Then listen again and repeat.

make a list of attendees

pick a date, time, and place

make a budget

assign responsibilities

plan an agenda

send out an announcement

arrange catering

set up the room

B Pair work Have you ever taken any of these steps to plan an event, such as a meeting or party? Which of the activities do you think you would be the best at doing? Use the Vocabulary.

A ◀») **Listen for main ideas** Listen to the conversation and answer the questions.

1 What kind of event are they planning?
   ..... a holiday party .....

2 How many people will come to the event?
   over a hundred people

3 Is it a formal or informal event?
   .... formal ....

4 Which of the following are mentioned as part of the event? (music / food / a lecture / dancing / meetings)
   ..... music, food .....

B ◀») **Listen for order of details** Listen again and number the activities in the order they will occur. Circle the activities she'll do herself.

2	make a list of attendees
1	pick a date and time
4	pick a location
3	make a budget
7	assign responsibilities
8	send out announcements
5	arrange catering
6	arrange music
9	set up the room

A 🔊 Vocabulary

Suggested teaching time:	4–6 minutes	Your actual teaching time:	

- Have students listen and study the phrases. Then have them listen and repeat chorally.

- To help students understand the Vocabulary, read the first item and have students look at the photo. Ask *What are attendees?* (The people who have been invited.) *Who will be the attendees at this event?* (Mike, Jeff, Ann, Beth, and Paul.) Then ask questions about the other photographs. You can say:
  ○ pick a date, time, and place: *What place has the person picked?* (The World Café.) *When is the event?* (On July 12.) *What time?* (At 8:00 P.M.)
  ○ make a budget: *What is a budget?* (A plan of how money will be spent.) *How much will be spent on food?* ($200.)
  ○ assign responsibilities: *What responsibilities have been assigned so far?* (Food: Mario and Karen; decorations: Louise and Pam; invitations: Bruno.)
  ○ plan an agenda: *What is an agenda?* (The list of things that will be done.) *What will happen at 10:30?* (Nancy will give a presentation / talk about customer relations.)
  ○ send out an announcement: *Who are announcements sent out to?* (The people who are invited. / The attendees.) *What is this announcement for?* (An international sales meeting.)
  ○ arrange catering: *What is catering?* (The activity of organizing and supplying food and drink for a party.)
  ○ set up the room: *Why do you need to set up a room?* (To prepare it for a meeting.) *What is the man doing?* (Arranging chairs.)

- To reinforce the Vocabulary, write the following words and draw the chart (without answers) on the board. Ask students to close their books. Then have them choose the words that go with the verbs and fill in the chart. Review with the class.

an agenda   a date   a budget   responsibilities
the invitations   a task   catering
the dining room   an announcement
a time   the conference room   a list of attendees

make	plan	pick	assign	set up	send out
a budget	an agenda	a date	responsibilities	the conference room	an announcement
a list of attendees	catering	a time	a task	the dining room	the invitations

ActiveTeach Multimedia Disc • Vocabulary Flash Cards

B Pair work

Suggested teaching time:	3–5 minutes	Your actual teaching time:	

- To help students prepare for the activity, write on the board: *What kind of event was it? When was it?*

- Have students choose two or three activities they have completed and write notes about them, using the questions on the board as a guide. Ask students to choose an activity they think they are good at doing and write notes to explain why.

- Form pairs. Walk around the room monitoring student's work. Then have several students tell the class activities they have completed or ones they are good at.

A 🔊 Listen for main ideas

Suggested teaching time:	10–12 minutes	Your actual teaching time:	

- Tell students they are going to listen to a conversation about planning an event.

- To prepare students for listening, have them read the questions so they know what information to listen for. If necessary, have students listen again to confirm their answers.

> **AUDIOSCRIPT** See page T35.

B 🔊 Listen for order of details

Suggested teaching time:	10–12 minutes	Your actual teaching time:	

- First have students read the list of activities. Tell them that the speaker sometimes has to go back and change the order during the conversation.

- Have students compare answers in pairs.

- Review the order of the steps with the class. Then ask students to include additional details they remember about some of the steps. For example, location: *They might have the party near the city market.*

 ActiveTeach Multimedia Disc • Learning Strategies

NOW YOU CAN Plan a meeting or a social event

A Frame your ideas

Suggested teaching time:	3–5 minutes	Your actual teaching time:

- Clarify that there are four tasks for Exercise A: Fill out the survey, add up the choices in each column, check the descriptions under the survey to find out which one describes you, and then compare answers with a partner.

- If necessary, explain the meaning of *team player* (Someone who works well with other people so the whole group is successful.) and *stick around* (To stay there.).

- Take a poll to see which students match the different descriptions. Ask several students if they agree with the results of their survey.

B Notepadding

Suggested teaching time:	10 minutes	Your actual teaching time:

- Have students look at the pictures in the *Some ideas* boxes. If necessary, clarify the meaning of a *TGIF party* (A party where people celebrate that the work week has ended because it's Friday.), *a talent show* (A party in which people show how well they sing, dance, tell jokes, etc.), and *a karaoke* (/kær·i·ˈoʊ·ki/) *show* (A party in which people sing to recorded music for fun.).

- Brainstorm and write on the board other social events the class might like to attend; for example, *having dinner, having a picnic, going dancing, going to a concert,* etc.

- Review the expressions in the *Be sure to recycle* . . . box. Have students write complete sentences for some of the expressions. Then have several students read one of their sentences aloud; for example, *Why don't we get someone to help us? Why don't you pick a location near the office? I think we should make a list of attendees first.*

- Form groups of three or four. Have each group choose one social event to plan. Encourage students to include as many details for the event as possible.

C Discussion

Suggested teaching time:	5–10 minutes	Your actual teaching time:

- As groups present their plans to the class, list the groups and types of events on the board; for example, *Group 1: Top Notch Pop karaoke show.*

- Encourage the class to ask questions. For example:
  Have you made a budget?
  How much money will you spend?
  What about food?
  Will you have a caterer?
  When will you send out the invitations?

- After all groups have presented their plans, have students raise their hands to vote for each of the events listed on the board. Keep a tally on the board to find out the best or most popular plan. You may want to hold the event if your students are enthusiastic about it.

Language and culture

- In the U.S. and Canada, people say *TGIF* (Thank goodness it's Friday!) to show they are happy the work or school week is finished and the weekend is beginning.

EXTRAS (optional)

- Workbook: Exercises 17–20
- Copy & Go: Activity 12

AUDIOSCRIPT for page T34 (**A** Listen for main ideas)

F: Ugh. My boss is making me plan the holiday party this year.
M: What's wrong with that? Sounds like fun.
F: It's a LOT of work. This is a pretty big event, you know. Over a hundred people! I don't even know where to begin.
M: Well, what needs to be done first?
F: Oh, I guess I could start by choosing the date and time.
M: Well, why don't you talk to your colleagues and get a sense of what they'd like to do?
F: Not a bad idea.
M: Then what?
F: Then I guess it's the location. I hated the place where they held the party last year. It was way too close to the office.
M: What was wrong with that?
F: Who wants to party near the office? I want to try something different—in a fun part of town. You know?
M: Oh, I get it. How about down around the city market? A lot of people have events around there.
F: Great idea! I'll make some phone calls tomorrow. And maybe I can get some of my colleagues to give me some more ideas.
M: Makes sense. So then what?
F: Well, with so many people coming, I guess the guest list would be the next thing to think about.
M: Come to think of it, you should probably make the guest list BEFORE you choose a place. You've got to know how many people you're going to have first.
F: Good point. I'll do that tomorrow before I make any phone calls.
M: What about food? You must get a big event like this catered, right?
F: Oh, definitely. This is a pretty formal event.
M: Well, that would be the next step. Once you know how many people are coming and where it's going to be. Who knows, you might want to have it right in a restaurant.
F: Right. . . Hey, wait a minute! We missed something important. I've got to make a budget first.
M: Like right after you've made your guest list, right?
F: Right. Because I'll know then how much I can spend per person. See what I mean? There's a lot to do!
M: So far so good. What's next?
F: Well, we've got to have music. So I'll need to find a DJ.
M: You know, one of the guys at work—his wife does that. Want me to get her number for you?
F: That would be great. Thanks. Oh, and decorations! They usually do a great job decorating the room for these parties. I'm sure I can get someone to take care of that. I'd better include it on my list so I don't forget.
M: Well . . . that sounds pretty much like everything, no?
F: I think so . . . Ah—invitations. They're going to want me to send out some nice invitations to get everyone in the mood.
M: OK, that should be everything. So—why don't you get some help from your colleagues? Surely you're not expected to do it all, right?
F: No, you're right. When I'm done I'll make a list and assign responsibilities. There are at least five people in the office who have already said they'd help. I'm sure I can get them to do the invitations and decorations. And I can take care of the rest.
M: Not too bad.
F: Thanks. That really helped.

Plan a meeting or a social event

A Frame your ideas Take the survey. Compare answers with a partner.

Check which event activities you would rather do. Choose from Column A or B.

What type of person are YOU?

Column A	Column B
○ make a budget	○ spend money
○ assign responsibilities	○ take responsibility
○ plan an agenda	○ be a presenter
○ arrange catering	○ cook food
○ get people to set up the room	○ set up the room
○ leave before cleanup	○ stick around to clean up

If you chose four or more from Column A, you're a BORN ORGANIZER!

If you chose four or more from Column B, you're a TEAM PLAYER!

B Notepadding In a group, plan a meeting or social event for your class. Choose the type of event and discuss what needs to be done. Write the activities and assign responsibilities. Discuss dates, times, and locations.

Type of event:	Location:
Date and time:	
Activity	**Name**

Some ideas

- A special meeting
- An English practice day

An end-of-year
New Year's Eve } party
A TGIF*
*Thank goodness it's Friday!

♲ **Be sure to recycle this language.**

Why don't we ___ ?	What needs to be done [first]?
Why don't you ___ ?	That's a [good idea. / great idea. /
How about ___ ?	good point.]
What about ___ ?	That would be great.
I think ___ .	That sounds ___ .

A talent]
A *Top Notch Pop* karaoke } show

C Discussion Present your plans to your class. Then choose the best plan.

Review

More Practice

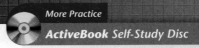

ActiveBook *Self-Study Disc*

grammar · vocabulary · listening
reading · speaking · pronunciation

A 2:16 🔊)) **Listening comprehension** Listen to each conversation.
Write a sentence to describe what the customer needs and when.
Listen again if necessary.

Example: He'd like to get his shoes shined by tomorrow morning.

1 She needs to get her dress dry-cleaned by Friday. ....
2 He needs to get his pants shortened by Wednesday. ....
3 She needs to get a sign printed by Wednesday. ....
4 He needs to get a picture framed by 4:00. ....

B Complete each question or request with any noun that makes sense with   Answers will vary, but may
the passive causative verb.   include the following:

1 Can I get my ....suit.................... dry-cleaned by tomorrow?
2 I'd like to have this ....skirt.................... lengthened.
3 Where can I get this ....jacket.................... shortened?
4 Can you tell me where I can get some ....reports.................... copied?
5 Where did she get her ....pictures.................... framed?
6 How much did he pay to have his ....shoes.................... repaired?
7 What's the best place to get some ....signs.................... printed?
8 Where can I go to get my ....package.................... delivered quickly?

2:17/2:18
🎵 **Top Notch Pop**
"I'll Get Back to You"
Lyrics p. 149

C Complete each causative statement in your own way. Remember   Answers will vary, but may
to use either the base form or the infinitive form of a verb.   include the following:

1 At the end of the meal, she had the waiter ....bring the bill....
2 We got the travel agent ....to reserve a car for us....
3 When I was young, my mother always made me ....clean my room....
4 When you arrive, you should get the hotel ....to make an appointment for you....
5 Don't forget to have the gas station attendant ....wash the windshield....
6 I can never get my friends ....to come with me....

D **Writing** Do you think being a procrastinator is a serious problem?
On a separate sheet of paper, explain your views by giving examples
from personal experience.

Some possible examples
• getting things repaired
• having things cleaned
• paying bills
• making plans for a vacation
• keeping in touch with people

WRITING BOOSTER ▸ p. 142

• *Supporting an opinion with
  personal examples*
• *Guidance for Exercise D*

Review

A 🔊 Listening comprehension

Suggested teaching time:	10 minutes	Your actual teaching time:

- Review the example with the class.
- Pause after each conversation to allow students time to write.
- Review by having students read the sentences aloud. Make any necessary corrections.

AUDIOSCRIPT

CONVERSATION 1
F: I'd like to get this dress dry-cleaned.
M: OK. It'll be ready on Monday.
F: I'm in a bit of a rush. Any chance I could get it done by Friday?
M: I'll see what we can do.

CONVERSATION 2
M1: I need to get these pants shortened. Can I get them back Wednesday?
M2: I don't know. We're pretty busy this week.
M1: I'd really appreciate it.
M2: We'll try. But it might not be ready till Thursday. OK?

CONVERSATION 3
F: I'd like to get a sign printed. Does it take long to do?
M: Just one sign? Not too long. You can have it by Thursday.
F: Gee. I'd appreciate it if you could get it done a little sooner. I'm on a bit of a tight schedule.
M: How about Wednesday? Is that OK?
F: That would be perfect. Thanks.

CONVERSATION 4 [F = Korean]
F: Can you do a rush job for me?
M: That depends. What do you need to get done?
F: I just need to get this picture framed. Can I get it by 4:00?
M: Today? I'm sorry. That wouldn't be possible. But I could have it for you first thing in the morning.
F: OK. That would be great.

B Complete each question . . .

Suggested teaching time:	3–5 minutes	Your actual teaching time:

- Encourage students to look at the verbs to help them decide how to complete each sentence. Have students compare answers with a partner.
- Ask several students for their information and make a list of possible answers on the board.

Option: [+5 minutes] To extend the activity, have volunteers reply to your statements with a passive causative question. *Why don't you ___?* Remind students to use the vocabulary from the unit and *get* or *have*. For example:

My pants are too long. (Why don't you have them shortened?)

The copier is broken. (Why don't you get it repaired?)

I've bought a beautiful painting. (Why don't you have it framed?)

My white jacket is stained with blue ink. (Why don't you have it dry-cleaned?)

I need fifty copies of this test a.s.a.p. (Why don't you get it copied at Quick Copy Service?)

I need a new sign for this room. (Why don't you have one printed?)

C Complete each causative . . .

Suggested teaching time:	2–5 minutes	Your actual teaching time:

- Write on the board:

I	got had made	my brother _____.

- To prepare students for the activity, ask them to create sentences; for example, *I got my brother to drive me to school. I had my brother buy my concert ticket.* Point out the corresponding structure: *get* + person + infinitive; *have* + person + base form.
- Review the function of the causative *make*: someone is obligated to do something.
- Then have students compare statements with a partner. Review with the class.

D Writing

Suggested teaching time:	10–15 minutes	Your actual teaching time:

- Review the ideas in the *Some possible examples* box. Point out that they are activities we can get done on time or put off until the last minute. Brainstorm other activities and write them on the board. For example:

buying gifts	reserving a table at a
sending holiday greetings	restaurant
buying tickets	replying to e-mails
packing before a trip	sending a thank-you card
planning parties	studying for a test

- To help students generate ideas, have them decide if they tend to do these activities right away or put them off until the last minute. Ask students to think of examples and write them down.
- Encourage students to start their writing by saying whether they think procrastinating is a serious problem or not, and then have them use their notes as a guide to give examples to support their statements. As students write, walk around the room and provide help as needed.

Option: **WRITING BOOSTER** (Teaching notes p. T142)

 **ActiveTeach Multimedia Disc** • **Writing Process Worksheets**

ORAL REVIEW

Before the first activity, give students a few minutes of silent time to explore the pictures and become familiar with them.

Game

Suggested teaching time:	10 minutes	Your actual teaching time:

- To help students prepare for the activity, tell them that they will play a memory game. They will take turns asking and answering questions about the pictures, using the causative.
- As students study the pictures, remind them to look at the time shown on each clock.
- If necessary, review what kinds of problems the man is having. (The copier doesn't work, he needs to get a package to L.A. right away, his pants are too long, he got in a car accident / he hit something with his car.)
- Form pairs. Review the example. Have students close their books and take turns asking and answering questions. Once students are finished, ask them to open their books and confirm their answers.

Possible responses ...

> What does the man need to get done at 9:00? Who is he talking to at 5:30? What happened at 6:30?

Option: [+5 minutes] For a different approach, ask students to share their own experiences in small groups. Have them describe a day in which they had to get lots of things done. Encourage students to ask questions to keep the conversation going.

Pair work

Suggested teaching time:	5 minutes	Your actual teaching time:

- Before students create the conversations, model a conversation with a student.
- Then have students choose roles. Finally, ask one or two pairs to role-play their conversations.

Possible responses ...

> **A:** Do you think I could get these documents copied by 9:30? **B:** 9:30? That might be difficult. The copier isn't working. **A:** I'm sorry, but I need them for a meeting. **B:** Well, I'll see what I can do. **A:** Thanks a million!
>
> **A:** Do you think you could get this package delivered to L.A. by the end of this week? **B:** That should be no problem. You can have it air expressed. **A:** When will it get there? **B:** On Friday morning. Is that OK? **A:** That would be perfect.
>
> **A:** Do you think I could get these pants dry-cleaned by tomorrow? **B:** Tomorrow? That might be difficult. **A:** I'm sorry, but it's pretty urgent. I need them for a party this weekend. **B:** Well, in that case, I'll see what I can do. **A:** I really appreciate it. Thanks!
>
> **A:** I need to get my car repaired a.s.a.p. **B:** What happened? **A:** Well, I hit a wall in the garage. **B:** Oh, no! What do you need to have done? **A:** I need to get a new headlight. Can you do it this week? **B:** I don't know. I'm very busy. **A:** Can you get it done next week? **B:** Yes. Next week would be fine.

Story

Suggested teaching time:	5–10 minutes	Your actual teaching time:

- Form small groups. Ask each student to contribute a sentence to the story.
- Remind students to use the causatives *have* and *get*. Then ask a group to retell the story to the class.

Option: [+5 minutes] To extend the activity, have students work in small groups and make up an ending to the story. Ask them to imagine what else happened to Paul that night. Walk around the room and provide help as needed. Then have several groups tell their story to the class.

Option: Oral Progress Assessment

Use the photographs on page 37. Encourage students to use the language practiced in this unit and prior units.

- Tell the student you are going to ask questions about the photographs and he or she should answer using the causative; for example, *What does Paul's colleague say about the copy machine? Why is Paul holding a package? What is Paul telling the tailor? Why is Paul talking on the phone?*
- Tell the student that together you are going to role-play a conversation between Paul and the tailor. The student should play Paul. Have the student start like this: *Do you think I could have these pants shortened by Friday?* Tell the student to continue the conversation and say as much as he or she can.
- Evaluate the student on intelligibility, fluency, correct use of target grammar, and appropriate use of vocabulary.

 • Oral Progress Assessment Charts

Option: *Top Notch* Project

Have students plan a social event for the class.

Idea: Ask students to make a list of the guests who will be invited. Form four groups and assign each group one of the following to think about and plan: food and drinks, music, invitations, and decorations. Encourage each group to take notes as they plan. Finally, have the groups report their ideas and suggestions to the class.

EXTRAS (optional)

- **Complete Assessment Package**
- **Weblinks for Teachers: pearsonlongman.com/topnotch/**

And on your ActiveTeach Multimedia Disc:
>   Just for Fun
>   Top Notch Pop Song Activities
>   Top Notch TV Video Program and Activity Worksheets
>   Supplementary Pronunciation Lessons
>   Audioscripts
>   Unit Study Guides

ORAL REVIEW

Game Study the pictures for one minute, paying attention to the time in each picture. Then close your books. Ask and answer questions about the photos, using the causative. Start like this:

What does Paul need to get done at 2:00?

Pair work Create a conversation for each situation. Start like this:

Do you think I could get this ___ by ___?

Story Close your books. In a small group, tell the story of Paul's day. Start like this:

At 9:00, Paul needed to get ___ ...

Paul's Difficult Day

For help:
Call 555-1212

NOW I CAN...

- [ ] Get someone else to do something.
- [ ] Request express service.
- [ ] Evaluate the quality of service.
- [ ] Plan a meeting or social event.

Packaging
Supplies

Bart's
AUTO
REPAIR

Reading for Pleasure

search | help | feedback

Looking for a good classic? Check out our recommendations. Click on a category for more.

FICTION

Novels	Mysteries	Thrillers	Romance	Science fiction	Short stories

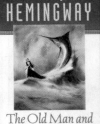  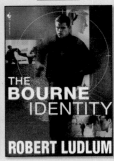 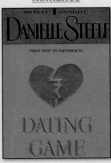  

Hemingway's exquisite novel. Read and reread by millions!

Who killed Charles McCarthy at the pool? And why? Detective Sherlock Holmes tries to solve another case.

A contemporary thriller that will have you on the edge of your seat!

No one does romance like Danielle Steele.

A strange object is found on the Moon. But who put it there? Arthur Clarke's masterpiece!

Beautiful short stories by the world's greatest and most beloved writers.

NON-FICTION

Biographies	Autobiographies	Travel	Memoirs	Self-help

  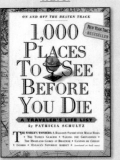  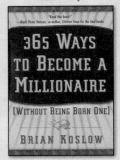

The true story of the amazing woman who inspired millions.

In Helen Keller's own words—her unforgettable story.

A must-read for real travelers—or even those who just dream about traveling!

The true story of writer Frank McCourt's surprising and funny experiences as a teacher in New York City.

Want to get rich? Brian Koslow shows you how.

A 🔊 **Vocabulary • *Types of books*** Read and listen. Then listen again and repeat.

fiction		non-fiction	
a novel	a romance novel	a biography	a memoir
a mystery	science fiction	an autobiography	a self-help book
a thriller	short stories	a travel book	

B **Discussion** Do you prefer fiction or non-fiction? Have you ever read a book in English? How about a magazine or a newspaper? If not, what would you like to read? Why?

UNIT 4

Reading for Pleasure

Preview

Suggested teaching time:	10 minutes	Your actual teaching time:	

Before Exercise A, give students a few minutes of silent time to look at the website.

- Ask students to review the books listed under *Fiction* and *Non-fiction* and ask *What is the difference between fiction and non-fiction?* (Fiction: books and stories about imaginary people and events; non-fiction: books and stories about real people and actual events.)

- To personalize, have students choose a book that they are interested in or one that attracted their attention and ask them what they liked about it; for example, *its author, its title, the type of book, the topic, the picture on the cover,* etc. Ask several students to tell the class which book they chose and why; for example, *I picked 1,000 Places to See Before You Die. I don't know the author, but I love traveling.*

- Take a poll to find out which books on the lists are the most popular choices in the class.

Language and culture

- *Contemporary* means modern or belonging to the present time; *on the edge of your seat* is waiting with great excitement to see what will happen next; *a must-read* is a piece of writing that is so interesting that everyone should read it; and *a masterpiece* is a work of art, piece of writing, or music etc., that is of very high quality.
- In British English, *blockbuster* is often used to describe a film, show, or book that is very successful.

A 🔊 Vocabulary

Suggested teaching time:	3–5 minutes	Your actual teaching time:	

- Have students listen to and study the descriptions of fiction and non-fiction book types. Then have students listen and repeat chorally.

- To help students figure out the meaning of unknown words, ask them to look at the website and read the descriptions of the books.

- To check comprehension, use the following information to describe a type of book. Have students say the type of book:
  - *A book about life on another planet.* (Science fiction.)
  - *A book about tips to stay healthy.* (A self-help book.)
  - *A book about a person who discovers a killer.* (A mystery.)
  - *A book with many stories, not just one.* (Short stories.)
  - *A book about people in love.* (A romance novel.)
  - *A book about one's own life.* (An autobiography.)
  - *A book about the life of an important person.* (A biography.)
  - *A book about invented people and events.* (A novel.)
  - *A book about visiting a foreign country.* (A travel book.)
  - *A book with an exciting story.* (A thriller.)
  - *A book about someone's personal experiences.* (A memoir.)

Language and culture

- There are many compound nouns with *book;* for example, *a travel book, a self-help book,* etc. However, do not say: *a novel book.* To describe in more detail what kind of novel it is, use an adjective; for example, *a romance novel, a historical novel, an autobiographical novel,* etc.
- An *autobiography* is a person's life story. A *memoir* is about a person's experiences in a specific situation; for example, *in a particular career* or *during a war.*
- **LEN** **From the Longman Corpus:** *Biography* and *autobiography* are frequently followed by the preposition *of* (a biography *of* Mahatma Gandhi, *The Autobiography of Nelson Mandela*).

 • Vocabulary Flash Cards

B Discussion

Suggested teaching time:	10–13 minutes	Your actual teaching time:	

- To help students prepare for the discussion, ask *How many students like to read books?* Then ask them to write the titles of some of their favorite books in any language and label them fiction or non-fiction. Then ask students to write the titles (or even types) of books they have read or tried to read in English. If students read English on the computer / on websites, they should include this information. Finally, ask students to write the names of the newspapers and magazines they like to read.

- Form small groups. Encourage students to give reasons for their choices and to ask each other follow-up questions. For example:
  Student A: *I try to read the newspaper The Herald Tribune at least once a week.*
  Student B: *Why only once a week?*
  Student A: *The vocabulary is difficult, so I use a dictionary. It takes me a week to read it.*

- To review, make a list on the board of books, magazines, or newspapers the students have read or would like to read in English.

C 🔊 Photo story

Suggested teaching time:	3–4 minutes	Your actual teaching time:

- To help students prepare for the Photo Story, have them cover the conversation and look at the pictures. Ask *Where are the women?* (In a bookstore.) *What do you think they are talking about?* (Possible answer: The types of books or magazines in the store.)

- After students read and listen, ask *What is Sophie shopping for?* (Gardening magazines for her mom.) *What has Lynn chosen?* (A biography of Helen Keller.) *What does Sophie say she's reading?* (A mystery.) *What does Lynn recommend?* (A new book by John Grisham.)

- Point out that *till the end* means *until the end*. If students have questions regarding vocabulary, tell them that the next exercise may clarify their questions.

Language and culture
- U.S. writer John Grisham is considered a master of the legal thriller. Graduating from law school and practicing law inspired him to write his first novel, *A Time to Kill*, in 1988. Grisham's books have been translated into twenty-nine languages, and seven have been turned into Hollywood movies.
- *I can't seem to . . .* is a colloquial way to say *I'm not able to. I can't seem to get into . . .* could also be stated as *I can't get into. . . .*

D Think and explain

Suggested teaching time:	5–10 minutes	Your actual teaching time:

- Encourage students to use the context of the conversation to figure out the meaning of the expressions.

- Have students compare answers with a partner. Then review with the class. Encourage them to use information from the story to explain their answers; for example, *I think can't get enough of means likes. If Sophie is buying some gardening magazines, that's because her mother likes them.*

- If necessary, clarify the meaning of the expressions *I can't put it down. / It's a real page-turner.* (I find it extremely interesting. / I can't stop reading it.) *I can't seem to get into it. / I can't get into it.* (I can't get interested in it.) *I can't get enough of it.* (I like it so much that I want a lot of it.) *They just aren't my thing.* (I don't like them.) *They put me to sleep.* (I am not interested, they are very boring.)

Option: [+5 minutes] To extend the activity, have students work in pairs and take turns briefly telling their partners about books or materials they have read or are reading using the expressions from the activity.

E Paraphrase

Suggested teaching time:	4–5 minutes	Your actual teaching time:

- Encourage students to identify who says each phrase and to use the context of the conversation to help figure out the meaning.

- To review answers, you may want to encourage students to say complete sentences. (Possible answers: 1. I've never [seen / met you] here. 2. I am just looking around. / I'm not looking for anything special. 3. I am buying some gardening magazines for my mom. 4. Do you think I could have it when you are done using / reading it? 5. I'd be happy to give it to you to use / read.)

F Group work

Suggested teaching time:	10–13 minutes	Your actual teaching time:

- Ask students to write notes about what they would include in the category *other*.

- Form groups. Ask students to give examples of what they are reading in each category. Encourage them to make relevant comments and ask follow-up questions; for example, *You spend a lot of your time reading magazines. When do you read them? / I also read a lot on the Internet! I like to read about things I can do to protect the environment.*

- To check comprehension, take a poll. Ask students to say which reading material they assigned the highest percentage to.

EXTRAS (optional)
- Workbook: Exercises 1–3

2:20 🔊 **Photo story** Read and listen to a conversation between two friends at a bookstore.

Lynn: Hey, Sophie! I've never run into you here before!

Sophie: Lynn! Good to see you. Looking for anything special?

Lynn: No, I'm just browsing. How about you?

Sophie: I'm just picking up some gardening magazines for my mom. She can't get enough of them . . . So, anything interesting?

Lynn: This one doesn't look bad. It's a biography of Helen Keller. What about you? Are you reading anything good these days?

Sophie: Well, I've got a new mystery on my night table, but I can't seem to get into it. I guess mysteries just aren't my thing.

Lynn: I know what you mean. They put me to sleep.

Sophie: Well, you're a big reader. I wonder if you could recommend something for me.

Lynn: Have you read the new John Grisham thriller?

Sophie: No, I haven't. I didn't know he had a new book out.

Lynn: Well, I can't put it down. It's a real page-turner.

Sophie: Thanks for the tip! Do you think I could borrow it when you're done with it?

Lynn: Of course. If you can wait till the end of the week, I'd be happy to lend it to you.

D **Think and explain** Classify each of the six underlined expressions from the Photo Story by its meaning. Explain your choices.

Likes	Doesn't like
can't get enough of them	can't seem to get into it
can't put it down	just aren't my thing
a real page-turner	put me to sleep

E **Paraphrase** Say each of the underlined verbs and phrasal verbs in your <u>own</u> way.

1 I've never <u>run into</u> you here before.   met

2 I'm just <u>browsing</u>.   looking around / not looking for anything special

3 I'm <u>picking up</u> some gardening magazines for my mom.   looking for and buying

4 Do you think I could <u>borrow</u> it when you're finished?   temporarily use / have it when you have finished

5 I'd be happy to <u>lend</u> it to you.   temporarily give

F **Group work** What percentage of your total reading time do you spend on the following reading materials? (Make sure it adds up to 100%!) Compare percentages with your classmates.

magazines		fiction	
newspapers		non-fiction	
the Internet		other	

GOAL | Recommend a book

Ways to describe a book

A 🔊 2:21 Read and listen. Then listen again and repeat.

It's **a page-turner.** *It's so interesting that you want to keep reading it.*

It's **a cliff-hanger.** *It's so exciting that you can't wait to find out what happens next.*

It's **a best-seller.** *It's very popular and everyone is buying copies.*

It's **a fast read.** *It's easy and enjoyable to read.*

It's **hard to follow.** *It's difficult to understand.*

It's **trash.** *It's very poor quality.*

B **Pair work** Discuss which types of books you find the most interesting. Use the Vocabulary from here and page 38.

> " I prefer thrillers. A thriller is usually a pretty fast read. It helps pass the time. "

GRAMMAR *Noun clauses*

A noun clause is a group of words that functions as a noun. A noun clause can be introduced by <u>that</u> and often functions as the direct object of a "mental activity" verb.

   I didn't know **that he wrote that book.**
   I think **that Junot Diaz's novels are fantastic.**
   She forgot **that Andrew Morton wrote biographies.**

When a noun clause functions as a direct object, <u>that</u> may be omitted.

   I didn't know **he wrote that book.**

In short answers, use <u>so</u> to replace a noun clause after the verbs <u>think</u>, <u>believe</u>, <u>guess</u>, and <u>hope</u>.

   A: Does Steven King have a new book out?
   B: I think **so.** / I believe **so.** / I guess **so.** / I hope **so.**
     (so = that Steven King has a new book out)

Other clauses with <u>that</u> often follow certain predicate adjectives. The word <u>that</u> can be omitted.

   We're both **disappointed** (that) his new book isn't very good.
   Were you **surprised** (that) the ending was sad?

Noun clauses and other clauses with <u>that</u> often follow these verbs and adjectives.

Verbs		Adjectives
agree	hear	disappointed
think	see	happy
believe	understand	sad
feel	hope	sorry
suppose	forget	sure
doubt	remember	surprised
guess	know	

Be careful!
I don't think **so.** / I don't believe **so.**
BUT I guess **not.** / I hope **not.**
NOT ~~I don't guess so.~~ / ~~I don't hope so.~~

GRAMMAR BOOSTER ▸ p. 126

• *More verbs and adjectives that can be followed by clauses with <u>that</u>*

Grammar practice On a separate sheet of paper, respond to each question with a clause using <u>that</u>. Use the prompts. *Answers will vary slightly, but may include the following:*

   What has the author Monica Ali been up to lately? (write / a new novel)

> *I think that she has written a new novel.*

1 Where does the story take place? (in London / I guess)
   I guess that it takes place in London.
2 What does Amy Tan usually write about? (mother-daughter relationships / I believe)
   I believe that she usually writes about mother-daughter relationships.
3 Where does Mario Vargas Llosa's novel *The Feast of the Goat* take place? (in the Dominican Republic / I hear)
   I hear that it takes place in the Dominican Republic.
4 What kind of book is Dan Brown going to write next? (another thriller / I hope)
   I hope that he is going to write another thriller.

VOCABULARY

A  Read and listen . . .

Suggested teaching time:	3 minutes	Your actual teaching time:

- Have students listen and study the words. Then have them listen and repeat chorally.

- To provide practice, write the Vocabulary and phrases on the board. Form pairs. Have students take turns reading a definition aloud and matching it with a word or phrase on the board. Ask one student in each pair to read three definitions. Have the other student keep his or her book closed and say the word or phrase.

ActiveTeach Multimedia Disc • Vocabulary Flash Cards

B Pair work

Suggested teaching time:	5 minutes	Your actual teaching time:

- To help students prepare for the activity, brainstorm different types of books. Write them on the board.

- Point out the speech balloon and read it to the class.

Option: [+3 minutes] For a different approach, if students are not regular readers, ask them which description they think would best match each type of book. For example, *I think a biography of a famous person might be a page-turner. It would be interesting to read.*

GRAMMAR

Suggested teaching time:	10–13 minutes	Your actual teaching time:

- Direct attention to the chart and have students read the first explanation and study the examples. Write on the board:

  I didn't know [something]. (direct object)
        that he was the author. (direct object noun clause)

- Point to the text on the board to clarify that a noun clause functions as a noun or pronoun.

- Tell students the underlined noun clause on the board is the direct object of the verb. It expresses the information you *know, believe, think,* etc.

- Have students read the second explanation and study the examples. Write on the board:

I	know, believe, guess	think, hope, suppose	*(that) she has a ticket.*

- Review the *Verbs* in the box and explain why they are called "mental activity" verbs. Note: Do not review the adjectives at this point.

- Tell students that when a noun clause is a direct object of the verb, the word *that* can be omitted. Point out that the omission of *that* is very common, especially in spoken English. To check comprehension of direct object noun clauses, ask several students to form such sentences; for

example, *I know [that] he passed the test. I believe [that] we're going to the mall. I guess [that] she left.*

- Have students read the third explanation and study the examples. Write on the board:

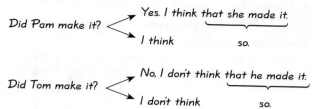

- To help clarify, say *Noun clauses can be replaced by so in short answers.*

- Review the negative forms in the *Be careful!* box.

- To check comprehension, ask questions and have several students reply with the verbs *think, believe, guess,* or *hope* and *so.* Ask *Did Frido Kahlo write an autobiography? Did Ernest Hemingway write short stories? Is The Bourne Identity a thriller? Did Helen Keller write novels?*

- Have students read the last explanation and study the examples.

- Write on the board: *I'm sure [that] you will like it.* Have students identify the adjective (Sure.) and the clause that follows it. (That you will like it.)

- Now review the *Adjectives* in the box. To check comprehension, have students use some of the adjectives to write sentences with noun clauses.

> **Language and culture**
>
> **LEN From the Longman Corpus:** A common learner error with noun clauses is using an incorrect tense when the main verb is in the past tense, for example: *I thought he ~~is~~ crazy.*

Option: **GRAMMAR BOOSTER** (Teaching notes p. T126)

ActiveTeach Multimedia Disc • Inductive Grammar Charts

Grammar practice

Suggested teaching time:	3–5 minutes	Your actual teaching time:

- First, review the example.

- Have students compare answers with a partner and then review with the class.

Option: [+10 minutes] To extend the activity, have students work in pairs and look at the books listed in the Preview on page 38 for two minutes. Then ask them to play a memory game and take turns asking and answering questions about the books. Have students use noun clauses or *so* in their answers. For example:

Student A: *What did Danielle Steele write?*
Student B: *I believe she wrote a romance novel.*
Student B: *Is Brian Koslow the author of a science-fiction book?*
Student A: *I don't think so. I think he wrote a self-help book.*

PRONUNCIATION

A 🔊 Read and listen . . .

Suggested teaching time:	3 minutes	Your actual teaching time:

- Have students listen and study the examples. Then have them listen and repeat.
- Ask students to take turns asking and answering the questions in the exercise. Remind them to use rising intonation for the questions.

B Pair work

Suggested teaching time:	5 minutes	Your actual teaching time:

- To help students generate ideas, draw the following diagram on the board (without the examples). Write *Weekend Activities* in the center circle. Brainstorm activities and write them in the surrounding circles.

- Read the speech balloon aloud with a student.
- Encourage students to use some of the activities on the board as they create their conversations. Remind students that *hope* and *guess* are followed by *not* in the negative. (I hope not. I guess not. NOT: ~~I don't hope so.~~ ~~I don't guess so.~~)

 • Pronunciation Activities

CONVERSATION MODEL

A 🔊 Read and listen . . .

Suggested teaching time:	2–3 minutes	Your actual teaching time:

This conversation strategy is implicit in the model:
- Use "Actually" to show appreciation for someone's interest in a topic.

- To set the scene for the conversation, ask *Where does this conversation take place?* (In a park.) *What is the woman holding?* (A book.)
- After students read and listen, check comprehension by asking *What kind of book is the woman reading?* (A thriller / fiction.) *Is it a good book?* (Yes, it's a cliff-hanger.) *What kind of book did the man read?* (A novel / fiction.) *Did he like it?* (Yes, a lot.)

- To point out the conversation strategy in the model, ask *How does the woman show her appreciation for the man's interest in what she is reading?* (She says *actually*.)

Language and culture
- Ernest Hemingway (1899–1961) was a U.S. novelist and short-story writer. *The Old Man and the Sea* earned him the Pulitzer Prize in fiction in 1953.

B 🔊 Rhythm and intonation

Suggested teaching time:	3 minutes	Your actual teaching time:

- Have students repeat each line chorally. Make sure students:
  - pause slightly before saying each book title.
  - use rising intonation for *Have you been reading anything interesting lately?* and *Is it any good?*
  - use falling intonation for *How about you?*
  - stress *highly* in *I highly recommend it.*

NOW YOU CAN Recommend a book

A Notepadding

Suggested teaching time:	5–10 minutes	Your actual teaching time:

- To review the vocabulary, ask students to name types of books. Then ask them to say reasons for recommending or not recommending a book. Elicit the vocabulary they have learned in this unit; for example, *Reasons for recommending a book: It's a page-turner. It's a cliff-hanger. It's a best-seller. It's a fast read. It's a must-read for [romance lovers]. Reasons for not recommending a book: It's hard to follow. It's trash. It put me to sleep. It's boring.*

B Pair work

Suggested teaching time:	6–10 minutes	Your actual teaching time:

- Be sure to reinforce the use of the conversation strategy. Encourage students to show appreciation by saying *actually.*

Don't stop! Extend the conversation. Review the ideas in the box. Ask students to write two more questions they could ask; for example, *Is it very long? Have you read other books by the same author?*

- To model the activity, role-play and extend the conversation with a more confident student.

 • Conversation Pair Work Cards
• Learning Strategies

EXTRAS (optional)
- Workbook: Exercises 4–9
- Copy & Go: Activity 13

A 🔊 2:22 Read and listen. Notice the stress on the verb in short answers with <u>so</u>. Then listen again and repeat.

1 Are there a lot of characters in the story? I THINK so.

2 Has she read that book yet? I don't THINK so.

3 Do you think this thriller will be good? I HOPE so.

4 Does the story have a happy ending? I beLIEVE so.

B **Pair work** Ask and answer <u>yes</u> / <u>no</u> questions about your future plans. Respond with short answers, using <u>think</u>, <u>believe</u>, <u>hope</u>, or <u>guess</u>.

> ❝ Are you going to read anything this weekend? ❞ ❝ I think so. ❞

CONVERSATION MODEL

A 🔊 2:23 Read and listen to someone recommend a book.

A: Have you been reading anything interesting lately?

B: Actually, I'm reading a thriller called *Don't Close Your Eyes*.

A: I've never heard of that one. Is it any good?

B: Oh, I think it's great. It's a cliff-hanger. How about you?

A: I've just finished a Hemingway novel, *The Old Man and the Sea*. I highly recommend it.

B 🔊 2:24 **Rhythm and intonation** Listen again and repeat. Then practice the Conversation Model with a partner.

NOW YOU CAN Recommend a book

A **Notepadding** Write some notes about a book you've read, or choose one of the books here.

Type of book:	
Title:	
Author:	
What is it about?	
Your recommendation:	

B **Pair work** Change the Conversation Model, using the Vocabulary and your notepad.

A: Have you been reading anything interesting lately?

B: Actually, ...

A: .... heard of that one. Is it any good?

B: Oh, I think .... It's .... How about you?

A: ....

> **Don't stop!**
> Ask questions about the book.
>   What's it about?
>   Where does it take place?
>   Why did you decide to read it?

FICTION

The Interpreter
by Charles Randolph

Silvia Broome is an interpreter at the United Nations who hears a secret plan to kill a state leader. But is she telling the truth?

The Time Machine
by H. G. Wells

A man builds a time machine and goes into the future, where he finds that people have become fearful, child-like creatures. But what are they afraid of?

NON-FICTION

New York
by Vicki Stripton

Every year, millions of tourists visit "the city that never sleeps." Read about its history, its sights, and its people.

Martin Luther King
by Coleen Degnan-Veness

In the U.S. in the 1950s and 60s, blacks did not have equal rights. But Martin Luther King had a dream —blacks and whites living together happily. He led peaceful protests and changed the country—and the world.

GOAL Offer to lend something

A 🔊 2:25 Read and listen to someone offering to lend a magazine.

A: Is that the latest issue of *Car Magazine*?

B: Yes, it is.

A: Could you tell me where you bought it? I can't find it anywhere.

B: At the newsstand across the street. But I think it's sold out.

A: Too bad. There's an article in there I'm dying to read.

B: You know, I'd be happy to lend it to you when I'm done with it.

A: Really? That would be great. Thanks!

B 🔊 2:26 **Rhythm and intonation** Listen again and repeat. Then practice the Conversation Model with a partner.

GRAMMAR *Noun clauses: embedded questions*

> **GRAMMAR BOOSTER ▸ p. 127**
> • Embedded questions:
>   ○ usage and common errors
>   ○ punctuation
>   ○ with infinitives
> • Noun clauses as subjects and objects

> **Noun clauses sometimes include embedded questions. Use if or whether to begin embedded yes / no questions. (If and whether have the same meaning.)**
>
> | Yes / no questions | Embedded yes / no questions |
> |---|---|
> | Is that magazine any good? | Tell me **if that magazine is any good**. |
> | Did he like the article? | I'd like to know **whether he liked the article**. |
> | Have you finished that newspaper? | Could you tell me **if you've finished that newspaper**? |
> | Can I borrow your brochure? | I wonder **whether I could borrow your brochure**. |
>
> **Use a question word to begin embedded information questions.**
>
> | Information questions | Embedded information questions |
> |---|---|
> | What's the article about? | Tell me **what the article's about**. |
> | Why did you decide to read it? | Could you tell me **why you decided to read it**? |
> | Who's the writer? | I wonder **who the writer is**. |
> | Who recommended the article? | Do you know **who recommended the article**? |
> | Who(m) is it written for? | Can you tell me **who(m) it's written for**? |
> | Whose magazine is it? | I'd like to know **whose magazine it is**. |
> | When was it written? | Would you tell me **when it was written**? |
> | Where is the writer from? | Do you know **where the writer is from**? |

> **Be careful!**
> Use normal word order (not question word order) in embedded questions.
> Don't say:
> I wonder ~~who is the writer~~.
> Do you know ~~where is the~~ writer from?

A **Find the grammar** Underline three examples of noun clauses in the Photo Story on page 39. Which two are embedded questions?

I wonder if you could recommend something [for] me. (Embedded question)
I didn't know he had a new book out.
Do you think I could borrow it when you're do[ne] with it? (Embedded question)

B **Grammar practice** Change the questions to embedded questions.

1 Does she like to read?

I wonder ....*if she likes to read*........ .

2 Where did you get that magazine?

Can you tell me ......*where you got that magazine*...... ?

3 Is he a John Grisham fan?

I've been wondering ......*if he's a John Grisham fan*...... .

4 Why don't you read newspapers?

I'm curious ......*why you don't read newspapers*...... .

5 Who told you about the article?

I was wondering ......*who told you about the article*...... .

6 When did you hear about the new website?

I'd like to know ......*when you heard about the new websi*[te] .

CONVERSATION MODEL

A 🔊 Read and listen . . .

Suggested teaching time:	3–5 minutes	Your actual teaching time:

These conversation strategies are implicit in the model:
• Soften a question with "Could you tell me . . . ?"
• Indicate disappointment with "Too bad."
• Use "I'm dying to . . ." to indicate extreme interest.
• Say "That would be great" to express gratitude for someone's willingness to do something.

• Have students look at the photo. Ask *What do you think the men are doing?* (Talking about a magazine.)

• To check comprehension after students read and listen, ask *What's the man reading?* (A magazine / *Car Magazine*) *What does the other man want to know?* (Where he bought it.) *What do you think "it's sold out" means?* (That there are no more copies.) *What does the other man offer to do?* (Lend it to him.)

• To point out some of the conversation strategies in the model, write on the board: *Where did you buy it?* Ask students to find a question in the conversation with the same meaning. (Could you tell me where you bought it?) Point out that a question starting with *Could you tell me . . .* is more polite than a direct question.

• Write *Thank you* on the board. Ask students to find another way in the conversation to express gratitude. (Really? That would be great. Thanks!)

Option: [+5 minutes] To extend the activity, have students work in pairs and say whether they sometimes lend or borrow reading materials or other things to friends or family members. If necessary, clarify the difference between *borrow* and *lend*; for example, *The giver* lends, *the receiver* borrows. Elicit the kinds of things they lend or borrow.

B 🔊 Rhythm and intonation

Suggested teaching time:	2–3 minutes	Your actual teaching time:

• Have students repeat each line chorally. Make sure students:
  ◦ use rising intonation for *Is that the latest issue of Car Magazine?* and *Could you tell me where you bought it?*
  ◦ stress *dying* in *I'm dying to read.*
  ◦ use extra stress on *great* in *That would be great.*

GRAMMAR

Suggested teaching time:	10–15 minutes	Your actual teaching time:

• Direct attention to the chart and have students read the first explanation and study the examples. Write on the board:
  1. *Is it a best-seller?*
  2. *I don't know if it is a best-seller.*

• To help clarify, point out the underlined words in sentence 2 and say *An embedded question is part of a larger sentence.* Then point to sentence 1 on the board and ask *Is this a yes / no question or an information question?* (A *yes / no* question.) Then point to sentence 2 and say *Embedded yes / no questions can start with if or whether.* Ask students to rewrite sentence 2, using *whether.* (I don't know *whether* it is a best-seller.)

• Write on the board:
  3. *Does he like the book?*
  4. *I don't know if he likes the book.*

• Point out that auxiliary verbs are not used in embedded questions. Then point out the verb form in sentence 4.

• Have students read the second explanation and study the examples. Write on the board:
  5. *Where did you buy it?*
  6. *Can you tell me where you bought it?*

• Point to sentence 5 and ask *Is this a yes / no question or an information question?* (An information question.) Say *Embedded information questions start with a question word.* Point out the underlined information in sentence 6.

• Have students look at the embedded information questions in the chart and underline the question words. (What, why, who, who, who(m), whose, when, where.)

• Review the *Be careful!* box. You can point out sentences 2, 4, 6 on the board. As a comparison, point out that inverted word order is used in regular *yes / no* or information questions.

Language and culture

LEN **From the Longman Corpus:** Learners across all language backgrounds commonly make errors with word order in embedded questions; for example, *Do you know ~~what are~~ the advantages of studying English?* Be sure students are aware of correct word order.

Option: GRAMMAR BOOSTER (Teaching notes p. T127)

 ActiveTeach Multimedia Disc • Inductive Grammar Charts

A Find the grammar

Suggested teaching time:	3–4 minutes	Your actual teaching time:

• To model the activity, find one of the noun clauses with the class.

• Have students identify whether the embedded questions are *yes / no* or information questions.

B Grammar practice

Suggested teaching time:	2–3 minutes	Your actual teaching time:

• Complete the first item with the class. Make sure students use the correct verb form (*likes*) and not the auxiliary verb *does* in the embedded question.

C Pair work

Suggested teaching time:	10 minutes	Your actual teaching time:	

- Before students take the survey, have them read it quickly to find out what it is about.

- To help students generate ideas, brainstorm other kinds of magazines students can include in the survey and write them on the board. Ask students for examples of magazines for each of the various types.

- Follow the same procedure for newspaper sections. What newspapers have these sections: *cartoons, letters to the editor, weather, movies, politics, technology, arts, TV, classifieds?*

- After students take the survey, read the speech balloons aloud with the class. Ask students to identify the embedded question in each one. Point out the normal (not inverted) word order.

- Have students exchange surveys with a partner so they can use them as a guide for their questions. Encourage students to ask as many embedded questions as they can.

Language and culture

- *Do-It-Yourself* magazines give advice for cooking, making or building things, etc. *Home* magazines give advice for decorating home interiors and exteriors. *Lifestyle* magazines give advice for healthy living. *Classifieds* are ads for jobs, apartments, etc.

NOW YOU CAN Offer to lend something

A Pair work

Suggested teaching time:	10 minutes	Your actual teaching time:	

- To prepare students for the activity, have them read the Conversation Model on page 42 again. You may also want to have students listen to the model.

- Brainstorm ideas to complete the first question and write them on the board. For example:

  Is that . . .

  > the latest issue of [Home] magazine?
  > today's issue of [The Buenos Aires Herald]?
  > the new [John Grisham thriller]?
  > a copy of [Cutting for Stone]?

- Be sure to reinforce the use of the conversation strategies; for example, encourage students to politely ask for information by using embedded questions.

Don't stop! Extend the conversation. Review the ideas in the box. Have students write two more questions they could ask to keep the conversation going. For example:

> *Could you tell me why you decided to read it?*
> *Do you know if it is a best-seller?*
> *I wonder where the writer is from.*

- To model the activity, role-play and extend the conversation with a more confident student.

- Walk around the room and provide help as needed. Encourage students to use the correct rhythm and intonation and to continue their conversations by asking follow-up questions.

 • **Conversation Pair Work Cards**

B Change partners

Suggested teaching time:	5–10 minutes	Your actual teaching time:	

- Remind students to use other magazines or newspapers. To challenge your students, you may want to encourage them to answer some of the questions with noun clauses or new embedded questions. For example:

  > *I don't know when it was written.*
  > *I guess it came out last week.*
  > *I don't remember where or when I bought it.*
  > *I think it was a birthday gift.*

EXTRAS (optional)

- **Workbook:** Exercises 10–15
- **Copy & Go:** Activity 14

C Pair work Complete the survey below. Then look at your partner's responses. Use embedded questions to learn more about your partner.

> " Tell me why you like to read photography magazines. "

> " I wonder what sections of the newspaper you like to read. "

What kinds of materials do you like to read?

MAGAZINES

- ○ World news
- ○ Sports
- ○ Photography
- ○ Computers and electronics
- ○ Entertainment
- ○ Music

- ○ Fashion
- ○ Economics
- ○ Health and fitness
- ○ Business
- ○ Food and cooking
- ○ Other _____

NEWSPAPER SECTIONS

- ○ World news
- ○ Local news
- ○ Sports
- ○ Business

- ○ Entertainment
- ○ Travel
- ○ Other _____

NOW YOU CAN | Offer to lend something

A Pair work Change the Conversation Model. Create a conversation in which you offer to lend your partner something that you are reading. Then change roles.

A: Is that .... ?

B: Yes, ...

A: Could you tell me where you bought it? I can't find it anywhere.

B: .... But I think it's sold out.

A: Too bad. ....

B: You know, I'd be happy to lend it to you when I'm done with it.

A: .... !

Don't stop!
Use more embedded questions.
 Could you tell me ___?
Do you know ___?
I wonder ___.

B Change partners Discuss and offer to lend another magazine, newspaper, or book.

43

BEFORE YOU LISTEN

A 🔊 2:27 **Vocabulary** • *Some ways to enjoy reading* Read and listen. Then listen again and repeat.

curl up with [a book]

read aloud [to someone]

listen to audio books

do puzzles

read [articles] online

skim through [a newspaper]

read electronic books / e-books

B Pair work Discuss which activities from the Vocabulary match the situations below. Explain your reasons.   See page T44 for answers.

- Is convenient for when you are driving
- Helps pass the time during a bus or train commute
- Is a good way to relax
- Is a way to keep up with the news

LISTENING COMPREHENSION

🔊 2:28 **Listen to take notes** Listen and take notes to answer these questions about each speaker. Listen again if necessary.

1 What kinds of reading material does he or she like?
2 When does he or she like to read?
3 Where does he or she like to read?

Su Yomei • Taiwan

1. novels, general fiction, short
   stories, books written by
   Japanese authors translated
   into Chinese
2. when she has a bit of quiet time
3. in bed, in a small room next to her living room

Ignacio Saralegui • Argentina

1. the paper, magazines,
   historical novels
2. on weekends
3. in bed, in the garden, in the bathroom

Vicki Patterson • U.S.A.

1. blogs, newspapers
2. during breakfast, when she
   gets back from work
3. on the sofa

BEFORE YOU LISTEN

A 🔊 Vocabulary

Suggested teaching time:	3–4 minutes	Your actual teaching time:

- Have students listen and study the phrases. Then have them listen and repeat chorally.

- To clarify the meaning of *curl up with [a book]*, direct attention to the way the woman is relaxing on the sofa. To clarify the meaning of *skim*, direct attention to the way the person is using his or her finger to read through a text quickly for the main ideas.

- Write on the board:
    1. *David enjoys word games.*
    2. *Steve is very busy, but wants to be informed.*
    3. *Maria has little children.*
    4. *John loves reading at night.*
    5. *Alex uses a laptop most of the time.*
    6. *Sarah drives to work every day.*
    7. *Brian always buys the latest technological gadgets.*

- To check comprehension and review drawing conclusions with *must*, form pairs and ask students to discuss each person's reading habits. (Possible answers: 1. David must like to do puzzles. 2. Steve must skim through the newspaper. 3. Maria must read aloud to her children. 4. John must curl up with a book at night. 5. Alex must read articles online. 6. Sarah must listen to audio books. 7. Brian must read electronic books / e-books.)

 **ActiveTeach** **Multimedia Disc** • **Vocabulary Flash Cards**

B Pair work

Suggested teaching time:	7–10 minutes	Your actual teaching time:

- Have students match each situation with one or more activities.

- To review, have several students describe some situations in which they enjoy reading.

Option: [+3 minutes] To extend the activity, encourage students to think of more situations. For example:
> *Doing puzzles is a great way to practice vocabulary if you are learning a foreign language.*
> *Reading articles online is the best way to find information when you do not have other materials available.*
> *Parents usually read aloud to their children before they go to sleep.*
> *Listening to audio books is convenient if you are busy. You can listen to them while you walk, drive, or exercise.*

Answers for Exercise B
Answers will vary, but may include the following:
- listen to audio books
- listen to audio books, do puzzles, read [articles] online, skim through [a newspaper], read electronic books / e-books
- curl up with [a book], read aloud [to someone], listen to audio books, do puzzles
- read [articles] online, skim through [a newspaper]

LISTENING COMPREHENSION

🔊 Listen to take notes

Suggested teaching time:	5–7 minutes	Your actual teaching time:

- To prepare students for the activity, brainstorm the different types of reading materials they've learned about in the unit.

- Before students listen, have them read the questions to know what information they should listen for.

- Stop after each section to allow students to complete their notes. You may want to play each section two or three times before moving on to the next one.

AUDIOSCRIPT

SU YOMEI [Chinese]
There is nothing I like more than curling up with a good book. I like all kinds of literature—novels, general fiction, short stories. . . . I also read a lot of books written by Japanese authors, translated into Chinese. My favorite author, though, is Chang Ailing. She's a very famous author from China. Her work has inspired women for many generations.

I like to read whenever I have a bit of quiet time—like early in the morning or during lunch hour—and at night when I'm lying in bed. I usually read in a small room next to my living room. It's like a small library with good natural sunlight. I really don't enjoy reading in coffee shops or other public places. I need a quiet space to read.

For me, reading is a spiritual experience that gives me great personal satisfaction. Television and movies can't do that. I can't understand why anyone doesn't enjoy reading. I can't think of any better way to relax, to forget the pressure of each day.

IGNACIO SARALEGUI [Spanish]
I really like to keep up with the news. I get the paper delivered on weekends, so that's when I enjoy reading it most. Pretty much from the first to the last page. During the week I enjoy skimming through the newspaper in a café. But the weekend is the best time. There's nothing like lying in bed with the paper, a good cup of coffee, and some croissants or toast. Or when the weather is nice, sitting in the garden and reading about what's going on in the world. And, well, I have to admit, one of my favorite places to read is in the, um, well, bathroom. . . . I can spend a good half-hour there reading the paper.

Aside from newspapers, I really enjoy stopping at newsstands and spending about five or ten minutes browsing through magazines. And, of course, I also enjoy going to bookshops and checking out the latest novels. Particularly historical novels. I just can't seem to read enough of those.

VICKI PATTERSON
I don't really consider myself to be a big reader, because I don't actually read a lot of books. Most of the reading I do is either on the Internet or in newspapers. I can't start my day without skimming through the newspaper during breakfast, checking out what's going on in local news, or maybe what's going on in business. Mainly I just look for the articles that look interesting, and I save them for later when I get back home from work. Then I like to curl up on the sofa with my newspaper and a good cup of tea.

The truth is I don't have a lot of time for reading books. And I don't have a lot of interest in reading them. Once in a while, I'll read one of the best-sellers or a good romance novel. But I spend a lot more time surfing the Internet, checking out my favorite blogs. That's where I get my information from—and my entertainment. It works for me.

 **ActiveTeach** **Multimedia Disc** • **Learning Strategies**

NOW YOU CAN Describe your reading habits

A Frame your ideas

Suggested teaching time:	10–15 minutes	Your actual teaching time:

- As students complete the survey, encourage them to look back into the unit if they need help with vocabulary.
- Have students either write complete sentences or just write short notes, such as *Not a big reader / Too busy.* Walk around, providing help as needed.

B Pair work

Suggested teaching time:	10–12 minutes	Your actual teaching time:

- Review the *Be sure to recycle . . .* box. Have students write sentences to complete some of the items. For example:
  I'd like to know if you consider yourself a big reader.
  Could you tell me if you have a favorite author?
  I guess I'm not a very good reader.
  I think I used to be a better reader when I was a child.
  I suppose [Stephenie Meyer] is one of my favorite authors.
- Encourage students to ask follow-up questions during the interview. For example:
  Student A: *When do you like to read?*
  Student B: *At night.*
  Student A: *Could you tell me why?*
  Student B: *I guess it helps me relax and go to sleep.*
- Walk around, providing help as needed.
- Then have students compare their reading habits; for example, **Student A:** *We both enjoy reading at night.*
  Student B: *Yes, but you like to read thrillers, and I like to read romance novels.*

Option: [+5 minutes] To extend the activity, ask students to interview a second student and then compare the reading habits of the two people they interviewed.

C Group work

Suggested teaching time:	10–12 minutes	Your actual teaching time:

- Form groups of four. Have students who've worked together in pairs for the previous activity join different groups for this activity.
- Review the speech balloon.
- Encourage students to compare their partner's reading habits and ask follow-up questions. For example:
  Student A: *[Carolyn] likes to read the newspaper every morning.*
  Student B: *[Andrew] also likes to read the newspaper in the morning. What newspaper does [Ellen] read?*
  Student A: *[Daily News]. And [Andrew]?*
  Student B: *He reads [The World Journal].*
- To check comprehension, have volunteers from different groups choose two of their partners' answers to share with the class.

Option: [+5 minutes] To extend the activity, as students talk about their partners' answers, take notes to help create questions to ask about the reading habits in the class; for example, *Who hates reading aloud? Who always skims newspapers and never reads them? Who collects newspaper clippings about impressive works of architecture?* Read the questions aloud and ask students to respond.

Option: [+10 minutes] To challenge students, have them write a paragraph describing their reading habits. Ask them to include the type of reading materials they like, examples of their favorite titles, ways they enjoy reading, and when they usually read. Have them use the information from the questionnaire. Draw the following diagram on the board (include the examples) or print it out from the ActiveTeach Multimedia Disc and distribute to students.

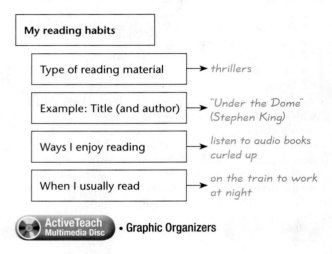

ActiveTeach Multimedia Disc • Graphic Organizers

EXTRAS (optional)

- Workbook: Exercises 16–18
- Copy & Go: Activity 15

A Frame your ideas Complete the questionnaire.

What are your reading habits?

1 Do you consider yourself to be a big reader? Why or why not?
_____
_____

2 Do you have any favorite authors? Who are they?
_____
_____

3 Do you prefer any particular types of books? Which types?
_____
_____

4 Are you a big newspaper reader? What sections of the
paper do you prefer to read?
_____
_____

5 Do you read a lot of magazines? What kind?
_____
_____

6 Do you spend a lot of time reading online? Why or why not?
_____
_____

7 Have you ever read aloud to someone? Has anyone ever
read aloud to you? When?
_____
_____

8 Do you listen to audio books? If so, do you like them?
_____
_____

9 When and where do you prefer to read the most?
_____
_____

10 Is there anything else you can add about your reading habits?
_____
_____

B Pair work Use the survey to interview your partner
about his or her reading habits. Take notes on a
separate sheet of paper.

C Group work Now tell your classmates about
your partner's reading habits.

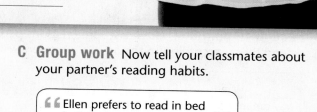

“ Ellen prefers to read in bed
before she goes to sleep . . . ”

 Be sure to recycle this language.

I'd like to know . . .	I guess (that) . . .
Could you tell me . . . ?	I think (that) . . .
	I suppose (that) . . .

45

BEFORE YOU READ

Warm-up Do you—or does anyone you know—read comics? Do you think there's any value in reading them?

READING   2:29 🔊)))

Comics: trash or treasure?

In Japan, they're known as *manga*; in Latin America, *historietas* or *historias em quadrinhos*; in Italy, *fumetti*. Some people call them "graphic novels." But no matter what you call them, comics are a favorite source of reading pleasure for millions in many parts of the world.

In case you're wondering how popular they are, the best-selling comic in the U.S. sells about 4.5 million copies a year. Mexico's comic titles sell over 7 million copies a week. But Japan is by far the leading publisher of comics in the world. *Manga* account for nearly 40 percent of all the books and magazines published in Japan each year.

Ever since comics first appeared, there have been people who have criticized them. In the 1940s and 50s, many people

In Japan, train station newsstands do a booming business selling *manga* during rush hour. And for true addicts, automatic vending machines that sell *manga* are everywhere.

believed that comics were immoral and that they caused bad behavior among young people. Even today, many question whether young people should read them at all.

They argue that reading comics encourages bad reading habits. In more recent years some comics have been criticized for including violence and sexual content.

On the other hand, some educators see comics as a way to get teenagers to choose reading instead of television and video games. And because of the art, a number of educators have argued that comics are a great way to get children to think creatively. Some recent research has suggested that the combination of visuals and text in comics may be one reason young people handle computers and related software so easily.

In many places, comics have been a convenient way to communicate social or political information. For example, in the 1990s, comics were used by the Brazilian health ministry to communicate

Spider-Man® is one of the world's most recognizable and celebrated comic superheroes. Fifteen million Spider-Man comics are sold each year in 75 countries and in 22 languages.

information about AIDS. In Japan, the Education Ministry calls comics "a part of Japan's national culture, recognized and highly regarded abroad." Comics are increasingly being used for educational purposes, and many publishers there see them as a useful way of teaching history and other subjects.

No matter how you view them, comics remain a guilty pleasure for millions worldwide.

Sources: Associated Press, Ananova News Service, PRNewswire

A Recognize points of view List some reasons people criticize comics and defend them, according to the article.   Answers will vary slightly, but may include the following:

Some reasons people criticize comics	Some reasons people defend comics
They are immoral and cause bad behavior. They encourage bad reading habits. They include violence and sexual content.	They get teenagers to choose reading instead of television and video games. They get children to think creatively. They help people handle computers and software. They can communicate social and political information. They can be used to teach history and other subjects.

BEFORE YOU READ

Warm-up

Suggested teaching time:	5 minutes	Your actual teaching time:

- To focus students' attention on the first question, take a poll to see who in the class reads comics and which of their family members read them as well.
- To help students generate ideas for the second question, write on the board:

  Reasons comics are or are not good reading material

- Ask students to brainstorm reasons; for example, *At least younger people are reading instead of watching TV. They are creative. It's good practice if the comic is in a foreign language. Comics can teach what's right and wrong (in society).* OR *They are not intelligent reading material. They are childish. Some are very sexist and violent.*

READING

Suggested teaching time:	10–15 minutes	Your actual teaching time:

- To draw on students' prior knowledge, have them look at the pictures and say what they already know about comics in their country and in other countries. (Possible answers: The Japanese are famous for their comics. Spider-Man is a superhero and famous around the world. Romantic comics are very popular in Mexico.)
- Have students read the title of the article. Ask them for the meanings of *trash* (Garbage or something that is of very poor quality.) and *treasure* (A very valuable or important object.). To help students focus on the Reading, ask them to find reasons why comics could be considered *trash* or *treasure* as they read and listen to the article.

Option: [+10 minutes] To extend the presentation, ask students to close their books. Write the following questions on the board:

1. *Which country sells the most comics a year?*
2. *Where can you buy* Shonen Jump *in Japan?*
3. *What opinion did many people have of comics when they first appeared?*
4. *What are four ways comics can help young people?*

Have students write the answers. Then have them read the text to confirm their answers. (1. Japan; 2. At newsstands and automatic vending machines; 3. Not very good—many people believed that they are immoral and caused bad behavior; 4. Comics get children to think creatively, they help teenagers use computers and software easily, they can give social or political information, and they can teach history—and other subjects.)

Option: [+15 minutes] To challenge students, draw the following chart (without the answers) on the board. Ask students to skim the text and complete the chart for each section with notes about the positive effects of comics. After students complete the chart, ask pairs to compare answers. Then review with the class.

Positive Effects of Comics	
Reading time	*help teenagers spend more time reading and less time watching TV and playing video games*
Social and political issues	*simple and effective ways to communicate social and political information*
Computer literacy	*help young people use computers and software easily*
Education	*a useful / successful way to teach history and other subjects*
Creative	*help children think creatively*

Language and culture

- A *publisher* is a person or company whose business is to print and sell books; *account for* means to be the reason for; *visuals* are drawings, diagrams, and other artwork; *AIDS* means Acquired Immune Deficiency Syndrome; *a guilty pleasure* means something you enjoy doing that you feel a bit ashamed for enjoying.

ActiveTeach Multimedia Disc
- Extra Reading Comprehension Questions
- Learning Strategies

A Recognize points of view

Suggested teaching time:	5 minutes	Your actual teaching time:

- Ask students to identify the paragraphs that give information about why people defend and criticize comics. (Reasons why people criticize comics: paragraphs 3 and 4; Reasons why people defend comics: paragraphs 5 and 6.)
- Have students underline the reasons in the paragraphs. Ask students to write the information they have underlined in each column.
- Ask students to compare answers with a partner. Then review with the class.

B Critical thinking

Suggested teaching time:	5 minutes	Your actual teaching time:

- First, have students write their own notes for each question. Then form small groups. Encourage students to use their notes as a guide as they discuss each question.
- To review, have several students from different groups answer one of the questions.

Option: [+5 minutes] To extend the activity, have students write notes about a popular comic they know. Include information such as the title, the story, and a few characters. Students can write about comics for adults, teenagers, or children. Form pairs. Encourage students to use their notes as they discuss comics and offer their own opinions.

NOW YOU CAN | **Discuss the quality of reading materials**

A Frame your ideas

Suggested teaching time:	10 minutes	Your actual teaching time:

- First, review the example.
- Write two columns on the board: *Treasure* and *Trash*. Brainstorm words and phrases to describe reading materials and place them in the appropriate column. Encourage students to use vocabulary from this and other units; for example, *Treasure: fun, interesting, exciting, useful, informative, a cliff-hanger, a page-turner, a fast read. Trash: boring, immoral, too conservative / radical, useless, silly, causes bad behavior.*

B Pair work

Suggested teaching time:	5–10 minutes	Your actual teaching time:

- Encourage students to ask each other questions to find out what they agree and disagree about. For example:
  Student A: *What do you think of comics?*
  Student B: *I think they're trash. The stories are so silly. Do you like them?*
  Student A: *No, not really. I think they cause bad behavior.*
- After pairs have chosen a type of reading material they both agree is trash and one they both agree is not, ask them to write a list of reasons to explain their opinions about each type.

C Group work

Suggested teaching time:	5–10 minutes	Your actual teaching time:

- Point out the *Be sure to recycle . . .* box and review the expressions. Have several students complete a sentence expressing an opinion; for example, *I think [that] some thrillers are real page-turners. I believe [that] horror magazines are useless. I guess [that] they are fun for teenagers. In my opinion, movie magazines are really interesting and exciting.*

Text-mining: Have students share their Text-mining examples and use them to create new statements with a partner.* For example:
  many people believed . . .
  they argue . . .
  some educators see comics as . . .
  some recent research has suggested . . .
  many publishers see them as . . .

*Follow the same procedure with students' Text-mining examples in other units.

- Have pairs combine to form groups of four. Encourage students to give examples and to ask each other follow-up questions. Also encourage them to politely express their views. You may want to write some useful language on the board:
  I see your point, but . . .
  You may be right, but . . .
  As I see it, . . .
  That's exactly what I think.
  I couldn't agree more.

FYI: The language of agreement and disagreement will be taught fully in Unit 9.

- Walk around the room and provide help as needed. To check comprehension, ask several groups to say whether they agreed with each other or not and to explain why.

EXTRAS (optional)

- Workbook: Exercises 19–21
- Copy & Go: Activity 16

B Critical thinking Discuss the following questions.

1 What point of view do you think the writer of the article has about comics? Explain your reasons.

2 Why do you think comics are so popular around the world? Why do you think Japanese *manga* are so popular outside of Japan?

3 Why do you think some people find reading comics "a guilty pleasure"?

On your *ActiveBook* Self-Study Disc:
Extra Reading Comprehension Questions

NOW YOU CAN Discuss the quality of reading materials

A Frame your ideas Complete the chart to explain your opinions about certain reading materials.

Types of materials	Who reads them?	Are they trash?		Your reasons
comics	boys, 12 to 17 years old	(Y)	N	I think they're violent and sexist.

Types of materials	Who reads them?	Are they trash?		Your reasons
comics		Y	N	
teen magazines		Y	N	
fashion magazines		Y	N	
sports magazines		Y	N	
movie magazines		Y	N	
romance novels		Y	N	
thrillers		Y	N	
horror magazines		Y	N	
sci-fi magazines		Y	N	
online blogs		Y	N	
newspapers		Y	N	
other:		Y	N	

B Pair work Compare the comments you wrote on your charts. Discuss your ideas. Then choose one type of reading material you both agree is trash and one you both agree is not. Prepare to explain your reasons to the class.

C Group work With a partner, compare the quality of two types of reading materials. Explain your reasons to your classmates.

Text-mining (optional):
Underline language in the Reading on page 46 to use in the Group Work.

For example: "Many people question whether …"

♻ **Be sure to recycle this language.**

Express an opinion
I think (that) . . .
I believe (that) . . .
I guess (that) . . .
In my opinion, . . .

Describe materials
I can't put ___ down.
I'm really into ___ .
I can't get enough of ___ .
They're a fast read.
I can't get into ___ .
___ aren't my thing.
___ don't turn me on.
___ are hard to follow.

47

Review

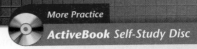
A 🔊 2:30 **Listening comprehension** Listen to each conversation and write the type of book each person is discussing. Then decide if the person likes the book. Explain your answer.

	Type of book	Likes it?	Explain your answer
1	mystery	Ⓨ N	he can't wait to get to the ending; it's a cliffhanger
2	travel	Y Ⓝ	he can't get into it; it's not a fast read
3	romance	Ⓨ N	she can't put it down; it's a page-turner
4	autobiography	Y Ⓝ	she's not really into it

B Write the name of each type of book.

1 A novel about people falling in love: .... romance novel ....

2 A book about a famous person: .... biography ....

3 A book that a famous person writes about his or her own life: .... autobiography ....

4 A very exciting novel with people in dangerous situations: .... thriller ....

5 Books that are about factual information: .... non-fiction ....

6 A strange fictional story about the future: .... science fiction ....

🎵 2:31/2:32
Top Notch Pop
"A True Life Story"
Lyrics p. 149

C Use the expressions in the box to change each question to an embedded question. (Use each expression once.)

> I was wondering . . .   Could you tell me . . .   I don't know . . .
>
> I can't remember . . .   Would you please tell me . . .

Answers will vary, but may include the following:

1 Where does the story take place?
Could you tell me where the story takes place?

2 Who is the main character in the novel?
I was wondering who the main character in the novel is.

3 How much was that newspaper?
I can't remember how much that newspaper was.

4 How do you say this in English?
Would you please tell me how you say this in English?

5 What does this word mean?
I don't know what this word means.

D **Writing** On a separate sheet of paper, write a review of something you've read—a book or an article from a magazine, a newspaper, or the Internet.

• Summarize what it was about.

• Make a recommendation to the reader.

WRITING BOOSTER ▸ p. 143

• *Summarizing*
• *Guidance for Exercise D*

Review

A 🔊 Listening comprehension

Suggested teaching time:	5 minutes	Your actual teaching time:

- First, have students listen for the type of book. Then have them listen again for the words or phrases that indicate whether the person likes the book or not. You may want to ask them to write the words they hear.

- Pause after each conversation to allow students time to write.

- Have students compare answers with a partner. Encourage them to use *I think* and a noun clause to discuss the answers; for example, **Student A:** *The speaker doesn't like the book.* **Student B:** *I think that he likes it. He said he can't wait to get to the ending.*

- Review with the class.

AUDIOSCRIPT

CONVERSATION 1
M: I'm reading a new mystery by Smithson.
F: Really? Is it any good?
M: Oh, it's a real cliff-hanger. I can't wait to get to the ending!
F: Then don't tell me how it ends. I might want to read it, too.
M: I'll let you borrow it.
F: Thanks!

CONVERSATION 2
F: How's that travel book you're reading?
M: Well, apparently it's a best-seller.
F: Oh, yeah? Must be good.
M: Actually, I can't get into it. It's not a fast read—at all.
F: Oh.

CONVERSATION 3
M: When are you going to finish that romance novel?
F: Pretty soon. To tell the truth, it's really trash. But you know something? I just can't put it down.
M: I don't get it. Why are you reading it if it's trash?
F: I can't help it. It's a page-turner. I've really been getting into it.

CONVERSATION 4
M: I'm reading an autobiography by a famous Italian artist.
F: Wow. That must be interesting.
M: I guess it should be. But I'm just not really into it.
F: Don't you like autobiographies?
M: Sure! I love them. Just not this one.

B Write the name . . .

Suggested teaching time:	5–6 minutes	Your actual teaching time:

- Complete the first item with the class.

- Have students compare answers with a partner. Then review with the class.

C Use the expressions . . .

Suggested teaching time:	3–5 minutes	Your actual teaching time:

- Remind students that embedded questions use normal word order. Tell students that they can only use each expression once.

- Call on students to share their answers with the class.

D Writing

Suggested teaching time:	10–15 minutes	Your actual teaching time:

- Point out that students can choose something they enjoyed or did not enjoy reading.

- To help students organize their ideas, have them begin by saying what they read and when or where they read it; for example, *Last week I read an interesting article in the newspaper. / I once read a story about a doctor in Africa. It was great!*

- To help students with the language, draw the following chart on the board (without the sentence starters) or print it out from the ActiveTeach Multimedia Disc and distribute to students.

Book or Article:
Summarize
It is about
It takes place
It tells the story of
Express your opinion
I enjoyed / didn't enjoy reading it because
I'd highly recommend it because
I think it's a must-read because
I would recommend it to

- Have students write the title of the book or article on the first line and then write the sentence starters on the board.

- As students complete the sentences, walk around the room and provide help as needed.

Option: [+10 minutes] To extend the activity, have students work in groups of three and read their reviews aloud. Encourage them to ask each other follow-up questions. Have students say if they would or would not like to read any of the recommendations and explain their reasons.

Option: **WRITING BOOSTER** (Teaching notes p. T143)

- Writing Process Worksheets
- Graphic Organizers

ORAL REVIEW

Before the first activity, give students a few minutes of silent time to explore the pictures and become familiar with them.

Pair work 1

Suggested teaching time:	5–7 minutes	Your actual teaching time:

- To set the scene for the conversation, ask *Where are the people?* (Possible answers: At a university, at language school, in a coffee shop, in a restaurant.)

- To prepare students for the activity, draw the following chart (without the answers) on the board.

Ask about what someone is reading	Comment on a book
Are you reading anything interesting (lately)? *Are you reading anything good (these days)?* *What's that you're reading?*	*I've heard about it. / I've never heard of that one.* *Is it any good? / Would you recommend it?* *I've always wanted to read that!*
Borrow a book or offer to lend it	**Recommend a book**
Do you mind if I borrow it when you're done? *Would you like to borrow it?* *I'd be happy to lend it to you when I'm done.*	*I highly recommend it.* *It's a (real) cliff-hanger.* *It's a (real) page-turner.* *It's a fast read.* *It's a best-seller.*

- Brainstorm ideas for each of the situations in the chart. Write them on the board as students say them. Before students create the conversations, choose a student and model the conversation.

> **Possible responses . . .**
> **A:** Are you reading anything interesting? **B:** Actually, I'm reading a [type of book] called [title of the book]. **A:** I've never heard about it. Is it any good? **B:** Oh, I think it's great. It's a real page-turner. **A:** Do you mind if I borrow it when you're done? **B:** Not at all.
>
> **A:** Are you reading anything good these days / lately? **B:** Well, I'm reading a [type of book] by [author of the book]. **A:** Really? I've always wanted to read that! **B:** I'd be happy to lend it to you when I'm done with it. **A:** That would be great. Thanks!

Pair work 2

Suggested teaching time:	5–7 minutes	Your actual teaching time:

- To prepare students for the activity, have them describe the reading habits shown in the circular pictures.

- Encourage students to keep the conversation going by asking follow-up questions. Point out that they can invent the information. For example:
  When do you usually do puzzles?
  Do you like reading in bed?
  Why don't you like listening to audio books?
  Do you skim through the newspaper every day?

> **Possible responses . . .**
> **A:** I usually like to curl up with a good book in bed. **B:** Really? I usually read on the sofa. **A:** What do you like to read? **B:** The newspaper. I always read it as I drink my morning coffee. How about you? **A:** Actually, I just skim through it every morning.

Option: [+5 minutes] For a different approach, ask students to work in pairs and share their own experiences. Have them take turns discussing their own reading habits; for example, *I love listening to audio books. I always listen to them on the train.*

Game

Suggested teaching time:	12–15 minutes	Your actual teaching time:

- Remind students to use noun clauses. They can start with *I think / believe / I guess* + a noun clause or *I'm sure* + a noun clause; for example, *I think it's the woman. I'm sure it's the woman.*

> **Option: Oral Progress Assessment**
>
> Use the illustrations on page 49. Encourage students to use the language practiced in this unit and previous units.
>
> - Ask the student to tell you about the woman's (or the man's) reading habits and to compare them with his or her own reading habits. (Possible answer: The woman likes to curl up in bed with a book. I like to . . .)
>
> - Tell the student that together you are going to role-play a conversation between the man and the woman. Have the student play the woman and offer to lend the book she is holding; start like this: *What are you reading?*
>
> - Evaluate the student on intelligibility, fluency, correct use of target grammar, and appropriate use of vocabulary.

 • Oral Progress Assessment Charts

Option: *Top Notch* Project
Have students create a literary review journal, a magazine containing reviews of books, magazines, and other reading materials.

Idea: Ask students to work in small groups. Encourage them to include their reviews from the Writing exercise on page 48 and add more reviews. Students can design a cover for their journal including the name of the journal, their names, and some decorative art.

EXTRAS (optional)

- Complete Assessment Package
- Weblinks for Teachers: pearsonlongman.com/topnotch/

And on your ActiveTeach Multimedia Disc:
  Just for Fun
  Top Notch Pop Song Activities
  Top Notch TV Video Program and Activity Worksheets
  Supplementary Pronunciation Lessons
  Audioscripts
  Unit Study Guides

Pair work

1 Create a conversation for the man and woman in which he asks about the book she is reading. She makes a recommendation. He asks if he can borrow the book. Start like this:

Are you reading anything interesting?

2 Use the pictures to create a conversation in which the man and woman discuss their reading habits. For example:

I usually like to curl up in bed with a good book.

Game Close your books. Make an "I" statement about the reading habits of the man or woman.
Your partner guesses if it's the man or the woman.
For example:

A: I like to do the puzzles in the newspaper.
B: I think it's the __.

NOW I CAN...

☐ Recommend a book.
☐ Offer to lend something.
☐ Describe my reading habits.
☐ Discuss the quality of reading materials.

49

Natural Disasters

GOALS After Unit 5, you will be able to:

1 Convey a message.
2 Report news.
3 Describe natural disasters.
4 Prepare for an emergency.

YESTERDAY AS THE APEX OF THE FIGHT AGAINST INFLUENZA WAS ... Fogarty, is shown in an unusual posture. He is sitting down while Mrs. Genevieve Murray is making ... Mrs. E. P. Stimpson and Mrs. Leone Phelps, leaders of Red Cross work, assigning "mothers" to care ... Mrs. Eugene H. Folsom (standing) and her Red Cross girls are caught in the picture to the right, in the midst of a busy day, making masks.

RED CROSS WORKERS SUCCEED IN MEETING HEAVY CALLS FOR AID IN BATTLE ON INFLUENZA

Women of Mother Kind Still Urgently Needed for Service in Stricken Homes; Mask Profiteers Scored;

OPEN AIR AND VACCINE WILL FIGHT DISEASE

300,000 Cases in State Are Feared Unless Patients Kept in Uncovered Hospitals

"Unless more drastic precautionary measures are taken and open-air hospitals generally established, the number of influenza cases in California will increase to 300,000," Dr. George ...

The influenza epidemic of 1918–1919 left an estimated 25 million people dead worldwide.

World Week
US EDITION

SNOWBOUND
Record snowfall paralyzes Washington D.C.

In February 2010, two major blizzards dumped historic levels of snow on the Washington D.C. area, causing travel delays, school closures, and power outages.

WORLD NEWS *Famine in Ethiopia*

In 1984, hungry communities in Ethiopia faced one of the worst food crises in history.

A Discussion Discuss one or more of the following topics about the content of the news.

1 Do you think or worry about epidemics, famines, and weather emergencies? When stories about these events appear in the news, are you interested in reading about them?

2 Why do newspapers often put this information on the front page?

3 What percentage of the news is about disasters and emergencies?

4 Not all disasters are natural disasters (caused by nature). What are some other kinds of disasters? How are they caused?

UNIT 5

Natural Disasters

Preview

Suggested teaching time:	5–10 minutes	Your actual teaching time:

Before Exercise A, give students a few minutes of silent time to look at the news items.

- To help students focus on key information and understand the content of the news, write on the board: *an epidemic / a blizzard / a famine*. Ask students to match the words to each news item using the pictures and the captions to help understand the meaning of the words. (Possible answers: Epidemic—a situation in which many people are sick with the same ailment; blizzard—a severe storm with a lot of snow and wind; famine—a situation in which a large number of people have little or no food for a long time and many people die.) As students read the items, they may need help with the following words: *call for* (Request.); *aid* (Help.); and *paralyzes* (Causes everything to stop.).

- Then write on the board: *What happened? / Where? / When?* Ask three volunteers to summarize the content of one news item using the questions on the board as a guide. (Possible answers: There was a worldwide influenza epidemic in 1918 and 1919. There was a giant blizzard in Washington, D.C., in February 2010. There was a famine in Ethiopia in 1984.)

A Discussion

Suggested teaching time:	10–15 minutes	Your actual teaching time:

- To help students prepare for the discussion, assign the following tasks:
  - For question 1, ask them to write information about any epidemics, famines, or weather emergencies they know about and to say whether they are worried about any of them. Also ask students to write notes about reasons why they are or are not interested in reading news stories about disasters.
  - For question 2, ask students to write one or two reasons. (Possible answers: So more people buy the newspapers. Because people are interested in shocking news. Because bad news attracts people's attention.)
  - For question 3, pass around one or more newspapers, depending on the size of your class, and have students look at them before they decide on a percentage.
  - For question 4, ask students to make a list of disasters that are not caused by nature. (Possible answers: Oil spills, pollution, traffic accidents, plane crashes, forest destruction, wars, terrorist attacks, waste dumping.) Walk around the room and help students with this vocabulary.

- Form small groups and have students use their notes as a guide to discuss the questions. Encourage students to draw conclusions for each question as a group.

- Then have volunteers from several groups share their conclusions with the class.

Language and culture

- *News* is an uncountable noun and needs a singular verb. *The news <u>is</u> often about disasters. Look at <u>this</u> news. The news* refers to a radio or television program that gives reports of recent events. *I saw it on the news. I watched the news last night.*

- The influenza epidemic of 1918 infected approximately one-fifth of the world's population, killing 25 million people. The epidemic broke out at the end of World War I. With the majority of doctors still working with the troops, the Red Cross had to recruit thousands of volunteers to help care for the people with influenza.

- A severe blizzard hit the Mid-Atlantic States in the eastern United States in February 2010. The combination of wet heavy snow and fifty-mile-an-hour winds toppled trees and power lines. Many people from Virginia to Pennsylvania were left with no power. Millions were affected by the storm. A snow emergency was declared in Washington, D.C., and many government offices and schools were closed.

- In 1981 a drought destroyed the harvests in Ethiopia. The local government warned that millions of people would be at risk of starvation, but the rest of the world was slow to get involved because of complicated political reasons. In October 1984, the death toll was estimated at 200,000. Eventually the public did get involved and foreign aid finally reached the people of Ethiopia in 1985.

B 🔊 Photo story

Suggested teaching time:	2–3 minutes	Your actual teaching time:

- To help students prepare for the Photo Story, brainstorm adjectives that describe the facial expressions and emotions of the two people in the photos. Write them on the board. (Possible answers: Worried, shocked, concerned, upset, confused.)

- After students read and listen to the conversation, check comprehension. Ask *Why is Rachel concerned?* (There is a flood in Slovakia.) *What does she know about the flood?* (It's in the middle of the city. Fifty percent of the houses are underwater.) *How will Rachel find out more about the flood?* (She will turn on CNN.)

Option: [+5 minutes] To extend the presentation, have students look back at the text to answer the following questions:

> *What does the word <u>enormous</u> describe?* (The flood in Slovakia.)
> *What could end up being huge?* (The death toll.)
> *What does Rachel say about property damage?* (Fifty percent of the houses in town are underwater.)
> *According to Rachel, what TV channel usually has breaking news?* (CNN.)

Language and culture

LEN From the Longman Corpus

- The three most common words to follow *oh, my* in spoken English are *God, gosh,* and *goodness,* in that order.
- The collocation *breaking news* is used most frequently to describe TV and radio news broadcasts. It is rarely used for other kinds of news.

C Focus on language

Suggested teaching time:	3–5 minutes	Your actual teaching time:

- Have students compare answers with a partner and then review their answers with the class.

- Be sure students understand that items 3 and 4 are referring to expressions formed by two words.

- To reinforce the language, tell students that the words in this exercise are typically used to talk about disasters. Other common words that are used in the conversation are *death toll* (The total number of people who die in an accident, disaster, or war.), *damage* (Physical harm.), and *injury* (Physical harm to a person.). For example:
  > *The death toll reached 10,000.*
  > *There was a lot of damage to buildings. / A lot of buildings were damaged.*
  > *There were some injuries. / Some people were injured.*

D Pair work

Suggested teaching time:	10–12 minutes	Your actual teaching time:

- Have students individually complete the *My news sources* column in the chart.

- Then ask students to work in pairs and take turns asking and answering questions to complete the *My partner's . . .* column. Encourage students to ask each other follow-up questions. For example:
  Student A: *I get most of my news from the Internet.*
  Student B: *Really? Do you like it better than reading a newspaper?*
  Student C: *I like to read a newspaper while I'm eating breakfast. It's relaxing.*
  Student D: *Which newspaper do you read?*

- Point out that in the last row of the chart, students should indicate the person who is the source of the news.

E Discussion

Suggested teaching time:	15 minutes	Your actual teaching time:

- To prepare students for the discussion, write three column heads on the board:
  > *Breaking news   Weather forecasts*
  > *Emergency information*

- As a class, brainstorm sources of information for each of the items on the board, but don't have students give reasons at this time. (Possible answers: Breaking news—TV, radio, Internet; Weather forecasts—TV, radio, Internet, newspaper; Emergency information—TV, radio, Internet, word of mouth.)

- Then have students form groups. Elicit examples of the sources they use or have used. Ask them to discuss the best sources for each situation and provide reasons and explanations.

- To review, take a poll to find out which sources students use for each type of news.

EXTRAS (optional)

- **Workbook:** Exercises 1 and 2

B 🔊 **Photo story** Read and listen to a conversation about a natural disaster.

Rachel: Oh, my goodness. Take a look at this!

Tom: Why? What's going on?

Rachel: There's this enormous flood in Slovakia—look at these people on the roof! The water's up to the second floor. And look at these cars. I sure hope there was no one in them.

Tom: That sounds horrendous. Any word on casualties?

Rachel: It says, "No reports of deaths or injuries so far . . . ." But it's in the middle of a city, for goodness sake. The death toll could end up being huge.

Tom: And can you imagine the property damage?

Rachel: Well, they estimate almost 50% of the houses in town are under water already.

Tom: What a disaster!

Rachel: I wonder how this flood compares to the one they had in New Orleans a few years back. Remember that?

Tom: You bet I do. How could anyone forget? And that flooded almost half the city too.

Rachel: Let's turn on CNN. They usually have breaking news about stuff like this.

C **Focus on language** Complete each statement with words or phrases from the Photo Story.

1 Two words that mean very big are ....enormous........ and ....huge........ .

2 The number of ......casualties...... indicates the number of people who are injured or killed in an event.

3 A two-word phrase that means the destruction of or harm to buildings, cars, and other things that belong to victims of an event is ....property damage.......... .

4 A two-word expression that is used to describe the first news reports of an important event that is happening at the present is ....breaking news.......... .

D **Pair work** Where do you get your news? Complete the chart with the news sources you and your partner use.

	My news sources	My partner's news sources
a newspaper		
a weekly news magazine		
TV newscasts		
radio news reports		
Internet news sites		
word of mouth		

E **Discussion** Which do you think are the best sources for breaking news? For weather forecasts? For emergency information? Explain your reasons. Give examples.

GOAL Convey a message

GRAMMAR *Indirect speech: imperatives*

To report what someone said without quoting the exact words, use indirect speech. Don't use quotation marks when you write indirect speech.

Direct speech: Peter said, "**Be careful if you go out during the storm.**"
Indirect speech: Peter said **to be careful if you go out during the storm.**

An imperative in direct speech becomes an infinitive in indirect speech.

They said, "**Read** the weather report." → They said **to read** the weather report.
She says, "**Don't go out** without a full tank of gas." → She says **not to go out** without a full tank of gas.

Change time expressions and pronouns in indirect speech as necessary.

She told Dan, "Call **me tomorrow**." → She told Dan to call **her the next day**.

> Indirect speech is a kind of noun clause. It is the direct object following a reporting verb such as <u>say</u>, <u>tell</u>, or <u>ask</u>.

GRAMMAR BOOSTER ▸ p. 129

• *Direct speech: punctuation rules*

A Grammar practice On a separate sheet of paper, rewrite each statement in indirect speech, making necessary changes.

1 Martha told me, "Be home before the snowstorm."

> Martha told me to be home before the snowstorm.

2 Everyone is saying, "Get ready for a big storm."
Everyone is saying to get ready for a big storm.
3 The radio says, "Get supplies of food and water in case the roads are closed."
The radio says to get supplies of food and water in case the roads are closed.
4 They told her, "Don't be home too late this afternoon."
They told her not to be home too late this / that afternoon.
5 Maria always tells him, "Don't leave your doors open."
Maria always tells him not to leave his doors open.

B Pair work For each sentence, say what you think the speaker's original words were. Take turns.

1 He told them to call him when it starts raining.

> ❝ Please call me when it starts raining. ❞

2 The police said to leave a window or door open when there's going to be a severe storm.
"Leave a window or door open when there's going to be a severe storm."
3 She told his parents to read the emergency instructions in the newspaper.
"Read the emergency instructions in the newspaper."
4 Ray told Allison to look for the story about him in the paper the next day.
"Look for the story about me in the paper tomorrow."
5 She asked him to pick up some supplies for her on the way home.
"Pick up some supplies for me on the way home."
6 They told me not to wait until the snow gets heavy.
"Don't wait until the snow gets heavy."

CONVERSATION MODEL

A 🔊 3:03 Read and listen to someone conveying a message.

A: I'm on the phone with your parents. Would you like to say hello?

B: I would, but I'm running late.

A: Anything you'd like me to tell them?

B: Yes. Please tell them to turn on the TV. There's a storm on the way.

A: Will do.

B 🔊 3:04 **Rhythm and intonation** Listen again and repeat. Then practice the Conversation Model with a partner.

GRAMMAR

Suggested teaching time:	10–15 minutes	Your actual teaching time:

- Direct attention to the chart and have students read the first explanation and study the examples. To help clarify, write on the board: *Steve said,* "<u>Ask</u> *Carol.*" / *Steve said to ask Carol.* Then say *Direct speech uses the exact words someone says. Indirect speech does not use the exact words.* Point out the quotation marks in direct speech. Clarify that they are placed at the beginning of the quoted information and after the period at the end.

- Have students read the second explanation and study the examples. To help clarify how the affirmative imperative changes in indirect speech, point out *ask* and *to ask* in the examples on the board. To check comprehension, tell students to change the following sentences into indirect speech starting with *The teacher said . . .*

  "*Do the homework.*" (The teacher said to do the homework.)

  "*Come to class on time.*" (The teacher said to come to class on time.)

  "*Have fun learning English!*" (The teacher said to have fun learning English!)

- To help clarify how the negative imperative changes in indirect speech, write on the board: *The guide said,* "<u>Don't touch</u> *it.*" / *The guide said <u>not to touch</u> it.* Point out that the negative imperative—*Don't touch*—becomes a negative infinitive—*not to touch*.

- Have students read the last explanation and study the examples. To help clarify, point out the change from *me* to *her* and from *tomorrow* to *the next day*.

FYI: Indirect speech with *say* and *tell* and tense changes is covered on page 54.

Option: [+3 minutes] To extend the presentation, point out other words that often change when using indirect speech; for example, *here* changes to *there*, and *this* changes to *that*. Write on the board: *Bart said,* "*Leave <u>this</u> book <u>here</u>.*" / *Bart said to leave <u>that</u> book <u>there</u>.*

> **Language and culture**
> - In British English the quotation marks around direct speech could be single quotes '/' or double quotes "/" as in American English.

Option:  **GRAMMAR BOOSTER** (Teaching notes p. T129)

- ActiveTeach Multimedia Disc • Inductive Grammar Charts

A Grammar practice

Suggested teaching time:	5 minutes	Your actual teaching time:

- To model the activity, review the example with the class. Remind students to change time expressions if necessary.

B Pair work

Suggested teaching time:	3 minutes	Your actual teaching time:

- To model the activity, read the speech balloon aloud. Point out the change in the pronoun *him* to *me*. Also point out the use of *please*, as it is a request.

- To review, ask volunteers for their answers.

Option: [+3 minutes] To extend the activity, form groups of three and ask students to talk about instructions or commands their parents give them or used to give them. For example:

Student A: *My mother told me not to be home late.*
Student B: *My mother tells me to be home before 10:00.*
Student C: *When my father lent me his car, he told me not to drive fast.*
Student A: *My father never lends me his car. He tells me to take the bus.*

CONVERSATION MODEL

A ◀)) Read and listen . . .

Suggested teaching time:	2 minutes	Your actual teaching time:

> These conversation strategies are implicit in the model:
> - Use "I would, but . . ." to politely turn down an offer.
> - Say "Will do" to agree to a request for action.

- To introduce the conversation, have students infer what is happening between the two people in the photograph. (Possible answers: The man is about to leave. There's a call for the man.)

- After students read and listen, ask *Why doesn't the man talk to his parents?* (Because he's in a hurry / he's late.) *What advice does he give?* (His parents should watch the news because there's going to be a storm.)

- Point out that there are other ways to say *Will do*, such as *I will, Sure,* or *OK*.

B ◀)) Rhythm and intonation

Suggested teaching time:	2–3 minutes	Your actual teaching time:

- Have students repeat each line chorally. Make sure students:
  ○ use rising intonation for *Would you like to say hello?*
  ○ pause after *would* in *I would, but I'm running late.*
  ○ use rising intonation for *Anything you'd like me to tell them?*
  ○ use falling intonation in *Will do.*

> **Language and culture**
> **LCN** **From the Longman Corpus:** *To be late* is more frequently used than *running late*, but *running late* is more informal.

PRONUNCIATION

A 🔊 Notice the rhythm . . .

Suggested teaching time:	3 minutes	Your actual teaching time:

- First listening: Have students listen and study the examples. Point out that in direct speech, the pause tells listeners they're going to hear the exact words. Point out that there is no pause in indirect speech.

- Second listening: Have students listen and repeat chorally. Make sure students pause before saying the exact words the speaker said and don't pause in sentences using indirect speech.

- Clarify that in written direct speech, a comma indicates the pause. Point out the comma after *said* and *parents* in the examples. Then point out that there is no comma in indirect speech.

B Pair work

Suggested teaching time:	3–5 minutes	Your actual teaching time:

- Have one student in each pair read the direct speech statement aloud and the other student read the corresponding indirect speech statement aloud. Then have pairs change roles.

- Walk around and encourage students to use correct rhythm.

 • Pronunciation Activities

NOW YOU CAN   Convey a message

A Notepadding

Suggested teaching time:	5 minutes	Your actual teaching time:

- Read the *Possible messages* aloud and have students write three more messages they might leave for a friend or relative on the phone. Point out that the messages can be related to the storm that is on the way or to any social situation. Remind students that they should use the affirmative or negative imperative. Point out the first words in the messages on the telephone display: *Watch*, *Turn*, and *Call*.

- To review, ask volunteers to share their messages with the class. You may want to write some of them on the board. For example:

  Come for lunch on Sunday.
  Buy a birthday gift for [Sam].
  Read the emergency instructions in the newspaper.
  Don't go out until the storm is over.

- Read the *Possible excuses* aloud and have students write three more reasons they might give for not being able to speak with someone on the phone.

- To review, ask volunteers to share their excuses with the class. You may want to write some of them on the board. For example:

  I have to be at the office at 10:00.
  If I don't leave now, I'll miss the train.
  I start school earlier today.

B Pair work

Suggested teaching time:	7–12 minutes	Your actual teaching time:

- Remind students that they should use indirect speech. If necessary, students can refer to Exercise A Grammar Practice on page 52 for help.

- Be sure to reinforce the use of the conversation strategies; for example, emphasize that they should sound willing when they say *Will do*. Remind students they can say *Will do*, *I will*, *Sure*, or *OK* to agree to a request for action.

> **Don't stop!** Extend the conversation. Review the ideas in the box. Have students give examples of what they can say for each of the items in the box. For example:
> *What time will you get back home?*
> *Could you do me a favor on your way to work?*
> *Can you call me later?*

- To model the activity, role-play and extend the conversation with a more confident student.

- Then walk around the room and provide help as needed. Encourage students to use the correct rhythm and intonation and to continue their conversations by asking follow-up questions.

 • Conversation Pair Work Cards

C Change partners

Suggested teaching time:	5–7 minutes	Your actual teaching time:

- Assign students new partners and have them create new messages.

- Walk around and provide help as needed. Remind students to use different messages and excuses.

EXTRAS (optional)

- Workbook: Exercises 3–6
- Copy & Go: Activity 17

3:05

A 🔊 Notice the rhythm of sentences in direct and indirect speech. Read and listen. Then listen again and repeat.

1 He said, [pause] "Be home before midnight." → He said to be home before midnight.

2 I told your parents, [pause] "Get a flu shot at the clinic." → I told your parents to get a flu shot at the clinic.

B **Pair work** Take turns reading aloud the sentences in the Grammar Practice on page 52. Read both the original sentences and the sentences you wrote, using correct rhythm for direct and indirect speech.

NOW YOU CAN   Convey a message

A **Notepadding** Read the possible excuses and messages. Then write three more excuses and three more messages.

B **Pair work** Change the Conversation Model. Role-play conveying a message. Use any of the excuses / messages on the telephone display. Then change roles.

    A: I'm on the phone with .... Would you like to say hello?

    B: I would, but ....

    A: Anything you'd like me to tell ....?

    B: Yes. Please tell .... to ....

    A: ....

Don't stop!
Continue the conversation.
Ask your partner:
• what time he or she will be home.
• to do you a favor.
• to call you later.

C **Change partners** Practice the conversation again. Use another message. Use another excuse.

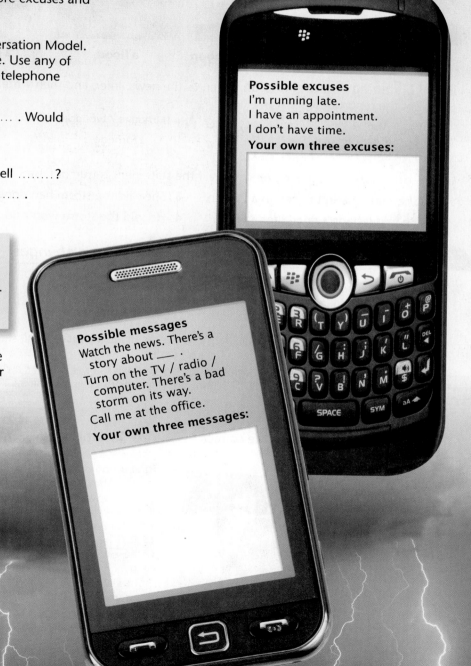

Possible excuses
I'm running late.
I have an appointment.
I don't have time.
Your own three excuses:

Possible messages
Watch the news. There's a story about ___ .
Turn on the TV / radio / computer. There's a bad storm on its way.
Call me at the office.
Your own three messages:

GOAL **Report news**

VOCABULARY *Severe weather and other natural disasters*

A ◀))) Read and listen. Then listen again and repeat.
3:06

a tornado

a hurricane / typhoon

a flood

a landslide

a drought

B ◀))) **Listening comprehension** Listen to the news. Infer, and then write the kind of
3:07
event the report describes.

1 .... a drought ....   3 .... a hurricane / typhoon ....

2 .... a flood ....   4 .... a tornado ....

C ◀))) Listen again. After each report, say if the statement is true or false.
3:08

1 She said it hadn't rained in a month.   3 She said the storm had done a lot of damage.

2 He said it hadn't rained for a week.   4 He said the storm won't do a lot of damage.

GRAMMAR *Indirect speech: say and tell—tense changes*

Use tell when you mention the listener. Use say when you don't.
Maggie **told her parents** to stay home. (listeners mentioned)
Maggie **said** to stay home. (listeners not mentioned)

When say and tell are in the past tense, the verbs in the indirect speech statement often change.
Present becomes past. Past becomes past perfect.
They said, "The weather **is** awful." → They said (that) the weather **was** awful.
Dan said, "We all **had** the flu." → Dan **said** (that) they all **had had** the flu.

GRAMMAR BOOSTER ▸ p. 129
• *Indirect speech: optional tense changes*

A **Grammar practice** Circle the correct
verbs for indirect speech.

My Great Grandmother Meets Hurricane Cleo

Hurricane Cleo struck the United States in August, 1964. My great grandmother, Ana, was traveling in Miami when the hurricane struck. She (1 said /(told)) me that she still remembers how scared everyone was.

She (2 said /(told)) me that the hotel (3 has called /(had called)) her room one morning and had (4 said /(told)) her that a big storm (5 is /(was)) on its way. They (6 (said)/ told) that all hotel guests (7 have to /(had to)) stay in the hotel until the weather service (8 tell /(said)) that it (9 is /(was)) safe to leave.

She stayed in her room and she didn't know what happened until the storm was over. When she turned on the TV, the reports (10 (said)/ told) that a lot of people (11 have been /(had been)) injured and that all the roads (12 are /(were)) flooded. She always (13 (says)/ said) that she still (14 (feels)/ felt) lucky to have survived Hurricane Cleo.

VOCABULARY

A ◀))) Read and listen . . .

Suggested teaching time:	2 minutes	Your actual teaching time:

- Ask students to listen and study the words. Then have students listen and repeat chorally.
- To check comprehension, write on the board:
  1. *strong winds and heavy rain*
  2. *a long period with no rain*
  3. *a lot of water covering an area*
  4. *earth and rocks falling down a mountain*
  5. *strong winds moving quickly in a circle*
- Have students work in pairs. Student A has the book open and says each vocabulary word (not in order). Student B says which definition on the board matches each word. (1. Hurricane or typhoon; 2. drought; 3. flood; 4. landslide; 5. tornado.)

> **Language and culture**
> - Hurricanes, typhoons, and cyclones are all the same severe weather event, but what they are called depends on where they are formed. Hurricanes are formed in the Atlantic and East Pacific Oceans, typhoons are formed in the West Pacific Ocean, and cyclones are formed in the Indian Ocean and the South Pacific.

 • Vocabulary Flash Cards

B ◀))) Listening comprehension

Suggested teaching time:	3–5 minutes	Your actual teaching time:

- To prepare students for the activity, point out that the reports do not use the actual vocabulary words from Exercise A. They describe the weather events instead. Encourage students to listen for the details about each event so they can infer which event is being described.

AUDIOSCRIPT

REPORT 1
F: Brazil farmers report the loss of dairy and beef cattle. There has been no measurable rainfall in three months, and the dry land cannot feed their animals.

REPORT 2
M: The rain hasn't stopped in a week, and people nearest the river are moving out of their houses because the roads are covered in water.

REPORT 3
F: The storm's winds reached a record 150 kilometers per hour, and the torrential rains are expected to continue for at least six more hours. Trees are down, and areas nearest the beaches are heavily damaged.

REPORT 4
M: A fast-moving, dark, funnel-shaped cloud is making its way across the eastern side of town, knocking down trees. Roofs on many houses have blown off. Residents are urged to immediately go underground and take cover until the danger has passed.

C ◀))) Listen to each report . . .

Suggested teaching time:	3–5 minutes	Your actual teaching time:

- To prepare students for the activity, have them read the four statements.
- Pause after each report and have students explain their answers.

GRAMMAR

Suggested teaching time:	10–15 minutes	Your actual teaching time:

- Direct attention to the chart and have students read the first explanation and study the examples. To check comprehension, write on the board:
  1. *She ____ to use her computer.*
  2. *He ____ us to listen to the news.*
  3. *They ____ John to buy the newspaper.*
  4. *Pete ____ to get the best tickets for the game.*
- Ask students to complete the sentences with *said* or *told*. Encourage students to identify a listener. (1. Said; 2. told / us; 3. told / John; 4. said.)
- Have students read the second explanation and study the examples. To help clarify, ask a student *What kind of music do you like?* **S:** *I like [pop music].* Then tell the class *[Carol] said that she <u>liked</u> [pop music].* Ask another student *What did you do last Saturday?* **S:** *I [visited some friends].* Then tell the class *[Amy] said that she <u>had</u> [visited some friends].* Point out that *that* can be omitted. Say *[Amy] said she had [visited some friends].*
- To point out the tense changes (backshifts), write on the board:

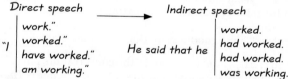

Direct speech → Indirect speech

"I work." / worked." / have worked." / am working." He said that he worked. / had worked. / had worked. / was working.

- Clarify that both the simple past tense and the present perfect change to the past perfect in indirect speech.

Option: **GRAMMAR BOOSTER** (Teaching notes p. T129)

 • Inductive Grammar Charts

A Grammar practice

Suggested teaching time:	4–7 minutes	Your actual teaching time:

- You may want to have students explain why *told* is the correct answer. (Because the listener, *me*, is mentioned.)
- If students need help, encourage them to figure out the exact words the speaker said and then report them.

FYI: In items 3 and 4 the answer choices don't include a past perfect option because that backshift is optional. (The Grammar Booster covers optional tense changes.)

B Grammar practice

Suggested teaching time:	4–6 minutes	Your actual teaching time:	

- To model the activity, review the example with the class. Have students identify the change in tense. (*Is* changes to *was*.)
- Before students complete the exercise, point out that they should change the verb tense in each item for this exercise.

Option: [+2 minutes] Have students complete the Grammar Booster exercises. Then ask them which items don't require a backshift.

Answers for Exercise B

2. He also said (that) it had caused the destruction of half the houses in the town.
3. My sister called and said (that) there was no electricity because of the hurricane.
4. The newspaper said (that) there had been a tornado in the central part of the country.
5. The paper said (that) the drought of 1999 was the worst natural disaster of the twentieth century.
6. After the great snowstorm in 1888, a New York newspaper reported that the blizzard of '88 had caused more damage than any previous storm.

CONVERSATION MODEL

A 🔊 Read and listen . . .

Suggested teaching time:	2 minutes	Your actual teaching time:	

> These conversation strategies are implicit in the model:
> - Use "Well" to begin providing requested information.
> - Say "What a shame" to show empathy for a misfortune.
> - Introduce reassuring contrasting information with "But, . . .".
> - Say "Thank goodness for that" to indicate relief.

- To clarify the expressions in the conversation, tell students that another way to say *What a shame* is *That's too bad*. Point out that *Thank goodness for that* means *I'm glad* or *That's good news*.

FYI: Speakers use the present *says* (rather than *said*) when discussing a publication one is reading.

B 🔊 Rhythm and intonation

Suggested teaching time:	3 minutes	Your actual teaching time:	

- Have students repeat each line chorally. Make sure students:
  - put extra stress on new information, such as, *terrible*, *storm*, and *south* in *Well, there was a terrible storm in the south*.
  - use rising intonation for *Really?*
  - put extra stress on *what* and *shame* in *What a shame*.

NOW YOU CAN   Report news

A Notepadding

Suggested teaching time:	5 minutes	Your actual teaching time:	

- Give students a few minutes of silent time to read the newspaper headlines.
- To help students prepare for the activity, review the events and vocabulary in the headlines by asking:
  What happened in Iran? (There was an earthquake.)
  What does the <u>Dar Post</u> say about a valley? (A river flooded it and people had to leave the area.)
  What is happening in Indonesia? (There is an Avian influenza epidemic and a lot of people died.)
  What does the <u>National News</u> say about a drought? (It caused severe famine and thousands of people died.)
  What happened in Kabul? (There was a dust storm that caused extreme damage to cars and buildings.)
- If necessary, clarify the meaning of *flee* (Escape.), *avian influenza* (An infectious disease of birds that can also infect pigs and humans.), and *elderly* (Old people.).
- Before students report what the headlines say, point out that headlines often use the *simple present* to refer to *past actions*. Students will need to change the verb to the past tense in reported speech; for example, *The <u>Dar Post</u> says that people fled the river valley.*
- You may also want to point out that headlines use the *simple present* to refer to *present actions*. Students won't need to change the verb to the past tense in reported speech if they use a reporting verb in the present; for example, *The <u>Mercury</u> headline says that influenza is causing many deaths.*

B Pair work

Suggested teaching time:	5 minutes	Your actual teaching time:	

- Review the *Be sure to recycle . . .* box to remind students of the language they can use to express their reactions.

> **Don't stop!** Extend the conversation. Review the ideas in the box. Have students give examples of questions they could ask to discuss the headlines. You may want to write some questions on the board. For example:
> *Where did that happen?*
> *How many people died?*
> *Why did so many people die?*

- To model the activity, role-play and extend the conversation with a more confident student.

 ActiveTeach Multimedia Disc
- **Conversation Pair Work Cards**
- **Learning Strategies**

C Change partners

Suggested teaching time:	4–5 minutes	Your actual teaching time:	

- Remind students to use a different headline when they change partners.

Option: [+5 minutes] For a challenge, ask students to extend the conversation by talking about events they remember; for example, recent earthquakes, floods, etc.

EXTRAS (optional)

- **Workbook:** Exercises 7–11
- **Copy & Go:** Activity 18

B Grammar practice Change each statement from direct speech to indirect speech, changing the verb tense in the indirect speech statement.

See page T55 for answers.

1 The TV reporter said, "The landslide is one of the worst in history."

The TV reporter said the landslide was one of the worst in history.

2 He also said, "It caused the destruction of half the houses in the town."

3 My sister called and said, "There is no electricity because of the hurricane."

4 The newspaper said, "There was a tornado in the central part of the country."

5 The paper said, "The drought of 1999 was the worst natural disaster of the twentieth century."

6 After the great snowstorm in 1888, a New York newspaper reported, "The blizzard of '88 caused more damage than any previous storm."

CONVERSATION MODEL

A 🔊 3:09 Read and listen to a conversation about the news.

A: What's going on in the news today?

B: Well, the *Times* says there was a terrible storm in the south.

A: Really?

B: Yes. It says lots of houses were destroyed.

A: What a shame.

B: But there haven't been any deaths.

A: Thank goodness for that.

B 🔊 3:10 **Rhythm and intonation** Listen again and repeat. Then practice the Conversation Model with a partner.

NOW YOU CAN Report news

A Notepadding Read each newspaper headline. Then write what it said on a separate sheet of paper, using indirect speech.

The Morning Herald says there was an earthquake in Iran.

B Pair work Use the newspaper headlines to report what each newspaper says. Then change roles and newspaper headlines.

A: What's going on in the news today?

B: Well, ... says ....

A: Really?

B: Yes. It says ....

A: ....

Don't stop!
Discuss all the facts in the headlines. Express your reactions to the news.

♻ **Be sure to recycle this language.**

Oh, no!
What a disaster.
That's enormous / gigantic / huge / horrendous.

C Change partners Practice the conversation again, using a different headline.

Morning Herald
20,000 killed in earthquake in Iran

DAR POST
People flee flooded river valley

MERCURY
Avian influenza epidemic causes record deaths in Indonesia
Doctors urge children and elderly to receive vaccinations

National News
Drought causes severe famine
Thousands die of hunger

Village Times
Severe dust storm hits Kabul suburbs
Extreme damage to cars, buildings

BEFORE YOU READ

A 🔊 **Vocabulary • Adjectives of severity**   Read and listen. Then listen again and repeat.

B Warm-up Have you or someone you know experienced a natural disaster? What kind of disaster was it? How severe was it? Tell the class about it.

READING 🔊

EARTHQUAKES

Earthquakes are among the deadliest natural disasters, causing the largest numbers of casualties, the highest death tolls, and the greatest destruction. In 1556 in China, the deadliest earthquake in history killed 830,000 people. But many other earthquakes have caused the deaths of more than 100,000 people, and it is not unusual, even in modern times, for an earthquake death toll to reach 20–30,000 people with hundreds of thousands left homeless and with countless injured. The floodwaters of the 2004 tsunami in Sumatra, which killed over 200,000 people, were caused by a catastrophic earthquake.

There are four factors that affect the casualty rate and economic impact of earthquakes: magnitude, location, quality of construction of buildings, and timing.

The 2008 earthquake in Sichuan Province, China, was one of the deadliest earthquakes in recent history.

Magnitude

The magnitude, or strength, of an earthquake is measured on the Richter scale, ranging from 1 to 10, with 10 being the greatest. Earthquakes over 6 on the Richter scale are often deadly, and those over 8 are generally catastrophic, causing terrible damage.

Location

A severe earthquake that is located far from population centers does not cause the same damage as a less severe one that occurs in the middle of a city. As an example, in 1960, the strongest earthquake ever recorded, 9.5 magnitude on the Richter scale, struck in the Pacific Ocean near the Chilean coastline, destroying buildings, killing over 2,000, and injuring another 3,000 in regional cities near the coast. If this quake had struck a city directly, it would have been catastrophic, and hundreds of thousands might have been killed. Similarly, in Alaska, in 1964, a magnitude 9.2 quake hit an area with few people, and the death toll was 117.

Quality of Construction

Modern building construction techniques can lessen the death toll and economic impact of a moderate earthquake that would otherwise cause severe destruction of older-style buildings. In

2010, a terrible earthquake in Port-au-Prince, the capital of Haiti, caused the destruction of a tremendous number of the city's buildings, mostly due to poor construction. In contrast, an even stronger earthquake later that year in Chile caused less destruction because of that country's use of earthquake-resistant construction.

Timing

Finally, the time of occurrence of an earthquake can affect the number of deaths and casualties. Earthquakes that occur in the night, when people are indoors, usually cause a greater death toll than ones that occur when people are outdoors.

Largest Earthquakes in the World Since 1950		
Place	**Year**	**Magnitude**
Off the coast of Chile	1960	9.5
Prince William Sound, Alaska, U.S.	1964	9.2
Off the west coast of northern Sumatra	2004	9.1
Kamchatka, Russia	1952	9.0
Chile	2010	8.8
Rat Islands, Alaska, U.S.	1965	8.7
Northern Sumatra, Indonesia	2005	8.6
Assam—Tibet	1950	8.6
Andreanof Islands, Alaska, U.S.	1957	8.6
Southern Sumatra, Indonesia	2007	8.5

Information source: worldbookonline.com

A Paraphrase Rewrite the following statements in your own words, changing the underlined word or phrase.

1 The <u>magnitude</u> of an earthquake is measured by the Richter scale.   strength

2 There are four <u>factors</u> that affect the destructive value of an earthquake.   parts / things

3 Good construction techniques can <u>lessen</u> the danger to people in buildings affected by an earthquake.   reduce

4 Damage is often <u>due to</u> poor construction.   caused by

5 If an earthquake occurs near a major <u>population center</u>, more people will be affected.   city

BEFORE YOU READ

A ◀))) Vocabulary

Suggested teaching time:	1–2 minutes	Your actual teaching time:

- Have students listen to the adjectives in the box. Then ask them to listen and repeat chorally.

- To help clarify, point out that the adjectives are graded from least damaging to most damaging, and that they are often used to describe types of disasters; for example, *a mild earthquake, a severe storm, a deadly epidemic.*

B Warm-up

Suggested teaching time:	3 minutes	Your actual teaching time:

- To help students organize their ideas, write on the board:
  Type of natural disaster: _____
  Where? When? How serious was it? What happened to buildings / people?

- Ask students to answer these questions with information about a disaster that they or people they know have experienced. Point out that they can also use information about a disaster they have only heard about.

- Form groups of four. Encourage students to use the vocabulary to describe the event.

- To review, have several students describe an event to the class.

READING ◀)))

Suggested teaching time:	10–15 minutes	Your actual teaching time:

- To practice the reading strategy of scanning, write these two topics on the board:
  1. The deadliest earthquakes in history
  2. The factors that determine the consequences of an earthquake

- Have students scan the text to decide which topic best describes what the article is about. Encourage students to support their choices by underlining the four factors in the text (magnitude or strength, location, quality of construction, timing). (Answer: 2.)

- Draw the following chart on the board (without the possible answers) or print it out from the ActiveTeach Multimedia Disc and distribute to students. Have them complete the chart with how the four factors determine the consequences of earthquakes.

	An earthquake will cause more damage if . . .	An earthquake will cause less damage if . . .
Magnitude	it measures low / below 6 (on the Richter scale)	it measures over 6
Location	strikes a city	strikes far from a city / in the ocean
Quality of construction	buildings are old	buildings are modern
Timing	it strikes at night	it strikes during the day

Option: [+10 minutes] To challenge students, have pairs create a series of *True* and *False* statements for another pair to answer using the information in the Reading; for example, *The strongest earthquake ever recorded was 9.5.* (True.) *Earthquakes that occur during the day cause more deaths.* (False.) Walk around the room and help students as needed. Then have pairs exchange their questions with other pairs and answer them.

Language and culture
- The Richter scale measures the intensity of earthquakes from 1 to 10. 1 = very weak, 10 = the strongest.

 ActiveTeach Multimedia Disc
- **Extra Reading Comprehension Questions**
- **Learning Strategies**
- **Graphic Organizers**

A Paraphrase

Suggested teaching time:	4–5 minutes	Your actual teaching time:

- To help students figure out the meaning of the underlined words, encourage them to find the paragraph in the Reading that includes the information in each statement.

- Then have students compare answers with a partner and review with the class.

B Confirm facts

Suggested teaching time:	2 minutes	Your actual teaching time:

- To model the activity, review the text in the speech balloon pointing out that it uses indirect speech.
- Have students look at the text and take notes for each question. Make sure they use indirect speech.

Option: [+5 minutes] For a challenge, have students play a memory game in small groups. Ask each student to write two questions starting with *What does the article say about . . .?* Then have students take turns asking and answering the questions. Remind them to use indirect speech.

Answers for Exercise B

2. The article said (that) the highest Richter scale reading was recorded near the Chilean coastline.
3. The article said (that) if an earthquake strikes far from population centers it causes less damage.
4. The article said (that) modern building construction techniques can lessen the destruction and economic impact.

C Identify cause and effect

Suggested teaching time:	2–3 minutes	Your actual teaching time:

- Form groups of four. Encourage students to support their views with examples from the article.
- Ask several students for their answers and opinions and write them on the board.

NOW YOU CAN Describe natural disasters

A Pair work

Suggested teaching time:	3–5 minutes	Your actual teaching time:

- Ask pairs to decide who is reading which fact sheet. Point out that the information is not factual. Give students a few minutes to read their fact sheets.
- To model the activity, review the speech balloon with the class.
- Encourage students to ask follow-up questions.

B Notepadding

Suggested teaching time:	10–15 minutes	Your actual teaching time:

- Review *Some historic disasters* in the box with the class. To draw on students' prior knowledge, ask them if they know about any of these disasters.
- Point out that students can also choose another disaster, one that they are familiar with.
- As students write details about the disaster they chose, encourage them to use the fact sheets in Exercise A as a model. Direct their attention to the *Be sure to recycle . . .* box in Exercise C, and ask them to include some of the vocabulary from this box.

Language and culture

- On April 18, 1906, an earthquake measuring 7.9 on the Richter scale struck San Francisco, California, in the United States. More than 3,000 people died, and there was a lot of damage to buildings and roads. More than half the population of 400,000 was left homeless. A three-day fire followed and caused more damage than the earthquake.
- An earthquake struck the city of Bam, Iran at dawn on December 26, 2003. Over 26,000 people died, and tens of thousands of people were injured and left homeless. Tents were set up on the outskirts of the city to provide water, food, and shelter for survivors. Bam is a historic city, with many buildings made of mud brick. This is the main reason why the earthquake caused so much property damage—it destroyed 70% of the city's buildings.
- An undersea earthquake in the Indian Ocean on December 26, 2004 generated a tsunami. The result was one of the deadliest disasters in modern history. Scientists now believe the earthquake registered 9.3 on the Richter scale. The death toll reached 300,000 people. Southeast Asia and nine other countries were the most directly impacted, but countries around the world were also affected because many holiday travelers were in the region.
- On August 29, 2005, Hurricane Katrina hit the south coast of New Orleans, Louisiana, in the United States, with winds of approximately 200 kilometers per hour. Much of New Orleans is below sea level, and the city is protected from flooding by a system of canals and levees (special walls to stop rivers from flooding). The hurricane caused breaches, or large gaps in the levees, and by August 30, 80% of New Orleans was underwater.
- A catastrophic 7.0 magnitude earthquake hit the south of Port-au-Prince, the capital of Haiti, on January 13, 2010. Over a million people were left homeless, 300,000 were injured, and the death toll reached 230,000. Important factors that contributed to the devastation caused by the earthquake were its magnitude, its location, and the quality of building construction.

C Group work

Suggested teaching time:	10 minutes	Your actual teaching time:

- To form groups, have students who have researched the same disaster work together and compare information.

Text-mining: Have students share their Text-mining examples and use them to create new statements with a partner.

- Then ask groups to write a script for their broadcasts or presentations. Suggest they include language from the *Be sure to recycle . . .* box and vocabulary they have learned in this unit.
- Ask groups to present their broadcasts or presentations to the class.

EXTRAS (optional)

- Workbook: Exercises 12–16
- Copy & Go: Activity 19

B Confirm facts Answer the questions, according to the information in the article. Use indirect speech. See page T57 for answers.

1 Where did the deadliest earthquake in history take place?
2 Which earthquake had the highest recorded Richter scale reading?
3 How can location affect the death toll of an earthquake?
4 What else can lessen the destruction and economic impact of an earthquake?

> " The article said the earthquake in 1556 was the deadliest in history. "

On your *ActiveBook* Self-Study Disc:
Extra Reading Comprehension Questions

C Identify cause and effect Discuss how magnitude and timing affect the casualty rate and economic impact of earthquakes. Explain your ideas by putting together information from the article.

NOW YOU CAN Describe natural disasters

A Pair work Partner A, read the fact sheet about the Jamaica hurricane. Partner B, read the fact sheet about the Philippines earthquake. In your own words, tell your partner about the disaster.

> " A hurricane hit Jamaica on September 20. There was a lot of property damage . . . . "

JAMAICA HURRICANE

Date:	September 20
Place:	Port Royal, Jamaica
Event:	hurricane

Property damage: many houses damaged by wind, flooding, and landslides

Casualties: hundreds homeless and missing

PHILIPPINES EARTHQUAKE

Date:	September 14
Place:	Manila, Philippines
Event:	earthquake, magnitude 6.7

Property damage: moderate in newer buildings, severe in older ones

Casualties: 200 deaths, many injuries, some severe and life-threatening

B Notepadding Choose one of the historic disasters from the list. Find information about it on the Internet, at a library, or in a bookstore. (Or choose a disaster you are already familiar with.) Write details about the disaster on your notepad.

Some historic disasters
• The San Francisco earthquake of 1906 (U.S.)
• The Bam earthquake of 2003 (Iran)
• The tsunami of 2004 (Indian Ocean)
• Hurricane Katrina 2005 (New Orleans, U.S.)
• The earthquake of 2010 (Haiti)
• A natural disaster of your choice: _____

Date:	
Place:	
Event:	
Property damage:	
Casualties:	

C Group work Make a news broadcast or presentation about the disaster you researched (or one of the disasters in A). Describe the natural disaster to your class.

♻ **Be sure to recycle this language.**

Type of disaster	Adjectives	Features
flood	mild	casualties
storm	moderate	injuries
landslide	severe	property damage
earthquake	deadly	death toll
flood	catastrophic	
famine		
epidemic		

Text-mining (optional)
Underline language in the Reading on page 56 to use in the Group Work.
For example:
" — was due to . . . "

GOAL | Prepare for an emergency

BEFORE YOU LISTEN

A 🔊 **3:13** **Vocabulary** • *Emergency preparations and supplies* Read and listen. Then listen again and repeat.

evacuate to remove all people from an area that is too dangerous

an emergency a very dangerous situation that requires immediate action

a power outage an interruption in the flow of electrical power over a large area

a shelter a safe place where people may go when the area they live in has been evacuated

a first-aid kit a small box or package containing supplies to treat minor injuries and illnesses

a flashlight a portable, battery-operated light

non-perishable food food that doesn't need refrigeration, such as canned and dried food

> A battery-operated flashlight is a must when there is a power outage.

> Be sure to have a first-aid kit with scissors and bandages.

B Pair work With a partner, write sentences using the Vocabulary words and phrases.

> *They tried to evacuate the entire population of the city before the flood, but lots of people refused to go.*

LISTENING COMPREHENSION

A 🔊 **3:14** **Listen for main ideas** Listen to an emergency radio broadcast. Write a sentence to describe the emergency the broadcaster is reporting.

Answers will vary, but may include the following:

A tropical storm with high winds and heavy rain is coming tomorrow morning and flooding is expected.

B 🔊 **3:15** **Listen for details** Listen again and correct each of the following false statements, using indirect speech.

Example: He said you should stand near windows during the storm.

> 🔊 No. He said _not_ to stand near windows during the storm. 🔊

1 He said you should turn your refrigerator and freezer off.
No. He said you should turn your refrigerator and freezer very cold.

2 He said that in case of a flood, you should put valuable papers on the lowest floor of your home.
No. He said that in case of a flood, you should put valuable papers on the highest floor of your home.

3 He said you should read the newspapers for the location of shelters.
No. He said you should listen to the radio for the location of the shelters.

BEFORE YOU LISTEN

A  Vocabulary

Suggested teaching time:	2–3 minutes	Your actual teaching time:

- Have students listen and study the words and the definitions. Then have students listen and repeat chorally.
- Direct students' attention to the photographs. Read the captions aloud. Write on the board:
  1. a portable light
  2. a small box with supplies to treat injuries
  3. a safe building
  4. a time with no electricity
  5. a dangerous situation
  6. foods that need no refrigeration
  7. to leave a dangerous place
- Have students close their books. Ask them to listen again and to provide a word or phrase for each definition.
- Ask students to compare answers with a partner. Then check their answers. (1. a flashlight; 2. a first-aid kit; 3. a shelter; 4. a power outage; 5. an emergency; 6. non-perishable food; 7. evacuate.)

Language and culture

- In British English a *flashlight* is called a *torch*. In American English a *torch* is a stick with fire at the end that also produces light.

ActiveTeach Multimedia Disc • Vocabulary Flash Cards

B Pair work

Suggested teaching time:	5 minutes	Your actual teaching time:

- To model the activity, review the example with the class.
- To help students generate ideas, encourage them to write about their own experiences or events they may be familiar with; for example, *I always keep my flashlight near me in case of an emergency. I remember a few years ago there was a power outage in [New York City].*

LISTENING COMPREHENSION

A  Listen for main ideas

Suggested teaching time:	3–5 minutes	Your actual teaching time:

- To help students prepare for the activity, draw the following diagram on the board:

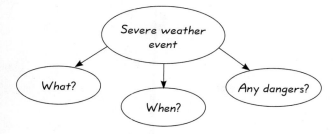

- Direct students' attention to the diagram and tell them to listen for the type of severe weather event the broadcaster is talking about, when it is expected, and what the dangers are.
- After students listen, have three students answer a question from the diagram. (Possible answers: *What?*—A tropical storm [Maria] with high winds and heavy rain. *When?*—October 12 between 9 and 11 A.M. *Any dangers?*—Floods.)
- Have students write their sentences using the diagram as a guide.

AUDIOSCRIPT

[M = U.S. regional]

M: Today is Monday, October 11. This is a Government Weather Service update on Tropical Storm Maria, which is approaching our area. The storm is expected to arrive between 9 and 11 A.M. tomorrow. This is an extremely dangerous storm with high winds and heavy rain. Flooding is expected, and evacuation may be necessary. The following are emergency procedures that all area residents should follow:

1. Fill your car with gas now, in case evacuation is necessary.
2. Bring outdoor furniture, tools, and other objects inside. They can be dangerous in high winds.
3. Close all windows and cover windows with wooden boards. When the storm hits, don't go near windows in case the wind causes the glass to break.
4. Turn your refrigerator and freezer to very cold and only open when necessary to preserve perishable food in the event of a power outage.
5. Buy extra batteries for flashlights in case there is a power outage or an evacuation.
6. If you don't have a portable battery-operated radio, buy one today, and have a good supply of extra batteries for the radio. Listen to the radio for official instructions in case evacuation is necessary.
7. Check your first-aid kit. Be sure it contains bandages, painkillers, and antiseptic in case of minor injuries.
8. Put valuable papers in a waterproof container on the highest floor of your home in case of flooding.
9. Get a supply of non-perishable food and water. You may have to stay indoors for several days, and local water supplies may be contaminated by flooding.

If evacuation becomes necessary:

1. Leave as soon as possible. Avoid flooded roads. Follow radio instructions for the best and safest evacuation route.
2. Listen to the radio for the location of shelters serving your neighborhood.
3. Take all emergency supplies and warm clothing and blankets to the shelter.
4. Lock your home and leave.

B  Listen for details

Suggested teaching time:	5–7 minutes	Your actual teaching time:

- To prepare students for the activity, first have them read the statements.
- To model the activity, play the recording and stop after the correct answer to the example sentence; review the text in the speech balloon.
- Have students listen to the rest of the program and make corrections as they listen.
- To review, read the statements aloud and have students correct them, using indirect speech.

C Paraphrase

Suggested teaching time:	10 minutes	Your actual teaching time:

- Have students read the questions. Form pairs and encourage students to complete the statements with the information they remember from the emergency broadcast.
- Have students listen again and complete any unfinished items.
- Review with the class. You may want students to listen again to review the corrected statements.

Option: [+5 minutes] For a different approach, have students choose two emergency procedures described by the announcer that they consider important. Form groups and have students discuss the procedures they have chosen and explain why.

 • Learning Strategies

NOW YOU CAN Prepare for an emergency

A Group work

Suggested teaching time:	10–15 minutes	Your actual teaching time:

- To prepare students for the activity, review *Kinds of emergencies* in the box. You may want to tell students that they can also choose to prepare for an emergency that is not on the list.
- Point out the example on the notepad. Ask students what kind of emergency the plan on the notepad could be for. (Possible answer: Flood, because water can become contaminated.)
- To help students generate ideas, brainstorm plans they will make. Write a list on the board. For example:

   Plans can be about:
   getting supplies
   deciding where to take shelter
   warning relatives or friends
   protecting one's property
   evacuating—where to go and what to take
   getting official information
   taking care of pets

- If necessary, brainstorm and write on the board a list of supplies; for example, *non-perishable food, a flashlight, a first-aid kit, wooden boards, warm clothing, blankets, a battery-operated radio, matches, gas.*
- Encourage students to write about at least four plans and indicate whether each plan is for a long-term or short-term emergency.
- As students write their plans, walk around the room and provide help as needed.

B Present your plans . . .

Suggested teaching time:	10–15 minutes	Your actual teaching time:

- Review the speech balloon with the class. You may wish to point out the indirect speech.
- As the groups present their plans, ask the class to take notes. The notes will help the class compare the plans. You may want to draw the following chart on the board or print one for each student from the ActiveTeach Multimedia Disc to help students organize their notes.

Group number	Type of emergency	Plans	Reasons
1			
2			
3			
4			
5			

- To compare the plans, encourage students to find at least one difference and one similarity between their plans and those of another group. Have volunteers share the differences and similarities with the class.

 • Graphic Organizers

EXTRAS (optional)

- Workbook: Exercises 17–21
- Copy & Go: Activity 20

C Paraphrase What did the radio announcer say in the emergency radio broadcast? With a partner, discuss the questions and complete each statement in indirect speech. Listen again if necessary.

1 What should you do to get your car ready for an evacuation?
He said to .....fill your car with gas now..

2 What should you do with outdoor furniture?
He said to .....bring it inside...

3 What should you buy for flashlights and portable radios?
He said to .....buy extra batteries...

4 What should you listen to in case of an evacuation?
He said to .....listen to the radio..

5 How should you prepare to have food and water in case you have to stay indoors for several days?
He said to .....get a supply of non-perishable food and water...

NOW YOU CAN | Prepare for an emergency

A Group work Choose an emergency from the list. Write plans for your emergency on the notepad. Provide a reason for each plan.

Plans	Reasons
Have 2 liters of water per person per day.	to have enough water in case the water is unsafe to drink

Type of emergency:

Plans	Reasons

Kinds of emergencies
• a flood
• a tornado
• a severe storm (blizzard, hurricane, typhoon)
• an epidemic
• a famine
• a drought
• a landslide
• an earthquake

batteries

matches

bottled water

B Present your plans to the class. Compare your plans.

" Our group prepared for a storm. We said to be sure cell phones were working. A power outage might occur. "

Review

A 3:16 🔊 **Listening comprehension** Listen to the report. The reporter describes three kinds of disasters. Listen carefully and check the ones that fall into the categories she describes. Listen again if necessary.

		Disaster	Place	Year	Killed
✓	1	epidemic	worldwide	1917	20,000,000
☐	2	famine	Soviet Union	1932	5,000,000
✓	3	flood	China	1931	3,700,000
✓	4	drought	China	1928	3,000,000
✓	5	epidemic	worldwide	1914	3,000,000
✓	6	epidemic	Soviet Union	1917	2,500,000
✓	7	flood	China	1959	2,000,000
✓	8	epidemic	India	1920	2,000,000
☐	9	famine	Bangladesh	1943	1,900,000
✓	10	epidemic	China	1909	1,500,000

The title above the table: **The 10 most deadly natural disasters of the 20th century**

Source: CRED (Center for Research on the Epidemiology of Disasters)

3:17/3:18
🎵 **Top Notch Pop**
"Lucky to Be Alive"
Lyrics p. 149

B Complete each statement with the name of the disaster or emergency.

1 In ......**a landslide**......, mud and soil cover the houses and can bury entire towns.

2 A widespread event in which many people become sick with the same illness is ......**an epidemic**...... .

3 A ......**flood**...... occurs when water from a river enters houses and roads.

4 A storm with high winds and rain is ......**a hurricane / typhoon**...... .

5 When there is no rain for a long period of time, ...**a drought**...... is said to occur.

6 In ......**a famine**......, there is not enough food and many people go hungry.

C Complete each indirect statement or question with <u>said</u> or <u>told</u>.

1 They ......**told**...... me to call the office in the morning.

2 The students ......**said**...... the test had been very difficult.

3 He ......**said**...... the storm was awful.

4 Who ......**told**...... us to get extra batteries?

D On a separate sheet of paper, rewrite the following indirect speech statements in direct speech.
See page T60 for answers.

1 She said they knew the reason there was so much property damage.

2 The radio announcer told the people to fill up their cars with gas before the storm.

3 I said not to tell the children about the storm.

4 He asked if the epidemic had been severe.

E On a separate sheet of paper, rewrite the following direct speech statements in indirect speech.
See page T60 for answers.

1 Robert told Marie, "Don't wait for the evacuation order."

2 Sylvia said, "I think the earthquake occurred during the night."

3 The emergency broadcast said, "Buy bottled water before the hurricane."

4 They told Marlene, "Call us the next day."

F **Writing** On a separate sheet of paper, write about how to prepare for an emergency. Choose an emergency and include information on what to do, what supplies to have, and what preparations to make.

WRITING BOOSTER ▸ p. 144

- *Organizing detail statements by order of importance*
- *Guidance for Exercise F*

Review

A 🔊 Listening comprehension

Suggested teaching time:	5–10 minutes	Your actual teaching time:

- To prepare students for listening, have them look at the chart. Ask *Which was the most deadly disaster of the twentieth century?* (The 1917 worldwide epidemic.) *What types of natural disasters does the chart include?* (Epidemics, famines, floods, and droughts.) *Which seems to be the most deadly type of disaster?* (Epidemics.)

- Before students do the activity, tell them they will listen to a general report, but that specific disasters are not mentioned. Ask them to listen for the vocabulary that identifies each type of disaster.

- First listening: Have students listen to the report and check the disasters they heard about. Ask students to take notes of key words that support their choices; for example, *lack of rainfall, too much water, sickness.*

- Second listening: Have students compare answers with a partner and listen again to confirm them.

- To review with the class, have students name the disasters they checked and explain their reasons.

AUDIOSCRIPT

[F = British English]
F: Good morning, listeners. Today we'll be discussing some of the worst natural disasters of the last century. It's hard to imagine events with death tolls over a million, but believe it or not, they're surprisingly common. Once, in the last century, a lack of rainfall killed over a million people. And twice, too much water has done the same thing. But the worst disasters by far are episodes of sickness that affect millions. Five were situations where over a million people died.

B Complete each statement . . .

Suggested teaching time:	2 minutes	Your actual teaching time:

- To model the activity, complete the first item with the class.

- Have students compare answers with a partner and then review with the class.

Option: [+5 minutes] To extend the activity, have pairs take turns making a statement that describes a disaster and guessing the type of disaster; for example, **Student A:** *It is very dry, and there has been no rain for a long time.* **Student B:** *A drought.* Have students continue until each one guesses three disasters. (Students learned the names of nine types of disasters in this unit: blizzard, tornado, hurricane, typhoon, flood, landslide, drought, earthquake, and epidemic.)

C Complete each indirect statement . . .

Suggested teaching time:	2 minutes	Your actual teaching time:

- Have students work individually and then compare answers with a partner. If necessary, remind students that we use a form of *tell* when we mention the listener and a form of *say* when we don't.

D On a separate sheet of paper . . .

Suggested teaching time:	3 minutes	Your actual teaching time:

- Explain that the verb tense changes (*knew* changes to *know*) and the pronoun changes (*she* changes to *I*) in a direct statement.

- Call on students to share their answers with the class.

Answers for Exercise D
1. "I know the reason there is so much property damage."
2. "Fill your cars with gas before the storm."
3. "Don't tell the children about the storm."
4. "Has the epidemic been severe?"

E On a separate sheet of paper . . .

Suggested teaching time:	3 minutes	Your actual teaching time:

- Point out that the imperative in direct speech (*Don't wait*) becomes an infinitive (*not to wait*) in indirect speech. If necessary, remind students that a backshift in tense can be necessary when reporting statements.

- Have several students read their sentences aloud.

Answers for Exercise E
1. Robert told Marie not to wait for the evacuation order.
2. Sylvia said she thought the earthquake had occurred during the night.
3. The emergency broadcast said to buy bottled water before the hurricane.
4. They told Marlene to call them the next day.

F Writing

Suggested teaching time:	10 minutes	Your actual teaching time:

- Brainstorm different types of emergencies students might experience in their area or city. Have students choose one to write about. If students need to review information or vocabulary about preparing for emergencies, have them look at Lesson 4.

- Ask students to write notes about:
    what to do
    what supplies to have
    what preparations to make

- Review ideas about how to organize their writing with the class; for example, you may want to encourage them to write a separate paragraph about each of the topics they made notes about.

- As students write, walk around the room and provide help as needed:

Option: **WRITING BOOSTER** (Teaching notes p. T144)

 • Writing Process Worksheets

ORAL REVIEW

Give students a few minutes of silent time to explore the pictures and become familiar with them.

Tell a story

Suggested teaching time:	10 minutes	Your actual teaching time:

- Suggest that students give each man a name to make discussing the action easier.
- Model the activity by reading the example aloud.
- To help students become familiar with the story, ask:
  What could the relationship between the two men be? (Father and son, grandfather and grandson, uncle and nephew, friends, neighbors.)
  What kind of disaster is expected? (A tropical storm.)
  What are possible consequences of the storm? (Flooding in coastal areas.)
  What supplies will the older man take to the shelter? (Possible answers: Non-perishable food, bottled water, a flashlight, a blanket, a first-aid kit.)
- To help students prepare their stories, write the following questions on the board:
  What are the people's names?
  What's the relationship between them?
  Why did the younger man call the older man?
  What did the older man do on Wednesday?
  How severe was the storm?
  What happened after the storm?
- Have students write notes for each question. Encourage them to use the language they learned. Ask students to invent an ending for their stories to answer the last question, *What happened after the storm?*
- Form groups of three and have students take turns telling their stories.

Pair work 1

Suggested teaching time:	5–10 minutes	Your actual teaching time:

- To model the activity, read the example aloud pointing out the indirect speech.
- Remind students to use indirect speech and make necessary changes to the words the announcer said.

Option: [+5 minutes] To challenge students, have pairs write four additional pieces of information the announcer could have given. Have them write the announcer's exact words. For example:
"Avoid flooded roads."
"Listen to the radio for instructions about what to do."
"Don't forget to cover windows with wooden boards."
"The storm is expected to hit the coast at 5:00."
Have pairs join other pairs and use indirect speech to report what the announcer said.

Pair work 2

Suggested teaching time:	5–10 minutes	Your actual teaching time:

- To model the activity, read the example aloud.

- Ask students to use the language they learned in this unit to create the conversation. Encourage them to invent information to keep the conversation going.

Possible responses . . .

A: Hello, [Dad]. Did you hear the weather report? **B:** No. What's up? **A:** A tropical storm is on its way. **B:** Really? **A:** Yes. Floods are expected in coastal areas. **B:** Did they say to prepare for an emergency? **A:** Yes. They said to get your car ready for evacuation.

A: Hi, [Dad]. There's going to be a bad storm. **B:** Really? **A:** Yes. The report said winds will be strong. It also said to buy extra food and water. **B:** I'll go to the store right away. **A:** And don't forget to check your first-aid kit. **B:** I will.

Option: [+10 minutes] To extend the activity, ask pairs to write a paragraph that describes the consequences of the storm. Encourage students to include the vocabulary about natural disasters that they learned in Lesson 3.

Option: Oral Progress Assessment

Use the illustrations on page 61. Encourage students to use the language practiced in this unit and previous units.

- Tell the student to answer your questions using indirect speech. Point out that he or she can invent the information. Start like this: **T:** *What did the report say about the weather?* **S:** *It said there was going to be a tropical storm. / It said a tropical storm was expected.*
- Point to the top picture (the two men speaking on the phone) and tell the student that together you are going to role-play a conversation. Ask him or her to use reported speech. Have the student take the role of the younger man. Start the conversation: *What's going on in the news today?*
- Evaluate the student on intelligibility, fluency, correct use of target grammar, and appropriate use of vocabulary.

 • Oral Progress Assessment Charts

Option: *Top Notch* Project
Have students make a presentation about a severe weather event or a disaster.

Idea: Encourage students to research information about a recent weather event or disaster *not* caused by nature. Ask them to use the Internet, newspapers, and magazines. Have students take notes, write about the event or disaster, and then present the information to the class.

EXTRAS (optional)

- **Complete Assessment Package**
- **Weblinks for Teachers:** pearsonlongman.com/topnotch/

And on your ActiveTeach Multimedia Disc:
  Just for Fun
  Top Notch Pop Song Activities
  Top Notch TV Video Program and Activity Worksheets
  Supplementary Pronunciation Lessons
  Audioscripts
  Unit Study Guides

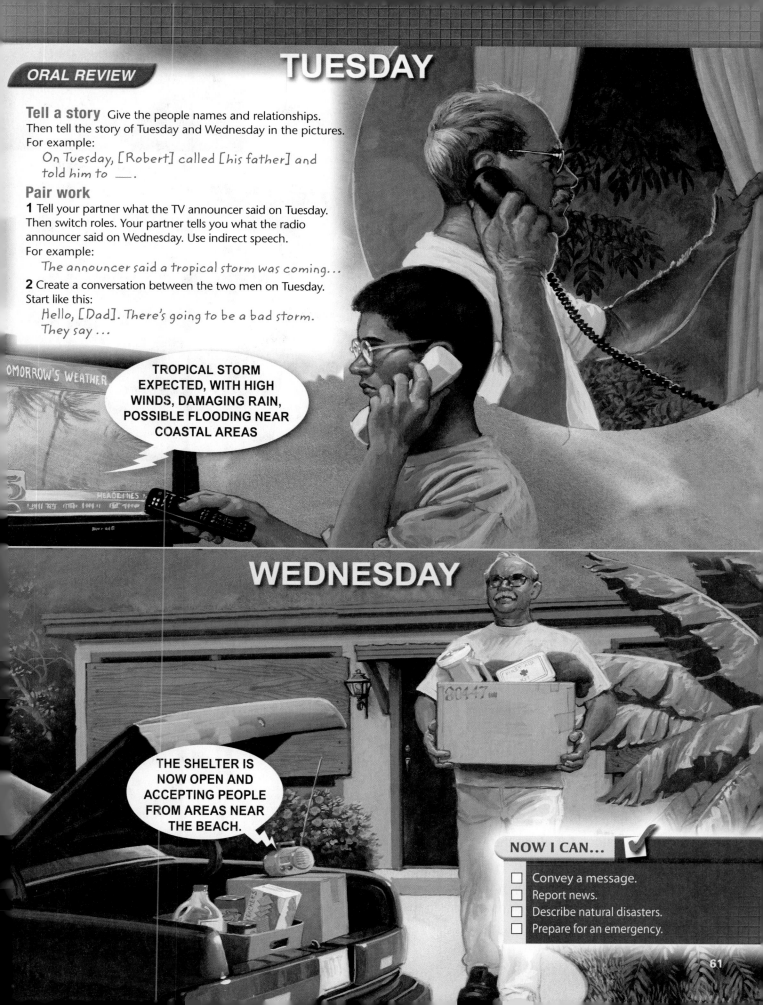

TUESDAY

Tell a story Give the people names and relationships. Then tell the story of Tuesday and Wednesday in the pictures. For example:

On Tuesday, [Robert] called [his father] and told him to ___.

Pair work

1 Tell your partner what the TV announcer said on Tuesday. Then switch roles. Your partner tells you what the radio announcer said on Wednesday. Use indirect speech. For example:

The announcer said a tropical storm was coming…

2 Create a conversation between the two men on Tuesday. Start like this:

Hello, [Dad]. There's going to be a bad storm. They say …

WEDNESDAY

NOW I CAN…

☐ Convey a message.
☐ Report news.
☐ Describe natural disasters.
☐ Prepare for an emergency.

Life Plans

GOALS After Unit 6, you will be able to:

1 Explain a change in life and work plans.
2 Express regrets about past actions.
3 Discuss skills, abilities, and qualifications.
4 Discuss factors that promote success.

What's the best career for you?

Take this preference inventory to see which fields are the best match for you. Check all the activities you like to do.

- ☐ work on experiments in a science laboratory
- ☐ write songs
- ☐ manage a department of a large business corporation
- ☐ repair furniture
- ☐ be a doctor and care for sick people
- ☐ design the stage scenery for a play
- ☐ teach adults how to read
- ☐ study a company's sales
- ☐ restore antique cars
- ☐ teach science to young people
- ☐ take a creative writing class
- ☐ read to blind people
- ☐ manage a company's sales representatives
- ☐ make clothes to sell
- ☐ interpret X-rays and other medical tests
- ☐ make paintings and sculptures
- ☐ help couples with marriage problems
- ☐ start my own business
- ☐ build houses

Write the number of check marks you have by each color.

Field: ☐ **BUSINESS**   ☐ **SCIENCE**   ☐ **CRAFTS**
        ☐ **SOCIAL WORK**   ☐ **ARTS**

A Discussion Talk about the following questions.

- Which field or fields did you have the most check marks in?
- Were you surprised by your results? Explain.
- What are some jobs or professions in that field?

UNIT 6

Life Plans

Preview

Suggested teaching time:	10 minutes	Your actual teaching time:

Before Exercise A, give students a few minutes of silent time to look at the preference inventory.

- Help students become interested in the topic. Ask *What is this inventory about?* (People's interests.) *How do you think it could be useful?* (It could help people choose a suitable occupation.) *What jobs or occupations do the pictures represent?* Elicit the jobs or occupations, not the objects that represent them. (Possible answers: Musician or composer, carpenter or builder, scientist or doctor, painter or artist, fashion designer.)

- Ask students if they have ever taken an inventory like this one before. Have volunteers tell the class about their experiences. Encourage students to describe the inventory and tell whether it was useful or not.

- Have students check the activities they are interested in, count up the check marks according to color, and write the totals at the bottom.

A Discussion

Suggested teaching time:	13–15 minutes	Your actual teaching time:

- Before students work together in groups, give them a few minutes to read the questions and write notes as they prepare their answers.

- As students discuss the questions, encourage them to give reasons for their choices and to ask each other follow-up questions. For example:
  Student A: *I really want to be a doctor.*
  Student B: *A doctor? Why?*
  Student A: *I like learning about the body and how it works.*
  Student C: *But are you interested in working with people?*
  Student A: *Yes. I especially want to work with children.*

- Take a poll to see which fields students have more jobs in or which fields students are most interested in.

- Have several volunteers tell the class why they were or weren't surprised by their results. Ask students if their present jobs match the results of their inventories. If your students have not yet entered the workforce, ask them to talk about someone they know or what kind of job or career they are thinking about in the future.

- To review the jobs and professions, draw the following chart on the board (without the possible responses). Have students say the jobs in each field and write them on the board.

Business	Science	Crafts
manager	scientist	woodworker
sales analyst	researcher	builder
accountant	doctor	carpenter
sales director	technician	architect
stockbroker	biologist	jewelry designer

Social Work	Arts	
social worker	musician	
therapist	painter	
marriage counselor	sculptor	
	fashion designer	
	graphic designer	

Option: [+5 minutes] To extend the activity, form small groups and have students take turns talking about the jobs and occupations of family members and friends; for example, *Are most of them happy in their jobs? Are they doing what they dreamed about when they were young?*

Language and culture

- Crafts include furniture, clothing, jewelry making, etc.
- Career inventories can help people get a better understanding of what their job or career options are. These inventories and assessments are designed to measure someone's interests or skills, indicate personality preferences, and identify work-related and life values. Career guidance companies and some schools use these tools with the goal of helping people make successful career choices.

B 🔊》 Photo story

Suggested teaching time:	7–10 minutes	Your actual teaching time:

- As a warm-up, have students cover the text and look at the pictures. Ask them to make predictions for the following questions: *Where are the women?* (Possible answers: In a doctor's office, in a hospital.) *Who are the two women?* (Possible answer: They could be friends or relatives.)

- To check comprehension after reading and listening, write on the board:

  1. What is the reason for Charlotte's visit?
  2. What does Dr. Miller suggest? Why?

- Have students discuss the questions in pairs and listen again to the Photo Story if necessary.

- To review, ask volunteers for their answers. (1. Charlotte needs some advice. She's interested in the health field, but wants to study something that doesn't take very long. 2. Dr. Miller suggests that she become a physical therapist because she can help people and there are always jobs available.)

C Focus on language

Suggested teaching time:	5–8 minutes	Your actual teaching time:

- Encourage students to identify who says the phrases and to use the context of the conversation to help figure out the meaning.

- Then have students compare answers with a partner and review with the class.

D Discussion

Suggested teaching time:	10–17 minutes	Your actual teaching time:

- To prepare students for the activity, review the list of areas in which people change their minds. As a class, brainstorm topics for the category *other* and write them on the board; for example, *buying a car, taking a trip, making an investment, buying a house or apartment, going to a particular school/university.*

- Have students check the areas and take notes of reasons why they have changed their mind.

- Then ask students to work in small groups and use their notes as a guide to talk about their experiences. Encourage the students who are listening to ask follow-up questions.

- To review, write the six areas on the board and take a poll to find out how many people have changed plans in each area. Have volunteers give a brief description of the plan they have changed and explain why.

Option: [+5 minutes] For a challenge, write on the board:

Think of something that has been on your mind for some time.
Think of reasons why you have been having trouble making up your mind.
Think of someone whose brain you could pick to help you make a decision.

Have students individually write notes to prepare to discuss the topics on the board and then tell a partner about their responses. Encourage students to use the language from the Photo Story. To review, have volunteers share their responses with the class.

Language and culture

- A *job* is something a person does to earn money. A *career* is a chosen profession that involves long-range planning and makes use of special skills, training, and education.

EXTRAS (optional)

- **Workbook:** Exercises 1–4

B))) **Photo story** Read and listen to a conversation about a career choice.

Charlotte: Dr. Miller, I wonder if I could pick your brain.

Dr. Miller: Sure, Charlotte. What's on your mind?

Charlotte: Well, I always thought I would go to engineering school, but now I'm not so sure anymore.

Dr. Miller: Well, it's not so unusual for a person your age to change her mind . . .

Dr. Miller: I must have changed mine ten times before I settled on medicine! Have you decided on something else?

Charlotte: Well, actually, I've developed an interest in the health field, and since you're a doctor . . .

Dr. Miller: Are you thinking of medicine?

Charlotte: Not specifically. Something related that doesn't take that long to study . . .

Charlotte: I know there are some good options, but I'm having trouble making up my mind.

Dr. Miller: Well, have you given any thought to becoming a physical therapist? It's a great field. You help people and there's always a job available.

Charlotte: Hmm. Physical therapy. I should have thought of that. I'll keep that in mind.

C **Focus on language** Look at the underlined expressions in the Photo Story. Then match each expression with its meaning.

....d.... **1** make up one's mind   **a** decide to do something else

....b.... **2** keep something in mind   **b** remember something

....c.... **3** be on one's mind   **c** think of something

....f.... **4** settle on   **d** decide to do something after considering conflicting choices

....a.... **5** change one's mind   **e** ask someone about something

....e.... **6** pick someone's brain   **f** make a final decision that won't change

D **Discussion** Is it common to change life or work plans before settling on something? Check any areas in which you have ever changed your mind. Then take a survey of the class. How many people have changed plans in each area? Discuss reasons people change their plans.

☐ a career or job choice

☐ a field of study

☐ a marriage

☐ a divorce

☐ the choice of a boyfriend or girlfriend

☐ other ....

GOAL Explain a change in life and work plans

CONVERSATION MODEL

A 🔊 3:20 Read and listen to a conversation about a change in plans.

A: So what are you doing these days?

B: Well, I'm in dental school.

A: No kidding! I thought you had other plans.

B: That's right. I was going to be an artist, but I changed my mind.

A: How come?

B: Well, it's hard to make a living as a painter!

B 🔊 3:21 **Rhythm and intonation** Listen again and repeat.
Then practice the Conversation Model with a partner.

GRAMMAR *Future in the past: was / were going to and would*

Was / were going to is the past form of **be going to**. It is used to express or ask about future plans or expectations someone had in the past. It is often used for plans that changed or weren't achieved.

I **was going to get** married (but I didn't).   They **were going to study** art (but they didn't).
Was she **going to take** the course?   **Were** you **going to study** with Dr. Mellon?

Weren't you **going to study** law? (Yes, I was. / No, I wasn't.)
Where **were** they **going to work**? (In Kuala Lumpur.)
Who **was going to teach** this class? (My sister was.)

Would is the past form of **will**. It can also express future in the past. Use **would** + the base form in a noun clause direct object that describes future plans or expectations.

She thought she **would be** a doctor (but she changed her mind).
We always believed they **would get** married (but they never did).
They said they **would pay** for their daughter's studies (but they didn't).

Note: Noun clause direct objects can also use **was / were going to** + the base form.

They said they **were going to arrive** before noon (but they didn't).

> **Be careful!** Don't use **would** + a base form alone to express future plans or expectations. Use **was / were going to** instead.
>
> She was going to be a doctor.
> NOT She ~~would be~~ a doctor.

> **GRAMMAR BOOSTER** ▸ p. 130
> • *Expressing the future: review*
> • *The future with will and be going to: review*

Grammar practice On a separate sheet of paper, write what each person said he or she was going to do. Write the sentences two ways, once with <u>was going to</u> and once with <u>said</u> and <u>would</u>.

See page T64 for answers.

❝I'm going to stop smoking.❞

❝I'm going to apply to law school.❞

❝I'm going to find a husband.❞

❝I'm going to marry Sylvia.❞

He was going to stop smoking. / He said he would stop smoking.

CONVERSATION MODEL

A 🔊 Read and listen . . .

Suggested teaching time:	2 minutes	Your actual teaching time:

> These conversation strategies are implicit in the model:
> • Say "No kidding!" to indicate delight or surprise.
> • Say "How come?" to ask for a reason.

• Point out to students the title of the lesson, *Explain a change in life and work plans.* Then have students look at the photograph and ask *What do you think the men are talking about?* (Possible answers: Someone wants to change his career or move to a different place.)

• After students read and listen, check comprehension by asking *What school is the man attending?* (Dental school.) *Why is his friend surprised?* (Because he thought he wanted to do something else.) *Why did the man change his mind?* (He wanted to make more money. / He wouldn't earn much money as a painter.)

B 🔊 Rhythm and intonation

Suggested teaching time:	3 minutes	Your actual teaching time:

• Have students repeat each line chorally. Make sure students:
  ◦ use falling intonation for *So what are you doing these days?* and *How come?*
  ◦ put extra stress on *other* in *I thought you had other plans.*

> **Language and culture**
>
> **LEN** **From the Longman Corpus:** A person can *make a living as a [doctor / cook, etc.]* or *make a living by [teaching / selling cars, etc.].* Use of *as* and a job title is said most frequently.

GRAMMAR

Suggested teaching time:	10–15 minutes	Your actual teaching time:

• Direct students' attention to the chart and have them read the first explanation and study the examples. To help clarify, say *Use the future in the past to talk about things you planned to do. Maybe you did or didn't do them.*

• To check comprehension, direct attention to the first example and ask *What plans did this person have?* (To get married.) *Did he or she get married?* (No.)

• To review how to form the future in the past, point out the words in blue. Write on the board: *was / were going to + base form of the verb.*

• To provide practice, have students work in small groups and say one thing they wanted to do, but didn't. Ask them to give the reason why they didn't. Encourage students to ask each other detailed questions using the future in the past. For example:

Student A: *We were going to go on vacation, but my sister broke her leg.*
Student B: *Where were you going to go?*

• Have students read the second explanation and study the examples. To help clarify, say *After verbs of belief or reporting verbs, you can use <u>would</u> followed by a base form to talk about things you planned to do.*

• To check comprehension, have students identify the verbs of belief (thought, believed) and the reporting verb (said) in the examples.

• To provide practice, write on the board:
  1. She thought he was going to the party.
  2. They knew they were going to be late.

• Ask students to rewrite these sentences using *would* + base form to express future in the past. (1. She thought he would go to the party. 2. They knew they would be late.)

• Direct attention to the *Be careful!* box. Be sure students understand that *would* can only be used to express future plans or expectations after verbs of belief or reporting verbs.

• Have students read the Note. To help clarify, say <u>Was / were going to</u> *can also be used after verbs of belief (thought, believed) and reporting verbs (said).*

• To provide practice, have students restate the examples from the second explanation using *was / were going to.* (She thought she was going to be a doctor. We always believed they were going to get married. They said they were going to pay for their daughter's studies.)

Option: **GRAMMAR BOOSTER** (Teaching notes p. T130)

 **ActiveTeach Multimedia Disc** • Inductive Grammar Charts

Grammar practice

Suggested teaching time:	5–7 minutes	Your actual teaching time:

• To model the activity, review the example with the class. Point out that *would* is used in a noun clause after *said.*

• Have students compare and explain their answers in pairs. Then review with the class.

Option: **[+5 minutes]** To extend the activity, form small groups and have students compare the plans and beliefs they had about their own futures at an earlier time in their lives; for example, **Student A:** *When I was a child, I thought I would be a teacher.* **Student B:** *That's interesting. I thought I was going to be a teacher, too, but I changed my mind.* To review, ask students from different groups to say whether they had similar or different beliefs and expectations.

Answers for Grammar practice
• She was going to apply to law school. / She said she would apply to law school.
• She was going to find a husband. / She said she would find a husband.
• He was going to marry Sylvia. / He said he would marry Sylvia.

VOCABULARY

A 🔊 Read and listen . . .

Suggested teaching time:	2 minutes	Your actual teaching time:

- Have students listen and read the sentences. Then have them listen and repeat chorally.

- To check comprehension, ask students to identify the vocabulary that corresponds to each of the statements:

  I studied really hard, but I failed the exam. (I didn't pass.)

  I have to work two jobs now to earn enough money. (It's hard to make a living.)

  I was going to travel, but my family thought I was crazy, so I'm not going. (My family talked me out of it.)

  I used to collect stamps; now I collect coins. (My tastes changed.)

  I was going to go out to dinner after class, but I think I'll just go home. (I just changed my mind.)

Language and culture

- In the United States, the person who practices law is called a *lawyer* or an *attorney*. In England and Wales, a *barrister* handles legal matters inside the court and a *solicitor* advises clients as to their legal rights. In Canada and Australia, the terms *lawyer, barrister,* and *solicitor* are all used. In India, the official term for *lawyer* is *advocate.*

LCN From the Longman Corpus: The phrase *change your mind* collocates most frequently with *about.* You can change your mind about something (*I changed my mind about that movie. It was actually good.*) or about doing something (*I changed my mind about marrying George*).

B Integrated practice

Suggested teaching time:	3–4 minutes	Your actual teaching time:

- To model the activity, complete the first item with the class. Point out that there can be many correct reasons.

Answers for Exercise B

1. Laura thought she would be a doctor, but she just changed her mind.
2. I thought I would become an astronaut, but I didn't pass the exam.
3. We were sure Bill and Stella would get a divorce, but their families talked them out of it.
4. Joe wanted to be a writer, but it's hard to make a living as a writer.

C 🔊 Listening comprehension

Suggested teaching time:	5–7 minutes	Your actual teaching time:

- Have students listen to the conversations and take notes about each person's plans. Then ask students to complete the gaps in each sentence.

AUDIOSCRIPT

CONVERSATION 1 [M = U.S. regional]
M: So what did you want to be when you grew up?
F: Me? I actually wanted to be a sculptor. And I was one for about five years.

M: Really? So how come you're an architect now?
F: I guess it was just impossible to make a living.
M: I can imagine.

CONVERSATION 2 [M = British English]
F: Weren't you going to marry that beautiful American dancer—what was her name—Jessica??
M: You remember! You're amazing!
F: Who could forget Jessica?
M: Hmmm. Well, she was gorgeous!
F: What made you change your mind?
M: I never really changed my mind. My parents convinced me not to do it.

CONVERSATION 3 [F = Russian]
M: I always thought you would become a lawyer.
F: What do you mean?
M: Well, you love to argue, and you love to win.
F: To tell you the truth, I really thought I would become a lawyer too, but I couldn't pass the entrance exam. I took it twice.
M: You're kidding!
F: Well, there's more to law than arguing and winning.

CONVERSATION 4
M: I remember that Romanian skier you were going to marry.
F: Oh, yes. Andrei. He was so cute.
M: Whatever happened?
F: When you get older, your tastes just change, I guess. That's why I married Jerome.

NOW YOU CAN Explain a change in life and work plans

A Notepadding

Suggested teaching time:	5 minutes	Your actual teaching time:

- Encourage students to write at least one plan for each category. Allow them to write about other types of plans if they want to.

B Pair work

Suggested teaching time:	5–10 minutes	Your actual teaching time:

- Be sure to reinforce the use of the conversation strategies; for example, make sure students express *No kidding!* with enthusiasm.

Don't stop! Extend the conversation. Have students give examples of questions they can ask. Remind them that they can also use tag questions. For example:

So where do you live now?

You don't get much free time, do you?

 ActiveTeach Multimedia Disc
- Conversation Pair Work Cards
- Learning Strategies

C Change partners

Suggested teaching time:	5 minutes	Your actual teaching time:

- Assign students new partners and remind them to use other life choices and plans.

EXTRAS (optional)

- Workbook: Exercises 5–10
- Copy & Go: Activity 21

A 🔊 3:22 Read and listen. Then listen again and repeat.

I wanted to be a rock star, but **my tastes changed**.

I was going to be an artist, but **it's hard to make a living as an artist**.

I thought I would be a lawyer, but **I didn't pass the exam**.

I wanted to become a firefighter, but **my family talked me out of it**.

I was going to marry George, but **I just changed my mind**.

B Integrated practice On a separate sheet of paper, complete each sentence, using <u>would</u> and a reason from the Vocabulary. Then compare reasons with a partner. See page T65 for answers.

1 Laura thought / be / a doctor, but . . . .

2 I thought / become an astronaut, but . . . .

3 We were sure / Bill and Stella / get a divorce, but . . . .

4 Joe wanted / a writer but . . . .

C 🔊 3:23 **Listening comprehension** Listen to the conversations. Complete each statement about the decision each person made. Then listen again and use the Vocabulary to write the reason each person changed his or her mind.

1 She wanted to be a ...sculptor..., but she changed her mind because ...it was impossible to make a living... .

2 He was going to ...marry... Jessica, but he didn't because ...his parents convinced him not to... .

3 He always thought she would become a ...lawyer..., but she didn't because ...she couldn't pass the entrance exam... .

4 She was going to ...marry... a Romanian named Andrei, but she didn't because ...her tastes changed... .

NOW YOU CAN Explain a change in life and work plans

A Notepadding On the notepad, write some life, study, or work plans you had in the past, but which you changed your mind about. Write the reasons for the changes, using the Vocabulary or other reasons.

B Pair work Change the Conversation Model, using the information on your notepad. Then change roles.

A: So what are you doing these days?

B: Well, ...

A: No kidding! I thought you had other plans.

B: That's right. I was going to .... , but ....

A: How come?

B: Well, ...

| life plans: |
| study plans: |
| work plans: |

Don't stop!
• Discuss where you live and work now.
• Discuss other aspects of life: marriage, work, studies, children, or other topics.

C Change partners Practice the conversation again about other life choices and plans.

| GOAL | Express regrets about past actions |

GRAMMAR   *Perfect modals*

Use perfect modals to express thoughts about past actions.

Express personal regret or judge another's actions: <u>should have</u> + past participle
I **should have studied** medicine. (But unfortunately, I didn't.)
She **shouldn't have divorced** Sam. (But unfortunately, she did.)

Express possibility or speculate: <u>may have</u>, <u>might have</u> + past participle
I **may** (or **might**) **have failed** the final exam. It was really hard.
He **may** (or **might**) **not have been** able to make a living as a painter.

Express certainty: <u>would have</u>, <u>could have</u> (for ability)
It's too bad he broke up with Anne. They **would have been** happy together.
He was the driver. He **could have prevented** the accident.

Draw conclusions: <u>must have</u> + past participle
Beth isn't here. She **must have gone** home early.
(I think that's what happened.)
They didn't buy the house. The price **must not have been** acceptable.
(I think that's the reason.)

GRAMMAR BOOSTER ▶ p. 131

Regrets about the past:
• <u>Wish</u> + the past perfect
• <u>Should have</u> and <u>ought to have</u>

Grammar practice   Choose the modal that logically completes each sentence.
Write the modal and the verb in the perfect modal form.

1 I don't know why she married him. He ....**must have been**.......... the only man available.
(must / should) be

2 I .....**should have studied**..... architecture. I .....**would have been**..... really good at it.
(should / may) study   (must / would) be

3 Jenna's not studying Chinese anymore. I guess it .....**would have been**..... too hard to learn Chinese
(should / would) be
and Japanese at the same time.

4 We didn't know we were going to have five children. We .....**should not have bought**..... such a small house.
(could not / should not) buy

5 Ella still loves Ben. She .....**should not have broken up**..... with him.
(must not / should not) break up

6 When I was young, everyone thought I was a great singer. But I decided to become a lawyer instead.
Looking back, I think I .....**may have decided**..... on the wrong career.
(may / should) decide

PRONUNCIATION   *Reduction of <u>have</u> in perfect modals*

A 🔊 **3:24** Notice the reduction of <u>have</u> in perfect modals. Read and listen.
Then listen again and repeat.

/ʃʊdəv/
1 I should have married Marie.

/naɾəv/
3 We may not have seen it.

/maiɾəv/
2 They might have left.

/kʊdəv/
4 She could have been on time.

B Pair work   Take turns reading the sentences with perfect modals in the
Grammar Practice above. Use correct reduction of <u>have</u>.

GRAMMAR

Suggested teaching time:	10–15 minutes	Your actual teaching time:

- Direct attention to the chart and have students read the first explanation. To point out how a perfect modal is formed, say *A perfect modal is a modal followed by have and the past participle.* Write on the board:

  perfect modal = modal + have + past participle

should may could	have gone

- Have students read the second explanation and study the examples. To help clarify meaning, write on the board: *I should have brought my raincoat.* Say *I didn't bring a raincoat. Now I regret it.* To check comprehension, ask students to turn to a classmate and use *should have* to express a regret; for example, *I should have studied more. I should have taken a taxi this morning.*

- Have students read the third explanation and study the examples. To help clarify meaning, write on the board: *I decided not to go sailing, but I may have enjoyed it.* Say *I didn't go sailing. Now I look back and think that I may have enjoyed it.* To check comprehension, say *I may have been a good nurse* and have students explain the meaning of your sentence. (You are not a nurse, but now you look back and think that if you were a nurse, maybe you would be a good one.) Be sure students understand that *may* and *might* have the same meaning and can be used interchangeably.

- Have students read the fourth explanation and study the examples. To help clarify meaning, write on the board:

  I should have taken the entrance exam.
  → 1. *I would have passed.*
  → 2. *I could have passed.*

- Ask *Did I take the entrance exam?* (No.) *In sentence 1, am I sure that I would have gotten a passing grade?* (Yes.) *And in sentence 2?* (No, maybe.)

- Have students read the last explanation and study the examples. To help clarify meaning, write on the board: *Susan didn't call back. She must have forgotten.* Tell students that using *must* means you are saying why you think or believe something happened or why someone did something.

- To check comprehension, write on the board: *[Lucy] was late for class today.* Ask students to turn to a classmate and draw conclusions about why that person was late to class today. Have students use *must*. (Possible answers: He or she must have come by car and not by bus. He or she must have missed the bus. He or she must have met a friend on his or her way. He or she must have overslept.)

- To point out how the negative is formed, say *The negative is formed by adding <u>not</u> after the modal.* Have students look back at the examples and identify negative statements. Write on the board: *I should have taken the train.* To provide practice, have students turn the sentence on the board into the negative. (I should not / shouldn't have taken the train.)

Option:  GRAMMAR BOOSTER (Teaching notes p. T131)

ActiveTeach Multimedia Disc • Inductive Grammar Charts

Grammar practice

Suggested teaching time:	3–5 minutes	Your actual teaching time:

- To model the activity, complete the first item with the class.

- Call on students to read their sentences aloud.

PRONUNCIATION

A 🔊 Notice the reduction . . .

Suggested teaching time:	2 minutes	Your actual teaching time:

- First listening: Have students listen and study the examples. Ask if they notice the reduction of *have*. To check understanding, direct attention to item 1 and ask *Is <u>should</u> <u>have</u> pronounced as two words or just one word?* (One word.) Direct attention to item 3. Point out that in negative perfect modals, *not* and *have* are pronounced together.

- Make sure students use reduced pronunciation of *have*.

Option: [+3 minutes] To extend the activity, have students practice saying items 1, 2, and 4 in the negative and item 3 in the affirmative.

B Pair work

Suggested teaching time:	3 minutes	Your actual teaching time:

- Before students practice, you may want to read the first item aloud and have students repeat chorally after you. Make sure students use the reduced pronunciation of *have*.

- Walk around and provide help as needed.

C Pair work

Suggested teaching time:	7–10 minutes	Your actual teaching time:	

- To model the activity, role-play the speech balloons with the class.
- Point out that students should provide three reasons for each of the items: they should speculate with *may have* or *might have*, draw a conclusion with *must have*, and state a possibility with *could have*.
- Call on pairs to share their responses with the class.

Language and culture
- The auxiliary *have* is reduced in spoken English because it is a function word. Function words—for example, auxiliaries (*have*), articles (*a, an, the*), prepositions (*on, in, at, for,* etc.), pronouns (*he, his, him,* etc.), conjunctions (*and, or, but,* etc.), and forms with *be* (*he's, they're,* etc.)—are often reduced because they do not provide important information in a sentence. Content words—such as nouns, verbs, adjectives, and adverbs—are generally not reduced.

 • Pronunciation Activities

CONVERSATION MODEL

A ◀)) Read and listen . . .

Suggested teaching time:	2 minutes	Your actual teaching time:	

These conversation strategies are implicit in the model:
- Express a regret with "I should have . . . ."
- Use "You never know . . ." to reassure someone.
- Accept another's reassurance by saying "True."

- To introduce the conversation, have students look at the photograph. Ask *Do you think the women are talking about something serious?* (Yes.) *Why?* (They are not smiling or laughing.)
- To check comprehension after students read and listen, ask *What does the first woman / speaker regret?* (That she didn't marry Steven.) *Why?* (She wants children. She thinks she would have children by now.)
- Point out that *Could be* means *That could be true.*

B ◀)) Rhythm and intonation

Suggested teaching time:	3 minutes	Your actual teaching time:	

- Have students repeat each line chorally. Make sure students:
  ◦ put extra stress on *Steven* in *I should have married Steven.*
  ◦ put extra stress on *that* in *Why do you think that?*
  ◦ pause slightly after *Well.*
  ◦ put extra stress on *know* in *But you never know.*

NOW YOU CAN | Express regrets about past actions

A Notepadding

Suggested teaching time:	10 minutes	Your actual teaching time:	

- Review the example with the class. Brainstorm more ideas for the last column and write them on the board. Encourage the use of different perfect modals; for example, *I would have made a lot of money. I may have traveled on business to different countries. I could have been a chef.*
- Encourage students to write three or four regrets. They can be real or imaginary. Remind students to use perfect modals to express how things might have been different. Walk around as students write and provide help as needed.

B Pair work

Suggested teaching time:	5–10 minutes	Your actual teaching time:	

- Be sure to reinforce the use of the conversation strategies; for example, encourage students to show interest about their partner's regret.

Don't stop! Extend the conversation. Review the language in the *Be sure to recycle . . .* box. Have several students provide options to speculate about what happened and complete the questions and suggestions. For example:
You could have had a quieter life.
You may not have been so busy.
You would have been happier.
Why didn't you get married?
Why don't you try to get a new job?
How about making up?

- To model the activity, role-play and extend the conversation with a more confident student.

Option: [+5 minutes] To challenge students, combine pairs to form groups of four and have students take turns reporting their partners' regrets and adding their opinions. For example:
Student A: *[Brandon] says he should have moved to the mountains. I think he might have had a boring life there.*
Student B: *But I think I might have been happier there than here in the city.*
Student C: *And you would have had a quieter life.*
Student D: *I agree.*

 • Conversation Pair Work Cards

EXTRAS (optional)

- Workbook: Exercises 11–15
- Copy & Go: Activity 22

C Pair work Provide three possible reasons for each of the statements below. Use <u>may</u> / <u>might have</u>, <u>must have</u>, and <u>could have</u>. Follow the example.

1 My brother never got married.
2 All the classes were canceled today.
3 Michael is forty and he just became a doctor.
4 Rachel grew up in New York, but now she lives in São Paulo.
5 They had one child and then they adopted three more.
6 They had their honeymoon in the U.S. instead of in France.

Example: John is late for dinner.

" He might have gotten stuck in traffic. "

" And he must not have taken his cell phone. "

" Or he could have had an important meeting at work. "

CONVERSATION MODEL

3:25

A 🔊)) Read and listen to a conversation between two people discussing a regret about the past.

A: I should have married Steven.

B: Why do you think that?

A: Well, I might have had children by now.

B: Could be. But you never know. You might not have been happy.

A: True.

3:26

B 🔊)) **Rhythm and intonation** Listen again and repeat. Then practice the Conversation Model with a partner.

NOW YOU CAN Express regrets about past actions

A Notepadding Write about some regrets you have about past actions. Say how you think things might have been different in your life today.

Past action	Regret	How might things have been different?
a job / career choice	I didn't take the job at MacroTech.	I might have been CEO by now!

Past action	Regret	How might things have been different?
a job / career choice		
a field of study		
a marriage / divorce		
a boyfriend / girlfriend choice		
a breakup		

B Pair work Change the Conversation Model. Discuss your regrets and speculate on how things might have been different. Use information from your notepad and past modals. Then change roles.

A: I should (*or* I shouldn't) have ....

B: Why do you think that?

A: Well, I ....

B: Could be. But you never know. You might ....

A: ....

Don't stop!
• Ask your partner more questions about his or her regrets.
• Speculate about what happened.
• Offer advice.

♻ **Be sure to recycle this language.**

Why did you / didn't you ___ ?
Why don't you ___ ?
How about ___ ?

must (not) have
may / might (not) have
could have

BEFORE YOU LISTEN

A 🔊 3:27 **Vocabulary • *Skills and abilities*** Read and listen. Then listen again and repeat.

talents   abilities in art, music, mathematics, etc., that you are born with
She was born with talents in both mathematics and art.

skills   abilities that you learn, such as cooking, speaking a foreign language, or driving
She has several publishing skills: writing, editing, and illustrating.

experience   time spent working at a job
Martin has a lot of experience in sales. He has worked at three companies.

knowledge   understanding of or familiarity with a subject gained from experience or study
James has extensive knowledge of the history of film. You can ask him which classics to see.

B **Think and explain** Explain the following in your own words. Use examples from your life.

- the difference between a talent and a skill
- the difference between experience and knowledge

LISTENING COMPREHENSION

A 🔊 3:28 **Listen for details** Listen to nine people being interviewed at an international job fair. Stop after each interview and match the interviewee with his or her qualification for a job.

Interviewee	Qualifications
..h.. **1** Sonia Espinoza	**a** a good memory
..d.. **2** Silvano Lucastro	**b** artistic ability
..f.. **3** Ivan Martinovic	**c** mathematical ability
..i.. **4** Agnes Lukins	**d** logical thinking
..e.. **5** Elena Burgess	**e** compassion
..b.. **6** Karen Trent	**f** manual dexterity
..g.. **7** Ed Snodgrass	**g** common sense
..c.. **8** Akiko Uzawa	**h** athletic ability
..a.. **9** Mia Kim	**i** leadership skills

B **Pair work** With a partner, classify each qualification from Exercise A. Do you agree on all the classifications? Discuss and explain your opinions.

a talent	a skill
athletic ability	

❝I think athletic ability is a talent. You're born with that.❞

❝I don't agree. I think if you train and work at it, you can develop into a great athlete. I think it's a skill.❞

LESSON 3

BEFORE YOU LISTEN

A  Vocabulary

Suggested teaching time:	1–2 minutes	Your actual teaching time:

- Have students listen and study the words and the definitions. Then have them listen and repeat chorally.

- To check comprehension, write the following sentences on the board and ask students to fill in the blanks with the vocabulary words:

  1. He has done this kind of job before, so he has ___.
  2. She types fast and knows at least five computer programs. She has the ___ we need for this position.
  3. She has many ___. She sings and plays the violin.
  4. They studied twentieth-century politics. I'm sure they have a lot of ___ about World War II.

  (1. experience; 2. skills; 3. talents; 4. knowledge)

ActiveTeach Multimedia Disc
- Vocabulary Flash Cards
- Learning Strategies

B Think and explain

Suggested teaching time:	3–4 minutes	Your actual teaching time:

- Have students work in pairs to explain the difference between the words. Encourage them to take notes and to contribute an example for each word.

- To help students give correct examples, point out the prepositions that usually follow the words. Write on the board:

  have skills in / at
  have knowledge of
  have experience in / with
  have a talent for

LISTENING COMPREHENSION

A  Listen for details

Suggested teaching time:	10–14 minutes	Your actual teaching time:

- After reading the direction line, point out that a *qualification* is a skill, personal quality, or experience that makes you right for a particular job.

- Have students listen to the first interview and review the example. Ask students to listen again for the information that supports the correct answer. (She plays tennis, golf, and she's on a basketball team. She's won a few swimming contests, and she teaches swimming.)

- Ask students to take notes as they listen to the other interviews. Have them listen for jobs the people are interested in and the qualifications for that job. Draw the following chart on the board (without the answers) or print it out from the ActiveTeach Multimedia Disc and distribute to students.

Conversation	Job applying for	Qualifications
Sonia Espinoza	*Director of a sports program*	*plays tennis, golf, basketball* *won swimming contests* *teaches swimming*
Silvano Lucastro		
Ivan Martinovic		
Agnes Lukins		
Elena Burgess		
Karen Trent		
Ed Snodgrass		
Akiko Uzawa		
Mia Kim		

Option: [+5 minutes] To extend the activity, have pairs tell each other which qualifications they have or don't have and give reasons; for example, *I have a good memory for numbers. I can easily remember people's phone numbers.*

ActiveTeach Multimedia Disc
- Graphic Organizers

AUDIOSCRIPT

[Interviewer = British English]

CONVERSATION 1 [F = Spanish]
- **M:** Good morning.
- **F:** Hello. I'm Sonia Espinoza. I'm interested in the job as director of the sports program. The one on the cruise ship.
- **M:** Do you have any experience with sports programs or any special athletic ability?
- **F:** Yes. I play tennis, golf, and I'm on a basketball team. I've won a few swimming contests, and I've been teaching swimming at a club for five years. I actually thought I would be an Olympic swimmer, but I'm not good enough for that.

CONVERSATION 2 [M2 = Italian]
- **M1:** Good morning. Please come in.
- **M2:** Thank you. I'm Silvano Lucastro. I'm interested in working in an international company, but I'm not sure what jobs might be available.
- **M1:** OK. Tell me something about yourself. What do you see as your strengths?
- **M2:** Well, I'm very logical. I can figure things out when other people can't. Whenever there is a problem, people bring it to me to look for an answer. I write everything down in a list and then think about every solution. It's a good way to solve problems.

AUDIOSCRIPT continues on page T69.

B Pair work

Suggested teaching time:	6–10 minutes	Your actual teaching time:

- To prepare students for the activity, review the difference between a talent and a skill by asking *Which one is an ability you learn?* (Skill.) *What is an example of a talent?* (Art, music.)

- Role-play the speech balloons with a student. Point out that it's not necessary to agree with your partner. Encourage students to give reasons why they chose *talent* or *skill* for each qualification.

- To review, have volunteers express their opinions.

NOW YOU CAN | Discuss skills, abilities, and qualifications

A Frame your ideas

Suggested teaching time:	5–10 minutes	Your actual teaching time:

- To help students familiarize themselves with the skills inventory before taking it, have them read it. Ask *What's this inventory for?* (To prepare you for a job interview or an interview for a school.) *What kind of information does it ask for?* (Your interests, your qualifications, your background experience.)
- Before students take the inventory, brainstorm and write on the board a list of useful skills; for example, *problem-solving skills, communication skills, planning skills, organizational skills.*
- As students take the inventory, walk around and help them with vocabulary they might need in order to write about their experiences.

B Notepadding

Suggested teaching time:	10 minutes	Your actual teaching time:

- Review the example with the class.
- Point out that there is a list of qualifications in the skills inventory in Exercise A. Brainstorm other qualifications with the class and write them on the board; for example, *time management, enthusiasm, motivation, professionalism, responsibility, reliability, honesty.*
- Encourage students to write four or five qualifications and examples for each.

C Pair work

Suggested teaching time:	5 minutes	Your actual teaching time:

- Form pairs and have students choose one role play from the list.
- Review the language in the *Be sure to recycle . . .* box.
- Encourage students to use their imaginations as well as the vocabulary and grammar from this unit. Remind them to include information from their skill inventories and notepads.

D Group work

Suggested teaching time:	5 minutes	Your actual teaching time:

- Read the speech balloon aloud.
- Form small groups and have students share what they learned about their partners. Encourage students to express their opinions. If their partners already have a job or are already taking a course, ask them to explain why they think their partners have / don't have the right job or are /aren't taking the right course. If their partners don't have a job or are not taking a course, ask students to offer some career advice or suggestions for the future.
- Ask several students to report the results of their interviews to the class.

EXTRAS (optional)

- Workbook: Exercises 16–20
- Copy & Go: Activity 23

AUDIOSCRIPT for page T68 (**A** Listen for details)

CONVERSATION 3 [M2 = Serbian]
M1: Hello. Please come in and have a seat.
M2: Thanks.
M1: Which job are you interested in?
M2: Well, I'm not sure. I don't have a family yet, and my English is pretty good. I'd love to work somewhere outside of the country for a while, but I don't have much work experience.
M1: That's OK. We have jobs for people at every level. Please tell me about your qualifications.
M2: Well, ever since I was a child, I've been great with my hands.
M1: Hmm. Manual dexterity . . . . Can you tell me a little more?
M2: Sure. People always tell me that I'm good at fixing things. I love to fix things that are broken.
M1: That's great. I actually know of a nice position that might be just right for you . . . in the U.S., working for a Ukrainian piano company. Let me get your personal information. Please spell your name.
M2: It's Ivan Martinovic. That's M-A-R-T-I-N-O-V-I-C.

CONVERSATION 4
M: Good afternoon.
F: Hi! I'm Agnes Lukins, and I'm a people person.
M: A people person. Could you please explain what you mean, Ms. Lukins?
F: I just love working with people. And, actually, people like working with me . . . and for me. They say I'm a good boss.
M: So would you say you have strong leadership qualities?
F: I guess so. I manage people well and my last two jobs have been in management. I'd like to know if there's anything available abroad . . . maybe in Mexico? I can speak Spanish.
M: Let's have a look at the possibilities there.

CONVERSATION 5 [F = Australian English]
M: Come in. You're Elena Burgess, aren't you?
F: Yes, that's right. I see you have two jobs available for psychologists. I just finished my studies, and I'm not sure which job to apply for. This would be my first job.
M: Well, please tell me about yourself. What do you see as your strengths?
F: Strengths? Hmm . . . Well, people say I have a lot of compassion.
M: You're compassionate? In what way?
F: I'm able to understand other people's feelings—to put myself in their shoes. I think I must have gotten that from my parents. Both my parents are psychologists, too.

CONVERSATION 6
M: Good afternoon. You must be Karen Trent.
F: Yes . . . I'm looking for a job.
M: Certainly, Ms. Trent. What kind of experience do you have?
F: Well, I'm a painter. I painted the murals at the new Design Center reception area.
M: Really? Those are beautiful! I understand they won a prize. You do have a lot of talent.
F: Thanks! I actually have a teaching certificate in art, and I'd love to work with children. Is there anything available in Europe? I speak French and German as well as English, and I'd love a chance to practice!

AUDIOSCRIPT continues on page T70.

A Frame your ideas Take the skills inventory.

Careers, Jobs, Advanced Studies *AND YOU*

Whether you're looking for a job or interviewing for a school, interviewers expect you to answer questions about your interests, talents, skills, and experience. Take this inventory to prepare yourself for those questions.

Interests
Check the fields that interest you:
- ☐ business
- ☐ science
- ☐ education
- ☐ art
- ☐ manufacturing
- ☐ other _____

Qualifications
Check the qualifications you believe you have:
- ☐ manual dexterity
- ☐ logical thinking
- ☐ mathematical ability
- ☐ common sense
- ☐ athletic ability
- ☐ artistic ability
- ☐ compassion
- ☐ a good memory
- ☐ leadership skills
- ☐ other _____

Experience
Briefly note information about your experience, skills, and any special knowledge you have.

Experience: _____

Skills: _____

Special knowledge: _____

B Notepadding On your notepad, write specific examples of your qualifications. Then share and discuss your skills, abilities, and qualifications with a partner.

Qualification	Example
mathematical ability	I'm great at number puzzles.

Qualification	Example

C Pair work Use the information on your notepad to do one of the following activities.

- Role-play an interview for a job.
- Role-play an interview for career advice.
- Role-play an interview for entry into a professional (or other kind of) school.

D Group work Tell your class what you learned about your partner in the interview.

"My partner has a lot of experience in . . ."

 Be sure to recycle this language.

Interviewer
Please come in / have a seat.
Please tell me something about your [skills].
Do you have any knowledge of [Arabic]?
What kinds of [talents] do you have?
What [work] experience do you have?

Interviewee
I have experience in [teaching].
I don't have much experience, but ___ .
I'm good at [math].
I have three years of [French].

69

GOAL Discuss factors that promote success

BEFORE YOU READ

A Warm-up How important do you think the following factors are to career success? Put the factors in order of importance. Make 1 the most important and 6 the least important.

- ☐ skills
- ☐ prior experience
- ☐ physical appearance, dress, etc.
- ☐ talent
- ☐ job knowledge
- ☐ work habits
- ☐ other ....

B Discussion Explain the reasons for your most important and least important choices. Use concrete examples.

READING 3:29

The Five Most Effective Work Habits
Advice to new workers from a CEO

If you are new to the working world, you are eager to demonstrate your skills and knowledge. However, in addition to those, some basic work habits may be even more effective in promoting your success. Read the following advice to new workers, written by the head of a company.

❶ Volunteer for assignments One of the best ways to signal that you are a keen learner and are not afraid of hard work is to volunteer for assignments. However, before volunteering for a task, be sure you have the skills and knowledge to accomplish it successfully.

❷ Be nice to people Be nice to people regardless of their rank or position. When you are nice to people, they go out of their way to help you, and every new worker needs help in order to get ahead.

❸ Prioritize your work We all love to start work on things that are close to our hearts. However, these may not be the most urgent and important in our list of tasks to do.
    Have a list of things to do according to their strategic importance to your company. When you prioritize your work, you are more

productive, and that increases your chances of career success.

❹ Stay positive As someone new in the working world, you are not used to office culture. And there may be office politics that complicate things. Try to stay above politics and remain positive in the face of challenges. When you are positive, you stay focused on your goals. You make better decisions and, therefore, get more things done.

❺ Highlight a problem but bring solutions Offer a solution each time you highlight a problem to your boss or management. You need to remember that when you bring problems and not solutions, people may think of you as a "complainer."

These five work habits, at first glance, may seem like common sense. However, in actual working environments, people tend to forget the basics. I counsel new workers in our company to internalize this behavior and consistently use it to increase their chances of career success.

Source: Adapted from www.career-success-for-newbies.com.

LESSON 4

BEFORE YOU READ

A Warm-up

Suggested teaching time:	2–3 minutes	Your actual teaching time:

- Give students a few minutes to put the career success factors in order of importance. Point out that there isn't one correct answer. For the last item, *other*, tell students they can also include one of the skills and qualifications they discussed in the previous lesson.

B Discussion

Suggested teaching time:	3–5 minutes	Your actual teaching time:

- Form small groups. Have students share their rankings and discuss their choices using the notes they made in the previous exercise.

- Have several students share their views with the class. Ask them to support their choices of the most important factor and the least important factor; for example, *I think that the most important factor for career success is having prior experience. If you have prior experience then you know what the job will be like.*

READING

Suggested teaching time:	10–15 minutes	Your actual teaching time:

- Before students read and listen, have them scan the text so they can answer the following questions: *What is it about?* (Effective work habits.), *Who wrote it?* (A CEO/the head of a company.), and *Who is it written for?* (New workers.)

- To access students' prior knowledge, draw the following diagram (without the possible answers) on the board and write *Good Work Habits* in the center circle. Have students close their books and give their own examples of good work habits and write them in the surrounding circles.

- After students read the article, have five volunteers each summarize a tip from the article and add them to the diagram on the board. Encourage students to be brief; for example, *you should volunteer for assignments.*

- Elicit opinions by having students explain why they think the work habits in the text are or aren't important.

Option: [+10 minutes] For a different approach, write the following questions on the board and have students listen for the answers:

1. *When should you not volunteer for assignments?*
2. *Why is it important to be nice to people?*
3. *Why shouldn't you start with the tasks you like?*
4. *What should you do so office politics don't affect you?*
5. *What should you do if you need to tell your boss about a problem?*

To review, have five volunteers each answer a question. (1. When you don't have the skills and knowledge to do them well. 2. Because they will go out of their way to help you. 3. You might become less productive because some tasks may not be important to the company. 4. Rise above them and be positive. 5. You should offer a solution.)

ActiveTeach Multimedia Disc
- Extra Reading Comprehension Questions
- Learning Strategies

AUDIOSCRIPT for page T68 (**A** Listen for details)

CONVERSATION 7 [M2 = U.S. regional]
M1: Please come in and have a seat.
M2: Thank you. I'm Ed Snodgrass, and I'm a student. I'm looking for some kind of a summer job . . . maybe in Thailand? Would that be possible?
M1: Asia. Well, let's see. Tell me something about your skills and abilities.
M2: Well, I'm pretty young, but people have always said I have a lot of common sense.
M1: Now that DOES sound good. What specifically do you mean?
M2: Well, I don't really have a lot of experience or skill, but I have a talent for just knowing what to do. Things seem pretty simple to me. I just seem to be able to figure out what to do when others can't.

CONVERSATION 8 [F = Japanese]
M: Please come in and have a seat.
F: Thank you very much. I'm Akiko Uzawa. I've been working as a computer programmer, but I'm interested in moving to information technology. I see there's a job available with a multinational.
M: Yes, that's right. This would be a change for you, Ms. Uzawa. What makes you feel you would be good at information technology?
F: Well, I went into programming because I was always good at math. I think with my background in mathematics I understand the needs and problems of people in IT.

CONVERSATION 9
M: Hello. Are you Mia Kim?
F: Yes, that's right. I'm currently working as a receptionist at a law firm, but I've just finished a course as a legal secretary and I'd like to apply for the opening in Paris.
M: Paris? Do you speak French?
F: Yes. I have a good knowledge of French. My parents both worked in France for a Korean company, and I went to a French-speaking school.
M: What do you see as your strengths?
F: Well, I have a great memory for details. Also for faces and facts. I hope you'll consider me for this job.

A Understand from context

Suggested teaching time:	5–7 minutes	Your actual teaching time:

- Ask students to underline the words in the article on page 70.
- If students need help writing the definitions, write the following sentences on the board and have students complete them:

    A habit is something that ___.
    If you find a solution to a problem, you ___.
    To volunteer for a task is to ___.
    To prioritize a task is to ___.

- Ask several volunteers to read their definitions aloud.

B Confirm content

Suggested teaching time:	5–10 minutes	Your actual teaching time:

- To help students prepare for the discussion, have them identify the sentences or paragraphs in the article that provide the answer to each question. Then have students write notes to support their answers.
- Form small groups. Encourage students to use their notes to support their answers with information from the article.
- To review, have students from several groups share their answers.

Answers for Exercise B

1. work habits
2. To show that they are keen learners and are not afraid of hard work.
3. Because if you are nice to people, they will go out of their way to help you.
4. You become more productive, and that increases your chance of career success.
5. You stay focused on your goals so you make better decisions, and get more things done.
6. People may think of you as a "complainer."

NOW YOU CAN | **Discuss factors that promote success**

A Notepadding

Suggested teaching time:	10 minutes	Your actual teaching time:

- Review the example with the class. Tell students that they can also talk about other people. Suggest ways that younger students can adapt this exercise; for example, *managing my home* could change to *managing my room / bedroom*.
- As students write notes, encourage them to include as many factors as possible. Ask them to think of specific examples that have helped and hurt them.
- Have students compare notepads with a partner. Encourage them to find differences and similarities.

B Discussion

Suggested teaching time:	10 minutes	Your actual teaching time:

- To prepare students for the discussion, review the language in the *Be sure to recycle . . .* box. Ask students to relate the language there to each area on their notepads. Start with the first area—my personal life—and provide options to complete some of the sentences; for example, *I thought I would get married, but I didn't. I should have been more patient with my [kids / parents].* Then ask students to think about the second area—managing my home—and do the same; for example, *I was going to have someone help me clean my house, but it was too expensive. I could have asked [my husband] to pay the bills.* Follow the same procedure with the third area—my studies / work; for example, *My parents talked me out of being a dancer. I might have been a good photographer. I could have studied French.*
- To help students have an organized discussion, ask them to discuss one area at a time. Remind students to talk about plans that changed and things they regret. Have students ask follow-up questions to find out why their partners changed their plans or why they regret something about the past. Encourage them to give their partners advice.

Option: [+5 minutes] To extend the activity, ask students from different groups to report about a past plan made by someone in their group that changed, or about a decision made by someone in their group that he or she regrets.

EXTRAS (optional)

- Workbook: Exercises 21–25
- Copy & Go: Activity 24

A Understand from context

Find the words below in the article on page 70. Use context to help you write a definition for each. Then compare definitions with a partner.

Answers will vary, but may include the following:

a habit	something that you often do, usually without thinking about it
a solution	a way to solve a problem
volunteer	offer to do something
prioritize	put your tasks in order of strategic importance

B Confirm content

Answer the following questions, according to what the CEO suggests.

See page T71 for answers.

1 Which is most important in determining a new worker's success: knowledge, work habits, or skills?

2 Why should workers volunteer to do tasks?

3 Why is "being nice" a valuable habit to develop?

4 What is the value of prioritizing tasks?

5 How does staying positive help you be more productive?

6 What's wrong with stating a problem without proposing a solution?

> On your *ActiveBook* Self-Study Disc:
> **Extra Reading Comprehension Questions**

NOW YOU CAN   Discuss factors that promote success

A Notepadding

On your notepad write some factors that have helped you be successful in your life, studies, or work, and some factors that have prevented you from being successful. (You can choose one, some, or all areas to comment on.) Then compare notepads with a partner.

Area	Factors that helped ☺	Factors that hurt ☹
my personal life	love, patience, common sense!	not listening to or paying attention to others

Area	Factors that helped ☺	Factors that hurt ☹
my personal life		
managing my home		
my studies / work		

B Discussion

Discuss factors that you think promote success and factors that don't. Use your notepad for support, but expand on it with specific examples from your life to illustrate each factor. Talk about plans that changed and any regrets you may have.

> ♻ **Be sure to recycle this language.**
>
> | Qualities | Changes of plans | Regrets |
> |-----------|-----------------|---------|
> | talents | I thought I would ___ , but ___ . | I should have ___ . |
> | skills | I was going to ___ , but ___ . | I could have ___ . |
> | experience | I changed my mind. | I might have ___ . |
> | knowledge | ___ talked me out of it. | I would have ___ . |
> | common sense | It's hard to make a living as ___ . | |
> | | My tastes changed. | |

Review

More Practice
ActiveBook *Self-Study Disc*

grammar · vocabulary · listening
reading · speaking · pronunciation

A ◀》 **Listening comprehension** Listen to the conversations between people talking about life changes. Write information on the notepad.

	Why did the person change his or her mind?	Any regrets?
1	His parents convinced him it would be hard to have a family.	No
2	She missed her opportunity.	Yes
3	She wasn't getting paid enough.	No
4	His English wasn't good enough.	Yes

B Explain the meaning of each of the following qualifications. Then write an occupation or course of study for a person with each qualification. Answers will vary, but may include the following:

	Qualification	Definition	Occupation or Study
1	athletic ability	able to play sports well	professional tennis player
2	artistic ability	showing skill and imagination in art	painter
3	mathematical ability	showing skill with numbers	mathematician
4	logical thinking ability	able to think carefully, using formal methods	philosophy professor
5	a good memory	able to recall information easily	scientist
6	leadership skills	be good at leading a team, organization, or country	business management

C Complete each statement of belief about the future, using <u>would</u>.

1 When I was a child, I thought I ....

2 My parents believed ....

3 My teachers were sure ....

4 When I finished school, I didn't know ....

D Read each sentence. On a separate sheet of paper, complete the statement in parentheses, using a perfect modal. See page T72 for answers.

1 Marie was very unhappy in her marriage. (She should . . .)

2 After Sylvia and David got separated, they discovered they were still in love. (They could . . .)

> She should have tried to communicate
> more with her husband.

3 My parents were sorry they sold their country house. (They shouldn't . . .)

4 I can't understand how she learned to speak Italian so fast. (She might . . .)

5 Look at John's car. It's all smashed up. (He must . . .)

3:31/3:32
🎵 **Top Notch Pop**
"I Should Have Married Her"
Lyrics p. 150

E Writing Write a short autobiography. Include information about one or all of the topics below. If you have any regrets, express them, using past modals.

- your birth
- your childhood
- your studies
- other aspects of your life

WRITING BOOSTER ▸ p. 145
- *Dividing an essay into topics*
- *Guidance for Exercise E*

Review

A 🔊 Listening comprehension

Suggested teaching time:	7–10 minutes	Your actual teaching time:

- To prepare students for listening, review the reasons for changing plans from the Vocabulary on page 65.

- Pause after each conversation to allow students time to write their answers. Encourage them to use vocabulary from this unit.

- To review, have students compare answers with a partner.

Option: **[+5 minutes]** To extend the activity, have students listen to the recording again and take notes about the plan that each person changed. (1. He was going to get married. 2. She was going to accept a bank manager's position. 3. She was going to be an art teacher. 4. He was going to be an interpreter at the United Nations.)

AUDIOSCRIPT

CONVERSATION 1
F: What happened? Weren't you going to get married?
M: Yes, but my parents were against the marriage.
F: How come?
M: My fiancée had to travel all the time for her work, and my parents convinced me that it would be hard to have a family. In the end, I agreed with them.
F: No regrets?
M: None.

CONVERSATION 2 [M = Spanish]
F: I really wish I'd accepted that bank manager's position last year.
M: I thought you were going to take it. Why didn't you?
F: Well, I'd already planned to spend a couple of weeks with my relatives in Canada, and I really didn't want to have to cancel that trip. By the time I got back, it was too late. They'd given the job to someone else.
M: Well, in any case, you've got a great job now.
F: True. But it'll take a long time before I get a job in management. I think I sort of missed the boat.

CONVERSATION 3
M: Didn't you use to teach painting?
F: Yes. I thought I would always teach art.
M: So how come you're a lawyer?
F: I have pretty expensive tastes. And I wasn't getting paid enough. . . . And it turns out that I really like law.
M: So all's well that ends well!
F: You bet!

CONVERSATION 4 [M = French]
F: I thought you were going to be an interpreter at the United Nations?
M: Well, I was, but I tried twice, and my English wasn't good enough, so I couldn't. The exam is extremely hard.
F: That's too bad.
M: Yes, I wish I had studied more.

B Explain the meaning . . .

Suggested teaching time:	5–8 minutes	Your actual teaching time:

- To help students with their definitions, write on the board: *If you have [athletic ability], you . . .* Have students complete the sentence on the board for the first item.

(Possible answer: If you have athletic ability, you are able to play sports well.) Encourage students to use the sentence on the board to write the definitions of the other qualifications. Then ask students to think of an occupation or field of study for each ability. (Possible answers are included in the teacher annotations within the chart. Other possible answers: 1. Professional athlete, athletic director; 2. photographer, artist, musician, designer; 3. engineer, architect; 4. lawyer, scientist; 5. doctor, salesperson, police officer; 6. manager, teacher.)

- Call on students to share their answers with the class.

C Complete each statement . . .

Suggested teaching time:	3–5 minutes	Your actual teaching time:

- To model the activity, brainstorm different options to complete the first sentence; for example, *When I was a child, I thought I would be a doctor / be famous / travel all over the world / be rich.*

- Then have students exchange papers with a partner. Have them ask questions if the statements are not clear.

D Read each sentence . . .

Suggested teaching time:	5–7 minutes	Your actual teaching time:

- Review the example with the class. Have students write other ways to complete the statement; for example, *She should have gotten divorced. She should have looked for professional advice. She should not have married that man.*

- Have students compare answers with a partner and review with the class.

Answers for Exercise D
Answers will vary, but may include the following:
2. They could have been happy together.
3. They shouldn't have sold it.
4. She might have taken a crash course.
5. He must have had an accident.

E Writing

Suggested teaching time:	10–15 minutes	Your actual teaching time:

- After reading the list of topics, brainstorm other aspects of life students can write about. List them on the board; for example, *trips, friends, celebrations, adventures, family reunions.*

- Have students choose the topics and take notes about them. Remind students to include information about any regrets they may have.

- Walk around as students write and provide help as needed.

Option:  **WRITING BOOSTER** (Teaching notes p. T145)

🔵 **ActiveTeach** Multimedia Disc • Writing Process Worksheets

ORAL REVIEW

Give students a few minutes of silent time to explore the pictures and become familiar with them.

Story in pairs

Suggested teaching time:	15 minutes	Your actual teaching time:

- To check comprehension, ask *Who are the main characters in the stories?* (Michael and Carlota.) *When do their stories start?* (When they were born in 1980.) *When do the stories end?* (Now, when they are grown-ups.)
- Form pairs and have each student choose a different character to tell about.
- To help students prepare their stories, draw the following chart on the board and tell them to write the name of the character they chose (Michael or Carlota).

The character I chose:	
Mother and father's dream for him or her	
Child's dream when he or she was young	
The actual choice and any regrets	
Reasons why he or she may have changed his or her mind	

- Have students copy the chart and write notes about the character they chose in the chart. Tell students that they will need to infer information from the pictures and use their imaginations. Encourage students to use the grammar from this unit to express Michael and Carlota's regrets and to offer reasons why they may have changed their minds. For example:

  Michael thinks he could have been a good pilot.
  His mother must have talked him out of being a pilot.
  Carlota thinks she would have enjoyed being a photographer.
  She might have thought it was hard to make a living as a photographer.

- Encourage students to use time expressions as they tell their stories; for example, *When Michael was a baby . . . / After graduating from medical school . . .*
- Walk around the room as students tell their stories and provide help as needed.
- Have students change partners and then describe the other character. Ask students to copy the chart again and write notes about the new character.
- Walk around the room as students tell their stories and provide help as needed.

Possible responses . . .

When Michael was born, his father thought he should be a pilot. His father must have been a pilot. Michael's mother thought he should be a doctor. She might have been a doctor. When Michael was a schoolboy he was going to be a pilot, but he did not become one. He might have just changed his mind. His mother must have persuaded him to become a doctor. Now Michael thinks he should have been a pilot. He thinks he would have been happier if he had become a pilot.

When Carlota was a baby, her mother thought she should be a photographer. Carlota's mother might have been a photographer. Carlota's father thought she should be a doctor. Carlota's father must have admired doctors. When Carlota was a young girl, she believed she would be a photographer, but she did not become one. She may have thought it was hard to make a living as a photographer. Her father must have talked her out of being a photographer. Now Carlota thinks she should have been a photographer. She thinks life would have been much more exciting.

Option: Oral Progress Assessment

Use the illustrations on page 73. Encourage students to use the language practiced in this unit and previous units.

- Tell the student you are going to ask questions about Michael's dreams and his parents' plans for him. Ask the student to answer in full sentences. Ask *What did Michael's father think Michael should be? What did his mother believe he should be? What did Michael think he would be when he was a boy?*
- Ask the student to choose a character and role play a discussion with you about his or her life choices and regrets. You play the other character. Start like this: **T:** *So what did you want to be when you were a child?*
- Evaluate the student on intelligibility, fluency, correct use of target grammar, and appropriate use of vocabulary.

 **ActiveTeach Multimedia Disc** • Oral Progress Assessment Charts

Option: *Top Notch* Project

Have small groups of students write job advertisements.

Idea: Ask students to research jobs on the Internet or in newspapers to use as models. Have them look for advertisements in their professions or in a field they would like to work in. Form groups of four. Ask each group to write two advertisements. Place the ads on the board, and have students walk around and read them. Then ask volunteers to say which job(s) they would apply for and why.

EXTRAS (optional)

- **Complete Assessment Package**
- **Weblinks for Teachers:** pearsonlongman.com/topnotch/

And on your ActiveTeach Multimedia Disc:
  Just for Fun
  Top Notch Pop Song Activities
  Top Notch TV Video Program and Activity Worksheets
  Supplementary Pronunciation Lessons
  Audioscripts
  Unit Study Guides

Story in pairs Choose one of the characters: Michael or Carlota. Look at the pictures for each of the three dates. Tell the story of your character to your partner. Then change partners and characters and tell the stories again.

Michael

Carlota

1980 Their parents' plans and dreams for them

1990 Their wishes and dreams for themselves

NOW Their actual choices and regrets

NOW I CAN... ✔

- [ ] Explain a change in life and work plans.
- [ ] Express regrets about past actions.
- [ ] Discuss skills, abilities, and qualifications.
- [ ] Discuss factors that promote success.

Holidays and Traditions

GOALS After Unit 7, you will be able to

1 Wish someone a good holiday.
2 Ask about local customs.
3 Exchange information about holidays.
4 Explain wedding traditions.

United States

Thanksgiving dinner in the United States, featuring the traditional main dish of roast turkey

Japan

People picnicking and viewing the cherry blossoms at a *Hanami* party in Japan

Mexico

Friends who have come together for *Quinceañera* to celebrate a girl's fifteenth birthday and her entry into adulthood in Mexico

Korea

A couple dressed in the traditional hanbok during the Korean holiday of *Chuseok*

Brazil

Dancers in the fantastic costumes of Brazil's world-famous yearly celebration of *Carnaval*

A Look at the photos. Which traditions are you already familiar with? Which ones would you like to know more about? Why?

B Discussion Why do people think it's important to keep traditions alive? Do you think it's important to learn about the customs and traditions of other cultures? Explain your reasons.

UNIT 7 Holidays and Traditions

Preview

Suggested teaching time:	3–5 minutes	Your actual teaching time:

Before Exercise A, give students a few minutes of silent time to look at the photos and the captions.

• To help students focus on main ideas, draw the following diagram on the board:

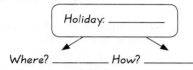

• Ask pairs to look at the photos and the captions to identify the name of each holiday, where it is celebrated, and how people celebrate it.

• To review, have volunteers describe a holiday; for example, *Carnaval is celebrated in Brazil. The dancers wear fantastic costumes and have a great time.*

A Look at the photos . . .

Suggested teaching time:	8–10 minutes	Your actual teaching time:

• To get students to share prior knowledge, have them turn to a partner and tell what they already know about the traditions pictured. You can also have them ask each other questions about the photos and captions. For example:

Student A: *Do you know when Thanksgiving is celebrated?*
Student B: *I think it is celebrated in November each year.*
Student C: *Do you know where in Brazil people celebrate Carnaval?*
Student D: *I think it is celebrated all over the country, but the most famous one is in Rio de Janeiro.*

• To review, ask several students to name one tradition they would like to know more about and why. For example:

I want to know more about Quinceañera because I'm interested in how people celebrate birthdays.
I'd like to know if Korean couples wear hanbok when they get married.
I'd like to know why the Japanese celebrate Hanami.

• Encourage students who may know the answers to their classmates' questions to raise their hands and provide the answers.

FYI: You may want to use the information in the *Language and Culture* box to answer some of the questions yourself.

Language and culture

• Hanami, or the Cherry Blossom Festival, is celebrated each spring when the trees are in bloom. It lasts for two weeks. It is a tradition for family and friends to visit parks, shrines, and temples to have picnics and view the flowers.

• In some Latin American countries, people celebrate a girl's transition from childhood to womanhood. They call this celebration the *Quinceañera* (/kin·sɛ·an·'yɛ·ra/), or 15th birthday. The girl and her friends get dressed up in formal clothes and the celebration ends with a party that often includes food, music, and dancing.

• (Chuseok or Chu Suk is described in the Photo Story on page 75.)

• Thanksgiving, is a national holiday in the United States. It is celebrated on the fourth Thursday in November. Families and friends get together and "give thanks" for all they have as they share a large meal. The traditional foods served on Thanksgiving—turkey, potatoes, and vegetables—are symbols of a successful harvest. Thanksgiving is also celebrated in Canada on the second Monday of October.

• Carnaval is an annual festival celebrated in Brazil, in February or March. It includes colorful parades with music and dancing. There are also similar types of carnivals in many other countries, including Venezuela, Argentina, Spain, and the United States.

B Discussion

Suggested teaching time:	10–15 minutes	Your actual teaching time:

• To help students prepare for the discussion, write on the board: *An old tradition in my country is ___.* Have students complete the sentence on a separate sheet of paper and write notes about the importance of the tradition.

• Brainstorm with the class reasons why we keep traditions alive. Write a list on the board. For example:
*Traditions bring families and communities together.
They remind or teach us about important historical events.
Traditions are dependable, something we can rely on.
They represent our culture.*

• Then discuss why it is important to learn about other cultures' customs and traditions; for example, *It can help us understand other cultures. Learning about others helps teach respect for different ways of thinking and doing things.*

• Have students work in small groups. Ask them to share their opinions about why it is important to keep traditions alive and learn about other people's traditions. Ask volunteers to share their responses with the class.

C 🔊)) Photo story

Suggested teaching time:	5–7 minutes	Your actual teaching time:

- To prepare students, have them look at the photographs and the first line of the dialogue. Ask *What are the women doing?* (Looking at a book / photographs together. Talking about something.) *Are they having a good time?* (Yes.) *Why do you think so?* (They are smiling and laughing.)

- After students read and listen, check comprehension by asking *How many holidays do the women talk about?* (Two.) *What are they called?* (Chuseok and Eid al-Adha.)

- To help students focus on details, have them read and listen again and look for the similarities between the two holidays.

- To review, have several students each name a similarity. Write their answers on the board. (Possible answers: People wear special clothes. They visit their relatives. They eat a lot. They visit the graves of their ancestors.)

- To personalize, ask students if they have any similar traditions. Encourage them to describe those traditions.

Language and culture
- Harvest is the time when crops (vegetables, fruits, grains, etc.) are ripe and then picked or taken from the field. Harvest is often a time for celebration in many different cultures all over the world.
- Eid al-Adha, or the Festival of Sacrifice, is a religious holiday celebrated by Muslims around the world. It commemorates the willingness of Ibraham (known as Abraham by Jews and Christians) to sacrifice his son as an act of obedience to God.

D Paraphrase

Suggested teaching time:	4–5 minutes	Your actual teaching time:

- Encourage students to identify who says the phrases and to use the context of the conversation to help figure out the meanings.

- To model the activity, complete the first item with the class.

- Have students compare answers with a partner and then review with the class.

E Focus on language

Suggested teaching time:	5–8 minutes	Your actual teaching time:

- To model the activity, review the example with the class.

- Before students write their sentences, write the following collocations on the board:
  takes place in [May] / [Spring]
  takes place on [date]
  get together with our friends / relatives / parents
  airports / stations / stores / streets are mobbed with people
  the traffic / airports / highways is / are impossible
  reminds me of [a celebration] / [a special dish] / [a time of the year] / my childhood

- Tell students they can use the words and phrases to describe one holiday or a few holidays. To review, have several students read one or two of their sentences aloud. You may want to write some of them on the board.

Language and culture
- Songkran marks the start of the Buddhist New Year in Thailand. It is a wild festival in which people of all ages have fun throwing water at each other.

F Pair work

Suggested teaching time:	10 minutes	Your actual teaching time:

- Have pairs write notes about a tradition.

- Then ask volunteers to present their information to the class. Elicit follow-up questions about what is new or unusual; for example, **Student A:** *In a Greek wedding, plates are smashed on the floor.* **Student B:** *Why?* **Student A:** *It's supposed to bring good luck.*

EXTRAS (optional)
- Workbook: Exercises 1–3

C ◀》 **Photo story** Read and listen to a conversation about holiday traditions.

ENGLISH FOR TODAY'S WORLD
connecting people from different cultures
and language backgrounds

Basma: Wow! That dress your sister's wearing is gorgeous! What was the occasion?

Mi-Cha: Oh, that was for Chuseok. The dress is called a hanbok.

Basma: Did you say Chuseok? What's that—a holiday?

Mi-Cha: That's right. It's a traditional Korean holiday. It takes place in September or October each year to celebrate the harvest.

Basma: So does everyone dress up like that?

Mi-Cha: Some people do.

Basma: So what else does everyone do on Chuseok?

Mi-Cha: We get together with our relatives. And we eat a lot!

Basma: Well, that sounds nice.

Mi-Cha: Not only that, but we go to our hometowns and visit the graves of our ancestors.

Basma: So I suppose the airports and train stations are mobbed with people, right?

Mi-Cha: Totally. And the traffic is impossible. It takes hours to get anywhere.

Basma: I think every country's got at least one holiday like that!

Mi-Cha: What holiday comes to mind for you?

Basma: It reminds me of Eid al-Adha, a four-day religious holiday we celebrate where I come from.

Mi-Cha: In what way?

Basma: Well, people put on their best clothes, and we eat a ton of great food. We also travel to be with our relatives and visit the graves of our loved ones who have died.

Mi-Cha: How about that! Sounds just like our holiday.

Basma: Arabic speaker, Mi-Cha: Korean speaker

D Paraphrase Say each of the underlined expressions from the Photo Story in your <u>own</u> way.

1 It takes place in September or October.
.... happens / occurs ....

2 We get together with our relatives.
.... visit / gather ....

3 The train stations are mobbed with people.
.... very crowded ....

4 The traffic is impossible.
.... very bad ....

5 It reminds me of Eid al-Adha.
.. makes me remember / brings memories of ..

E Focus on language Write five sentences about a holiday or a tradition in your country, using the underlined language from Exercise D.

> Songkran takes place in April.

F Pair work Complete the chart about traditions in your country. Present your information to the class.

A special type of clothing	Explain when it is worn.
A type of music	Explain when it is played.
A special dish	Explain when it is eaten.
A traditional dance	Explain when it is danced.
A special event	Explain what happens.

GOAL | **Wish someone a good holiday**

CONVERSATION MODEL

4:03

A))) Read and listen to a conversation about a holiday.

A: I heard there's going to be a holiday next week.

B: That's right. The Harvest Moon Festival.

A: What kind of holiday is it?

B: It's a seasonal holiday that takes place in autumn. People spend time with their families and eat moon cakes.

A: Well, have a great Harvest Moon Festival!

B: Thanks! Same to you!

4:04

B))) **Rhythm and intonation** Listen again and repeat.
Then practice the Conversation Model with a partner.

4:05

))) **Types of holidays**
seasonal
historical
religious

a moon cake

VOCABULARY   *Ways to commemorate a holiday*

4:06

A))) Read and listen. Then listen again and repeat.

set off fireworks

march in parades

have picnics

pray

send cards

give each other gifts

wish each other well

remember the dead

wear costumes

B **Pair work** Match the Vocabulary with holidays and celebrations you know.

66 Everyone wears costumes on . . . 99

CONVERSATION MODEL

A ◄)) Read and listen . . .

Suggested teaching time:	2–4 minutes	Your actual teaching time:

These conversation strategies are implicit in the model:
• Show friendliness by wishing someone a good holiday.
• Reciprocate good wishes with "Thanks! Same to you!"

• To prepare students for the Conversation Model, review the seasons (winter, spring, summer, fall / autumn). Have students call them out and write them on the board.

• To check comprehension, after students read and listen to the conversation, ask *What's special about next week?* (It's a holiday, the Harvest Moon Festival.) *What do people do during this holiday?* (They spend time with their families / get together with their relatives and eat moon cakes.)

• Have students read and listen to the different types of holidays listed in the box. Then have students listen again and repeat. To clarify the meaning of a seasonal holiday, ask *What kind of holiday is the Harvest Moon Festival?* (Seasonal.) *Why?* (Because people celebrate it each year in autumn.)

Option: [+3 minutes] To extend the activity, form small groups and have students write one or two examples they know for each type of holiday. To review, write students' responses on the board.

Language and culture
• In China, the Harvest Moon Festival celebrates the end of the summer harvesting season, under the biggest, brightest full moon of the year. Other Asian countries have their own versions of this holiday, such as Chuseok in Korea.
LEN **From the Longman Corpus:** *With, in,* and *on* are the prepositions that most frequently follow *spend time.* It is also common to say *spend time (doing something).*

B ◄)) Rhythm and intonation

Suggested teaching time:	3 minutes	Your actual teaching time:

• Have students repeat each line chorally. Make sure students:
  ◦ use falling intonation for *What kind of holiday is it?*
  ◦ stress new and important information such as *seasonal* and *autumn* in *It's a seasonal holiday that takes place in autumn.*

VOCABULARY

A ◄)) Read and listen . . .

Suggested teaching time:	2–3 minutes	Your actual teaching time:

• Have students listen and study the vocabulary. Then have them listen and repeat chorally.

• To provide practice and reinforce collocations, have pairs play a game: Student A says a verb from the exercise. Student B does not look at the book and says the verb plus a phrase to go with that verb; for example, **Student A:** *march.* **Student B:** *march in parades.* **Student B:** *wear.* **Student A:** *wear costumes.*

Language and culture
• The people in the photo are praying in the Muslim tradition.
• The people in the photo for *wish each other well* are dressed for a New Year's Eve party in the U.S.
• The people in the photo for *wear costumes* are celebrating Halloween—a U.S. holiday mainly for children every October 31st. Many adults also enjoy dressing up in costumes for Halloween parties. In British English a *fancy dress* is the term used for a *costume.*
LEN **From the Longman Corpus:** While both are used, *have a picnic* is used more frequently than *go on a picnic.*

 **ActiveTeach Multimedia Disc**
• Vocabulary Flash Cards
• Learning Strategies

B Pair work

Suggested teaching time:	5–7 minutes	Your actual teaching time:

• To model the activity, read the speech balloon aloud and brainstorm ways to complete it.

FYI: The example uses the preposition *on,* but students can make any necessary changes for local or other holidays; for example, *Everyone wears costumes on Halloween / at Carnaval / when its Halloween.*

• Encourage pairs to write down one occasion or holiday for each vocabulary phrase.

• To review, ask students to say their examples in complete sentences; for example, *We set off fireworks and march in parades on Independence Day.*

Option: [+5 minutes] To extend the activity, have pairs discuss some of their favorite traditions for special events or holidays. Encourage students to use the vocabulary and their own ideas; for example, *going on a picnic for [my birthday], preparing traditional food for [a holiday], wearing traditional costumes on [a holiday], visiting my relatives on [a holiday], setting off fireworks on [a holiday], sending cards to [relatives].* To review, have volunteers share their favorite traditions with the class. You may want to make a list on the board.

C ◄)) Listening comprehension

Suggested teaching time:	5–7 minutes	Your actual teaching time:

- To prepare students for listening, have them study the chart. If there is a world map in the classroom, point out the countries indicated.
- As students listen, stop the recording after each description to allow them time to write.

AUDIOSCRIPT See page T80.

GRAMMAR

Suggested teaching time:	12–15 minutes	Your actual teaching time:

- Direct attention to the chart and have students read the first explanation and study the examples. To check comprehension, write on the board: *My sister is the girl who is wearing a costume.* Have students identify the adjective clause and underline it. (Who is wearing a costume.) Then ask *Who is the adjective clause giving more information about?* (The girl.) *Can that be used instead of who to introduce the clause?* (Yes.) Add *that* below *who* on the board.
- Have students read the second explanation and study the examples. To check comprehension, write on the board: *The Harvest Moon Festival is a holiday that takes place in autumn.* Have students identify the adjective clause and underline it. (That takes place in autumn.) Then ask *What is the adjective clause giving more information about?* (The holiday.) *Can who be used instead of that to introduce this clause?* (No.)
- Have students read the *Be careful!* note and study the example. To check comprehension, write on the board:
  1. *Carnaval is a holiday that usually comes in February.*
  2. *My brother is the boy who he is carrying the flag.*
- Have students correct the sentences by crossing out the unnecessary word in each adjective clause. (1. it; 2. he.)

Option: **GRAMMAR BOOSTER** (Teaching notes p. T131)

ActiveTeach Multimedia Disc • Inductive Grammar Charts

A Understand the grammar

Suggested teaching time:	3–5 minutes	Your actual teaching time:

- Before students start the exercise, write on the board: *The costume is for the person who leads the parade.* Have students identify the clause, *who leads the parade.*

Language and culture
- Ramadan is a religious holiday that is celebrated for a month of the year by Muslims around the world. (See the Reading on page 80 for more information.)

- On April Fool's Day people play tricks on one another. It takes place on April 1 in various English-speaking countries, such as the United Kingdom, the United States, Australia, and Canada.
- The Dragon Boat Festival originated in China. People race in boats that are decorated with a Chinese dragon head and tail while someone beats a drum.

B Grammar practice

Suggested teaching time:	5–6 minutes	Your actual teaching time:

- To model the activity, read the examples aloud.
- To review, encourage students to focus on adjective clauses and relative pronouns as they correct each other's sentences.

NOW YOU CAN   Wish someone a good holiday

A Pair work

Suggested teaching time:	3–5 minutes	Your actual teaching time:

- To reinforce the use of the conversation strategies, be sure that students sound friendly when wishing someone a good holiday. Point out the *some ways . . .* box. Explain that good wishes are appropriate for only celebratory holidays, not for a serious holiday.

Don't stop! Extend the conversation. Have students give examples of questions they can ask. Encourage them to use the vocabulary on page 76. For example:
Do people give each other gifts?
What kinds of costumes do they wear?
Where do people have picnics?
Then have students give examples of sentences that use adjective clauses to provide extra information about a holiday; for example, *It is a seasonal holiday that takes place in spring. Children put up decorations that they make with paper.*

- Before students role-play the conversation, you may want to ask them to write notes about the holiday they will describe.
- Choose a more confident student and role-play and extend the conversation.

ActiveTeach Multimedia Disc • Conversation Pair Work Cards

B Change partners

Suggested teaching time:	5 minutes	Your actual teaching time:

- Assign students new partners. Remind them to use other holidays.

EXTRAS (optional)

- Workbook: Exercises 4–8
- Copy & Go: Activity 25

C 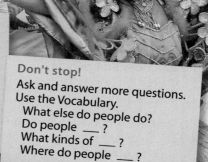 ◀))) **Listening comprehension** Listen and use the Vocabulary to complete the chart.

	Type of holiday	What people do to celebrate
Mardi Gras (U.S.)	religious	wear costumes, have a parade
Bastille Day (France)	historical	dance in the streets, eat all kinds of foods, military parades, fireworks
Tsagaan Sar (Mongolia)	seasonal	wear new clothes, clean house, make traditional food, give gifts

GRAMMAR   *Adjective clauses with subject relative pronouns <u>who</u> and <u>that</u>*

Adjective clauses identify or describe people or things. Introduce adjective clauses about people with <u>who</u> or <u>that</u>.

A mariachi singer is someone   **who (or that) sings** traditional Mexican music.
Carnaval is a great holiday for people   **who (or that) like** parades.
Anyone   **who (or that) doesn't wear a costume** can't go to the festival.

Use <u>that</u>, not <u>who</u>, for adjective clauses that describe things.

Thanksgiving is a celebration   **that takes place in November.**
The parade   **that commemorates Bastille Day** is very exciting.

Be careful! Don't use a subject pronoun after the relative pronouns <u>who</u> or <u>that</u>.
Don't say: Thanksgiving is a celebration that ~~it~~ takes place in November.

> **GRAMMAR BOOSTER** ▸ p. 131
> - Adjective clauses: common errors
> - Reflexive pronouns
> - <u>By</u> + reflexive pronouns
> - Reciprocal pronouns: <u>each other</u> and <u>one another</u>

A Understand the grammar Underline the adjective clauses and circle the relative pronouns. Then draw an arrow from the relative pronoun to the noun or pronoun it describes.

1 Ramadan is a religious tradition that falls on a different day every year.
2 Chuseok is a Korean holiday that celebrates the yearly harvest.
3 The woman who designed our Halloween costumes for the parade was really talented.
4 The celebrations that take place in Brazil during Carnaval are a lot of fun.
5 People who celebrate April Fool's Day have a lot of fun every April 1st.
6 The Dragon Boat Festival in China is a celebration that takes place on the fifth day of the fifth moon, in May or June.

B Grammar practice On a separate sheet of paper, write five sentences with adjective clauses to describe some holidays and traditions in your country.

> . . . is a religious tradition that . . .
>
> . . . is a great holiday for people who . . .

NOW YOU CAN   **Wish someone a good holiday**

A Pair work Use your holiday chart from page 75 to role-play the Conversation Model with a visitor to your country. Wish each other a good holiday. Then change roles.

A: I heard there's going to be a holiday next ....
B: That's right. ....
A: What kind of holiday is it?
B: It's a .... holiday that takes place in .... People ....
A: Well, have a .... !
B: Thanks! Same to you!

Some ways to exchange good wishes on holidays

Have a { nice / good / great / happy } [holiday]!

Enjoy yourself on [Chuseok]!
You too!
Same to you!

Don't stop!
Ask and answer more questions.
Use the Vocabulary.
What else do people do?
Do people ___ ?
What kinds of ___ ?
Where do people ___ ?

B Change partners Exchange wishes about other holidays.

GOAL Ask about local customs

CONVERSATION MODEL

A 🔊⟩⟩ 4:08 Read and listen to a conversation about local customs.

A: Do you mind if I ask you about something?

B: Of course not. What's up?

A: I'm not sure about the customs here. If someone invites you for dinner, should you bring the host a gift?

B: Yes. It's a good idea. But the gift that you bring should be inexpensive.

A: Would it be appropriate to bring flowers?

B: Definitely!

A: Thanks. That's really helpful.

B 🔊⟩⟩ 4:09 **Rhythm and intonation** Listen again and repeat. Then practice the Conversation Model with a partner.

GRAMMAR *Adjective clauses with object relative pronouns* who, whom, *and* that

In some adjective clauses, the relative pronoun is the subject of the clause.
The person **who comes for dinner** should bring a gift.
(**who** = subject / **The person** comes for dinner.)

In other adjective clauses, the relative pronoun is the object of the clause.
The person **who** (or **whom** or **that**) **you invite for dinner** should bring a gift.
(**who** = object / You invite **the person** for dinner.)

When the relative pronoun is the object of the clause, it may be omitted.
The person **you invite for dinner** should bring a gift.

Be careful!
When the relative pronoun is the subject of the clause, it can NOT be omitted.
Don't say: ~~The person comes for dinner~~ should bring a gift.
Do not use an object pronoun after the verb.
Don't say: The person who you invite ~~them~~ for dinner . . .

> **Relative pronouns**
> • Use <u>who</u> or <u>that</u> for a subject of a clause.
> • Use <u>who</u>, <u>whom</u>, or <u>that</u> for an object of a clause.
> Note: <u>Whom</u> is very formal.

GRAMMAR BOOSTER ▸ p. 133
• *Adjective clauses:* <u>who</u> *and* <u>whom</u> *in formal English*

A Understand the grammar Correct the error in the adjective clause in each sentence. Explain each correction.

1 Putting butter on a child's nose is a birthday tradition ~~who~~ *that* people observe on the Atlantic coast of Canada.   **❝** Only use <u>who</u> for people. **❞**

2 On the Day of the Dead, Mexicans remember family members who ~~they~~ have died.
   They is not necessary because <u>who</u> is the subject of the clause.

3 The tomatoes that people throw ~~them~~ at each other during La Tomatina in Buñol, Spain, make a terrible mess.   Do not use an object pronoun after the verb.

4 The performer ^who^ sang that traditional holiday song is world-famous. You cannot omit the relative pronoun when it is the subject of the clause.

5 The fireworks people set ~~them~~ off during the summer festivals in Japan are very beautiful.
   Do not use an object pronoun after the verb.

CONVERSATION MODEL

A 🔊 Read and listen . . .

Suggested teaching time:	2–3 minutes	Your actual teaching time:

These conversation strategies are implicit in the model:
- Preface a potentially sensitive question with "Do you mind if I ask you . . .".
- Ask about socially appropriate behavior in order to avoid embarrassment.
- Express appreciation with "Thanks. That's really helpful."

- After students read and listen, ask *What custom is the man asking about?* (The customs for dinner guests.) *What kind of gift does the woman say he should bring?* (An inexpensive one.) *What is the woman's opinion about giving flowers?* (She thinks it's a very good idea.)

FYI: It's acceptable to answer affirmatively (such as with *Sure*) to a question with *Do you mind if I ask you . . .*

B 🔊 Rhythm and intonation

Suggested teaching time:	2 minutes	Your actual teaching time:

- Have students repeat each line chorally. Make sure students:
  - use rising intonation for *Do you mind if I ask you about something?*
  - stress *really* and *helpful* in *That's really helpful.*

GRAMMAR

Suggested teaching time:	10–15 minutes	Your actual teaching time:

- Direct students' attention to the chart and have them read the first explanation and study the example. To help clarify, write on the board: 1. *The friend who sent me flowers lives in Paris.* Ask students to identify and underline the adjective clause. (Who sent me flowers.) Ask students to identify the subject of the verb *sent* in the clause. (Who.) Circle *who* and add the word *subject* below *who* on the board:

   1. The friend (who) sent me flowers lives in Paris.
               subject

- Have students read the second explanation and study the example. To help clarify, write on the board: 2. *The flowers that he sent me are really beautiful.* Ask students to identify and underline the adjective clause. (That he sent me.) Ask students to identify the subject of the verb *sent* in the clause. (He.) Circle *he* and add the word *subject* below *he* on the board. Then circle *that* and add the word *object* below *that* on the board.

   2. The flowers (that) (he) sent me are really beautiful.
         object subject

- Point out that in this sentence, the relative pronoun is not the subject, but the object, of the sentence. Write on the board: *He sent me flowers. (that = flowers)*

- Have students read the third explanation and study the example. Direct students' attention to example 2 on the board. Point out that *that* can be omitted because it is the object of the clause. Then read the example aloud without it.

- Have students read the information in the relative pronouns box. To check comprehension, write the following sentences on the board and have students say which pronouns are correct and why.

   3. *The guest that / who / whom was late brought the host a gift.*
   4. *The woman that / who / whom I met at the party is from Canada.*
   (3. That / who; because the relative pronoun is the subject of the clause; 4. that / who / whom; because the relative pronoun is the object of the clause.)

- Have students read the *Be careful!* notes. To check comprehension of the first note, direct students' attention to example 1 on the board. Ask *Can who be omitted in example 1?* (No.) *Why not?* (Because it is the subject of the clause.) To check comprehension of the second note, write on the board: 5. *The gift that I bought it is a traditional decoration.* Have students indicate the unnecessary word in the sentence. (It.)

Language and culture
- Both *who* and *whom* can be used in the object position, but *who* is much more common in everyday speech.
- **LEN** **From the Longman Corpus:** *That* is used much more frequently as a subject relative pronoun than *who*.

Option: **GRAMMAR BOOSTER** (Teaching notes p. T133)

 **ActiveTeach Multimedia Disc** • Inductive Grammar Charts

A Understand the grammar

Suggested teaching time:	6–10 minutes	Your actual teaching time:

- To model the activity, review the speech balloon and the first item with the class. Have students explain why *who* is not correct. (Because *who* is only for people.)

- Remind students that if the relative pronoun is the subject of the clause, we don't need another pronoun as subject. Similarly, if the relative pronoun is the object of the clause, we don't need another pronoun as object.

Language and culture
- The Day of the Dead is a holiday that is celebrated primarily in Mexico and Central America on November 1st and 2nd. It is a festive time in which people honor the memory of their dead ancestors and decorate their graves.
- La Tomatina is a wild week-long festival held at the end of August in the Valencia region of Spain with music, parades, dancing, and fireworks. On the last day of the festival, people throw tomatoes at each other.

B Grammar practice

Suggested teaching time:	5 minutes	Your actual teaching time:

- To help students understand, review the first item with the class. Ask students if the pronoun can be omitted. (No, because *who* is the subject of the clause.)
- Have students compare answers with a partner and then review with the class.

Option: [+5 minutes] To extend the activity, write the following statements on the board:

  1. Carnaval is a holiday that is very popular in Brazil.
  2. Carnaval is a holiday that I have always enjoyed.
  3. I gave her the flowers that I picked from my garden.
  4. I can't find the gift that she gave me.
  5. I saw some friends who were marching in a parade.

Ask students to identify and cross out relative pronouns that can be omitted. (Sentences 1 and 5: relative pronouns can't be omitted; sentences 2, 3, 4: they can be omitted.)

> **Language and culture**
> - Anzac Day is a day of remembrance in Australia and New Zealand that takes place on April 25. *Anzac* stands for <u>A</u>ustralian and <u>N</u>ew <u>Z</u>ealand <u>A</u>rmy <u>C</u>orps. It marks the day in which these two military forces fought at Gallipoli in Turkey during the First World War.

PRONUNCIATION

A 🔊 "Thought groups" . . .

Suggested teaching time:	2–3 minutes	Your actual teaching time:

- First listening: Have students listen and study the examples. Ask students if they noticed the pauses between the *thought groups* as they listened.
- Clarify that a *thought group* is a group of words said together in the rhythm of a sentence in order to help convey meaning. Point out that adjective clauses form natural *thought groups*.
- Second listening: Have students listen and repeat. Be sure students pause slightly between *thought groups*.

B Practice reading . . .

Suggested teaching time:	2 minutes	Your actual teaching time:

- To model the activity, call on a student to read the sentence aloud. Make any necessary corrections.
- To review, have volunteers read a sentence aloud.

 • Pronunciation Activities

---

NOW YOU CAN Ask about local customs

A Pair work

Suggested teaching time:	6–10 minutes	Your actual teaching time:

- Have students read the *Ideas* in the box and ask them to write a question someone might ask about each situation. Write a list on the board. For example:

  Someone invites you out for dinner: Should I offer to pay the check? Should I invite the person out for dinner the next week?

  Someone invites you to a party: Should I bring the host a gift? Should I let the person know if I'm coming or not?

  Someone gives you a gift: Should I open it in front of the person? Should I put it away without opening it?

  Someone makes a special effort to help you: Should I give the person a gift? Should I send a thank-you card?

- Ask students to suggest more ideas and write them on the board.
- Be sure to reinforce the use of the conversation strategies; for example, make sure students sound like they mean it when they express appreciation.
- Brainstorm answers to the question *Do you mind if I ask you about something?* (Possible answers: Sure. Not at all. No problem.)

Don't stop! Extend the conversation. Elicit examples of more questions students can ask. For example:
  Is it OK if I take off my shoes?
  Would it be possible to leave earlier?
  Should I eat everything on my plate?

- Choose a more confident student and role-play and extend the conversation.

 • Conversation Pair Work Cards
• Learning Strategies

B Change partners

Suggested teaching time:	10 minutes	Your actual teaching time:

- Tell students to form new pairs by working with the person on their left. Remind them to ask about local customs in other situations.
- Walk around and provide help as needed. Make note of any errors you hear. Write some errors on the board and ask the class to correct them.

EXTRAS (optional)

- Workbook: Exercises 9–12
- Copy & Go: Activity 25

B Grammar practice Complete the adjective clause in each sentence, using the cues. Omit the relative pronoun when possible.

1 People .... *who visit other countries* .... should find out the local customs.
   People visit other countries.

2 The man .... **you were talking with** .... plays in a mariachi band.
   You were talking with the man.

3 The young people .... **you saw in the parade** .... were all wearing traditional costumes.
   You saw the young people in the parade.

4 The traditional Chinese dress .... **that she's wearing** .... is called a cheongsam.
   She's wearing the dress.

5 Anzac Day is a holiday .... **that people celebrate in Australia** .... to remember the soldiers who died in wars.
   People celebrate the holiday in Australia.

A Chinese woman wearing a traditional cheongsam

PRONUNCIATION   *"Thought groups"*

4:10

A ◀)) "Thought groups" clarify the meaning of sentences. Notice how sentence rhythm indicates how thoughts are grouped. Listen and repeat.

1 The person who comes for dinner should bring flowers.

2 The man we invited to the party is from Senegal.

3 The song that you were listening to is fado music from Portugal.

4 The Cherry Blossom Festival is a tradition that people observe in Japan every spring.

B Practice reading the sentences you completed in B Grammar Practice, breaking the sentences into thought groups.

NOW YOU CAN   Ask about local customs

A Pair work Change the Conversation Model. Role-play a conversation in which you ask about local customs. Use the ideas from the box below. Then change roles.

A: Do you mind if I ask you about something?

B: .... What's up?

A: I'm not sure about the customs here. If .... , should .... ?

B: ....

A: Would it be appropriate to .... ?

B: ....

A: Thanks. That's really helpful.

Ideas
• someone invites you out for dinner
• someone invites you to a party
• someone gives you a gift
• someone makes a special effort to help you
• your own idea: ___

Don't stop!
Ask and answer other questions.
   Is it OK if ___ ?
   Would it be possible to ___ ?
   Should I ___ ?

B Change partners Ask about local customs in other situations.

BEFORE YOU READ

Preview Look at the photos and the names of the holidays in the Reading. How would you categorize each holiday—historical, seasonal, or religious? Are you familiar with any of these holidays? What do you know about them?

READING 4:11

Holidays Around the World

Ramadan, the Month of Fasting

"May you be well throughout the year" is the typical greeting during Ramadan, the ninth month of the Islamic calendar, a special occasion for over one billion Muslims throughout the world. According to Islamic tradition, Ramadan marks the time when Muhammad received the word of God through the Koran. Throughout the month, Muslims fast—totally abstaining from food and drink from the break of dawn until the setting of the sun. It is also a time of increased worship and giving to the poor and the community. Ramadan ends with the festival of Eid ul-Fitr—three days of family celebrations—and eating!

Worshippers pray during Ramadan.

The Chinese New Year

The Chinese New Year is celebrated by Chinese around the world and marks the beginning of the first month in the Chinese calendar. The celebration usually takes place in February and lasts for fifteen days. Before the holiday begins, families clean out their houses to sweep away bad luck and they decorate their doors with red paper and big Chinese characters for happiness, wealth, and longevity. The night before, families gather together for a delicious meal. Outside, people set off firecrackers that make loud noises all through the night. In the morning, children wish their parents a healthy and happy new year and receive red envelopes with money inside. It is customary for people to give each other small gifts of fruits and sweets and to visit older family members. In the street, lion and dragon dancers set off more firecrackers to chase away evil spirits.

Dragon dancers chase away evil spirits.

Simón Bolívar's Birthday

Simón Bolívar was born on July 24, 1783 in Caracas, Venezuela. He is known throughout Latin America as "The Liberator" because of his fight for independence from Spain. He led the armies that freed Venezuela, Bolivia, Colombia, Ecuador, Peru, and Panama. He is memorialized in many ways, but two countries celebrate his birthday every July 24th—Venezuela and Ecuador. On that day, schools and most general businesses are closed and there are military parades and government ceremonies. But the malls are open and people usually use the holiday to go shopping.

Bolívar led the fight for independence

Sources: www.muhajabah.com and www.colostate.edu

BEFORE YOU READ

Preview

Suggested teaching time:	5 minutes	Your actual teaching time:

- Have pairs of students look at the photos and read the captions to determine what type of holidays the Reading will describe. (Religious, seasonal, historic.) Remind them not to read the text yet. Encourage them to explain their choices.

- To review, have three volunteers say how they would categorize each holiday. Ask them to support their choices. For example:

    The first photo shows a religious holiday, Ramadan. I think it is a religious holiday because the people are praying.

    The second photo shows a seasonal holiday in China. People are celebrating the beginning of a new year.

    The third photo shows an important man in the history of a country. His name is Simón Bolívar. Celebrating his birthday must be a historical holiday.

- To elicit prior knowledge, ask students to say what they may already know about each holiday. Encourage them to be brief. For example:

    Ramadan is celebrated by Muslims.

    Simón Bolívar is an important man in the history of some Latin American countries.

    People set off fireworks on the Chinese New Year.

READING 🔊

Suggested teaching time:	10–15 minutes	Your actual teaching time:

- To help students focus on the main ideas as they read, draw the following chart on the board. After students read and listen, have them complete the chart with notes from the Reading.

Name of holiday	Time of the year	Location	Reason

- To review, ask students to give their answers in complete sentences. (Possible answers: Ramadan takes place in the ninth month of the Islamic calendar. It is celebrated by Muslims around the world. It commemorates the time when Muhammad received the word of God through the Koran. / The Chinese New Year takes place in February each year. It is celebrated by Chinese people around the world. It marks the beginning of the first month in the Chinese calendar. / Simón Bolívar's birthday is celebrated on July 24th in Venezuela and Ecuador. People honor him because he won independence for their country.)

Language and culture

- The *Koran* is the holy book of Islam. To *abstain* means to not do something or to stop doing something. *Longevity* means long life. A *liberator* is a person who frees another person or country from someone's control.

ActiveTeach
Multimedia Disc
- Extra Reading Comprehension Questions
- Learning Strategies

AUDIOSCRIPT for page T77 (**C** Listening comprehension)

LISTENING 1

M: There are Mardi Gras celebrations in many places in the world, but the Mardi Gras celebrations in New Orleans in the United States are world-famous. Mardi Gras means "fat Tuesday," and usually occurs in February. It began as a religious holiday in which people could really enjoy themselves before the more solemn Catholic celebration of Lent. Now it's considered to be "the biggest party in the world," and people travel from all over to enjoy the celebrations. On this day, people wear really wild costumes and dance in a huge parade to New Orleans' famous jazz music. Along the parade route, people in the parade throw purple-, green-, and gold-colored necklaces, candy, and other things to the people who are watching.

LISTENING 2

F: Celebrated on July 14th, Bastille Day is France's most important national holiday. It celebrates the attack on the hated Bastille prison, which marked the beginning of the French Revolution that led to modern France. It's a joyous holiday in which people celebrate being French. You can see people dancing in the streets together and eating all kinds of food. Usually in the morning there are military parades with French flags flying all over. And in the evening, fireworks are set off and families sit together to watch them.

LISTENING 3

M: Tsagaan Sar—or White Month—is a celebration of the lunar new year in Mongolia. It's held for three days in February or March. Before the first day of the celebration, families clean every corner of their house. During this time, people wear new clothes—usually traditional Mongolian clothing—and they make lots of traditional foods. They also give each other gifts, and especially enjoy giving gifts to their children. One of the ways Mongolians really enjoy themselves during this holiday is to watch wrestling matches and horse races. All these activities symbolize starting the new year clean, rich, and happy.

A Scan for facts

Suggested teaching time:	10 minutes	Your actual teaching time:

- To help students practice the reading strategy of scanning, ask them to scan the article for the traditions that people observe for each celebration. You may want to ask students to underline the information.
- Have students complete the chart individually and then compare answers with a partner.
- To review, have volunteers each explain one tradition. Encourage them to support their answers, giving additional information about each tradition; for example, *The Chinese give each other gifts. They give each other small gifts of fruits and sweets.*

B Compare and contrast

Suggested teaching time:	3 minutes	Your actual teaching time:

- Encourage students to think of reasons to support their choices. You may want to ask them to make notes of the reasons. Have pairs compare choices with a partner.
- Review one holiday at a time and have students who made the same choice share their reasons with the class; for example, *I find Ramadan a very interesting holiday. It's a long holiday and it's a time in which people pray and give to others.*

C Relate to personal experience

Suggested teaching time:	2 minutes	Your actual teaching time:

- Have students work in pairs to match the traditions in the chart with holidays they know. Encourage them to write sentences; for example, *We give each other gifts at Christmas.*
- Then have several students give their own examples for the same tradition.

NOW YOU CAN Exchange information about holidays

A Notepadding

Suggested teaching time:	10–15 minutes	Your actual teaching time:

- Encourage students to write notes rather than complete sentences on the notepad.
- Ask students to use the vocabulary they learned in this unit. Point out that they can use the chart on this page and the Vocabulary on page 76 for reference.
- You may want to encourage students to point out what they like or dislike about the customs and traditions of holidays as they write about them on their notepads.
- Walk around and provide help as needed.

B Group work

Suggested teaching time:	5–10 minutes	Your actual teaching time:

- Form groups of three to six students.
- Review the language in the *Be sure to recycle . . .* box. Brainstorm ways to complete the sentences. For example:
  Traditionally, people decorate their homes with the national flag.
  It's customary to get together with relatives.
  It's probably best not to go into town because the traffic is impossible.
  It's offensive to open someone's gift when you receive it.
  Purple is taboo. You shouldn't give purple flowers.
  It's impolite to leave food on your plate.
- Brainstorm questions students can ask to find out more about the holidays. For example:
  How many days is it?
  What kinds of gifts do people give each other?
  Do people go out for dinner with their families?
  What kinds of food do they eat?
  Do people go to their hometowns / travel to see their relatives?
  Is the traffic impossible?
  Are train and bus stations or airports mobbed with people?
  Do people wear their best clothes?
  Do children wear costumes?

Option: [**+5 minutes**] Take a poll to find out which holidays your students chose to write notes about. Then have a few volunteers say what they like about those holidays.

EXTRAS (optional)

- Workbook: Exercises 13–15
- Copy & Go: Activity 27

A Scan for facts Complete the chart. Check the holidays on which each tradition is observed, according to the information in the Reading. Explain your answers.

On this holiday, people...	Bolívar's Birthday	Chinese New Year	Ramadan
give each other gifts.	○	☑	○
wear costumes.	○	☑	○
pray.	○	○	☑
wish each other well.	○	☑	○
get together with their families.	○	☑	○
perform traditional dances.	○	☑	○
decorate their homes.	○	☑	○
celebrate for several days.	○	☑	○
give away money.	○	○	☑
have parades.	☑	○	○
avoid eating during the day.	○	○	☑

Which holiday is celebrated in more than one country?

☑ Simón Bolívar's Birthday   ○ Chinese New Year   ○ Ramadan

B Compare and contrast Which holiday or traditions from the Reading do you find the most interesting? Why?

C Relate to personal experience Name one holiday you know for each tradition in the chart.

> On your *ActiveBook* Self-Study Disc:
> **Extra Reading Comprehension Questions**

NOW YOU CAN   Exchange information about holidays

A Notepadding With a partner, choose three holidays in your country. Discuss the traditions of each holiday and write notes about them on your notepads.

	A historical holiday	A seasonal holiday	A religious holiday
name of holiday			
purpose			
typical food			
typical music			
typical clothing			
other traditions			

B Group work Choose one of the holidays from your notepad and give an oral report to your classmates. Each student has to ask you one question.

♻ **Be sure to recycle this language.**

Traditionally, people ___ .   It's offensive to ___ .
It's customary to ___ .   ___ is taboo.
It's probably best to ___ .   It's impolite to ___ .

GOAL   Explain wedding traditions

BEFORE YOU LISTEN

A 🔊 4:12 **Vocabulary • *Getting married*** Read and listen. Then listen again and repeat.

The events

an engagement an agreement to marry someone—**get engaged** *v.*

a (marriage) ceremony the set of actions that formally makes two single people become a married couple—**get married** *v.*

a wedding a formal marriage ceremony, especially one with a religious service

a reception a large formal party after a wedding ceremony

a honeymoon a vacation taken by two newlyweds after their wedding

The people

a fiancé a man who is engaged

a fiancée a woman who is engaged

a bride a woman at the time she gets married

a groom a man at the time he gets married

newlyweds the bride and groom immediately after the wedding

B **Discussion** Read about wedding traditions in many English-speaking countries. How are these similar or different from traditions practiced in your country?

The bride throws the bouquet after the wedding ceremony. The woman who catches it is believed to be the next to get married.

The newlyweds cut the cake together at the wedding reception.

The groom carries the bride "across the threshold," through the doorway to their new home. Soon after the wedding, they go on their honeymoon.

LISTENING COMPREHENSION

A 🔊 4:13 **Listen for the main idea** Listen to Part 1 of a lecture about a traditional Indian wedding. Which of the following statements best summarizes the information?

☐ **a** An Indian couple gets engaged long before the wedding.

☑ **b** There's a lot of preparation before an Indian wedding.

☐ **c** An Indian wedding lasts for days.

B 🔊 4:14 **Listen for details** Listen again to Part 1 and circle the best way to complete each statement.

1 A traditional Hindu wedding celebration can last for more than (two / (five)) days.

2 The bride's and groom's birthdates are used to choose the (engagement / (wedding)) date.

3 Before the wedding, musicians visit the (bride's / (groom's)) home.

4 The (bride / (groom)) is washed with oil.

5 An older relative offers the (bride / (groom)) money.

6 Relatives spend a lot of time painting the ((bride's) / groom's) skin.

BEFORE YOU LISTEN

A 🔊 Vocabulary

Suggested teaching time:	3–5 minutes	Your actual teaching time:

- Have students listen and study the words that describe *The events*. Then have students listen and repeat chorally.

- Follow the same procedure for the words that describe *The people*.

- To check comprehension, write the following phrases on the board: *a reception, an engagement, a honeymoon, a wedding*. Have students close their books and put these events in the order in which they take place. Ask volunteers to explain the order of the events. (1. An engagement; 2. a wedding; 3. a reception; 4. a honeymoon.)

- To review, have several students explain the order of the events using the Vocabulary. For example:
  The engagement comes first because it is when a man and a woman agree to marry.
  After the engagement, the couple becomes the fiancé and the fiancée.
  The wedding comes next. / This is the occasion when the bride and the groom get married.
  After the wedding, the newlyweds are given a reception.
  After the wedding, the couple takes a trip called a honeymoon.

 • Vocabulary Flash Cards

B Discussion

Suggested teaching time:	7–10 minutes	Your actual teaching time:

- Have students look at the photographs and read the captions.

- To check comprehension, ask:
  What does the bride do after the wedding ceremony? (She throws the bouquet and a woman catches it.)
  What do the newlyweds do at the reception? (They cut the cake together.)
  What does the groom do after the reception? (He carries the bride through the doorway to their new home.)
  Where do they go after that? (On their honeymoon.)

- Form small groups. Encourage students to find differences and similarities with the traditions that are familiar to them. To help students generate ideas, write these questions on the board:
  Do newlyweds go on a honeymoon?
  Does the groom carry the bride through the doorway?
  Do the bride and groom cut the cake together?
  Does the bride throw the bouquet?

LISTENING COMPREHENSION

A 🔊 Listen for the main idea

Suggested teaching time:	3 minutes	Your actual teaching time:

- To help students prepare for listening, have them read the statements. Point out that all of the statements may be true, but students should decide which one is the best summary.

- To review, have students support their choices. (The best summary is "b" because the lecture gives information about the different activities that the couple and their families do before the wedding.)

AUDIOSCRIPT

PART 1

F: In India, Hindu wedding traditions vary from state to state. But most families are known to go out of their way to make a wedding a huge celebration which can last for as long as five days or more. It is common for wedding preparations to start a year before the actual date. After a couple gets engaged to be married, the date for the wedding is chosen very carefully based on the bride and groom's birthdays—and other details—to bring good luck.

Two days before the wedding, celebrations begin at the groom's home. This is called "Making the Groom." Musicians visit his home as early as four in the morning and play traditional music while the groom's relatives and neighbors come to see him. While there, they make decorations from mango leaves, which will later be used at the wedding ceremony. Next, someone washes the groom with coconut or olive oil. His face is painted with a black dot on each cheek and a spot between his eyes. Then an older person in the family offers the groom money as a gift.

The bride goes through a ceremony before the wedding called "Making the Bride." Her face, arms, hands, and feet are painted attractively by her relatives, leaving her skin a red color. This process takes many hours to do and requires a lot of patience.

B 🔊 Listen for details

Suggested teaching time:	3 minutes	Your actual teaching time:

- To prepare students for the activity, have them read the statements before listening again.

- Ask students to compare answers with a partner and then review with the class.

- Ask students what other details they can add from the listening passage. They can listen again if necessary.

C 🔊 **Listen for the main idea**

Suggested teaching time:	2 minutes	Your actual teaching time:

- Follow the same procedure as in Exercise A Listen for the Main Idea on page 82.

- To review, have students support their choices. (The correct answer is "a" because the lecture gives information about the traditions that are observed during the wedding ceremony—from beginning to end.)

AUDIOSCRIPT

PART 2

F: The wedding ceremony is usually held in the evening. When the bride and groom arrive, there is a lot of noise and music. Members of the family wash their feet and sprinkle flowers and water on them. The couple sits in chairs under a special roof made of leaves and flowers. While the bride is seated behind a cloth so the groom can't see her, the guests eat and enjoy the wedding feast. Then when it's near the end of the feast, the cloth is removed and the music is played again. It is considered bad luck to sneeze at this moment. All the guests clap their hands while the music is playing. Then one by one the guests come to the couple and throw rice grains at their heads for prosperity. Everyone wishes the couple well. Then the couple gives each other rings made of flowers and handfuls of rice. The groom places a golden necklace over the bride's neck.

Finally, the groom places a second necklace around the bride's neck to signify the end of the wedding.

D 🔊 **Listen for details**

Suggested teaching time:	3 minutes	Your actual teaching time:

- Follow the same procedure as in Exercise B Listen for Details on page 82.

- Ask students what other details they recall from the listening passage. Permit them to listen again if necessary.

Option: **[+10 minutes]** To challenge students, have pairs discuss which tradition from the listening passage was the most interesting. Encourage students to offer follow-up comments; for example, *I think it's interesting and fun that the wedding celebration lasts so long, especially for guests who have to travel far to get there.* To review, have volunteers share their views with the class.

 • **Learning Strategies**

NOW YOU CAN **Explain wedding traditions**

A **Frame your ideas**

Suggested teaching time:	6–10 minutes	Your actual teaching time:

- Before students read the sayings and proverbs, point out the difference in meaning between a *wedding* or *marriage ceremony* and *marriage* by itself. Call on a student to describe what a *wedding* or *marriage ceremony* is. (The ceremony in which two people become married.) Explain that the word *marriage* on its own refers to the relationship between two people who are married; for example, *After the wedding, they had a long and happy marriage.*

- To review, encourage pairs to use some of the vocabulary on page 82 to discuss what the sayings and proverbs mean. Then have volunteers each explain a proverb or saying. (Possible answers: Italian saying—It's easier to find a wife for a son than to find a husband for a daughter. Irish saying—Getting married is easy; it's living together that's difficult. South African proverb—Having children makes a marriage more complete. Polish saying—Women cry before the wedding because they are happy and emotional; men cry after because they regret their decision to marry. British saying—The newlyweds will have a happy marriage if the bride has these things, for good luck.)

Language and culture

- The proverb from the U.K. expresses superstitions associated with weddings. If the bride wears something old, her old friends will remain close during the marriage. If she wears something new, the newlyweds will have a prosperous future. If someone from the bride's family lends her something to wear, the couple will have a happy marriage. If the bride wears something blue, the couple will be faithful to each other.

B **Discussion**

Suggested teaching time:	7–10 minutes	Your actual teaching time:

- To personalize, have students choose two proverbs and write notes about why they agree or don't agree with them and why they find or don't find them offensive.

- To draw on students' prior knowledge, ask them to share other proverbs, sayings, or superstitions they know about weddings and marriage.

C **Notepadding**

Suggested teaching time:	5–7 minutes	Your actual teaching time:

- As students complete their notepads individually, encourage them to use the vocabulary they learned in this unit.

D **Pair work**

Suggested teaching time:	6–7 minutes	Your actual teaching time:

- To model the activity, review the speech balloons with the class.

- Before students create their role play, brainstorm questions "the visitor" can ask. You may want to write some of them on the board. For example:

  How do the bride and the groom choose the date?
  How long is the wedding ceremony?
  What do the bride and the groom usually wear?
  Are there any things to avoid?
  What happens during the reception?
  Do the newlyweds go on honeymoon trips?

EXTRAS (optional)

- **Workbook:** Exercises 16–18
- **Copy & Go:** Activity 28

C 🔊 **Listen for the main idea** Now listen to Part 2 of the lecture. What is the information mainly about?

☑ **a** the wedding ceremony ☐ **b** the honeymoon ☐ **c** the reception after the wedding

D 🔊 **Listen for details** Listen again to Part 2 and check the statements that are true. Correct the statements that are false.

☐ **1** Relatives wash the bride's and groom's ~~hands~~. _feet_

☑ **2** The bride is seated behind a cloth so the groom cannot see her.

☑ **3** Relatives throw rice grains at the bride and groom.

☑ **4** The couple gives each other rings made of flowers.

☐ **5** The groom places a ~~flower~~ _golden_ necklace around the bride's neck.

NOW YOU CAN **Explain wedding traditions**

A Frame your ideas With a partner, read each saying or proverb about weddings and marriage. Discuss what you think each one means.

"The woman cries before the wedding and the man after."
Poland

"Marry off your son when you wish. Marry off your daughter when you can."
Italy

"Marriages are all happy. It's having breakfast together that causes all the trouble."
Ireland

"Marriage is just friendship if there are no children."
South Africa

Advice to the bride: "Wear something old and something new, something borrowed, and something blue."
United Kingdom

B Discussion Do you find any of the sayings or proverbs offensive? Why or why not? What sayings or proverbs about weddings do you know in your own language?

C Notepadding On your notepad, make a list of wedding traditions in your country. Compare your lists with those of other groups.

D Pair work Role-play a conversation in which you describe local wedding traditions to a visitor to your country. Ask and answer questions about the details.

❝ So how does a couple get engaged here? ❞

❝ Well, before they get engaged, they have to . . . ❞

Before the wedding:
At the wedding ceremony:
After the wedding:

Review

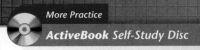

More Practice
ActiveBook *Self-Study Disc*

grammar · vocabulary · listening
reading · speaking · pronunciation

A 🔊 4:17 **Listening comprehension** Listen to each conversation and
circle the occasion or the people they are talking about. Then circle T
if the statement is true or F if it is false. Correct any false statements.

1 an engagement / a reception / (a honeymoon)   (T) F   The man who is speaking is the groom.
2 (an engagement) / a reception / a honeymoon   (T) F   The man who is speaking is the groom.
3 (a bride) / a groom / relatives   T   (F) The woman who is speaking is ~~the bride~~.   a guest
4 a bride / a groom / (relatives)   (T) F   The woman who is speaking is a guest.

B Complete each statement, using the unit Vocabulary. Then write the name of a holiday or celebration you
know for each statement.

Name a holiday when people . . .	Examples
1 ......set off...... fireworks.	Answers will vary.
2 ......march...... in parades.	
3 ......have...... picnics.	
4 ......spend...... time with their families.	
5 wear ......costumes...... .	
6 give ......each other...... gifts.	
7 ......wish each...... other well.	

🎵 4:18/4:19
Top Notch Pop
"Endless Holiday"
Lyrics p. 150

C Complete each sentence with an adjective clause. Answers will vary, but may include the following:

1 A groom is a man *who has just gotten married* .
2 Eid al-Adha is a religious holiday *that lasts four days* .
3 A honeymoon is a vacation *that people take after they get married* .
4 A hanbok is a traditional dress *that Korean people wear during Chuseok* .
5 A wedding reception is a party *that people give after the wedding ceremony* .
6 Chuseok is a holiday *that people celebrate in Korea* .

D On a separate sheet of paper, answer each question in your <u>own</u> way.

1 What's your favorite holiday? What kind of holiday
is it (seasonal, historical, religious)?

2 What's the longest holiday in your country? How
long is it?

3 What's the most interesting wedding tradition in
your country?

My favorite holiday is Semana Santa. It's a
religious holiday that takes place for a week
in March or April.

E **Writing** On a separate sheet of paper, describe two different holidays that are
celebrated in your country. Include as many details as you can about each.

- What kind of holiday is it?
- When is it celebrated?
- How is it celebrated?
- What do people do / eat / say / wear, etc.?

WRITING BOOSTER ▸ p. 146

- *Descriptive details*
- *Guidance for Exercise E*

A 🔊 Listening comprehension

Suggested teaching time:	5 minutes	Your actual teaching time:	

- To review the vocabulary, you may want to call on volunteers to give a brief definition or description of each word.

- First listening: Have students listen and circle the occasion or people mentioned. Pause after each conversation to allow students time to write their answers.

- Second listening: Have students listen and decide if the statements are true or false.

- To review, have students support their answers. (1. The groom is talking about his honeymoon in Tahiti. 2. The man is going to be a groom, but there is no date yet. 3. The woman who is speaking is a guest. 4. The woman is talking about the bride's family.)

Language and culture
- *Tie the knot* is an informal expression meaning "to get married."

AUDIOSCRIPT

CONVERSATION 1
M: Check out these pictures we took in Tahiti.
F: Oh, these are really nice! Is that your wife?
M: Yes. We took off right after the reception.
F: How romantic! How long were you there?
M: Ten days.

CONVERSATION 2
F: Hey, congratulations! I heard the news!
M: Thanks. I guess everyone knows now.
F: That's great! So when's the date?
M: In September. We've got a lot of planning to do.
F: Well, the great thing is that you've decided to tie the knot. Congratulations!

CONVERSATION 3
M: Is it true what I hear—that you caught the bouquet?
F: Uh-huh. She threw it right to me.
M: Well, you've been great friends since childhood, right?
F: Yeah, we have. I'm so happy for her!

CONVERSATION 4
F: Can you believe how much money they paid for this reception?
M: I know. It's unbelievable! It must have cost a fortune.
F: I heard the parents and the grandparents all wanted a really big wedding. They must have a lot of money!
M: Well, you know what they say. Weddings are really for the family.
F: I guess so. Everyone does seem to be having a wonderful time.

B Complete each statement . . .

Suggested teaching time:	3–5 minutes	Your actual teaching time:	

- To model the activity, complete the first item with the class.

- As students do the activity, tell them that they can refer to the Vocabulary on page 76 if necessary.

C Complete each sentence . . .

Suggested teaching time:	2–3 minutes	Your actual teaching time:	

- Review the example with the class.

- Have students read their complete sentences aloud. Make necessary corrections.

D On a separate sheet of paper . . .

Suggested teaching time:	5 minutes	Your actual teaching time:	

- Review the example first.

- Encourage students to write two or three sentences for each question.

- Then have students share their answers with a partner. Ask several students to read their answers aloud.

Language and culture
- In British English the word *favorite* is spelled *favourite*. Many American English words that end in *-or* such as *color, favor,* and *honor* are spelled with *-our* such as *colour, favour,* and *honour* in British English.

E Writing

Suggested teaching time:	10–12 minutes	Your actual teaching time:	

- To help students prepare for writing, brainstorm the kind of information that can be used to answer each question:
  - *What kind of holiday is it?* (Seasonal, religious, historical.)
  - *When is it celebrated?* (Date / time of the year; how long it lasts.)
  - *How is it celebrated?* (Do people celebrate in public places? Do they celebrate in their homes? Do they get together with their families? Do they travel long distances to see their relatives? Do they decorate their homes? Are there any parades / fireworks?)
  - *What do people do / eat / say / wear, etc.?* (Do people give each other gifts? Do they send each other cards? Do they perform any ceremonies? Do they eat traditional foods? What do they say to wish each other a good holiday? Do they wear traditional costumes?)

- Encourage students to write a paragraph for each question. You may want to tell them to finish each paragraph by saying what people enjoy the most about each holiday.

Option:  **WRITING BOOSTER** (Teaching notes p. T146)

🔘 **ActiveTeach**
Multimedia Disc • Writing Process Worksheets

ORAL REVIEW

Pair work challenge

Suggested teaching time:	5–10 minutes	Your actual teaching time:	

- To model the activity, review the example with the class. Have students brainstorm questions about a holiday. (Possible answers: What kind of holiday is it? Where do people celebrate it? How long does it last? What do people do? What do they eat?)
- Form pairs and divide the class into Students A and Students B. Students A will read about *Songkran* and Students B will read about *Mexican Independence Day*.
- To begin, ask students to open their books and look at the fact sheet and photos for one minute.
- Then have students close their books and discuss the holidays in pairs.

Pair work 1

Suggested teaching time:	5 minutes	Your actual teaching time:	

- To prepare students for the first conversation, have them work in pairs. Tell each pair to imagine that one of them is a visitor to Thailand or Mexico and wants to know more about a local holiday. The other student is from, or working or studying in, that country.
- Encourage students to ask what kind of holiday it is, when it takes place, and what people do. Remind them to wish each other a good holiday.

Possible responses . . .

A: I heard there's going to be a holiday. B: That's right. Mexican Independence Day. A: What kind of holiday is it? B: It's a historical holiday that takes place in September each year. People march in parades and perform traditional dances. A: Do they set off fireworks? B: Lots of them. A: Well, have a great Independence Day! B: Thank you!

A: I heard there's going to be a holiday. B: *That's right. It's Songkran next week.* A: What kind of holiday is it? B: It's a seasonal holiday that lasts for three days. People have lots of fun throwing water at each other in the streets. A: Well, enjoy yourself on Songkran! B: Thanks!

Pair work 2

Suggested teaching time:	5 minutes	Your actual teaching time:	

- Follow the same procedure as in Pair Work 1. Direct attention to the Notes at the end of each fact sheet.
- Have students discuss the holiday they did not use for the first conversation. Point out that students should ask if a custom is appropriate.

Possible responses . . .

A: Do you mind if I ask you about something? B: Of course not. What's up? A: I'm not sure about the customs here. I know that people throw water at each other during Songkran. Is it OK to throw water at a complete stranger? B: Definitely! You should feel free to throw water at anyone. People never get offended. A: Thanks. That's really helpful.

A: Do you mind if I ask you about something? B: Sure. What's up? A: I'm not sure about the customs here. I know that people shout "Viva México" to celebrate their country's independence. Would it be appropriate for a foreigner to shout it also? B: Definitely! Even if you're not Mexican, you can join in. A: Thanks. That's really helpful.

Group presentation

Suggested teaching time:	5–10 minutes	Your actual teaching time:	

- Review the example with the class.
- Ask students to write as many statements as they can about the holidays using adjective clauses.
- Have students give a presentation to their group or to the class using the sentences they wrote as a guide.

Option: [+10 minutes] To challenge students, ask them to write eight statements about the holidays, some of which should be false. Have them keep their books closed. Students then exchange sheets of paper with a partner and mark the statements *true* or *false*.

Option: Oral Progress Assessment

Use the photographs on page 85. Encourage students to use language practiced in this unit and previous units.

- Tell the student to describe the holidays and the pictures using three adjective clauses; for example, *Songkran is a seasonal holiday that people celebrate in Thailand. In the first picture, there is a woman who is making an offering. In the second picture, there are people who are throwing water at each other.*
- Ask the student to choose one of the pairs of people in the photos. Tell the student that together you are going to role-play a conversation.
- Evaluate the student on intelligibility, fluency, correct use of target grammar, and appropriate use of vocabulary.

 • Oral Progress Assessment Charts

Option: *Top Notch* Project

Have students create a presentation about a holiday or a wedding tradition.

Idea: Have students work in small groups and choose a holiday or wedding tradition from another country. Ask each group to use the library or the Internet to research information. Ask groups to include visuals such as photographs from magazines or the Internet.

EXTRAS (optional)

- **Complete Assessment Package**
- **Weblinks for Teachers:** pearsonlongman.com/topnotch/

And on your ActiveTeach Multimedia Disc:
- **Just for Fun**
- **Top Notch Pop Song Activities**
- **Top Notch TV Video Program and Activity Worksheets**
- **Supplementary Pronunciation Lessons**
- **Audioscripts**
- **Unit Study Guides**

Pair work challenge For one minute, look at the photos and Fact Sheet for one of the holidays. Your partner looks at the other holiday. Then close your books. Ask and answer questions about each other's holidays. For example:

Why do people celebrate Songkran?

Pair work Create conversations for the people.

1 Ask about one of the holidays. Start like this:

I heard there's going to be a holiday.

2 Ask about local customs during the holiday. Start like this:

Do you mind if I ask you something?

Group presentation Choose one of the holidays and give a presentation to your group or class. Use adjective clauses.

Songkran is a seasonal holiday that . . .

At Songkran . . .

Songkran Water Festival

Celebrated in Thailand. Lasts for three days.

Marks the . . .
- *start of the Buddhist New Year.*
- *beginning of the farming season.*

People . . .
- *clean their homes.*
- *make offerings at temples.*
- *sing and dance in the street.*
- *throw lots of water at each other!*

NOTE: *Don't worry! It's customary for people to throw lots of water at complete strangers on this holiday.*

Mexican Independence Day

Celebrated on September 15 and 16.

Commemorates . . .
- *the beginning of the War of Independence.*
- *Mexico's independence from Spain.*

People . . .
- *march in parades.*
- *perform traditional music and dances.*
- *decorate with the colors of the Mexican flag (red, white, and green).*
- *set off fireworks.*
- *eat special dishes (sometimes red, white, and green).*

NOTE: *It's customary for people to shout, "Viva México!" Even if you are not Mexican, you can join in.*

On Mexican Independence Day . . .

NOW I CAN... ✓

- ☐ Wish someone a good holiday.
- ☐ Ask about local customs.
- ☐ Exchange information about holidays.
- ☐ Explain wedding traditions.

85

Inventions and Discoveries

GOALS After Unit 8, you will be able to:

1 Describe technology.
2 Take responsibility for a mistake.
3 Describe how inventions solve problems.
4 Discuss the impact of inventions/discoveries.

the wheel

the steam locomotive

the mosquito net

penicillin: the first "wonder drug"

the automobile

the television

A Discussion Most of the pictures represent inventions. Do you know which one resulted from a discovery? How would you explain the difference between an invention and a discovery? Provide some examples of inventions and discoveries.

UNIT 8

Inventions and Discoveries

Preview

Suggested teaching time:	10–15 minutes	Your actual teaching time:

Before Exercise A, give students a few minutes of silent time to look at the pictures and read the captions.

- To draw on students' prior knowledge, have pairs share what they know about the inventions or discoveries represented in the pictures. Encourage students to imagine what life was like before these inventions or discoveries. For example:

  Before cars and the steam locomotive were invented, horses were used to carry people and things on land.

  Many people used to die of diseases that now can be cured with penicillin.

  The wheel was invented thousands of years ago. Before the wheel, people had to carry things themselves or on animals.

  Before the invention of the television, people got their news from the radio or newspapers.

- To review, have volunteers explain the importance of one of these inventions / discoveries; for example, *To me, penicillin is important because it has saved and continues to save millions of lives. I think the television is an important invention because it shows us what is happening all over the world.*

Language and culture

- Alexander Fleming in London, England, accidentally discovered penicillin in 1928. The use of penicillin (once also called the "miracle drug") to treat diseases and illness began in the 1940s.
- The oldest wheel, discovered in Mesopotamia, has been dated back to 4000–3500 B.C.E. Before the discovery of the wheel, people moved heavy objects by placing logs under them and pushing and pulling.
- British inventor Richard Trevithick built the first successful steam locomotive in 1804. This invention not only enabled the transportation of products over long distances more quickly but led to the growth of many industries.
- Inventors from Germany, England, Russia, and the United States contributed to the invention of the television. In 1926, Scottish inventor John Logie Baird was the first to transmit a live moving image. Televisions have been available to the public since the 1930s.
- Karl Benz built the first gasoline-powered motorcar in 1886 in Germany. In 1908, Henry Ford of the United States began to mass-produce the Model T, a relatively inexpensive car that was accessible to the average person.

A Discussion

Suggested teaching time:	10 minutes	Your actual teaching time:

- Have students discuss the questions in small groups. If students need help explaining the difference between an *invention* and a *discovery*, write the following definitions on the board:

  Something that was designed or created for the first time

  Something that already existed but was not known before

- Ask students to match the definitions with the correct terms. (Invention / discovery.)
- To review, draw the following chart on the board (without the possible responses):

Inventions	Discoveries
steam locomotive	fire
automobile	gold
television	gravity
computer	dinosaurs
airplane	the cell
telephone	that the Earth is round

- Have volunteers classify the objects represented by the pictures and place them under the correct headings. Then ask students to give their own examples. List them in the correct column.

B 🔊 Photo story

Suggested teaching time:	3–5 minutes	Your actual teaching time:

- Before students read and listen to the Photo Story, ask questions about the photos. *What are the women doing?* (Shopping.) *How can you tell?* (They are in a shopping mall. They are carrying shopping bags.)

- To check comprehension after students read and listen, ask *What happened during Leslie's trip?* (She was bitten by mosquitoes. / She got a lot of mosquito bites.) *What product does Jody say Leslie should have brought?* (Insect repellent.) *Did Leslie bring some?* (Yes.) *Why didn't it work?* (Because it had no poison.)

- To personalize, ask students if they've ever gotten a lot of mosquito bites. Encourage them to say where they were and whether they could have prevented the bites.

C Paraphrase

Suggested teaching time:	7–10 minutes	Your actual teaching time:

- Encourage students to identify which woman says each of the phrases and to use the context of the conversation to help figure out their meaning.

- Have students compare answers with a partner and then review with the class. Students should support their answers with a reason based on the Photo Story.

Answers for Exercise C
1. got a lot of mosquito bites
2. bit us a lot
3. That must have been terrible.
4. a lot of
5. have to use it even if you don't like it
6. won't use it
7. I'm taking

D Think and explain

Suggested teaching time:	5 minutes	Your actual teaching time:

- Have students answer the questions individually. You may want to ask them to underline the information that supports their answers.

- To review, have volunteers read their answers aloud.

Answers for Exercise D
1. itching
2. in the mountains
3. through a hole in the screen
4. because it isn't organic or natural
5. mosquito nets to hang over the bed

E Opinion survey

Suggested teaching time:	10–15 minutes	Your actual teaching time:

- Ask students to rank the items and take notes about why they ranked them the way they did. Tell students they can base their choices on what is important for them or for people in general. Clarify that both criteria are valid as long as they can support their choices.

- To review, write the items on the board and keep a tally of the invention / discovery that students consider the most important. Then have volunteers explain their choices of the most important inventions.

EXTRAS (optional)

- Workbook: Exercises 1–4

AUDIOSCRIPT for page T88 (B Listening comprehension)

ADVERTISEMENT 1
M: Need the newest technology? The Strawberry palmtop is a smart phone with 10,000 applications, and room enough for 10,000 more. Get the latest technology for the lowest price—now that's smart!

ADVERTISEMENT 2
F: For the most reliable workhorse in digital office phones, order the classic and traditional Blackstone. The Blackstone uses familiar, time-proven technology—no gimmicks or hard-to-understand buttons. No other office phone provides unfailing service and sound quality that's clear enough for a conference call with 50 people in the room.

ADVERTISEMENT 3
M: The Micro Scanner enables you to scan images from a remote source. Clear-as-a-bell color images transmitted from anywhere in your phone network can be instantly uploaded onto your PC. No more old-fashioned two-step processes. The Micro Scanner is simple and inexpensive and makes all low-tech scanners obsolete.

ADVERTISEMENT 4
F: What's better than a camera phone? What about a phone camera? The Digicon B1X Beta permits you to talk to people on site in wide angle and telephoto scenes, permitting you to direct them to get the best shot. Talk right into the lens. It's always ready. This all-in-one device uses ideas that most people haven't yet imagined. And it's available today for people who simply have to have all the latest applications.

ADVERTISEMENT 5 [M = British English]
M: Available today from Teknicon: the 17-inch LCD monitor—the latest in Teknicon's award-winning monitors. This model has a beautiful, sleek design and enhanced virtual surround-sound speakers. Impress your guests! They'll know just by seeing it that you have purchased the very best in the Teknicon line.

◀)) Photo story Read and listen to a conversation about how an invention might have helped someone.

Leslie: This itching is driving me crazy!

Jody: Look at your arm! Are those mosquito bites?

Leslie: Yeah. Ben and I got eaten alive last weekend. We went away for a second honeymoon at this cute little bed and breakfast in the mountains, but the mosquitoes were brutal.

Jody: That doesn't sound very romantic. Didn't they have screens in the windows?

Leslie: Well, they did, but ours had a big hole and we didn't realize it until the middle of the night. What a nightmare!

Jody: Too bad you didn't bring any insect repellent. There are tons of mosquitoes in the mountains this time of year. Hello?

Leslie: We actually did have some, but it just didn't work that well. You know how Ben is—everything has to be organic and natural.

Jody: Well, with all due respect to Ben, you just have to bite the bullet once in a while and use the stuff that works. Whether you like it or not, the poison _is_ effective.

Leslie: I agree, but Ben won't hear of it. You know, next time we go away for a romantic weekend, I'm packing one of those mosquito nets to hang over the bed.

C Paraphrase Say each of the underlined expressions from the Photo Story in your _own_ way.
See page T87 for answers.

1 "Ben and I got eaten alive last weekend."

2 ". . . the mosquitoes were brutal."

3 "What a nightmare!"

4 "There are tons of mosquitoes in the mountains this time of year."

5 ". . . you just have to bite the bullet once in a while and use the stuff that works."

6 "I agree, but Ben won't hear of it."

7 ". . . I'm packing one of those mosquito nets to hang over the bed."

D Think and explain Answer the following questions, according to the Photo Story.
See page T87 for answers.

1 What effect does a mosquito bite cause?

2 Where were Leslie and Ben when they got the mosquito bites?

3 How did mosquitoes get into their bedroom?

4 Why would Ben object to "the stuff that works"?

5 What is another preventive measure against mosquitoes?

E Opinion survey Rank the inventions and discoveries in order of importance from 1 (most important) to 10 (least important). Explain the reason for ranking one the most important.

Rank	Item	Rank	Item
	air travel		pasteurization of milk products
	antibiotics		the Internet
	cell phones		vaccination
	insect repellents		water purification systems
	mosquito nets		other:

GOAL   Describe technology

Describing manufactured products

A 🔊 4:21 Read and listen. Then listen again and repeat.

Uses new technology		Offers high quality		Uses new ideas	
high-tech	OR	high-end	OR	innovative	OR
state-of-the-art	OR	top-of-the-line	OR	revolutionary	OR
cutting-edge		first-rate		novel	

B 🔊 4:22 **Listening comprehension** Listen to the ads. Choose the correct word or phrase to describe the product.

1 The Strawberry smart phone is (state-of-the-art / top-of-the-line).

2 The Blackstone is a (revolutionary / high-end) device.

3 The Micro Scanner is a (high-end / cutting-edge) product.

4 The Digicon B1X Beta is a (novel / first-rate) camera.

5 The 17-inch LCD Monitor is (innovative / top-of-the-line).

> **GRAMMAR BOOSTER ▸ p. 134**
> - *Real and unreal conditionals: review*
> - *Clauses after wish*
> - *Unless in conditional sentences*

Conditional sentences: review

Real (or "factual") conditionals
If you **want** a fuel-efficient car, you **need** something smaller.
If you **buy** the Alva, you**'ll get** great fuel efficiency and a top-of-the-line car.
Remember: Never use a future form in the if- clause.
  Don't say: If you ~~will buy~~ the Alva . . .

Unreal conditionals
If I **were** you, I **wouldn't buy** the Digicom.
(unreal: I'm not you.)
If Blueberry **had** a cutting-edge smart phone, it **would outsell** Strawberry. (unreal: It doesn't.)
Remember: Never use <u>would</u> in the if- clause.
  Don't say: If Blueberry ~~would have~~ . . .

A Understand the grammar Check the statements that describe unreal conditions.

☐ **1** If they see something first-rate, they buy it.

☐ **2** If we take the bus to town, we save a lot of time.

☑ **3** If you turned off your cell phone in the theater, it wouldn't bother the other theatergoers.

☐ **4** If I rent the Alva, I'll save a bundle of money on gas.

☐ **5** They won't be able to upload the photos if they don't have a good Internet connection.

☑ **6** If she were here, she would explain how to use the Digicon remote telephone.

☑ **7** If the doctor prescribed an antibiotic, I would take it.

B Grammar practice Choose the correct form.

1 If the Teknicon 17-inch monitor (were / would be) on sale, I (will / would) buy it right away.

2 Most people (buy / will buy) state-of-the-art products if they (have / will have) enough money.

3 If they (would invent / invented) a safe way to text-message while driving, people (will / would) be very happy.

4 If she (knew / would know) about the Pictopia phone camera, she (uses / would use) it on her next work assignment.

VOCABULARY

A 🔊 Read and listen . . .

Suggested teaching time:	2 minutes	Your actual teaching time:

- To introduce the topic, tell students they will learn words to describe manufactured products. Point out that manufactured products are goods or items such as cameras and cars that are made in large quantities in factories. Ask students to name additional examples.

- Point out that the words are all adjectives (words that describe nouns); for example, *a cutting-edge monitor, a revolutionary camera, a novel invention*. Explain that the words in each column are synonyms with no real difference in meaning.

Language and culture
- Compound adjectives are hyphenated when they precede nouns. *I want a high-tech computer. She bought a first-rate camera.* However, they are not hyphenated when they are subject complements. *My computer is high tech. Her camera is first rate.*
- *Top-of-the-line* and *state-of-the-art* are usually hyphenated both before nouns and after the *be* verb.

 • Vocabulary Flash Cards

B 🔊 Listening comprehension

Suggested teaching time:	5–7 minutes	Your actual teaching time:

- First listening: Ask students to take notes of the key words that might support their choices. Stop after each ad to allow them time to choose the correct adjectives.

- Second listening: Have students listen again to confirm their choices and make any necessary corrections.

AUDIOSCRIPT See page T87.

GRAMMAR

Suggested teaching time:	10–15 minutes	Your actual teaching time:

- Direct students' attention to the chart and have them study the examples of real (or factual) conditionals. Write on the board:

Present real conditional
1. If you <u>buy</u> first-rate products, you <u>spend</u> more money.
        If clause   *Result clause*

Future real conditional
2. If he <u>gets</u> a raise, he'll <u>buy</u> lots of high-tech products.
    If clause   *Result clause*

- To review conditional sentences, point out the *if* clauses and the *result* clauses. You may also want to point out the comma after the *if* clause and tell students that if the *if* clause is second, a comma is not used.

- To review the verb forms of present real conditionals, ask *What verb form does sentence 1 use in the if clause?* (Simple present.) *And in the <u>result</u> clause?* (Simple present.) To clarify, say *We use the present real conditional to express habits or general truths.*
  - To provide practice, ask several students to say what they usually do if they get up early; for example, *If I get up early, I go running. If I get up early, I make breakfast.*

- To review the verb forms of future real conditionals, ask *What verb form does sentence 2 use in the if clause?* (Simple present.) *And in the <u>result</u> clause?* (Will + base form.) To clarify, say *We use the future real conditional to say what will happen under a certain condition.* Then ask *What is the condition in sentence 2?* (Getting a raise.) *And its result?* (Buying lots of high-tech products.)
  - To provide practice, ask several students to say what they will do this weekend if it rains; for example, *If it rains, I'll stay at home. If it rains, I'll go shopping.* Ask a student to read aloud the *Remember* note.

- Have students study the examples of unreal conditionals. Add to the board:
  3. If I <u>needed</u> a new car, I would <u>buy</u> a high-end model.

- To review the verb forms of unreal conditionals, ask *What verb form does sentence 3 use in the if clause?* (Simple past.) *And in the <u>result</u> clause?* (Would + base form.)

- To review, say *We use the unreal conditional to express an imagined condition and its imagined result.* Then ask *What is the imagined condition?* (Needing a car.) *And its imagined result?* (Buying one.)
  - To provide practice, ask several students to say which car they would buy if they had enough money to buy a new top-of-the-line car; for example, *If I had enough money for a new car, I'd buy a Futura 360.* Have students read the *Remember* note.

Option: **GRAMMAR BOOSTER** (Teaching notes p. T134)

 • Inductive Grammar Charts

A Understand the grammar

Suggested teaching time:	3–5 minutes	Your actual teaching time:

- To model the activity, complete the first item with the class. Have students identify the verb forms in each clause. (Simple present.) and which type of conditional sentence it is. (Present real conditional.)

Language and culture
- In American English, the fuel for a car is *gasoline*, or *gas*. In British English, *gas* only refers to something to cook with or heat a home. *Petrol* is the fuel for cars.

B Grammar practice

Suggested teaching time:	3 minutes	Your actual teaching time:

- To review answers, ask several students to read a sentence aloud. Make necessary corrections.

C Grammar practice

Suggested teaching time:	4–5 minutes	Your actual teaching time:

- To model the activity, brainstorm different ways to complete the first item; for example, *If money were not a problem, I'd travel around the world / I'd buy a new house / I'd make big donations to charities.*

- As students complete the activity, encourage them to identify the type of conditional sentence for each item before completing the sentence.

- Have students explain their sentences to a partner and then review with the class.

Option: **[+5 minutes]** To extend the activity, have pairs take turns saying where they would travel if they could go anywhere in the world, and then have them ask follow-up questions. For example:

Student A: *If I could go anywhere in the world, I would go to Greece.*

Student B: *Really? Why would you go there?*

To review, have volunteers share their travel wishes with the class.

CONVERSATION MODEL

A ◀)) Read and listen . . .

Suggested teaching time:	1–2 minutes	Your actual teaching time:

This conversation strategy is implicit in the model:
- Congratulate someone for a major new purchase.

- After students read and listen, ask *What kind of car did the woman buy?* (The Alva 500 / a top-of-the-line Alva.) *Would her friend like to buy a new car?* (Yes, if she had the money.)

Language and culture
- *To treat oneself to something* is to buy something special for yourself. *She treated herself to a state-of-the-art computer.* You can also treat someone else to something; for example, *He treated us to dinner.*

B ◀)) Rhythm and intonation

Suggested teaching time:	2–3 minutes	Your actual teaching time:

- Have students repeat each line chorally. Make sure students:
  - use falling intonation for *What kind?*
  - put extra stress on *myself* in *I'd get a new car myself.*

NOW YOU CAN Describe technology

A Notepadding

Suggested teaching time:	5–8 minutes	Your actual teaching time:

- Review the example with the class. Have students identify the product (Hairdryer/cell phone.) and the adjective to describe it (State-of-the-art.). Ask students to say other adjectives that describe a product that uses new technology. (Cutting-edge, high-tech.)

- Before students complete their notepads, encourage them to be creative and invent new products. Point out that they can write about *dream products* they would like to have.

- Remind students to use the vocabulary they learned in this unit. Walk around and provide help as needed.

B Pair work

Suggested teaching time:	5 minutes	Your actual teaching time:

- To reinforce the use of the conversation strategy, remind students that they need to display enthusiasm when they congratulate someone.

- Direct attention to the last sentence in the conversation and remind students that they should use the unreal conditional to say what they would do. Brainstorm ways to complete the sentence. Encourage students to use contractions. You may want to write some examples on the board:

  If I needed a [phone], I'd buy that one, too.
  If I could afford it, I'd get the [Alva 700].
  If I had the money, I'd go [to Japan].

Don't stop! Extend the conversation. Have students give more examples of questions they can ask. For example:

Where did you buy it?
Have you tried it?
That's a first-rate product, isn't it?
Is it easy to use?
Was it expensive?
Was it on sale?
Did you buy it online?

- To model the activity, role-play and extend the conversation with a more confident student. As students interact, walk around the room and provide help as needed.

 • Conversation Pair Work Cards

C Change partners

Suggested teaching time:	5 minutes	Your actual teaching time:

- Make sure students personalize the activity and use other products.

EXTRAS (optional)

- **Workbook:** Exercises 5–8
- **Copy & Go:** Activity 29

5 If I (**have** / will have) an Internet connection in my hotel room, I (send / **will send**) you the report by tomorrow morning.

6 What (**will** / would) you do if your laptop (**breaks** / will break)?

7 I (won't / **wouldn't**) buy a Lunetti phone if I (have / **had**) all the money in the world. No one needs such a high-end phone in the office.

C Grammar practice With a partner, complete each statement with an <u>if-</u> clause or a result clause. Then share and explain some statements with your class.

1 If money were not a problem, . . .

2 People would stop getting infected with diseases if . . .

3 If people are not careful when they choose new products, . . .

4 I would stay up all night tonight if . . .

CONVERSATION MODEL

4:23

A 🔊» Read and listen to a conversation about new technology.

A: I just got a new car.

B: No kidding! What kind?

A: The Alva 500. The 500 model is top-of-the-line. I thought I'd treat myself.

B: Well, congratulations! If I had the money, I'd get a new car myself.

4:24

B 🔊» **Rhythm and intonation** Listen again and repeat. Then practice the Conversation Model with a partner.

NOW YOU CAN Describe technology

A Notepadding Write one product you've recently gotten (or would like to have) for each category.

Quality	Product name	Adjective
Uses new technology:	the Whisper combination hairdryer / cell phone	state-of-the-art

Quality	Product name	Adjective
Uses new technology:		
Offers high quality:		
Uses new ideas:		

B Pair work Role-play a new conversation, changing the Conversation Model with one of the products and adjectives on your notepads. Use the unreal conditional. Then change roles.

A: I just got ....

B: No kidding! What kind?

A: .... It's .... I thought I'd treat myself.

B: Well, congratulations! If I .... , I'd ....

> **Don't stop!**
>
> Discuss another product and use other adjectives.
>
> Ask questions about it:
> • What does it look like?
> • How does it work?
> • How fast / accurate / powerful is it?
> • Does it work well?
> • Is it guaranteed?

C Change partners Personalize the conversation again, using other products on your notepads.

GOAL Take responsibility for a mistake

CONVERSATION MODEL

A 🔊 **4:25** Read and listen to someone taking responsibility for a mistake.

A: Sorry I'm late. I thought the meeting was tomorrow.

B: What happened?

A: I'm ashamed to say I just forgot to put it on my calendar.

B: Don't worry. That can happen to anyone.

A: Well, if I had written it down, I wouldn't have forgotten.

B: No harm done. We were just getting started.

B 🔊 **4:26** **Rhythm and intonation** Listen again and repeat.
Then practice the Conversation Model with a partner.

GRAMMAR *The past unreal conditional*

The past unreal conditional describes unreal or untrue conditions and results.
Use the past perfect in the if- clause. Use <u>would have</u> or <u>could have</u> in the result clause.

If she **had rented** a more economical car, she **wouldn't have spent** so much money on gas. (unreal condition: She <u>didn't</u> rent a more economical car.)

If Jonas Salk **hadn't invented** a vaccine to protect people against polio, many more people **would have gotten** the disease. (unreal condition: He <u>did</u> invent a vaccine.)

Questions and answers
Could they **have prevented** the accident if they **had known** the tires were so old?
(Yes, they **could have.** / No, they **couldn't have.**)

How many people **would have been injured or killed** if air bags **hadn't been invented**? (No one knows exactly, but a lot.)

> **Be careful!**
> **Don't use <u>would</u> or <u>could</u> in the if- clause.**
> Don't say: "If Jonas Salk ~~wouldn't have invented…~~"

> **GRAMMAR BOOSTER ▸ p. 135**
> *The unreal conditional: variety of forms*

A Understand the grammar Choose the meaning of each past unreal conditional sentence.

1 I wouldn't have gone to class if I had known I had the flu.
(a) I went to class.   **b** I didn't go to class.

2 If we had used our GPS, we wouldn't have gotten lost.
(a) We got lost.   **b** We didn't get lost.

3 If they hadn't planted those new genetically engineered tomatoes, they would have lost this year's crop.
a They lost this year's crop.   (b) They didn't lose this year's crop.

4 The airline wouldn't have canceled the flight if they hadn't had a program to predict engine failure.
(a) They canceled the flight.   **b** They didn't cancel the flight.

B Grammar practice Choose the correct forms to complete each past unreal conditional sentence.

1 What ....**would**.... you ..**have done**.. if you ....**hadn't had**........ a phone in your car?
        do   not / have

2 We **couldn't have been able to have** this digital video conference if an Internet connection ....**hadn't been**.... available.
   cannot / have   not / be

3 If our old film camera ....**hadn't broken**.........., we ....**wouldn't have bought**........ this digital one.
                not / break   not / buy

4 If she ....**had taken**.... her smart phone with GPS, she ....**wouldn't have been**.... late for the dinner.
        take   would not / be

5 If instrument navigation ....**hadn't been invented**........, intercontinental air travel ....**wouldn't have developed**.... .
              not / be invented   not / develop

CONVERSATION MODEL

A 🔊)) Read and listen . . .

Suggested teaching time:	2 minutes	Your actual teaching time:

> These conversation strategies are implicit in the model:
> • Apologize for lateness and provide an explanation.
> • Indicate regret for a mistake by beginning an explanation with "I'm ashamed to say . . .".
> • Reduce another's self-blame with "That can happen to anyone." and "No harm done."

• Have students look at the photograph. Ask *How many people are in the photograph?* (Three.) *Where are they?* (At work. In a meeting.)

• To check comprehension after students read and listen, ask *Why was the man sorry?* (Because he was late for the meeting.) *What was his colleague's reaction?* (He said not to worry.) *Why was he late for the meeting?* (Because he forgot to put it on his calendar.)

> **Language and culture**
> • It is common to say "Sorry I'm late" instead of "I'm sorry I'm late."

B 🔊)) Rhythm and intonation

Suggested teaching time:	3 minutes	Your actual teaching time:

• Have students repeat each line chorally. Make sure students:
  ◦ put extra stress on *happen* and *anyone* in *That can happen to anyone.*
  ◦ pause slightly after *well* in *Well, if I had written it down.*
  ◦ put extra stress on *wouldn't* and *forgotten* in *I wouldn't have forgotten.*

GRAMMAR

Suggested teaching time:	10–13 minutes	Your actual teaching time:

• Direct attention to the chart and have students read the first explanation and study the examples. Write on the board:
  If he had remembered the meeting, he would have arrived on time.

• To review the verb forms of the past unreal conditional, ask *What form do you see in the if clause?* (Past perfect.) *And the result clause?* (Would + have + past participle.) Point out that *could + have* + past participle is also possible. To clarify, say *We use the unreal conditional to talk about an unreal or untrue condition and its possible result.* Then ask *What is the unreal condition in the example?* (That he remembered the meeting—unreal, because he didn't.) *And its result?* (He didn't arrive on time.)

• To provide practice, ask students to say how they would have reacted if they had been the man's boss. For example:
  If I had been his colleague:

I would have gotten angry, but I wouldn't have let him know.
I would have told him not to worry.
I would have understood.

• Have students read the *Questions and answers.* To provide practice, have pairs take turns asking each other if they would have made up an excuse or told the truth if they had been the man who was late for the meeting. For example:
  Student A: *Would you have made up an excuse?*
  Student B: *Maybe I would have blamed the traffic. And you? Would you have made up an excuse?*
  Student A: *No, I wouldn't have. I would have told the truth.*

• Have students read the *Be careful!* box. Point out that this is a common error.

Option: [+5 minutes] To challenge students, write the following sentences on the board and ask them to correct the mistakes in the past unreal conditional.
  1. *If I had remembered it was her birthday, I would call her.*
  2. *If I would have had my credit card, I would have bought it.*
  3. *What would you have done if you knew the truth?*
Review with the class. (1. Would <u>have called</u>; 2. <u>had had</u>; 3. <u>had known</u>.)

FYI: The use of *might + have* + past participle in the *result clause* for past unreal conditional sentences is covered in *Summit.*

> **Language and culture**
> **LEN** From the Longman Corpus: A common error of learners across all language backgrounds is to say *would had* instead of *would have,* and *had have* instead of *had had.*

Option:  **GRAMMAR BOOSTER** (Teaching notes p. T135)

🔘 **ActiveTeach Multimedia Disc** • Inductive Grammar Charts

A Understand the grammar

Suggested teaching time:	2–5 minutes	Your actual teaching time:

• To model the activity, complete the first item with the class. You may want to ask *Why did she go to class?* (Because she didn't know she had the flu.)

B Grammar practice

Suggested teaching time:	3–5 minutes	Your actual teaching time:

• To review, ask several volunteers to share their answers with the class.

Option: [+5 minutes] To extend the exercise, ask pairs to imagine past unreal conditions and take turns saying how their lives would have been different. For example:
  If I had gone to another school, I wouldn't have learned any English.
  If I had bought that new sports car, I would have made a big mistake.

C Grammar practice

Suggested teaching time:	5–10 minutes	Your actual teaching time:

- To clarify the task, say *Read each situation aloud and discuss what you would have done.*

- To model the activity, read the first situation aloud and ask several students to say what they would have done. (Point out that they can change the verb *seen* in the example if necessary.) For example:

  If I had seen the article before Monday, I wouldn't have bought the car.

  If I had seen the article in the newspaper, I would have chosen another car.

  If I had checked the facts, I would have known.

  If I had suspected that the information was not true, I would have tried to find out more.

- Encourage students to give reasons for the actions they would have taken.

PRONUNCIATION

A ◀)) Notice the reduction . . .

Suggested teaching time:	2 minutes	Your actual teaching time:

- Explain that these contractions represent spoken English, but are not used in writing.

- First listening: Have students listen and study the examples. Be sure students notice that *Where'd, Who'd,* and *we'd* are pronounced as one syllable and that there is an additional syllable in *It'd.*

- Second listening: Have students listen and repeat chorally. Make sure students pronounce the reductions properly.

B ◀)) Listening comprehension

Suggested teaching time:	5 minutes	Your actual teaching time:

- To clarify the task, tell students that they will listen to contracted forms, but they will write full forms.

- First listening: To model the activity, pause after the first item and have students repeat what they hear. (Where'd they go?) Ask *What verb is the 'd a reduction of in Where'd?* (Did.) Then have a volunteer write the full question on the board. (Where did they go?)

- Before students write their sentences, remind them that the reductions they hear can be *had, would,* or *did.*

- Second listening: Have students listen and write the remaining sentences.

AUDIOSCRIPT

1
F: Where'd they go?
2
M: Who'd they talk to?
3
F: When'd you buy that car?
4
M: If I'd wanted that laptop, we would have gotten it.

5
F: If we'd known we couldn't use that scanner, we wouldn't have tried.
6
M: Why'd they try to fix the coffee maker?

 • Pronunciation Activities

NOW YOU CAN | Take responsibility for a mistake

A Pair work

Suggested teaching time:	8–10 minutes	Your actual teaching time:

- Review the list of mistakes and reasons for making them in the *Ideas* box. Encourage students to think of more mistakes and more reasons. You may want to write some on the board. For example:

  Mistakes: *You broke something you borrowed.*
  You forgot to bring your host a gift.

  Reasons: *You accidentally dropped it.*
  You left home in a hurry.

- To help students generate ideas, ask them to use the unreal conditional to explain how things could have been different for some of the mistakes. For example:

  You were late:
  If I had gotten up earlier, I wouldn't have been late.
  You forgot someone's birthday:
  If I had looked at the calendar, I would have remembered.
  You forgot to pay a bill:
  If I were more organized, I wouldn't have forgotten to pay it.
  You forgot to call someone:
  If I had written it down, I wouldn't have forgotten.
  You broke something you borrowed:
  If I'd been more careful, I wouldn't have dropped it.

- To reinforce the use of the conversation strategies, brainstorm ways to respond to an apology and to reduce someone's self-blame; for example, *It can happen to anyone. Don't worry. It's not a problem. It's OK.*

- Choose a more confident student and role-play a conversation.

 • Conversation Pair Work Cards

B Change partners

Suggested teaching time:	5 minutes	Your actual teaching time:

- Pair students with classmates they don't usually talk to in class. Remind them to take responsibility for a different mistake.

EXTRAS (optional)

- Workbook: Exercises 9–13
- Copy & Go: Activity 30

C Grammar practice

With a partner, take turns reading each situation and completing each statement. Use the past unreal conditional. More than one answer is possible.

1 On Monday you bought a new Blendini sports car because its advertising said it was very economical. However, you didn't check the facts. Then on Friday you saw an article in the newspaper: "Blendini Company fined for lying about statistics. Car uses more fuel than all others of its class."

If I had seen ....

....

2 You forgot to close the windows in your house before a weekend trip. There was a terrible rainstorm. When you got home, some of your furniture was damaged by the water. Your family blamed you because you were the last to leave the house.

If I hadn't forgotten ....

....

3 There was a big sale at the Morton Street Mall. Everything in every store was half-price. You didn't know and you went shopping somewhere else. When you got home, a friend called to tell you about all the bargains she got.

If I ....

....

4 You bought some insect repellent for a trip to the mountains. When you got there, the mosquitoes were brutal. Before you sprayed the repellent on yourself and your children, you looked at the label. It said, "Caution. Not for use on children under 12."

If I ....

....

PRONUNCIATION *Contractions with 'd in spoken English*

A 4:27 🔊 Notice the reduction of <u>had</u>, <u>would</u>, and <u>did</u>. Read and listen. Then listen again and repeat.

1 Where did you go? → Where'd you go?* /wɛrd/

2 Who did you see? → Who'd you see?* /hud/

3 It would be OK. → It'd be OK.* /ɪtəd/

4 If we had had a map, we wouldn't have gotten lost. → If we'd had a map, we wouldn't have gotten lost. /wid/

* **Note:** <u>Where'd</u>, <u>Who'd</u>, and <u>It'd</u> are contracted in speech, but not in writing.

B 4:28 🔊 **Listening comprehension** Write the sentences you hear. Write full, not contracted, forms.

1 Where did they go?

2 Who did they talk to?

3 When did you buy that car?

4 If I had wanted that laptop, we would have gotten it.

5 If we had known we couldn't use that scanner, we wouldn't have tried.

6 Why did they try to fix the coffee maker?

NOW YOU CAN Take responsibility for a mistake

A Pair work Change the Conversation Model. Role-play a conversation, taking responsibility for a mistake. Use the ideas (or your own mistake and reason) and the past unreal conditional. Then change roles.

A: Sorry I ....

B: What happened?

A: I'm ashamed to say I just ....

B: Don't worry. That can happen to anyone.

A: Well, if I had .... , I .... have ....

B: No harm done. ....

B Change partners Take responsibility for another mistake.

Ideas

Some mistakes you can make
• You were late for something.
• You forgot to do something.
• You missed a meeting.
• You missed someone's birthday.
• You didn't call someone.
• You didn't return someone's call.

Some reasons for a mistake
• You accidentally deleted an e-mail.
• You forgot to write something down.
• You wrote down the wrong date or time.
• You just got too busy and it slipped your mind.
• You had an emergency.

GOAL Describe how inventions solve problems

BEFORE YOU LISTEN

A 🔊 4:29 **Vocabulary** • *More descriptive adjectives* Read and listen. Then listen again and repeat.

low-tech / high-tech

wacky

unique

efficient / inefficient

B Complete the chart with the correct adjective and one product or invention you know.

Definition	Adjective	A product or invention
the only one of its kind	unique	Answers will vary.
pretty silly	wacky	
doesn't use modern technology	low-tech	
uses modern technology	high-tech	
doesn't waste time, money, or energy	efficient	
wastes time, money, or energy	inefficient	

LISTENING COMPREHENSION

A 🔊 4:30 **Listen for main ideas** Listen and then write each problem in your own words.

1 The cats woke her up three times last night.

2 The floor is dirty and they have one hour to clean up.

3 Cars splashed water on her skirt.

4 He has to get the soil ready for the tomatoes, and he has a lot of work to do in the home.

B 🔊 4:31 **Listen to associate** Listen again and write the number of the conversation next to the invention each person should have had.

THE ROBO-TILLER

The All Body Umbrella

The Pet Exit

The VAC-BOT

C **Discussion** Describe each of the inventions. Use one or more of the adjectives from the Vocabulary above and from page 88.

> " It's not a novel idea, but the Pet Exit is both low-tech and efficient. It doesn't need electronics or machinery. "

BEFORE YOU LISTEN

A 🔊 Vocabulary

Suggested teaching time:	2–3 minutes	Your actual teaching time:

- Have students listen to and study the phrases. Then have students listen and repeat chorally.

- To check comprehension of the vocabulary, ask the following questions and have students look at the pictures and answer them.

    Why is the fan low tech? (Because it is simple and old fashioned.)

    Why is the air conditioner high tech? (Because it uses modern technology.)

    Why do you think the glasses are wacky? (Because they are silly and have windshield wipers.)

    Why is the red car unique? (Because it has an unusual shape and it is not like the others.)

    Why is the machine efficient? (Because it can decorate many cakes in an orderly way.)

    Why is the man inefficient? (Because he is decorating just one cake at a time and making a mess.)

Language and culture

- *Wacky* is an informal word mainly used in spoken English.

- **LEN** From the Longman Corpus: The adjective *unique* is frequently modified by adverbs such as *very* and *really* in spoken English.

- **Vocabulary Flash Cards**
- **Learning Strategies**

B 🔊 Complete the chart . . .

Suggested teaching time:	3–5 minutes	Your actual teaching time:

- Have students complete the chart individually. Point out that they can refer to brands to describe the products in the last column. They can write about products they have or products they know about.

- Ask students to compare answers with a partner.

- To review, have students say complete sentences; for example, *My new Xenox printer is very efficient. At home I have a twenty-year-old low-tech radio.*

LISTENING COMPREHENSION

A 🔊 Listen for main ideas

Suggested teaching time:	3–5 minutes	Your actual teaching time:

- Pause after each conversation to allow students time to write each problem. Encourage them to write short, simple sentences.

- Have students compare answers with a partner and then review with the class.

AUDIOSCRIPT See page T93.

B 🔊 Listen to associate

Suggested teaching time:	2–4 minutes	Your actual teaching time:

- To prepare students for listening, have them look at the pictures and say what each invention does. (Possible answers: The Robo-Tiller—It prepares the soil / ground / earth for planting. It's a garden tool. The All-Body Umbrella—It protects your whole body from the rain because it reaches the floor. The Pet Exit—It's a small door for pets to come in and go out of by themselves. The Vac-Bot—It is a vacuum cleaner that cleans by itself without someone pushing it.)

- As students listen, ask them to write the number of the conversation for each invention and take notes to support their answers.

- To review with the class, have students explain their choices. (Possible answers: Conversation 1—The woman should have had the Pet Exit because the cats woke her up three times last night. Conversation 2—They should have had the Vac-Bot because the floor was dusty / dirty, and they had just one hour to clean up. Conversation 3—The woman should have had the All-Body Umbrella because cars had splashed water on her skirt. Conversation 4—The man should have had the Robo-Tiller because he had to get the soil ready for tomatoes, and he had a lot of work to do in his home.)

Language and culture

- In British English, a *vacuum cleaner* is called a *hoover*.

C Discussion

Suggested teaching time:	5–8 minutes	Your actual teaching time:

- To help students prepare for the discussion, read the speech balloon aloud and ask them to write a few sentences describing each invention. Encourage them to use the vocabulary.

- Divide students into small groups. In their discussions, encourage group members to say if they would use the inventions and to explain why.

- To review, have volunteers describe the inventions and say if they would use them if they had them. (Possible answers—The Robo-Tiller is high tech. It looks fast and efficient. I wouldn't use it if I had it because my garden is very small. The All-Body Umbrella is really wacky. But it's also low tech and efficient. If I had it, I wouldn't use it because I don't want to look silly. The Pet Exit is low tech and efficient. I don't have a pet, so I wouldn't use it if I had one in my house. The Vac-Bot is unique. It looks very efficient! I would use it if I had it because I don't have much time to clean my house.)

NOW YOU CAN | Describe how inventions solve problems

A Frame your ideas

Suggested teaching time:	10 minutes	Your actual teaching time:

- Review the example first. Point out the impersonal use of *you*, which students might also want to use to describe their new inventions. Say *So you don't fall asleep while driving* means the same as *so people don't fall asleep while driving.*

- Encourage students to check at least two boxes for each category and to use a dictionary if needed.

B Project

Suggested teaching time:	10–15 minutes	Your actual teaching time:

- To review adjectives, draw the following graphic organizer on the board or print it out from the ActiveTeach Multimedia Disc and distribute it to students.

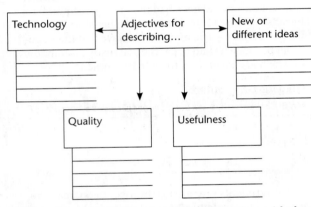

- Have students complete the graphic organizer with the adjectives from the *Be sure to recycle . . .* box. (Possible answers: Technology—high-tech, state-of-the-art, cutting-edge, low-tech. Quality—top-of-the-line, high-end, first-rate. Usefulness—efficient, inefficient, practical. New or different ideas—innovative, wacky, unique, novel, revolutionary.)

- To review real and unreal conditionals, read the examples and have students identify the type of conditional used in each. (The first example uses the future real conditional and the second example uses the past unreal conditional.) Have students suggest other conditional sentences; for example, *If you had our cutting-edge Smart Planner, your weekdays would be as organized as ever. / No time for cooking? If you get the revolutionary Efficient Home Cook, you'll get your meals done in no time.*

- To help students organize, write the following steps on the board:
  1. Choose an invention.
  2. Give it a name.
  3. Draw a picture of it.
  4. Choose adjectives to describe it.
  5. Write an advertisement. Include real and unreal conditionals.

 • Graphic Organizers

C Group work

Suggested teaching time:	10 minutes	Your actual teaching time:

- Have groups present their ads to the class. Encourage the class to ask follow-up questions. For example:
  Is it expensive?
  Does it use high-end technology?
  How does it work?
  What does it look like?
  Is it guaranteed?
  Where can you get it?
  Does it use batteries?

- To finish, have several students say which products they would like to have and why.

EXTRAS (optional)

- **Workbook:** Exercises 14 and 15
- **Copy & Go:** Activity 31

AUDIOSCRIPT for page T92 (**A** Listen for main ideas)

CONVERSATION 1
F1: I'm going crazy. I didn't sleep a wink last night.
F2: How come?
F1: It's my cats again. If they're out, they want to come in. And if they're in, they want to go out. Like T.S. Eliot said: "They're on the wrong side of every door." Last night they woke me up three times.

CONVERSATION 2
F: Oh, no! Look at the time! It's already six o'clock and your mother is coming at seven!
M: This place is a mess. Look at the dust on the floor! What'll we do?
F: Relax. I'll clean up while you make dinner.
M: We'll never be ready in time. Maybe she won't notice the dust.

CONVERSATION 3 [F2 = French]
F1: Georgette! What happened to your skirt? You look like you fell in the river.
F2: I might as well have. I had to wait a long time for the bus, and every car that passed by splashed water on me.
F1: Yeah! The puddles from the rain are enormous.
F2: And filthy!

CONVERSATION 4
M: Thanks so much for the tomato plants! I love homegrown tomatoes.
F: You're welcome. Just be sure to plant them within a couple of days. They're getting a little too big for their pots.
M: I will. See you soon!
F: Bye now.
M: Oh, my gosh. I don't have time to get the soil ready for so many plants! I have a lot of work to do in the house this weekend.

NOW YOU CAN Describe how inventions solve problems

A Frame your ideas Check the boxes to show where you think new inventions are needed. Then complete the chart with ideas.

At home and in the car	New invention needed	Benefit of the invention
☑ for safety in the car	a wake-up alarm	so you don't fall asleep while driving

	New invention needed	Benefit of the invention
At home and in the car		
☐ for safety in the car		
☐ for safety at home		
☐ for organizing things		
☐ for cooking and preparing food		
☐ for raising children		
☐ for taking care of pets		
☐ for relaxing		
In the office		
☐ for writing		
☐ for organizing papers		
☐ for training staff		
☐ for communicating		
☐ for eating lunch or snacking		
In English class		
☐ for learning new words		
☐ for learning grammar		
☐ for getting more speaking practice		
☐ for preparing to take tests		

B Project In small groups, discuss and choose one invention from someone's chart. Give the invention a name. (The invention can be low-tech, high-tech, wacky, or even impossible! The name can be funny.) Draw a picture of the invention. Then write an advertisement for your invention. Include real and unreal conditional sentences in your ad.

 Be sure to recycle this language.

top-of-the-line	wacky
high-tech / low-tech	practical
high-end	unique
state-of-the-art	efficient / inefficient
cutting-edge	novel
first-rate	revolutionary
innovative	

If you get our revolutionary "Drive Awake" alarm, you'll never again fall asleep while driving!

BEEP!!!

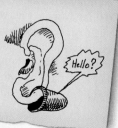

If she had brought the state-of-the-art "EAR-RINGS," she would have gotten your phone call.

Hello?

C Group work Present your ads to the class.

BEFORE YOU READ

Warm-up Of the following inventions that help people communicate in words, which do you think was the most important: the printing press, the telephone, the radio, the television, or the Internet? Explain your opinion.

READING 4:32

The Printing Press

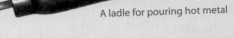
A ladle for pouring hot metal

Until the 6th or 7th century, all books had to be written by hand.

If you asked a large number of people what the most important invention has been, many would say the wheel. But many others would say the printing press. It's debatable which altered history more. But without a doubt, the printing press ranks within the top two or three inventions in history.

Long before the telephone, the television, the radio, and the computer, the written word was the only way to communicate ideas to people too far away to talk with. Until the sixth or seventh century, all books had to be written by hand. For that reason, very few books existed and, therefore, very few people read them.

In the sixth and seventh centuries, the Japanese and Chinese invented a way to print pages by carving characters and pictures on wooden, ivory, or clay blocks. They would put ink on a block and then press paper onto the ink, printing a page from the block. This process is called letterpress printing. The invention of letterpress printing was a great advance in communication because each block could be inked many times and many copies of each page could be made. Many books could now be made. Therefore, many people could read the same book.

Carved print blocks

Later, in the eleventh century, another great advance occurred. The Chinese invented "movable" type. Each character was made as a separate block which could be used many times in many texts. This meant that pages could be created by putting together these individual characters rather than having to have each whole page carved. Movable type was much more efficient than the earlier Japanese and Chinese print blocks because books could be created much more quickly by people with less skill.

In Europe, movable type was used for the first time in the fifteenth century.

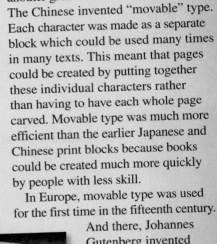

And there, Johannes Gutenberg invented typecasting, a way to make movable type much more quickly, by melting metal and pouring it into the forms of the letters. This greatly increased the speed of printing because letters could now be used more than one time on a page. Eventually, movable type made books available to many more people.

Information source: Eyewitness Books: *Invention*. By Lionel Bender, Alfred A. Knopf, New York, © 1991.

BEFORE YOU READ

Warm-up

Suggested teaching time:	6–10 minutes	Your actual teaching time:

- Before students decide on the most important invention, discuss the uses of each invention with the class. (Possible answers: The printing press is a machine used for making books / newspapers / magazines. The telephone is useful for communicating with our family / our friends / the people we work with. We use the radio for listening to music / getting our news / listening to different kinds of programs. We use the television for getting our news / watching movies and all sorts of programs. We use the Internet for communicating with people / doing research / getting our news.)

- Have several students explain their choices of the most important invention to the class. (Possible answers: To me, the most important invention is the printing press. After its invention, people created books more easily and knowledge became available to many people. / I think the printing press is the most important invention of the past, but the Internet was the most important invention of the twentieth century. I use the Internet every day. I just couldn't live without it.)

READING

Suggested teaching time:	10–15 minutes	Your actual teaching time:

- Encourage students to identify events that led to the invention of the printing press.

- After students read, draw the following diagram on the board (without the answers) and have students complete it with the events and dates that led to the invention of the printing press. To review with the class, complete the diagram on the board as students provide the answers.

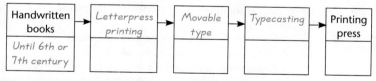

| Handwritten books | → | Letterpress printing | → | Movable type | → | Typecasting | → | Printing press |
| Until 6th or 7th century | | | | | | | | |

FYI: Students will be discussing these events in detail in the exercises that follow.

Option: [+10 minutes] To challenge students, ask them to scan the text to find the sentences that give information about each picture. Have students compare answers with a partner and then review with the class. (Possible answers: Man writing a book by hand / second paragraph—Until the sixth or seventh century, all books had to be written by hand. Carved print blocks / third paragraph—. . . the Japanese and Chinese invented a way to print pages by carving characters on wooden, ivory, or clay blocks. Ladle / Last paragraph—. . . Johannes Gutenberg invented typecasting, a way to make movable type much more quickly, by melting metal and pouring it into the forms of letters.)

Language and culture

- To *carve* means to cut shapes (e.g., letters) into hard surfaces such as wood or stone; *ivory* is the hard yellowish-white substance from the tusks of elephants; to *melt* means to heat a hard substance to a high enough temperature to make it become liquid.

ActiveTeach
Multimedia Disc
- **Extra Reading Comprehension Questions**
- **Learning Strategies**

LESSON PLAN

A Infer information

Suggested teaching time:	4–5 minutes	Your actual teaching time:

- Before students answer the questions, encourage them to identify the paragraph from the Reading that provides each answer and to underline relevant information.
- To review, have students take turns reading their answers with a partner.

Answers for Exercise A

1. The telephone, the television, the radio, and the computer.
2. Because they were made by hand.
3. For letterpress printing a whole page was carved on a block. Movable type used characters carved on small blocks that were put together to print a page.
4. Movable type was more efficient. People with less skill created books more quickly.
5. Revolutionary.
6. It became faster because letters could be used more than one time on a page.

B Identify cause and effect

Suggested teaching time:	4–5 minutes	Your actual teaching time:

- To review with the class, discuss the answers with the students. (Possible answers: 1. If typecasting hadn't been invented, people would have passed stories from one generation to the next only verbally / orally. 2. If the printing press hadn't been invented, scientific and technological advances would have been impossible. If books didn't exist, we wouldn't know much about the past. If we didn't have newspapers, we wouldn't have known about events in different places.)

NOW YOU CAN Discuss the impact of inventions / discoveries

A Frame your ideas

Suggested teaching time:	5 minutes	Your actual teaching time:

- Have students look at the pictures and read the captions. If necessary, clarify vocabulary: *crops* (Plants you grow to eat or make things.); and *DNA* (A substance that carries genetic information in a cell.).
- To check comprehension, ask the following questions about each invention. Encourage students to answer in their own words.
  What is a plow used for? (Getting the soil / land ready for planting crops.)
  Why are vaccinations important? (Because they protect people from serious diseases.)
  Why do people prefer zippers to buttons? (Because they are easier to use.)
  Why is the invention of the computer important? (Because it started a new era of communications.)
  Why is the discovery of the structure of DNA important? (Because it helps scientists understand human genes.)

B Notepadding

Suggested teaching time:	8–10 minutes	Your actual teaching time:

- To help students generate ideas, write the following questions on the board and have students use them as a guide to complete their notepads.
  How did it improve the quality of (daily) life?
  Did it lead to other inventions? Which ones?
  Did it create economic growth? How?
  What other positive outcomes did the invention create?

Text-mining: Have students share their Text-mining examples and use them to create new statements with a partner.

- Walk around the room as students write their notes, providing help as needed. (Possible answers: Plow—(life before) people had to dig by hand using a simple tool; (life after) people could use more land to grow things. Vaccines—(life before) a lot of people died of infectious diseases; (life after) saved a lot of lives, many diseases were stopped from spreading. Zipper—(life before) more time-consuming to get dressed, it took longer to make clothes because people had to sew on many buttons and make button holes; (life after) it made getting dressed easier, it took less time to make clothes because zippers are easier to sew on. Computer—(life before) research not available to everyone and harder to get, more difficult to share information and ideas; (life after) communication improved throughout the world, making it more accessible and faster. Discovery of the structure of DNA—(life before) scientists did not understand the genetic information contained in human DNA; (life after) scientists can study genetic diseases, crops can be made stronger, it can help us solve crimes.

C Group report

Suggested teaching time:	8–10 minutes	Your actual teaching time:

- Read the speech balloon aloud.
- To help students organize, write the following steps on the board:
  1. Share the information on your notepads.
  2. Choose an invention or discovery.
  3. Create a report: Include information about its impact (life before and after the invention) and a conclusion (what life would have been like without it).
  4. Share your report with the class.
- Encourage students to use the unreal conditional; for example, *If the plow hadn't been invented, farms would have remained small.* Point out that students can also use the past unreal conditional *if* clause with information about the present; for example, *If the plow hadn't been invented, farmers would still need a lot of time to prepare the fields.*

EXTRAS (optional)

- **Workbook:** Exercises 16–19
- **Copy & Go:** Activity 32

A Infer information Answer the following questions in your <u>own</u> words, using information from the Reading. See page T95 for answers.

1 What modern forms of communication don't depend on the "written word"?

2 Why were there so few books before the invention of printing?

3 What's the difference between letterpress printing and printing using movable type?

4 What advantages did movable type have over letterpress printing?

5 How would you describe Gutenberg's invention?

6 How did typecasting improve the process of printing?

B Identify cause and effect Discuss these questions. Use the conditional when possible.

1 If typecasting hadn't been invented, how would ideas have traveled great distances prior to the invention of the telephone?

2 If the printing press hadn't been invented, how would the world be different today?

> On your *ActiveBook* Self-Study Disc:
> **Extra Reading Comprehension Questions**

NOW YOU CAN Discuss the impact of inventions/discoveries

A Frame your ideas Look at some key inventions and discoveries and how they changed people's lives.

2000 B.C.E.: The plow loosens and turns the soil so crops can be planted efficiently.

1796: The discovery by Edward Jenner of the process of vaccination made the first successful vaccine possible.

1914: The modern zipper permits the opening and closing of clothes without buttons and buttonholes.

1940–1945: The first electronic computers, the size of a large room, manipulated data according to a set of instructions. The computer opened a new era of communications and research technology.

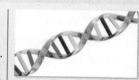

1953: James Watson, Francis Crick, and Rosalind Franklin clarified the basic structure of DNA, the genetic material for expressing life in all its forms. This discovery made the possibilities of genetic engineering practical for the first time.

B Notepadding Write your ideas about how life was before and after each invention or discovery.

	Life before	Life after
the plow		
vaccination		
the zipper		
the computer		
the DNA molecule		

> **Text-mining (optional):** Underline language in the Reading on page 94 to help you with your report. For example: "Before ___, ___ was the only way to ..."

C Group report Present a report about an invention or a discovery to your class. Describe its impact in history. Use the past unreal conditional.

> 66 After the plow was invented, farmers could plant large areas. If it hadn't been invented, they couldn't have planted enough food to sell. 99

Review

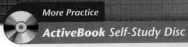
More Practice
ActiveBook *Self-Study Disc*
grammar · vocabulary · listening
reading · speaking · pronunciation

A ◄)) **Listening comprehension** Listen to people talking about new products. Match the name of each product with the best adjective to describe it.

Name of product	Adjective
__d__ **1** The Ultraphone	**a** top-of-the-line
__c__ **2** Dinner-from-a-distance	**b** unique
__b__ **3** Kinder-TV	**c** efficient
__a__ **4** Ten Years Off	**d** cutting-edge

B Check the statement that is true for each situation.

1 We wouldn't have gotten lost if we had remembered to bring our portable GPS device.
- ☐ We brought it, and we got lost.
- ☐ We brought it, and we didn't get lost.
- ☑ We didn't bring it, and we got lost.
- ☐ We didn't bring it, and we didn't get lost.

2 If the salesclerk were here, she would explain how the Omni works.
- ☐ The salesclerk is here, so she will explain how the Omni works.
- ☐ The salesclerk is here, but she won't explain how the Omni works.
- ☐ The salesclerk isn't here, but she will explain how the Omni works.
- ☑ The salesclerk isn't here, so she won't explain how the Omni works.

3 If Ron had bought the Ultraphone, he would already have sent those e-mails.
- ☐ Ron bought the Ultraphone, and he has already sent those e-mails.
- ☐ Ron bought the Ultraphone, but he hasn't sent those e-mails yet.
- ☐ Ron didn't buy the Ultraphone, but he has already sent those e-mails.
- ☑ Ron didn't buy the Ultraphone, so he hasn't sent those e-mails yet.

4:34/4:35
♪♪ **Top Notch Pop**
"Reinvent the Wheel"
Lyrics p. 150

C Complete each conditional sentence. Answers will vary, but may include the following:

1 If the computer hadn't been invented, ... I wouldn't have been able to book my vacation online ....

2 If I had to decide what the most important scientific discovery in history was, ... I would say it was penicillin ....

3 If most people cared about the environment, ... there wouldn't be so much pollution ....

4 If gasoline, heating oil, and other products that come from fossil fuels become scarce, ... we will start using ...... other sources of energy ....

5 If I could invent an inexpensive yet innovative low-tech solution to a problem, ... I would become rich ....

D **Writing** Choose one of the following inventions: the car, the television, or the Internet, or another invention. On a separate sheet of paper, describe the advantages, disadvantages, and historical impact of the invention you chose.

WRITING BOOSTER ▸ p. 146
- *Summary statements*
- *Guidance for Exercise D*

A 🔊 Listening comprehension

Suggested teaching time:	4–5 minutes	Your actual teaching time:

- To prepare students for listening, have them read the information in the lists. Point out that they will hear descriptions of the products, not the adjectives in the list.

- Pause after each conversation to allow students time to match the products and the adjectives.

- Have students listen again and write information that supports their answers; for example, *Ten Years Off is top-of-the-line because it is the best one Lake makes.* Ask students to compare their answers and reasons with a partner. Review with the class.

Option: [+5 minutes] To extend the activity, have students listen again and identify each product and what it does. (1. A phone that can read your lips and permits you to create documents in your office. 2. A machine operated by a remote (control) that keeps food cold and then cooks it. 3. A special TV that permits you to remove the programs you don't want your children to watch. 4. A face cream that makes you look younger.)

AUDIOSCRIPT

CONVERSATION 1
M: I want one of those phones that does everything: takes pictures, does e-mail, pays bills . . . . I'm tired of my old-fashioned phone. All you can do is call people and talk!
F: Well, have you seen the Ultraphone? It's got the latest technology. You just talk into it, and it can create documents at your office.
M: How does it do that?
F: It can read your lips. You just speak into the lens of the camera so it can see your lips.
M: You're pulling my leg. That sounds impossible!
F: No. Just step this way. I'll show you how it works.
M: Wow! The Ultraphone . . .

CONVERSATION 2
F1: I need a faster way to get dinner ready. It takes too long to start after I get home from work.
F2: Well, let me show you something better—remote-controlled cookware. You combine the ingredients the night before and just plug it in. The cookware keeps everything cold until you press the button on this remote. Then the cookware heats up and cooks everything. When you get home, dinner is ready!
F1: "Dinner-from-a-Distance" sounds like a lot less work in a lot less time!

CONVERSATION 3 [M2 = U.S. regional]
M1: We're worried about what our children are watching on TV. There are so many terrible programs. What can we do?
M2: Well, have you heard about Kinder-TV? It takes the worry out of TV for parents.
M1: No. What's that?
M2: Well, you buy this special TV and then you register by e-mail. Once a week, you receive an e-mail describing daytime TV programs for that week. You just check off the programs you don't want and Kinder-TV simply removes them.
M2: It's absolutely the only one that exists.

CONVERSATION 4
F1: This face cream is great. It makes me look ten years younger.
F2: You DO look great. What's it called?
F1: "Ten Years Off."
F2: Who makes it?
F1: Lake.
F2: Well, Lake is the best brand, so I'm not surprised that "Ten Years Off" is great.
F1: They make a lot of creams, but they told me "Ten Years Off" is absolutely the best one they make.

B Check the statement . . .

Suggested teaching time:	2–3 minutes	Your actual teaching time:

- Remind students that the present and past unreal conditionals express imagined conditions and results—things that do / did not actually happen / happened.

- Have students compare answers with a partner and then review with the class.

C Complete each conditional . . .

Suggested teaching time:	5 minutes	Your actual teaching time:

- Model item 1 by saying a sentence; for example, *If the computer hadn't been invented, we would have to send letters by mail.*

- To review, call on students to read their sentences aloud.

D Writing

Suggested teaching time:	9–12 minutes	Your actual teaching time:

- Encourage students to write two paragraphs. Have one paragraph describe the advantages and disadvantages of the invention. Have the other paragraph explain the historical impact, what would have happened if it hadn't been invented.

- If necessary, have students review the grammar for conditionals on pages 88 and 90.

- You may want to ask students to conclude their writing with a third paragraph about their own use of the invention. Walk around and provide help as needed.

Option:  **WRITING BOOSTER** (Teaching notes p. T146)

🔘 **ActiveTeach Multimedia Disc** • Writing Process Worksheets

ORAL REVIEW

Before the first activity, give students a few minutes of silent time to explore the pictures and become familiar with them.

Contest

Suggested teaching time:	10–15 minutes	Your actual teaching time:	

- After the task, ask students to compare their sentences in small groups.
- When students have finished the contest, review the uses of the wheel with the class. Students earn one point for each correct sentence. (Possible answers: Men use logs as wheels to move heavy objects. Carts have two wheels and are used to transport people and things. Egyptian chariots use wheels. The potter's wheel is used to make pottery / vases. Cars have four wheels.)

> ### Language and culture
> - A *potter's wheel* enabled potters to make pots in less time and with less effort. The earliest known use of a potter's wheel was in Mesopotamia around 4000–3500 B.C.E. Some scholars have suggested that it could have been invented even earlier in Egypt or China.

Pair work 1

Suggested teaching time:	5–10 minutes	Your actual teaching time:	

- To model the activity, read the example aloud.
- Have pairs choose one use of the wheel and discuss life before and after its invention. You may want to ask them to write a few sentences.
- To review, have several students present their ideas to the class. (Possible answers: Before the invention of the wooden wagon wheel, it took a long time to travel short or long distances. People used animals to carry and move things or carried things on their back. After the invention of the wheel, people could travel long distances more quickly. People could use carts to transport things, thereby expanding trade. Before the invention of the car, people traveled by tram or train. After the invention of the car, people started using public transportation less often.)

Pair work 2

Suggested teaching time:	10 minutes	Your actual teaching time:	

- To prepare students for this exercise, direct their attention to the picture of the people in the car and brainstorm reasons they are going to be late. (Possible answers: They were delayed by the rain or a storm. They got stuck in traffic. There was an accident on the highway. They forgot about the invitation. The man or woman had to work late. The man or woman had a problem at work.)
- As students role-play, walk around the room monitoring their work. Encourage students to use the conditional.

Possible responses . . .

> **A:** Hello, Mom. I'm sorry. We're going to be late. If I hadn't had to work late, we would have been there already. **B:** Don't worry. Your father hasn't gotten home yet. **A:** We'll be there soon. **B:** That'll be fine.
>
> **A:** Hello, Mom. I'm sorry. We're going to be late. **B:** What happened? **A:** There was an accident on the highway. If there hadn't been we would have been there on time. **B:** That's OK. It's still early. Dinner is at 8:00. **A:** Great.

Option: Oral Progress Assessment

Use the pictures on page 97. Encourage students to use the language practiced in this unit and previous units.

- Tell the student to look at the *Uses of the Wheel* and answer these questions: *Is the wheel an invention or a discovery?* (An invention.) *Why do you think it is an important invention?* (Because before the invention of the wheel, it was very difficult to carry heavy objects and it took a very long time to travel great distances.) Then ask the student to use some of the adjectives from this unit to describe the two-wheeled cart and the car. (The two-wheeled cart is low-tech, but very useful. The car in the picture is a first-rate car.)
- Point to the second picture. Ask the student to tell a short story about what happened.
- Evaluate the student on intelligibility, fluency, correct use of target grammar, and appropriate use of vocabulary.

 • Oral Progress Assessment Charts

Option: *Top Notch* Project

Ask students to prepare a presentation about an invention or discovery that appeared during their lifetimes that has changed their lives. Encourage students to do some research on the invention or discovery.

Idea: Point out that the invention can be a small and simple product that affected them in some way. Ask students to create visuals for the presentation (photographs, drawings, charts, etc.). Tell them to include the following details in their presentation:

- Name of the invention
- How old they were when it was invented
- Why it changed their lives / Why it is important for them
- How their lives would be different if it hadn't been invented

EXTRAS (optional)

- **Complete Assessment Package**
- **Weblinks for Teachers:** pearsonlongman.com/topnotch/

And on your ActiveTeach Multimedia Disc:
> **Just for Fun**
> **Top Notch Pop Song Activities**
> **Top Notch TV Video Program and Activity Worksheets**
> **Supplementary Pronunciation Lessons**
> **Audioscripts**
> **Unit Study Guides**

Uses of the Wheel

logs used as wheels

two-wheeled carts

a wooden wagon wheel

a horse-drawn chariot

a potter's wheel

an automobile

Contest Look at the pictures about the uses of the wheel for one minute. Then close your books and try to remember all the uses of the wheel in the pictures. You get a bonus point for thinking of another use.

Pair work

1 Choose one use of the wheel. Discuss how it changed history and people's lives. Present your ideas. For example:

The log helped people move heavy objects over great distances. They could build more easily with stone.

2 The family in the second picture is late. Create a conversation for the two women. Start like this:

A: Hello, Mom. I'm sorry. We're going to be late. If . . .

NOW I CAN... ✔

- ☐ Describe technology.
- ☐ Take responsibility for a mistake.
- ☐ Describe how inventions solve problems.
- ☐ Discuss the impact of inventions/discoveries.

Controversial Issues

GOALS After Unit 9, you will be able to:

1 Bring up a controversial subject.
2 Discuss controversial issues politely.
3 Propose solutions to global problems.
4 Debate the pros and cons of issues.

How politically literate are you?

Test yourself to find out.

Choose the correct term for each definition. Then look at the answers to see how you did.

1 The group of people who govern a country or state
   - ● a government
   - ○ a constitution

2 The art or science of government or governing
   - ○ a constitution
   - ● politics

3 A set of basic laws and principles that a country is governed by, which cannot easily be changed by the political party in power
   - ● a constitution
   - ○ a democracy

4 An occasion when people vote to choose someone for an official position
   - ○ a government
   - ● an election

5 Show by marking a paper or using a machine, etc., which person you want in a government position
   - ○ govern
   - ● vote

6 Lead or take part in a series of actions intended to win an election for a government position
   - ● campaign
   - ○ vote

7 A system of government in which every citizen in the country can vote to elect its government officials
   - ○ a monarchy
   - ● a democracy

8 The system in which a country is ruled by a king or queen
   - ○ a dictatorship
   - ● a monarchy

9 Government by a ruler who has complete power
   - ○ a democracy
   - ● a dictatorship

10 A country ruled by a king or a queen whose power is limited by a constitution
   - ○ a dictatorship
   - ● a constitutional monarchy

ANSWERS: 1 a government 2 politics 3 a constitution 4 an election 5 vote 6 campaign 7 a democracy 8 a monarchy 9 a dictatorship 10 a constitutional monarchy

A 🔊 5:02 **Vocabulary** • *Political terminology* Read and listen. Then listen again and repeat.

a government	a constitution	vote	a democracy	a dictatorship
politics	an election	campaign	a monarchy	a constitutional monarchy

B **Pair work** How much do you know about world politics? On the chart, discuss and write the name of at least one country for each type of government. Then compare charts with other classmates.

A democracy	A monarchy	A constitutional monarchy	A dictatorship

UNIT 9

Preview

Controversial Issues

Suggested teaching time:	10–15 minutes	Your actual teaching time:

Before Exercise A, give students a few minutes of silent time to look at the test.

- Direct students' attention to the unit title. Elicit or explain that *controversial issues* are problems or topics that can cause a lot of disagreement because people have strong personal opinions about them. Ask students to name some topics that they feel are controversial; for example, *politics, family traditions, values, religious beliefs, environmental problems, smoking in public places,* etc. Explain any unfamiliar words or topics.

- Give students a few minutes to answer the questionnaire and check the answer key.

- Ask students how well they did.

A ◀)) Vocabulary

Suggested teaching time:	2 minutes	Your actual teaching time:

- Ask students to listen and study the words. Then have them listen and repeat chorally.

- To provide practice, write the Vocabulary words on the board and have pairs take turns reading definitions from the questionnaire aloud and matching the words. Ask the student who is identifying the words to keep his or her book closed. Point out that students don't need to give the complete definition. For example:
   Student A: *A set of laws and principles that cannot easily be changed.*
   Student B: *A constitution.*
   Student A: *A country that is ruled by a king.*
   Student B: *A monarchy.*

Option: [+5 minutes] To extend the activity, play a memory game with the class. Have students look back at the questionnaire for one minute as you write the following questions on the board:
   1. Which four words are systems of government?
   2. Which three words are related to a democracy?
   3. Which word means a set of laws?
   4. Which word means a group of people who govern?
   5. Which word means the art or science of governing?
Then have students close their books and write the answers for each question. Ask students to compare answers with a partner. (1. Democracy, monarchy, constitutional monarchy, dictatorship; 2. election, vote, campaign; 3. constitution; 4. government; 5. politics.)

Language and culture

- *Democracy, dictatorship,* and *monarchy* can be used to describe both a form of government (non-count noun) and a country having that form of government (count noun); for example, *Some countries are slowly moving toward democracy. Argentina is a democracy.*
- The United Kingdom of Great Britain and Northern Ireland is an example of a *constitutional monarchy.* A *monarch* is the head of state. Democratic elections choose the government, including a prime minister who is the head of the government

 **ActiveTeach Multimedia Disc** • Vocabulary Flash Cards

B Pair·work

Suggested teaching time:	3–5 minutes	Your actual teaching time:

- Encourage pairs to write one to three countries for each type of government.

- To review, draw the chart on the board and complete it as students call out names of countries. If you or your students are unsure about a country, ask them to research the question for the next time the class meets. (Possible answers: democracy—The United States, France, Argentina, Switzerland, Mexico, Brazil, India, Turkey; monarchy—Brunei, Oman, Saudi Arabia; constitutional monarchy—The United Kingdom, Spain, Morocco, Japan, Norway, Swaziland; dictatorship—North Korea, Myanmar (Burma), Libya, Niger.)

C 🔊 Photo story

Suggested teaching time:	3–5 minutes	Your actual teaching time:

- To help students focus on main ideas, write the following questions on the board:
    1. *What situation does Sam need help with?*
    2. *What does San-Chi say?*

- After students read and listen to the Photo Story, have pairs discuss the questions.

- Then ask volunteers to say their answers aloud. (Possible answers: 1. He wants to know if he can talk about politics at the dinner table with a Taiwanese family. 2. He says it is OK to talk about politics, but not to argue about it.)

> **Language and culture**
> - *Do* can be used before a verb or verb phrase to emphasize it, especially when what is being said is surprising. *I do tend to be a little opinionated.*
> **LCN** From the Longman Corpus
> - While *call someone* and *give (someone) a call* mean the same thing, *give (someone) a call* is used much more frequently in spoken English.
> - *Do* is used most frequently for emphasis before the verbs *have*, *need*, and *know*.

D Paraphrase

Suggested teaching time:	7–8 minutes	Your actual teaching time:

- To practice the reading skill of understanding vocabulary from context, encourage students to use the information in the text to help them figure out the meaning of words or expressions.

- To model the activity, complete the first item with the class. Review other ways to ask about someone's life: *What's new? How's everything? What's new and interesting in your life?*

- Have students compare answers with a partner and then review with the class.

E Think and explain

Suggested teaching time:	5–10 minutes	Your actual teaching time:

- Have students answer the questions individually and then discuss them with a partner.

Answers for Exercise E
Answers will vary slightly, but may include the following:
1. Because he is surprised to meet the person he had been meaning to call.
2. Because he is from Taiwan.
3. Because he does not know if it is acceptable to talk about politics at the dinner table in Taiwan. / Because he belongs to a different culture and does not know about the customs in Taiwan.
4. Because he knows Sam has strong opinions about politics and it wouldn't be polite to argue.

F Discussion

Suggested teaching time:	15 minutes	Your actual teaching time:

- To help students prepare to discuss question 1, have them write notes about reasons why they like or don't like to talk about politics and why politics is or isn't a good topic for discussion at someone's home.

- To help students prepare to discuss question 2, draw the following graphic organizer on the board or print it out from the ActiveTeach Multimedia Disc and distribute it to students.

Forms of government			
Democracy	Dictatorship	Monarchy	Constitutional monarchy
+			
–			

- Have students think of some advantages and disadvantages for each form of government and write notes in the chart.

- As students discuss the questions in groups, remind them that they don't have to agree. Encourage them to give reasons for their answers and ask each other follow-up questions. For example:
    Student A: *I don't like to talk about politics.*
    Student B: *Really? Why not?*

- To review, ask several students to say if they think every country should have the same form of government. (Possible answers: Every country couldn't have the same form of government because people's values and beliefs affect the way in which they want to be governed. All countries don't have the same form of government because they all have a different history.)

- Then ask several students to say which form of government they think is best and to give their reasons.

- To finish the activity, ask several students to say what they would tell a visitor to their country about talking about politics at the dinner table.

 • Graphic Organizers

EXTRAS (optional)

- **Workbook:** Exercises 1–3

C 🔊)) **Photo story** Read and listen to a conversation about discussing politics.

San-Chi: So what are you up to these days, Sam?

Sam: Hi, San-Chi! What a coincidence. I've been meaning to give you a call. I need some cultural advice.

San-Chi: What about?

Sam: Well, I'm having dinner at Mei-Li's house tonight, and her parents are in from Taiwan.

San-Chi: Really?

Sam: Mm-hmm. And you know how much I love to talk politics. Would it be rude to bring that up at the dinner table?

San-Chi: Uh . . . Well, not really. Most people from Taiwan like to talk about politics, too. But it would not be cool to argue with them if you don't agree with what they say.

Sam: How well you know me! I do tend to be a little opinionated.

San-Chi: Well, in that case, I'd advise you to talk about something else!

San-Chi: Chinese speaker

D Paraphrase Say each of the following statements from the Photo Story in your <u>own</u> way.

1 "So what are you up to these days, . . .?" What have you been doing lately?

2 "I've been meaning to give you a call." I was planning to call you.

3 "Would it be rude to bring that up at the dinner table?" Would it be impolite to talk about that at the dinner table?

4 ". . . it would not be cool to argue with them . . ." It wouldn't be OK to argue with them.

5 "I do tend to be a little opinionated." I express my beliefs strongly.

E Think and explain Answer the following questions, based on the Photo Story. See page T99 for answers.

1 Why does Sam say, "What a coincidence" when San-Chi greets him?

2 Why does Sam choose San-Chi to ask his cultural question?

3 Why do you think Sam is concerned about the dinner-table conversation at Mei-Li's house?

4 Why does San-Chi suggest Sam talk about something other than politics at Mei-Li's?

F Discussion

1 Do you like to talk about politics? Do you think politics is a good topic for discussion when you are invited to someone's home? Explain.

2 Review the types of government from page 98. Do you think every country should have the same form of government? Why don't all countries have the same form of government? In your opinion, is there a "best" form of government? Explain.

Do you like to discuss politics at the dinner table?

GOAL Bring up a controversial subject

VOCABULARY *A continuum of political and social beliefs*

A 🔊 5:04 Read and listen. Then listen again and repeat.

radical *adj.* supporting complete political or social change —**a radical** *n.*

liberal *adj.* supporting changes in political, social, or religious systems that respect the different beliefs, ideas, etc., of other people —**a liberal** *n.*

moderate *adj.* having opinions or beliefs, especially about politics, that are not extreme and that most people consider reasonable or sensible —**a moderate** *n.*

conservative *adj.* preferring to continue to do things as they have been done in the past rather than risking changes —**a conservative** *n.*

reactionary *adj.* strongly opposed to political or social change —**a reactionary** *n.*

B 🔊 5:05 **Listening comprehension** Listen to each conversation. Then, with a partner, complete the chart. Listen again if necessary to check your work or settle any disagreements.

	radical	liberal	moderate	conservative	reactionary
1 He's	●	○	○	○	○
2 She's	○	○	○	●	○
3 He's	○	○	●	○	○
4 She's	○	○	○	○	●
5 He's	○	○	●	○	○

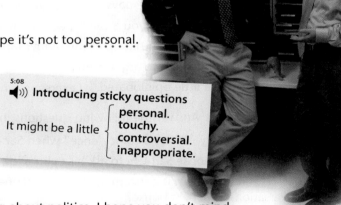

CONVERSATION MODEL

A 🔊 5:06 Read and listen to a conversation about politics.

A: Do you mind if I ask you a political question? I hope it's not too personal.

B: No problem. What would you like to know?

A: Well, are you a liberal or a conservative?

B: Actually, I'm neither. I like to make up my mind based on the issue.

A: So would you say you're an independent?

B: I guess you could say that.

> 🔊 5:08 **Introducing sticky questions**
>
> It might be a little { personal.
> touchy.
> controversial.
> inappropriate.

If you don't want to answer . . .

B: No offense, but I feel a little uncomfortable talking about politics. I hope you don't mind.

A: Absolutely not. It's a good thing I asked.

B 🔊 5:07 **Rhythm and intonation** Listen again and repeat. Then practice the Conversation Model with a partner.

PRONUNCIATION *Stress to emphasize meaning*

A 🔊 5:09 Listen to the different intonations of the same sentence. Then listen again and repeat.

1 Are you a conservative? (normal stress—no special meaning)

2 **ARE** you a conservative? (I think you're a conservative, but I'd like to be sure.)

3 Are **YOU** a conservative? (I'm surprised that you, among all people, would be a conservative.)

4 Are you a con**SERV**ative? (I'm surprised that you would have such a belief.)

VOCABULARY

A 🔊 Read and listen . . .

Suggested teaching time:	2–3 minutes	Your actual teaching time:

- To help students understand the Vocabulary, draw the following diagram on the board (without the answers) and clarify that a continuum shows different degrees of something. Have students copy the diagram:

Strong supporter of change ←——————————————→ *Strong opposer of change*

radical   liberal   moderate   conservative   reactionary

- Ask students to listen and study the Vocabulary. Then have them listen and repeat chorally.

- To check comprehension, ask students to name the two words that are defined in the diagram. (Strong supporter of change: radical; Strong opposer of change: reactionary) Have students add the words to the diagram.

- Then ask students to close their books. Say the remaining words: *moderate, conservative, liberal* and have students write them in the correct order on the continuum.

> **Language and culture**
> - The vocabulary words are both adjectives and nouns; for example, *She has radical views. She's a radical.*
> - *Left-wing (radical, liberal), centrist,* and *right-wing (reactionary, conservative)* are also common ways to describe political beliefs. *Liberal, moderate,* and *conservative* are used to describe beliefs that are not extreme.

 • **Vocabulary Flash Cards**

B 🔊 Listening comprehension

Suggested teaching time:	3–5 minutes	Your actual teaching time:

- Before students listen, point out that they should pay attention to the pronouns at the beginning of each statement to identify which person's opinions they are evaluating.

- For the first listening, stop after each conversation to ask students to identify the topic of each discussion. (1. marriage; 2. an election; 3. roles for men and women; 4. violence in movies / rules for children; 5. an election.)

- Have students listen again to confirm their answers.

- To review with the class, ask students to give reasons for their choices. (Possible answers: 1. He's a radical because he wants to end the institution of marriage. 2. She's conservative because she wants to vote for a political party that doesn't make any changes. 3. He's liberal because he thinks change that helps people is good. 4. Her views are reactionary because she thinks the old laws should be brought back. 5. His views are moderate because he's not going to vote for a liberal, but for someone who is not so extreme.)

FYI: Answers may vary depending on personal judgment.

AUDIOSCRIPT See page T106.

CONVERSATION MODEL

A 🔊 Read and listen . . .

Suggested teaching time:	2 minutes	Your actual teaching time:

> These conversation strategies are implicit in the model:
> - Ask for permission when bringing up a sticky subject.
> - Politely indicate unwillingness with "No offense, but . . .".
> - Apologize for refusing with "I hope you don't mind."

- To introduce the conversation, have students look at the photograph. Ask *Do the men look serious?* (Yes.)

- To check comprehension after students read and listen, ask *What does the man want to know about his colleague?* (If he's a liberal or a conservative.) *Does he ask the question right away?* (No, he asks if he can ask a political question first.)

- Direct attention to the box about ways to introduce *sticky questions*. Ask students what they think a sticky question is. (Possible answers: A question that might be uncomfortable to answer. A question that the other person may not want to answer.)

- Have students listen and repeat the ways to introduce sticky questions. If necessary, clarify the meaning of *touchy* (something that might make the other person upset or angry), *controversial* (something that deals with a subject that people might disagree about), and *inappropriate* (something not acceptable to a particular person or a certain situation).

B 🔊 Rhythm and intonation

Suggested teaching time:	3 minutes	Your actual teaching time:

- Have students repeat each line chorally. Make sure students:
  - use falling intonation for *What would you like to know?*
  - use rising intonation for *Do you mind if I ask you a political question?*
  - use rising intonation for *Well, are you a liberal* and falling intonation for *or a conservative?*
  - use rising intonation for *So would you say you're an independent?*

PRONUNCIATION

A 🔊 Listen to the different intonations . . .

Suggested teaching time:	3 minutes	Your actual teaching time:

- First listening: Have students listen and study the examples. Review the information in parentheses and be sure students understand that changing the stress in a sentence affects its meaning. Point out that as speakers they should try to stress the right words to give the correct message, and as listeners they should pay attention to stress to understand the correct message.

- Second listening: Have students listen and repeat chorally. Be sure that students stress the right words.

B Pair work

Suggested teaching time:	2–3 minutes	Your actual teaching time:

- To prepare students for the activity, write the question on the board and identify three words or word parts you want students to stress as they practice:
    1. *Would YOU say you're an independent?*
    2. *Would you say YOU're an independent?*
    3. *Would you say you're an indePENdent?*

- Have students take turns asking the question and identifying the information that is stressed. Encourage students to discuss the different meanings.

- To review, discuss the meanings with the class. (1. Other people might say you're an independent, but what is your opinion—would you say the same? 2. Other people say they are independent. But what about you? 3. I am surprised that you would consider yourself an independent, so I'm asking this question to confirm it.)

Option: [+5 minutes] To extend the activity, write on the board:
1. *Did TOM buy a car?*
2. *Did Tom BUY a car?*
3. *Did Tom buy a CAR?*
4. *Did Tom buy a SPORTS car?*

Ask pairs to write possible answers for each of the questions based on the stressed information. Complete the first item with the class. Point out the stress is on TOM, which means the speaker is surprised (or clarifying that) it was Tom who bought a car. Write on the board: *No, Tim bought a car.* (Possible answers: 2. No, he rented a car. 3. No, he bought a motorcycle. 4. No, he bought a convertible.)

 • **Pronunciation Activities**

GRAMMAR

Suggested teaching time:	10 minutes	Your actual teaching time:

- To draw on students' prior knowledge, ask them to say non-count nouns they already know and write them on the board; for example, *butter, money, bread, love.* Ask *Do these nouns have a plural form?* (No.) *Do they need singular or plural verbs?* (Singular verbs.) You may want to ask students to use them in sentences.

- Have students read the explanation and study the correct and incorrect examples. Ask *Why is the wrong in the first example?* (Because non-count nouns cannot be preceded by *a, an,* or *the.*) *What's wrong with the second example?* (Non-count nouns have no plural form and need a singular verb.) Do the same with the last two examples.

- Review the nouns in the *Abstract idea nouns* box. To provide practice, have pairs write three simple sentences with nouns from the box.

- Review the nouns *democracy, monarchy, dictatorship,* and *government* and point out that they can be count or non-count, depending on how they are being used; for example, *The best system of government is democracy. There are many democracies in the world today.*

Option:  **GRAMMAR BOOSTER** (Teaching notes p. T136)

 • **Inductive Grammar Charts**

A Grammar practice

Suggested teaching time:	2–3 minutes	Your actual teaching time:

- To model the activity, complete the first item with the class.

B Correct the errors . . .

Suggested teaching time:	3–5 minutes	Your actual teaching time:

- Review the example with the class.

- Ask students to read aloud their paragraphs to a partner.

NOW YOU CAN Bring up a controversial subject

A Which questions . . .

Suggested teaching time:	5–10 minutes	Your actual teaching time:

- Have students check the questions individually. Point out that there are no wrong answers.

- Have pairs of students explain their choices; for example, *I think the last question is OK if you're not in a work situation. / I think that question is very personal.*

B Pair work

Suggested teaching time:	5–8 minutes	Your actual teaching time:

- Be sure to reinforce the conversation strategies; for example, make sure students use appropriate and polite tone for asking and responding to sticky questions.

Don't stop! Extend the conversation. Encourage students to ask more questions. Write these prompts on the board.
   What don't you like about ___?
   Why don't ___?
   Do you think ___ will win the election?

- Point out that Partner B can decline the question, in which case Partner A can ask for permission to ask a different question.

- To model the activity, role-play and extend the conversation with a more confident student.

 • **Conversation Pair Work Cards**
• **Learning Strategies**

C Change partners

Suggested teaching time:	5 minutes	Your actual teaching time:

- Remind students to discuss another controversial subject.

EXTRAS (optional)

- Workbook: Exercises 4–8
- Copy & Go: Activity 33

B Pair work Practice varying the stress in this statement: "Would you say you're an independent?" Discuss the different meanings.

GRAMMAR · *Non-count nouns that represent abstract ideas*

GRAMMAR BOOSTER ▸ p. 136

- Count and non-count nouns: review and extension

Nouns that represent abstract ideas are always non-count nouns.

Education is an important issue.
NOT: ~~The~~ education is an important issue.
NOT: ~~Educations are~~ an important issue.
The news* about politics is always interesting.
NOT: The news about ~~the~~ politics is always interesting.
NOT: The news about politics ~~are~~ always interesting.

Abstract idea nouns

advice	patience
crime	peace
education	politics
health	poverty
help	progress
information	proof
investment	success
justice	time
news	work

*The word <u>news</u> is always singular. When it refers to a report in the press, on radio, TV, or the Internet, it is commonly referred to as <u>the news</u>.

A Grammar practice Complete each statement by choosing the correct form of the nouns and verbs.

1 Our (advice / advices) to you (is / are) to avoid discussing politics.
2 (Poverty / The poverty) (was / were) the topic of the international conference.
3 Both candidates have programs for (the health / health) and (educations / education).
4 Making (peace / the peace) takes a lot of (work / works) and a long time.
5 Good news (is / are) hard to find in the newspaper these days.

B Correct the errors.

Here's some political ~~informations~~ *information* about the election. The good news ~~are~~ *is* that both candidates have programs for ~~the~~ education. The liberal candidate, Bill Slate, says financial ~~helps~~ *help* for the schools ~~are~~ *is* a question of ~~the~~ justice. ~~The poverty~~ *Poverty* has affected the quality of the schools, and students from schools in poor areas don't have ~~a~~ success. Joanna Clark, the conservative candidate, disagrees. She believes ~~a~~ progress has been made by investing in ~~the~~ teacher education. Her ~~advices are~~ *advice is* to keep the old policy. "Creating better schools takes ~~the~~ time and ~~a~~ patience," she says.

NOW YOU CAN · Bring up a controversial subject

A Which questions are too personal or controversial?

- ❏ What advice would you like to give the president / prime minister / king / queen?
- ❏ What do you think about the president / prime minister / king / queen?
- ❏ What should be done to decrease poverty?
- ❏ What would be necessary for peace in ___ ?
- ❏ What do you think about our ___ policy?
- ❏ Are you liberal or conservative?
- ❏ Who are you voting for in the election?

B Pair work Change the Conversation Model to bring up a topic that might be controversial. Partner B can decline to discuss the question. Then change roles.

A: Do you mind if I ask you a political question? I hope it's not too ....

B: No problem. What would you like to know?

A: Well, ... ?

B: Actually, ...

Don't stop!
Ask other questions that you don't think are too personal.

C Change partners Discuss another controversial subject.

GOAL Discuss controversial issues politely

CONVERSATION MODEL

A ◀))) 5:10 Read and listen to a polite conversation about a controversial issue.

A: How do you feel about capital punishment?

B: I'm in favor of it. I believe if you kill someone you deserve to be killed. What about you?

A: Actually, I'm against the death penalty. I think it's wrong to take a life, no matter what.

B: Well, I guess we'll have to agree to disagree!

B ◀))) 5:11 **Rhythm and intonation** Listen again and repeat. Then practice the Conversation Model with a partner.

C **Discussion** Are you in favor of capital punishment? Explain.

> 5:12
> ◀))) **Agreement**
> I agree with you on that one.
> I couldn't agree more.
> I couldn't have said it better myself.
> That's exactly what I think.

> 5:13
> ◀))) **Disagreement**
> I guess we'll have to agree to disagree.
> Really? I have to disagree with you there.
> Do you think so? I'm not sure I agree.
> Well, I'm afraid I don't agree.
> No offense, but I just can't agree.

VOCABULARY *Some controversial issues*

A ◀))) 5:14 Read and listen. Then listen again and repeat.

censorship of books and movies

compulsory military service

lowering the driving age

raising the voting age

prohibiting smoking indoors

CONVERSATION MODEL

A 🔊 Read and listen . . .

Suggested teaching time:	2 minutes	Your actual teaching time:

These conversation strategies are implicit in the model:
- Use "How do you feel about . . ." to invite someone's opinion.
- Offer an explanation for one's opinion.
- Use "Well," to introduce a different point of view.
- Use "So . . ." to begin a question clarifying someone's statement.

- Before students read and listen to the Conversation Model, ask them to look at the photograph. Ask *Where are the women?* (In a living room.) *What is the woman on the left holding?* (A newspaper.)
- To check comprehension after students read and listen, ask them to summarize how each woman defends her opinion. (Possible answers: Speaker A thinks there is never a good reason for killing someone. Speaker B believes the death penalty is the right way to punish someone for killing another person.)
- Point out that the expression *No matter what* means "in any or all circumstances or situations" and that *death penalty* (the legal punishment of being killed) and *capital punishment* are synonyms.
- Have students listen and read ways to express agreement and disagreement. Then have them repeat what they heard.

Option: [+5 minutes] To extend the activity and practice the ways to agree and disagree, have pairs take turns role-playing short discussions: Student A makes a *position statement* for a controversial issue. Student B agrees or disagrees. Then they change roles. Point out that the purpose of the activity is <u>not</u> to express personal opinions, but to practice the expressions. For example:

Student A: *I believe monarchies are the best form of government.*
Student B: *Really? I have to disagree with you there.*

Student B: *I think this country needs a radical change.*
Student A: *I couldn't agree more.*

Language and culture
- *Death penalty* is almost always preceded by *the* (the death penalty) but *capital punishment* is a non-count noun.

B 🔊 Rhythm and intonation

Suggested teaching time:	3 minutes	Your actual teaching time:

- Have students repeat each line chorally. Make sure they:
  ○ use falling intonation for *How do you feel about capital punishment?*
  ○ use emphatic stress with *against* in *I'm against the death penalty.*

C Discussion

Suggested teaching time:	3–5 minutes	Your actual teaching time:

- To help students prepare for the discussion, ask them to take notes about the reasons why they are in favor of or against capital punishment.
- As students discuss in small groups, encourage them to use the ways to agree and disagree from the boxes.

VOCABULARY

A 🔊 Read and listen . . .

Suggested teaching time:	2–3 minutes	Your actual teaching time:

- Have students listen, study the phrases, and look at the pictures. Then have students listen and repeat chorally.
- To check comprehension, ask:
  Do you know of any books that have been censored?
  Is military service compulsory in this country?
  What's the driving age in this country?
  When can people vote in this country?
  When did smoking become a controversial issue?
- Then take a poll and ask each student to say which controversial issue concerns him or her the most.

Language and culture

LEN From the Longman Corpus: *Prohibit* and *compulsory* are formal words that are used more frequently in writing than in speech. It is more common in spoken English to say that something is *not allowed* or that someone *can't (do something)* than that something is *prohibited*. And it is more common to say that someone *has to (do something)* than that something is *compulsory*.

 ActiveTeach Multimedia Disc • Vocabulary Flash Cards

AUDIOSCRIPT for page T103 (**B** Listening comprehension)

1
F: Oh, no! I can't believe how inconsiderate people are. My eyes are burning, and I can't taste the food. I really think smoking should be outlawed in restaurants.

2 [M = French]
M: I'm a pacifist. I am against all wars, no matter what. I really think governments would be less likely to go to war if there weren't so many soldiers to send! Let's change the law so the government doesn't have such a large military force.

3
F: Look at this article in the newspaper. It says research has proved that 16-year-olds are not mature enough to drive cars. People shouldn't be permitted to drive until they're at least eighteen. I think we should change the driving age.

4
M: I think it's ridiculous that people can go in the army at eighteen, but they can't vote until they're twenty-one. Eighteen-year-olds are smart enough to vote.

5 [F = Indian]
F: Some of the things you see on TV these days are horrible. I don't want my children watching so much violence and immoral behavior. Can't we stop the TV stations from showing such terrible stuff?

B 🔊 Listening comprehension

Suggested teaching time:	5 minutes	Your actual teaching time:

- To prepare students for listening, point out that they will not hear the exact phrases from Exercise A. Instead, they will listen to people giving their opinions of the issues.
- Have students listen for the issues and complete the first column in the chart, using the exact phrases from Exercise A.

AUDIOSCRIPT See page T102.

C 🔊 Now listen again . . .

Suggested teaching time:	5 minutes	Your actual teaching time:

- Have students listen for each person's opinion and check the correct column in the chart. You may want to ask students to take notes to support their choices.

GRAMMAR

Suggested teaching time:	5–10 minutes	Your actual teaching time:

- Direct students' attention to the chart and have them read the explanation and study the examples. To check comprehension, write the following sentences on the board:
  1. I _agreed_ to plan the party.
  2. I _advised_ him to stay home.
  3. I _reminded_ them not to be late.
  4. I _pretended_ not to see her.
- Ask *Which verbs are followed directly by an infinitive?* (Agreed, pretended.) *Which verbs are followed by an object before an infinitive?* (Advised, reminded.)
- Point out that in items 3 and 4 on the board the negative is formed by adding *not* before the infinitive.
- To provide practice, have pairs write new simple sentences with the verbs on the board; for example, *I agreed to leave earlier. She advised him to go.* To review, have several students read their sentences aloud.
- Ask students to study the lists of verbs in the boxes.

Language and culture

LÉN **From the Longman Corpus:** In the list *Verbs followed by an object before an infinitive*, learners across all language backgrounds make the most errors with the verbs *permit, allow,* and *advise*.

Option: *GRAMMAR BOOSTER* (Teaching notes p. T137)

 • Inductive Grammar Charts

A Grammar practice

Suggested teaching time:	2 minutes	Your actual teaching time:

- To model the activity, read the first item aloud.
- Have students compare answers with a partner.

B On a separate sheet . . .

Suggested teaching time:	3–5 minutes	Your actual teaching time:

- Have students choose verbs from the boxes and write sentences, using their own ideas.

Option: [+10 minutes] To extend the activity, write the following statements on the board.
  1. I _decided_ ___ the train.
  2. I _reminded_ ___ the invitations.
  3. I _can't afford_ ___ that car.
  4. I _warned_ ___ to strangers.
  5. I _convinced_ ___ on vacation with us.

Have students decide whether to use an infinitive or an object and an infinitive after the underlined verbs, and then complete the statements with their own ideas. If necessary, students can look for the verbs in the lists under the Grammar chart. (Possible answers: 1. I decided (not) to take the train. 2. I reminded him to send the invitations. 3. I can't afford to buy that car. 4. I warned her not to talk to strangers. 5. I convinced them to come on vacation with us.)

NOW YOU CAN | Discuss controversial issues politely

A Pair work

Suggested teaching time:	5–10 minutes	Your actual teaching time:

- Review the *Issues* in the box. Brainstorm other topics students can discuss and write them on the board. You may want to classify them into *Personal and social issues* and *Environmental issues*. Help students with words they might not know in English. (Possible answers: Personal and social issues—divorce, drug addiction, discrimination, genetic engineering; Environmental issues—pollution, animal testing.)
- Review the language in the *Be sure to recycle . . .* box.
- To reinforce the use of the conversation strategies, remind students to explain why they are in favor of or against an issue.

Don't stop! Extend the conversation. Before they practice have students brainstorm more examples of questions they can ask. For example: *How do you feel about ___? Are you in favor of ___?*

- As students interact, walk around the room and provide help as needed.

 • Conversation Pair Work Cards

B Change partners

Suggested teaching time:	10 minutes	Your actual teaching time:

- Assign students new partners. Remind them to discuss another issue.

EXTRAS (optional)

- Workbook: Exercises 9–13
- Copy & Go: Activity 34

B ◀)) 5:15 **Listening comprehension** Listen to people's opinions about controversial issues. Complete the chart with the issue they discuss. Use the Vocabulary.

C ◀)) 5:16 Now listen again and check <u>For</u> or <u>Against</u> in the chart, according to what the person says.

	Issue	For	Against
1	prohibiting smoking in restaurants	✓	
2	cumpulsory military service		✓
3	raising the driving age	✓	
4	lowering the voting age	✓	
5	censorship of TV programs	✓	

GRAMMAR *Verbs followed by objects and infinitives*

GRAMMAR BOOSTER ▸ p. 137
• Gerunds and infinitives: review
  ◦ form and usage
  ◦ usage after certain verbs

Certain verbs can be followed by infinitives, but some verbs must be followed by an object before an infinitive.

The newspaper reminded **all 18-year-olds** to vote.
We urged **them** <u>to write</u> letters against the death penalty.

Verbs followed directly by an infinitive:

agree	decide	manage	pretend
appear	deserve	need	refuse
can't afford	hope	offer	seem
can't wait	learn	plan	

Verbs followed by an object before an infinitive:

advise	convince	permit	request	urge
allow	encourage	persuade	require	warn
cause	invite	remind	tell	

For a review of gerunds and infinitives, open **Reference Charts** on your *ActiveBook* Self-Study Disc.

A **Grammar practice** Complete each statement or question with an object and an infinitive.

1 The newspaper advised ...*all voters to register*... early for the next election.
   _{all voters / register}

2 Did you remind ...*your daughter to complete*... her voter registration card?
   _{your daughter / complete}

3 We persuaded ...*our friends to vote*... for our candidate.
   _{our friends / vote}

4 Our teacher always encourages ...*students to study*... every night, not just the day before the exam.
   _{students / study}

5 Can't we convince ...*legislators to lower taxes*... on property?
   _{legislators / lower taxes}

B On a separate sheet of paper, write two sentences using verbs that can be followed directly by an infinitive and two sentences with verbs that must have an object before an infinitive.

NOW YOU CAN **Discuss controversial issues politely**

Issues
• censorship
• compulsory military service for men and / or women
• lowering / raising the voting or driving age
• prohibiting smoking indoors
• Your own issue _____

A **Pair work** Use an issue from the list to change the Conversation Model. Use the Agreement and Disagreement Vocabulary from page 102. Then change roles and issues. Start like this:

A: How do you feel about .... ?

B: ....

Don't stop!
Ask your partner's opinion of other issues. Provide reasons to support your point of view.

♻ **Be sure to recycle this language.**
I'm against ___.
I'm in favor of ___.
I think / believe / feel:
   it's wrong.
   it's right.
   it's OK under some circumstances.
   it's wrong, no matter what.
   it depends.

B **Change partners** Discuss another issue, giving reasons to support your opinion.

GOAL   Propose solutions to global problems

Explore your ideas What is the difference between a problem and a global problem? Do you think your generation faces more serious global problems than the generation of your parents or grandparents? Explain.

READING 5:17 **The following issues were most frequently mentioned in a global survey about current world problems.**

Corruption People all over the world complain about the corruption of police, government officials, and business leaders. Two examples of corruption are:

- A police officer takes money (a "bribe") from a driver so he doesn't give the driver a ticket for speeding.

- A company that wants to do business with a government agency offers a public official money or a gift to choose that company for the job.

Some people feel that power promotes corruption and that corruption is unavoidable. But an independent media—for example, non-government-backed newspapers, television stations, and Internet blogs—can also play an important role in exposing corruption.

Poverty Approximately one-fifth of the world's population, over 1 billion people, earns less than US $1.00 a day. Each day, over a billion people in the world lack basic food supplies. And according to UNICEF, each day, 25,000 children under the age of five die of starvation or preventable infectious disease.

There are many causes of poverty, ranging from catastrophic natural events to bad economic and agricultural policies, so there's no one solution to poverty worldwide. Some people feel that wealthy nations must send aid to poorer nations, while others are concerned that nothing will help unless local corruption is reduced and bad government policies are changed.

Terrorism Every day, we see or hear about suicide bombings and other violent acts committed against innocent people for religious or political reasons. Many ask why terrorism is on the rise.

Some social scientists believe that television and movies may contribute to growing anger. They claim that some people may feel frustrated and powerless when they measure their lives against the lives of extremely wealthy people they see in the media.

However, views about what causes terrorism can be very controversial, and many people disagree about its causes or possible solutions. While some feel that terrorism can be met with military force, others believe that people's extreme poverty and powerlessness must be reduced to make a difference.

Racism and discrimination Racism (the belief that one's own race or ethnic group is superior to others) and racial and ethnic discrimination (treating members of other groups unfairly) exist in many places. These two common problems cause human rights violations all over the world. In some cases a more powerful ethnic or racial group justifies the domination and, horribly, even the complete destruction of ethnic or racial minorities they consider to be inferior. When taken to this extreme, genocides such as the European Holocaust and the massacre in Sudan have threatened to wipe out entire peoples.

Can racism and discrimination be eliminated—or are these simply unfortunate features of human nature? Many people believe that education can help build tolerance of the "other" and may contribute to creating a more peaceful world.

A Activate language from a text Based on the information in the Reading, cross out the one word or phrase that is unrelated to the others. Explain your reasoning.

1	people	~~politics~~	ethnic groups	races
2	money	property	income	~~racism~~
3	bribe	corruption	discrimination	~~money~~
4	hunger	starvation	~~domination~~	lack of food
5	racism	~~business~~	discrimination	prejudice

BEFORE YOU READ

Explore your ideas

Suggested teaching time:	2–3 minutes	Your actual teaching time:

- Give students a few minutes to think about the questions individually.

- Then ask a student to explain the difference between a problem and a global problem. (Possible answer: A global problem affects the whole world.)

- Have students brainstorm issues they consider to be serious and make a list on the board. For example:

education	epidemics	wars
vaccination	famine	pollution
censorship	clean water	poverty
infectious diseases	natural disasters	genetic manipulation

- To finish, have several students evaluate which issues they consider to be the most serious, today.

READING

Suggested teaching time:	10–15 minutes	Your actual teaching time:

- Ask students to scan the text for the four problems discussed in the article. (Corruption, poverty, terrorism, racism / discrimination.)

FYI: If students do not know the meanings of the words, tell them that they will learn the meanings in the Reading.

- To give students a focus for reading, ask them to find information that describes causes and solutions for each problem. You may want to ask them to underline this information as they read.

- To review, draw the following graphic organizer (without the answers) on the board or print it out from the ActiveTeach Multimedia Disc and distribute it to students. Complete it with the class as you get feedback.

Causes ⟹	Global problem	⟸ Solutions
• having power • human nature	corruption	• independent media can help expose it
• catastrophic natural events • bad economic and agricultural policies	poverty	• sending aid • reducing corruption • changing bad government policies
• growing anger due to frustration and powerlessness	terrorism	• using military force • reducing extreme poverty and powerlessness
• believing that one race is superior to other races	racism and discrimination	• educating to build tolerance of others

Option: [+5 minutes] As an alternate approach, use the Reading as a listening activity. Ask students to close their books. Write the following questions on the board and have students listen for the answers.

1. *Corruption:* What are two common examples?
2. *Poverty:* What are some consequences of this problem?
3. *Terrorism:* What is a possible reason why it might be increasing?
4. *Racism:* What are some consequences of this belief?

Encourage students to take notes as they listen. Then have students reread the text to check their answers. (Possible answers: 1. A driver gives money to a police officer so he doesn't get a ticket. A company gives money to a public official so the company is chosen for a job. 2. A lot of people die of starvation or infectious diseases. 3. Some people may feel frustrated and powerless when they measure their lives against the lives of wealthy people they see in the media. 4. The domination over ethnic and racial minorities and possibly genocide.)

Language and culture

- *Starvation* is suffering or death due to the lack of food; *unavoidable* means impossible to prevent; *powerlessness* is the inability to stop or control something because one does not have the power or strength to do it.

- *Genocide* is a count noun in the Reading because it refers to specific occurrences of genocide in history.

ActiveTeach Multimedia Disc
- Extra Reading Comprehension Questions
- Learning Strategies
- Graphic Organizers

A Activate language from a text

Suggested teaching time:	3–5 minutes	Your actual teaching time:

- To model the activity, complete the first item with the class. Elicit or explain that *politics* does not refer to people. Then ask, *Which issue from the Reading are the remaining words related to?* (Racism and discrimination.)

- As students complete the activity, encourage them to write notes to support their choices.

- Have students compare answers with a partner. To review with the class, ask students to give the reason for each answer. (Possible answers: 2. Other words are related to money; 3. other words are things that are illegal; 4. other words are related to not having food; 5. other words refer to negative attitudes or actions against people.)

Language and culture

- *Domination* is the power or control over someone or something; *prejudice* is an unreasonable dislike and distrust of people who are different from you in some way, especially because of their race, sex, or religion.

B Understand from context

Suggested teaching time:	2–3 minutes	Your actual teaching time:

- Have students find the words in the text. Encourage them to complete the items they know first.
- Have students compare answers with a partner. Then review with the class.

C Critical thinking

Suggested teaching time:	5–10 minutes	Your actual teaching time:

- Give students a few minutes to look back at the text and take notes for each question individually.
- As students discuss the questions in small groups, encourage them to use the vocabulary they learned on page 102 to agree and disagree.
- To review, have students from different groups share their views with the class.

NOW YOU CAN Propose solutions to global problems

A Frame your ideas

Suggested teaching time:	3–4 minutes	Your actual teaching time:

- Have students rank the ideas individually. Then ask them to share their rankings and explain their reasons with the class.
- Take a poll to find out which issues ranked highest in importance and highest in difficulty to accomplish.

B Notepadding

Suggested teaching time:	10 minutes	Your actual teaching time:

- Point out that students can include solutions for local or global problems. They can also include some of the solutions offered in the text on page 104.
- Encourage students to write notes, not full sentences. (Possible answers: reducing poverty and hunger—help poor countries grow food, raise money for the poor, teach the poor how to use their land; preventing terrorism—change foreign policy, reduce poverty, promote freedom in all countries, guarantee human rights in all countries; avoiding war—promote peace, respect others; ending or reducing corruption—promote moral values, enforce stricter legal punishments; wiping out racism and ethnic discrimination—teach children to respect others, teach children to value diversity; protecting human rights—teach democratic values, help international organizations that protect them.)
- As students write their notes, walk around and provide help as needed.

C Discussion

Suggested teaching time:	10 minutes	Your actual teaching time:

- Before students begin, ask them to review the Conversation Model on page 102 for ways to agree and disagree.
- Encourage students to use their rankings from Exercise A to give their opinions of the most important issues and their notes from Exercise B to give their suggestions for solutions to the problems.

Text-mining: Have students share their Text-mining examples and use them to create new statements with a partner.

- As students discuss the questions in small groups, remind them to acknowledge their partner's opinion (agree / disagree), give their reasons, and state their own opinion and reason(s). For example:

    Student A: *I'm very concerned about poverty and hunger. I think it's shocking that some people die of starvation while others throw away food.*

    Student B: *I agree with you on that one. Governments could spend less money on wars and use that money to help prevent this problem.*

    OR

    Student C: *To me, the most important issue is preventing terrorism.*

    Student D: *Really? I'm afraid I don't agree. Many more people die of hunger.*

    Student C: *That may be true, but . . .*

Option: **[+10 minutes]** To extend the activity, choose ideas from the list in Exercise A and ask several groups for solutions they discussed. Make a list on the board.

Option: **[+15 minutes]** For a challenge, have students write a paragraph about one or more topics from Exercise A. Ask them to explain the problem and suggest solutions.

EXTRAS (optional)

- Workbook: Exercises 14–16
- Copy & Go: Activity 35

B Understand from context Match each definition with a word from the box.

..c.. **1** a lack of necessary money to survive

..b.. **2** the attempt to destroy all members of a racial or ethnic group

..e.. **3** judging or harming people because of their racial or ethnic heritage

..a.. **4** money paid or some other reward given to a person to perform a dishonest or unethical act or to provide a favor

..d.. **5** the abuse of power by people in government or business

..f.. **6** the belief that other racial or ethnic groups are inferior to one's own

a	a bribe
b	genocide
c	poverty
d	corruption
e	discrimination
f	racism

C Critical thinking Discuss each of the following.

1 Reread the section on corruption in the Reading. What do all acts of corruption have in common? Do you think it is possible to end corruption, or do you feel that it is an "unavoidable part of human nature"? Use specific examples in your discussion.

2 What are some of the causes of poverty, and what are its effects? How is the problem of poverty related to all of the other problems mentioned in the Reading?

3 In your opinion, why do people engage in acts of terrorism? Is terrorism an expression of power or powerlessness and frustration? Provide examples to support your opinion.

4 What reasons do people have to hate other groups? Is hatred of another group ever understandable, appropriate, or justified? Explain the reasons for your opinion.

On your *ActiveBook* Self-Study Disc:
Extra Reading Comprehension Questions

NOW YOU CAN Propose solutions to global problems

A Frame your ideas On a scale of 1 to 6, put the ideas in order of importance and their difficulty to accomplish (1= most important or most difficult).

B Notepadding Write some possible solutions to global problems.

Problem	Possible solutions

Order of importance   **Order of difficulty to accomplish**

○ reducing poverty and hunger ○

○ preventing terrorism ○

○ avoiding war ○

○ ending or reducing corruption ○

○ wiping out racism and ethnic discrimination ○

○ protecting human rights ○

C Discussion Discuss the solutions to the global problems you proposed. Do you all have the same concerns?

Text-mining (optional)
Underline language in the Reading on page 104 to use in your discussion. For example:
"There's no one solution to ___."

GOAL **Debate the pros and cons of issues**

A 🔊 5:18 **Vocabulary** • *How to debate an issue politely* Read and listen. Then listen again and repeat.

1

❝ I think smoking is a disgusting habit. ❞

❝ **That may be true, but** if you only smoke in your own house, you're not hurting anyone but yourself. ❞

2

❝ I think more people should be active in politics. That way, we would have better governments. ❞

❝ **I see what you mean, but** it's not realistic to expect everyone to care. ❞

3

❝ I think our president is doing an excellent job. ❞

❝ **Well, on the one hand,** he's not corrupt. **But on the other hand,** he hasn't done much to improve the country. ❞

4

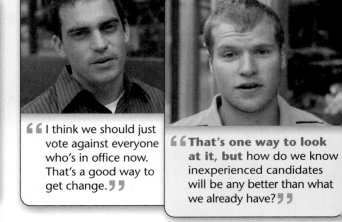

❝ I think we should just vote against everyone who's in office now. That's a good way to get change. ❞

❝ **That's one way to look at it, but** how do we know inexperienced candidates will be any better than what we already have? ❞

B **Pair work** Take turns saying and responding to each opinion. Use the Vocabulary above to disagree politely. Or, if you agree with the opinion, use the language of agreement from page 102. For example:

1 "In some countries, dictatorship has helped stop corruption."

> ❝ I couldn't agree more. Countries with dictatorships are better off. ❞   **OR**   ❝ That may be true, but no one should have to live under a dictatorship. ❞

2 "There is no real democracy. All governments are controlled by a few powerful people."

3 "I think moderates are the only people you can trust in government."

4 "I'm not going to vote. All the candidates are corrupt."

BEFORE YOU LISTEN

A 🔊 Vocabulary

Suggested teaching time:	5 minutes	Your actual teaching time:

- Have students listen and study the captions. Then have students listen and repeat the phrases chorally.

- Point out that the phrases in boldface type are used by the second speaker to tell the first speaker that he or she disagrees with the first speaker's opinion.

- To reinforce the Vocabulary, write a position on the board; for example, *I feel that military action is the only way to stop terrorism.* Encourage students to disagree with you politely using the vocabulary they have learned. (Possible answers: That may be true, but I'm against violence. / Well, that's one way to look at it. I think that it might be better to fight its causes.)

Language and culture

- *On the one hand* is always used together with *on the other hand*. However, *on the other hand* is often used alone to present a conflicting idea.

B Pair work

Suggested teaching time:	5–10 minutes	Your actual teaching time:

- Review the first item and speech balloon with the class. Point out that students can agree or disagree with each other.

- You may want to have students review ways to agree and disagree from page 102.

AUDIOSCRIPT for page T100 (**B** Listening comprehension)

CONVERSATION 1

M: I'm completely against marriage. I don't think a piece of paper means anything!

F: What piece of paper are you talking about?

M: A marriage license. What good is it? Everyone today is getting divorced anyway. I think we should simply end the institution of marriage! Marriage is a thing of the past.

F: Those are pretty extreme ideas.

CONVERSATION 2

M: Well, you're finally old enough to vote, Marianne. Who are you going to vote for?

F: I'm going to vote for the Constitution Party.

M: The Constitution Party? Wow, is that a surprise! You're so young. Don't you want to see change? The Constitution Party just has the same old ideas election after election.

F: So? What's wrong with the same ideas? They're better than some of the new ones! I think it's safer to stick with policies that have been successful. If it isn't broke, don't fix it.

CONVERSATION 3

M: You know—I used to be afraid of change. I thought there was only one way to look at things. That the way we did things when I was young was the only way.

F: How have you changed?

M: Well, for instance, I used to think there should be certain roles for men and certain roles for women. Now I've come to think I was silly.

F: You mean you're turning out to be a radical in your old age?

M: Come on. I'm no radical, just more thoughtful. I'm not in favor of big changes, but a little change is good. Especially when it makes people more free.

F: That sounds reasonable.

CONVERSATION 4

F: I can't imagine bringing children into this twenty-first century world.

M: What do you mean?

F: Well, there are no rules anymore. You can buy anything . . . anywhere. You can see all kinds of disgusting stuff on TV and in the movies: violence, sex, whatever! Anything goes. There's no respect.

M: I can't believe anyone so young can have such old ideas!

F: I think we should bring back some of the old laws.

CONVERSATION 5

F: Who are you going to vote for?

M: I think I'm going to vote for Bartlett Nardone.

F: I thought you liked Al Smith.

M: No. He's too liberal for me. But Nardone, he's not so extreme. He's a pretty sensible guy.

LISTENING COMPREHENSION

🔊 Listen to summarize

Suggested teaching time:	10 minutes	Your actual teaching time:

- **First listening:** To provide practice with listening for main ideas, have students listen and write down which form of government is discussed in each conversation. Review with the class. (Conversation 1: dictatorship; Conversation 2: democracy; Conversation 3: monarchy.)

- **Second listening:** To provide practice with listening for details, have students listen for the arguments for and against the different types of government and take notes. Stop the recording after each conversation to allow students time to write.

AUDIOSCRIPT

CONVERSATION 1

M: You know, I feel that some countries don't deserve democracy. The citizens are just incapable of living in peace.
F: Well, what form of government would be best for them?
M: I hate to say it, but some places need dictatorships. Even military dictatorships. They're effective. They're efficient. They make people live in peace.
F: I totally disagree. I believe dictatorships are morally wrong. The people have no rights in a dictatorship. If the government does something terrible, the people can't replace it.

CONVERSATION 2 [F = Australian English]

F: Which party are you going to vote for in the election?
M: The Liberal Party.
F: Why?
M: Because they want to change the election laws so there can be only two candidates for president.
F: But that's not democratic. This is a democracy. The people have the power. They can vote for who they like. That's what's good about democracy.
M: That's one way to look at it. But one of the disadvantages of democracy is that we can get a president who only has a small percentage of the votes. We're supposed to have majority rule, not minority rule.

CONVERSATION 3 [F = Dutch]

M: How do you feel about the royal family?
F: Me? Well, on the one hand, I like the royals as people—they do a lot of important charity work, like visiting sick children and raising money for hospitals. But on the other hand, I believe that in this day and age, monarchy is wrong. The monarchs aren't the real government and they cost us a lot of money.
M: That's true, but if you didn't have the monarchy, you'd lose your tradition and your history.
F: I see what you mean, but with all the problems we have, we should use all that money to help people with their problems.

Answers for Listen to summarize
Answers will vary, but may include the following:
Dictatorship: In favor—effective, efficient, and people live in peace; Against—morally wrong, people have no rights.
Democracy: In favor—people have the power to vote for who they want; Against—a president who only has a small percentage of the votes.
Monarchy: In favor—traditions and history; Against—not the real government, costs a lot of money.

 • Learning Strategies

---

NOW YOU CAN   Debate the pros and cons of issues

A Group work

Suggested teaching time:	5–10 minutes	Your actual teaching time:

- Ask students for suggestions about political issues or other issues to add to the choices.

- Take a poll to see which issue will be debated.

FYI: If you think your students will find it difficult to debate, use Exercises B and C to help prepare them.

B Notepadding

Suggested teaching time:	5–10 minutes	Your actual teaching time:

- Encourage students to use the vocabulary and grammar from this unit to write their reasons. Tell students to include specific examples to support their arguments.

C Debate

Suggested teaching time:	15 minutes	Your actual teaching time:

- Before dividing the class in half, point out that students will be supporting one of the arguments— regardless of their personal opinion.

- Review the language in the *Be sure to recycle . . .* box.

- To help students plan their debate, draw the following graphic organizer on the board or print it out from the ActiveTeach Multimedia Disc and distribute it to students. Ask students to write notes about the pros and cons of the issue they have chosen.

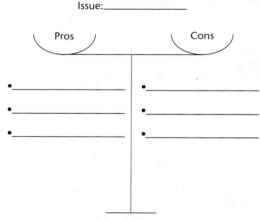

- Encourage a friendly and polite debate.

FYI: If students are role-playing, have them work in groups of two or three. Ask them to role-play a debate for each topic. Then ask several groups to perform in front of the class.

 • Learning Strategies
• Graphic Organizers

EXTRAS (optional)

- **Workbook:** Exercises 17 and 18
- **Copy & Go:** Activity 36

5:19

🔊)) **Listen to summarize** Listen to three conversations about dictatorship, democracy, and monarchy. Then listen again, and on a separate sheet of paper, take notes about the arguments in favor of and against each system of government. Then, work in pairs. Partner A: Summarize the arguments in favor. Partner B: Summarize the arguments against. See page T107 for answers.

NOW YOU CAN   Debate the pros and cons of issues

A Group work Choose an issue that you'd like to debate.

- Banning text-messaging while driving
- Decriminalizing the use of illegal drugs
- Preventing children from going to movie theaters to see extremely violent movies
- Using the military to fight terrorism
- Permitting people to say or write anything as long as it doesn't cause physical danger
- Your own local or political issue:
  _____

B Notepadding On your notepad, write arguments in favor and against.

Issue:

Arguments in favor:

Arguments against:

C Debate Divide the group into two teams, with one team in favor and the other team against. Take turns presenting your views. Use the Vocabulary. Sit or stand with the people on your team. Take turns and disagree politely. Then continue the discussion.

♻ **Be sure to recycle this language.**

Discuss controversies	Express agreement	Express disagreement
Are you in favor of ___ ?	I agree with you on that one.	We'll have to agree to disagree!
It's not cool to ___ .	I couldn't agree more.	I have to disagree with you there.
I tend to be a little opinionated.	I couldn't have said it better myself.	I'm not sure I agree.
I'm opposed to / in favor of ___ .	That's exactly what I think.	I'm afraid I don't agree.
I think / believe / feel:		No offense, but I can't agree.
it's wrong.		
it's right.		
it's OK under some circumstances.		
it's wrong, no matter what.		

Review

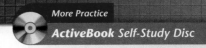

More Practice
ActiveBook *Self-Study Disc*

grammar · vocabulary · listening
reading · speaking · pronunciation

A 5:20 **Listening comprehension** Listen to the news report about four news stories. Then listen again and complete each statement.

1 Sorindians and Ramays are two ((ethnic groups)/ governments) that occupy land areas next to each other.

2 ((Sorindians)/ Ramays) want to be able to observe their dietary laws and traditional clothing customs.

3 The problem between the Sorindians and the Ramays is an example of (corruption /(ethnic discrimination)).

4 A package left in the bathroom at the central post office raised fears of ((terrorism)/ corruption).

5 Poor people are migrating into the ((city from the countryside)/ countryside from the city).

6 Another story in the news is the reported ((corruption)/ poverty) of a police captain.

B Complete the paragraph about an election, using verbs and count and non-count nouns correctly.

Many ....**candidates**.... running for election make ....**promises**.... about ....**education**....
⎵1 candidate / candidates ⎵2 promise / promises ⎵3 education / the education
But ....**progress**.... comes slowly, and ....**information**.... ....**is**.... hard to get.
⎵4 progress / the progress ⎵5 information / informations ⎵6 is / are
Voters would like to see ....**proof**.... that their ....**advice**.... ....**is**....
⎵7 proof / proofs ⎵8 advice / advices ⎵9 is / are
being followed. For instance, we are just now receiving ....**news**.... of education statistics and
⎵10 news / the news
....**it's**.... not very good. ....**Help**.... is needed, and ....**time**.... is necessary
⎵11 it's / they're ⎵12 Help / The help ⎵13 the time / time
to improve our schools.

C Complete each sentence.

1 The law doesn't allow the president ....**to change**.... (change) the Constitution.

2 Our friends advised us ....**not to be**.... (not / be) disappointed about the election.

3 The Constitution requires senators ....**to leave**.... (leave) office after two terms.

4 The election committee permitted the candidates ....**to speak**.... (speak) about their educational policies.

D Disagree politely with the following statements, using a different way to disagree for each. Then add a reason why you disagree with each statement.

That's one way to look at it, but . . .

1 Monarchies are dictatorships.

(YOU) ....
....

2 There's no such thing as a real democracy anywhere in the world.

(YOU) ....
....

5:21/5:22
Top Notch Pop
"We Can Agree to Disagree"
Lyrics p. 150

3 All people with power are corrupt.

(YOU) ....
....

E **Writing** On a separate sheet of paper, write at least two paragraphs about one of the following issues: compulsory military service, capital punishment, or censorship of books and movies. Include both the pros and cons of the issue.

WRITING BOOSTER ▸ p. 147
• *Contrasting ideas*
• *Guidance for Exercise E*

Review

A 🔊 Listening comprehension

Suggested teaching time:	5–7 minutes	Your actual teaching time:

- To prepare students for listening, review words for global problems that were discussed in this unit; for example, *corruption, terrorism, racism, discrimination, poverty, war, hunger, drug abuse,* etc.
- Pause after each report to allow students time to choose their answers.
- To review, have students compare answers with a partner and then with the class.

> **AUDIOSCRIPT**
>
> **F:** Good evening. Fighting has broken out again tonight on the border between the Sorindian and Ramay provinces. Ethnic Sorindians say they are not permitted to observe their dietary laws and that their children are not permitted to wear traditional dress at school.
>
> On another note, a package containing a large amount of explosive material was discovered at the central post office today. Authorities are searching for the person or persons who left it in the men's restroom.
>
> In the central city, volunteers are opening soup kitchens to feed the large numbers of homeless poor who have recently arrived from the countryside. The government is making funds available to help this growing population.
>
> And finally, a police captain in Spartock has been accused of taking bribes to permit engineers to build buildings that don't conform to safe construction laws. A report will be issued tomorrow.

B Complete the paragraph . . .

Suggested teaching time:	3–5 minutes	Your actual teaching time:

- To prepare students for the activity, review what they learned about non-count nouns. Ask *Are nouns that refer to abstract ideas count or non-count?* (Non-count.) *Do non-count nouns have plural forms?* (No.) *Are they normally used with articles?* (No.) *Do they need plural or singular verbs?* (Singular verbs.)
- Point out that not all the nouns in the paragraph are non-count nouns.
- Ask volunteers to read their paragraphs aloud.

C Complete each sentence . . .

Suggested teaching time:	2–3 minutes	Your actual teaching time:

- Complete the first item with the class.
- Have students compare answers with a partner.

D Disagree politely . . .

Suggested teaching time:	4–5 minutes	Your actual teaching time:

- To prepare students for the activity, read the example aloud. Then have volunteers say the phrases that they remember to express agreement and disagreement. For example:

  I agree with you on that one.
  I couldn't agree more.
  I have to disagree with you there.
  I'm not sure I agree.

- To review with the class, have several students express their views about each issue.

E Writing

Suggested teaching time:	7–10 minutes	Your actual teaching time:

- Ask students to write notes about the pros and cons of the issue they have chosen.
- Walk around the room as students write, helping as needed.
- Encourage students to finish their paragraphs with their opinion of whether they are for or against the issue.

Option:  (Teaching notes p. T147)

🔘 **ActiveTeach** Multimedia Disc • **Writing Process Worksheets**

ORAL REVIEW

Before the first activity, give students a few minutes of silent time to explore the pictures and become familiar with them.

Contest

Suggested teaching time:	6 minutes	Your actual teaching time:	

• Clarify the task. Tell students they will look at the pictures for one minute and then turn to a partner and take turns identifying what the people are talking about in each picture.

• After students have finished the contest, review the news with the class by having several students say as much as they can about the pictures. (Possible answers: In the first picture, the people are talking about a case of corruption. A judge took bribes. It was discovered and he was sent to prison. In the second picture, the women are talking about terrorism. A car exploded in a public place. A lot of innocent people were hurt. An unknown terrorist group seems to be responsible. In the third picture, the men are discussing elections in Senegal. Senegal is a democracy. A president will be elected.)

Pair work 1

Suggested teaching time:	6–8 minutes	Your actual teaching time:	

• Encourage students to express their concerns about the problem and about how it could be solved.

• Remind students to use the ways to agree and disagree they learned in this unit.

Possible responses ...
A: Look at this article. It says a judge who was taking bribes in court is being sent to prison. **B:** A judge? I'm concerned about so much corruption. I think we need stricter laws to reduce it. **B:** I see what you mean, but we also need to teach traditional moral values. **A:** I couldn't agree more.

Pair work 2

Suggested teaching time:	6–8 minutes	Your actual teaching time:	

• Encourage students to express their concerns about the problem, and discuss its causes and possible solutions.

Possible responses ...
A: Look! Another terrorist bombing. **B:** That's terrible! Why would anyone do something like that? **A:** Well, I think some people in poorer countries feel angry about their poverty and that makes them violent. **B:** That may be true, but I believe we need to bring back capital punishment.

Pair work 3

Suggested teaching time:	6–8 minutes	Your actual teaching time:	

• Review the vocabulary to describe the continuum of political and social thought. (Radical, liberal, moderate, conservative, reactionary.) Ask students to choose where their character belongs on the continuum.

• As students role-play, encourage them to express their opinions based on their own choices.

Possible responses ...
A: I'm voting for Leon Mubumba because he's a moderate. He's against radical change but he thinks a little change will be good. Who are you voting for? **B:** I'm not sure, but I think I'm going to vote for Sam Bombasa. **A:** Are you a conservative? **B:** Not really, but I don't want too much change. Things are not so bad right now. **A:** Well, that's one way to look at it, but how will things ever get better?

Option: [+5 minutes] For a challenge, ask students to role-play a conversation between the elected candidate and the TV reporter. Have the student playing the TV reporter ask the candidate how his party is planning to solve different world problems.

Option: Oral Progress Assessment

Use the illustrations on page 109. Encourage students to use the language practiced in this unit and previous units.

• Tell the student to choose one of the world issues the people are talking about: *corruption, terrorism,* or *elections.* Give the student one minute to propose some solutions to one of the problems; for example, *I believe that teaching moral values to young people can help stop corruption. Children should be taught the importance of being honest at school.* Ask two follow-up questions about the student's proposed solutions.

• Evaluate the student on intelligibility, fluency, correct use of target grammar, and appropriate use of vocabulary.

 • Oral Progress Assessment Charts

Option: *Top Notch* Project

Ask students to make a presentation about an international organization.

Idea: Have students form small groups. Ask each group to research an international organization; for example, the United Nations, the World Bank, or Oxfam. Ask students to visit the organization's website and international news websites, such the BBC or CNN, to gather information. Find out how these organizations are trying to solve some of the problems discussed in this unit. Ask students to take notes so that they can report their findings to the class. Encourage them to explain whether they agree or disagree with what the organization is doing and give supporting reasons.

EXTRAS (optional)

• Complete Assessment Package
• Weblinks for Teachers: pearsonlongman.com/topnotch/

And on your ActiveTeach Multimedia Disc:
  Just for Fun
  Top Notch Pop Song Activities
  Top Notch TV Video Program and Activity Worksheets
  Supplementary Pronunciation Lessons
  Audioscripts
  Unit Study Guides

ORAL REVIEW

Contest Look at the pictures for one minute. Then close your books and name the three issues depicted in the news.

Pair work

1 Create a conversation between the man and woman in Picture 1. Continue the conversation, discussing corruption in general. Start like this:

> Look at this article about the judge who was taking bribes in court.

2 Create a conversation between the two women in Picture 2. Start like this and continue the conversation, discussing terrorism in general:

> A: Look! Another terrorist bombing.
> B: Terrible! What do you think causes this?

3 Create a conversation between the two men discussing the election in Senegal in Picture 3. Start like this and continue the conversation:

> I'm for Leon Mubumba. I'm a moderate. I think ...

CITY POST
Judge to prison for taking bribes.

Daily Gazette
Car bomb explodes near open-air market.
Numerous casualties. Unknown group claims responsibility.

ELECTION IN SENEGAL

NOW I CAN...

- [ ] Bring up a controversial subject.
- [ ] Discuss controversial issues politely.
- [ ] Propose solutions to global problems.
- [ ] Debate the pros and cons of issues.

Beautiful World

GOALS | After Unit 10, you will be able to:

1 Describe a geographical location.
2 Warn about a possible risk.
3 Describe a natural setting.
4 Discuss solutions to global warming.

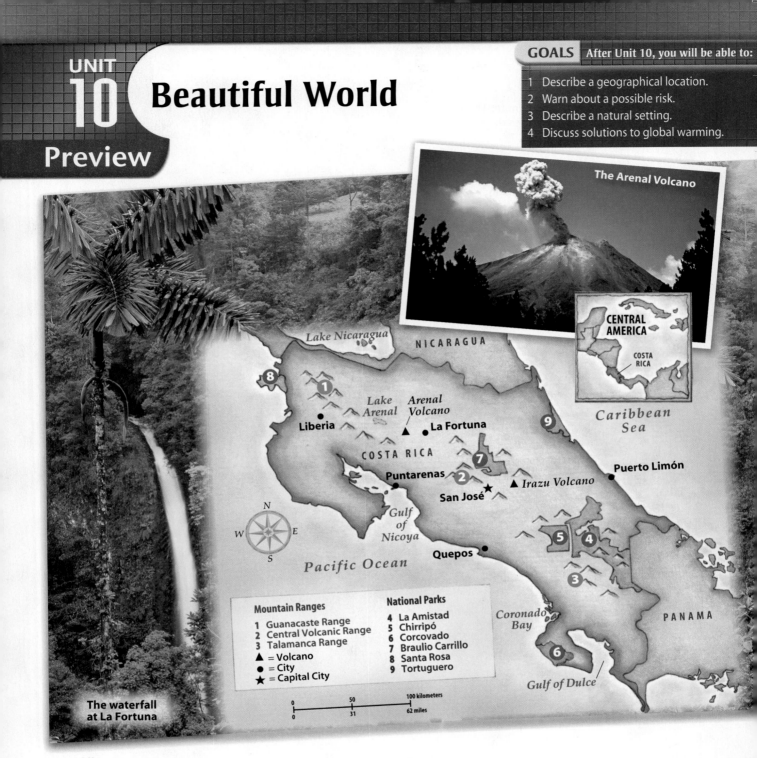

The Arenal Volcano

CENTRAL AMERICA

COSTA RICA

Caribbean Sea

Lake Nicaragua

NICARAGUA

8

1

Lake Arenal

Arenal Volcano

Liberia

La Fortuna

COSTA RICA

9

Puerto Limón

7

Puntarenas

2

San José

▲ Irazu Volcano

Gulf of Nicoya

5

4

Quepos

3

Pacific Ocean

Coronado Bay

PANAMA

6

Gulf of Dulce

Mountain Ranges
1 Guanacaste Range
2 Central Volcanic Range
3 Talamanca Range
▲ = Volcano
● = City
★ = Capital City

National Parks
4 La Amistad
5 Chirripó
6 Corcovado
7 Braulio Carrillo
8 Santa Rosa
9 Tortuguero

0	50	100 kilometers
0	31	62 miles

The waterfall at La Fortuna

A 🔊 5:23 **Vocabulary** • *Geographical features* Read and listen. Then listen again and repeat.

a gulf	a lake	a sea	a mountain range
a bay	an ocean	a volcano	a national park

B Use the map to answer the questions about Costa Rica. See page T110 for answers.

1 What two countries share a border with Costa Rica?

2 In what mountain range is Costa Rica's capital located?

3 What is Costa Rica's largest national park?

4 What is Costa Rica's largest lake?

5 Approximately how far is Puntarenas from San José?

6 What bodies of water are on Costa Rica's two coasts?

UNIT 10

Beautiful World

Preview

Suggested teaching time:	10–15 minutes	Your actual teaching time:

Before Exercise A, give students a few minutes of silent time to look at the maps and the photos.

- Ask students to study the map legend and encourage them to use the map labels, photos, and captions to figure out the meaning of unknown words.
- To check comprehension, ask:
  What country is featured on the map? (Costa Rica.)
  What other countries are there on the map? (Nicaragua and Panama.)
  What are some cities in Costa Rica? (Liberia, La Fortuna, Puntarenas, San José, Puerto Limón, Quepos.)
  What does a star indicate? (The capital city.)
  What symbol shows a volcano? (A triangle.)
  What is a mountain range? (A group of mountains.)
  How many mountain ranges are there in Costa Rica? (Three.)
  How many national parks are shown on the map? (Six.)
- Point out the scale for distance under the legend. Ask *Is Costa Rica a small or a large country?* (A small country.)
- To draw on students' prior knowledge, ask them what they know about Costa Rica. Then have students share their impressions or experiences with the class.

Language and culture
- Costa Rica, which means "Rich Coast," is a tropical country with a variety of habitats and microclimates. Over a million people visit Costa Rica annually. It is a popular spot for eco-tourists, who come to see the diverse flora and fauna—mountains, rainforests, volcanoes, 850 species of birds, and 200 species of mammal.
- In American English, some words that end in -ter, such as *kilometer*, *center*, and *theater* are spelled with -tre in British English; *kilometre*, *centre*, and *theatre*.

A ◀))) Vocabulary

Suggested teaching time:	2–3 minutes	Your actual teaching time:

- Have students listen and study the words. Then ask them to listen and repeat chorally.
- To provide practice, have pairs take turns saying a vocabulary word and giving an example from the map; for example, **Student A:** *sea.* **Student B:** *Caribbean Sea.*

Language and culture
- A *sea* is a large body of salt water that is smaller than an ocean or is enclosed by land; a *gulf* or *bay* is an inlet of the sea almost surrounded by land. A *bay* is usually, but not always, smaller than a gulf.

B Use the map . . .

Suggested teaching time:	3–5 minutes	Your actual teaching time:

- Have students answer the questions individually and then compare answers with a partner. For question 5, point out that students should figure out the approximate distance by using the scale.
- Review the answers with the class.

Option: [+5 minutes] For a challenge, have pairs take turns describing a location on the map and guessing that location. For example:
  Student A: *This national park is between Coronado Bay and the Gulf of Dulce.*
  Student B: *Corcovado.*

Answers for Exercise B
1. Nicaragua and Panama
2. Central Volcanic Range
3. La Amistad
4. Lake Arenal
5. Approximately 80 km / 48 miles
6. The Pacific Ocean and the Caribbean Sea

C 🔊 Photo story

Suggested teaching time:	5 minutes	Your actual teaching time:

- Before students read and listen to the conversation, have them look at the photos. Ask *Where are the men?* (At a resort. By the pool.)
- After students read and listen, ask:
    Where are Max and Frank from? (Max is from Italy and Frank is from Hong Kong.)
    What places is Max planning to visit? (The La Fortuna waterfall and the Arenal Volcano.)
    Is the waterfall worth visiting? (Yes, it's spectacular.)
    What does Frank warn Max about? (The path down to the bottom of the falls—it can get wet and slippery.)
    What's Frank's opinion about visiting both places in the same day? (He doesn't think it's a problem.)
- To personalize, direct students' attention to the pictures of the La Fortuna waterfall and the Arenal Volcano on page 110. Have students turn to a partner and say if they would like or wouldn't like to visit these places and give reasons. To review, have several volunteers share their opinions with the class. (Possible answers: I'd love to visit the waterfall. It looks really beautiful. / I'd like to go to the waterfall, but I'm not sure I'd enjoy getting there. It might be difficult.)

> **Language and culture**
> - *You wouldn't happen to know . . . , would you?* is used to make the question seem less direct than *Do you know,* and therefore more polite.
> **LEN** **From the Longman Corpus:** *Get a look, take a look,* and *have a look* at something mean the same thing, but *take a look* is the most frequently used.

D Paraphrase

Suggested teaching time:	5–7 minutes	Your actual teaching time:

- Encourage students to identify which person says each of the phrases and to use the context of the conversation to help figure out the meaning.
- Have students support their answers with a reason based on the Photo Story, and then have them compare answers with a partner.

E Pair work

Suggested teaching time:	10 minutes	Your actual teaching time:

- Encourage students to write the names of one or two places for each geographical feature. Point out that they can name places in different countries. Students should include names in English if they know them.
- To review with the class, draw the following diagram on the board. Then draw lines from each circle and write the names of places as you get feedback from students.

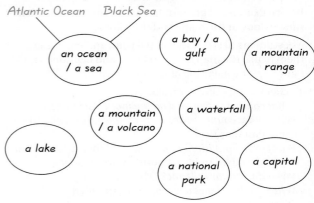

F Guessing game

Suggested teaching time:	10–15 minutes	Your actual teaching time:

- To prepare students for the activity, ask them to think of three geographical features and write sentences to describe them. Point out that if students choose a place in a country not their own, they should include the country's name in their descriptions.
- To model the activity, read the speech balloons and brainstorm ways to complete them. (Possible answers: It's a beautiful lake. It's between two mountain ranges / a mountain range and a small town. It's a volcano. It's near a big city / the sea.)
- Form small groups and have students take turns describing the places and guessing the names. Walk around, monitoring students' work.

EXTRAS (optional)
- Workbook: Exercises 1–4

C 🔊 **Photo story** Read and listen to two tourists talking about Costa Rica.

Max: Have you folks been here long?

Frank: A little over a week. Unfortunately, we've only got two days left. You?

Max: We just got here yesterday, actually.

Frank: I'm Frank, by the way. Frank Lew. From Hong Kong.

Max: Max Belli. From Labro, Italy. Have you heard of it?

Frank: I can't say I have.

Max: It's a very small town about 20 kilometers north of Rome.

Max: Hey, you wouldn't happen to know anything about the La Fortuna waterfall, would you? We plan on driving up there this weekend.

Frank: Actually, we just got back from there yesterday.

Max: What a coincidence! Was it worth seeing?

Frank: Spectacular. You don't want to miss it.

Frank: But be sure to take it slow on the path down to the bottom of the falls. It can get pretty wet and slippery.

Max: Thanks for the warning. What if we want to get a look at the Arenal Volcano, too? Do you think that's doable in two days?

Frank: No problem. The volcano's only about twenty minutes west of La Fortuna by car. So I'm sure you could handle them both.

Max: Italian speaker / Frank: Chinese speaker

D Paraphrase Say each of the following statements from the Photo Story in your <u>own</u> way. Use the context of the story to help you restate each one.

1 "I can't say I have." No, I haven't.

2 "What a coincidence!" Really?

3 "Was it worth seeing?" Was it worth the trouble of visiting?

4 "You don't want to miss it." You should go.

5 ". . . be sure to take it slow." . . . go slowly / take your time

6 "Do you think that's doable in two days?" Can I do that in two days?

7 ". . . I'm sure you could handle them both." I'm sure you can do them both.

E Pair work Brainstorm and write the names of places you know for each of the following geographical features.

an ocean or sea		a national park	
a bay or gulf		a lake	
a mountain or volcano		a waterfall	
a mountain range		a capital	

F Guessing game Describe a geographical feature of your country. Your classmates guess what place it is.

❝It's a beautiful lake. It's between . . .❞

❝It's a volcano. It's near . . .❞

GOAL Describe a geographical location

GRAMMAR *Prepositions of geographical place*

GRAMMAR BOOSTER ▸ p. 138
- *Prepositions of place: more usage*
- *Proper nouns: capitalization*
- *Proper nouns: use of the*

Look at the map and study the examples.
Mexico is north **of** (OR **to** the north **of**) Guatemala.
Honduras and El Salvador are located **to** the south.

Tikal is **in** the north. Guatemala City is **in** the south.
Cobán is located **in** the central part **of** Guatemala.

Champerico is **on** the west coast **of** Guatemala.
Flores is **on** the south shore **of** Lake Petén Itzá.
El Rancho is located **on** the Motagua River.

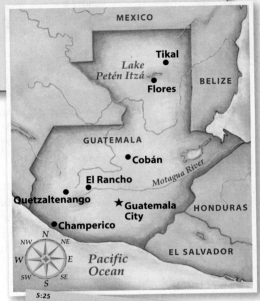

A Grammar practice Complete the sentences with the correct prepositions.

1 Vladivostok is located …**on**… the eastern coast …**of**… Russia.

2 Barranquilla is …**in**… the northern part …**of**… Colombia.

3 Haikou is …**on**… the northern coast …**of**… Hainan Island in China.

4 Machu Picchu is located about 100 kilometers northwest …**of**… Cuzco.

5 Vietnam is located south …**of**… China.

6 Kota Kinabalu is …**on**… the north coast of Borneo, a part of Malaysia.

7 Manaus is located …**on**… the Amazon River in Brazil.

8 Canada is …**to**… the north …**of**… the United States.

B Pair work On a separate sheet of paper, write and discuss the locations of five places in or near your country.

5:25
◀))) **Directions**
N = north   NE = northeast
S = south   NW = northwest
E = east   SE = southeast
W = west   SW = southwest
Note: the **east** coast (OR **eastern** coast)

PRONUNCIATION *Voiced and voiceless th*

5:26
A ◀))) Read and listen. Then listen again and repeat.

Voiced **th**	Voiceless **th**
1 the west	1 north
2 this way	2 northeastern
3 northern	3 south
4 southern	4 southwestern

B Pair work Take turns reading the sentences you wrote in Exercise B Pair Work above, paying attention to voiced and voiceless **th** sounds.

GRAMMAR

Suggested teaching time:	10–15 minutes	Your actual teaching time:

- Direct students' attention to the chart and have them study the examples and find the places on the map.

- Ask students to read the *Directions* box. Have them listen and repeat. Then have students find the directions on the compass on the map.

- Direct students' attention to the note in the *Directions* box. Be sure students understand that there is no change in meaning between *the east coast* and *the eastern coast*. The same applies to the other directions.

- To provide practice with prepositions and directions, ask questions about the map: *Where is Guatemala—to the south of Mexico or to the north of Mexico?* (To the south of Mexico.) *Is Guatemala City in the north or in the south of the country?* (In the south.) *Is Champerico on the eastern coast or on the western coast?* (On the western coast.) *Is Flores on the southern shore or on the northern shore of a lake?* (On the southern shore of a lake.)

Language and culture

- *North, south, east,* and *west* can be used as nouns (They live in the east.) or as adjectives (They live on the east coast.). *Northern, southern, eastern,* and *western* are only used as adjectives (They live on the eastern coast, *not* They live in the ~~eastern~~.).

LCN From the Longman Corpus: It is a common error for learners across all language backgrounds to use *from* instead of *of* in directions (It is a small city west ~~from~~ Munich.). Be sure students use *of* instead.

Option:  **GRAMMAR BOOSTER** (Teaching notes p. T138)

ActiveTeach Multimedia Disc • Inductive Grammar Charts

A Grammar practice

Suggested teaching time:	3 minutes	Your actual teaching time:

- To model the activity, complete the first item with the class. Point out that students can refer to the information in the grammar box if necessary.

- Have students compare answers with a partner. Then review with the class.

B Pair work

Suggested teaching time:	5–7 minutes	Your actual teaching time:

- To prepare students for the activity, brainstorm geographical places with locations that students can describe. Make a list on the board. (Possible answers: mountain, mountain range, volcano, lake, gulf, bay, river, city, town, capital, national park.)

- To model the activity, give some examples. *Cancún is located on the eastern coast of Mexico. New York is north of Washington, D.C. Mt. Fuji is located west of Tokyo.*

- Have pairs discuss the locations and then write sentences about the location of five or more places.

- To review with the class, have several students describe the location of a place.

PRONUNCIATION

A ◄»)) Read and listen . . .

Suggested teaching time:	2 minutes	Your actual teaching time:

- Have students read and listen to the examples. Point out that if a sound is voiced, there is vibration in the throat and that if a sound is voiceless, there is no vibration. You may want to have students put a hand on their throats to compare the vibration with the voiced *th-* (the) and the lack of vibration with the voiceless *th-* (thanks). (See the *Language and culture* box below.)

- Have students listen again and repeat chorally. Be sure students pronounce the sounds correctly.

B Pair work

Suggested teaching time:	3 minutes	Your actual teaching time:

- Before students practice reading the sentences, ask them to identify the voiced and voiceless *th-* sounds. Have them circle the voiced sounds and underline the voiceless sounds. Be sure students have circled and underlined the sounds correctly.

Option: [+5 minutes] To extend the activity, draw the chart and write the words *Thursday, that, those, breathtaking, these, path, think,* and *breathe* on the board.

Voiceless *th-*	Voiced *th-*

Ask students to write the words in the correct columns. Then have pairs take turns reading the words. (Answers: Voiceless *th—Thursday, breathtaking, path, think*; Voiced *th—that, breathe, those, these*.)

Language and culture

- Students often have difficulty pronouncing the sound /ð/, as in *there*, and substitute a sound like /z/ or /d/. Demonstrate the position of the tongue: The tongue is placed loosely between the upper and lower teeth. The tip of the tongue lightly touches the upper teeth and vibrates. The sound /ð/ is voiced, which means the vocal cords vibrate, and the voice is used to produce the sound. Also difficult for many students is the voiceless *th– sound* /θ/, as in *thin*. They often substitute a sound like /s/ or /t/. To pronounce the sound /θ/, the tongue is placed between the upper and lower teeth. The tip of the tongue very lightly touches the upper teeth (and doesn't vibrate). The sound /θ/ is voiceless; the vocal cords do not vibrate and the voice is not used. Although it is worthwhile to help students create these sounds, their mispronunciation rarely interferes with comprehensibility.

ActiveTeach Multimedia Disc • Pronunciation Activities

CONVERSATION MODEL

A 🔊 Read and listen . . .

Suggested teaching time:	2 minutes	Your actual teaching time:	

These conversation strategies are implicit in the model:
- Show interest in someone's plans by asking follow-up questions.
- Indicate possible intention with "I've been thinking about it."

- Before listening to the conversation, have students describe what is in the thought bubble. (A map of Japan. The location of Sanzen-In temple.)

- Have students listen and read the *Recommendations* and *Criticisms* boxes. If necessary, clarify the meaning of the expressions: *It's a must-see* and *You don't want to miss it.* (It is so good, exciting, interesting, etc., that you think people should not fail to see it or visit it.) *It's overrated.* (It is not as good or important as some people say it is.) *It's a waste of time.* (It is not worth the time that you would spend to go visit it.)

- To personalize, ask students to use the expressions in the boxes to describe things they have seen and places they have visited; for example, *[Name of a movie] is overrated—I fell asleep watching it.*

Language and culture
- It is possible to say *plan to do something* or *plan on doing something.*
- *Sanzen-in Temple* is the main attraction of Ohara, a small village north of Kyoto, the old capital city of Japan. It was built in 784 and it is famous for its beautiful gardens.

B 🔊 Rhythm and intonation

Suggested teaching time:	3 minutes	Your actual teaching time:	

- Have students repeat each line chorally. Make sure students:
  ○ use falling intonation for *Where exactly is the temple located?*
  ○ put extra stress on *Kyoto* in *About fifteen kilometers north of Kyoto.*
  ○ stress both *must* and *see* in *It's a must-see.*

NOW YOU CAN Describe a geographical location

A Pair work

Suggested teaching time:	10–15 minutes	Your actual teaching time:	

- To draw on students' prior knowledge, ask them to say what they already know about Australia. Encourage students to make simple sentences. (Possible answers: Australia is a country and a continent. There is a famous theater, the Opera House, in Sydney.)

- To help students become familiar with the places shown in the photos, have pairs write sentences about them. Encourage students to write one sentence describing what they can see and one sentence describing what they think can be done in that place. (See the *Language and culture* box below.) For example:
  Ayers Rock is a big red rock in the middle of a desert. It is a good place for climbing.
  In the Great Barrier Reef you can see colorful fish. It is a great place for scuba diving.
  In the Kakadu National Park there are trees, rocks, and a river. It must be a great place for hiking.
  The Snowy Mountains reach high up into the air. They must be a good place for hiking and climbing.

- To reinforce the use of the conversation strategies, remind students to ask follow-up questions with interest and enthusiasm.

Don't stop! Extend the conversation. Have students give more examples of questions a tourist could ask. For example:
  It isn't overrated, is it?
  What are some activities you can do?
  What's the best way to get there?
  What kinds of animals are there?
Encourage students to be creative and point out that if necessary, they can invent the answers to the questions as they role-play.

 ActiveTeach Multimedia Disc
- Conversation Pair Work Cards
- Learning Strategies

B Change partners

Suggested teaching time:	7–10 minutes	Your actual teaching time:	

- Make sure students switch roles when they change partners and describe other places.

Language and culture
- Canberra is the capital of Australia. Sydney, the largest city in Australia, is known as an important seaport and commercial center. It is home of the famous Sydney Opera House. Melbourne is the second largest city and the cultural center of the country. Perth is a modern isolated city on the west coast of Australia with beautiful beaches and great surfing.
- Ayers Rock is 348 meters (1,142 feet) high and changes color according to the time of the day.
- The Great Barrier Reef is 2,000 kilometers (1,243 miles) long. There are many types of beautiful coral and fish.
- In Kakadu National Park, you can go hiking, boating, or fishing but canoes are prohibited because of crocodiles.
- In the Snowy Mountains you can enjoy spectacular views.
- In Tasmania, there are several national parks that offer beautiful scenery.

EXTRAS (optional)
- Workbook: Exercises 5–9
- Copy & Go: Activity 37

A 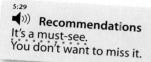 Read and listen to someone describing a geographical location.

5:27

A: Where exactly is the temple located?

B: About fifteen kilometers north of Kyoto. Are you planning to go there?

A: I've been thinking about it.

B: It's a must-see. Be sure to take pictures!

5:29
🔊 **Recommendations**
It's a must-see.
You don't want to miss it.

5:30
🔊 **Criticisms**
It's overrated.
It's a waste of time.

B 🔊 **Rhythm and intonation** Listen again and repeat.
Then practice the Conversation Model with a partner.

5:28

NOW YOU CAN   Describe a geographical location

A Pair work Change the Conversation Model
to talk about the location of an interesting
place. Use the map and the pictures or a map
of your own country. Then change roles.

A: Where exactly is .... located?

B: .... Are you planning to go there?

A: I've been thinking about it.

B: ....

Don't stop!
• **Ask more questions about the place.**
  Is it worth seeing?
  Is it doable in [one day]?
• **Ask about other places.**

AYERS ROCK

THE GREAT BARRIER REEF

KAKADU NATIONAL PARK

THE SNOWY MOUNTAINS

B Change partners Describe other places.

113

GOAL Warn about a possible risk

VOCABULARY *Describe possible risks*

A ◀))) 5:31 Read and listen. Then listen again and repeat.

It can be quite **dangerous**.

It can be very **rocky**.

It can be extremely **steep**.

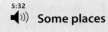
◀))) 5:32 **Some places**

a path

a cliff

a cave

It can be so **slippery**.

It can be pretty **dark**.

It can be terribly **exhausting**.

It can be really **foggy**.

◀))) 5:33 **Dangerous animals and insects**
Watch out for [snakes].
Keep an eye out for [bears].

a snake   a shark

a jellyfish   a bear

a scorpion   a mosquito

B ◀))) 5:34 **Listening comprehension** Listen to the conversations. Check if the speaker thinks the place is safe or dangerous.

	Safe	Dangerous
1 He thinks hiking around the waterfall is . . .	☐	☑
2 She thinks climbing the mountain is . . .	☐	☑
3 She thinks swimming in the bay is . . .	☑	☐
4 He thinks walking on the cliffs is . . .	☐	☑

C ◀))) 5:35 Listen again. Complete each statement with the dangers.

1 He warns that the path is ....pretty steep.... and there may be ....mosquitoes.... .

2 She warns that there may be .....bears..... and that the path can be ....quite exhausting.... .

3 He's worried that there will be a lot of ....mosquitoes.... and there may be ....jellyfish.... .

4 He warns that the cliffs are ....really steep.... and there may be ....snakes.... .

LESSON PLAN

VOCABULARY

A ◀)) Read and listen . . .

Suggested teaching time:	7–10 minutes	Your actual teaching time:

- Have students study the pictures and read the captions at the top of the page. Then ask them to listen and repeat chorally.

- Write the following continuum on the board and tell students that the adverbs express different degrees of intensity. (Note: these degrees can vary depending on the speaker's intonation.)

```
        (+)              (++)              (+++)
─────────────────────────────────────────────────▶
pretty / quite   very / really / so   extremely / terribly
```

- Have students read the *Some places* box. Then ask them to listen and repeat chorally.

- To provide practice with adjective and adverb placement, draw the following diagram on the board and have pairs make different combinations to describe places. Encourage students to write four or five combinations.

pretty / quite very / really extremely / very	+	adjective	+	path cliff cave your idea: ___

- To review with the class, have several students read their combinations. You may want to write some of them on the board; for example, *an extremely steep cliff, a very dark cave, a pretty slippery path, a quite dangerous road.*

- Have students listen to *Dangerous animals and insects.* Then have them listen and repeat chorally.

- Draw students' attention to the warnings *Watch out for . . .* and *Keep an eye out for . . . .* Give examples and explain their meanings: *Watch out for snakes.* (Be careful because there are snakes in the area.) *Keep an eye out for bears.* (Be careful because there may be bears.)

- To provide practice, write the sentences on the board and have pairs complete them with their own ideas.

    In [place], you should watch out for ___. / keep an eye out for ___.

Option: **[+10 minutes]** For a challenge, form small groups and have students take turns describing places and experiences, using the vocabulary in Exercise A. Ask the other students to guess the place.

Language and culture

- *Jellyfish* is both the singular and plural form (a jellyfish / many jellyfish).
- Scorpions and jellyfish sting. Snakes and sharks bite. Mosquitoes bite. Bees and wasps sting.
- *Watch out* can also be used without *for* to mean "be careful;" for example, *Watch out! There's a snake!*

 **ActiveTeach** Multimedia Disc • Vocabulary Flash Cards

B ◀)) Listening comprehension

Suggested teaching time:	2–5 minutes	Your actual teaching time:

- To prepare students for listening, point out that each conversation is between a man and a woman. Ask students to pay attention to the *He* or *She* at the beginning of each statement, and listen to this person's opinion of each place.

- As students listen, stop after each conversation to allow them time to choose their answers.

FYI: Do not go into details at this stage. Students will be discussing the reasons why each place is safe or dangerous in the next exercise.

AUDIOSCRIPT

CONVERSATION 1 [F = Spanish]
F: I can't wait to see the waterfall. They say it's beautiful.
M: It is. You don't want to miss it.
F: I'm going to take a lot of pictures.
M: Well, watch out on your way down. The path is pretty steep.
F: Don't worry. I'll be careful.
M: And make sure you bring something for the mosquitoes. They can be terrible at this time of year.
F: Thanks.

CONVERSATION 2 [M = Korean]
M: Well, I'll be heading off for Sorak Mountain tomorrow morning.
F: Wow! That's great. First time?
M: Uh-huh.
F: Well, keep an eye out for bears, OK? They say it's good to make a lot of noise while you're hiking there.
M: I'll do that.
F: And make sure you bring a lot of water. They say that hiking the path can be quite exhausting if you're not used to it.
M: OK.

CONVERSATION 3 [M = Australian English]
M: Is it OK to go swimming in the bay here?
F: Oh, it's beautiful. The water is great.
M: I heard there are a lot of mosquitoes, though. Is that true?
F: On the beach? I don't think so.
M: Are you sure it's OK? Someone told me they were terrible.
F: Who told you that? We go swimming there all the time.
M: What about jellyfish?
F: Don't worry about it. We've been going swimming there for years and we've never had a problem.

CONVERSATION 4 [F = U.S. regional]
F: I'd like to take a walk north of the town to see the cliffs.
M: The views of the ocean are fantastic. But make sure you stay on the path, OK? The cliffs are really steep and it's dangerous to stand too close to the edge.
F: Thanks for the warning.
M: One other thing. I'm sure you won't have a problem, but keep an eye out for snakes.
F: You're kidding. For real?
M: Well, there are snakes in the area. Just be careful and I'm sure you'll be fine.

C ◀)) Listen again . . .

Suggested teaching time:	3–5 minutes	Your actual teaching time:

- To help students focus on the correct details, ask them to listen for the reasons why each place is or might be dangerous.

- Have students compare answers with a partner.

GRAMMAR

Suggested teaching time:	10 minutes	Your actual teaching time:

- Direct students' attention to the chart and have them read the first explanation and study the examples. To help clarify, write on the board:

  It's too foggy to drive fast.

  ↓   ↓   ↓

  too + adj. + infinitive

- Point out that *too* + an adjective + an infinitive is used to give an explanation, reason, or warning. Restate the sentence on the board: *Don't drive fast because it is very foggy.*

- To provide practice, write the following ideas on the board and have pairs write sentences, using *too* to give reasons for not doing these activities.

  1. climb Mt. Everest
  2. swim across the Atlantic Ocean
  3. hike in the mountains at night

- Review with the class by having several students read their sentences aloud. (Possible answers: 1. Mt. Everest is too steep / high to climb. 2. It's too far to swim across the ocean. 3. It's too dangerous / dark to hike in the mountains at night.)

- Have students read the second explanation and study the examples. To help clarify, use *for* + the person or people for whom the explanation or warning is given. Point out that when a pronoun is used after *for*, an object pronoun must be used. Write on the board:

  It's too dangerous for | *children to climb that mountain.*
  | *them (NOT they).*

- Direct students' attention to the *Be careful!* box. Point out that *cliffs* and *them* refer to the same thing, so *them* is not necessary.

Option:  *GRAMMAR BOOSTER* (Teaching notes p. T140)

ActiveTeach Multimedia Disc • Inductive Grammar Charts

Grammar practice

Suggested teaching time:	3–5 minutes	Your actual teaching time:

- After students complete the exercise, have them check answers with a partner.

CONVERSATION MODEL

A 🔊 **Read and listen . . .**

Suggested teaching time:	2 minutes	Your actual teaching time:

These conversation strategies are implicit in the model:
- Qualify a positive response with "Sure, but . . .".
- Elaborate further information with "Well, . . .".
- Express gratitude for a warning.

- Direct students' attention to the illustration of the undertow. If necessary, explain that an *undertow* is a current under the water's surface that pulls away from the land when a wave comes onto the shore; it can pull a swimmer out to sea.

> **Language and culture**
>
> **LCN** **From the Longman Corpus:** The verbs *tell*, *show*, and *know* are frequently used with the noun *way*. You can *know the way* (to a place) or *tell* or *show someone the way*.

B 🔊 **Rhythm and intonation**

Suggested teaching time:	3 minutes	Your actual teaching time:

- Have students repeat each line chorally. Make sure students:
  ○ use rising intonation for *Can you tell me the way to the beach?*, *Is it safe to go swimming there?*, and *Really?*
  ○ pause slightly after *That way.* and *Sure.*

NOW YOU CAN   Warn about a possible risk

A **Pair work**

Suggested teaching time:	10 minutes	Your actual teaching time:

- Be sure to reinforce the use of the conversation strategies; for example, make sure students sound like they mean it when they express gratitude for a warning.

- Make sure students use *the* in the first blank in the conversation, unless they use a proper noun that doesn't require *the*.

Don't stop! Extend the conversation. Have students give more examples of questions they can ask. For example:
  Are the cliffs [dangerous]?
  Should I keep an eye out for [snakes / scorpions]?
Then have students give examples of dangers they can warn others about. Encourage students to provide examples using the vocabulary from page 114 or *too* + adjectives + infinitives. For example:
  Keep an eye out for bears.
  It's too dangerous to go swimming because of the sharks.

- Model the conversation and extend it with a more confident student.

ActiveTeach Multimedia Disc • Conversation Pair Work Cards

B **Change partners**

Suggested teaching time:	5–10 minutes	Your actual teaching time:

- To review, ask a few students *What did your partner warn you about?*

EXTRAS (optional)

- Workbook: Exercises 10–15
- Copy & Go: Activity 38

Use <u>too</u> + an adjective and an infinitive to give a warning or an explanation.
It's **too dark to go** hiking now. = You'd better not go hiking now because it's dark.
Those cliffs are **too steep to climb.** = You'd better not climb those cliffs because they're very steep.

Use a <u>for</u> phrase to further clarify a warning or explanation.
It's too dangerous **for children** to go swimming there.
(Only adults should swim there.)

Be careful!
DON'T SAY: Those cliffs are too steep to climb them.

Grammar practice Complete the sentences, using <u>too</u> + an adjective and an infinitive with a <u>for</u> phrase.

1 It's ..... too dangerous for you to go ..... to that neighborhood alone.
  dangerous / you / go

2 The pyramid at Teotihuacán is ..... too steep for older tourists to climb ..... .
  steep / older tourists / climb

3 It's ..... too late for your friends to catch ..... the last train to the capital.
  late / your friends / catch

4 The path is ..... too rocky for your children to walk on ..... safely.
  rocky / your children / walk on

5 It's really ..... too hot for us to go ..... hiking to the waterfall today.
  hot / us / go

6 Don't you think this map is ..... too confusing for them to understand ..... ?
  confusing / them / understand

CONVERSATION MODEL

undertow

5:36
A 🔊 Read and listen to someone warning about a risk.

A: Excuse me. Can you tell me the way to the beach?

B: That way. It's not very far.

A: Thanks. Is it safe to go swimming there?

B: Sure, but be careful. There's sometimes an undertow.

A: Really?

B: Well, it's too dangerous for children to go swimming there. But I'm sure you'll be fine.

A: Thanks for the warning.

5:37
B 🔊 **Rhythm and intonation** Listen again and repeat.
Then practice the Conversation Model with a partner.

NOW YOU CAN **Warn about a possible risk**

A Pair work Change the Conversation Model. Ask for directions to another place. Warn about possible risks. Then change roles.

A: Excuse me. Can you tell me the way to .... ?

B: ....

A: Thanks. Is it safe to .... there?

B: ....

B Change partners Warn about another place.

Don't stop!
• **Ask for more information.**
  Do I need to watch out for snakes?
  Are there a lot of mosquitoes?
  Is the path very [steep]?
  Is it worth [seeing]?
• **Warn about other dangers.**
  Watch out for [jellyfish].
  It's too ___ [for ___] to ___ .

Places to go	Things to do
a waterfall	swim
a path	hike
a cave	walk
a beach	climb
cliffs	bike
	ski

GOAL **Describe a natural setting**

BEFORE YOU LISTEN

5:38

A 🔊 **Vocabulary** • *Describing the natural world* Read and listen. Then listen again and repeat.

5:39

🔊 **Strong positive adjectives**
The scenery was **breathtaking**.
The views were **spectacular**.
The sights were **extraordinary**.

Geographic nouns

a forest   a jungle   a valley   a canyon   an island   a glacier

Geographic adjectives

mountainous   hilly   flat   dry / arid   lush / green

B **Pair work** Talk about places you know, using the nouns and adjectives from the Vocabulary.

❝ The north of this country is pretty arid, but in the south there are lots of spectacular forests. ❞

LISTENING COMPREHENSION

5:40

A 🔊 **Listen for main ideas** Read the questions and listen to Kenji Ozaki describe a memorable trip he once took. Then answer the questions.

1 What country did Mr. Ozaki visit? The United States

2 What kind of a place did he visit? A National Park, Yosemite

3 What do you think he liked best about it? He liked the size of it and the natural beauty. He felt like he was part of nature.

4 What geographical adjective best describes the place? Mountainous

BEFORE YOU LISTEN

A ◀)) Vocabulary

Suggested teaching time:	3–5 minutes	Your actual teaching time:

- Have students look at the photographs and read the geographic nouns. Then have them listen and repeat chorally.

- To provide practice with the nouns, describe a place. Ask students to call out the noun.
  It's an area of land completely surrounded by water. (An island.)
  It's a large mass of ice. (Glacier)
  It's between two mountains or mountain ranges. (A valley.)

- Have students look at the photographs and read the geographic adjectives. Then have them listen and repeat chorally.

- To provide practice with the adjectives, describe a type of geography. Ask students to call out the adjective.
  When it hardly ever rains and there are very few plants. (Dry / arid.)
  When there are no mountains or hills. (Flat.)

- Have students read the *Strong positive adjectives*. Ask them to listen and repeat. To clarify the meaning of the adjectives, point out that they all mean *very impressive* or *exciting*. To clarify the meaning of the nouns, point out that *scenery*, *view*, and *sights* are often used to describe nature. If necessary, provide definitions of the nouns: *scenery* (The natural features of a place, such as mountains, forests, and deserts.); *view* (The area that you can see from a place.); and *sights* (Things that you can see.).

Language and culture

LCN **From the Longman Corpus:** The adjective *lush* frequently collocates with the adjective *green* (*lush green valleys / lawns / hills*).

 ActiveTeach Multimedia Disc
- Vocabulary Flash Cards
- Learning Strategies

B Pair work

Suggested teaching time:	7–10 minutes	Your actual teaching time:

- To model the activity, read the speech balloon with the class.

- Encourage students to talk about places they know or other places they may have read about. You may want to ask pairs to write four or five sentences describing these places.

- To review, have several students describe the places they discussed.

LISTENING COMPREHENSION

A ◀)) Listen for main ideas

Suggested teaching time:	5 minutes	Your actual teaching time:

- To prepare students for listening, have them read the questions to know what information to listen for.

- Encourage students to take notes as they listen.

- To review, have students compare answers with a partner and then review with the class.

AUDIOSCRIPT

KENJI OZAKI [Japanese]

About two years ago, I went to the United States on vacation with friends. We drove everywhere—about 190 miles east from San Francisco to Yosemite National Park. I'd say it took about six hours to get there.

Yosemite National Park was huge!!! I mean REALLY huge. I was so excited to be there surrounded by those beautiful mountains—with so many things to see. In Yosemite Valley, there were these super-high cliffs . . . and spectacular waterfalls. There's this one spot called the Mariposa Grove—it's an ancient forest with literally hundreds of giant sequoias—the sequoia's one of the biggest and most extraordinary trees there is. We also visited Glacier Point, which has breathtaking views of Yosemite Valley and all the mountains around it.

What I can't forget is the fresh air . . . the smell . . . it was so clean. Everything was just so great. And I was really surprised when I saw some people way up high on the cliffs—they were actually climbing—they looked so small to me. Someone told me that it would actually take them more than a couple of days to get to the top.

What I liked best about Yosemite National Park was the size of it. And the natural beauty. I had never ever seen a park that big and so . . . well . . . untouched. At least it seemed that way to me. Since I grew up in Japan, I had never imagined there could be such a place. I felt like I was a part of nature.

 ActiveTeach Multimedia Disc
- Learning Strategies

B 🔊 Listen for details

Suggested teaching time:	3–5 minutes	Your actual teaching time:	

- Review the adjectives and the nouns in the box.
- Ask students to match the words as they listen. Then have them listen again to confirm their choices and take notes to support their answers.
- To review, have pairs compare their answers and support their choices. Then review with the class.

C Summarize

Suggested teaching time:	7–10 minutes	Your actual teaching time:	

- To help students focus on main ideas, have them review their answers in Exercises A and B.
- On the board, write the names of some of the places.

  Yosemite National Park   Mariposa Grove
  Yosemite Valley   Glacier Point

- If necessary, play the recording again while students take notes about each place.

Option: [+10 minutes] To extend the activity, ask several volunteers to present their summaries to the class.

NOW YOU CAN   Describe a natural setting

A Frame your ideas

Suggested teaching time:	5 minutes	Your actual teaching time:	

- To prepare students for the activity, ask them to look at the photographs. Call out a place and brainstorm words (nouns and adjectives) to describe it. Students should say words or phrases rather than complete sentences; for example, **T:** *The Galapagos Islands.* **S:** *lush, green, fresh, natural, beauty.*
- Encourage students to use the vocabulary they learned in this unit.

Language and culture

- The Galapagos Islands, a group of volcanic islands in the Pacific Ocean, are located about 1,050 kilometers (650 miles) to the west of Ecuador (South America). Some wildlife species, such as giant tortoises and lizards, are found only on these islands.
- Tibet is considered the highest place on Earth, with an average height of 4,000 meters (12,000 feet) above sea level. Potala Palace (shown in the picture), is located in Llasa, Tibet's capital.
- Alaska, the largest state in the U.S., has spectacular scenery, with mountains, glaciers, volcanoes, and forests.
- Tahiti, an island in the southern Pacific Ocean, is a popular tourist destination. Mountains, waterfalls, and lush vegetation cover the island.
- Iguazu Falls is located between Brazil (Iguaçu) and Argentina (Iguazú). It means "big water." It is considered to be one the most spectacular waterfalls in the world.

B Notepadding

Suggested teaching time:	5–10 minutes	Your actual teaching time:	

- Point out that students can write about a place they have visited or read about.
- To help students generate ideas, brainstorm the kinds of information that can be included under the headings *Description* and *Things you can do there*. Write on the board (without the possible answers):

Description	Things you can do there
location	places to go: towns,
natural features	waterfalls, mountains,
adjectives to describe	beaches, cliffs, caves, paths,
the features	forests
wildlife	activities: hiking, climbing,
weather	swimming, taking pictures,
advice	canoeing, resting, relaxing,
warnings	snorkeling, diving, skiing,
	surfing, lying on the beach

- As students complete their notepads, walk around the room, providing help as needed.

C Pair work

Suggested teaching time:	10 minutes	Your actual teaching time:	

- Review the language in the *Be sure to recycle . . .* box. Remind students to use the language they learned in this unit.
- Encourage the students who are listening to ask their partner follow-up questions.

Option: [+10 minutes] For a challenge, have students give presentations about the places they chose to the class. Ask them to use their notepads as a guide. Have their classmates ask follow-up questions.

EXTRAS (optional)

- Workbook: Exercises 16–18
- Copy & Go: Activity 39

B 🔊)) **Listen for details** Listen again to how Mr. Ozaki describes the natural features he saw on his trip. Complete each phrase with a word from the box.

1 beautiful ....mountains..........
2 super-high ....cliffs............
3 spectacular ....waterfalls.........
4 an ancient ....forest.............

5 extraordinary ....trees............
6 breathtaking ....views............
7 fresh ....air..............
8 natural ....beauty...........

forest	air
waterfalls	beauty
canyon	water
mountains	cliffs
views	trees

C **Summarize** In your own words, describe Mr. Ozaki's trip by restating key details. Listen again if necessary.

NOW YOU CAN | Describe a natural setting

A **Frame your ideas** Choose a photo. Describe the place and what a person could do there. Your partner guesses which place you chose.

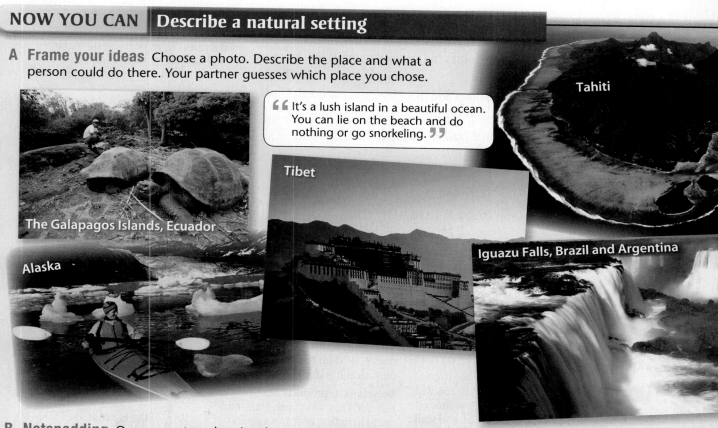

❝ It's a lush island in a beautiful ocean. You can lie on the beach and do nothing or go snorkeling. ❞

Tahiti

Tibet

The Galapagos Islands, Ecuador

Alaska

Iguazu Falls, Brazil and Argentina

B **Notepadding** On your notepad, write about a spectacular place you know or a place you'd like to visit. What does it look like? What can you do there?

Name of place:	Things you can do there:
Description:	

C **Pair work** Tell your partner about the place you wrote about on your notepad. Use the Vocabulary.

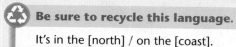 **Be sure to recycle this language.**

It's in the [north] / on the [coast].	You don't want to miss it.
It's located on the [Orinoco River] / the east coast / shore of [Lake Victoria].	[Bash Bish Falls] is overrated, but [Niagara Falls] is breathtaking.
It's south of ___.	[Saw Valley] is a waste of time, but [Pine Valley] is extraordinary.
It's in the central part of ___.	It's very rocky / steep / slippery.
It's a must-see.	

117

GOAL Discuss solutions to global warming

BEFORE YOU READ

A 5:42 **Vocabulary** • *Ways to talk about the environment* Read and listen. Then listen again and repeat.

the environment *n.* the air, water, and land in which people, animals, and plants live

pollution *n.* the act of causing air, water, or land to become dirty and unhealthy for people, plants, and animals

power *n.* electricity or other force that can be used to make machines, cars, etc., work

renewable energy *n.* power for heat and machines, such as wind power or solar power from the sun, that can be reused and never run out

energy-efficient *adj.* uses as little power as possible

increase *v.* to become larger in amount
an increase in [temperature] *n.*

decrease *v.* to become smaller in amount
a decrease in [pollution] *n.*

B **Discussion** What do you already know about global warming? What causes it? What effect is it having on the environment?

READING 5:43

Choose Clean Energy and Help Curb Global Warming

Fossil fuels such as oil, coal, and natural gas—provide energy for our cars and homes, but increase the amount of carbon dioxide (CO_2) in the air, contributing to global warming. However, there are choices we can make that can lessen their negative impact on the environment.

Get Moving—Take good care of your car and keep your tires properly inflated with air. You will use less gasoline and save money. Better yet, skip the drive and walk, take public transportation, or ride a bicycle when you can.

Upgrade—Replace your old refrigerator or air-conditioner with a new energy-efficient model. Not only will you save money on your electric bill, but you'll contribute to cutting back on the pollution that causes global warming.

See the light—Use new energy-saving compact fluorescent light bulbs. They produce the same amount of light as older incandescent bulbs, but they use 25% less electricity and last much longer.

Cut back—Try to reduce the amount of water you use for showers, laundry, and washing

dishes. And turn the temperature on your hot water heater down.

Recycle—Use products that are recycled from old paper, glass, and metal to reduce energy waste and pollution by 70 to 90%. And before you toss things in the garbage, think about what you can reuse.

Think local—Shipping foods over long distances is a waste of energy and adds to pollution. In addition, the pesticides and chemicals used to grow them are bad for the environment. So buy locally grown fruits and vegetables instead.

Speak out—Talk to lawmakers about your interest in curbing global warming. Support their attempts to improve standards for fuel efficiency, to fund renewable and clean energy solutions, such as wind and solar power, and to protect forests.

Information source: www.sierraclub.org

Compact flourescent light bulbs use less electricity.

The expected effects of global warming

• An increase in floods, droughts, tornadoes, and other extreme weather conditions

• A rise in sea levels, causing flooding in coastal areas

• Higher sea surface temperatures, endangering sea life

• The shrinking of glaciers, leading to a decrease in fresh water for rivers and less energy production

• A loss of tropical forests, an increase in arid lands, more forest fires, and a loss of animal and plant species

• A decrease in agricultural yields, leading to famine

Clean energy solutions like wind power can help curb global warming.

LESSON 4

BEFORE YOU READ

A  Vocabulary

Suggested teaching time:	2–3 minutes	Your actual teaching time:

- Ask students to read the words and their definitions. Then have them listen and repeat chorally.

- Follow the same procedure with the words in the small box. Point out the change in stress between the verb forms and noun forms. (The verb forms have the stress on the second syllable. The noun forms have the stress on the first.)

- To check comprehension, write the following definitions on the board.
  1. *uses little power*
  2. *force that makes machines work*
  3. *to become larger in amount*
  4. *air, water, and land*
  5. *power that doesn't run out*
  6. *act of damaging air, water, or land*
  7. *to become smaller in amount*

- Ask students to study the vocabulary words for a minute and then close their books. Ask them to work in pairs to write the correct word for each definition. To review, have them open their books and check their answers. (1. Energy-efficient; 2. power; 3. increase; 4. the environment; 5. renewable energy; 6. pollution; 7. decrease.)

ActiveTeach Multimedia Disc • Vocabulary Flash Cards

B Discussion

Suggested teaching time:	3–5 minutes	Your actual teaching time:

- Ask students what global warming is. (Possible answer: *Global warming is an increase in Earth's temperature.*)

- To help students visualize the main points of their discussion, write the following on the board:
  Global Warming
  Causes   Effects

- In small groups, have students discuss global warming's causes and effects. Encourage them to take notes, using the Vocabulary from Exercise A.

- To review, call on students from different groups to share their ideas with the class. As you get feedback from students, list some causes and effects on the board. (Possible answers: Causes—pollution, cars, and factories. Effects—storms are worse, oceans rise, summers are hotter.)

Language and culture
- The term *global warning* is increasingly being referred to as *climate change*.

READING

Suggested teaching time:	10–15 minutes	Your actual teaching time:

- To help students practice the reading strategy of skimming, write the following questions on the board and have students skim quickly through the text to decide which question best describes what the article is about. Then review with the class.
  1. *What is global warming?*
  2. *What are the main causes and effects of global warming?*
  3. *What can be done to reduce global warming?*
  4. *Why is Earth's temperature rising so quickly?*
  (Question 3.)

- After students have read the article, call attention to the sidebar. Review the expected effects of global warming. Ask students if any of these match the effects listed in Exercise B.

Option: [+5 minutes] To extend the activity, write on the board the following tips for helping to curb global warming. Have students read the tips and then put them in the order in which they occur in the Reading. Ask students to reread the text to confirm their answers.
  1. *Buy recycled products and recycle the products you already have.*
  2. *Try to use less water.*
  3. *Express your concern and support those who take action.*
  4. *Try to use less gasoline.*
  5. *Get new lightbulbs that use less electricity.*
  6. *Buy foods that are produced locally.*
  7. *Get a new energy-efficient refrigerator or air conditioner.*
  (4, 7, 5, 2, 1, 6, 3)

ActiveTeach Multimedia Disc • Extra Reading Comprehension Questions • Learning Strategies

A Understand from context

Suggested teaching time:	3–5 minutes	Your actual teaching time:	

• Ask students to find and underline the words in the text. Encourage them to complete the items they are confident about first.

• Have students compare answers with a partner. Then review with the class. Ask students to explain why they made their choices.

B Critical thinking

Suggested teaching time:	5–7 minutes	Your actual teaching time:	

• Give students a few minutes to look back through the text and take notes for each question individually.

• As students discuss the questions in small groups, encourage them to use the Vocabulary in Exercise A on page 118.

• For question 2, if necessary, clarify the meaning of *disaster relief.* (Food and clothes given to people who need help after a natural disaster.)

• To review, have students from different groups share their answers with the class.

C Summarize

Suggested teaching time:	5 minutes	Your actual teaching time:	

• To prepare students for the activity, have them look back at the text and count the number of ways to curb global warming given in the article. (Seven.)

• Elicit these ways from students and write them on the board. Have students use them as a guide to write their summaries.

• Walk around as pairs write their summaries, providing help as needed. Make sure students use their own words rather than copy from the article.

• Ask students to include other ways to curb global warming.

NOW YOU CAN Discuss solutions to global warming

A Notepadding

Suggested teaching time:	5 minutes	Your actual teaching time:	

• Have students include activities that increase energy waste and pollution. Encourage students to write at least two ideas for each category on their notepads. (Possible answers: At home—I use old light bulbs. I don't have an energy-efficient refrigerator. I don't always buy locally-grown products. I keep my home too warm. I take long showers. I use a lot of water to wash dishes and clothes every day; At work—We never turn the lights off when we leave. We use a lot of energy for air conditioning; At school—We don't recycle paper. We put lots of things in the garbage without considering if they can be reused; Transportation—I never walk or ride my bike to school. I usually drive to work. I never take public transportation; Other—I buy things with a lot of packaging. I don't usually express my concerns about the environment.)

B Pair work

Suggested teaching time:	5 minutes	Your actual teaching time:	

• To model the activity, review the speech balloons with the class.

• To help students with the language they will need for the activity, you may want to write some ways to give suggestions on the board:
  (Maybe) you should . . .
  Why don't you try. . .?
  You should / could . . .
  If I were you, I'd . . .
  Have you ever thought of . . .?
  You might want to . . .

• As students share their ideas, encourage them to give each other as many suggestions as they can.

C Discussion

Suggested teaching time:	7–10 minutes	Your actual teaching time:	

• To prepare students for the activity, review the language in the *Be sure to recycle . . .* box.

Text-mining: Have students share their Text-mining examples and use them to create new statements with a partner.

• As students discuss the questions in small groups, remind them to acknowledge their partner's opinions and state their own opinions and reasons.

• Ask volunteers from different groups to report their conclusions to the class.

EXTRAS (optional)
• Workbook: Exercises 19–23
• Copy & Go: Activity 40

A **Understand from context** Find each of the following words or phrases in the Reading. Then use your understanding of the words to write definitions.

1 curb .... limit ....
2 fossil fuels .... oil, coal, natural gas ....
3 a negative impact .... a bad effect ....

4 inflated .... filled ....
5 reduce .... make smaller in amount ....
6 rise .... increase ....

B **Critical thinking** Discuss the following questions.

1 The article mentions fossil fuels as a major source of energy. What two other sources of energy are mentioned? How are they different from fossil fuels?

2 Look at the list of the effects of global warming in the Reading. What impact could they have on these aspects of your country's economy: tourism, food production, housing, and disaster relief?

C **Summarize** Review the article again. Then close your book. With a partner, discuss and make a list of the ways the article suggests you can help curb global warming.

> On your *ActiveBook* Self-Study Disc:
> **Extra Reading Comprehension Questions**

NOW YOU CAN | Discuss solutions to global warming

A **Notepadding** What do you do in your daily life that might contribute to the energy waste and pollution that causes global warming? Make a list on your notepad.

at home:
at work:
at school:
transportation:
other:

C **Discussion** Do you agree with the suggestions in the article? Discuss the value of trying to take personal actions to help curb global warming. Talk about:

- what you are doing now.
- what you'd like to do in the future.
- what you think is not worth doing.

♻ **Be sure to recycle this language.**

Are you in favor of ___ ?
I think / don't think it's a good idea to ___ .
I'm against ___ .
That's true, but ___ .
I see what you mean, but ___ .
On the one hand, ___ . But on the other hand, ___ .
That's one way to look at it, but ___ .
That depends.
We'll have to agree to disagree.

Text-mining: (optional)
Underline language in the Reading on page 118 to use in your discussion.
For example:
"___ is a waste of energy …"

B **Pair work** Compare notepads with a partner. Discuss what you think each of you could do to help cut down on energy waste and pollution.

❝ I don't really recycle right now, but I'd like to. I think it would be better for the environment if I did. ❞

❝ I want to buy energy-efficient light bulbs, but they're so much more expensive than the regular kind. ❞

Review

A ◀)) **Listening comprehension** Listen to the
conversations and, using the word box, write the
type of place each person is talking about. Then check
whether or not the person recommends going there.

| a canyon | cliffs | a glacier | a volcano |
| a cave | a desert | a valley | a waterfall |

Type of place	Recommended?	Type of place	Recommended?
1 a canyon	☐ yes ☑ no	**3** an island	☑ yes ☐ no
2 a waterfall	☑ yes ☐ no	**4** a valley	☐ yes ☑ no

B Look at the pictures. Complete the warnings about each danger, using <u>too</u>.

1  **2**  **3**  **4**

1 That road .... is too rocky .... to ride on if you're not careful.

2 Those steps .... are too slippery to .... climb safely after a rain.

3 .... It's too dark to .... go in the cave without a flashlight.

4 .... It's too dangerous to .... go swimming in the bay.

5:45/5:46
♪ **Top Notch Pop**
"It's a Beautiful World"
Lyrics p. 150

C Complete the locations, using the map.

1 The town of Saint-Pierre .... is on .... an island.

2 Grand Barachois Bay ...... is south of ...... the village of Miquelon.

3 The island of Saint-Pierre .... is southeast of .... Langlade.

4 The village of Miquelon .... is .... about
.... 33 km / 21 miles .... from the town of Saint-Pierre.

5 The beaches .... are on .... the .... eastern .... coast.

D **Writing** On a separate sheet of paper, write a description
of your country, state, or province. Include the location and
description of major cities, geograpical features, national
parks, and other points of interest. Use adjectives to provide
details that help the reader see and feel what the places are like.

quiet / noisy	humid / dry	spectacular
crowded	flat	breathtaking
hot / warm	hilly	beautiful
cold / cool	mountainous	gorgeous

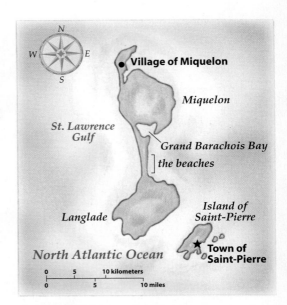

WRITING BOOSTER ▸ p. 148

- *Organizing by spatial relations*
- *Guidance for Exercise D*

Review

A ◀)) Listening comprehension

Suggested teaching time:	5–7 minutes	Your actual teaching time:

- To prepare students for listening, review the words in the box.
- As students listen, pause after each conversation to allow them time to answer.
- To review, have students compare answers with a partner.

Option: [+5 minutes] To extend the activity, have students listen to the passage again and write the speakers' negative or positive comments about each place. Encourage students to listen for the expressions they learned in this unit. (1. It's a little overrated. 2 It's a must-see. 3. You don't want to miss it. 4. It's a waste of time.)

AUDIOSCRIPT

CONVERSATION 1
F: Have you ever gone to Morton's Pass?
M: Oh, yeah.
F: I heard it's a pretty nice canyon to visit. How far is it?
M: Oh, I'd say about fifty miles south of the city.
F: Would you recommend it?
M: Well, if you ask me, it's a little overrated. I'd pick something else to see, instead.
F: Thanks for letting me know.

CONVERSATION 2
M: Terry tells me that you've been to Bash Bish Falls.
F: Did she tell you that?
M: Yeah. I'm thinking of going next week. I love waterfalls. So what do you think? Is it worth it?
F: In my opinion, it's a must-see. You'd be crazy not to go.
M: Really!

CONVERSATION 3
F: Have you ever been to Treasure Island?
M: A bunch of times. Why?
F: Well, I'm wondering if it's worth a trip. I'm not sure if I'd like being on an island.
M: In my opinion?
F: Yes, I'd love to hear your opinion.
M: You don't want to miss it.
F: That's all you have to say?
M: That's all I have to say.

CONVERSATION 4
M: So in the last days of my vacation I'm thinking of spending some time in Pipo Valley. Tom told me it was spectacular.
F: Oh, yeah?
M: What do you mean, "Oh, yeah?"
F: Well, if you ask me, I'd say it was a waste of time.
M: You've been there?
F: I've been there. There's Mount Pi on one side. And Mount Po on the other side.
M: And?
F: I still don't think it's worth it. But to each his own.

B Look at the pictures . . .

Suggested teaching time:	3–4 minutes	Your actual teaching time:

- To model the activity, complete the first item with the class. Point out that students should use *too* + adjective + infinitive.
- Have students compare answers with a partner and then review with the class.

C Complete the locations . . .

Suggested teaching time:	3–4 minutes	Your actual teaching time:

- Before students begin the activity, tell them that Saint-Pierre and Miquelon are small rocky islands off the coast of Newfoundland, Canada. They are the last possessions of France.
- Point out that they also need to write the correct form of *be*.
- Call on students to share their answers with the class.

D Writing

Suggested teaching time:	10–15 minutes	Your actual teaching time:

- Have students choose the country, state, or province they want to write about.
- To help students generate ideas, write the following checklist on the board.

  Location   Wildlife
  Cities   Activities
  Geographical feature   Possible risks

- Before they write, ask students to take notes about the ideas they have checked. Encourage them to use the adjectives in the box and to refer to the grammar and vocabulary from the unit.
- Walk around the room and provide help as needed.

Option: **WRITING BOOSTER** (Teaching notes p. T148)

🔘 **ActiveTeach Multimedia Disc** • **Writing Process Worksheets**

ORAL REVIEW

Before the first activity, give students a few minutes of silent time to explore the map, chart, and pictures and become familiar with them.

Game

Suggested teaching time:	12–15 minutes	Your actual teaching time:

- To model the activity, review the examples with the class.

- To prepare students, ask them to write four sentences describing a location or a natural feature. Point out that there are many ways to describe a place.

- Form small groups and have students use the sentences they wrote to play the guessing game. (Possible answers: It's located south of Katmai National Park. (Kodiak Island.); It's to the east of Alaska. (Canada.); It's a large area of water southwest of Alaska. (The Bering Sea.); It's a capital. (Juneau.); It's north of Anchorage. (Denali National Park / Fairbanks.); It's a large area of water to the north of Alaska. (The Arctic Ocean.))

- To review, say *Juneau* and have several students share with the class a sentence they used to describe it. (Possible answers: It's a capital city. It's a city to the east of a park. It's on the coast of Alaska. It's near some glaciers.) Follow the same procedure with the other cities and geographical features shown on the map.

Pair work

Suggested teaching time:	12–15 minutes	Your actual teaching time:

- To prepare students for the conversation, ask them to imagine that they are visitors to Alaska; one of them asks directions to a place and the other explains the way and warns about a possible risk.

- Direct attention to the icons under *Explore Alaska!* and have students name the risks or lack of risks in each place. (Possible answers: Watch out for bears in Denali National Park. There are a lot of mosquitoes in Katmai National Park. Don't worry, there aren't any snakes on Kodiak Island.)

- Ask students to choose one of the places under *Explore Alaska!* for their conversations.

Possible responses ...

A: Where is Katmai National Park? **B:** About three hours southwest of Anchorage by car. Are you planning to go there? **A:** I've been thinking about it. **B:** You don't want to miss it. Be sure to take some insect repellent. **A:** Are there mosquitoes? **B:** Yes, a lot. You'll get eaten alive if you don't have any.

Possible responses ...

A: Excuse me. Could you tell me the way to Denali National Park? **B:** That way. It is about 100 kilometers north of here. **A:** I'm thinking of going today. Is it worth it? **B:** Absolutely. The views are spectacular. **A:** Is it safe to go to the park with children? **B:** Sure, but keep an eye out for bears. There are a lot in the area. **A:** Really? **B:** Yes. Just be careful.

Option: [+10 minutes] For a challenge, ask students to visit the official websites of the Denali National Park or the Kodiak National Wildlife Refuge and find and report interesting information about them.

Language and culture

- Alaska is the largest state in the United States.
- Anchorage, the largest city in Alaska, is a modern city, but you can see wild animals such as moose wandering around town. Fairbanks is the second largest city.
- The tallest mountain in North America, Mt. McKinley (or Denali), is in Denali National Park.
- Katmai National Park is an ideal place for viewing brown bears in their natural habitat.
- Glacier Bay National Park has spectacular mountain ranges, beaches, and glaciers. Visitors go kayaking, river rafting, glacier viewing, and whale watching.
- Kodiak Island is a beautiful island with rugged mountains and the largest brown bears in North America.

Option: Oral Progress Assessment

Use the illustrations on page 121. Encourage students to use the language practiced in this unit and previous units.

- Tell the student to look at the map and pictures and describe the geographical features of Alaska.

- Tell the student to give at least three warnings about the risks in Alaska, using the pictures, the *Explore Alaska!* brochure, and his or her imagination. Ask the student to also use *too* if possible. For example:
  The mountains at Glacier Bay National Park are too high to climb.

- Evaluate the student on intelligibility, fluency, correct use of target grammar, and appropriate use of vocabulary.

 • Oral Progress Assessment Charts

Option: *Top Notch* Project

Form small groups of three or four students and have them create a travel brochure.

Idea: Ask students to choose a place from this unit, or another interesting place. Have them do research and take notes. Then ask students to prepare a brochure that includes pictures and maps. Encourage students to give reasons why their classmates should plan a trip to that particular place. Then have groups present their brochures to the class.

EXTRAS (optional)

- Complete Assessment Package
- Weblinks for Teachers: pearsonlongman.com/topnotch/

And on your ActiveTeach Multimedia Disc:
  Just for Fun
  Top Notch Pop Song Activities
  Top Notch TV Video Program and Activity Worksheets
  Supplementary Pronunciation Lessons
  Audioscripts
  Unit Study Guides

Game Using the map and the pictures, describe a location or natural features. Your classmates guess the place. For example:

It's located south of Denali National Park. **OR** It has spectacular glaciers.

Pair work Use the map and the "Explore Alaska!" chart to create conversations for the man and the woman. Start like this:

Where exactly is __? **OR** Excuse me. Could you tell me the way to __?

Glacier Bay National Park

Katmai National Park

Arctic Ocean

Alaska

Fairbanks

Denali National Park

CANADA

Anchorage

Katmai National Park

Juneau

Bering Sea

Kodiak Island

Glacier Bay National Park

Gulf of Alaska

0   500 miles

0   300 kilometers

Explore Alaska!

	bears	mosquitos	snakes	fog
Denali National Park	✓	✓	✗	✓
Kodiak Island	✓	✓	✗	✓
Katmai National Park	✓	✓	✗	✗
Glacier Bay National Park	✗	✗	✗	✓

NOW I CAN...

- [ ] Describe a geographical location.
- [ ] Warn about a possible risk.
- [ ] Describe a natural setting.
- [ ] Discuss solutions to global warming.

Grammar Booster

The Grammar Booster is optional. It is not required for the achievement tests in the *Top Notch Complete Assessment Package*. If you use the Grammar Booster, there are extra Grammar Booster exercises in the Workbook in a separate labeled section.

Tag questions: short answers

Look at the affirmative and negative short answers to the tag questions from page 4.

You're Lee, **aren't you**?	Yes, I am. / No, I'm not.
You're not Amy, **are you**?	Yes, I am. / No, I'm not.
She speaks Thai, **doesn't she**?	Yes, she does. / No, she doesn't.
I don't know you, **do I**?	Yes, you do. / No, you don't.
He's going to drive, **isn't he**?	Yes, he is. / No, he isn't.
We're not going to eat here, **are we**?	Yes, we are. / No, we aren't.
They'll be here later, **won't they**?	Yes, they will. / No, they won't.
It won't be long, **will it**?	Yes, it will. / No, it won't.
You were there, **weren't you**?	Yes, I was. / No, I wasn't.
He wasn't driving, **was he**?	Yes, he was. / No, he wasn't.
They left, **didn't they**?	Yes, they did. / No, they didn't.
We didn't know, **did we**?	Yes, you did. / No, you didn't.
It's been a great day, **hasn't it**?	Yes it has. / No, it hasn't.
She hasn't been here long, **has she**?	Yes, she has. / No she hasn't.
Ann would like Quito, **wouldn't she**?	Yes, she would. / No, she wouldn't.
You wouldn't do that, **would you**?	Yes, I would. / No, I wouldn't.
They can hear me, **can't they**?	Yes, they can. / No, they can't.
He can't speak Japanese, **can he**?	Yes, he can. / No, he can't.

A Complete each conversation by circling the correct tag question and completing the short answer.

1 A: Mary would like to study foreign cultures (would /(wouldn't)) she?
   B: Yes, _____she would_____.

2 A: It's a long time until dinner, (is /(isn't)) it?
   B: No, _____it isn't_____.

3 A: We met last summer, (did /(didn't)) we?
   B: Yes, _____we did_____.

4 A: They're starting the meeting really late, (haven't /(aren't)) they?
   B: No, _____they aren't_____.

5 A: There weren't too many delays in the meeting, (wasn't it /(were there))?
   B: No, _____there weren't_____.

6 A: You don't know what to do, ((do)/ don't) you?
   B: No, _____I don't_____.

7 A: There isn't any reason to call, ((is)/ isn't) there?
   B: No, _____there isn't_____.

8 A: It's awful to not have time for lunch, ((isn't it)/ aren't you)?
   B: Yes, _____it is_____.

9 A: When you know etiquette, you can feel comfortable anywhere, (can /(can't)) you?
   B: Yes, _____you can_____.

10 A: It's really getting late, (is it /(isn't it))?
   B: No, _____it isn't_____.

B Correct the error in each item.

1 They'd both like to study abroad, ~~would~~ they?   *wouldn't*

2 It's only a six-month course, ~~is it~~?   *isn't*

3 Clark met his wife on a rafting trip, didn't ~~Clark~~?   *he*

4 Marian made three trips to Japan last year, ~~hasn't~~ she?   *didn't*

5 There were a lot of English-speaking people on the tour, ~~wasn't it~~?   *weren't there*

6 The students don't know anything about that, ~~don't~~ they?   *do*

7 There isn't any problem with my student visa, ~~isn't~~ there?   *is*

8 It's always interesting to travel with people from other countries, ~~aren't they~~?   *isn't it*

9 With English, you can travel to most parts of the world, ~~can~~ you?   *can't*

10 I'm next, ~~don't~~ I?   *aren't*

Grammar Booster

Note about the Grammar Booster

Many will elect to do the Grammar Booster as self-study. However, if you choose to use the Grammar Booster with the classroom activity instead, teaching notes are included here.

UNIT 1   Lesson 1

Tag questions: short answers

Suggested teaching time:	5–7 minutes	Your actual teaching time:

- Have students study the presentation and the examples.
- To check comprehension, write the following on the board:

  He is Canadian, isn't he?   Yes, he is. / No, he isn't.
  He went to Brazil, didn't he?   Yes, he did. / No, he didn't.

- Ask students to name the main verb in the first statement (Is.) and the verbs used in the short answers. (Is, isn't.) Follow the same procedure with the second statement. (Went, did, didn't.)
- Point out that the tense of the verb or auxiliary in the short answer should match the verb tense in the statement.
- Be sure students understand that the listener should agree or disagree with the information in the statement, not in the tag question.

A Complete each conversation . . .

Suggested teaching time:	3–5 minutes	Your actual teaching time:

- Remind students that when the statement is affirmative, the tag question is negative, and that when the statement is negative, the tag question is affirmative.

B Correct the error . . .

Suggested teaching time:	3–5 minutes	Your actual teaching time:

- Write the following on the board: Sam isn't here, is he?
- Point out Sam in the statement and he in the tag question. Remind students that pronouns rather than names or nouns are used in tag questions.
- Point out that affirmative statements with I am require negative tag questions with aren't, as in item 10.
- As students complete the exercise, encourage them to underline the verb or verb phrase (auxiliary plus main verb) in each statement to help them write the correct tag question. (1. 'd like; 2. 's; 3. met; 4. made; 5. were; 6. don't know; 7. isn't; 8. 's; 9. can travel; 10. 'm.)

Verb usage: present and past (review)

Suggested teaching time:	15–20 minutes	Your actual teaching time:	

The simple present tense . . .

- Have students read the first rule and examples.

- To review, ask *Which sentence expresses a scientific fact?* (Water boils at 100°.) *What do the other two sentences express?* (Things that happen regularly.)

- To check comprehension, ask pairs to write two examples of facts and two examples of regular occurrences.

- Ask groups to read their sentences aloud.

- Ask students to name the frequency adverb in the second example. (Never.) Elicit other examples of frequency adverbs: *usually, often, sometimes, occasionally, rarely.*

- Have students find the two time expressions in the statement. (Before 6:00 / on weekdays.) Then elicit other time expressions; for example, *at night, in the morning, after lunch, at weekends, on Saturdays.*

- Have pairs make sentences using the simple present tense for future actions; for example, *The train leaves at 2:00 tomorrow. The meeting starts at 6:00 tonight.*

The present continuous . . .

- Write on the board:
  1. *this Friday / next weekend*
  2. *this week / month / year*
  3. *now / right now*

- To check comprehension, have students match each set of time expressions on the board with the three uses of the present continuous presented. (1. Future actions; 2. actions occurring during a time in the present; 3. actions happening now.)

The present perfect / present perfect continuous

- Point out that with *for* or *since,* there is no difference in meaning between the present perfect and the present perfect continuous. Write the following on the board:
  since I was born
  for a long time

- Have pairs make statements about themselves, using the phrases on the board and the present perfect or the present perfect continuous; for example, *I've lived / I've been living in the same house since I was born. I've studied / I've been studying English for a long time.*

The present perfect (but NOT . . .

- Have volunteers tell the class how many meals or snacks they have had so far today.

The simple past tense

- Point out that past time expressions help make it clear when that action happened; for example, *We went to Tokyo last year. We were at the game on Sunday.*

- Write the following on the board: *What did you do [past time expression]?*

- Have pairs take turns asking and answering questions using the simple past tense. For example:
  A: *What did you do last June?*
  B: *Last June I took a trip to Paris.*

The past continuous

- To review, ask *How do we form the past continuous?* (*Was* or *were* plus the present participle.)

- To check comprehension, say *At 8:00 this morning I was eating breakfast.* Then ask several students *What were you doing at 8:00 this morning?*

The past continuous and the simple past . . .

- Point out that the action in the simple past tense interrupts the action in the past continuous.

- To check comprehension, ask several students to say what they were doing when you— or another person— arrived earlier today; for example, *I was talking with Sarah when you walked into the classroom. I was taking out my books when you came in.*

Use to / used to

- Point out the affirmative *used to* + base form of the verb. (Smoke.) Then point out the negative form *didn't* + *use to* and make sure students notice the spelling.

- To check comprehension, ask several students to say something they did in the past but no longer do now.

The past perfect

- Point out that the past perfect is used for the event that happened / finished first.

- To review how to form the past perfect, ask *How do we form the past perfect?* (*Had* + past participle.)

- Have students share with the class what they had done by [10:00 o'clock] this morning; for example, *By ten o'clock this morning I had walked the dog and read the newspaper.*

A Correct the verbs . . .

Suggested teaching time:	3–5 minutes	Your actual teaching time:	

- Ask students to think about what each statement expresses—a fact, a regular occurrence, an action happening now, a description of a schedule, OR a future action.

- Encourage students to take note of frequency adverbs, time expressions, and stative verbs.

Option: **[+5 minutes]** To provide more practice, write the following on the board:
  1. *Right now we*
  2. *She always*
  3. *This Saturday*
  4. *Winter*
  5. *The morning bus*
  6. *This month*

Have pairs complete the sentences using the simple present tense or the present continuous. (Possible answers: 1. Right now we are doing an exercise. 2. She always arrives first. 3. This Saturday we are going to the movies. 4. Winter starts in December. 5. The morning bus leaves at 8:00. 6. This month he is living in France.)

Verb usage: present and past (review)

The simple present tense (but NOT the present continuous):
- **for facts and regular occurrences**
  I **study** English. Class **meets** every day. Water **boils** at 100°.
- **with frequency adverbs and time expressions**
  They never **eat** before 6:00 on weekdays.
- **with stative ("non-action") verbs**
  I **remember** her now.
- **for future actions, especially those indicating schedules**
  Flight 100 usually leaves at 2:00, but tomorrow it **leaves** at 1:30.

The present continuous (but NOT the simple present tense):
- **for actions happening now (but NOT with stative [non-action] verbs)**
  They're **talking** on the phone.
- **for actions occurring during a time period in the present**
  This year I'm **studying** English.
- **for some future actions, especially those already planned**
  Thursday I'm **going** to the theater.

The present perfect or the present perfect continuous:
- **for unfinished or continuous actions**
  I've **lived** here since 2007. OR I've **been living** here since 2007.
  I've **lived** here for five years. OR I've **been living** here for five years.

The present perfect (but NOT the present perfect continuous):
- **for completed or non-continuing actions**
  I've **eaten** there three times.
  I've never **read** that book.
  I've already **seen** him.

The simple past tense:
- **for actions completed at a specified time in the past**
  I **ate** there in 2010. NOT I've eaten there in 2010.

The past continuous:
- **for one or more actions in progress at a time in the past**
  At 7:00, we **were eating** dinner.
  They **were swimming** and we **were sitting** on the beach.

The past continuous and the simple past tense:
- **for an action that interrupted a continuing action in the past**
  I **was eating** when my sister **called**.

<u>Use to</u> / <u>used to</u> :
- **for past situations and habits that no longer exist**
  I **used to smoke**, but I stopped.
  They **didn't use to require** a visa, but now they do.

The past perfect:
- **to indicate that one past action preceded another past action**
  When I arrived, they **had finished** lunch.

Stative (non-action) verbs

appear	notice
be	own
believe	possess
belong	prefer
contain	remember
cost	see
feel	seem
hate	smell
have	sound
hear	suppose
know	taste
like	think
look	understand
love	want
need	weigh

A **Correct the verbs in the following sentences.**

1 I ~~talk~~ on the phone with my fiancé right now. *am talking*

2 ~~She's~~ usually ~~avoiding~~ sweets. *She avoids*

3 They ~~eat~~ dinner now and can't talk on the phone. *are eating*

4 Every Friday ~~I'm going~~ to the gym at 7:00. *I go*

5 Burt ~~is wanting~~ to go home early. *wants*

6 Today we ~~all study~~ in the library. *are all studying*

7 The train ~~is never leaving~~ before 8:00. *leaves*

8 Water ~~is freezing~~ when the temperature goes down. *freezes*

9 ~~We're liking~~ coffee. *We like*

10 On most days ~~I'm staying~~ home. *I stay*

Throughout the Grammar Booster, accept full or contracted forms for answers.

B **Complete each sentence with the present perfect continuous.**

1 We ___'ve been coming___ to this spa for two years.
   come

2 *Slumdog Millionaire* ___has been playing___ at the Classic Cinema since last Saturday.
   play

3 Robert ___has been waiting___ for an admissions letter from the language school for a week.
   wait

4 The tour operators ___have been worrying about___ weather conditions for the rafting trip.
   worry about

5 I ___'ve been talking about___ that tour with everyone.
   talk about

C **Check the sentences and questions that express unfinished or continuing actions. Then, on a separate sheet of paper, change the verb phrase in those sentences to the present perfect continuous.**

The Averys have lived in New York since the late nineties.

The Averys have been living in New York since the late nineties.

☐ 1 Their relatives have already called them.

   been waiting
☑ 2 We have ~~waited~~ to see them for six months.

☐ 3 I haven't seen the Berlin Philharmonic yet.

☐ 4 This is the first time I've visited Dubai.

   been eating
☑ 5 We have ~~eaten~~ in that old Peruvian restaurant for years.

☐ 6 Has he ever met your father?

   been studying
☑ 7 How long have they ~~studied~~ Arabic?

☐ 8 My husband still hasn't bought a car.

☐ 9 The kids have just come back from the soccer game.

UNIT 2   Lesson 1

Other ways to draw conclusions: *probably*; *most likely*

Two other ways to draw conclusions are with <u>probably</u> and <u>most likely</u>. These indicate less certainty than <u>must</u>.

<u>Probably</u> frequently occurs after the verb <u>be</u> or when <u>be</u> is part of a verb phrase.
   They're **probably** at the dentist's office.
   It's **probably** going to rain.

Use <u>probably</u> before <u>isn't</u> or <u>aren't</u>. With <u>is not</u> or <u>are not</u>, use <u>probably</u> before <u>not</u>.
   She **probably** isn't feeling well.
   She's **probably** not feeling well.

Use <u>probably</u> before other verbs.
   He **probably** forgot about the appointment.
   The dentist **probably** doesn't have time to see a new patient.

> **Be careful!** Don't use <u>probably</u> after verbs other than <u>be</u>.
> Don't say: He ~~forgot probably~~ about the appointment.

You can also use <u>Probably</u> or <u>Most likely</u> at the beginning of a sentence to draw a conclusion.
   Probably she's a teacher. / **Most likely** she's a teacher.
   Probably he forgot about the appointment. / **Most likely** he forgot about the appointment.

On a separate sheet of paper, rewrite each sentence with <u>probably</u> or <u>most likely</u>. See page T124 for answers.

1 He must have a terrible cold.

2 She must be feeling very nauseous.

3 They must not like going to the dentist.

4 The dentist must not be in her office today.

5 Acupuncture must be very popular in Asia.

6 A conventional doctor must have to study for a long time.

B Complete each sentence . . .

Suggested teaching time:	3–4 minutes	Your actual teaching time:

- This exercise provides practice with the present perfect continuous.
- To review, ask *When do we use the present perfect continuous?* (For unfinished or continuing actions.)
- After students complete the exercise, have them compare answers. Then review with the class.

Option: [+3 minutes] To provide more practice, ask students to change phrases with *for* to *since* and phrases with *since* to *for* in items 1, 2, and 3. (Possible answers: 1. We have been coming to this spa since [2008]. 2. *Slumdog Millionaire* has been playing at the Classic Cinema for [one week]. 3. Robert has been waiting for an admissions letter from the language school since [last month].)

C Check the sentences . . .

Suggested teaching time:	5–6 minutes	Your actual teaching time:

- Review the instructions with the class to make sure students understand that there are two tasks: identifying items with actions that are unfinished or continuing and then changing the tense in the identified sentences.
- Review the example with the class. Point out that *have lived* and *since* tells us that the Averys are still living in New York. (An unfinished / continuing action.) Point out that the present perfect continuous tells us that an action started in the past and is still happening now. (Have been living.)
- Complete item 1 with the class. Point out that *already* tells us that the call was made and it's finished. Point out that the present perfect continuous is not used for finished actions.
- Have students compare answers with a partner. Then review with the class.

UNIT 2 Lesson 1

Other ways to draw conclusions: . . .

Suggested teaching time:	7–10 minutes	Your actual teaching time:

- Have students study the rules, the examples, and the *Be careful!* note.
- To check comprehension of the use of *probably* with the verb *be*, write the following on the board:
    1. *He's probably in his office.*
    2. *He's probably going to come.*
    3. *He probably isn't going to see a doctor.*
    4. *He's probably not going to see a doctor.*
- Ask *Do we use <u>probably</u> to express facts or draw conclusions?* (To draw conclusions.)
- Direct students' attention to the first two examples. Ask *Does <u>probably</u> come before or after <u>be</u>?* (After.)

- Direct students' attention to the next two examples. Ask *Are these affirmative or negative statements?* (Negative.) *Where does <u>probably</u> come in negative sentences?* (Before *isn't* OR between *is* and *not*.)
- To provide practice, write the following on the board: *They're going to make a new appointment.* Ask students to write the sentence inserting *probably* and then rewrite it in the negative. (They're probably going to make a new appointment. They probably aren't going to make a new appointment. OR They're probably not going to make a new appointment.)
- To check comprehension of the placement of *probably* with other verbs, write the following on the board: *She probably got a prescription.*
- Ask *Does <u>probably</u> come before or after verbs that are not <u>be</u>?* (Before.)
- To review the use of *most likely*, write the following on the board: *Most likely he is at the doctor's office right now.*
- Point out that we can also use *most likely* to draw a conclusion. Ask *Where does <u>most likely</u> come?* (At the beginning of a sentence.)
- Point out that *probably* can also be used at the beginning of a sentence.

On a separate sheet of paper, . . .

Suggested teaching time:	5 minutes	Your actual teaching time:

- Complete the first item with the class. Have students provide the three possible answers.
- Point out that students can choose to use *probably* at the beginning or in the middle of sentences.
- Review with the class.

Answers for Unit 2, Lesson 1
1. He probably has a terrible cold.
   Most likely he has a terrible cold.
   Probably he has a terrible cold.
2. She's probably feeling very nauseous.
   Most likely she's feeling very nauseous.
   Probably she's feeling very nauseous.
3. They probably don't like going to the dentist.
   Most likely they don't like going to the dentist.
   Probably they don't like going to the dentist.
4. The dentist probably isn't in her office today.
   Most likely the dentist isn't in her office today.
   Probably the dentist isn't in her office today.
5. Acupuncture is probably very popular in Asia.
   Most likely acupuncture is very popular in Asia.
   Probably acupuncture is very popular in Asia.
6. A conventional doctor probably has to study for a long time.
   Most likely a conventional doctor has to study for a long time.
   Probably a conventional doctor has to study for a long time.

UNIT 2 Lesson 2

Expressing possibility with _maybe_

Suggested teaching time:	3–5 minutes	Your actual teaching time:

- To check comprehension, write the following on the board:
    1. _She may need a blood test._
    2. _Maybe she needs a blood test._

- Ask _Do both examples have the same meaning?_ (Yes.) _Do they express certainty or possibility?_ (Possibility.) _Which example uses a modal?_ (1) _Is_ _maybe_ _a modal, too?_ (No.) _Where does_ _maybe_ _usually appear in a sentence?_ (At the beginning.)

- To summarize, write the following on the board:
    maybe
    ○ _expresses possibility_
    ○ _is not a modal_
    ○ _occurs at the beginning of a sentence_

On a separate sheet of paper, . . .

Suggested teaching time:	3–5 minutes	Your actual teaching time:

- Complete the first item with the class. Remind students to spell _maybe_ as one word (_maybe_ not _may be_).

- Review with the class.

Answers for Unit 2, Lesson 2
1. Maybe his doctor uses herbal therapy.
2. Maybe conventional medicine is the best choice.
3. Maybe the doctor wants to take a blood test.
4. Maybe she prefers to wait until tomorrow.
5. Maybe they are afraid to see a dentist.

UNIT 3 Lesson 1

Let to indicate permission

Suggested teaching time:	5–7 minutes	Your actual teaching time:

- Point out that _let_ is used to talk about giving or asking for permission.

- Remind students that _let_ is an irregular verb: the base form, the simple past, and the past participle are all _let_.

- Write the following on the board: _They let me go._

- Ask _How is this sentence formed?_ (_Let_ + object + base form.)

- Point out that the object can be a noun (or noun phrase) or object pronoun. Provide an example with a noun and a noun phrase: _He let Kate go. He let his daughter go._

- To provide practice, ask several students _What did your parents let you do when you were a child? What didn't they let you do?_ (Possible answers: My parents let me walk to school by myself. They let me go to bed late on Saturday nights. They didn't let me ride my bike in the street. They didn't let me stay out late at night.)

A On a separate sheet of paper, . . .

Suggested teaching time:	4 minutes	Your actual teaching time:

- As students work on the exercise, remind them to pay attention to necessary changes in verb forms.

- Have students compare answers with a partner. Then review with the class.

Answers for Exercise A
1. Don't let your younger brother open the oven door.
2. You should let your little sister go to the store with you.
3. We don't let our daughter eat a lot of candy.
4. I wouldn't let my youngest son go to the mall alone.
5. Why don't you let your children see that movie?
6. You should let them make their own decision.
7. We always let him stay out late.

Causative _have_: common errors

Suggested teaching time:	3–5 minutes	Your actual teaching time:

- Before students study the presentation, write the following on the board: _I have them fix it._

- Review with students that the causative can occur in different tenses. Ask _In what tense is the statement on the board?_ (Simple present.)

- Have students change the statement on the board to the simple past (I had them fix it.) and then to the future. (I will have them fix it.)

- Have students study the _Be careful!_ note and examples in the presentation.

- To check comprehension, ask _In the first example, who called before 10:00?_ (They / the other people.) _In the second example, who called before 10:00?_ (The speaker / I.) _Which example uses the simple past tense causative?_ (The first.) _What tense does the second example use?_ (The past perfect.)

- Write the following on the board:
    1. _Steven had the air conditioner repaired before the party._
    2. _Steven had repaired the air conditioner before the party._

- Ask students to explain the difference between the two examples on the board. (1. Someone else repaired the air conditioner for Steven. 2. Steven repaired the air conditioner himself.)

B Who did what? Read each . . .

Suggested teaching time:	4–5 minutes	Your actual teaching time:

- Review the first example with the class. Ask _Did the people fix the car themselves, or did someone else do it?_ (Someone else.)

- Ask students to explain how we know that _had_ is causative in the first sentence. (Because it is followed by an object and a base form.)

- Have students compare answers with a partner. Then review with the class.

Expressing possibility with *maybe*

Maybe most frequently occurs at the beginning of a sentence.
   Maybe he needs an X-ray. (= He may need an X-ray.)

> **Be careful!** Don't confuse **maybe** and **may be**.
> She **may be** a doctor.
> NOT She ~~maybe~~ a doctor.
> **Maybe** she's a doctor.
> NOT ~~May be~~ she's a doctor.

On a separate sheet of paper, rewrite each sentence with maybe.   See page T125 for answers.

1 His doctor may use herbal therapy.

2 Conventional medicine may be the best choice.

3 The doctor may want to take a blood test.

4 She may prefer to wait until tomorrow.

5 They may be afraid to see a dentist.

Let to indicate permission

Use an object and the base form of a verb with **let**.
         object   base form
She **let her sister wear** her favorite skirt.

> **Be careful!**
> Don't say: She let her sister ~~to wear~~ her favorite skirt.

Let has the same meaning as **permit**.
Use **let** to indicate that permission is being given to do something.
   My boss **let** me **take** the day off.
   I **don't let** my children **stay** out after 9:00 P.M.
   Why **don't** you **let** me **help** you?

On a separate sheet of paper, rewrite each sentence, using let.   See page T125 for answers.

1 Don't permit your younger brother to open the oven door.

2 You should permit your little sister to go to the store with you.

3 We don't permit our daughter to eat a lot of candy.

4 I wouldn't permit my youngest son to go to the mall alone.

5 Why don't you permit your children to see that movie?

6 You should permit them to make their own decision.

7 We always permit him to stay out late.

Causative *have*: common errors

Be careful! Don't confuse the simple past tense causative have with the past perfect auxiliary have.
   I **had** them **call** me before 10:00.   (They called me.)
   I **had called** them before 10:00.   (I called them.)

Who did what? Read each sentence. Complete each statement. Follow the example.

We had them fix the car before our trip.   _They_ fixed _the car_ .

We had fixed the car before our trip.   _We_ fixed _the car_ .

1 Janet had already called her mother.   _Janet_ called _her mother_ .

Janet had her mother call the train station.   _Her mother_ called _the train station_

2 Mark had his friends help him with moving.   _His friends_ helped _Mark_ .

Mark had helped his friends with moving.   _Mark_ helped _his friends_

3 My father had signed the check for his boss.   _My father_ signed _the check_

My father had his boss sign the check.   _His boss_ signed _the check_ .

4 Mr. Gates had them open the bank early.   _They_ opened _the bank_ .

Mr. Gates had opened the bank early.   _Mr. Gates_ opened _the bank_ .

The passive causative: the by phrase

Use a by phrase if knowing who performed the action is important.
I had my dress shortened **by the tailor** at the shop next to the train station.

If knowing who performed the action is not important, you don't need to include a by phrase.
I had my dress shortened ~~by someone~~ at the shop next to the train station.

On a separate sheet of paper, use the cues to write advice about services, using <u>you should</u> and the passive causative <u>get</u> or <u>have</u>. Use a <u>by</u> phrase if the information is important. Follow the example.

See page T126 for answers.

shoe / repair / Mr. B / at the Boot Stop

You should get your shoes repaired by Mr. B at the Boot Stop.

1 picture / frame / Lydia / at Austin Custom Framing

2 hair / cut / Eva / at the Curl Up Hair Salon

3 photos / print / at the mall

4 a suit / make / Luigi / at Top Notch Tailors

5 sweaters / dry-clean / at Midtown Dry Cleaners

Verbs that can be followed by clauses with that

The following verbs often have noun clauses as their direct objects. Notice that each verb expresses a kind of "mental activity." In each case, it is optional to include <u>that</u>.

She	agrees thinks believes feels	(that) the students should work harder.	I	assume suppose doubt guess	(that) they made reservations.
We	hear see understand hope	(that) the government has a new plan.	He	forgot noticed realized remembered knew	(that) the stores weren't open.
They	decided discovered dreamed hoped learned	(that) everyone could pass the test.			

Adjectives that can be followed by clauses with that

Use a clause with <u>that</u> after a predicate adjective of emotion to further explain its meaning.

I'm	afraid angry	(that) we'll have to leave early.	He's	sorry unhappy	(that) the flight was cancelled.
We're	worried ashamed	(that) we won't be on time to the event.	She's	surprised disappointed	(that) the news spread so fast.
They're	happy sad	(that) the teacher is leaving.			

UNIT 3 Lesson 2

The passive causative: the by phrase

Suggested teaching time:	3–5 minutes	Your actual teaching time:

- Before students study the presentation, write the following on the board:

  I had the document copied.
    got

- Review the passive causative by asking *How do we form the passive causative?* (*Have* or *get* + object + the past participle.)

- Review the use of the passive causative by brainstorming everyday services the students use; for example, *have a document copied, get a sweater dry-cleaned, have your house cleaned,* etc.

- Then have students study the first rule and example.

- Point out that the *by* phrase in the example sentence (*by the tailor*) adds important and necessary information. The listener learns who performed the action.

- Point out that if students want to say the location where a service is received, they need to use *at;* for example, *at the garage, at the bank, at the hair salon.*

- To review the structure, ask *Where do we place the by (or at) phrase in the sentence?* (After the past participle.)

- Write the following on the board:

  photos printed
  hair colored
  car repaired
  documents copied
  clothes cleaned
  checks cashed

- To check comprehension, ask students to say who offers these services or where they can get them done. You may want to point out they can use *by* plus a person or *at* plus a place; for example, *I have my photos printed by my sister. I have my photos printed at the drugstore.*

- Have students study the second rule and example.

- Point out that the *by* phrase in the example *(by someone)* does not add any specific or helpful information, so it is not necessary.

On a separate sheet of paper, . . .

Suggested teaching time:	3–4 minutes	Your actual teaching time:

- Review the example with the class. Point out that the example includes *by* plus a person and *at* plus a place.

- To review, ask several students to read their sentences aloud. Make necessary corrections.

Option: [+5 minutes] To extend the activity, have students form groups of three. Ask them to share good or bad experiences they have had arranging a service; for example, *I got my report copied by Quick Copy. But it was two days late.* To finish the activity, ask a few volunteers to share one of their experiences with the class.

Answers for Unit 3, Lesson 2

1. You should have that picture framed by Lydia at Austin Custom Framing.
2. You should have your hair cut by Eva at the Curl Up Hair Salon.
3. You should have your photos printed at the mall.
4. You should have a suit made by Luigi at Top Notch Tailors.
5. You should have your sweaters dry-cleaned at Midtown Dry Cleaners.

UNIT 4 Lesson 1

Verbs that can be followed by clauses with that

Suggested teaching time:	3–5 minutes	Your actual teaching time:

- Have students study the presentation and the examples.

- Write the following on the board: *I dreamed that I was sailing around the world.*

- Have students identify the noun clause and underline it. (That I was sailing around the world.)

- Ask students to identify the verb of mental activity in the example. (Dreamed.) You may want to remind students that the noun clause functions as the direct object of the verb of mental activity.

- Ask students *Can that be omitted?* (Yes.) Write parentheses ( ) around *that* on the board.

- To check comprehension, say or write verbs from the list one by one and ask students to make sentences with the verb and a noun clause. Make necessary corrections.

- You may prefer to have students complete this activity in pairs or small groups.

Adjectives that can be followed by clauses . . .

Suggested teaching time:	3–5 minutes	Your actual teaching time:

- Have students study the presentation and the examples.

- Point out that predicate adjectives of emotion follow verbs such as *be;* for example, *I'm afraid that I won't finish the project.* Write the following on the board:

  I + am + afraid + that I won't finish the project.

- Then write the following on the board:

  1. They were sure that they would miss the plane.
  2. I'm sorry to hear that you didn't get the job.

- Have students identify the adjectives and the noun clauses in the examples. (1. sure + [that] they would miss the plane; 2. sorry + [that] you didn't get the job.)

Option: [+3 minutes] If students need more controlled practice before starting the next exercise, write the following sentences on the board:

  We hear that the class ____.
  I noticed that the teacher ____.
  He forgot that the assignment ____.
  We hope that everyone ____.

Ask students to complete the noun clauses; for example, *We hear that the class is difficult.* You may want to write their sentences on the board as well.

On a separate sheet of paper, . . .

Suggested teaching time:	3–5 minutes	Your actual teaching time:	

- Have students compare their answers.
- Review with the class by having several students read one of their sentences aloud. Make necessary corrections.

Option: [+5 minutes] To provide more practice, ask students to work in pairs or small groups and think about important moments and first-time experiences in their lives; for example, their first day of school or college, their first job interview, their first day at work, their first time on an airplane, etc. Write the following on the board:

I was __ that __.
My parents were __ that __.

Ask students to take turns expressing their feelings about these moments or experiences by completing the sentences on the board. Encourage students to use the expressions in the presentation; for example, *When I started my new job, I was afraid that I would make mistakes. My parents were disappointed that I didn't want to play sports in school.* Walk around and provide help as needed.

Answers for Unit 4, Lesson 1
Answers will vary, but may include the following:
1. (that) I would be tall one day.
2. (that) I would go back to school.
3. (that) I can play the piano pretty well.
4. (that) I had a doctor's appointment.
5. (that) they were planning a trip.
6. (that) we go on an exciting vacation.
7. (that) I enjoy learning new languages.
8. (that) I liked to cook.
9. (that) I used to ride horses.
10. (that) I was traveling to the moon.

UNIT 4 Lesson 2

Embedded questions: usage and common errors

Suggested teaching time:	7–10 minutes	Your actual teaching time:	

- Have students study the presentation and the examples.
- To review embedded questions, ask students to read and underline the embedded question in each statement. (If we're late, what time it is, why it isn't working, where the bathroom is, how I get to the bank.)
- Have students read the *Be careful!* note.
- To check comprehension, write the following on the board:
  1. *I know where he is.*
  2. *I know where is he.*
  3. *I don't know what did he buy.*
  4. *I don't know what he bought.*
- Ask students to say which statements on the board are correct. (1 and 4.) Remind students that embedded questions require normal word order—no inversion and no auxiliaries.
- Have students study the phrases that are often followed by embedded questions.

- Point out that phrases with embedded questions are more polite than direct questions. They are often used when asking for a favor, for information, or when talking to people we don't know.
- To provide practice, ask several students to make statements using a phrase with an embedded question; for example, *I don't know when they are coming. I wonder where I put my jacket. Can you tell me what time it is?*

Option: [+3 minutes] To provide more practice with embedded questions, write the following on the board:
I remember (who, what, where, when, why).
I don't remember (who, what, where, when, why).

Ask students to think about their childhood. Ask them to say what they remember / don't remember using embedded questions. For example:
I remember where we used to go on vacation. It was to the beach . . .
I remember what my first grade classroom was like. It was sunny and . . .
I don't remember who my first teacher was.

Option: [+3 minutes] For a different approach, have students take turns role-playing a tourist visiting this city or town and someone who lives here. Encourage the tourist to use embedded questions; for example, **Student A:** *Hello. Can you tell me how to get to the train station from here?* **Student B:** *Sure. Walk up this street two blocks.*

Embedded questions: punctuation

Suggested teaching time:	5–7 minutes	Your actual teaching time:	

- Have students study the presentation and the examples.
- Write the following on the board:
  1. *Do you know why she's not here*
  2. *I wonder why she's not here*
- To check comprehension, ask students to tell which punctuation is needed for each item. (1. a question mark; 2. a period.)

A On a separate sheet of paper, . . .

Suggested teaching time:	3–5 minutes	Your actual teaching time:	

- Complete the first item with the class.
- Have students compare answers. Then review with the class.

B On a separate sheet of paper, . . .

Suggested teaching time:	3–5 minutes	Your actual teaching time:	

- Review the example with the class.
- Tell students they can refer to the presentation for phrases to use. Also point out that more than one phrase can be correct for each item.
- Review with the class by having several students write their questions on the board. Make necessary corrections.

On a separate sheet of paper, complete each sentence in your own way. Use clauses with <u>that</u>.

See page T127 for answers.

1 When I was young, I couldn't believe . . .

2 Last year, I decided . . .

3 This year, I was surprised to discover . . .

4 Last week, I forgot . . .

5 Recently, I heard . . .

6 In the future, I hope . . .

7 Now that I study English, I know . . .

8 In the last year, I learned . . .

9 Not long ago, I remembered . . .

10 Recently, I dreamed . . .

11 (your own idea)

12 (your own idea)

UNIT 4   Lesson 2

Embedded questions: usage and common errors

You can use an embedded question to ask for information more politely.

Are we late? → Can you tell me if we're late?

What time is it? → Can you tell me what time it is?

Why isn't it working? → Could you explain why it isn't working?

Where's the bathroom? → Do you know where the bathroom is?

How do I get to the bank? → Would you mind telling me how I get to the bank?

Be careful!   Do not use the question form in embedded questions.

Do you know why she won't read the newspaper?

Don't say: Do you know why ~~won't she~~ read the newspaper?

Can you tell me if this bus runs express?

Don't say: Can you tell me ~~does this bus run~~ express?

Phrases that are often followed by embedded questions

I don't know . . .

I'd like to know . . .

Let me know . . .

I can't remember . . .

Let's ask . . .

I wonder . . .

I'm not sure . . .

Do you know . . . ?

Can you tell me . . . ?

Can you remember . . . ?

Could you explain . . . ?

Would you mind telling me . . . ?

Embedded questions: punctuation

Sentences with embedded questions are punctuated according to the meaning of the whole sentence.

If an embedded question is in a sentence, use a period.

I don't know (something). → I don't know **who she is**.

If an embedded question is in a question, use a question mark.

Can you tell me (something)? → Can you tell me **who she is**?

A On a separate sheet of paper, complete each sentence with an embedded question. Punctuate each sentence correctly.

1 Please let me know (When does the movie start?)   Please let me know when the movie starts.

2 I wonder (Where is the subway station?)   I wonder where the subway station is.

3 Can you tell me (How do you know that?)   Can you tell me how you know that?

4 We're not sure (What should we bring for dinner?)   We're not sure what we should bring for dinner.

5 They'd like to understand (Why doesn't Pat want to come to the meeting?)   They'd like to understand why Pat doesn't want to come to the meeting.

6 Please tell the class (Who painted this picture?)   Please tell the class who painted this picture.

B On a separate sheet of paper, rewrite each question more politely, using noun clauses with embedded questions. Begin each one with a different phrase. Follow the example.   Answers will vary slightly, but may include the following:

Where's the airport? *Can you tell me where the airport is?*

1 What time does the concert start?   Would you mind telling me what time the concert starts?

2 How does this new MP3 player work?   Could you explain how this new MP3 player works?

3 Why is the express train late?   Do you know why the express train is late?

4 Where is the nearest bathroom?   Can you tell me where the nearest bathroom is?

5 Who speaks English at that hotel?   I wonder who speaks English at the hotel.

6 When does Flight 18 arrive from Paris?   I'm not sure when Flight 18 arrives from Paris.

Grammar Booster   **127**

C Correct the wording and punctuation errors in each item.

1 Could you please tell me ~~does~~ this train ~~go~~ to Nagoya~~?~~ *(whether)* *(goes)*

2 I was wondering ~~can~~ I get your phone number~~?~~ *(if)* *(can)*

3 I'd like to know what time ~~does~~ the next bus arrive~~?~~ *(s)*

4 Can you tell me how much ~~does~~ this magazine cost~~?~~ *(s)*

5 Do you remember where ~~did~~ he use to live?

6 I'm not sure why ~~do~~ they keep calling me.

7 I wonder ~~will~~ she come on time~~?~~ *(if)* *(will)*

See page T128 for answers.

Embedded questions with infinitives

In embedded questions, an infinitive can be used to express possibility (**can** or **could**) or advice (**should**).
You can use an infinitive after the question word. The following sentences have the same meaning.

I don't know **where I can get** that magazine. = I don't know **where to get** that magazine.
I'm not sure **when I should call** them. = I'm not sure **when to call** them.
She wanted to know **which train she should take**. = She wanted to know **which train to take**.

You can also use an infinitive after **whether**.

I can't decide **whether I should read** this book next. = I can't decide **whether to read** this book next.

Be careful! Don't use an infinitive after **if**. Use **whether** instead.

I can't decide **if I should read** this book next. = I can't decide **whether to read** this book next.
Don't say: I can't decide ~~if to read~~ this book next.

D On a separate sheet of paper, rewrite each sentence with an infinitive. See page T128 for answers.

1 Could you tell me whose novel I should read next?

2 I'd like to know where I can buy Smith's latest book.

3 Can you remember who I should call to get that information?

4 I'd like to know which train I can take there.

5 Let me know if I should give her the magazine when I'm done.

6 I wasn't sure when I could get the new edition of her book.

7 Let's ask how we can get to the train station.

Noun clauses as subjects and objects

A noun clause can function as either a subject or an object in a sentence.

As a subject	As an object
What he wrote inspired many people.	I like **what he wrote**.
Where the story takes place is fascinating.	I want to know **where the story takes place**.
How she became a writer is an interesting story.	They are inspired by **how she became a writer**.
That she wrote the novel in six months is amazing.	I heard **that she wrote the novel in six months**.
Who wrote the article isn't clear.	I wonder **who wrote the article**.

E On a separate sheet of paper, use the prompts to write sentences with noun clauses.

1 People always ask me (Why did I decide to study English?) People always ask me why I decided to study English.

2 (She wrote science fiction novels.) has always fascinated me. That she wrote science fiction novels has always fascinated me.

3 We all wanted to know (Where did she go on vacation?) We all wanted to know where she went on vacation.

4 (What websites do you visit?) is important information for companies who want to sell you their products. What websites you visit is important information for companies who want to sell you their products.

5 Can you tell me (Who did you invite to dinner?) Can you tell me who(m) you invited to dinner?

6 (How did you decide to become a teacher?) is an interesting story. How you decided to become a teacher is an interesting story.

C Correct the wording . . .

Suggested teaching time:	3–4 minutes	Your actual teaching time:

- Point out that the first sentence could also be *Could you please tell me if . . .*

- Have students compare answers. Then review with the class.

Embedded questions with infinitives

Suggested teaching time:	5–7 minutes	Your actual teaching time:

- Have students study the first rule and examples.

- Point out that the infinitive can be used to express possibility (First two examples.) and to express advice. (Third example.)

- Have students study the second rule and example.

- Then have students read the *Be careful!* note.

- To check comprehension, say the following sentences and ask students to restate them using infinitives.
  Let me know where I can find that information. (Let me know where to find that information.)
  I'm not sure who(m) I should talk to. (I'm not sure who(m) to talk to.)
  I'd like to know how I can repair it. (I'd like to know how to repair it.)
  I don't know whether I should ask for my money back. (I don't know whether to ask for my money back.)
  I don't know if I can watch that horror movie. (I don't know whether to watch that horror movie.)

- You may want to write the sentences on the board and have students write their answers.

D On a separate sheet of paper, . . .

Suggested teaching time:	5 minutes	Your actual teaching time:

- Complete the first item with the class.

- Review with the class by having students read their sentences aloud or write them on the board.

Option: [+5 minutes] To provide more practice, ask students to work in pairs or small groups and choose a place to go on vacation. Write the following on the board: *We should find out ___.*

Have students write at least four sentences about what they should find out before they go. For example:
We should find out where to stay.
We should find out interesting things to do there.
We should ask where to go for the best local food.
We should find out whether to bring warm clothes.

Combine pairs / groups and ask them to share their information. Encourage students to make necessary corrections.

Answers for Exercise D
1. Could you tell me whose novel to read next?
2. I'd like to know where to buy Smith's latest book.
3. Can you remember who(m) to call to get that information?
4. I'd like to know which train to take there.
5. Let me know whether to give her the magazine when I'm done.
6. I wasn't sure when to get the new edition of her book.
7. Let's ask how to get to the train station.

Noun clauses as subjects and objects

Suggested teaching time:	4–5 minutes	Your actual teaching time:

- Have students study the rule and examples.

- Ask students to look at the examples and name the words that can introduce a noun clause. List them on the board: *what, where, how, that, who.*

- Point out that other words are also possible. Write them on the board: *why, when, how much, how many, how often.* Provide examples: *I wonder why she is late. How many pictures he painted is still a mystery.*

- Write the following on the board:
  1. That he isn't here is surprising.
  2. I don't know why he isn't here.

- Have students identify and underline the clauses in the examples. (1. That he isn't here; 2. why he isn't here.)

- Direct attention to item 1. Ask *Is the clause the subject or the object of the sentence?* (The subject.) Then direct students' attention to item 2 and ask the same question. (The object.)

E On a separate sheet of paper, . . .

Suggested teaching time:	4–5 minutes	Your actual teaching time:

- Point out that word order is the same in noun clauses when used as a subject or object of a sentence. Remind students that embedded questions require normal word order (not question word order).

- Have students compare answers with a partner. Then review with the class.

UNIT 5 Lesson 1

Direct speech: punctuation rules

Suggested teaching time:	4–5 minutes	Your actual teaching time:

- Have students study the rules and examples.
- Remind students that in direct speech we are quoting the exact words someone said.
- Write two incorrect direct speech sentences on the board:
    1. Sandra "said don't call me before six.".
    2. He said, I have a meeting next Monday.
- Have pairs identify the errors and rewrite the sentences correctly. (1. Sandra said, "Don't call me before six." 2. He said, "I have a meeting next Monday.")
- Review with the class.

A On a separate sheet of paper, . . .

Suggested teaching time:	4–5 minutes	Your actual teaching time:

- Before students start the exercise, write the following on the board:
    1. Brandon said, "I'm hungry."
    2. Brandon said he was hungry.
- Ask *Do the two sentences on the board have the same meaning?* (Yes.) *What's the difference between them?* (Item 1 uses direct speech— the exact words the speaker said; item 2 uses indirect speech.)
- Read the example aloud. Have students compare answers with a partner. Then review with the class.

Answers for Exercise A
1. Martin told me, "Don't get a flu shot."
2. My daughter said, "Please pick me up after school."
3. The English teacher said, "Read the newspaper tonight and bring in a story about the weather."
4. We said, "Please don't forget to listen to the news."
5. They said, "Don't buy milk."
6. We told them, "Please call us in the morning."
7. She said, "Please tell your parents I'm sorry I can't talk right now."

B Look at each statement . . .

Suggested teaching time:	4–5 minutes	Your actual teaching time:

- Complete the first item with the class.
- Have students compare answers with a partner. Then review with the class.

Option: [+5 minutes] Ask students to think about instructions they heard today or on a previous day. Encourage them to write three or four statements using direct speech. Have pairs read each other's sentences and make any necessary corrections; for example, *This morning my father said, "Don't forget your umbrella." My boss told me, "I need the report right now."*

Answers for Exercise B
1. "Be home before midnight."
2. "Pack emergency supplies before the storm."
3. "Turn on the radio and listen to the news about the flood."
4. "Don't call us before 9 A.M."
5. "Don't go downtown this afternoon."

UNIT 5 Lesson 2

Indirect speech: optional tense changes

Suggested teaching time:	5–7 minutes	Your actual teaching time:

- Have students study the first rule and examples.
- Emphasize that the change in verb tense is optional. Point out that students should be able to understand and even produce both forms.
- To check comprehension, say several sentences and have students work in pairs to make sentences in reported speech. Encourage students to use both *say* and *tell* as well as *teacher, she / he,* and *just.* For example:
    1. *School is closed tomorrow.* (The teacher said the school was closed tomorrow. OR The teacher said the school is closed tomorrow.)
    2. *The weather report says there will be rain tomorrow.* (She said that the weather report said there will be rain tomorrow. OR She said that the weather report says there will be rain tomorrow.)
    3. *You need to work on increasing your active vocabulary.* (The teacher told us we needed to work on increasing our active vocabulary. OR The teacher told us we need to work on increasing our active vocabulary.
- Have students study the *Be careful!* note.
- Point out that a reporting verb in the present tense is appropriate if the information is recent or is still true.

Direct speech: punctuation rules

When writing direct speech, use quotation marks to indicate the words the speaker actually said. Put final punctuation marks before the second quotation mark.

Jeremy said, "Don't answer the phone."

Use a comma after the verb or verb phrase that introduces the quoted speech.

They said, "Call me after the storm."

Begin the quoted speech with a capital letter.

I said, "Please come to dinner at nine."

A On a separate sheet of paper, write and punctuate each of the following statements in direct speech. Follow the example. See page T129 for answers.

They said tell us when you will be home

They said, "Tell us when you will be home."

1 Martin told me don't get a flu shot

2 My daughter said please pick me up after school

3 The English teacher said read the newspaper tonight and bring in a story about the weather

4 We said please don't forget to listen to the news

5 They said don't buy milk

6 We told them please call us in the morning

7 She said please tell your parents I'm sorry I can't talk right now

B Look at each statement in indirect speech. Then on a separate sheet of paper, complete each statement. Using the prompt, make the indirect speech statement a direct speech statement. Use correct punctuation.

See page T129 for answers.

1 They told us to be home before midnight. (They told us)

2 The sign downtown said to pack emergency supplies before the storm. (The sign downtown said)

3 Your daughter called and told me to turn on the radio and listen to the news about the flood. (Your daughter told me)

4 Your parents said not to call them before 9 A.M. (Your parents said)

5 Mr. Rossi phoned to tell me not to go downtown this afternoon. (Mr. Rossi phoned to tell me)

Indirect speech: optional tense changes

When the reporting verbs <u>say</u> or <u>tell</u> are in the simple past tense, it is not always necessary to use a different tense in indirect speech from the one the speaker used. The following are three times when it's optional:

When the statement refers to something JUST said:

I just heard the news. They said a storm **is** coming.

OR I just heard the news. They said a storm **was** coming.

When the quoted speech refers to something that's still true:

May told us she **wants** to get a flu shot tomorrow.

OR May told us she **wanted** to get a flu shot tomorrow.

When the quoted speech refers to a scientific or general truth:

They said that English **is** an international language.

OR They said that English **was** an international language.

Be careful! Remember that when the reporting verb is in the present tense, the verb tense in indirect speech does not change.

They **say** a big storm **is** expected to arrive tomorrow morning.

Don't say: They say a big storm ~~was~~ ...

On a separate sheet of paper, write each direct speech statement in indirect speech. Change the verb in the indirect speech only if necessary. See page T130 for answers.

1 Last Friday my husband said, "I'm going to pick up some things at the pharmacy before the storm."

2 Last year my parents said, "We're going to Spain on vacation this year."

3 She told them, "This year's flu shot is not entirely protective against the flu."

4 He just said, "The danger of a flood is over."

5 We always say, "It's easier to take the train than drive."

6 When I was a child, my parents told me, "It's really important to get a good education."

7 The National Weather Service is saying, "Tonight's weather is terrible."

8 Your parents just told me, "We want to leave for the shelter immediately."

UNIT 6 Lesson 1

Expressing the future: review

The present continuous
My tooth has been killing me all week. I'm **calling** the dentist tomorrow.
What are you doing this afternoon? I'm **going** to the beach.

The simple present tense
The office is usually open until 9:00, but it **closes** at 6:00 tomorrow.

Modals <u>should</u>, <u>could</u>, <u>ought to</u>, <u>may</u>, <u>might</u>, <u>have to</u>, and <u>can</u>
You **could** catch the next bus. We **should** call her next week.

A **Read each sentence. Check the sentences that have future meaning.**

☐ **1** Hannah is studying English this month.

☐ **2** Nancy studies English in the evening.

☑ **3** You should call me tomorrow.

☑ **4** He might have time to see you later.

☑ **5** My parents are arriving at 10:00.

☑ **6** I'm taking my daughter out for dinner tonight.

☐ **7** I'm eating dinner with my daughter. Can I call you back?

☐ **8** The class always starts at 2:00 and finishes at 4:00.

☑ **9** We may stay another week in Paris.

The future with <u>will</u> and <u>be going to</u>: review

Use <u>will</u> or <u>be going to</u> to make a prediction or to indicate that something in the future will be true.
There is no difference in meaning.
Getting a new car **will cost** a lot of money.   Getting a new car **is going to cost** a lot of money.

Use <u>be going to</u> to express a plan.
My tooth has been killing me all week. I'm **going to call** a dentist. NOT I will call a dentist.

**Be careful! <u>Will</u> is also used for willingness. This use of <u>will</u> doesn't have a future meaning.
<u>Be going to</u> cannot be used for willingness.**
A: Is it true that you **won't go** to the dentist?
B: **I'll go** to the dentist, but I don't like fillings. NOT I'm going to go…

On a separate sheet of paper, . . .

Suggested teaching time:	4–5 minutes	Your actual teaching time:

- Complete the first item with the class. Remind students that the verb tense needs to change because it doesn't meet the three criteria of optional changes in the presentation on page 129.
- Have students compare answers with a partner. Encourage them to discuss why the verb tense changes or not based on the presentation.
- Then review with the class.

Answers for Unit 5, Lesson 2
1. Last Friday my husband said he was going to pick up some things at the pharmacy before the storm.
2. Last year my parents said they were going to Spain on vacation this year.
3. She told them this year's flu shot was not entirely protective against the flu.
4. He just said the danger of a flood is over.
5. We always say it's easier to take the train than drive.
6. When I was a child, my parents told me it's really important to get a good education.
7. The National Weather Service is saying that tonight's weather is terrible.
8. Your parents just told me they want to leave for the shelter immediately.

UNIT 6   Lesson 1

Expressing the future: review

Suggested teaching time:	5–7 minutes	Your actual teaching time:

- Have students study the examples of the present continuous.
- Then have them find and say the time words in the examples. (Tomorrow, this afternoon.)
- Point out that including time words when using the present continuous for the future is common but not necessary, unless they are needed for clarity.
- To provide practice, say the following statements and have students restate them using the present continuous for the future. Students should add a time word each time; for example, *I'm going to travel to Spain.* (I'm traveling to Spain [next week].) *I'm going to see Sue.* (I'm seeing Sue tomorrow [at 3:00].) *He's going to leave.* (He's leaving [after supper].)
- Have students study the example of the simple present tense.
- To check comprehension, write the following on the board:
  1. Our Friday meetings usually start at 10:00.
  2. This Friday our meeting starts at 11:00.

- Ask *Which example shows the simple present tense used with future meaning?* (2) *How do you know?* (Because it says *This Friday.*)
- Have students study the modals that can be used with future meaning and the examples.
- Although time words are not necessary to give modals future meaning, provide practice by saying each modal and asking several students to make a sentence including time words to give it future meaning. For example:
  You should see her tomorrow.
  Maybe we could go to Canada next summer.
  He may be late to class on Monday.
  She might find a surprise when she gets home.
  You have to finish this by Friday.
  I can help you with your homework after dinner.

A Read each sentence . . .

Suggested teaching time:	4–5 minutes	Your actual teaching time:

- Ask students to underline the time words that give the statements future meaning. (3. tomorrow; 4. later; 5. at 10:00; 6. tonight.)
- If necessary, point out that in item 1, *this month* refers to an action occurring during a present period of time.
- Ask students to find a statement in which the future meaning is given by the context only. (9)
- Have students compare answers with a partner. Then review with the class.

The future with will and be going to: review

Suggested teaching time:	5–7 minutes	Your actual teaching time:

- Have students study the presentation and the examples.
- Be sure students understand that both *will* and *be going to* can be used for predictions. *Be going to* is used for plans. *Will* is used for decisions made at the moment of speaking.
- To review, ask students to work in pairs and provide examples for *will* and *be going to* to express predictions and *be going to* to express plans. Encourage students to give feedback to each other.
- Walk around and provide help as needed.
- Have students study the *Be careful!* note. Make sure students understand that this use of *will* does not refer to the future. It indicates what the person is / is not willing to do.

B Complete the conversations, . . .

Suggested teaching time:	4–5 minutes	Your actual teaching time:

- Complete the first item with the class. Review the correct answers: A: *I'm going to leave*—The person has a plan. B: *'ll meet*—The person has no plan. He / She makes a decision at the moment of speaking.
- Have students compare answers with a partner. Then review with the class.

Option: [+5 minutes] To extend the activity, write the following on the board:

1. A: *Are you free this Friday?*
   B: *No, I ___.*
2. A: *Did you hear the weather report for tomorrow?*
   B: *Yes, it ___.*
3. A: *I don't know how to use this copier. Can you give me a hand?*
   B: *Sure. I ___.*

Have students work in pairs. Ask them to complete the conversations using *will* or *be going to*. To review, ask several pairs to perform one of their conversations. (Make sure students use: 1. *be going to*—prior plan; 2. *will / be going to*—prediction; 3. *will*—no plan, decision made at the moment of speaking.)

UNIT 6 Lesson 2

Regrets about the past: <u>wish</u> + the . . .

Suggested teaching time:	5–7 minutes	Your actual teaching time:

- Before students study the presentation, write: *I wish I had a car.* Ask students, *Does this sentence express a present or a past regret?* (A present regret.)
- Tell students that to express a present regret, we use the simple past tense after *wish*.
- Then write: *I wish I had gone to the party.* Ask *Does this sentence express a regret about the present or the past?* (A regret about the past.)
- Point out that the past perfect follows *wish* to express a past regret.
- Have students study the first rule and examples.
- Ask several students to make sentences using *I wish* about past actions or decisions they regret; for example, *I wish I had never moved to the city. I wish I had married my first boyfriend.*
- Have students study the second rule and examples.
- Point out that both *should have* and *ought to have* express regret.
- To provide practice, ask students to work in pairs. Student A uses *I wish* to express a past regret. Then Student B says the same sentence using *I should have* or *I ought to have.* For example:

  Student A: *I wish I had listened to my parents about studying.*

  Student B: *I should have listened to my parents about studying.* OR *I ought to have listened to my parents about studying.*

- Make sure to point out the Note. In American English *should have* is more common than *ought to have* in negative statements and in questions.

On a separate sheet of paper, . . .

Suggested teaching time:	4–5 minutes	Your actual teaching time:

- Review the first item with the class.
- Have students compare answers with a partner. Then review with the class.

Option: [+5 minutes] Write the following on the board:

studies   trips   work / job

Have students form pairs. Ask students to take turns using *wish, should have,* or *ought to have* to talk about past decisions they regret making, using the topics on the board. (Possible answers: I wish I had gone to college. I should have finished my studies. I ought to have gone on vacation when I had the chance. I wish I hadn't spent so much money on my vacation. I should have accepted the first job I was offered. I ought to have taken a part-time job while I was at college.)

UNIT 7 Lesson 1

Adjective clauses: common errors

Suggested teaching time:	4–5 minutes	Your actual teaching time:

- To review adjective clauses, write the following on the board: *I just took a trip that I will never forget.*
- Ask students to find and say the adjective clause in the statement. (That I will never forget.)
- Then ask *What do adjective clauses give additional information about?* (A noun / a person or thing.) *What does the clause on the board give additional information about?* (A trip.)
- Have students study the rules and examples.
- To check comprehension, write the following on the board:
  1. *Mexico is a country who I would like to visit.*
  2. *I don't like the food that it is served in that restaurant.*
- Ask students what's not correct in each sentence. Have pairs decide why they are wrong, based on the presentation.
- Review with the class. (1. *That* and not *who* is used for adjective clauses that describe things. 2. The subject *it* is not necessary because *that* is the subject of the clause.)

B **Complete the conversations, using <u>will</u> or <u>be going to</u>.**

1 A: Would you like to go running in the park? I <u> 'm going to leave </u> in about half an hour.
leave

   B: That sounds great. I <u> 'll meet </u> you there.
meet

2 A: It's midnight. Why are you still reading?

   B: We <u> 're going to have </u> a test tomorrow.
have

3 A: Do you have plans for tomorrow?

   B: Yes. I <u> 'm going to see </u> a chiropractor for the first time.
see

4 A: I hope you can come tomorrow night. We'd really like you to be there.

   B: OK. I <u> 'll come </u> .
come

5 A: I'm thinking about getting a new laptop.

   B: Really? Well, I <u> 'll show </u> you mine. I love it.
show

UNIT 6 Lesson 2

Regrets about the past: <u>wish</u> + the past perfect; <u>should have</u> and <u>ought to have</u>

<u>Wish</u> + the past perfect
I wish I **had married** later. And I wish I **hadn't married** Celine!
Do you wish you **had bought** that car when it was available?

<u>Should have</u> and <u>ought to have</u> + past participle
<u>Ought to have</u> has the same meaning as <u>should have</u>.
I **should have married** later = I **ought to have married** later.
I **shouldn't have married** Celine. = I **ought not to have married** Celine.

Note: American English speakers use <u>should have</u> instead of <u>ought to have</u> in negative statements and in questions.

On a separate sheet of paper, rewrite the statements and questions, changing <u>wish</u> + the past perfect to <u>should have</u> or <u>ought to have</u>.

1 She wishes she had had children. (ought to) She ought to have had children.

2 Do you wish you had studied Swahili? (should) Should you have studied Swahili?

3 I wish I had gone to New Zealand instead of Australia. (ought to) I ought to have gone to New Zealand instead of Australia.

4 Do you wish you had taken the job at the embassy? (should) Should you have taken the job at the embassy?

5 I wish I hadn't studied law. (should) I shouldn't have studied law.

UNIT 7 Lesson 1

Adjective clauses: common errors

Remember:
Use the relative pronouns <u>who</u> or <u>that</u> for adjectives that describe people. Use <u>that</u> for adjective clauses that describe things.
Don't say: Feijoada is a dish ~~who~~ is famous in Brazil.

Don't use a subject pronoun after the relative pronoun.
Don't say: Feijoada is a dish that ~~it~~ is famous in Brazil.

A On a separate sheet of paper, combine the two sentences into one, making the second sentence an adjective clause. Use <u>who</u> whenever it is possible. When it isn't possible, use <u>that</u>. Follow the example.

The hotel clerk was very helpful. / He recommended the restaurant. See page T132 for answers.

The hotel clerk who recommended the restaurant was very helpful.

1 My cousin lives in New Zealand. / She called today.

2 We have a meeting every morning. / It begins at 9:30.

3 The celebration is exciting. / It takes place in spring.

4 The teacher is not very formal. / She teaches the grammar class.

5 Patients might prefer homeopathy. / They want to avoid strong medications.

6 The copy shop is closed on weekends. / It offers express service.

7 The hotel is very expensive. / It has three swimming pools.

8 Do you like the teacher? / He teaches advanced English.

Reflexive pronouns

Reflexive pronouns	
myself	itself
yourself	ourselves
himself	yourselves
herself	themselves

A reflexive pronoun should always agree with the subject of the verb.

People really enjoy **themselves** at Brazil's Carnaval celebrations.

My sister made **herself** sick from eating so much.

Common expressions with reflexive pronouns

believe in oneself	If you **believe in yourself**, you can do anything.
enjoy oneself	We **enjoyed ourselves** on our vacation.
feel sorry for oneself	Don't sit around **feeling sorry for yourself**.
help oneself (to something)	Please **help yourselves** to dessert.
hurt oneself	Paul **hurt himself** when he tried to move the fridge.
give oneself (something)	I wanted to **give myself** a gift, so I got a massage.
introduce oneself	Why don't you **introduce yourselves** to your new neighbors?
be proud of oneself	She was **proud of herself** for getting the job.
take care of oneself	You should **take** better **care of yourself**.
talk to oneself	I sometimes **talk to myself** when I feel nervous.
teach oneself (to do something)	Nick **taught himself** to use a computer.
tell oneself (something)	I always **tell myself** I'm not going to eat dessert, but I do.
work for oneself	Oscar left the company and now he **works for himself**.

B Complete the sentences with reflexive pronouns.

1 My brother and his wife really enjoyed _____themselves_____ on their vacation.

2 My uncle has been teaching _____himself_____ how to cook.

3 The food was so terrific that I helped _____myself_____ to some more.

4 Instead of staying at home and feeling sorry for _____myself_____ after the accident, I stayed in touch with all my friends.

5 I hope your sister's been taking good care of _____herself_____.

6 I was too shy to introduce _____myself_____ to anyone at the party.

7 Mr. Yu hurt _____himself_____ while lighting firecrackers for the Chinese New Year.

C Complete each sentence with one of the common expressions with reflexive pronouns. Then add two more sentences of your own.

1 When did your brother _____teach himself_____ how to play the guitar?

2 You'd better tell your daughter to stop playing near the stove or she'll _____hurt herself_____.

3 I really hope you _____enjoy yourself_____ when you're on vacation.

4 _____

5 _____

A On a separate sheet of paper, . . .

Suggested teaching time:	4–5 minutes	Your actual teaching time:

- Review the example with the class.
- Remind students that they should use *who* whenever it is possible.
- Have students compare answers with a partner. Review with the class.

Option: [+5 minutes] To extend the activity, form groups of three. Ask students to use adjective clauses to make sentences about different people they have seen or talked to recently and several things they did this past week. For example:

The friend who / that I saw yesterday used to be my neighbor.

The movie that opened on Saturday was not very good.

Answers for Exercise A

1. My cousin who lives in New Zealand called today.
2. We have a meeting that begins at 9:30 every morning.
3. The celebration that takes place in the spring is spectacular.
4. The teacher who teaches the grammar class is not very formal.
5. Patients who want to avoid strong medications might prefer homeopathy.
6. The copy shop that offers express service is closed on weekends.
7. The hotel that has three swimming pools is very expensive.
8. Do you like the teacher who teaches advanced English?

Reflexive pronouns

Suggested teaching time:	5 minutes	Your actual teaching time:

- Point out the reflexive pronoun in the phrase *Enjoy yourself on Chuseok!* in the *Some ways . . .* box on page 77.
- Ask students to read the reflexive pronouns in the box in this presentation.
- To check comprehension, write the following on the board: ____ *looked at* ____ *in the mirror.*
- Say subject pronouns in random order and have volunteers use each pronoun plus a reflexive pronoun to complete the sentence on the board; for example, **T:** *He.* **S1:** *He looked at himself in the mirror.* **T:** *We.* **S2:** *We looked at ourselves in the mirror.*
- Have students study the common expressions and the examples.
- Answer any questions students may have. Students will practice these expressions in Exercise C.

B Complete the sentences . . .

Suggested teaching time:	3–4 minutes	Your actual teaching time:

- Have students find and underline the subject of the verb *enjoyed.* (My brother and his wife.) Make sure students understand that the correct answer is *themselves* because *My brother and his wife* can be replaced by *They.*
- Have them compare answers with a partner. Then review with the class.

C Complete each sentence . . .

Suggested teaching time:	3–4 minutes	Your actual teaching time:

- Complete the first item with the class.
- Have students compare answers with a partner. Then review with the class.

Option: [+3 minutes] For a challenge, ask several students questions using the expressions with reflexive pronouns in the presentation on page 132. Point out that students should use the expressions in their answers. For example:

Have you ever hurt yourself badly?

How can we help children feel good about themselves?

Have you ever taught yourself to do something?

Do you ever talk to yourself?

Would you like to work for yourself?

Do you ever give yourself gifts?

By + reflexive pronouns

Suggested teaching time:	3–4 minutes	Your actual teaching time:

• To check comprehension, ask students if they can think of other things they or others can and can't do by themselves; for example, *I can't drive by myself yet; I'm still taking driving lessons. My grandparents can't live by themselves anymore; they need help now.*

D Complete each sentence . . .

Suggested teaching time:	3 minutes	Your actual teaching time:

• Complete the first item with the class.

• Have students compare answers with a partner. Then review with the class.

Reciprocal pronouns: each other and . . .

Suggested teaching time:	5–7 minutes	Your actual teaching time:

• Call students' attention to the Vocabulary on page 76. Point out that *give each other gifts* and *wish each other well* use reciprocal pronouns.

• Write the following on the board:
  <u>Friends</u> send <u>each other</u> cards.
  <u>Friends</u> send <u>one another</u> cards.

• Point out that the subject *Friends* and the reciprocal pronouns *each other* and *one another* refer to the same people. Tell students that using reciprocal pronouns shows that everyone is doing the same action.

• To provide practice, ask students *When do people give each other gifts in your family or in your circle of friends? When do we send one another cards / write letters?* Encourage students to respond in full sentences and use reciprocal pronouns; for example, *In our family, we give each other gifts on [our birthdays]. My friends and I send one another [postcards] when we go on vacation.*

• Have students study the *Be careful!* note and the examples.

• To help clarify, write the following on the board:
  1. *They looked at themselves in the mirror.*
     A ——→ A   B ——→ B
  2. *They looked at each other.*
     A ←——→ B

• Say *In item 1, A looked at A and B looked at B. In item 2, A looked at B and B looked at A.*

E On a separate sheet of paper, . . .

Suggested teaching time:	3–5 minutes	Your actual teaching time:

• Review the example with the class.

• Have students compare answers with a partner. Then ask several students to write their sentences on the board.

Option: [+5 minutes] To provide more practice, have students think about someone they know. Form pairs. Have students take turns asking each other questions about their partner's choice. Students should use reflexive pronouns in their questions and answers. Write some example questions on the board to guide the students.
  1. *Where did you meet each other?*
  2. *How do you keep in touch with each other?*
  3. *What do you usually tell each other about?*
  4. *Do you send each other cards or gifts?*
  5. *Do you ever see each other?*

Answers for Exercise E
1. On New Year's Eve, in New York City, people wait in Times Square for midnight to come so they can kiss each other and wish one another a happy new year.
2. During the Thai holiday *Songkran*, people throw water at each other on the street.
3. During the Tomato Festival in Buñol, Spain, people have a lot of fun throwing tomatoes at each other for about two hours.
4. After a day of fasting during Ramadan, Muslims around the world invite one another to eat in their homes that evening.

UNIT 7   Lesson 2

Adjective clauses: who and whom . . .

Suggested teaching time:	5–7 minutes	Your actual teaching time:

• Point out that most native speakers use *who* instead of *whom*. *Whom* is considered very formal.

• To check comprehension, write on the board:
  1. *The woman who wanted to see you is here.*
  2. *The woman whom you wanted to see is here.*

• Ask students to make two sentences out of each example. (1. The woman is here. She wanted to see you. 2. The woman is here. You wanted to see her.)

• Underline *who* in item 1 and point out that it is the subject of the clause. Underline *you* in item 2 and point out that it is the subject of the clause. Then underline *whom* and point out that it is the object of the clause. Point out that *whom* can be omitted because it is the object of the clause.

• To provide practice, ask students to use these sentence starters to write two sentences:
  The man / woman who . . .
  The man / woman whom . . .

• Review with the class. (Possible answers: The man whom you met is my brother. The woman whom you wanted to talk to is here. The man who really influenced me in life was my grandfather. The woman who just called is my mother.)

Complete each (formal) sentence . . .

Suggested teaching time:	3–4 minutes	Your actual teaching time:

• Remind students to use *whom* for object relative pronouns (not *who*) in this exercise.

• Have students compare answers with a partner. Then review with the class.

By + reflexive pronouns

Use **by** with a reflexive pronoun to mean "alone."
You cannot put on a kimono **by yourself**. You need help.
Students cannot learn to speak English **by themselves**. They need practice with others in English.

D Complete each sentence with **by** and a reflexive pronoun.

1 Very young children shouldn't be allowed to play outside _____ by themselves _____.

2 Did your father go to the store _____ by himself _____?

3 When did you learn to fix a computer _____ by yourself _____?

4 We got tired of waiting for a table at the restaurant, so we found one _____ by ourselves _____.

Reciprocal pronouns: *each other* and *one another*

Each other and **one another** have the same meaning, but **one another** is more formal.
People give **each other** (or **one another**) gifts.
Friends send **each other** (or **one another**) cards.

> **Be careful!**
> Reciprocal pronouns don't have the same meaning as reflexive pronouns.
> They looked at **themselves**. (Each person looked in a mirror or at a photo.)
> They looked at **each other**. (Each person looked at the other person.)

E On a separate sheet of paper, rewrite each underlined phrase, using a reciprocal pronoun. Then add one sentence of your own. Follow the example. See page T133 for answers.

On Christmas, in many places in the world, people <u>give and receive</u> presents.
On Christmas, in many places in the world, people give each other presents.

1 On New Year's Eve, in New York City, people wait in Times Square for midnight to come so they can <u>kiss other people</u> and <u>wish other people</u> a happy new year.

2 During the Thai holiday *Songkran*, people <u>throw water at other people</u> on the street.

3 During the Tomato Festival in Buñol, Spain, people have a lot of fun <u>throwing tomatoes at other people</u> for about two hours.

4 After a day of fasting during Ramadan, Muslims around the world <u>invite other people</u> home to have something to eat that evening.

5 (Your own sentence)

UNIT 7   Lesson 2

Adjective clauses: *who* and *whom* in formal English

In formal written or spoken English, use **who** for subject relative pronouns and **whom** for object relative pronouns.

	subject	
The singer was terrible.	+	**He** sang in the restaurant.
The singer		**who sang in the restaurant** was terrible.

	object	
The singer was terrible.	+	We heard **him** last night.
The singer		**whom we heard last night** was terrible.

> **Remember:** An object relative pronoun can be omitted.
> The singer we heard last night was terrible.

Complete each (formal) sentence with **who** or **whom**.

1 The concierge _who_ works at that hotel is very helpful.

2 The man _whom_ I met on the plane has invited us to lunch.

3 The manager _who_ lives in Singapore may apply for the job.

4 I'm very satisfied with the dentist _whom_ you recommended.

5 The guests _whom_ we invited to the dinner were an hour late.

6 The sales representative _whom_ you are going to call speaks English.

7 The singer _whom_ you told me about is performing tonight.

8 My friend _who_ works at the bank can help you.

9 Is your colleague someone _whom_ I can ask to help me?

Real and unreal conditionals: review

Remember: Conditional sentences have two clauses: an <u>if</u>-clause and a result clause.

- **Real (or "factual") conditionals express the present or future results of real conditions.**

  Present or everlasting results: Use the present of <u>be</u> or the simple present tense in both clauses.

  If I **speak** slowly, people **understand** me.

  If the temperature of water **rises** above 100 degrees Celsius, it **turns** to steam.

  Future results: Use the present of <u>be</u> or the simple present tense in the <u>if</u>-clause. Use a future form (future with <u>will</u> or present continuous for the future) in the result clause.

  If I'm late, I'**ll disturb** the others at the meeting.

  Remember: The order of the clauses can be reversed. It's customary to use a comma after the <u>if</u>-clause when it comes first.

  If you **buy** a smart phone, you **won't need** both a cell phone and a PDA.

  You **won't need** both a cell phone and a PDA if you **buy** a smart phone.

  Remember: Don't use a future form in the <u>if</u>-clause. Don't say: If I ~~will be~~ late, I'll disturb the others at the meeting.

- **Unreal conditionals express the results of conditions that don't exist. Use the simple past tense or <u>were</u> in the <u>if</u>-clause. Use <u>would</u> + a base form in the result clause. The order of the clauses can be reversed.**

  If I **bought** a more economical car, I **wouldn't worry** so much about the price of gasoline.

  If he **were** here, he **would tell** us about his trip.

  Remember: Don't use the conditional in the <u>if</u>-clause. Don't say: If he ~~would be~~ here, he would tell us about his trip.

A Correct the errors in the conditional sentences.

1 If you ~~will~~ take a good picture, it can preserve memories of times you might forget.
2 If I ~~was~~ ^{were} you, I would send them an e-mail right away.
3 If you ~~would~~ go out today, you'll need an umbrella.
4 Most people would eat healthy food if they ~~understand~~ ^{understood} the consequences of eating too much junk food.
5 These speakers will be OK if you ~~used~~ ^{use} them in a smaller room.
6 If the weather ~~will be~~ ^{were} better, I'd go for a swim.
7 If I ~~would have~~ ^{had} a chance, I would work shorter hours.
8 ~~Will~~ ^{Would} you ride a bicycle to work if your car broke down?
9 What would you do if I ~~would ask~~ ^{asked} you to make dinner?
10 He ~~won't~~ ^{wouldn't} eat at that restaurant if they ~~would tell~~ ^{told} him he had to wear formal clothes.

Clauses after <u>wish</u>

Use <u>were</u> or the simple past tense after <u>wish</u> to express a regret about something that's not true now.

I **wish** my laptop **were** top-of-the-line. (But it's not top-of-the-line.)

I **wish** I **had** a Brew Rite digital coffee maker. (But I don't have one.)

Remember: Use the past perfect after <u>wish</u> to express a regret about something that was not true in the past.

Sean **wishes** he **hadn't sold** his car. (But he did sell it.)

Sean **wished** he **hadn't sold** his car. (But he did.)

Use the conditional (<u>would</u> or <u>could</u> + a base form) after <u>wish</u> to express a desire in the present that something will occur in the future or on an ongoing basis.

I **wish** it **would rain**. (a desire for a future occurrence)

I **wish** it **would rain** more often. (a desire for something to occur on an ongoing basis)

Use <u>would</u> and a base form after <u>wished</u> to express a wish one had in the past for a future occurrence.

Yesterday I **wished** it **would rain**, but it didn't. (a past wish for a future occurrence)

Real and unreal conditionals: review

Suggested teaching time:	10–12 minutes	Your actual teaching time:

- Have students read the first rule and examples.
- To check comprehension, draw the following chart on the board (without the answers).

		If-clause	Result clause
Real conditionals	Present results of real conditions	present of be or simple present	present of be or simple present
	Future results of real conditions	present of be or simple present	will or present continuous
Unreal conditionals	Results of conditions that don't exist	were or simple past	would + a base form

- Write *Present results of real conditions* in the first row of the second column, and complete the items for the *if*-clause and the result clause in the first row with the class.
- Have students read the rule about future results and the examples.
- Write *Future results of real conditions* in the second row of the second column, and complete the items for the *if*-clause and the result clause in the second row with the class.
- Have students read the two *Remember* notes.
- To check comprehension, write the following examples on the board (do not erase the chart) and have students find the mistake in each example.
  1. If the price is good I will buy it.
  2. I will go shopping, if it rains.
  3. If I will have time, I will call her.
- Review with the class. (1. A comma is needed after *good*. 2. No comma is needed after *shopping*. 3. The simple present form *have* is needed in the *if*-clause.)
- Have students read the rule about unreal conditionals and the examples.
- Write *Results of conditions that don't exist* in the third row of the second column, and with the class, complete the items for the *if*-clause and the result clause in the third row.

A Correct the errors . . .

Suggested teaching time:	4–5 minutes	Your actual teaching time:

- Complete the first item with the class. Ask *Does this sentence express a real condition or an unreal condition?* (A real condition.) *Can we use will in the if-clause?* (No.) *What form is needed?* (The simple present tense, *take*.)
- Have students compare answers with a partner. Then review with the class.

Clauses after wish

Suggested teaching time:	7–10 minutes	Your actual teaching time:

- Have students study the first rule and examples.
- Remind students that *were* is used for all persons; for example, *I wish I were rich.* (NOT *I wish I was rich.*)
- To check comprehension, ask several students to make (simple) sentences with *I wish + were*; for example, *I wish I were on vacation. I wish my car were faster. I wish laptops were cheaper.*
- Have students study the second rule and examples.
- To check comprehension, write the following on the board:
  I wish I had (not) ___.
  I wished I had (not) ___.
- Ask several students to complete the sentences. Check to make sure they use the past participle; for example, *I wish I had studied more for the test today. John wished he hadn't spent all his money on a new car. I wish I had tried to make my hotel reservations earlier.*
- Have students study the third rule and examples.
- To check comprehension, write the following on the board:
  I wish ___ would ___.
- Ask several students to complete the sentence. They can make sentences about themselves or about someone they know. Tell students they should say two sentences: their wish plus the reason or information why they wish it. For example:
  I wish it would be hot and sunny today. I want to go to the beach.
  I wish he would come home earlier. I get worried when he's out so late.
- Have students study the fourth rule and the example.
- To check comprehension, ask volunteers to express wishes they had in the past for the future; for example, *When I was on vacation last summer, I wished the week would never end. When I was in college, I wished I would find a girlfriend.*

LESSON PLAN

B Complete each statement . . .

Suggested teaching time:	3–4 minutes	Your actual teaching time:

- Review the first item with the class. Ask students to say what the clause after *wish* expresses. (A desire in the present that something will occur in the future.)
- Before students write their answers, encourage them to figure out which of the four uses in the presentation on page 134 each item refers to.
- Have students compare answers with a partner. Then review with the class.

Option: [+5 minutes] To extend the activity, write the following on the board:

1. something you have but you wish you didn't have
2. something you don't have but you wish you had
3. something you did but you wish you hadn't done
4. something you didn't do but you wish you had done
5. something you have to do but you wish you wouldn't have to do

Ask students to think about each situation and write brief notes for each one. Form small groups. Have students take turns talking about their wishes and regrets using their notes as a guide. Walk around and help as needed.

Unless in conditional sentences

Suggested teaching time:	4–5 minutes	Your actual teaching time:

- Have students study the presentation and the examples.
- Point out that *unless* has the same meaning as *if . . . not*.
- To check comprehension, write the following on the board:
  1. If you don't hurry, you'll be late.
  2. Unless ____, you'll be late.
  3. He won't buy it if it's not on sale.
  4. He won't buy it unless ____.
- Ask students to complete items 2 and 4. (Possible responses: 2. you hurry; 4. it's on sale.)

C On a separate sheet of paper, . . .

Suggested teaching time:	3–5 minutes	Your actual teaching time:

- Review the example with the class.
- Point out the comma in the example. Remind students to include a comma after the *if*-clause or *unless* clause when they come at the beginning of the sentence.
- Have students compare answers with a partner. Then review with the class.

Answers for Exercise C
1. Unless you are in a hurry, you should walk.
2. Unless you care about special features, you shouldn't consider getting the top-of-the-line model.
3. She won't go running in the park unless her friends go with her.
4. Claire won't buy a car unless it has a high-tech sound system.

The unreal conditional: variety of forms

Suggested teaching time:	5–7 minutes	Your actual teaching time:

- Have students study the rule and examples.
- To check comprehension of active and passive forms, write the following on the board:
  1. If they had advertised the job, he would have applied for it.
  2. If he had applied for the job, they would have hired him.
- Ask pairs to rewrite the sentences, changing the verbs in the underlined clauses into the passive.
- Review with the class. (1. If the job had been advertised, he would have applied for it. 2. If he had applied for the job, he would have been hired.)
- To check comprehension of continuous verb forms, write the following on the board:
  1. If the car hadn't broken down, we would have been ____.
  2. If we had been ____, we would have heard the news.
- With students, complete the sentences with continuous verb forms and add any other necessary information. (Possible answers: 1. dancing OR swimming at the beach OR playing golf; 2. watching TV OR listening to the radio OR paying attention.)
- To check comprehension of past conditions with present results, write the following on the board:
  1. If she had taken part, she would have won.
  2. If he had gotten a degree, he would have a better job now.
- Ask *Which example expresses the present result of a past condition?* (2)
- You may want to have students give their own examples of past conditions with present results.

T135

B Complete each statement or question with the correct form of the verb.

1 I wish my favorite author _____would write_____ a new book. I've read all her old books so many times.
write

2 Pat wished she _____had spent_____ more time test-driving cars before she bought that SUV.
spend

3 Most people wish they _____were_____ rich.
be

4 I wish it _____had been_____ possible for me to get a better camera when I bought this one.
be

5 They wished they _____had known_____ sooner that their computer couldn't be fixed.
know

6 When I was a child, my parents wished I _____would become_____ a doctor.
become

7 Do you wish you _____had_____ a more comfortable car for the trip tomorrow?
have

8 Don't they wish they _____had studied_____ German?
study

9 I wish I _____had married / could marry_____ a mechanic. My car keeps breaking down.
marry

Unless *in conditional sentences*

You can use __unless__ (in place of __if__ + __not__) in negative __if__-clauses.

__Unless__ they buy a freezer, they'll have to go shopping every day. (= If they don't buy a freezer,…)
She wouldn't go for a long drive __unless__ she had a cell phone with her. (= …if she didn't have a cell phone with her.)
Martin doesn't buy electronics __unless__ they're state-of-the-art. (= … if they're not state-of-the-art.)

C On a separate sheet of paper, rewrite the sentences, changing __if not__ statements to __unless__ and making any necessary changes. Follow the example. See page T135 for answers.

If you don't buy the Brew Rite coffee maker, you'll have to spend a lot more money on another brand.

Unless you buy the Brew Rite coffee maker, you'll have to spend a lot more money on another brand.

1 If you aren't in a hurry, you should walk.

2 If you don't care about special features, you shouldn't consider getting the top-of-the-line model.

3 She won't go running in the park if her friends don't go with her.

4 Claire won't buy a car if it doesn't have a high-tech sound system.

UNIT 8 *Lesson 2*

The unreal conditional: variety of forms

Unreal conditional sentences can have a variety of active and passive forms in either clause.

If she **had worn** a seat belt, she **wouldn't have been** hurt.
If the car **had been totaled**, he **would have bought** a new one.
If the automobile **hadn't been invented**, we **would** still **be using** horses.
If horses **were** still **being used**, our high-speed highway system **would never have been created**.
If Marie Claire **were getting** married today, she **wouldn't marry** Joe.
If she **had married** Joe, she **would have children** today.

On a separate sheet of paper, complete the following unreal conditional sentences in your own way, using active and passive forms. Refer to the presentation on page 135 for some possibilities. Answers will vary, but may include the following:

1 If I were elected ruler of a country, . . . I would raise taxes.

2 The car would have been invented earlier if . . . people had had more free time.

3 If I were looking for a high-tech smart phone, . . . I would buy one online.

4 If this laptop had been available when I was looking for one, . . . I would have bought it.

5 . . . , I wouldn't be studying English now. If I didn't want to travel

6 If I were going to take a commercial space flight today, . . . I would be very excited.

UNIT 9 Lesson 1

Count and non-count nouns: review and extension

Count nouns name things that can be counted individually. They have singular and plural forms.

a president / presidents	a liberal / liberals	a candidate / candidates
a government / governments	an election / elections	a monarchy / monarchies

Non-count nouns name things that are not counted individually. They don't have singular or plural forms and they are not preceded by a or an. To express a specific quantity of a non-count noun, use unit expressions.

a piece of news   a cup of tea   a kilo of rice   a time of peace   an act of justice

Many nouns can be used as count or non-count nouns, but the meaning is different.

She studied **government** at the university. (= an academic subject)
That country has had four **governments** in ten years. (= a group of people who rule the country)

Democracy is the best form of government. (= a type of government)
After the revolution, the country became **a democracy**. (= a country with a democratic system)

I love **chicken**. (the food, in general)
I bought **a chicken**. (the actual whole bird)

She has blond **hair**. (in general = all of her hair)
She got **a hair** in her eye. (= one individual strand of hair)

Complete each sentence with the correct form of each noun.

1 The government has made _____progress_____ with the economic situation.
     progress

2 They've given a lot of _____importance_____ to making the banks stable.
     importance

3 Unfortunately, (the) radicals / a radical changed the law.
          radical

4 _____Peace_____ can only come if people stop making war.
     peace

5 _____Moderates_____ don't favor extreme change.
     moderate

6 He's _____a reactionary_____ who would like to outlaw freedom of speech.
     reactionary

7 If I could give you one piece of _____advice_____, it would be to vote.
          advice

8 If more people don't find _____work_____, people will elect a different president.
          work

9 Some _____governments_____ are more liberal than others.
     government

10 It's impossible to end all _____poverty_____.
          poverty

On a separate sheet of paper, . . .

Suggested teaching time:	3–4 minutes	Your actual teaching time:

- Have students share answers with a partner.
- Then review with the class by having several students write their sentences on the board.

UNIT 9   Lesson 1

Count and non-count nouns: . . .

Suggested teaching time:	7–10 minutes	Your actual teaching time:

- Have students study the first rule and examples.
- Ask the class to give examples of other count nouns. Have students give the singular form using *a* or *an* and then the plural form; for example, *a book—books, an umbrella—umbrellas, a season—seasons*, etc.
- Have students study the second rule and examples.
- Point out that abstract ideas are also non-count nouns; for example, *progress, help, importance, health, education*.
- Point out that fields of study, some foods, and materials are also non-count nouns; for example, *law, biology, chocolate, juice, wood, cotton, plastic*.
- Write the following on the board:
  1. paper   3. water
  2. bread   4. furniture
- Ask students to say or write unit expressions for each item. (Possible answers: 1. a piece of; 2. a loaf of, a piece of; 3. a glass of, a pitcher of, a bottle of; 4. a piece of.)
- Have students study the third rule and examples.
- Write the following on the board:
  1. I don't like <u>coffee</u>.
  2. I had a <u>coffee</u>.
  3. I saw a <u>chicken</u>.
  4. I ate <u>chicken</u>.
  5. Turn on the <u>light</u>.
  6. There's very little <u>light</u> in this room.
- Ask students to work in pairs. Have them discuss how the meaning of the underlined words is different in each pair of sentences. Ask students to say if an item is count or non-count.
- Review with the class. (1. Non-count; 2. count; 3. count; 4. non-count; 5. count; 6. non-count.)

Complete each sentence . . .

Suggested teaching time:	3–4 minutes	Your actual teaching time:

- Point out that students might need to complete each sentence with a noun and they might need to include an article or the plural form of the noun.
- Have students compare answers with a partner. Then review with the class.

Option: [+5 minutes] If you feel your students need more practice, have them write sentences with the words in the presentation, as well as any words you may have written on the board during the presentation.

UNIT 9 Lesson 2

Gerunds and infinitives: review . . .

Suggested teaching time:	10–12 minutes	Your actual teaching time:	

- Have students read the spelling rules for gerunds and the examples.
- To check comprehension, write the following on the board:
  1. write
  2. play
  3. allow
  4. vote
  5. put
  6. stop
  7. admit
  8. mix
- Ask pairs to turn the base forms into gerunds, and refer to the presentation if necessary.
- Review with the class. (1. Writing; 2. playing; 3. allowing; 4. voting; 5. putting; 6. stopping; 7. admitting; 8. mixing.)
- Have students read the rule about how infinitives are formed.
- To check comprehension, call on volunteers to name some infinitives. (Possible answers: To write, to play, to allow, etc.)
- Have students study the rule about uses of gerunds and the examples.
- Clarify any questions students might have about the grammatical functions; for example, subjects precede verbs in statements; direct objects follow verbs; objects of prepositions follow prepositions; subject complements follow *be*.
- Write the following on the board:
  1. You should avoid talking to strangers.
  2. Skiing is his passion.
  3. I'm not interested in discussing politics.
  4. Her favorite pastime is sailing.
- To check comprehension, ask students to underline the gerunds and identify their function. Ask students to compare answers with a partner.
- Review with the class. (1. *Talking*: direct object; 2. *skiing*: subject; 3. *discussing*: object of preposition *in*; 4. *sailing*: subject complement.)
- Have students study the rule about uses of infinitives and the examples.
- Write the following on the board:
  1. I hope to see her this weekend.
  2. My plan is to go on vacation in July.
  3. To be informed is important.
- Ask pairs to underline the infinitives and identify their function.
- Review with the class. (1. *To see*: direct object; 2. *to go*: subject complement; 3. *to be*: subject.)

A Using the sentences in the box . . .

Suggested teaching time:	3–4 minutes	Your actual teaching time:	

- Encourage students to refer to the presentation if they need help.
- To review, you can have students compare answers and do peer correction. Students should exchange papers and focus on checking for the correct usage of gerunds and infinitives.

Answers for Exercise A
Answers will vary, but may include the following:
1. a Voting is a right people have in democratic countries.
   b He felt like voting for the radical candidate.
2. a She quit smoking last month.
   b I look forward to smoking a cigarette.
3. a She is in favor of censoring books.
   b His occupation is censoring movies.
4. a To permit eighteen-year-olds to vote wouldn't be a wise decision.
   b They don't want to permit that kind of behavior.
5. a They need to lower the driving age.
   b To lower the amount of fat in your diet is an excellent idea.

Gerunds and infinitives: review . . .

Suggested teaching time:	5–7 minutes	Your actual teaching time:	

- Have students read the first rule and the list of verbs.
- If students do not know the meaning of a verb, you may want to give an example with an explanation.
- Form pairs or small groups. Ask students to take turns making sentences using the verbs and gerunds.
- Have students read the second rule and the list of verbs.
- Answer any questions about meaning.
- Ask students to find new partners and take turns making sentences with infinitives.
- Have students read the third rule and the list of verbs.
- You may want to give examples: *Yesterday I began crying for no reason. Yesterday I began to cry for no reason.*
- Ask students to find new partners. Encourage them to make two sentences, one with a gerund and the other with an infinitive; for example, *I felt really sick, but I continued working. Even though I was sick, I continued to work.*

Gerunds and infinitives: review of form and usage

Form

Gerunds: A gerund is a noun formed from a verb. All gerunds end in -**ing**. To form a gerund, add -**ing** to the base form of a verb.

discuss → discuss**ing**

If the base form ends in a silent -**e**, drop the -**e** and add -**ing**.

vote → voting

In verbs of one syllable, if the last three letters are a consonant-vowel-consonant* (CVC) sequence, double the last consonant and then add -**ing** to the base form.

C V C
s i t → sitting

| * Vowels = a, e, i, o, u |
| * Consonants = b, c, d, f, g, h, j, k, l, m, n, p, q, r, s, t, v, w, x, y, z |

BUT: If the base form of the verb ends in -**w**, -**x**, or -**y**, don't double the final consonant.

blow → blowing **fix** → fixing **say** → saying

If a base form has more than one syllable and ends in a consonant-vowel-consonant sequence, double the last consonant only if the spoken stress is on the last syllable.

permit → permitting BUT order → ordering

Infinitives: An infinitive is also a verbal noun. It is formed with **to** + the base form of a verb.

elect → to elect persuade → to persuade

Usage

Gerunds can be subjects, objects, and subject complements within sentences.

Discussing politics is my favorite activity. (subject)
I love **reading** about government. (direct object of verb **love**)
I read a book about **voting**. (object of preposition **about**)
My favorite pastime is **watching** TV news. (subject complement after **be**)

Infinitives function as subjects, direct objects, and subject complements.

To hang out all day discussing politics would be my favorite weekend activity. (subject)
I love **to guess** who's going to win elections. (direct object of verb **love**)
My greatest dream for the future is **to work** in the government. (subject complement after **be**)

A Using the sentences in the box above as a model, write pairs of sentences on a separate sheet of paper, using the gerunds and infinitives in the two ways shown. See page T137 for answers.

1 voting
 a (as the subject of a sentence)
 b (as a direct object)

2 smoking
 a (as a direct object)
 b (as an object of the preposition to)

3 censoring
 a (as the object of the preposition of)
 b (as a subject complement)

4 to permit
 a (as the subject of a sentence)
 b (as a direct object)

5 to lower
 a (as a direct object)
 b (as a subject of a sentence)

Gerunds and infinitives: review of usage after certain verbs

Certain verbs are followed by gerunds:
 avoid, can't stand, discuss, dislike, enjoy, feel like, (don't) mind, practice, quit, suggest

Other verbs are followed by infinitives:
 agree, choose, decide, expect, hope, learn, need, plan, seem, want, wish, would like

Other verbs can be followed by either a gerund or an infinitive:
 begin, continue, hate, like, love, prefer

For a review of gerunds and infinitives, open **Reference Charts** on your *ActiveBook* Self-Study Disc.

B Complete the paragraph with gerunds or infinitives. When either a gerund or an infinitive is correct, fill in the blank with both forms.

I hope ___to make___ some positive changes in my life, and I would like ___to start___ right away.
      1 make   2 start

I have observed that a lot of people enjoy ___complaining___ about the political situation, but they don't like
                                               3 complain

___to do / doing___ anything about it. They love ___to watch / watching___ the news and ___to say / saying___ they care
   4 do   5 watch   6 say

about all the poor people who don't have enough to eat, but they don't feel like ___doing___ anything to
                                                                                      7 do

change the situation. They worry about poverty, but they don't mind ___wasting___ money on stupid things
                                                                        8 waste

they don't need ___to have___ . Well, I'm sick of ___reading___ about how people are suffering, and I've
                   9 have   10 read

agreed ___to join___ a political action group. I simply hate ___to not do / not doing___ anything!
          11 join   12 not do

UNIT 10   Lesson 1

Prepositions of place: more usage

It's in {
Cheju Province.
the Rocky Mountains.
the Central Valley.
the Sahara Desert.
the Atlantic Ocean.
the state of Jalisco.
}

It's on {
the Nicoya Peninsula.
Easter Island.
the Hudson River.
Coronado Bay.
the coast.
Lake Placid.
the Gulf of Aqaba.
}

It's in the central part
It's southwest
It's about 50 kilometers north
} of Madrid.

A Write the correct prepositions of place.

1 Pisco is __on__ the Pacific coast of Peru.

2 Tianjin, in China, is __in__ Hebei Province.

3 Desaguadero is __on__ Lake Titicaca in Bolivia.

4 The island of Bahrain is __in__ the Persian Gulf.

5 Cabimas is __on__ Lake Maracaibo in Venezuela.

6 Sapporo is __on__ Hokkaido Island in Japan.

7 Riobamba is __on__ the Pastaza River in Ecuador.

8 Taiwan's Jade Mountain National Park is east __of__ the city of Alishan.

9 Fengkang is __in__ the southern part __of__ Taiwan.

10 The city of Budapest, Hungary, is __on__ the Danube River.

11 Denmark is north __of__ Germany.

12 The capital of Chile, Santiago, is located __in__ the Central Valley.

Proper nouns: capitalization

Capitalize names of:

places	Bolivia, the United Kingdom, Kyoto
languages / nationalities	French, Korean, Arabic
buildings and public places	the Paramount Theater, the Tower of London, the Golden Gate Bridge
organizations	the U.N., the World Bank, Amnesty International
names and titles	Mary, Mary Smith, Dr. Mary Smith
days / months / holidays	Monday, January, the Moon Festival
religions	Christianity, Islam, Buddhism
historic times or events	the Cold War, the Middle Ages, the Edo Period

When a proper noun has more than one word, each word is capitalized, except for articles (the) and prepositions (of).

Panama City	the Gulf of Aqaba	the City of Chicago
the University of Buenos Aires	Niagara Falls	the Bay of Biscayne

Capitalize all the words of a title, except for articles and prepositions that have fewer than four letters. If an article or a preposition is the first word of a title, capitalize it.

The Story of English	Looking Back on My Life
The International Herald Tribune	I Know Why the Caged Bird Sings

B Complete the paragraph . . .

Suggested teaching time:	4–5 minutes	Your actual teaching time:

- Point out that students can refer to the list in the presentation on page 137 or an expanded list in the Reference Charts on the ActiveBook Self-Study Disc.
- Have students compare answers with a partner. Then review with the class.

UNIT 10 Lesson 1

Prepositions of place: more usage

Suggested teaching time:	5–7 minutes	Your actual teaching time:

- Have students read the examples with *in*. Provide more examples: *The Galápagos Islands are in the Pacific Ocean. There are many active volcanoes in Ethiopia.* Then ask students to create their own examples.
- Have students read the examples with *on*. Provide more examples: *Cairo is on the Nile River. I spent my vacation on an island in the Caribbean.* Then ask students to create their own examples.
- Have students read the examples with *of*. Provide more examples: *Chile is west of Argentina. Mongolia is north of China.* Then ask students to create their own examples.

A Write the correct prepositions of place.

Suggested teaching time:	4–5 minutes	Your actual teaching time:

- Complete the first item with the class. Remind students that an island is *in* a body of water, not *on* it.
- Have students compare answers with a partner and then review with the class.

Option: [+5 minutes] To provide more practice, have students choose a place they know well and use the prepositions to describe that place. Students can work in pairs or small groups. Encourage the class to focus on prepositions and to give each other feedback.

Proper nouns: capitalization

Suggested teaching time:	5–7 minutes	Your actual teaching time:

- Have students study the list of names that need capitalization. Say each category aloud and ask for more examples. Make necessary corrections.
- Have students study the information about proper nouns and the examples.
- Ask the class for any examples they know of proper nouns with more than one word; for example, *the Eiffel Tower, Times Square, the Great Wall, Ipanema Beach,* etc.
- Have students study the last explanation and the examples.
- Write the following on the board:
  1. the story of my life
  2. six legends to remember
  3. adventures in the mountains
  4. tales of the jungle
- Tell students to imagine the phrases on the board are titles of books. Ask students to say which words should be capitalized. (1. The Story of My Life; 2. Six Legends to Remember; 3. Adventures in the Mountains; 4. Tales of the Jungle)

B On a separate sheet of paper, . . .

Suggested teaching time:	4–5 minutes	Your actual teaching time:

- Review the example with the class.

- Have students compare answers with a partner. Encourage them to refer to the presentation on page 138 if necessary.

- Review with the class.

Answers for Exercise B

1. My cousins are studying French.
2. The Leaning Tower of Pisa is in northern Italy.
3. It's on the southern coast of Australia.
4. I visit the City Museum of Art every Saturday.
5. My uncle Jack works for the United Nations.
6. The Channel Tunnel between England and France was completed in 1994.
7. She graduated from the University of Washington.
8. We liked the movie about the Great Wall of China.
9. My son is in the College of Sciences.
10. His father speaks Korean and Japanese fluently.
11. Their grandson was born last **March**.

Proper nouns: use of _the_

Suggested teaching time:	7–10 minutes	Your actual teaching time:

- Have students study the explanations and the examples.

- Point out the last use of _the_ in the presentation and explain that an acronym is a word made up from the first letters of the names of something.

- Write the following on the board:
  1. the Indian Ocean
  2. the World Meteorological Organization
  3. South Korea
  4. the Czech Republic
  5. the Pyrenees
  6. the Bay of Biscay
  7. NASA

- Ask students to number the rules in the presentation from 1 to 7. Then have them match the examples with the explanations. (1. 4; 2. 6; 3. 5; 4. 2; 5. 3; 6. 1; 7. 7)

Option: [+5 minutes] To provide more practice, form groups of three or four. Bring in newspapers in English. (If no newspapers in English are available, and there's an Internet connection, students can visit the CNN or BBC websites.) Student A scans the text to find three names of countries, organizations, or geographical areas. Then he / she writes them on a slip of paper with no capitalization. If the names include _the_, they can be written with or without _the_. Then he / she gives the slip of paper to Students B and C, who capitalize the names and add _the_ wherever necessary. Student A corrects his / her partners' work. Then students change roles.

B On a separate sheet of paper, rewrite each sentence with correct capitalization.
Follow the example. See page T139 for answers.

i'm reading one hundred years of solitude.

I'm reading One Hundred Years of Solitude.

1 my cousins are studying french.

2 the leaning tower of pisa is in northern italy.

3 it's on the southern coast of australia.

4 i visit the city museum of art every saturday.

5 my uncle jack works for the united nations.

6 the channel tunnel between england
and france was completed in 1994.

7 she graduated from the university of washington.

8 we liked the movie about the great wall of china.

9 my son is in the college of sciences.

10 his father speaks korean and japanese fluently

11 their grandson was born last march.

Proper nouns: use of *the*

When a proper noun includes the word of, use the.

with the	without the
the Republic of Korea	Korea
the Gulf of Mexico	Mexico City
the Kingdom of Thailand	Thailand

When a proper noun uses a political word such as republic, empire, or kingdom, use the.

the United Kingdom   the British Empire   the Malagasy Republic

When a proper noun is plural, use the.

the Philippines	the United States
the Netherlands	the Andes Mountains

When a proper noun includes a geographical word such as ocean, desert, or river, use the. BUT do not use the with the following geographical words: lake, bay, mountain, island, or park.

with the	without the
the Atlantic Ocean	Crystal Lake
the Atacama Desert	Hudson Bay
the Yangtze River	Hainan Island
the Iberian Peninsula	Ueno Park
the Persian Gulf	Yellow Mountain

When words like east or southwest are used as the name of a geographical area, use the. Do not use the when they are used as adjectives.

with the	without the
the Middle East	Western Europe
the Far East	East Timor
the West	Northern Ireland

When a proper noun includes a word that is a kind of organization or educational group, use the. Do not use the with a university or college (unless the name uses of).

with the	without the
the International Language Institute	Columbia College
the United Nations	Chubu University
the World Health Organization	
the University of Adelaide	

Do not use the with acronyms.

U.C.L.A. (the University of California, Los Angeles)
NATO (the North Atlantic Treaty Organization)
OPEC (the Organization of Petroleum Exporting Countries)

C **Correct the errors in the following sentences. Explain your answers.**

1 When she went to ~~the~~ Malaysia, she brought her husband with her.

2 A lot of people from ^the^ United States teach English here.

3 ~~The~~ Haiti is the closest neighbor to ^the^ Dominican Republic.

4 When we arrived in ~~the~~ Berlin, I was very excited.

5 ~~The~~ Jordan is a country in ^the^ Middle East.

6 I introduced our visitors to ^the^ University of Riyadh.

7 I lived in ^the^ People's Republic of China for about two years.

8 Mr. Yan is a student at ^the^ College of Arts and Sciences.

9 She is the director of ^the^ English Language Institute.

10 She's the most famous actress in ^the^ Netherlands.

11 He's interested in cultures in ^the^ Middle East.

12 ~~The~~ Poland was one of the first countries in ~~the~~ Eastern Europe to change to democracy.

UNIT 10 *Lesson 2*

Infinitives with <u>enough</u>

You can use an infinitive after an adjective and <u>enough</u> to give an explanation.
She's **old enough** to vote.   He's not **busy enough** to complain.

Be careful! <u>Too</u> comes before an adjective, but <u>enough</u> comes after an adjective.
It's **too far** to walk.
It isn't **close enough** to walk. NOT It isn't ~~enough close~~ to walk.

A **On a separate sheet of paper, complete each statement in your own way, using an infinitive.**

See page T140 for answers.

1 He's tall enough . . .

2 He isn't strong enough . . .

3 She's thirsty enough . . .

4 She isn't hungry enough . . .

5 The movie was interesting enough . . .

6 The movie wasn't exciting enough . . .

B **On a separate sheet of paper, write ten sentences, using your choice of adjectives from the box. Write five using <u>too</u> and an infinitive and five using <u>enough</u> and an infinitive.**

early	heavy	important	old	young	long
expensive	high	loud	sick	scary	short

Answers will vary, but may include the following:
My sister is too young to vote.
They're too sick to come with us.
This smart phone is too expensive to buy.
It's too early to eat lunch.
The meeting is too important to miss.
The window is too high for us to reach with the ladder.
The volume is not loud enough to hear.
She's not old enough to watch that movie.
That costume is not scary enough to wear on Halloween.
The table is not long enough to seat so many people.

C Correct the errors . . .

Suggested teaching time:	5 minutes	Your actual teaching time:

- Complete the first item with the class.
- Have students compare answers with a partner. Then review with the class.

UNIT 10 *Lesson 2*

Infinitives with *enough*

Suggested teaching time:	5–7 minutes	Your actual teaching time:

- Have students study the presentation and the examples.
- To check comprehension, write the following on the board:

  1. strong   *a. stay home*
  2. tall   *b. reach the shelf*
  3. sick   *c. drive on his / her own*
  4. old   *d. lift that suitcase*

- Ask students to work in pairs and match a numbered adjective with a lettered phrase to write statements using *enough* + an infinitive.
- Ask several pairs to read their answers. Make necessary corrections. (Possible answers: 1. He's not strong enough to lift that suitcase. 2. She's tall enough to reach that shelf. 3. I'm sick enough to stay home. 4. She's not old enough to drive on her own.)
- Draw attention to the *Be careful!* note.
- To check comprehension, write the following on the board:

  1. She's very young. She cannot vote. (young)
  2. He's 21 years old. He can vote. (old)

- Have students combine the sentences using the words in parentheses and *too* or *enough*, as needed. (1. She's too young to vote. 2. He's old enough to vote.)
- Review with the class.

A On a separate sheet of paper, . . .

Suggested teaching time:	3–4 minutes	Your actual teaching time:

- Complete the first item with the class. You may want to write students' ideas on the board; for example, *He's tall enough to be a model. He's tall enough to reach the shelf.*
- Have students compare answers with a partner.
- To review with the class, call on volunteers to read their sentences aloud.

Option: [+3 minutes] To provide more practice, ask students to describe people in their family, friends, or other people they know using *too* or *enough* plus an infinitive; for example, *My sister is beautiful enough to be a model. My brother is too lazy to get a job.*

Answers for Exercise A
Answers will vary, but may include the following:
1. He's tall enough to reach the shelf.
2. He isn't strong enough to lift that box by himself.
3. She's thirsty enough to drink three glasses of water.
4. She isn't hungry enough to eat now.
5. The movie was interesting enough to keep me awake.
6. The movie wasn't exciting enough to see again.

B On a separate sheet of paper, . . .

Suggested teaching time:	5 minutes	Your actual teaching time:

- You may want to have students write the sentences in pairs.
- To review, ask each pair / student to read a sentence. Encourage the class to make necessary corrections.
- You may want to write the correct sentences on the board.

Writing Booster

Note about the Writing Booster

These teaching notes and suggested teaching times are provided if you choose to use the Writing Booster in class.

UNIT 1 Formal e-mail etiquette

Suggested teaching time:	10–15 minutes	Your actual teaching time:	

- Have students read the presentation about e-mails.
- To check comprehension, ask *What is acceptable when communicating with a friend, but unacceptable when writing a business e-mail?* (Making spelling errors, making grammar errors, using emoticons, using abbreviations, writing in informal style.)
- Have students read the *Do's* and *Don'ts* for formal e-mails.
- To check comprehension, write the following on the board:
  1. salutation
  2. sentences
  3. spelling
  4. capital and lowercase letters
  5. punctuation
  6. complimentary close
  7. ending your message
  8. emoticons and abbreviations
  9. dating your e-mail
- Ask students to close their books. Call on volunteers to choose a topic from the board and explain a rule for writing formal e-mails; for example, *If you are on a first-name basis, you can use a person's first name in the salutation.*

FYI: Point out that e-mail can be used as a count noun or a non-count noun; for example, *I sent her an e-mail.* (count) *E-mail is fast and convenient.* (non-count)

A Circle all the formal e-mail . . .

- Have students compare answers with a partner.
- Encourage students to use the information in the box to explain the errors.

Answers for Exercise A
Use "Dear" and "first name" and a colon: "Dear Glenn:"
Don't use abbreviations: "You"
Don't write sentence fragments.
Don't use informal language: "in your office"
Don't use numbers to replace words: "to"
Don't make spelling errors: "discuss"
Use a period at the end of sentences. "I know you love long meetings."
Don't use abbreviations or informal language: "Let me know if you want to change the time."
Use a complimentary close and end with your name.

B Guidance for Writing (page 12)

- After students have written their e-mail messages, have them use the *Do's* and *Don'ts* as a checklist to edit their writing.
- Encourage students to make any necessary corrections.

UNIT 2 Comparisons and contrasts

Suggested teaching time:	20–30 minutes	Your actual teaching time:	

- Have students study the presentation about comparisons.
- To check comprehension, have pairs write a sentence expressing the similarities between two people, cars, restaurants, etc. For example:
  My sister and I are alike in some ways. We both like to sing.
  My sister likes dancing and I like it, too.
- To review, call on pairs to share their sentences with the class.

Writing Booster

The Writing Booster is optional. It is intended to orient students to the elements of good writing. Each unit's Writing Booster is focused both on a skill and its application to the Writing topic from the Review page.

UNIT 1 Formal e-mail etiquette

Social e-mails between friends are informal and have almost no rules. Friends don't mind seeing spelling or grammar errors and use "emoticons" and abbreviations.

Emoticons
☺ = I'm smiling.
☹ = I'm not happy.

Abbreviations
LOL = "Laughing out loud"
LMK = "Let me know"
BTW = "By the way"
IMHO = "In my humble opinion"

However, because e-mail is so fast and convenient, it is commonly used in business communication and between people who have a more formal relationship. When writing a more formal e-mail, it is not acceptable to use the same informal style you would use when communicating with a friend.

For formal e-mails . . .

Do:
- Use title and last name and a colon in the salutation, unless you are already on a first-name basis:
  Dear Mr. Samuelson:
  Dear Dr. Kent:
  If you are on a first-name basis, it's appropriate to address the person with his or her first name:
  Dear Marian:
- Write in complete sentences, not fragments or run-on sentences.
- Check and correct your spelling.
- Use capital and lowercase letters correctly.
- Use correct punctuation.
- Use a complimentary close as in a formal letter, such as:
  Sincerely, Cordially, Thank you, Thanks so much.
- End with your name, even though it's already in the e-mail message bar.

Don't:
- Use emoticons.
- Use abbreviations such as "LOL" or "u" for "you."
- Use all lowercase letters.
- Date the e-mail the way you would a written letter. (The date is already in the headings bar.)

A Circle all the formal e-mail etiquette errors in the following e-mail to a business associate. Then explain your reasons.

See page T141 for answers.

Glenn, it was nice to see u yesterday at the meeting. I was wondering if we could continue the meeting sometime next week. Maybe on Tuesday at your place? There's still a lot we need 2 discus. I know you love long meetings LMK if u wanna change the time.

B Guidance for Writing (page 12) Use the do's and don'ts to check the two e-mail messages you wrote for Exercise D.

UNIT 2 Comparisons and contrasts

COMPARISONS: Use this language to compare two things:

To introduce similarities
- **be alike**
  Herbal medicine and homeopathy **are alike** in some ways.
- **be similar to**
  Homeopathy **is similar to** conventional medicine in some ways.

To provide details
- **both**
  Both herbal medicine and homeopathy are based on plants. / Herbal medicine and homeopathy are **both** based on plants.
- **and . . . too**
  Herbal medicine is based on plants **and** homeopathy is **too**.
- **and . . . (not) either**
  Herbal medicine doesn't use medications **and** homeopathy **doesn't either**.
- **also**
  Many of the medications in conventional medicine **also** come from plants.
- **as well**
  Many of the medications in conventional medicine come from plants **as well**.
- **Likewise,**
  Herbs offer an alternative to conventional medications. **Likewise,** homeopathy offers a different approach.
- **Similarly,**
  Similarly, homeopathy offers a different approach.

CONTRASTS: Use this language to contrast two things:

To introduce differences

- **be different from**
  Conventional medicine **is different from** acupuncture in a number of ways.

To provide details

- **but**
  Herbal medicine treats illness with herbs, **but** acupuncture mainly treats illness with needles.

- **while / whereas**
  Herbal medicine treats illness with herbs **while** (or **whereas**) acupuncture treats illness with needles. OR **While** (or **Whereas**) herbal medicine treats illness with herbs, acupuncture treats illness with needles.

- **unlike**
  Spiritual healing involves taking responsibility for one's own healing, **unlike** conventional medicine. OR **Unlike** conventional medicine, spiritual healing involves taking responsibility for one's own healing.

- **However,**
  Conventional doctors routinely treat heart disease with bypass surgery. **However,** acupuncturists take a different approach.

- **In contrast,**
  Herbal doctors treat illnesses with teas made from plants. **In contrast,** conventional doctors use medicines and surgery.

- **On the other hand,**
  Conventional medicine is based on modern scientific research. **On the other hand,** herbal therapy is based on centuries of common knowledge.

A **On a separate sheet of paper, make comparisons, using the cues in parentheses.** See page T142 for answers.

1 There's nothing scarier than having a toothache while traveling. Feeling short of breath while on the road can be a frightening experience. (likewise)

2 Many painkillers can be bought without a prescription. Many antihistamines can be bought without a prescription. (both)

3 A broken tooth requires a visit to the dentist. A lost filling requires a visit to the dentist. (and . . . too)

4 You may have to wait for the results of an X-ray. The results of a blood test may not be ready for several days. (similarly)

5 An X-ray doesn't take much time to do. A blood test doesn't take much time to do. (and... not / either)

B **On a separate sheet of paper, make contrasts, using the cues in parentheses.** See page T142 for answers.

1 If you feel pain in your back, you can try taking a painkiller. If you have pain in your chest, you should see a doctor. (on the other hand)

2 Homeopathy is fairly common in Europe. It is not as popular in the United States. (while)

3 Spiritual healing uses the mind or religious faith to treat illnesses. Other types of treatments do not. (unlike)

4 Conventional medicine and acupuncture have been used for thousands of years. Homeopathy was only introduced in the late 18th century. (whereas)

5 Many people choose conventional medicine first when they need medical help. About 80% of the world's population uses some form of herbal therapy for their regular health care. (however)

C **Guidance for Writing (page 24)** On a separate sheet of paper, write three statements that show similarities in the two medical treatments you chose to write about in Exercise E and three statements that contrast them. Use the language of comparison and contrast in each statement. Use these statements in your writing.

UNIT 3 *Supporting an opinion with personal examples*

Use these expressions to state your opinions. Follow the punctuation style in the examples.

- **In my opinion,**
  In my opinion, there's nothing wrong with being a procrastinator. People just have different personalities.

- **To me,**
  To me, it's better to be well-organized. Being a procrastinator keeps a person from getting things done.

- **From my point of view,**
  From my point of view, if you aren't well-organized, you're going to have a lot of problems in life.

- **I believe**
  I believe that people who are procrastinators have other strengths such as creativity.

- **I find**
  I find being well-organized helps a person get more done.

> **Note:** All of these expressions can be used either at the beginning of a sentence or at the end. Use a comma before the expression when you use it at the end of a sentence.
> There's nothing wrong with being a procrastinator, **in my opinion**.
> Being well-organized helps a person get more done, **I find**.

- Have students study the presentation about contrasts.
- To check comprehension, have the same pairs write new sentences expressing the differences between the two items they previously discussed. Encourage them to provide details. For example:

  I'm also different from my sister in a number of ways. I like singing and dancing in public, but my sister doesn't. I like to wear dresses and skirts. In contrast, my sister wears jeans and sneakers.

- To review, call on pairs to share their sentences with the class.

FYI: You may want to point out that although it is often heard, it is not correct to say *different than* instead of *different from* since *different* is not a comparative form.

A On a separate sheet of paper, . . .

- Complete the first item with the class.
- Have students compare answers with a partner. Then review with the class.

Answers for Exercise A
1. There's nothing scarier than having a toothache while traveling. Likewise, feeling short of breath while on the road can be a frightening experience.
2. Both painkillers and antihistamines can be bought without a prescription.
3. A broken tooth requires a visit to the dentist and a lost filling does too.
4. You may have to wait for the results of an X-ray. Similarly, the results of a blood test may not be ready for several days.
5. An X-ray doesn't take much time to do and a blood test doesn't either.

B On a separate sheet of paper, . . .

- Complete the first item with the class.
- Have several students write their answers on the board.

Option: [+10 minutes] For further practice of the language of comparisons and contrasts, write the following chart on the board (without the questions):

Food	Getting around	Vacations
How do you like your coffee? Do you like international food?	Do you take the train to work? Do you enjoy driving?	What do you like to do when you are on vacation? What is your favorite destination?

With the class, brainstorm simple interview questions for each topic and write them on the chart. Have pairs of students take turns asking and answering the questions in the chart as well as asking other follow-up questions. Then have students report their findings, using the language of comparisons and contrasts from the presentation on pages 141–142. For example:

Hans doesn't take sugar in his coffee and Joanna doesn't either.

Unlike me, Sheila loves Mexican food.

Samuel enjoys visiting crowded cities. However, Sandra loves going to quiet, isolated places.

Answers for Exercise B
Answers will vary slightly, but may include the following:
1. If you feel pain in your back, you can try taking a painkiller. On the other hand, if you have pain in your chest, you should see a doctor.
2. While homeopathy is fairly common in Europe, it is not as popular in the United States.
3. Unlike other types of treatments, spiritual healing uses the mind or religious faith to treat illnesses.
4. Conventional medicine and acupuncture have been used for thousands of years, whereas homeopathy was only introduced in the late 18th century.
5. Many people choose conventional medicine first when they need medical help. However, about 80% of the world's population uses some form of herbal therapy for their regular health care.

C Guidance for Writing (page 24)

- Draw the following chart on the board:

	Treatment 1: _____	Treatment 2: _____
Similarities	1. 2. 3.	1. 2. 3.
Differences	1. 2. 3.	1. 2. 3.

- Have students copy the chart to write notes about the similarities and differences between the two treatments they chose. Ask them to use the ideas in their charts to write their sentences.
- Walk around the room and provide help as needed.

UNIT 3 *Supporting an opinion . . .*

Suggested teaching time:	20–30 minutes	Your actual teaching time:

- Have students read the expressions and the examples.
- Ask *Which expressions are followed by a comma?* (In my opinion, / To me, / From my point of view.) *Which expressions are followed by a clause?* (I believe / I find.) Point out that *that* can be omitted after both *I believe* and *I find.*
- To provide practice, call on several students to express their opinions about procrastinating; for example, *In my opinion, putting things off is not a problem as long as you get them done in the end. / I believe you can't do a good job if you're not well organized.*
- Draw students' attention to the Note. Explain that a comma is used for all of the expressions when the expression is at the end of the sentence.

- Have students read the personal examples.
- To check comprehension, write the following on the board:

  I leave things for the last minute. For example, . . .
  For instance, . . .
  Whenever . . .
  Every time . . .
  When I . . .

- Have pairs complete the sentences on the board with actions; for example, *paying bills, exercising, writing a report, buying gifts, fixing the car, finishing my homework,* etc. Encourage students to be creative.
- To review, call on a few volunteers to share their sentences with the class.
- Draw attention to the *Be careful!* and the *Remember* note. Tell students to use a period before *For example* and *For instance* and a comma before *such as*.

FYI: It is also permissable to use a semicolon before *for example* and *for instance*. In that case, *for* is not capitalized. However, because many learners tend to overuse semicolons and use them incorrectly, it is recommended that they separate two sentences with a period.

A On a separate sheet of paper, . . .

- Have students answer the questions individually. You may want to encourage them to support their views with an example.
- Have students compare answers with a partner.
- To review with the class, have several students share their answer to each question.

Answers for Exercise A
Answers will vary, but may include the following:
1. From my point of view, children should study the arts in school because it gives them the chance to express themselves freely.
2. In my opinion, extroverts aren't better people than introverts, but they are probably friendlier and more fun to be with.
3. I believe it's OK to wear casual clothes in an office as long as you look clean and neat.

B On a separate sheet of paper, . . .

- Complete the first item with the class. Encourage several students to give examples. You may want to write them on the board; for example, *Every time I start working on a new project, I write a to-do list. For example, I always plan my vacations months ahead.*
- To review with the class, have several students share their examples.

Option: [+5 minutes] For further practice, have students write a sentence describing an aspect of their personality and have them support it with an example. Form pairs and have students share their sentences. To review, call on students to describe their partner, using the information they previously shared. Encourage the use of examples.

Answers for Exercise B
Answers will vary, but may include the following:
1. For example, I always make to-do lists on my calendar.
2. Whenever they have a lot of things to do, they do the easiest things first.
3. When I get a bill, I put it on a shelf, and I often forget about it.
4. I've never had a hard time doing things on time, such as paying bills or calling people on their birthdays.

C Guidance for Writing (page 36)

- Ask students to write a sentence stating their opinion on the topic they chose.
- Encourage them to use different expressions to introduce examples from the presentation on pages 142–143.
- Walk around the room and provide help as needed.
- Encourage students to use all or some of their examples in their writing.

UNIT 4 *Summarizing*

Suggested teaching time:	15–20 minutes	Your actual teaching time:

- Have students read the presentation about how to write a good summary.
- Direct attention to item 1. With the class, choose a story all students know, such as a fairy tale. One by one, ask the basic *Who?, What?, When?, Where?, Why?,* and *How?* questions about the story. Call on volunteers to answer them.
- Direct students' attention to item 2. Call on volunteers to identify the main ideas of the story they discussed in the previous activity. Then ask them to share a few details.
- Finally, direct students' attention to the basic information questions in the note on the right.

A Practice answering basic information . . .

- Have students work in pairs. Have pairs choose a movie they have both seen.
- Ask students to read the questions and then write their own question about the movie.
- Elicit answers to as many questions in the exercise as possible.
- To review with the class, have pairs use the questions as a guide to tell the class about the movie they discussed.

Use personal examples to make your opinions clear and interesting to readers.

- **For example,**
  I'm usually on time in everything I do. **For example,** I always pay my bills on time.
- **For instance,**
  My brother is usually on time in everything he does, but sometimes he isn't. **For instance,** last week he completely forgot to get our mother a birthday gift.
- **…, such as …**
  There are a few things I tend to put off, **such as** paying bills and studying for tests.
- **Whenever**
  Some people have a hard time paying their bills on time. **Whenever** my husband receives a bill, he puts it on the shelf and forgets about it.
- **Every time**
  Every time I forget to pay a bill, I feel terrible.
- **When I was …**
  I had to learn how to be well-organized. **When I was** a child, my parents did everything for me.

> **Be careful!**
> Do not use <u>for example</u> or <u>for instance</u> to combine sentences.
> Don't write: I'm usually on time for everything I do, ~~for example,~~ I always pay my bills on time.

> **Remember:**
> Use a comma before <u>such as</u> when it introduces a dependent clause.

A On a separate sheet of paper, write a sentence expressing your personal opinion in response to each of the following questions.   See page T143 for answers.

1 Do you think children should study the arts in school?

2 Do you think extroverts are better people than introverts?

3 Do you think it's OK to wear casual clothes in an office?

B On a separate sheet of paper, provide a personal example for each of the following statements.
See page T143 for answers.

1 I'm (I'm not) a very well-organized person.

2 Some (None) of the people I know procrastinate.

3 I always (don't always) pay my bills on time.

4 I've always (never) had a hard time doing things on time.

C Guidance for Writing (page 36) On a separate sheet of paper, state your opinion on the topic in Exercise D. Then list at least five personal examples to support your view. Use the examples in your writing.

UNIT 4   *Summarizing*

A good summary provides only the main ideas of a much longer reading, movie, or event. It should not include lots of details. Here are two effective ways to write a summary:

1 **Answer basic information questions:** For a longer reading, one approach to writing a summary is to think about the answers to basic questions of: Who?, What?, When?, Where?, Why?, and How?

2 **Focus on main ideas instead of details:** For a shorter reading, identify the main ideas. Sentences that are main ideas provide enough information to tell the story. After you have identified the sentences that express the main ideas, rewrite them in your own words.

> **Some basic information questions:**
> **Who was the book about?**
> The book I read is about Benito Juárez.
> **Who was Juárez?**
> Juárez was the president of Mexico from 1867 to 1872.
> **Why was he important?**
> He restored the Republic and modernized the country.

A Practice answering basic information questions. Think of a movie you really like. On a separate sheet of paper, write any answers you can to the following questions.

1 Who is the movie about?

2 When does the movie take place?

3 Where does the movie take place?

4 In three to five sentences, what is the movie about?

5 What actors are in the movie? Who is the director?

6 (Add your own information question)

B Practice focusing on main ideas. In the following article, underline any sentences you think are main ideas. Cross out any sentences that you think are details.

Thirty years ago, most people in the United States, Canada, and Europe didn't think about what to wear to work in an office. Men always wore suits and ties. Women wore suits or conservative skirt outfits. But in the 1990's, that started to change.

It began with "casual Fridays." During the summer, some companies invited their employees to "dress down," or wear more casual clothes to work on Fridays. The policy quickly became popular with employees. After this, it didn't take long for employees to start dressing more casually every day of the week.

Many employees welcomed the new dress policy and the more comfortable work environment that came with it. Etiquette had definitely changed, and suits and ties were rarely seen in many offices. Some employees went as far as wearing jeans, T-shirts, and sneakers to the office.

Then some people began to change their minds about casual dress at work. Many managers felt that casual dress had led to casual attitudes toward work. Now the etiquette for dress in many companies is beginning to change back again.

After you have completed Exercise B, read this summary of the article. How does it compare with the sentences you underlined in the article?

Thirty years ago, most people in the United States, Canada, and Europe didn't think about what to wear to work in an office. But in the 1990's, that started to change. During the summer, some companies invited their employees to "dress down," or wear more casual clothes to work on Fridays. Then some people began to change their minds about casual dress at work. Now the etiquette for dress in many companies is beginning to change back again.

C Guidance for Writing (page 48) Answer each question if you can. If you cannot answer a question, answer the next one. Then use your answers to write the summary within your review.

1 What is the title of the reading material you chose?

2 Who is the writer?

3 Who is it about?

4 What is it about?

5 Where does it take place?

6 When does it take place?

7 Why was it written?

8 Why is it important?

9 Did you like it? Why or why not?

10 Would you recommend it to others? Why or why not?

UNIT 5 *Organizing detail statements by order of importance*

One way to organize supporting details within a paragraph is by **order of importance**, usually beginning with the most important and ending with the least important. Or, if you wish, it is possible to reverse the order, beginning with the least important and building to the most important.

Imagine you are writing an essay about how to prepare for a trip. Use words and expressions that indicate the relative importance of details to the reader.

First, [or **First and most important,**] make sure your passport is up-to-date. Nothing can be worse than arriving at the airport and not being able to get on the plane.

Second, [or **Next,** or **Following that,**] check the weather for your destination. This will ensure that you bring the right clothes. It's terrible to arrive somewhere and find out that the weather is unusually cold for this time of year. The last thing you want to do is to have to go shopping!

Last, [or **Finally,**] write a list of important phone numbers and e-mail addresses of people you have to contact. It can be hard to get that information if you are out of your own country.

Following are two ways to construct the paragraph:

1 **Write a topic sentence stating the main idea of the paragraph and then begin describing the details in order of importance.**

The severity of an earthquake is determined by several factors. **First and most important** is the magnitude of the quake. Really strong earthquakes cause lots of damage, even to well-constructed buildings, no matter where or when they occur. Earthquakes with a Richter reading of 9 or over are uniformly catastrophic. **The second most important** factor is location, …etc.

2 **Write a topic sentence that states the details in the order of importance.**

The severity of an earthquake is determined by four factors, in order of importance: magnitude, location, quality of construction, and timing. The magnitude of an earthquake is by far the most significant factor in its destructive power… etc.

B Practice focusing on main ideas. . . .

- Have students read the article for meaning. Ask them to read it again and underline the main ideas.
- Then have students read it a third time to confirm the main ideas they underlined and then cross out any sentences that are really just details.
- Finally, have students read the summary on the right.
- Ask students to work in pairs. Have them compare the main ideas they underlined with the information in the summary.

C Guidance for Writing (page 48)

- Have students answer as many questions as they can. You may want to ask them to answer the questions in note form instead of in complete sentences.
- Move around the room and provide help as needed.
- Have students use their answers to write the summary within their reviews.

UNIT 5   *Organizing detail statements . . .*

Suggested teaching time:	15–20 minutes	Your actual teaching time:

- Have students read the presentation about organizing details by order of importance.
- Point out that we can order details by beginning with the most important one first. Ask *What expressions can we use to introduce the most important detail?* (First, First and most important.) *What expressions can we use to introduce details that come next in importance?* (Second, Next, Following that.) *What expressions can we use to introduce details that are less important than the ones already mentioned?* (Last, Finally.)

- Point out that it is also possible to start with the least important detail and build to the most important.
- Have students read the ways to construct a paragraph in the note on the right.
- Ask *What is a topic sentence?* (A sentence that gives information about the main ideas or details contained in a paragraph.) *What are two ways to construct a paragraph that includes supporting details?* (We can state the main idea in the topic sentence and then explain the details in the sentences that follow. OR We can state the details in order of importance in the topic sentence and then give more information about them.)

A On a separate sheet of paper, . . .

- To help students prepare for the exercise, ask them to recall the expressions they have learned that help organize the importance of details. Write them on the board:

First	*Second*	*Last*
First and most	*Next*	*Finally*
important	*Following that*	

- Ask students to read the paragraph for meaning.

- Have them read it again and insert words from the board into the paragraph.

- Then have students compare answers with a partner. Finally, review with the class.

Option: [+5 minutes] Form small groups. Have students take turns telling their partners about something they know how to do. It can be a simple activity, such as driving a car or making a sandwich. Encourage them to use the words they practiced in this unit; for example, *Driving a car with an automatic transmission is not difficult. First, check that the car is in "park" and start the engine. Next, put your foot on the brake pedal and move the gear shift to "drive." Finally, put your foot on the accelerator and press gently.*

Answers for Exercise A
Answers will vary, but may include the following:
Here are some things not to forget when preparing for an emergency. [First / First and most important,] call your relatives who live in other places, telling them where you are so they don't worry. [Second / Next / Following that,] have a discussion with all family members about the importance of listening to emergency broadcasts. [Last / Finally,] keep a supply of blankets and warm jackets in case of power outages or flooding. Be sure to follow all emergency instructions carefully: your life and the life of your family could depend on it.

B Guidance for Writing (page 60)

- Have students complete the chart individually.

- Place students who have chosen the same or a similar type of emergency in small groups. Ask them to compare their charts and explain their choices.

- Encourage students to use the information in their charts as a guide when writing about how to prepare for an emergency.

UNIT 6 *Dividing an essay into topics*

Suggested teaching time:	20–30 minutes	Your actual teaching time:

- Ask students to look at the pictures in the Oral Review on page 73. Ask *What story do these pictures tell about?* (The lives of Michael and Carlota.)

- Have students read the presentation.

- Have students look at the pictures again. Call on a volunteer to read the headings aloud. (1980. Their parents' plans and dreams for them. / 1990. Their wishes and dreams for themselves. / Now. Their actual choices and regrets.)

- Ask *Why are these headings useful?* (Because they help organize the information in the story.)

- Then ask *In a piece of writing, why are headings useful?* (Because they indicate the topic of each paragraph and they help the reader understand the text.)

A Read the following short biography . . .

- Have students read the biography for meaning.

- Review the example with the class. Ask *Why is <u>Early life</u> an appropriate heading for this paragraph?* (Because it is about Van Gogh's early days—where and when he was born, his childhood, and what he did as he grew up.)

- Have partners discuss the main ideas in each paragraph before writing their own topic headings. Students can write the headings individually or in pairs.

- Review with the class.

B Guidance for Writing (page 72)

- Review the headings in the box.

- Brainstorm other headings with the class. Write them on the board: *My home, My favorite pastimes, My friends, School days, Changes.*

- Ask students to choose suitable headings for their autobiographies and then write notes for each heading they chose. Move around the room and provide help as needed.

- Encourage students to refer to their notes as they write their autobiographies.

A On a separate sheet of paper, rewrite the following paragraph, inserting words to indicate the relative importance of each item. See page T145 for answers.

> Here are some things not to forget when preparing for an emergency. Call your relatives who live in other places, telling them where you are so they don't worry. Have a discussion with all family members about the importance of listening to emergency broadcasts. Keep a supply of blankets and warm jackets in case of power outages or flooding. Be sure to follow all emergency instructions carefully: your life and the life of your family could depend on it.

Type of emergency: _____

Supplies and resources	Notes
non-perishable food:	
bottled water	
batteries	
cell phones	
smart phones	
GPS devices	
medications	
phone numbers	

B Guidance for Writing (page 60) **Look at the list of supplies and resources. Number them in order of their importance for the emergency you chose. Write notes about why each one is important. Use your notes to help you write about how to prepare for your emergency.**

UNIT 6 *Dividing an essay into topics*

Look at the picture in the Oral Review on page 73. The picture tells the story of the lives of Michael and Carlota. It is divided into three topics, each with a date and a topic heading. The headings help the viewer see at a glance how the story will be organized.

Similarly, if a piece of writing contains more than one section or topic, it is sometimes helpful to include **topic headings** each time a new section begins. Each topic heading signals the topic of the paragraph or section in the way a table of contents tells a reader what the sections of a book will be.

A **Read the following short biography of famous Dutch painter Vincent Van Gogh. Write your own topic headings to divide the biography into sections.** Answers will vary, but may include the following:

Early Life

Vincent Van Gogh was born in a small village in Holland on March 30, 1853. He was an introverted child and he didn't have many friends. But his younger brother, Theo, was one of them. As he grew up, Vincent became interested in drawing—and he was very good at it.

Becoming a Painter / Life in Paris

In 1886, Vincent Van Gogh moved to Paris to live with his brother, Theo, who collected and sold paintings. In Paris, he met other artists and was influenced by their work. He also became interested in Japanese art and collected woodblock prints.

Hard Times / Life in Arles

In 1888, he moved to Arles, a town in southern France. The artist Paul Gauguin moved there too, and they became good friends. But they didn't have much money. Van Gogh often became sad and could not paint.

A Sad Ending

After a while, Van Gogh recovered and began to paint again. He sent some paintings to Paris, but he could not sell them. Then, in 1890, early on a Sunday evening, Van Gogh went out to the countryside with his paints. He took out a gun and shot himself in the chest. In his short, sad life, Van Gogh painted 200 paintings. He sold only one of them.

B Guidance for Writing (page 72) **On a separate sheet of paper, write these headings to divide into topics the autobiography you plan to write. Under each heading, write notes of facts that belong in that section. Then refer to those notes as you write your autobiography.**

Some headings:
My parents   My birth   My childhood
My studies   (other)

To describe an event, be sure to provide descriptive details that express the four senses:

sight   The fireworks are like beautiful red and yellow flowers in the sky.
There is a huge parade with thousands of people, and everyone is smiling.

sound   As you walk down the street, you can hear music and people singing.
The fireworks are as loud as thunder, and you have to cover your ears.

smell   You can smell the meat grilling on the street.
Everything smells delicious, and you can't wait to eat!

taste   The pastries are as sweet as honey, and you can't stop eating them.
The dish has the sour taste of lemon.

Try using these patterns in some of your details.

like
This traditional dessert looks **like** a beautiful white cloud.
as ... as
When it is in season, this local fruit is **as sweet as** sugar.
so ... that
The decorations in the street are **so colorful that** you feel like a child seeing them for the first time.

A   **On a separate sheet of paper, write a sentence that expresses one of the four senses for each of the following topics. Try to use** underline{like}, underline{as . . . as}, **and** underline{so . . . that} **in some of your sentences.**

1   Describe a smell in someone's kitchen.

2   Describe a sound in your classroom.

3   Describe the taste of your favorite food.

4   Describe the taste of something you liked as a child.

5   Describe something you see early in the morning.

6   Describe something you hear at a park.

7   Describe something you see at a park.

B   **Guidance for Writing (page 84) On a separate sheet of paper, write the names of the two holidays you chose for Exercise E. Then, under the name of each holiday make a list of sights, sounds, smells, and tastes associated with it. Use these details in your writing.**

When a piece of writing contains several paragraphs, the ideas are often summarized in a paragraph at the end. Including a final **summary statement** reminds the reader of the main ideas that were presented. Read the short essay to the right. Notice the summary statement at the end.

After a problem or a breakdown, many drivers say, "If I had only had a spare tire, I would have been able to fix it and be on my way in a few minutes."

Here are the things responsible drivers should never forget: A flashlight with working batteries can help you repair your car in the dark. A spare tire can save you hours of waiting for help. And remember: you can't change that tire without a jack. If your car breaks down at night, flares can warn oncoming traffic that you are stopped. And if your battery dies, jumper cables can help you start the car again.

No matter how high-tech a car you have, breakdowns can happen at a moment's notice. However, we can plan ahead and be equipped with some simple technology to prevent a problem from becoming worse.

A   **Read the following piece and underline the main ideas. Then write your own summary statement.**

There are a number of excellent presentation graphics technologies available today. Two well-known ones are Microsoft Office's PowerPoint™ and Macintosh's Keynote™. No matter which technology you use, here are some do's and don'ts that will make your presentation more successful.

First, the do's: Keep your slides concise. Keep the amount of text to a minimum because it's hard for the audience to focus on your main points if there's too much text. Use large letters (from 18 to 48 points) and simple, easy-to-read fonts. Use bullets to separate items in a list. Use just a few colors and keep that color scheme consistent throughout the presentation. If your presentation will be in a bright room, light-colored text on dark backgrounds will be easiest to read.

What should a presenter avoid? Don't use all capital letters. They are hard to read. Never use dark letters on a dark background. The presentation will be hard to see. Don't use sound effects that are unrelated to the meaning of your presentation and avoid distracting transitions.

When presenting from a PowerPoint or Keynote presentation, look at your computer screen or handheld notes, not the screen the audience is looking at—to do that you would have to turn away from your audience and you would lose contact with the people you are presenting to.

Your summary statement:

There are a number of do's and don'ts you should consider when preparing a PowerPoint

or Keynote presentation. Bearing them in mind will help you make your presentation more successful.

UNIT 7 Descriptive details

Suggested teaching time:	15–20 minutes	Your actual teaching time:

- Have students read the presentation and study the examples.
- Ask pairs to write an additional example for each of the four senses.
- To review, call on volunteers to read their examples aloud.
- Draw students' attention to the patterns in the box.
- Write the following on the board:
  1. *The clouds / sky / sun looks like ____.*
  2. *The buildings / shops / flowers are as ____ as ____.*
  3. *The people / beaches / streets are so ____ that ____.*
- Have pairs complete each sentence with their own ideas.
- To review, call on volunteers to share their sentences with the class.

A On a separate sheet of paper, . . .

- Complete the first item with the class; have several students share their ideas and write them on the board; for example, *Her kitchen always smells like a freshly-baked apple pie.*
- Have students write their sentences individually or in pairs.
- Review with the class by having students share their sentences.

Option: [+5 minutes] For further practice, have pairs choose one of the pictures on page 74 and write a description of what is happening in the picture. Encourage them to use their imaginations and include descriptive details and some of the patterns they learned in this section. To review, call on volunteers to read their descriptions aloud.

B Guidance for Writing (page 84)

- Remind students to use the patterns they previously learned to express some of the details.
- Encourage students to write as many sentences as they can, and then choose the ones they want to include in their writing. Walk around the room and provide help as needed.

UNIT 8 Summary statements

Suggested teaching time:	15–20 minutes	Your actual teaching time:

- Ask students to read the presentation.
- To check comprehension, ask *Why is it a good idea to include a summary statement at the end of an essay?* (Because it reminds the reader of the main ideas that were presented.)
- Have students read the short essay on the right.
- To check comprehension, ask *What is the essay about?* (How to plan ahead and prepare for a problem with your car.)
- Have students read the summary statement again. Help them become aware that the main idea of the essay is expressed in the summary statement.

A Read the following piece . . .

- Ask students to read the text for meaning.
- Have students read the text again and underline the main ideas.
- Then ask students to compare the sentences they underlined with a partner.
- Review the main ideas with the class.
- Have students write their summary statements individually or in pairs. Then review with the class.

B Guidance for Writing (page 96)

- Ask students to identify the main ideas in their paragraphs. Encourage them to underline one or two sentences in each paragraph.
- Have students use the information they underlined to write their summary statements in a final paragraph.

UNIT 9   *Contrasting ideas*

Suggested teaching time:	20–30 minutes	Your actual teaching time:

- Have students read the presentation.
- To check comprehension, ask *What words can we use to tell the reader that a contrasting idea will follow?* Write them on the board as students say them.

  in contrast
  on the one hand / on the other hand
  however
  nevertheless
  even though

- Clarify any questions students may have about the words.
- Then ask *How can we organize an essay that contrasts ideas?* (We can write the pros in one paragraph and the cons in another paragraph. OR We can write the pros and cons in the same paragraph, using contrasting sentences.)

Option: [+5 minutes] To provide practice of the language used for contrasting ideas, have pairs choose contrasting items from each list (pros and cons) and write sentences using some of the words in the box or their own ideas. For example:

  On the one hand, the government should not interfere in the decisions of adults. But on the other hand, if they don't, people who don't have good judgment may make the wrong decision.

  Some people think that wearing a helmet messes up their hair. In contrast, other people think that a helmet looks cool.

A The following essay . . .

- Have students read aloud the lists of *Pros* and *Cons* to the right of the presentation.
- Then have students read each paragraph for meaning.
- Encourage students to write a summary of about 50 words. You can have students write it individually or in pairs.
- To review with the class, call on volunteers to read their summaries aloud.

B Guidance for Writing (page 108)

- Encourage students to write 4–5 items on each list. Walk around the room and provide help as needed.
- Before students write about the issue they chose, ask them to decide if they will present the pros and cons together using contrasting sentences, or write the pros in one paragraph and the cons in the other.

B Guidance for Writing (page 96) **After you have completed writing about the advantages and disadvantages of your invention, circle the main ideas in each paragraph. Use the main ideas to write a summary statement for your final paragraph.**

The following language helps organize information by contrasting it. It signals to the reader that a contrasting idea will follow.

in contrast
on the one hand / on the other hand
however
nevertheless
even though

A technique to help organize contrasting ideas is to make two lists: **pros** (arguments in favor) and **cons** (arguments against).

To the right are handwritten notes a student made to prepare an essay that presents arguments for and against the mandatory use of a motorcycle helmet. The actual essay can be organized in two ways:

1) as paragraphs in which each of the pros and cons are presented together in contrasting sentences, or
2) as two paragraphs with the ideas in favor in one paragraph and ideas against in another.

Pros
—injuries will be less serious in case of accidents
—lives will be saved
—medical costs will be lower in case of accidents
—people don't have good judgment, so the government has to make decisions for them
—looks cool

Cons
—it limits a person's freedom
—people should drive carefully to prevent most accidents
—if people think they are protected and safe from injury when they use a helmet, they might not drive carefully
—the government shouldn't interfere in the decisions of adults
—messes your hair

A **The following essay is organized into two paragraphs. Read the essay and write the main idea of each paragraph.**

Should motorcycle drivers be required to wear helmets?

Main idea: Some arguments for requiring helmet laws.

Many cities and countries have laws requiring motorcycle drivers to wear a helmet. In some ways these laws are good and effective. For example, it is well known that motorcycle driving is very dangerous. If a motorcycle collides with another vehicle, the driver of the motorcycle has no protection and is often injured or killed. Most fatal injuries are caused by the driver's head hitting the pavement. On the one hand, such injuries are often not survivable. But on the other hand, if a driver is wearing a helmet, the chance of fatal head injury is reduced. Unfortunately, even though drivers know that helmet use could save their lives, many think an accident won't happen to them. However, if there is a law requiring drivers to wear helmets, a lack of judgment won't matter. Drivers will have no choice but to wear the helmet.

Main idea: Some arguments against compulsory helmet-use laws.

Nevertheless, there are arguments against compulsory helmet-use laws. Some people feel that wearing a helmet causes drivers to have a false sense of security. In other words, drivers may feel that when they are wearing a helmet, they don't have to drive carefully. With a helmet, they feel they have a justification for reckless driving. In contrast, other people object to helmet laws because they feel that the government shouldn't interfere with the decisions of adults. They argue that if they get hurt, it's their own responsibility and if they die, it doesn't hurt anyone but themselves. People who have this opinion often complain about government intrusion in personal freedom.

B Guidance for Writing (page 108) **On a separate sheet of paper, write the issue you chose and make a list of pros and cons. Use your notes to organize and write your essay.**

To describe a place, organize details according to spatial relations. Choose a starting point (for example, the capital city or the largest city). Describe its location.

> Lima is the capital of Peru. It is located on the west coast, **on** the Pacific Ocean.
>
> The largest city in China is Shanghai. It is located in the southeast, **along** the South China Sea.

Describe where things are located in relation to that point. Choose a logical order to follow, such as north to south or west to east, so it is easy for the reader to understand.

- **To the [north] of**
  To the north of São Paulo is the city of Campinas.
- **In the [south] of**
  In the south of the island is the city of Kaosiung.
- **[East] of**
  East of Tokyo is the city of Chiba.
- **Next to**
  Next to Washington, D.C. is the city of Baltimore.
- **In the middle / center of**
  In the center of the country is the city of Madrid.

- **Along the [coast / river]**
  Along the coast, and west of the capital, are the cities of Valparaíso and Viña del Mar.
- **At the start of**
  At the start of the Pan-American Highway is the city of Fairbanks, Alaska.
- **At the end of**
  At the end of the Volga River is the Caspian Sea.

A On a separate sheet of paper, write a description for each of these places, using the language above. Use the maps of Guatemala (page 112), Australia (page 113), and Alaska (page 121).

1 Cobán (page 112) **3** Sydney (page 113) **5** Alice Springs (page 113)

2 Denali National Park (page 121) **4** Mexico (page 112) **6** Juneau (page 121)

B Guidance for Writing (page 120) On a separate sheet of paper, draw a simple map of the place you chose in Exercise D. Write numbers on your map for at least two important places, beginning with 1 for the location you will start from, 2 for the next location, and so on. Then, use your map to help you write your descriptions, using the language of spatial relations.

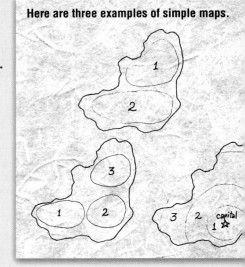

Here are three examples of simple maps.

Suggested teaching time:	20–30 minutes	Your actual teaching time:

- Have students read the presentation and the examples.
- Summarize the ideas in the box by writing the following on the board:

    1. Choose a point: [a city, state, province, etc.]

    2. Describe its location. [It is on the west coast, on the Pacific Ocean.]

    3. Describe other things in relation to that point. [To the southeast of ____ is the city of ____.]

- Use an example from your country to give a description using the patterns on the board.
- Have pairs write their own examples for each item.
- To review, call on volunteers to give descriptions of places using the information they wrote.

A On a separate sheet of paper, . . .

- Ask students to find the places on the maps in Unit 10.
- Complete the first item with the class. Write students' ideas on the board.
- Have students write their sentences individually and then compare them with a partner.
- Review with the class.

Answers for Exercise A
Answers will vary, but may include the following:

1. In the middle of the country is the city of Cobán.
2. To the north of Anchorage is Denali National Park.
3. Along the coast are the cities of Sydney and Canberra.
4. To the north of Guatemala is Mexico.
5. In the center of the country is the city of Alice Springs.
6. East of Glacier Bay National Park is the city of Juneau.

B Guidance for Writing (page 120)

- Point out the examples of the simple maps on the right.
- Have students draw their own maps individually and divide them into sections as they would organize their writing. Encourage students to include as many details as possible such as key cities / towns, lakes, mountains, parks, etc.
- To help students prepare for writing, form pairs and have students take turns describing to their partners the places they chose as they point to the map they have drawn.
- Remind students to use the language of spatial relations.
- Encourage students to use their maps as they write, organizing their ideas by spatial relations.

🎵 Top Notch Pop Lyrics

🔊 It's a Great Day for Love [Unit 1]

Wherever you go,
there are things you should know,
so be aware
of the customs and views—
all the do's and taboos—
of people there.
You were just a stranger in a sea of new faces.
Now we're making small talk on a
first-name basis.

(CHORUS)
It's a great day for love, isn't it?
Aren't you the one I was hoping to find?
It's a great day for love, isn't it?
By the time you said hello,
I had already made up my mind.

Wherever you stay
be sure to obey
the golden rules,
and before you relax,
brush up on the facts
you learned in school.
Try to be polite and always be sure to get
some friendly advice on proper etiquette.

(CHORUS)

And when you smiled at me
and I fell in love,
the sun had just appeared
in the sky above.
You know how much I care, don't you?
And you'll always be there, won't you?

(CHORUS)

1:33/1:34

🔊 X-ray of My Heart   [Unit 2]

Thanks for fitting me in.
This heart is killing me.
Oh, that must hurt.
Are you in a lot of pain?
Yes, I thought I'd better
see someone right away.
It might be an emergency—
could you try to explain?

(CHORUS)
Give me something to keep me
from falling apart.
Doctor, won't you please
take an x-ray of my heart.

You know, I'm here on business,
and today I saw a guy …
Why don't you have a seat
while I do some simple tests?
Thanks. As I was saying,
he walked by without a word.
So that's what's bothering you—
just go home and get some rest!

(CHORUS)
The minute that I saw him
I felt weak in the knees.
Are you dizzy, short of breath?
Does it hurt when you sneeze?
Yes, I have all those symptoms—

and a pain in my chest.
Well, love at first sight
can have painful side effects.
Now, I might not be able
to go to work today.
Could I get a prescription
for some kind of medicine?
Well, let's have a look now.
You might have to heal yourself,
or try another treatment
for the kind of pain you're in.

(CHORUS)

2:17/2:18

🔊 I'll Get Back to You   [Unit 3]

Your camera isn't working right.
It needs a few repairs.
You make me ship it overnight.
Nothing else compares.
You had to lengthen your new skirt,
and now you want to get
someone to wash your fancy shirts
and dry them when they're wet.
Come a little closer—
let me whisper in your ear.
Is my message getting across
to you loud and clear?

(CHORUS)
You're always making plans.
I'll tell you what I'll do:
let me think it over and
I'll get back to you.

You want to get your suit dry-cleaned.
You want to get someone
to shorten your new pair of jeans
and call you when they're done.
I guess I'll have them print a sign
and hang it on your shelf,
with four small words in one big line:
"Just do it yourself."
Let me tell you what this song
is really all about.
I'm getting tired of waiting while you
figure it out.
I've heard all your demands,
but I have a life, too.
Let me think it over and
I'll get back to you.
I'm really reliable,
incredibly fast,
extremely helpful
from first to last.
Let me see what I can do.
Day after day,
everybody knows
I always do what I say.

(CHORUS)

2:31/2:32

🔊 A True Life Story   [Unit 4]

The story of our lives
is a real page-turner,
and we both know
what it's all about.

It's a fast read,
but I'm a slow learner,
and I want to see
how it all turns out.

(CHORUS)
It's a true life story.
I can't put it down.
If you want to know who's in it,
just look around.

The story of our lives
is a real cliffhanger.
It's hard to follow,
but boy, does it pack a thrill—
a rollercoaster ride
of love and anger,
and if you don't write it,
baby, then I will.

(CHORUS)

You can't judge a book by its cover.
I wonder what you're going to discover.
When you read between the lines,
you never know what you might find.
It's not a poem or a romance novel.
It's not a memoir or a self-help book.
If that's what you like, baby, please
don't bother.
If you want the truth, take another look.

(CHORUS)

3:17/3:18

🔊 Lucky to Be Alive   [Unit 5]

(CHORUS)
Thank you for helping me to survive.
I'm really lucky to be alive.

When I was caught in a freezing snowstorm,
you taught me how to stay warm.
When I was running from a landslide
with no place to hide,
you protected me from injury.
Even the world's biggest tsunami
has got nothing on me,
because you can go faster.
You keep me safe from disaster.
You're like some kind of hero—
you're the best friend that I know.

(CHORUS)

When the big flood came with the
pouring rain,
they were saying that a natural
disaster loomed.
You just opened your umbrella.
You were the only fellow who kept calm
and prepared.
You found us shelter.
I never felt like anybody cared
the way that you did when you said,
"I will always be there—
you can bet your life on it."
And when the cyclone turned the day
into night,
you held a flashlight and showed me the safe
way home.

Top Notch Pop Lyrics   **149**

You called for help on your cell phone.
You said you'd never leave me.
You said, "Believe me,
in times of trouble you will never be alone."
They said it wasn't such a bad situation.
It was beyond imagination.
I'm just glad to be alive—
and that is no exaggeration.

(CHORUS)

3:31/3:32
🔊 I Should Have Married Her [Unit 6]

She was born with talents
in both literature and art.
It must have been her love of books
that first captured my heart.
We both had experience
with unhappiness before.
I thought we would be together
for rich or for poor.

(CHORUS)

I should have married her.
She was the love of my life,
but now she's someone else's wife.
I thought we would be happy.
I thought our love was so strong.
I must have got it all wrong.

It's hard to make a living
when you're living in the past.
I wish we could have worked it out,
but some things just don't last.
I wonder what she's doing
or if she thinks of me.
One day she just changed her mind.
The rest is history.

(CHORUS)

It's too late for regrets.
She's gone forever now.
We make our plans,
but people change,
and life goes on somehow.

(CHORUS)

4:18/4:19
🔊 Endless Holiday [Unit 7]

Day after day,
all my thoughts drift away
before they've begun.
I sit in my room
in the darkness and gloom
just waiting for someone
to take me to a tourist town,
with parties in the street and people dancing
to a joyful sound.

(CHORUS)

It's a song that people sing.
It's the laughter that you bring
on an endless holiday.
It's the happiness inside.
It's a roller coaster ride
on an endless holiday.

I try and I try
to work hard, but I
get lost in a daze,
and I think about
how sad life is without
a few good holidays.

I close my eyes, pull down the shade,
and in my imagination I am dancing in a
big parade,
and the music is loud.
I get lost in the crowd
on an endless holiday.
It's a picnic at noon.
It's a trip to the moon
on an endless holiday,
with flags and confetti,
wild costumes and a great big
marching band,
as we wish each other well
in a language we all understand.
The sky above fills with the light
of fireworks exploding, as we dance along
the street tonight.

(CHORUS)

4:34/4:35
🔊 Reinvent the Wheel [Unit 8]

You've got your digi-camera with
the Powershot,
Four mega pixels and a memory slot.
You've got your e-mail and your Internet.
You send me pictures of your digi-pet.
I got the digi-dog and the digi-cat,
the "digi" this and the "digi" that.
I hate to be the one to break the news,
but you're giving me the "digi" blues,

(CHORUS)

And you don't know
the way I really feel.
Why'd you have to go and
reinvent the wheel?

You've got your cordless phone and
your microwave,
and your Reflex Plus for the perfect shave.
It's super special, top of the line,
with the latest new, cutting edge design.
You've got your SLR and your LCD,
your PS2 and your USB.
I've seen the future and it's pretty grim:
they've used up all the acronyms.

(CHORUS)

I keep waiting for a breakthrough innovation:
something to help our poor communication.
Hey, where'd you get all of that high-tech taste?
Your faith in progress is such a waste.
Your life may be state of the art,
but you don't understand the human heart.

(CHORUS)

5:21/5:22
🔊 We Can Agree to Disagree [Unit 9]

I believe that dogs should be
allowed to wander free.
That may be true, but don't you think
that people have rights, too?
I believe that time has come
for true dog liberty.
I see what you mean, but I don't
share your point of view.

(CHORUS)

We can agree to disagree
about what's wrong and right.

It wouldn't be cool for you and me
to fight when we don't see eye to eye.

I think my cat deserves to eat
a treat, no matter what.
Well, on the one hand, yes,
but on the other hand, well, no.
Don't you feel that every meal
should be shared with a pet?
That's one way to look at it,
but I don't think so.

(CHORUS)

You can be a radical.
You can be conservative.
My dog doesn't care, and he won't ask you
to leave.
You can be a moderate.
You can be a liberal.
You can believe what you want to believe.
I urge you to think it over
before you decide.
That your dog is very nice,
I couldn't agree more.
I believe that you and I
should be the best of friends.
That's exactly what I think.
Why weren't we friends before?

(CHORUS)

5:45/5:46
🔊 It's a Beautiful World [Unit 10]

The path is located
half an hour west of here.
I heard it's a must-see,
and that it goes pretty near
to a breathtaking beach
a little farther up the coast.
That's the one that everybody
seems to like the most.

(CHORUS)

It's a beautiful world.
Be careful as you go.
The road is dark and dangerous.
Be sure to take it slow.
Yes, it's a beautiful world,
from the mountains to the seas.
Through life's lonesome valleys,
won't you come with me?

Are you planning on going
to see the waterfall?
I've been thinking about it,
and I want to do it all!
Would you happen to know
anything about Rocky Cave?
How do you get there?
Can you show me the way?

(CHORUS)

I can't wait.
I don't want to miss it.
There isn't a place worth seeing
that I don't want to visit.

(CHORUS)

Top Notch TV
Teaching Notes

For some general guidelines on using the *Top Notch TV* sitcom and interviews, see the Teaching Ideas document in the *Top Notch TV* Activity Worksheets folder on the ActiveTeach Multimedia Disc. **Note:** The Answer Keys provide answers to the Activity Worksheet exercises from the ActiveTeach Multimedia Disc.

UNIT 1

Sitcom: *I'm a little early, aren't I?*

Social language
- Make small talk
- Ask how someone would like to be addressed
- Explain customs

Grammar
- Tag questions

SCENE 1

PREVIEW
- Ask students these questions:
  Have you ever pronounced someone's name incorrectly?
  Do you usually ask people how to pronounce their name if you aren't sure?
  How do you feel when someone mispronounces your name?

REVIEW
- Ask comprehension questions. Play the video episode again if necessary.
  What is Marie doing? (preparing information for Mr. Rashid's group)
  Is she in a rush? (yes)
  What is slowing Marie down? (Mrs. Beatty is talking to her.)
  What is Marie's family name? (LePage)
  Does Mrs. Beatty pronounce it correctly? (no)
  What is Marie's title? (Ms.)
  What does Mrs. Beatty want to call Marie? (Ms. LePage) Why? (She loves the way it sounds.)
  Where is Marie from? (Paris, France)
  When Cheryl comes back, does Marie have the information for her? (no)
  What does Cheryl do to help her? (She takes Mrs. Beatty to Mr. Evans's office.)

EXTENSION
Oral work
- Pair work: role play. Ask *How does Marie feel in this video? (stressed) Does Mrs. Beatty realize this? (no)* Have students role-play Marie and Mrs. Beatty and reenact their exchange in the video episode.
- Discussion. Ask *What does Marie tell Mrs. Beatty she can call her? (by her first name—Marie)* Then ask individual students *What do your friends call you? Your boss? Your colleagues? Your clients, if any?* As a class, make a list on the board of situations when it is appropriate to call people by their title and family names. Then make a list of situations when it is appropriate to call people by their first names.

Written work
- Pair work. Have students work in pairs to summarize the story in the video episode. Write these sentences on the board to help students begin:
  Marie was working very hard on information for Mr. Rashid's group when Mrs. Beatty came into the office. Mrs. Beatty was early for her appointment with Mr. Evans . . .
- Pair work. Have students work in pairs to continue the conversation between Mrs. Beatty and Cheryl for a few more exchanges. Encourage students to use tag questions, especially for Mrs. Beatty's lines. Invite pairs to read their conversations to the class.

VIDEO SCRIPT
Marie is working very hard to finish something, but she is constantly interrupted by Mrs. Beatty.

Cheryl: Marie, can I have that information for Mr. Rashid's group? He'll be here in a few minutes.
Marie: I'm working as fast as I can. *(to Mrs. Beatty)* Mr. Evans will be with you very soon.
Mrs. Beatty: That's fine. I'm a little early, **aren't I**?
Marie: Just a few minutes.
Mrs. Beatty: Is your last name pronounced "Le-PAIGE"?
Marie: It's "Le-PAHGE," actually.
Mrs. Beatty: Oh, that's beautiful.
Marie: Thank you.
Mrs. Beatty: Now, is it Ms. LePage or Mrs. LePage?
Marie: Um, it's Ms., but you can call me by my first name.
Mrs. Beatty: Do you mind if I call you Ms. LePage? I love the way it sounds.
Marie: That's fine.
Mrs. Beatty: I'm keeping you from your work, **aren't I**?

Marie: I'm sorry. I'd love to talk, but I really have to get this done right away.

Mrs. Beatty: I understand. You're not from here, **are you**?

Marie: Excuse me?

Mrs. Beatty: Your accent. You come from France, **don't you**?

Marie: Yes. Paris, actually.

Mrs. Beatty: That's nice. It sure is a beautiful day, **isn't it**?

Marie: Mmm-hmm.

Cheryl: Can I have that information?

Marie: I'm not quite done.

Cheryl: What's taking so long? *(to Mrs. Beatty)* Mrs. Beatty, I can take you to Mr. Evans's office. He'll be here shortly.

Mrs. Beatty: Why, thank you. Beautiful day, **isn't it**?

Cheryl: Yes, it is.

ANSWER KEY

A. 1. c 2. b 3. c 4. a 5. b 6. a

B. 1. You're not from here 2. You come from France 3. It sure is a beautiful day

C. *Following are the expected answers. Students may produce variations that are also correct.*
1. information for Mr. Rashid's group 2. Mrs. Beatty is talking to her 3. Mr. Evans's office

SCENE 2

PREVIEW

- Tell students to imagine they are traveling to a country they have never been to. Ask *What can you do to learn about the etiquette of the country?* (for example, *talk to a person from the country or someone who has been to the country; read books; look up information on the Internet*)

REVIEW

- Ask comprehension questions. Play the video episode again if necessary.
  Who has traveled to India many times? (Mr. Rashid)
  Why does Paul need to learn Indian etiquette? (because a tourist group from India is coming next week)
  How does Paul greet Mr. Rashid? (with a handshake)
  Is this OK in Indian culture? (no) Why not? (It can be insulting, especially for women, since men and women generally do not touch.)
  In Indian culture, what does waving one's hand mean? (It means "Go away.")
  How should Paul greet the tourists from India? (He should fold his hands and say "Namaste.")
  Is pointing with one's finger OK? (no) Why not? (It's considered impolite.)

What should Paul point with? (his chin)
Does Mr. Rashid say Paul is doing well learning the etiquette? (yes)

EXTENSION

Oral work

- Pair work: role play. Play the video with the sound off. Have students look at Paul's and Mr. Rashid's body language and identify what they are talking about. Then have students work in pairs to role-play Paul and Mr. Rashid in this episode.

- Discussion. Have students name the various things Paul learns from Mr. Rashid and write them on the board. Ask these questions:
  Are any of the gestures Paul uses considered impolite in your culture?
  What gestures are considered impolite in your culture?
  Have you ever seen a tourist in your country use a gesture that was impolite?
  Do you think it is important to learn the etiquette of a country before traveling there?

Written work

- Pair work. Pair students. Tell pairs that they will write information about etiquette in India for a travel website. Have them make a list of do's and don'ts using what they have learned from the video episode.

- Pair work. Have students work in pairs to write a thank-you letter for Paul to thank Mr. Rashid for what he has taught him.

LANGUAGE AND CULTURE NOTE: The *Namaste* is a gesture and bow used when greeting or parting with someone. It is also an expression of respect. The word *Namaste* in Sanskrit means *bowing to you.*

VIDEO SCRIPT

Mr. Rashid teaches Paul how to greet people from India.

Mr. Evans: Paul, we have our first group from India coming next week. Since Mr. Rashid has traveled to India many times, I've asked him to talk to you about etiquette in India. Mr. Rashid?

Mr. Rashid: Paul, why don't you greet me as if I were an Indian tourist? Ask me to come with you and show me to the tour bus.

Paul: OK. Hi, there! I'm Paul.

Mr. Rashid: If I were an Indian woman, you would have just insulted me. Women and men generally do not touch.

Paul: OK. Uh, hi, there.

Mr. Rashid: You just told me to go away.

Paul: Oh, I'm sorry.

Mr. Rashid: Oh, too close. You should stand this far away from someone. Instead of shaking hands, do this and say "Namaste."

Paul: Namaste.

Mr. Rashid: Excellent. Now tell me to come with you to the tour bus.

Paul: OK. Come with me.

Mr. Rashid: This is a rude gesture in India. Do it like this.

Paul: Come with me.

Mr. Rashid: Good.

Paul: . . . to the bus over there. I know. I've just insulted you.

Mr. Rashid: Pointing with your fingers is considered impolite. Use your chin instead.

Paul: . . . to the bus over there. I'm never going to get this.

Mr. Rashid: You're doing wonderfully.

Paul: Oh, thank you, Mr. Rashid.

Mr. Rashid: Oh, too close.

Top Notch Pop and Karaoke: *It's a Great Day for Love*

UNIT 2

Sitcom: *Are you OK?*

Social language
- Describe symptoms
- Show concern

Grammar
- Modals *may, might, must*
- *Be able to*

SCENE 1

PREVIEW

- On the board, write *Laughter is the best medicine.* Ask students *Have you ever heard this saying in English before? Do you think laughter can be the best medicine? In what situations?*

REVIEW

- Ask comprehension questions. Play the video episode again if necessary.
  What is wrong with Paul? (He is sick; he feels awful.)
  What does Marie suggest? (He may have to go see a doctor.)
  Does Paul like doctors? (no)
  What does Bob suggest Paul is allergic to? (work)
  What does Bob say he used to want to be? (a doctor)
  Who is meeting with Mr. Evans in the café? (Dr. Anderson)
  Why does Cheryl want to ask Dr. Anderson to come up? (to take a look at Paul)
  What does Bob say is the best medicine? (laughter)
  Does Paul agree? (No. He says it hurts.)

EXTENSION

Oral work

- Group work: role play. Play the video episode with the sound off. Have students look at Paul's body language and identify the ailments and symptoms he is talking about. Then have them focus on the nonconventional medicine Bob jokingly suggests to Paul. Call on volunteers to role-play the episode.

- Discussion. Create a list on the board of the ailments and symptoms Paul has. *(He has a cold; he is sneezing; his back hurts; he has pain in his hip; his neck is bothering him; he has a stomachache.)* Ask individual students *What suggestion would you give Paul? Do you ever try nonconventional medical treatments?*

Written work

- Ask students to name the different nonconventional medical treatments Bob recommends to Paul and write them on the board *(acupuncture, an herbal remedy, spiritual healing).* Then have students write a paragraph stating what would be best for Paul.

- Have students write a list of questions that a doctor might ask Paul to find out what is causing his symptoms.

LANGUAGE NOTE: *My back is killing me* means *My back hurts very much.*

VIDEO SCRIPT

Paul is not feeling well, and Cheryl, Marie, and Bob try to give him suggestions.

Cheryl: Let's get Ms. Novak's tickets ready. She **may be** stopping by this afternoon.

Marie: Paul, are you OK?

Paul: No. I feel awful.

Cheryl: What's wrong?

Paul: I've got this horrible cold. I'm sneezing, and my back is killing me. I've got this pain in my hip. My neck has been bothering me all day. And I have a stomachache.

Marie: You **may have to go** see a doctor.

Paul: No! I hate doctors.

Cheryl: I wonder what could be wrong?

Bob: Maybe he's allergic to work.

Paul: I'm not kidding here. I'm in pain.

Bob: I used to want to be a doctor, you know. Say "Ahhh."

Paul: Ahhh-choo!

Bob: Now I remember why I didn't become a doctor.

Cheryl: Paul, you really **must get** some medical help.

Bob: A little acupuncture **might help** you feel better.

Paul: Stay away from me.

Cheryl: Dr. Anderson is meeting Mr. Evans downstairs in the café. Should we ask her to come up? She **may be able to help**.

Marie: Great idea. I'll go get her.

Bob: You **might prefer** an herbal remedy.

Paul: Stop it.

Cheryl: How long have you been feeling this way?

Paul: I got the cold last night, and the pain in my back started this morning.

Bob: Want to try a little spiritual healing?

Paul: You're making me laugh.

Bob: Laughter is the best medicine, you know.

Paul: But it hurts!

ANSWER KEY

A. 1. awful 2. see a doctor 3. work 4. the café 5. Dr. Anderson 6. nonconventional 7. last night 8. this morning

B. 1. cold 2. sneezing 3. back 4. hip 5. neck 6. stomachache

C. 1. acupuncture 2. herbal remedy 3. spiritual healing

SCENE 2

PREVIEW

• Ask *If you have a cold, should you stay home? Do you take medications when you have a cold? If yes, which ones?* Write a list of cold medications on the board.

REVIEW

• Ask comprehension questions. Play the video episode again if necessary.

> *Where does Dr. Anderson examine Paul? (in the Top Notch Travel office)*
> *Does Paul have a cold? (yes)*
> *Has Paul taken any medications lately? (yes) Which ones? (pain killer, cold tablets, nasal spray, cough medicine, vitamins, antacid, decongestant)*
> *What does Dr. Anderson say about the medicine? (Paul has taken too much medicine in one day.)*

> *Has Paul spent time with (or been with) someone who is sick? (yes—his friend Don)*
> *How long has Don had a cold? (all week)*
> *What did Paul do with Don yesterday? (lifted weights and ran)*
> *Does Paul usually exercise this much? (no, he just started this exercise routine yesterday)*
> *So why is Paul in a lot of pain? Is it because of his cold? (No. Paul is in a lot of pain because he exercised too much.)*

EXTENSION

Oral work

• Discussion. Have students recall the list of medications Paul has taken. Write them on the board (*pain killer, cold tablets, nasal spray, cough medicine, vitamins, antacid, decongestant*). Ask students these questions:

> *For which symptoms do you think Paul took the different medications?*
> *Which of these medications do you take when you are sick?*
> *Have you ever taken too many different medications as Paul did? How did you feel?*

• Pair work. Ask students *What advice do you think Dr. Anderson will give Paul?* Have students work in pairs to continue the conversation between Dr. Anderson and Paul for a few more exchanges. Invite students to perform their scenarios for the class.

Written work

• Tell students to imagine they are Dr. Anderson. Tell them to write up a report of her examination of Paul.

• Pair work. Pair students. Tell students they will create True and False quizzes. Have each pair write true and false statements about the video episode. Then combine pairs into groups of four and have them exchange quizzes and answer them. Finally, have the writers of each quiz check the answers.

VIDEO SCRIPT

Dr. Anderson comes to examine Paul.

Dr. Anderson: Say "Ahhh."

Bob: Cover your face, doc.

Paul: Ahhh.

Dr. Anderson: Well, you have a cold, that's for sure.

Cheryl: What about the other stuff? The pain in the back and the side . . . ?

Dr. Anderson: Have you taken any medications lately?

Paul: Just some over-the-counter stuff—pain killer, cold tablets, nasal spray.

Dr. Anderson: That sounds OK.

Paul: And some cough medicine, vitamins, antacid.

Dr. Anderson: That's a lot of medicine.

Paul: And some decongestant.

Dr. Anderson: That's too much medicine in one day.

Marie: That **must be** why you're feeling so bad.

Dr. Anderson: Have you been around anyone else who's sick?

Paul: My friend Don has had a cold all week. We lifted weights last night for about an hour and ran five miles. He had to walk the last mile.

Dr. Anderson: Is that your usual exercise routine?

Paul: Yep. I started it yesterday.

Dr. Anderson: Well, that explains it. You exercised too much.

Paul: That's all?

Dr. Anderson: That's all.

Bob: A little chiropractic treatment **might help** you.

Paul: Stay away from me.

ANSWER KEY

A. 1. False 2. False 3. True 4. True 5. False
   6. True 7. False
B. 1. pain killer 2. cold tablets 3. nasal spray
   4. cough medicine 5. vitamins 6. antacid
   7. decongestant
C. *Following are the expected answers. Students may produce variations that are also correct.*
   1. He took too much medication 2. He got a cold from his friend Don 3. He exercised too much

Interview: *Are you traditional in your medical ideas?*

PREVIEW

- On the board, create two columns titled *Traditional medicine* and *Nontraditional medicine*. Ask students to give examples for each category. Take a poll of which type of medicine students use more.

REVIEW

- Ask comprehension questions. Play the video segment again if necessary.
   Does Joe use nontraditional medical treatments often? (no)
   Does he think they could be good? (yes)
   Does James use nontraditional medical treatments? (no)

What types of medicines does Vanessa prefer? (natural herbal medicines)

Is James comfortable with Western medicine and surgery? (yes) Why? (because of the research and proven facts behind it)

What does Joe think are disadvantages of Western medicine? (It sometimes makes a problem worse instead of better.)

Does Lisa use any nontraditional therapies? (yes) What kind? (She drinks a lot of tea.)

What does Vanessa do when she feels like she is coming down with something? (She takes an herbal medicine and drinks orange juice for the vitamin C.)

What does Vanessa do when she actually feels really sick? (She takes cough medicine.)

EXTENSION

Oral work

- Pair work: role play. Have students work in pairs to choose one of the interviewees and role-play the short conversation between the interviewer and the interviewee.

- Discussion. On the board, write the first interview question: *Are you traditional in your medical ideas?* Have students discuss the interviewees' answers and say who they are most like. Tell students to give examples of their preferences.

Written work

- Ask *Do you agree with Joe's statement that Western medicine can make a problem worse instead of making it better?* Have students write a paragraph explaining their point of view.

- On the board, write *What are the advantages of traditional Western medicine and surgery?* Have students write a paragraph answering this question. Tell them to say whether they agree with James's comment.

LANGUAGE NOTES: Joe says that *there's probably a lot of merit* in nontraditional treatments. This means there is probably a lot of value to them.

To come down with something means to get sick.

VIDEO SCRIPT

Interviewer: Are you traditional in your medical ideas? That is, do you kind of believe in Western medicine, or do you like to explore nontraditional treatments, such as acupuncture or homeopathic medicine?

Joe: I don't explore nontraditional treatments as much as I would probably like to. I think there's probably a lot of merit in them, and they haven't been studied enough.

James: I'm more traditional than anything else in my medication, in my medical practices.

Vanessa: I'm more for the naturalistic approach. I like, you know, more natural herbal medicines.

Interviewer: In your opinion, what are the advantages of traditional Western medicine and surgery?

James: I think the enormous amount of research and . . . and . . . proven fact that's behind our medicine just makes it . . . makes me feel more comfortable with it.

Interviewer: What do you see as maybe some disadvantages of Western medicine?

Joe: I think at times Western medicine can make the problem worse than trying to make the problems better.

Interviewer: Are there any nontraditional therapies that you use?

Lisa: I drink a lot of tea actually, so I guess that's pretty nontraditional.

Vanessa: Usually when I feel myself coming down with something, I will take an echinacea, which is an herbal medicine. I'll probably drink a lot of orange juice because vitamin C helps you. But if I feel really sick, then I'll take cough medicine.

ANSWER KEY

A. 1. b 2. c 3. a

B. takes an herbal medicine, drinks a lot of orange juice

C. *Following are the expected answers. Students may produce variations that are also correct.*
   1. *advantages:* There's an enormous amount of research and proven fact behind Western medicine. 2. *disadvantages:* At times Western medicine can make a problem worse, instead of making it better.

 Top Notch Pop and Karaoke:
X-ray of My Heart

UNIT 3

Sitcom: *I need to get a package to Australia a.s.a.p.!*

Social language

- Request express service
- Recommend a service provider
- Plan a social event

Grammar

- Causatives

SCENE 1

PREVIEW

- Ask students *Have you ever been in an emergency situation where you needed express service? What was the situation? What was the express service?*

REVIEW

- Ask comprehension questions. Play the video episode again if necessary.
  Who made the mistake with the travel documents? (Mr. Evans)
  What did he do? (He was supposed to give them to Mr. Wells, but he gave them to Mr. Rashid by mistake.)
  When does Mr. Wells need the documents? (the day after tomorrow)
  Why does he need them? (His group is flying in on Thursday.)
  What does Marie say she will do? (She will call the courier.)
  What will Paul do? (He will reprint the tour information.)
  Will Paul also print the travel guides? (no) Why not? (because he can't print twenty-five copies that fast)
  Where will they have the travel guides printed? (at Harper's)
  Why won't they have the travel guides printed at Copies To Go? (because Harper's is faster and much more reliable)
  What will Bob do? (He will reprint the tickets.)
  Who is Mr. Evans calling? (his tailor) Why? (because his sleeves are too long)

EXTENSION

Oral work

- Discussion. Ask students these questions:
  Do you think Mr. Evans has a good staff?
  Do they handle the problem well?
  Which workers are more active?
  Which are less active?
  Which of the workers are you most like? Why?

- Group work: role play. Divide the class into groups of four. Tell students to imagine that Marie, Cheryl, Paul, and Bob are having dinner after their hectic afternoon getting the package of travel documents out. Have students role-play the four friends to talk about what happened. To help students begin, write on the board:
  Cheryl: Can you believe that Mr. Evans was calling his tailor during the meeting?

Written work

- Pair work. Have students work in pairs to summarize the story in the video episode. Write this sentence on the board to help them begin:
  Mr. Evans had a meeting with his staff this afternoon . . .

- Pair work. Pair students. Have students focus on Mr. Rashid. Tell them to imagine that he arrives in Lebanon and opens the big white envelope Mr. Evans gave him. He calls Mr. Evans to tell him about the mistake. Write these lines to help students begin. Have them continue for a few more exchanges.

 Mr. Rashid: Hello, Mr. Evans? This is Mr. Rashid.
 Mr. Evans: Hello! How are you? I was expecting your call, actually.

VIDEO SCRIPT

Mr. Evans misplaced some travel documents, and the staff scrambles to reproduce the documents and have them sent to the right client.

Mr. Evans: Now, about the travel documents for the Australian group. We**'ve had** everything **mailed** to them, right?

Cheryl: Mr. Evans, we gave you the package of travel documents to give to Mr. Wells the other night at dinner, before he flew home to Sydney.

Mr. Evans: A white envelope about this big?

Cheryl: Yes.

Mr. Evans: I gave it to Mr. Rashid before he left for Lebanon.

Cheryl: Oh, Mr. Wells needs those documents the day after tomorrow! His group is flying in on Thursday.

Marie: I'll call the courier. If they can pick up a package by 5:00 P.M., we should be OK.

Paul: That gives us an hour. I'll reprint the tour information, but what about the travel guides? I can't print twenty-five copies that fast.

Cheryl: I'll call Copies To Go and **have** them **reprint** the travel guides.

Marie: They can't do a rush job. Call Harper's instead. They're faster and much more reliable. *(on the phone)* Hello, National Express? I need to get a package to Australia a.s.a.p.!

Paul: If Harper's can't make the color copies that fast, we'll take black and white.

Cheryl: Bob, are you reprinting the tickets?

Bob: Yep.

Cheryl: *(on the phone)* Hello. I need to **get** twenty-five color documents **printed** right away.

Mr. Evans: *(on the phone)* Yes, it's very much a hurry.

Cheryl: Who are you calling, Mr. Evans?

Mr. Evans: What's that? Oh, uh . . . my tailor.

Cheryl: Your tailor?

Mr. Evans: These sleeves are too long, and they're driving me crazy.

ANSWER KEY

A. 1. c 2. c 3. c 4. b 5. a 6. b
B. 1. Marie 2. Cheryl 3. Paul 4. Bob

C. *Following are the expected answers. Students may produce variations that are also correct.*
1. have the package picked up / have them pick up the package 2. have the travel guides reprinted / have them reprint the travel guides 3. they're faster and much more reliable 4. his tailor, his sleeves are too long

LANGUAGE NOTE: *a.s.a.p.* means <u>a</u>s <u>s</u>oon <u>a</u>s <u>p</u>ossible.

SCENE 2

PREVIEW

- Ask individual students *Imagine you have to organize a party or dinner for your company. Which is better? To do everything yourself, or to ask for help? Why?*

REVIEW

- Ask comprehension questions. Play the video episode again if necessary.
 Who is the party next week for? (Mr. Wells's group)
 Who has Mr. Evans asked to organize a party? (Cheryl)
 What does Cheryl ask Marie to do? (choose a restaurant)
 What does Cheryl ask Bob to do? (choose the menu)
 What does Cheryl ask Paul to do? (plan the music)
 Is it difficult for Marie to choose a restaurant? (no) Why not? (She only has to choose between two restaurants.)
 What is the name of the restaurant she chooses? (The Green Room)
 What does Bob want on the menu? (steak and potatoes)
 What does the client want? (fish or chicken)
 Which does Bob choose? (chicken)
 Is it difficult for Paul to plan the music? (no) Why not? (Cheryl already has a list of music choices.)
 Is Paul happy? (no) Why not? (because he does not have much to do)
 Does Mr. Evans think Cheryl did a good job? (yes)

EXTENSION
Oral work

- Discussion. Ask students *Is anyone here like Cheryl when it comes to organizing? If you were Marie, Bob, or Paul, would you mind Cheryl doing all the work?*
- Group work: role play. Divide the class into groups of four. Have students role-play Cheryl, Marie, Bob, and Paul and reenact the meeting in the video episode. Encourage students role-playing Marie, Bob, and Paul to use their facial expressions to convey the characters' feelings.

Written work

- Have students write Cheryl's to-do list after Mr. Evans asked her to plan the party. Tell students to use information from the video episode. For example, *Call Mr. Wells and ask for food preference. Call restaurants for prices for a party room.*
- Pair work. Tell students their boss has asked them to plan a party. Have students work individually to create a list of restaurants, a choice of menus, and a selection of music. Then have students exchange papers with a partner and select a restaurant, a menu, and music for the party.

VIDEO SCRIPT

Bob, Paul, and Marie help Cheryl plan a party for a client.

Mr. Evans: Thank you, everyone, for fixing my mistake with Mr. Wells. Now. I've asked Cheryl to plan a party for his group next Friday. I'd like for everyone to help. Cheryl, do you have a plan?

Cheryl: Yes, I do. Marie, I'd like to **have** you **choose** a restaurant for the party.

Marie: I'd love to!

Cheryl: Bob, I'll let you choose the menu.

Bob: You will?

Cheryl: Paul, could you plan the music?

Paul: Yes!

Cheryl: Good. Now, Marie, I called ten restaurants and **had** them **give** us a price for a party room. These two had the best prices.

Marie: The Green Room is a nice restaurant.

Cheryl: Great! That's my favorite, too. Now, Bob, about the food . . .

Bob: I was thinking steak and potatoes and . . .

Cheryl: Well, the client asked for fish or chicken. So I **had** the restaurant **put** together a menu with each. Which do you like better?

Bob: I like chicken more than fish, I guess.

Cheryl: Great! Chicken it is. Now Paul . . .

Paul: Let me guess. You have a list of music choices.

Cheryl: Yes!

Paul: These look fine.

Cheryl: Great! I think we're all done.

Mr. Evans: You see how easy it is to plan something when we do it all together?

Marie: So glad we could help.

ANSWER KEY

A. 1. True 2. True 3. False 4. False 5. True
B. 1. c 2. a 3. c 4. c 5. b 6. a 7. b
C. 1. choose a restaurant for the party 2. choose the menu 3. plan the music

---

 Top Notch Pop and Karaoke: *I'll Get Back to You*

UNIT 4

Sitcom: *May I ask you what you're reading?*

Social language
- Agree to lend something
- Describe reading material

Grammar
- Noun clauses

SCENE 1

PREVIEW

- Ask students these questions:
  Are comic books popular in your country?
  Do you read comic books?
  With what age group are comics most popular?

REVIEW

- Ask comprehension questions. Play the video episode again if necessary.
  Is Bob eating alone? (No. Paul and Marie went to get newspapers.)
  What does Bob say he is reading? (A History of the World)
  Why is Mr. Evans surprised? (because Bob is reading nonfiction over lunch; he heard that it's a very difficult book)
  Does Bob agree that it's a very difficult book? (No. He says it's a pretty easy read.)
  What kind of books does Mr. Evans usually prefer? (fiction—thrillers, mysteries, and science fiction)
  Why is Bob surprised? (because Mr. Evans also reads science fiction)
  Does Bob say he is learning a lot from his book? (yes)
  What does he say he is reading about? (Great Britain)
  What happens when Mr. Evans looks at the book? (He sees that Bob is actually reading a comic book.)
  What does Mr. Evans want to borrow from Bob? (A History of the World)
  What does Bob think Mr. Evans wants to borrow? (the comic book he's reading)

EXTENSION

Oral work

- Pair work: discussion. Write on the board *I usually prefer _____ myself. You know, _____, _____ . . . There's nothing like curling up with a good _____, is there?* Ask students to fill in the blanks with words

Mr. Evans says. (*I usually prefer <u>fiction</u> myself. You know, <u>thrillers</u>, <u>mysteries</u> . . . There's nothing like curling up with a good <u>science fiction novel</u>, is there?*) Then have students work in pairs to read the sentence with their own preferences and discuss.

- Pair work: role play. Tell students to imagine that Cheryl comes into the restaurant and catches Bob reading his comic book. Have students work in pairs to role-play a conversation between Bob and Cheryl.

Written work

- Ask *Why do you think Bob is surprised that Mr. Evans reads science fiction? Why do you think Mr. Evans tells him not to tell anyone?* Have students write a paragraph to explain Bob's and Mr. Evans's reactions and their own opinion of science fiction.

- Have students summarize the story in the video episode. Write these sentences on the board to help them begin: *Mr. Evans joins Bob for lunch. Bob is reading a book . . .*

LANGUAGE NOTE: Bob says, "Cheryl hates when I read comics." The more grammatically accurate expression should be "Cheryl hates *it* when I read comics." The word *it* is dropped because it's casual speech.

VIDEO SCRIPT

Bob is reading a book and eating lunch in the café when Mr. Evans enters to join him.

Mr. Evans: Hello, Bob. Dining alone?
Bob: Paul and Marie went to get newspapers.
Mr. Evans: Do you mind **if I join you**?
Bob: Please, sit down.
Mr. Evans: May I ask **what you're reading**?
Bob: Um . . . *A History of the World.*
Mr. Evans: The bestseller? I'm very impressed! Reading nonfiction over lunch! I hear **that it's a very difficult book**.
Bob: Oh . . . uh, no. It's a pretty easy read. I . . . I can't put it down, actually.
Mr. Evans: A real page-turner, huh? Do you think **I could borrow it** when you're done?
Bob: Sure.
Mr. Evans: I usually prefer fiction myself. You know, thrillers, mysteries . . . There's nothing like curling up with a good science-fiction novel, is there?
Bob: You read science fiction, too?
Mr. Evans: Don't tell anyone. Are you learning a lot from your book?
Bob: Uh, yes. I think so.
Mr. Evans: So tell me **what you're reading about right now**.
Bob: Um . . . this part is about Great Britain.

Mr. Evans: Really? Do you mind **if I take a look**?
Bob: Cheryl hates when I read comics.
Mr. Evans: Then I can understand **why you can't put the book down**. Do you think **that I could borrow it**, then?
Bob: I'm still reading this one, but I have another one I can loan you.
Mr. Evans: I meant this one.
Bob: Oh, help yourself.

ANSWER KEY

A. 1. False 2. True 3. False 4. True 5. True
   6. False
B. 1. b 2. b 3. a 4. b
C. 1. what you're reading about right now 2. if I take a look 3. why you can't put the book down 4. that I could borrow it

---

SCENE 2

PREVIEW

- Ask students *Do you read newspapers? If yes, what kind? Can you believe everything you read in them?*

REVIEW

- Ask comprehension questions. Play the video episode again if necessary.
    What is the first story Paul mentions from his paper? (A tornado carried a woman 300 miles and she lived to tell about it.)
    What does Marie ask Paul? (if he knows that the story is not true)
    How does he reply? (He says that it's in the paper, so it must be true.)
    What does Marie say Paul should read for real news? (the paper she is reading)
    What does Paul say about her paper? (that it's boring)
    What does Marie say about the headlines in Paul's paper? (that they are offensive)
    What does Paul say about the headlines in Marie's paper? (that they are offensive)
    Do Bob and Mr. Evans say what paper they read? (no) Why not? (They don't want to be part of Paul and Marie's argument.)

EXTENSION
Oral work

- Discussion. Ask *Would you read newspapers similar to the newspaper Paul reads? Why or why not?* Have students express and discuss their opinions.

- Pair work: role play. Have students work in pairs to role-play Marie and Paul and reenact what happened in the video episode. Encourage students to make up their own headlines.

Written work

- Pair work. Ask students to imagine that Mr. Evans and Bob actually responded to Marie's question about the type of newspapers they read. Have students work in pairs to write a conversation. Write this line on the board to help students begin:

  Mr. Evans: Well, I agree with . . .

- Pair work. Have students recall all the newspaper headlines from the video episode and write them on the board. Then have students work in pairs to choose one headline and write a newspaper story for it.

CULTURE NOTE: The newspaper Paul reads is a tabloid paper, which is designed to entertain and to report sensational stories that are often not true.

VIDEO SCRIPT

Over lunch in the café, Paul and Marie argue about newspapers.

Paul: Look at this. The paper says **that a tornado carried a woman for 300 miles**, and she lived to tell about it.

Marie: I'm not sure **if you know this**, but that story isn't true.

Paul: It's in the paper. It must be true.

Marie: That paper is trash. I can't believe **you're reading it**.

Paul: What do you mean?

Marie: It's fiction, not news. Nothing in there is true. If you want real news, you have to read this paper.

Paul: That paper is boring. This one's much more interesting.

Marie: "Woman Gives Birth to Cow!" "Man Builds House from Bread!" "Baby with Two Heads!" Come on. This is offensive.

Paul: "Storm Kills 100 in Texas." "Train Accident Kills Five, Injures More." "Man Kills Wife and Son." I'm sorry, but all that death and destruction is pretty offensive to me.

Marie: I know **that these things happened**. And I know **that those didn't**.

Paul: You don't know that. You just assume **that it's true**.

Marie: Let's ask Bob and Mr. Evans **what paper they read**. Never mind. Let's just read.

Paul: That sounds good to me. Look at this! "A Man with Four Legs!"

ANSWER KEY

A. 1. Paul's 2. Paul's 3. Marie's 4. Marie's
5. Marie's 6. Paul's 7. Paul's
B. 1. Paul 2. Marie 3. Marie 4. Paul 5. Paul

C. *Individual responses may include variations like the following:*
1. Marie thinks that Paul's paper is trash
2. Paul thinks that Marie's newspaper is boring
3. Bob and Mr. Evans don't give their opinions about the newspapers

---

Interview: *Do you do a lot of reading?*

PREVIEW

- Ask students to name different kinds of books and write them on the board—for example, *novel, mystery, science fiction, memoir, biography*. Ask students about their favorite types of books to read.

REVIEW

- Ask comprehension questions. Play the video segment again if necessary.

  Does Herb do a lot of reading? (no) Does Blanche? (yes)

  What does she like to read? (novels, mystery stories, and travel stories)

  Does Lorayn get books from the library? (no) Where does she get her books? (She buys them and then trades them with her friends.)

  Does Blanche like books on tape? (no) Why not? (because they put her to sleep)

  Did Dan like the book he's just read? (yes) Why? (It was probably the funniest book he has ever read.)

  What type of magazines does Alvino like to read? (fashion)

  What type of magazines does Lorayn buy for her husband? (how-to)

  Which sections of the newspaper are most important to Dan? (the front page and "Arts and Leisure")

EXTENSION

Oral work

- Pair work: interviews. On the board, write the following interview questions that the interviewer asks the people:

  Do you do a lot of reading?

  Do you buy books or get them from the library?

  Do you like books on tape?

  Who are some of your favorite authors?

  Do you read newspapers and magazines? If yes, which ones?

  If you read a newspaper, which part is most important to you?

  Do you read how-to magazines?

  Pair students and have them take turns asking and answering the questions.

- Discussion. Tell students to recall the different types of reading materials mentioned in the video (*novels, mystery stories, travel stories, newspapers, magazines, how-to magazines*). Have students discuss how their reading habits are similar to or different from those of the interviewees.

Written work

- Pair work. Have students work in pairs to write summaries of the interviewees' reading habits.

- Pair work. Tell students they will create True and False quizzes. Have them work in pairs to write true and false statements about the video segment. Then combine pairs into groups of four and have them exchange quizzes and answer them. Finally, have the writers of each quiz check the answers.

LANGUAGE NOTES: The interviewer asks "Do you folks do a lot of reading?" *Folks* means *people*. *You folks* is an informal way of saying *all of you* or *both of you*.

To tend to do something means to be likely to do something.

Put me to sleep means *make me fall asleep*.

A belly laugh is a deep laugh. When Dan says "belly laughs on every page," he means every page made him laugh very hard.

CULTURE NOTE: Alvino says he reads fashion magazines. He mentions *Details*. This is the name of a popular fashion magazine for men in the United States.

OOPS! The interviewer says, "And what part of the newspapers *are* most important to you?" The grammatically correct sentence should be "And what part of the newspapers *is* most important to you" because the subject *part* is a singular noun.

VIDEO SCRIPT

Interviewer: Do you folks do a lot of reading?
Herb: She does.
Blanche: I do, particularly. I like to read novels and mystery stories, sometimes travel stories.
Interviewer: Do you buy books, or do you get them from the library?
Lorayn: I buy books, and I tend to trade them with friends.
Interviewer: How about books on tape?
Blanche: I tried that. They put me to sleep.
Interviewer: So, novels. You like to read fiction. Who are some of your favorite authors?
Dan: I just read Nick Hornby—*How to Be Good*—which was probably the funniest book I've ever read.
Interviewer: Would you say it's a real page-turner?
Dan: Absolutely. Absolutely. I mean, belly laughs on every page.

Interviewer: So, do you read anything else like newspapers, magazines?
Alvino: I do read magazines, yes.
Interviewer: Could you tell me, let's see, what sorts of magazines you like to read?
Alvino: Fashion. I enjoy fashion—*Details*, actually.
Interviewer: How about how-to magazines? Do you ever buy magazines about home repair or cooking, for instance?
Lorayn: I buy my husband magazines on . . . how-to magazines. He's the one that's good at fixing things and repair, even cooking.
Interviewer: How about newspapers? Do you read newspapers?
Dan: The *New York Times* when I'm home.
Interviewer: And what part of the newspapers are most important to you?
Dan: The front page and "Arts and Leisure."

ANSWER KEY

A. 1. False 2. True 3. False 4. True 5. False
   6. False
B. 1. Dan 2. Alvino 3. Dan 4. Lorayn
C. 1. novels, mystery stories, travel stories
   2. funny 3. fashion 4. front page, Arts and
   Leisure 5. fixing, repair, cooking

 Top Notch Pop and Karaoke: *A True Life Story*

UNIT 5

Sitcom: *I want to go someplace different.*

Social language

- Express fear of disasters
- Reassure someone
- Convey a message

Grammar

- Indirect speech

SCENE 1

PREVIEW

- Have students name some severe weather events— for example, *tornadoes, hurricanes, monsoons, floods, landslides, droughts.* Ask *What parts of the world have these problems often?*

REVIEW

- Ask comprehension questions. Play the video episode again if necessary.

  Where does Mrs. Beatty usually travel? (to major cities in Europe)

  Where does she want to travel now? (someplace away from the city)

  What does Mrs. Beatty say about California? (that there are earthquakes)

  Thailand? (that there's a monsoon)

  Australia? (that there are tornadoes)

  Jamaica? (that there are hurricanes)

  South Africa? (that there are floods)

  Hawaii? (that there are landslides)

  What does Mr. Evans finally suggest? (Finland)

  What does Mr. Evans say about Finland? (that it's wild and beautiful and that nothing bad ever happens there)

  Does Mrs. Beatty agree to go to Finland? (yes)

EXTENSION

Oral work

- Discussion. Have students discuss the different destinations Mr. Evans suggests to Mrs. Beatty. Ask *Do you think Mrs. Beatty has a reason to be so worried about natural disasters? Do you worry about such things when you travel or choose travel destinations?*

- Pair work: role play. Pair students. One student should role-play Mr. Evans, and the other student should be a client. Have Mr. Evans suggest travel destinations and see which ones the client would like to visit most. Have the client make up excuses why he / she does not want to go to some places.

Written work

- Pair work. Have students work in pairs to create Mrs. Beatty's to-do list before she goes on her trip. Write eight to ten things she needs to do.

- Pair work. Have pairs of students write a letter from Mrs. Beatty to one of her friends about her travel plans and how she came to that decision.

VIDEO SCRIPT

Mr. Evans tries to come up with a place for Mrs. Beatty's vacation—a place that does not have natural disasters.

Mr. Evans: So, Mrs. Beatty, you're looking for an exciting place for your next vacation.

Mrs. Beatty: I usually travel to major cities in Europe, but this time I want to go someplace different—someplace away from the city—as long as it's safe.

Mr. Evans: How about California? The Big Sur area is spectacular.

Mrs. Beatty: California has lots of earthquakes, doesn't it?

Mr. Evans: Well, they have earthquakes occasionally, but not very often.

Mrs. Beatty: But it *does* have earthquakes.

Mr. Evans: Yes.

Mrs. Beatty: I'm not going.

Mr. Evans: OK. How about someplace in Asia? A beach in Thailand? Ko Chang has beautiful beaches, and it's very quiet there.

Mrs. Beatty: A quiet beach sounds nice. But they **said** on the news **there's** a monsoon in Thailand.

Mr. Evans: But the monsoon will be over by the time you go.

Mrs. Beatty: What else can you recommend?

Mr. Evans: Australia. The Australian outback is amazing.

Mrs. Beatty: I've heard they have tornadoes in Australia.

Mr. Evans: Well, some parts . . .

Mrs. Beatty: Where else?

Mr. Evans: Jamaica?

Mrs. Beatty: Hurricanes.

Mr. Evans: South Africa?

Mrs. Beatty: Floods.

Mr. Evans: Hawaii?

Mrs. Beatty: Landslides.

Mr. Evans: You know a lot about natural disasters, don't you, Mrs. Beatty? Let's see. What about Finland?

Mrs. Beatty: Finland?

Mr. Evans: It's wild, beautiful, and very different from other parts of Europe. And nothing bad ever happens in Finland.

Mrs. Beatty: Finland sounds good. I'll go to Finland.

Mr. Evans: Great. I'll book your tickets.

ANSWER KEY

A. 1. c 2. a 3. c 4. b 5. c

B. California, Thailand, Australia, Jamaica, South Africa, Hawaii, Finland

C. 1. California, it has earthquakes 2. Thailand, it has monsoons 3. Australia, it has tornadoes
4. Jamaica, it has hurricanes 5. South Africa, it has floods 6. Hawaii, it has landslides

SCENE 2

PREVIEW

- Ask students *Are you ever afraid when you travel somewhere? If yes, what are you afraid of? (for example, flying, getting sick, having documents stolen) Do you ever let your fears stop you from doing what you want to do?*

REVIEW

- Ask comprehension questions. Play the video episode again if necessary.

    Why does Marie interrupt Mr. Evans and Mrs. Beatty? (She has an urgent phone call.)

    Who's calling? (Mr. Woods, a client)

    What is the problem? (He is traveling, and there is some sort of epidemic.)

    What kind of epidemic is there? (the new influenza)

    Was Mr. Woods vaccinated before he left? (yes)

    What does Mr. Woods want from Mr. Evans? (He wants to fly home today.)

    What information does Mr. Evans get from the Internet? (that only three people are sick)

    What does Mrs. Beatty ask? (where Mr. Woods is traveling)

    What does Mr. Evans tell her? (that she'll get vaccinated and she'll be fine)

    Does Mrs. Beatty feel better in the end? (no) Why not? (She's afraid of getting hit by a bus.)

EXTENSION

Oral work

- Pair work: role play. Have students work in pairs to role-play the telephone conversation between Mr. Woods and Marie. Tell students to use their imagination and the information from the video episode.

- Discussion. Ask students these questions:

    Do you agree with Mrs. Beatty? Would you travel to Finland for vacation if you knew there was a flu epidemic there?

    Do you agree with Mr. Evans's final comment?

    Has anyone had a similar experience to Mrs. Beatty's? What did you do?

Written work

- Pair work. Have students work in pairs to write an imaginary phone conversation between Mr. Evans and Mr. Woods. Tell students to use their imagination and the information from the video episode.

- Tell students to imagine that Mrs. Beatty left Top Notch Travel too scared to think about another trip. Mr. Evans writes her a letter to apologize for scaring her and to encourage her to think about traveling somewhere again. Tell students to suggest a few very safe destinations.

VIDEO SCRIPT

After Mr. Evans has booked Mrs. Beatty's vacation, something happens that changes Mrs. Beatty's mind.

Mr. Evans: OK, I just booked your tickets to Helsinki, Finland. You'll be staying at the Palace Hotel.

Mrs. Beatty: That's great.

Marie: Excuse me, Mr. Evans?

Mr. Evans: Yes, Marie?

Marie: Mr. Woods is on the phone. He **told me to tell you it's** urgent.

Mr. Evans: Urgent?

Marie: He's traveling, you know.

Mr. Evans: Yes?

Marie: He **said there's** some kind of epidemic.

Mr. Evans: What kind of epidemic?

Marie: It sounds like it's that new influenza.

Mr. Evans: But he was vaccinated for that before he left.

Marie: I know. But he **told me to tell you** that he **wants** to fly home today.

Mr. Evans: On the Internet it **says** only three people **are** sick. That is not an epidemic. And it's not like anybody's dying from this flu.

Marie: He **said** he **didn't want** to be the first.

Mrs. Beatty: Where is he traveling, may I ask?

Marie: He's in Finland.

Mrs. Beatty: Finland? I just booked tickets to Finland!

Mr. Evans: Mrs. Beatty, everything will be fine. You'll get vaccinated, and you'll have nothing to worry about.

Mrs. Beatty: I'm not going to Finland. You **told me** nothing bad ever **happens** in Finland.

Mr. Evans: Mrs. Beatty, I can't think of anywhere in the world you can go and be completely safe. Right here in this city you could go outside and get hit by a bus. But you can't let that stop you from doing the things you want to do. Look, why don't we go to lunch and we'll talk it over?

Marie: I don't think she's going anywhere.

ANSWER KEY

A. 1. False 2. True 3. False 4. True 5. False
   6. False

B. 1. c 2. b 3. a 4. a 5. b

C. *Following are the expected answers. Students may produce variations that are also correct.*

   1. was urgent, an epidemic in Finland, wants to fly home today, doesn't want to be the first to die from the flu

   2. had been vaccinated for the flu before he left, there is no epidemic in Finland, nobody is dying from the flu

 Top Notch Pop and Karaoke: *Lucky to Be Alive*

UNIT 6

Sitcom: *I could have been a great dancer...*

Social language
- Explain life choices
- Express regrets

Grammar
- The future in the past
- Perfect modals

SCENE 1

PREVIEW

- Ask students *When you were growing up, what did you want to be?* Write students' responses on the board.

REVIEW

- Ask comprehension questions. Play the video episode again if necessary.

  What did Cheryl think she would be when she was young? (a chef)

  Why didn't she become a chef? (Her mother talked her out of it—she thought Cheryl would always have to work late, and she was afraid Cheryl would never meet a man and get married.)

  Does Paul think Cheryl would have met Bob if she had become a chef? (no) Why not? (because Bob only ate fast food before he met her)

  What was Bob going to be when he was younger? (a dancer)

  Did Marie and Paul know this? (no)

  Where did Bob dance when he was young? (in the state ballet)

  Why didn't he become a dancer? (The diet was too hard.)

  What food was hardest for Bob to stop eating? (bread and butter)

  Does Bob enjoy watching ballet now? (no) Why not? (It makes him hungry.)

EXTENSION

Oral work

- Group work: role play. Have students work in groups to role-play the characters and reenact what happened in the video episode.

- Group work: role play. Have students work in groups to role-play the characters in the conversation. Have them continue the story for a few more exchanges in which Marie and Paul add what they were going to be when they were young. To help students begin, write on the board:

  Cheryl: So, Marie, what did you think you were going to be when you were younger?

Written work

- Have students write a summary of the story in the video episode. To help students begin, write this sentence on the board: *After dinner in Cheryl's apartment, the friends talk about what they wanted to be when they were younger...*

- Review that Bob wanted to be a dancer, but this required a very strict diet, and he decided not to continue this dream. Have students write a paragraph about what they wanted to be when they were younger. Tell them to include details of what was required to achieve this dream. Finally, have them say whether they continued with the dream. If they changed their minds, have them describe what they became and explain why.

LANGUAGE NOTE: *To talk someone out of something* means to convince someone not to do something.

VIDEO SCRIPT

After dinner in Cheryl's apartment, Cheryl and Bob talk about their future plans when they were younger.

Marie: Another wonderful dinner, Cheryl. Thank you.

Cheryl: You're welcome. I really enjoy cooking. Actually, when I was young, I thought I **was going to be** a chef.

Paul: You could be a chef. These cookies are fantastic!

Marie: Why didn't you become a chef?

Cheryl: My mother talked me out of it. She thought I **would** always **have to work** at night. She was afraid I **would** never **meet** a man and get married.

Paul: She was probably right. If you were a chef, you **wouldn't have met** Bob.

Cheryl: How do you know?

Paul: Before he met you, Bob only ate fast food.

Bob: It's true.

Mr. Evans: Your mother **must have been** very happy when you and Bob got engaged.

Cheryl: She was. Hey, you'll never guess what Bob **was going to be**.

Bob: Cheryl...

Marie: A rock musician?

Paul: A basketball player?

Cheryl: No, Bob **was going to be** a dancer. He was actually in the state ballet when he was young.

Marie: No kidding!

Paul: You never told me this!

Bob: I **could have been** a great dancer.

Paul: What made you change your mind?

Bob: The diet was too hard. I had to stop eating everything—chocolate cake, fried chicken, potato chips. I tried. I **might have been** able to do it. But then they said no more bread and butter. Bread and butter! Can you believe it? And that was the end.

Marie: Wow, Bob. I never knew. Do you enjoy watching ballet at all?

Bob: I can't. I'd like to, but as soon as the music starts, I get very, very . . . hungry.

ANSWER KEY

A. 1. wouldn't have 2. must have 3. could have 4. might have

B. 1. fast food 2. a dancer 3. state 4. diet 5. bread and butter 6. hungry

C. 1. was going to be a chef 2. would always have to work 3. would never meet a man

SCENE 2

PREVIEW

• Ask students *Do you give your honest opinion to someone who's not good at singing? How about acting? cooking? dancing?*

REVIEW

• Ask comprehension questions. Play the video episode again if necessary.

> *What did Mr. Evans think he was going to be? (He thought he was going to be a television etiquette teacher.)*
>
> *Why did he want to do this? (He has always loved etiquette.)*
>
> *Why does Cheryl think Mr. Evans would be good at this job? (because he is very polite)*
>
> *What reason does Bob give? (Mr. Evans always knows which fork to use at a restaurant.)*
>
> *What reason does Paul give? (Mr. Evans has taught Paul a lot about the customs of other cultures.)*
>
> *Is Mr. Evans's performance good? (no)*
>
> *Does everyone give their honest opinion of the performance? (no) Why not?*

EXTENSION

Oral work

• Pair work. Call on a volunteer to role-play Mr. Evans's performance as a TV host. Then ask *What is the topic of the program? (dinner conversation) What topics are acceptable at the dinner table in this country?* Have students work in pairs to prepare a TV program on dinner conversation. Tell them to use information they know about etiquette in their own culture and in other cultures. Have each pair perform their TV program for the class.

• Pair work. Pair students. On the board, write

> *I have always loved* _____. *I thought I would have made a great* _____.

Have students fill in the blanks and say the lines to their partner. Have the partner respond whether he / she thinks the person could still do this and explain why or why not. For example, *I think you could still do it. It's perfect for you.*

Written work

• Pair work. Have students work in pairs to summarize the story in the video episode. Write these sentences on the board to help them begin:

> *Mr. Evans said he'd always loved etiquette. He thought he would have made a great TV etiquette teacher . . .*

• Have students write a list of qualifications a person must have to apply for a job in television, as Mr. Evans would like to do. Then have students write a paragraph explaining why they think Mr. Evans would or would not be good for the job.

LANGUAGE NOTE: *To give something a try* means to try something.

VIDEO SCRIPT

Mr. Evans tries his hand at being a TV host for etiquette.

Marie: What about you, Mr. Evans? What did you think you **were going to be** when you were younger?

Mr. Evans: If I tell you, will you try not to laugh?

Marie: Of course.

Mr. Evans: I always thought I **would have** my own television program to talk about etiquette.

Cheryl: I didn't know you were so interested in etiquette.

Mr. Evans: I have always loved etiquette. I think I **would have made** a great television etiquette teacher.

Cheryl: Well, I think you could still do it. It's perfect for you.

Mr. Evans: Really? Why?

Cheryl: Well, you're very polite, for one thing.

Bob: You always know which fork to use at a restaurant. That's a real talent.

Paul: You've taught me a lot about the customs of other cultures.

Mr. Evans: Maybe I could still give it a try. "Today's topic: dinner conversation. If your international guests look offended and are leaving the table early, you've probably chosen a topic that's taboo in their home country. Find out what's acceptable and what's not . . . coming up on *International Etiquette with Evans*." What do you think?

Bob: Wow.

Cheryl: Amazing.

Marie: Unforgettable.

Paul: You have a real . . . talent all right.

Mr. Evans: Thank you.

Interview: *How would you describe your skills and abilities?*

PREVIEW

- Ask students to name different abilities they have and write them on the board. Then ask individual students *Do you think you were born with these abilities, or did you learn them?*

REVIEW

- Ask comprehension questions. Play the video segment again if necessary.
    What is Rita's occupation? (teacher)
    What will Matt's career be in? (marketing)
    What does San do? (She works in television.)
    What does she want to do in the future? (produce and direct TV programs)
    When Matt was a child, what did he think he would do when he grew up? (He thought he would be president of the United States or drive a fire truck.)
    What made teaching a good career for Rita? (She loves children and the idea of sharing knowledge with them.)
    What skills does San have? (She has artistic ability.) Matt? (He comes up with new creative ideas.)
    Does San think talents and abilities are genetic? (She thinks they are a combination of genetics and environment.)

EXTENSION

Oral work

- Pair work: interviews. On the board, write the following interview questions:
    Could you tell me what your career will be?
    Did you think you'd be in this career when you were a child?
    Is _____ a good career for you?
    (if yes) What makes _____ a good career for you?
    (if no) What would be a good career for you?

  Pair students and have them take turns asking and answering each of the questions.

- Pair work: role play. Have students work in pairs to choose San or Rita from the video segment and role-play the short conversations between the interviewee and the interviewer. Tell students to try to include all the information they talked about.

Written work

- Ask *Do you think talents and abilities are genetic?* Tell students to write a paragraph explaining whether they agree or disagree with San's comment.

- Tell students that Matt is applying for a job at a company and that he needs to write an e-mail describing his skills and talents. Tell students to write this e-mail, using information from the video segment and making up details.

LANGUAGE NOTES: *To impart knowledge* means to teach.

A *buzz* is a slang term for a strong feeling of excitement or interest.

VIDEO SCRIPT

Interviewer: Could you tell me what your career or occupation is?
Rita: I'm an elementary school teacher.
Matt: My career path will be in marketing, helping companies build their brand and help market products to the general consumer.
San: I work in television, and I would like to eventually produce and direct.
Interviewer: Did you think that you'd be in marketing when you were a child?
Matt: No. I thought I'd be president of the United States or drive a fire truck.
Interviewer: What made teaching a good career for you?
Rita: First of all, I love children, and I liked the idea of imparting some of my knowledge to young ones.
Interviewer: Everybody has skills, talents, and abilities, so, you know, some people are artistic, others have mechanical ability. What would you say are some of your skills?
San: I would say I have a lot of artistic ability. I did a lot of art in school.
Matt: Good question. My skills and talents would be coming up with new ideas, different ideas, creative ideas that kind of build a buzz around a product.
Interviewer: Do you think that talents and abilities are genetic?
San: I think they're a combination of both genetics and environment. I think that you are born with certain qualities that your parents I think have, and just living with some people around you and learning from your teachers and those that you're constantly interacting with, you pick up certain skills.

 Top Notch Pop and Karaoke:
I Should Have Married Her

UNIT 7

Sitcom: *I want a large wedding.*

Social language
- Discuss a wedding
- Discuss holiday traditions

Grammar
- Adjective clauses

SCENE 1

PREVIEW

- Tell students to recall weddings they have
  attended or their own wedding. Ask *Do you prefer
  large or small weddings? Why?*

REVIEW

- Ask comprehension questions. Play the video
  episode again if necessary.

   *What are Bob and Cheryl talking about? (their
   wedding)*
   *What is the problem? (They can't agree on several
   things.)*
   *Where does Bob want to get married? (outdoors, in a
   park or at the beach)*
   *What about Cheryl? (indoors) Why? (so she won't
   get wet if it rains)*
   *What type of music does Cheryl prefer? (traditional)
   Bob? (contemporary)*
   Does Bob want a long ceremony? (no) Cheryl? (yes)
   *What type of reception does Bob want? (huge)
   Cheryl? (short)*
   *What does Marie suggest doing about the size and
   location of the wedding? (She suggests making the
   wedding large enough to fit all of Cheryl's family.
   She also suggests having the ceremony in the park
   on Oak Street that has a building they can go to if
   it rains.)*

*What does Marie suggest about the music? (She
suggests having traditional music in the ceremony
and contemporary music at the party.)*
*What does Marie suggest about the cakes? (She
suggests having two cakes—one white and one
chocolate.)*
Do Bob and Cheryl like Marie's suggestions? (yes)

EXTENSION

Oral work

- Discussion. On the board, write *size, location,
  music, length of ceremony, reception,* and *cake.* Have
  students discuss Bob's and Cheryl's preferences
  and then say who they agree with more on the
  different points.

- Group work: role play. Divide the class into groups
  of three. Have students role-play Cheryl, Bob, and
  Marie and reenact what happened in the video
  episode.

Written work

- Have students imagine that Cheryl has just
  e-mailed them her dilemma about the wedding
  planning. Tell students to write her an e-mail with
  advice different from the advice Marie gave them.

- Pair work. Have students work in pairs to write a
  list of things Cheryl and Bob need to do to prepare
  for the wedding. Tell them to use information from
  the video episode—for example, *get permission from
  the park to have their wedding there, order two cakes
  from the bakers.*

VIDEO SCRIPT

*In the café, Marie helps Cheryl and Bob plan their
wedding.*

Bob: I don't know. I didn't know that planning a
      wedding would be so hard.
Cheryl: Marie, could you give us your opinion on
         a few things?
Marie: I'd love to!
Cheryl: First, how many people should we
         invite? Bob wants a small wedding.
Bob: Twenty guests would be nice.
Cheryl: I want a large wedding. About 300
         people.
Bob: Three hundred?! Yesterday you said 200!
Cheryl: I have a lot of relatives **who want to come**.
Bob: Then there's the location. I always thought I
      would get married in a park or at the beach.
Marie: That's so romantic!
Cheryl: I would like to get married indoors,
         where **I won't get wet** if it's raining.
Marie: That makes sense.
Cheryl: I prefer traditional music in the
         ceremony.

Bob: Contemporary music.

Cheryl: I'd like a long ceremony, and a short reception.

Bob: I want a short ceremony, and a huge celebration afterwards.

Cheryl: I want a white cake.

Bob: And I want . . .

Marie: A chocolate cake, I know.

Bob: How are we ever going to agree on this?

Marie: Don't hurt yourself. Here's an idea **that might work**. Plan a wedding **that's big enough to include all of Cheryl's family** . . . sorry, Bob . . . in the park on Oak Street **that has that building where you can go if it rains**. You can have traditional music in the ceremony and contemporary music at the party, and you could have two cakes at the reception—one white and one chocolate.

Bob: Sounds OK to me.

Cheryl: Me, too.

Bob: Hey! We did it!

Cheryl: Yeah! I'm so happy.

Marie: Excuse me.

Cheryl: Oh, Marie, thank you so much.

Bob: You're amazing! We couldn't have done it without you.

ANSWER KEY

A. 1. False 2. False 3. True 4. True 5. False 6. True 7. True

B.

	Bob	Cheryl
Size of wedding	small	large
Location	in a park or at the beach	indoors
Music	contemporary	traditional
Length of ceremony	short	long
Length of reception	huge (or long)	short
Cake	chocolate	white

C. 1. that might work 2. that's big enough to include all of Cheryl's family 3. that has that building where you can go

SCENE 2

PREVIEW

- Ask students *What are some popular holidays in your culture?* Write students' responses on the board. Ask individual students *Which is your favorite holiday? Are there any new holidays you'd like to see?*

REVIEW

- Ask comprehension questions. Play the video episode again if necessary.

    Why does Paul come to the restaurant? (to tell everyone to come back to the office)

    Why doesn't Bob want to go back to work? (He's too tired from planning the wedding.)

    What does Paul suggest? (making today a holiday)

    What holiday does Paul suggest? (National Wedding Day)

    Does he say what happens on National Wedding Day? (no) Why not? (He doesn't know.)

    What holiday does Marie suggest? (National Singles Day)

    What happens on this holiday? (Married people give gifts to their single friends.)

    Does Bob like Marie's holiday idea? (no) Why not? (because buying gifts is hard work)

    What holiday does Cheryl suggest? (Red Day)

    What happens on this holiday? (People wear red clothes, and there's dancing in the streets all night.)

    What holiday does Bob suggest? (National Buy-Your-Friend-Another-Cup-of-Coffee Day)

    What holiday does Mr. Evans suggest? (National On-Time Day)

    What happens on this holiday? (People remind each other to come back to work on time.)

EXTENSION

Oral work

- Group work. Point out that Paul does not have an idea for what could happen on National Wedding Day. Have students work in groups to discuss what could happen on National Wedding Day. Then bring the class together and have groups share their ideas.

- Group work: role play. Divide the class into groups of four. Have students role-play Paul, Bob, Marie, and Cheryl. Tell each student to suggest one more holiday before Mr. Evans comes to the café.

Written work

- Tell students to imagine that Cheryl, Marie, Paul, and Bob have been coming back to work from lunch late all week. When Mr. Evans returns from his lunch, he sends everyone an e-mail about not returning late anymore. Tell students to write this e-mail.

- Pair work. Review what Cheryl said about Red Day. (*Everyone wears red, and there's dancing in the street that goes on all night.*) Tell students they are in charge of organizing their town's Red Day this year. Have students work in pairs to write a list of things they need to do in preparation. On the board, write *location, advertising, music, food* to give students hints of the kinds of things they need to think about.

Paul, Marie, Cheryl, and Bob each tries to come up with a holiday.

Paul: Hi. Lunchtime is over. Are you coming up to the office?

Bob: I'm too tired to go back to the office. Planning a wedding is hard work. I need a holiday.

Paul: Let's make today a holiday. We'll tell Mr. Evans we can't come back to work.

Bob: That's a great idea.

Marie: What are we celebrating?

Paul: You're getting married. How about National Wedding Day?

Bob: What happens on National Wedding Day?

Paul: I don't know. Why am I the one **who has to think of everything**?

Marie: Why don't we make it National Singles Day instead? All the married people give gifts to their single friends.

Bob: No. Buying gifts is hard work. I want to enjoy myself on our new holiday.

Cheryl: What about a Red Day? Everybody wears red clothes, and there's dancing in the street **that goes on all night**.

Bob: How about National Buy-Your-Friend-Another-Cup-of-Coffee Day?

Paul: Nice try.

Mr. Evans: How about National On-Time Day?

Bob: What happens on National On-Time Day?

Mr. Evans: You remind one another to come back to work on time.

Paul: Happy holiday.

Mr. Evans: Waitress!

ANSWER KEY

A. 1. a 2. c 3. b 4. b
B. 1. e 2. c 3. b 4. a 5. d
C. *Individual responses may include variations like the following:*
1. *National Singles Day:* All the married people give gifts to their single friends. 2. *Red Day:* Everybody wears red clothes, and there's dancing in the street that goes on all night. 3. *National On-Time Day:* People remind one another to come back to work on time.

Interview: *Could you please describe a typical wedding in your country?*

PREVIEW

- Ask students *What are some wedding traditions in this culture?* Write students' responses on the board.

REVIEW

- Ask comprehension questions. Play the video segment again if necessary.

  What comes first in a German wedding—the civil ceremony or the religious ceremony? (the civil ceremony)
  Where does the civil ceremony happen? (at City Hall)
  Where does the religious ceremony happen? (traditionally at a church)
  What happens after the religious ceremony? (People wait for the bride and groom to come out and throw rice and flowers at them.)
  Is there a reception afterwards? (yes)
  What do people wear for traditional African weddings? (special clothing and outfits)
  How long does a traditional African wedding last? (two days sometimes)
  What happens during the reception? (a lot of traditional dancing and eating lots of food)
  Do people give speeches? (yes) About what? (about the bride and groom; about advice on how to be together)

EXTENSION
Oral work

- Discussion. Have students compare German wedding customs with those in their own country and discuss whether any of the traditions in their culture are similar to those in Germany.

- Discussion. Invite students to share what they think is a perfect wedding. Tell them to refer to the traditions Jessica and Emma spoke about and say whether any of them would fit into their idea of a perfect wedding.

Written work

- Tell students to write a summary of Jessica's description of a wedding in Germany or of Emma's description of a wedding in Ghana.

- Have students write a paragraph comparing wedding traditions in their culture and those in Germany or Ghana. Encourage them to refer to traditions Jessica and Emma spoke about and if there are any similarities.

OOPS! Jessica talks about the *broom* and bride. She means *groom*.

VIDEO SCRIPT

Interviewer: You're from Germany. What is a wedding like in Germany?

Jessica: Well, first of all, you have to have a civil ceremony where you go to the City Hall, and . . . well, you make everything official. And then traditionally, you go to church and have the religious ceremony.

Interviewer: And is there a wedding reception afterwards?

Jessica: Usually there is, of course. After church when everybody's waiting for the broom and the bride coming out and throwing rice at them and flowers, and then the whole crew's going to a nice place and having dinner and having a party.

Interviewer: You mentioned that your family is originally from Ghana.

Emma: Yes.

Interviewer: Could you tell me a little bit about the courtship and marriage ceremonies of your country?

Emma: There's a traditional . . . sometimes they do involve, like the American type of wedding, the very traditional. You walk down the aisle. But they also, there's also the traditional part in African culture. You wear the clothing and the outfits. It's much longer. Sometimes it can go into the next day. Some people extend.

Interviewer: Tell me about the reception.

Emma: They find a place to go to, or it's outside sometimes, there's a big tent. It just depends on the bride and groom, what they want. And there's tons of dancing, traditional dancing, eating, lots of food. Sometimes you have somebody come in and talk about how they know him and how good he is and what he's done and, you know, people giving lots of wisdom of how to be together. It's just . . . it's just really a great thing.

ANSWER KEY

A. 1. False 2. True 3. True 4. False 5. True
B. There's a lot of traditional dancing. People eat a lot of food. People give speeches about the groom. People give advice to the couple about how to be together.
C. 1. City Hall, civil ceremony 2. church, religious ceremony 3. (wedding) reception

 **Top Notch Pop and Karaoke: Endless Holiday**

UNIT 8

Sitcom: *Technology today is amazing!*

Social language
- Describe innovative products
- Offer advice

Grammar
- Conditionals: review
- The past unreal conditional

SCENE 1

PREVIEW
- Ask students *What are some of the latest inventions on the market today? What inventions would you like to see?* Write students' replies on the board.

REVIEW
- Ask comprehension questions. Play the video episode again if necessary.
  What is Bob wearing? (TV glasses)
  What is Bob doing? (watching TV)
  What is he watching? (a basketball game)
  Why does Bob scream "Yes!"? (because his team is winning)
  What does Cheryl think of the TV glasses? (She thinks they are great.)
  What does Marie wish people would invent? (something that would make people who talk on cell phones quieter)
  What does Bob start laughing at? (a guy on TV)
  What would Cheryl invent for Bob? (something that would automatically charge him when he goes over the speed limit)
  What would make Bob slow down? (if he had to pay)
  Why does Bob scream "No!"? (He wants Cheryl to leave his car alone.)

EXTENSION
Oral work
- Discussion. Ask students *What does Cheryl think of Bob's TV glasses? Would you mind if someone you spend a lot of time with watched TV glasses all the time? Why or why not?*
- Discussion. Ask students *What do you think of Cheryl's and Marie's ideas for inventions? Do you think these inventions would be valuable to society?*

Written work
- Pair work. Have students work in pairs to create a commercial for Bob's TV glasses. Tell students to use information from the video episode. Then have pairs present their commercials to the class.

- Pair work. Ask *If you could invent something, what would it be? Why do you think it is necessary?* Have students work in pairs to write a paragraph describing their invention. Then invite pairs to present their inventions to the class.

LANGUAGE NOTE: A *speed limit* is the maximum speed at which drivers are permitted to drive on a road.

VIDEO SCRIPT

In Cheryl's apartment, Marie, Bob, and Cheryl talk about technology and inventions.

Marie: What are those wacky glasses you are wearing?

Bob: These are ultra high-tech, top-of-the-line, state-of-the-art, cutting-edge TV glasses.

Marie: And you're actually watching TV right now?

Bob: Yeah. Right here on the corner.

Marie: What are you watching?

Bob: The basketball game.

Marie: Unbelievable. And Cheryl doesn't mind this?

Bob: Yes!

Marie: What?

Bob: Sorry. My team's winning.

Marie: This new invention doesn't bother you?

Cheryl: Are you kidding? If I **had known** how happy they would make him, I **would have bought** those glasses for Bob long ago.

Marie: Technology today is amazing. You know, I **wish** they**'d invent** something that would make people who talk on cell phones quieter. This guy in the café today was so loud, I couldn't hear myself talking.

Bob: Ha-ha-ha . . .

Marie: It wasn't funny.

Bob: What? Oh, sorry. I was laughing at this guy on TV.

Cheryl: If I **could invent** something, it **would be** a thing for Bob's car that would automatically charge him when he goes over the speed limit. He drives so fast sometimes, but he**'d slow down** if he **had to pay**.

Bob: No!

Marie: Is your team losing?

Bob: No. I heard what you said. You just leave my car alone.

ANSWER KEY

A. ultra high-tech, top-of-the-line, state-of-the-art, cutting-edge

B. 1. had known 2. would make 3. would have bought 4. invent 5. would make 6. could invent 7. would be 8. would 9. charge 10. slow down

C. 1. Bob says "Yes!" because his team is winning 2. Bob is laughing at the guy on TV

SCENE 2

PREVIEW

- Ask individual students *Have you ever bought a product that did not work or turned out to be dangerous? What was the product, and what did you do?*

REVIEW

- Ask comprehension questions. Play the video episode again if necessary.

   What is the problem with Paul's cell phone? (Whenever he is traveling with a group, he can never hear his cell phone ring or feel it vibrate.)

   What did he do about it? (He got a new invention that lets him know when his phone is ringing.)

   Where does he keep this invention? (He wears it on his arm.)

   How does it work? (It buzzes him.)

   Does the buzz hurt? (yes)

   Does Paul know who called him? (No. There is no answer.)

   What does Marie suggest Paul do? (She suggests that Paul take the invention back to the store before he hurts himself.)

   What does Marie say after Paul leaves? (that she hopes he will be able to drive)

   How does Bob know that Paul will be fine? (because he will stop calling him)

EXTENSION

Oral work

- Group work. Have students work in groups to come up with a more effective and less dangerous invention that would solve Paul's problem. Then have groups share their ideas with the class.

- Pair work: role play. Tell students that Paul returns to the store where he purchased this invention to complain. Have students work in pairs to role-play a conversation between Paul and the salesperson at the store.

Written work

- On the board, write *If I were Paul and I couldn't hear my cell phone ring or feel it vibrate, I would . . .* Have students write a paragraph describing what they would do.

- Pair work. Imagine Paul bought his invention on the Internet, not in the store. He decides to e-mail the company right away to complain about it. Have students work in pairs to write this e-mail.

VIDEO SCRIPT

Paul enters the apartment to show his new cell phone.

Cheryl: Hi, Paul.

Paul: Wait 'til you see what I've got.

Bob: What is it?

Paul: Well, I have this problem with my cell phone. Whenever I'm traveling with a group, I can never hear it ring or feel it vibrate. So I got this thing that lets me know whenever my phone is ringing.

Marie: How does it do that?

Paul: It buzzes me.

Marie: Buzzes?

Paul: You know, bzzz, bzzz. So I can feel it.

Cheryl: Does it work?

Paul: I don't know. No one's called me yet . . . Ow!

Marie: What?!

Paul: Someone's calling me! Hello? Hello? No one's there. Wow. That was a big buzz. That almost hurt.

Cheryl: Maybe it isn't working right.

Paul: It's working fine . . . Ooh! Ow! Another phone call. Hello? Hello? That's strange. Man, if I ever **get used to** that, I**'ll** always **know** whenever my phone is ringing . . . Ahhhhhhh! Stop calling me!

Marie: Paul. If I **were** you, I **would take** that thing back to the store before you hurt yourself.

Paul: I'm going. I'll see you later.

Marie: I hope he can drive OK.

Bob: He'll be fine.

Cheryl: How do you know?

Bob: I'll stop calling him.

ANSWER KEY

A. 1. True 2. False 3. True 4. False 5. True

B. 1. hear 2. feel 3. buzzes 4. hurts 5. Bob

C. 1. 'll always know whenever my phone is ringing 2. would take that thing back to the store 3. he can drive OK

 Top Notch Pop and Karaoke: *Reinvent the Wheel*

UNIT 9

Sitcom: *Can we please avoid discussing politics?*

Social language
- State an opinion
- Disagree politely about controversial issues
- Discuss politics

Grammar
- Non-count nouns for abstract ideas
- Verbs followed by objects and infinitives

SCENE 1

PREVIEW

- Ask students these questions:
  Are you interested in politics?
  Do you like to discuss politics with your friends? Why or why not?
  If not, what do you like to talk about with your friends?

REVIEW

- Ask comprehension questions. Play the video episode again if necessary.
  According to Paul, what are politicians planning to do? (raise taxes)
  What has the government decided to spend money on? (building a stronger military)
  What two things does Marie think they should spend more money on? (education and eliminating poverty)
  Who does not want to discuss politics? (Cheryl) Why? (because they always argue when they discuss politics)
  What does Bob think they should spend more money on? (fighting corruption) Why? (If they were able to stop corrupt officials, they wouldn't need to raise taxes.)
  Who thinks the government should spend more money on the military? (Paul)
  What does Cheryl think the government should spend more money on? (cooking schools) Why? (because most people can't cook well)
  Is she serious? (no)
  How does everyone react? (They get mad at her.)
  Why does Cheryl say this? (to show that they always get mad at each other when discussing politics)

EXTENSION

Oral work

- Group work: discussion. Have groups of students join Bob, Paul, and Marie's discussion and talk about what they think the government should spend more money on. Tell students to refer to the characters in the video if they agree with their points of view.

- On the board, write *Should the government raise taxes to build a stronger military?* Debate. Divide the class in half. Have students choose whether they want to argue yes or no. Even out the teams. Have students prepare their arguments for or against spending more money on the military. Encourage them to use arguments that Paul, Bob, and Marie made in the video. Then have students make their arguments and invite members of the opposing group to respond. Finally, as a class, decide which group had the strongest argument.

Written work

- Write on the board *Do you agree with Cheryl that it's better not to discuss politics with friends?* Have students write a paragraph to express their opinions. Tell students to give examples from their own lives.

- Pair work. Have students work in pairs to write a letter to a local politician suggesting things that need to be done in the community or complaining about government policies.

VIDEO SCRIPT

In Cheryl's apartment, Paul, Bob, and Marie are talking about politics, while Cheryl tries to avoid the topic.

Paul: Did you see the politicians expect to raise taxes again?

Bob: Really? What has the government decided to spend our money on now?

Paul: They're planning to build a stronger military.

Marie: It's wrong to spend so much on the military. They should spend it on **education** instead.

Cheryl: Can we please avoid discussing **politics**?

Marie: Why?

Cheryl: Every time we begin talking about **politics**, people get mad at each other.

Bob: They should spend more money on fighting **corruption**. If they were able to stop corrupt officials, maybe they wouldn't need to raise our taxes.

Paul: That's true, but I think we need to spend more money on the military. Without a strong military, the world won't be very safe.

Marie: That's one way to look at it. But maybe the world would be safer—and better—if we tried to eliminate **poverty**.

Bob: What do you think, Cheryl?

Cheryl: I think that if I say what I really think, you'll get all mad and call me crazy or ridiculous.

Marie: Cheryl. Don't be so afraid. We're only talking.

Cheryl: I think that the government should spend more money on cooking schools.

Marie: What?

Cheryl: Most people don't know how to cook well. I think the government should help teach them.

Marie: That's ridiculous!

Bob: Are you crazy?

Paul: Use our taxes to pay for cooking schools?

Cheryl: Of course not! But look at you. You're all mad at me. This is why I never discuss **politics** with friends. But don't let me stop you from getting mad at each other.

SCENE 2

PREVIEW

- Write on the board the names of different political beliefs: *radical, liberal, moderate, conservative, reactionary.* Ask students *Do you usually think of people you know as liberal, conservative, moderate, and so on? Are you ever wrong?*

REVIEW

- Ask comprehension questions. Play the video episode again if necessary.

    What does Marie call Paul? (a conservative) Why? (because he always wants things to be just like they used to be)
    Does he agree with her? (no)
    What does Paul call Marie? (a radical) Why? (because she always wants to change everything)
    Does she agree with him? (no)
    What does Bob call Marie? (a liberal)
    Does Marie agree that Bob is liberal? (no) Why not? (because she thinks he is a moderate)
    Why does Marie think Bob is a moderate? (because Bob is always in the middle)
    Why does Paul call Marie a little dictator? (because she tells Bob he can't be one thing and call it something else)
    How does Marie know so much about political beliefs? (She studied politics in school.)
    Does anyone know Cheryl's political beliefs? (no) Does she share them? (no)
    What does Cheryl say? (that she believes the chips are the best she has ever tasted)

EXTENSION

Oral work

- Group work: role play. Divide the class into groups of four. Have students role-play Marie, Bob, Cheryl, and Paul and reenact what happened in the video episode.

- Discussion. Ask students these questions:
    Do you think Cheryl is interested in politics at all?

If you were Cheryl, would you be able to stay quiet during a discussion like they are having?
Who in the video are you most like? Why?

Written work

- Tell students that the government has recently announced that the education system in their country will be restructured. Have students individually take the role of Marie, Bob, or Paul and write a letter to the government to make some suggestions. Tell students to keep in mind each person's political beliefs while writing the letter.

- Pair work. Have students work in pairs to write a conversation between Marie and Cheryl. Marie knows Cheryl does not like to talk about politics, so she decides to carefully ask her some questions in a regular conversation to try to find out her political beliefs. Have pairs share their conversations with the class.

VIDEO SCRIPT

Marie, Paul, and Bob continue to express their political and social beliefs, while Cheryl stays above the fray.

Marie: Paul, I never knew you were so conservative.

Paul: I'm not conservative.

Marie: Sure you are. You always seem to **want things to be** just like they used to be.

Paul: That's not conservative. That's just smart. *(to Cheryl)* Thanks.

Marie: That's the definition of conservative.

Paul: Really? Well, I didn't know you were so radical.

Marie: What makes you think I'm radical?

Paul: You always want to change everything.

Marie: No, I don't. I just **want our government to realize** that it's the twenty-first century and they need new ways of doing things. *(to Cheryl)* Thank you.

Paul: That sounds radical to me.

Marie: Bob, tell him I'm not a radical.

Bob: She's not a radical. She's a liberal. Like me.

Marie: I wouldn't call you a liberal.

Bob: Oh, really?

Marie: I'd say you're more of a moderate. You're always in the middle.

Bob: If I want to be a liberal, I'll be a liberal. (to Cheryl) Thank you, honey.

Marie: You can be whatever you want, you just can't be one thing and call it something else.

Paul: Listen to you. You're like a little dictator.

Marie: I studied **politics** in school. I know something about the definitions of political beliefs.

Paul: Is that so? So what is Cheryl? A radical? Moderate? Conservative?

Marie: Who knows? She's not saying.

Paul: Cheryl, what are you? Would you mind telling us that much?

Cheryl: OK. You want to know what I believe? I believe . . . I believe . . . I believe these are the best chips I have ever tasted.

ANSWER KEY

A. 1. True 2. True 3. False 4. True 5. False

B. *Following are the expected answers. Students may produce variations that are also correct.*
1. conservative, he always seems to want things to be just like they used to be 2. radical, she always wants to change everything
3. moderate, he's always in the middle

C. *Individual responses may include variations like the following:*
1. The government should realize that it's the twenty-first century, and they need new ways of doing things 2. Because she studied politics in school 3. Cheryl says she believes that the chips she's eating are the best chips she's ever tasted

---

Interview: *How do you feel about . . . ?*

PREVIEW

- Ask students *What do you think are the biggest problems in the world today?* Write students' responses on the board. Leave them there for the oral work.

REVIEW

- Ask comprehension questions. Play the video segment again if necessary.

  Is Ian a smoker? (yes)
  What does he think about prohibiting smoking indoors? (He doesn't appreciate it all the time, but he understands why.)
  Do you think Christiane is a smoker? (probably not)
  What does she say about restaurants where smoking is prohibited? (The food tastes better, and your clothes don't smell.)
  Is Stephan in favor of censorship of books or movies? (no) Why not? (He thinks that censorship creates fear and prevents people from getting information that should be available to them.)
  What does Christiane think are two big problems in the world? (war and racism)
  What is the most important way to prevent these problems? (communication)

EXTENSION
Oral work

- Discussion. Ask *Do you agree with Christiane that the two big problems in the world are war and racism?*

Encourage students to discuss other problems and solutions, referring to the list on the board from the preview.

- Discussion. Ask students these questions:

    Who do you agree with about prohibiting smoking indoors—Ian or Christiane?

    What are some other benefits of prohibiting smoking indoors?

    What are some disadvantages for smokers?

Written work

- Have students summarize Christiane's comments about ways to solve the problems of war and racism in the world. Then have students write some additional solutions.

- Have students write a paragraph explaining why they agree or disagree with Stephan's views on censorship.

OOPS! Christiane talks about sitting down *on* a table. She means sitting down *at* a table.

VIDEO SCRIPT

Interviewer: How do you feel about prohibiting smoking indoors?

Ian: As a smoker I don't appreciate it all the time, but I can understand why.

Christiane: I think it's fantastic. I think it's great. If you go to restaurants and nobody can smoke, the food tastes better and your clothes don't smell.

Interviewer: How about censorship of books or movies by a government?

Stephan: I am 100 percent against censorship of any books or movies or any expression of creativity, and I feel that when governments try to censor books or movies, then it creates a sort of atmosphere of fear, and people don't get to . . . don't have ready access to information that should be available to them.

Interviewer: If you could tell me maybe two things that you think are big problems in the world today . . . .

Christiane: I think one of the biggest problems is war. And I think another big problem is racism in this world.

Interviewer: And of those, could you tell me, you know, a little bit more about what you think could be done to alleviate these problems?

Christiane: I think, actually with both problems, it's mostly about understanding each other and sitting down on a table and . . . talk, get to know each other and be able to make more compromises and understand different cultures and reasons why people do certain

things certain ways. And I think we would all be much happier.

Interviewer: Communication.

Christiane: Communication. That's the clue. Exactly. Yeah.

ANSWER KEY

A. war, racism

B. understand different cultures, make more compromises, communicate better

C. 1. books, movies 2. governments 3. information

D. *Individual responses may include variations like the following:*

1. Ian doesn't appreciate prohibiting smoking indoors because he's a smoker 2. Christiane thinks prohibiting smoking indoors is fantastic because the food in restaurants tastes better and clothes don't smell

---

 Top Notch Pop and Karaoke: *We Can Agree to Disagree*

UNIT 10

Sitcom: *We weren't going to tell you this, but . . .*

Social language

- Warn about risks and dangers
- Describe the natural world

Grammar

- Prepositions of location
- *Too* + adjective and infinitive

SCENE 1

PREVIEW

- Ask students these questions:

    Do married couples in your country usually go on a honeymoon after a wedding?

    Do you know any popular honeymoon destinations?

    What do you think would be the best honeymoon destination?

REVIEW

- Ask comprehension questions. Play the video episode again if necessary.

    What do Cheryl and Bob need help with? (choosing a destination for their honeymoon)

Does Bob want to go anywhere special? (No. He doesn't like to travel, so he will go anywhere Cheryl wants to go, as long as the hotel has nice bathrooms and a TV.)
What is the first place Cheryl says she wants to go? (Cozumel, off the Yucatán Peninsula)
Does Paul recommend this place? (yes)
What does Marie say to discourage Cheryl and Bob from going there? (She says there are too many sharks to go swimming there.)
What is the second place Cheryl says she wants to go? (Tierra del Fuego in the south of Argentina and Chile)
Does Paul recommend this place? (yes)
What does Marie say to discourage Cheryl and Bob from going there? (She says that in June it's too dark to do very much there.)
What is the third place Cheryl says she wants to go? (jungles and rain forests in Malaysia)
What does Paul say to discourage Cheryl and Bob from going there? (He says that some people feel the scorpions make it too dangerous to hike.)
Where does Bob suggest they go? (to the hotel on Grand Street) Why? (because they have really nice bathrooms and big televisions)

EXTENSION

Oral work

- Discussion. Ask students these questions:
    Why do you think Marie keeps interrupting Paul when he says nice things about Cheryl's ideas for the vacation?
    Are you familiar with the places Cheryl mentions? Would you like to go to any of the places for vacation? Why or why not?

- Group work: role play. Have students work in groups to come up with a honeymoon destination for Cheryl and Bob. Tell students to give a description of the location. Then have each group continue the conversation for several more exchanges. Have students role-playing Mr. Evans recommend the honeymoon destination to Cheryl and Bob.

Written work

- Have students write a description of Bob's ideal honeymoon vacation, using the information they know about his dislike for travel.
- Pair work. Ask students *Do you think Cheryl and Bob will have fun on their honeymoon if Cheryl wants to see exciting things and Bob is most interested in a nice hotel and a big TV?* Have students work in pairs to choose a destination and write a postcard to Mr. Evans from Bob and Cheryl on their honeymoon.

VIDEO SCRIPT

In the café, Cheryl and Bob ask the rest of the Top Notch Travel staff to help them decide on a location for their honeymoon.

Cheryl: Everyone, we'd like to ask your opinion about something.
Mr. Evans: What is that?
Cheryl: We're trying to decide where to go on vacation after the wedding, for our honeymoon.
Bob: We thought you might be able to help us decide on a location.
Mr. Evans: An excellent idea. Where are you thinking of going?
Cheryl: Well, Bob doesn't really like to travel, so he's agreed to go wherever I want to go, as long as the hotel has nice bathrooms and a TV.
Mr. Evans: That sounds fair. What's your first choice?
Cheryl: I've always wanted to go to Cozumel, **off** the Yucatán Peninsula.
Paul: Cozumel is spectacular. The island itself is pretty flat, but the beaches are beautiful and the ocean is so blue.
Marie: Aren't there **too** many sharks **to go** swimming there?
Paul: No! It's very safe. What? Oh! But it's somewhat overrated.
Bob: You just said . . .
Mr. Evans: What else are you thinking of?
Cheryl: What about Tierra del Fuego **in** the south **of** Argentina and Chile?
Paul: The scenery is extraordinary! The mountain ranges and national parks are breathtaking.
Marie: But in June, won't it be **too dark to do** very much?
Paul: No! Plenty of people go there in June to go skiing or . . . But, of course, it's probably not romantic enough for a honeymoon.
Cheryl: I've heard the jungles and rain forests **in** Malaysia are a must-see.
Paul: They're so lush. . . . Of course, some people feel that the scorpions make it **too dangerous to hike**.
Bob: We could go to that hotel **on** Grand Street **along** the river.
Cheryl: Stay in town? For our honeymoon?
Bob: Well, I heard the rooms have really nice bathrooms and big televisions.

ANSWER KEY

A. 1. b 2. c 3. a 4. b
B. 1. b 2. c 3. a
C. 1. off 2. too many sharks to go swimming
   3. in the south of 4. too dark to do 5. must-see
   6. too dangerous to hike

SCENE 2

PREVIEW

- Ask students *What do you know about Tahiti? Do you think Tahiti is a good honeymoon destination?*

REVIEW

- Ask comprehension questions. Play the video episode again if necessary.

    How did Marie know Cheryl wants to go to Tahiti? (Cheryl told her once.)

    Do Mr. Evans, Paul, and Marie all recommend Tahiti as a honeymoon destination? (yes)

    What does Bob say about Tahiti? (that it's too expensive)

    How does he know? (Mr. Rashid traveled there.)

    Does Cheryl remember how expensive Mr. Rashid's trip was? (yes)

    What does Mr. Evans say about a vacation in the South Pacific? (He thinks it would be perfect.)

    Why does Cheryl think they can't go there? (because it's too expensive)

    What does Mr. Evans tell them? (that he, Marie, and Paul would like to send them to Tahiti as a wedding present)

    How long will the vacation be? (two weeks)

    What does Mr. Evans tell Bob? (that the hotel has a spectacular bathroom and a big TV)

EXTENSION

Oral work

- Group work: role play. Divide the class into groups of five. Have students role-play a conversation in which Bob and Cheryl tell everyone about their honeymoon in Tahiti.

- Group work: role play. Divide the class into groups of five. Have students imagine that Mr. Evans tells Bob that unfortunately there is no TV in the hotel room, and the bathroom is just a regular bathroom. Have students role-play Bob's reaction and continue the conversation for several more exchanges.

Written work

- Group work. Have students work in groups to create a Tahiti travel brochure. Encourage students to describe why Tahiti would be a perfect location for a honeymoon.

- Pair work. Have students work in pairs to write a thank-you letter from Bob and Cheryl to Mr. Evans, Paul, and Marie from Tahiti, where they are on their honeymoon.

LANGUAGE NOTE: *I'm out of ideas* means *I can't think of any more ideas.*

VIDEO SCRIPT

The rest of the Top Notch Travel staff give Bob and Cheryl a surprise wedding gift.

Marie: Cheryl, you once told me that you wanted to go to Tahiti.

Cheryl: That's right. I forgot about that.

Mr. Evans: You would love Tahiti.

Paul: One of the most beautiful places on earth.

Marie: And very, very romantic.

Cheryl: Really? You all think Tahiti is a good idea?

Mr. Evans: I think you'd love it.

Bob: It's too expensive.

Cheryl: How expensive?

Bob: Well, do you remember how much Mr. Rashid's vacation to Tahiti cost?

Cheryl: Yes, I do.

Bob: He traveled cheaply.

Cheryl: Well, that's it. I'm out of ideas. I guess we'll go someplace boring.

Mr. Evans: We weren't going to tell you until a couple of months from now, but Paul, Marie, and I were talking, and we thought a vacation **in** the South Pacific would be perfect.

Cheryl: I just wish we could afford it.

Mr. Evans: So we decided that as our wedding gift to you, we would like to send you to Tahiti. All expenses paid.

Cheryl: You're kidding!

Mr. Evans: We've booked your flights and a hotel **on** the southern coast for two weeks.

Cheryl: I don't know how to thank you!

Bob: But the . . .

Mr. Evans: And the hotel room has a spectacular bathroom and a TV this big.

Bob: I don't know how to thank you!

Cheryl: Thank you so much! I'm so excited!

ANSWER KEY

A. 1. False 2. True 3. False 4. True 5. True
B. 1. c 2. a 3. b
C. 1. a vacation in the South Pacific 2. All expenses paid 3. flights 4. on the southern coast

 Top Notch Pop and Karaoke:
It's a Beautiful World

Top Notch ActiveTeach DVD-ROM

For Windows:

- Insert the **Top Notch ActiveTeach** disc into the DVD-ROM drive of your computer. On most computers, the ActiveTeach menu will open automatically. On most computers, the DVD video program will also open automatically (using your default DVD software player). Close the application you do not want to use.

If *ActiveTeach* does not begin automatically:

- Open "**My Computer.**"
- Right-click on the TN_3_ActiveTeach icon. Click on **Open**.
- Double-click on the TN_3_ActiveTeach.exe file to start the application. Do not remove the DVD-ROM from the DVD-ROM drive while using ActiveTeach.
- On the opening screen, click on the book image to start ActiveTeach.
- To watch the DVD video program, open the default DVD Player software installed on your computer.

For MAC:

- Insert the **Top Notch ActiveTeach** disc into the DVD-ROM drive of your computer.
- Double-click on the TN_3_ActiveTeach icon on your desktop.
- Double click on the TN_3_ActiveTeach launch file. Do not remove the DVD-ROM from the DVD-ROM drive while using ActiveTeach.
- On the opening screen, click on the book image to start ActiveTeach.
- To watch the DVD video program, open the default DVD Player software installed on your computer.

Note: The original *Top Notch ActiveTeach* disc must be in the DVD-ROM drive when you use this application. This application cannot be copied or used without the original DVD-ROM.

ON A DVD PLAYER

You can also watch the video program using a DVD player connected to a TV.

ActiveTeach System Requirements		
	For PC-Compatible Computers	**For Macintosh Computers**
Operating System	Microsoft Windows® XP, Vista, Windows 7	Mac OSX v. 10.4.x
Processor	Intel Pentium® IV 1000MHz or faster processor (or equivalent)	PowerPC & Intel processor 500MHz or faster processor (or equivalent)
RAM	512 MB RAM minimum or higher	512 MB RAM minimum or higher
Internet Browser	Microsoft Internet Explorer® 7.x or Mozilla Firefox™ 3.x, or higher	Safari® 3.x, Mozilla Firefox™ 3.x, or higher
Plug-ins	Adobe PDF 8	Adobe PDF 8
Hardware	Computer DVD-ROM drive, Sound card and speakers or headphones. External DVD Player can also be used to watch available video.	Computer DVD-ROM drive, Sound card and speakers or headphones. External DVD Player can also be used to watch available video.
Monitor Resolution	1024x768	1024x768

TECHNICAL SUPPORT

For Technical Product Support, please visit our support website at www.PearsonLongmanSupport.com. You can search our **Knowledgebase** for frequently asked questions, instantly **Chat** with an available support representative, or **Submit a Ticket/Request** for assistance.